THE POETICAL WORKS
OF
ROBERT
BROWNING

Volume II

STRAFFORD
SORDELLO

EDITED BY

IAN JACK

AND

MARGARET SMITH

CLARENDON PRESS · OXFORD
1984

Oxford University Press, Walton Street, Oxford OX2 6DP
London Glasgow New York Toronto
Delhi Bombay Calcutta Madras Karachi
Kula Lumpur Singapore Hong Kong Tokyo
Nairobi Dar es Salaam Cape Town
Melbourne Auckland

and associated companies in
Beirut Berlin Ibadan Mexico City Nicosia

Published in the United States
Oxford University Press, New York

British Library Cataloguing in Publication Data
Browning, Robert
The poetical works of Robert Browning. —
(Oxford English texts)
Vol. Two
I. Title   II. Jack, Ian
III. Smith, Margaret
821'.8   PR4201
ISBN 0–19–812317–5

Library of Congress Cataloging in Publication Data
Browning, Robert, 1812–1889.
The poetical works of Robert Browning.
(Oxford English texts)
Includes bibliographical references.
Contents: v. 1. Pauline; Paracelsus—v. 2. Strafford; Sordello.
I. Jack, Ian Robert James.   II. Smith, Margaret, Middleton.   III. Title.
PR4203.J3 1982   821'.8   84–12603
ISBN 0–19–812317–5

Typeset by Phoenix Photosetting, Chatham
and Printed in Great Britain by
Thomson Litho Ltd, East Kilbride

CONTENTS

INTRODUCTION TO 'STRAFFORD'

After a season . . . it is settled, by majority of votes, that such
and such a 'Crossing of the Rubicon,' an 'Impeachment of
Strafford,' a 'Convocation of the Notables,' are epochs in the
world's history, cardinal points on which grand world-
revolutions have hinged.

CARLYLE.[1]

BROWNING'S interest in the drama began early. We do not
know how old he was when he read Nathaniel Lee's tragedy,
Caesar Borgia, which he later described as 'the first play I ever
read',[2] but it is clear that he was already a reader of plays during
his days at Mr. Ready's school, when he wrote plays of his
own and persuaded his schoolfellows to act in them. The
continuing importance of the drama to him is shown by the
fact that Edmund Kean's acting of the part of Richard III
prompted the writing of *Pauline*, as well as the formation of a
whole series of further projects: 'I don't know whether I had
not made up my mind to *act*, as well as to make verses, music,
and God knows what'.[3] It is not surprising that his meeting
with William Charles Macready, the celebrated actor-
manager, confirmed his interest in the drama and led to his
writing for the stage.

Macready's *Diaries*[4] provide a great deal of information. On
6 September 1835 he read 'the extracts from a poem called
Paracelsus' in the *Examiner* and considered them 'of great
merit'. On 27 November he met Browning at the home of the
Rev. William Fox: 'I was very much pleased to meet him. His
face is full of intelligence . . . I took Mr. Browning on, and
requested to be allowed to improve my acquaintance with
him. He expressed himself warmly, as gratified by the proposal; wished to send me his book; we exchanged cards and

---

[1] 'Thoughts on History', *Fraser's Magazine*, November 1830: reprinted in *The Works* (Centenary Edition), xxvii. 87.
[2] See a signed note on the title-page of the edition of 1736 now in Balliol College Library: it is dated 'Apr. 28. '73.'
[3] Cf. Vol. I, p. 3.
[4] *The Diaries of William Charles Macready 1833–1851*, ed. William Toynbee, 2 vols. 1912.

parted.' On the 7th and 8th of December he read *Paracelsus*, 'a work of great daring, . . . but occasionally obscure', and concluded that its author 'can scarcely fail to be a leading spirit of his time'. He noted, among other merits, 'a most subtle and penetrating search into the feelings and impulses of our nature'. On the last day of the year Browning was one of a small group who joined Macready in pouring out 'a libation as a farewell to the old year and a welcome to the new': he noted that Browning 'looks and speaks more like a youthful poet than any man I ever saw'. The scene was set for Browning's initiation into the theatre.

On 1 February 1836 Macready commented that John Forster (the author of the notice in the *Examiner*) 'was talking much of Browning, who is his present *all-in-all*'. A fortnight later Forster read him 'passages from a poem by Browning', probably *Sordello*, and the following day the two men called on Macready 'and talked over the plot of a tragedy which Browning had begun to think of: the subject, Narses.[1] He said that I had *bit* him by my performance of *Othello*,[2] and I told him I hoped I should make the blood come. It would indeed be some recompense for the miseries, the humiliations, the heart-sickening disgusts which I have endured in my profession if, by its exercise, I had awakened a spirit of poetry whose influence would elevate, ennoble, and adorn our degraded drama. May it be so!' On 26 May there occurred the famous party at Talfourd's, after the first night of his *Ion*, at which Macready found himself 'very happily placed between Wordsworth and Landor, with Browning opposite'. According to Mrs. Sutherland Orr,[3] 'Toasts flew right and left. Mr. Browning's health was proposed by Serjeant Talfourd as that of the youngest poet of England, and Wordsworth responded to the appeal with very kindly courtesy. The conversation afterwards turned upon plays, and Macready . . . overtook Mr. Browning as they were leaving the house, and said, "Write a play, Browning, and keep me from going to America." The

---

[1] 'a passing fancy', Browning noted later: 'one difficulty in the subject was insuperable, I soon saw': *Letters*, p. 296. Gibbon gives an account of Narses, the eunuch who conquered Italy for Justinian, in the later part of his Chapter XLI.

[2] Macready had acted Othello on 3 February: Browning came into his dressing-room afterwards, and 'seemed much delighted' (*Diaries*, i. 273).

[3] *Life*, p. 82.

reply was, "Shall it be historical and English? what do you say to a drama on Strafford?"' Two days later Browning prophesied that the work on which he was engaged was 'nearly done': 'from the first of July I shall be free: if, before then, any subject shall suggest itself to you—any character or event with which you are predisposed to sympathize—I will give my whole heart & soul to the writing a Tragedy on it to be ready by the first of November next: should I be unequal to the task, the excitement and extreme effort will have been their own reward:—should I succeed, my way of life will be very certain, and my name pronounced along with yours'.[1]

Sordello was not to be so easily completed, and we know from the preface to the first edition of *Strafford* that his 'eagerness to freshen a jaded mind by diverting it to the healthy natures of a grand epoch' led Browning to write the play before returning to the poem on which he had already been working for several years. His offer to write on 'any subject' proposed by Macready explains DeVane's doubt whether he had suggested Strafford on 26 May; yet it is perfectly likely that 'Strafford, as a dramatic subject, had been occupying his thoughts', as Mrs. Orr states:

The subject was in the air, because Forster was then bringing out a life of that statesman, with others belonging to the same period. It was more than in the air, so far as Browning was concerned, because his friend had been disabled, either through sickness or sorrow, from finishing this volume by the appointed time, and he, as well he might, had largely helped him in its completion.[2]

The Life of Strafford appeared with that of Sir John Eliot[3] in 1836 as Volume II of the 'Lives of Eminent British Statesmen' in the Biography section of *The Cabinet Cyclopædia*, a long series of books published between 1829 and 1849 under the general editorship of the Rev. Dionysius Lardner. Volumes III–IV and VI–VII were also by Forster, III comprising Lives

[1] MS letter inserted in 'Copy 3' of *Strafford* in the Berg Collection. The text in *New Letters*, p. 12, unaccountably omits 'any character . . . to sympathize—'.
[2] *Life*, p. 82. Forster disappears from Macready's *Diaries* from 1 March to 16 April 1836, so this was probably the time of his indisposition.
[3] On p. 104 Forster quotes lines i. 765–70 of *Paracelsus* as the work of 'the poet, whose genius has just risen amongst us', adding in a note: 'There would be little danger in predicting that this writer will soon be acknowledged as a first-rate poet. He has already proved himself one'.

of Pym and Hampden and IV Lives of Sir Henry Vane the
Younger and Henry Marten, while VI and VII are devoted to a
longer Life of Oliver Cromwell, described by Carlyle as 'a
crown to all the modern Biographies.'[1]

While the fact that Browning helped Forster with his Life of
Strafford is beyond all doubt, the extent of his help has been
much debated. In the *Pall Mall Gazette* for 12 April 1890 F. J.
Furnivall wrote as follows:

The poet set to work, completed Strafford's life on his own lines, in
accordance with his own conception of Strafford's character, but
generously said nothing about it till after Forster's death. Then he
told a few of his friends . . . On my telling Prof. Gardiner of this, I
found that he knew it, and had been long convinced that the conception of Strafford . . . was not John Forster's, but was Robert Browning's. The other day [he] urged me to make the fact of Browning's
authorship public.[2]

Furnivall appealed to Smith, Elder to reprint the Life as one of
Browning's works, and it was presumably after their refusal
that it was 'Publisht for The Browning Society By Kegan
Paul, Trench, Trübner & Co.' in 1892, in a similar format to
that of the *Poetical Works*, with an introduction by C. H. Firth
and 'Forewords' by Furnivall himself. Furnivall states that
Browning had spoken to him about the Life on three occasions, once saying that 'very few people had any idea of how
much he had helpt John Forster in it', and once that he 'had
written almost all Forster's *Life of Strafford*': on the other
occasion he had told Furnivall, 'at length' and with more
detail, 'that one day he went to see Forster and found him very
ill, and anxious about the *Life* . . . , which he had promist to
write at once, to complete a volume . . . for Lardner's *Cabinet
Cyclopædia*. Forster had finisht the Life of Eliot—the first in
the volume—and had just begun that of Strafford, for which
he had made full collections and extracts; but illness had come
on, he couldn't work, the book ought to be completed forthwith, as it was due in the serial issue of volumes; what *was* he to
do? "Oh," said Browning, "don't trouble about it. I'll take
your papers and do it for you". Forster thankt his young friend
heartily, Browning put the Strafford papers under his arm,

[1] *The Works of Thomas Carlyle* (Centenary Edition), vi. 19.   [2] p. 3.

walkt off, workt hard, finisht the Life, and it came out to time in 1836, to Forster's great relief, and past under his name.'[1]

In the year before the Browning Society edition of the Life, Mrs. Sutherland Orr had published her *Life and Letters of Robert Browning*, in which she stated that Browning 'had largely helped' Forster in the 'completion' of the Life of Strafford;[2] while in a note to the 'New Edition' of her book which appeared in 1908, 'Revised and in part Rewritten by Frederic G. Kenyon', Kenyon quoted from Elizabeth Barrett's reference to 'your "Strafford"—Mr. Forster's "Strafford". I beg his pardon for not attributing to him other men's works'.[3] The context of the remark is to be found in her correspondence with Browning at this time. 'Don't forget to bring me my "Statesmen"', she wrote on 21 May 1846. Four days later she wrote again: 'I gave up the early poems because I felt contented to read them afterwards—but listen . . my Statesmen, I *will not give up*. Now listen—I expect nothing at all from them—they were written for another person, & under peculiar circumstances . . they are probably as bad as anything written by you, can be. Will *that* do? . . . And *may* I see them?' It is clear that he gave in, for a few days later we find her writing: 'Oh, but I find you out in the Statesmen . . for all the dim light'. On 2 June she told him that she had read the Statesmen 'with a peculiar sort of pleasure, coming & going as I see you & miss you. There is no mistaking your footsteps along the sands'; and five days later she wrote the sentence quoted above from Kenyon's revision of Mrs. Orr's *Life*.

Whatever share Browning may have had in the other Lives, it is clear that he played a most important part in the composition of the *Strafford*, since he was (as Kenyon pointed out) 'incapable of claiming what did not belong to him'. When Browning wrote to Forster in 1854 he recalled 'the *Strafford* crisis', mentioning Forster's 'Pym-like build . . . , which made chairs creak and floors groan when we turned over books together'.[4] The most loyal of men, Browning wished the matter kept a complete secret at the time, although later he was prepared to tell one or two people what had happened. 'Tell Professor Gardiner by all means', he wrote to Miss Hickey in 1883, '—with the same entreaty for a discretion in the use of

[1] pp. v–vi.   [2] p. 88.   [3] p. 82 n.   [4] *New Letters*, p. 76.

the fact. He will understand that I had no notion of scribbling anything but as a rough piece of work which F. might fill up, file away, and make his own: he had no time to do as much in that way as both he and I expected.'[1] When he sat down to write his play, therefore, he was well versed in all the principal sources for the life of his protagonist.

When Forster told Macready of Browning's choice of subject for a play, on 3 August 1836, the latter commented in his *Diary* that 'he could not have hit upon one that I could have more readily concurred in'. Subsequent events are chronicled by Macready. On 4 October he was alarmed to hear from Forster that Browning had completed his play 'in ten days (!)', and commented: 'I cannot put faith in its dramatic qualities—the thing seems, not to say incredible, but almost impossible. *I cannot place reliance on the world*'. When Browning told him, six days later, that the play was not in fact completed he considered this 'a circumstance to rejoice at'. On the last day of the month Browning reported that the play was 'finished', and on 1 November Macready made a prophetic comment: 'Forster told me of Browning's play which he praised most highly; but I fear he has such an interest in the individual characters, the biographies of whom he has written, that he is misled as to its dramatic power; character to him having the interest of action. *Nous verrons!*' On 3 November the three men 'settled next Wednesday sennight for the reading of the *Earl of Strafford*'. On 12 November we hear that 'Dow was enchanted with the last act',[2] but when, a week later, Browning and Dow came with the tragedy 'the fourth act was incomplete.' Macready accordingly 'requested him to write in the plot of what was deficient'. This was done, and when he read the play the following day Macready 'was greatly pleased'. The following day Browning came again, 'in some anxiety to have my opinion'. Macready 'told it frankly, and he was very much pleased, agreeing in my objections, and prom-

---

[1] Ibid., pp. 353–4. We are in general agreement with 'A Re-Examination of *Robert Browning's Prose Life of Strafford*', by W. S. Peterson (*Browning Newsletter*, Fall 1969); and cf. M. Hancher in the same periodical for Spring 1970. The letters by Forster's widow and Pen Browning in *Literary Anecdotes of the Nineteenth Century*, ed. W. Robertson Nicoll and Thomas J. Wise (vol. i, 1895), pp. 396–7 do not materially affect the issue. Cf. Berdoe, pp. 526 ff.

[2] W. A. Dow, who persuaded Browning to write the 'Lines to the Memory of James Dow': see Vol. I, Appendix F.

ising to do everything needful to the play's amendment. He sat very long'. The manuscript was delivered by Forster the following day. On the 23rd there is another important entry: 'Began *very attentively* to read over . . . *Strafford*, in which I find more grounds for exception than I had anticipated. I had been too much carried away by the truth of character to observe the meanness of plot, and occasional obscurity'. The next day he told Browning that he 'could not look at his play again until Bulwer's was produced, in which he acquiesced'.

About this time Browning sent an undated letter to Macready of which only a fragment is known to survive: 'I propose leaving the 4th act with you on the night of "La Valliere" . . . I have taken a cursory look at your *addissions* [sic] in "Strafford", seeing it on the table. I shall remedy every oversight I am sure out of an after crop of thoughts!'[1] In fact Browning 'left . . . the omitted scenes in his play' with Macready on 20 December, well before the first night of Bulwer's *The Duchess de la Vallière* on 4 January 1837. Having read them, however, Macready concluded that *Strafford* was 'still not up to the high-water mark', and we hear no more until March.

The Diaries for 18 March and the following days contain important references:

Elstree, March 18th.—Received a note from Forster, appointing Monday for the visit of himself and Browning about *Strafford* . . . Read before dinner a few pages of *Paracelsus*, which raises my wonder the more I read it . . . Looked over two plays . . . utter trash . . . Read some scenes in *Strafford*, which restore one to the world of sense and feeling once again.

March 19th.—Read *Strafford* in the evening, which I fear is too historical; it is the policy of the man, and its consequence upon him, not the heart, temper, feelings, that work on this policy, which Browning has portrayed—and how admirably.

March 21st.—Browning came with me into the study, and with much interruption over the discussion of points and passages, we read through his tragedy of *Strafford*; I must confess my disappointment at the management of the story—I doubt its interest . . . After dinner . . . resumed our conversation . . . , and I resolved—seeing no other course—to read it again to-night—after tea I did so, but I am by no means sanguine, I lament to say, on its success.

[1] *Checklist*, 37:8.

March 22nd.—Resumed with Browning the conversation of last night on *Strafford*; showed the necessity—as far as Mr. Osbaldiston is concerned—of his direct declaration, yes or no, as to his ability to give the finished play on Saturday. After some deliberation he decided in the negative, and preferred withholding the play till my Benefit. He seemed to think much of the objections and suggestions I had offered.

On the following day he 'Wrote to Browning on a thought that had struck me for the last scene',[1] and on the 28th Browning and Forster 'walked to chambers' with him and they 'sat discussing the plot of Strafford until two o'clock'. When he delivered the play next day Browning 'looked very unwell, jaded and thought-sick'. After an interruption Macready 'Went through the alterations . . . , and proceeded to the theatre', where he talked to Osbaldiston about the play, and 'appointed eleven to-morrow to read it to him.' He wrote to Browning, at Forster's request, 'mentioning my opinion of the play. Read over attentively, noting down my objections . . . ; it consumed much time'.

When Macready read the play to Osbaldiston, however, he 'caught at it with avidity',

agreed to produce it without delay on his part, and to give the author £12 per night for twenty-five nights, and £10 per night for ten nights beyond. He also promised to offer Mr. Elton[2] an engagement to strengthen the play. Browning and Forster came in; I had the pleasure of narrating what had passed . . . , and of making Browning very happy; I went over the memoranda I had made of corrigenda in his MS.; the suggestion of the children's voices being heard in the pause following the announcement of Strafford's death he was quite *enraptured* with; he took the book and promised to work hard. Forster is trying to induce the Longmans to publish it; I doubt his success.[3] Browning asked me if I would allow him to dedicate the play to me. I told him, of course, how much I should value such an honour, which I had not anticipated or looked for.

Macready's close interest in the play continued throughout April:

London. April 3rd.—. . . Browning and Forster accompanied me to

---

[1] See the last footnote to the play.
[2] He did not act in it, but cf. p. 16 n below.
[3] Longmans accepted the play, however.

my chambers, drank a bottle of champagne which I found for them, and read the two last acts of *Strafford*, discussing the alterations in it. Browning left them with me, and took notes of what was yet to do. They left me a little after three, and I got to bed about four!! . . .
April 4th.—. . . Browning called in with alterations, etc.; sat and talked whilst I dined. A young [Greek] gentleman came in . . . I introduced Browning to him as a great tragic poet . . . Read over three copied acts of *Strafford*.
April 5th.—After thinking in bed of the want of connection in the scenes of Browning's play . . . I rose and sent for Forster; explained to him the dangerous state of the play, and the importance it was of to remedy this defect. We sat down to work . . . We went over the play . . . , altered, omitted, and made up one new scene; we were occupied from eleven till four o'clock; the day entirely surrendered to it. Went to the theatre to procure the two last acts . . . Began Forster's life of Strafford . . . Forster and Dow called with the MS. of *Strafford*. Read and marked to read, etc., the four acts they left us.

Two days later Forster and Browning called again, the latter 'with some of the passages to be supplied—very feebly written. Forster and he had rather a warm altercation—Browning, as I understood him, asserting that no change had been made in the conduct of the play since its first draught, which was not, in my mind, correct'.

On the 8th of April Browning accompanied Macready to the theatre, where the actor 'Read over *Strafford* to the persons in the green-room,[1] but did not produce the impression [he] had hoped—it dragged its slow length along'. When he read it to his daughters at home he was sorry to find that they too 'were oppressed by a want of action and lightness', adding the comment: '*I fear it will not do*'. Three days later he read it through with Forster, who 'evidently felt all the objections that I had stated—was obliged to acknowledge the feebleness and heaviness of the play'. The next day he gave Forster the manuscript, 'which [he] had cut', and 'Spoke to Osbaldiston about *Strafford*, . . . having been anxious to find some of the actors restive about their parts, to furnish Browning with a decent excuse to withdraw the play'. To his disappointment, however, they were agreed to proceed with it. Shortly

---

[1] 'I suppose he [Browning] was nervous', Lady Martin (then Helen Faucit) was later to comment, 'for I remember Mr. Macready read the play to us in the green-room': cf. p. 12 n below.

Forster called, and went twice over the play . . . approving of all the
omissions and expressing himself much raised in hope by the alterations. He thought my view of the work quite a clear one, and in the
most earnest spirit of devotion set off to find and communicate with
Browning on the subject—a fearful rencontre . . . Called at Forster's
chambers, whence Browning and he came to mine. There were
mutual complaints—much temper—sullenness, I should say, on the
part of Forster, who was very much out of humour with Browning,
who said and did all that man could do to expiate any offence he
might have given. Forster (who has behaved most nobly all through
the matter of this play—no expression of praise is too high) showed
an absence of sense and generosity in his behaviour which I grieved
to see. There was a *scene* . . . Browning assented to all the proposed
alterations, and expressed his wish, that *coûte que coûte*, the hazard
should be made, and the play proceeded with.

'Bulwer would scarcely have done this', Macready adds in a
particularly interesting comment, 'and in playing the great
game he has before him he [Browning] should regard this as a
trivial offence, and so dismiss it'.

Browning was not prepared to take any such view of the
matter, however, and the comedy of his tragedy continued the
following day:

April 14th.—Calling at Forster's, met Browning, who came upstairs
and who produced some scraps of paper with hints and unconnected
lines—the full amount of his labour upon the alterations agreed on. It
was too bad to trifle in this way, but it was useless to complain; he
had wasted his time in striving to improve the fourth act scene,[1]
which was ejected from his play as impracticable for any good result.
We went all over the play *again* (!) very carefully, and he resolved to
bring the amendments suggested by eleven o'clock this evening.
Met Browning at the gate of my chambers; he came upstairs and,
after some subjects of general interest, proceeded to that of his
tragedy. He had done nothing to it; had been oppressed and incapable of carrying his intentions into action. He *wished* to *withdraw it*. I
cautioned him against any precipitate step—warned him of the
consequences, and at last got him to offer to go and bring Forster,
whom I wished to be a party to all this business. He came with
Browning, and we turned over all the pros and cons—for acting or
not acting the play. They both decided on its performance, Browning to have more time than he had asked for the completion of his

---

[1] Cf. p. 16 below.

alterations. It was fixed to be done. Heaven speed us all! I thank God I felt quite satisfied with my conduct throughout this delicate affair of Browning.

As the date of the rehearsal approached Macready's troubles and worries multiplied. On the 15th he went to Covent Garden Theatre and 'spoke to the copyist about *Strafford*. We were obliged to make arrangements—very tardy in their effects—subservient to the parsimonious regulations of Mr. Osbaldiston'. His spirits remained low on the 20th, when after dinner he 'read over *Strafford*, which I strongly fear *will fail*—it is *not good*'. The next few entries are exclusively concerned with the play:

April 22nd.—Browning came to breakfast, very pale, and apparently suffering from over-excitement. I think it is unfortunate that without due consideration and time for arranging and digesting his thoughts on a work so difficult as a tragedy, he should have committed himself to the production of one. I should be too glad of any accident that would impede its representation, and give me a *fair* occasion for withdrawing it; but this I cannot now do without incurring the suspicion of selfishness and of injustice to him, and therefore, though I feel convinced that the performance of this play on my Benefit night will cause much dissatisfaction . . . yet still, *coûte que coûte*, Browning shall not have the power of saying that I have acted otherwise than as a true friend to his feelings.

Elstree, April 23rd.—Took up the part of Strafford, at which I continued . . . during the entire morning to dinner-time. The more I consider the play the lower my hopes smile upon it; I expect it will be damned—grievously hissed at the end—from the unintelligibility of the motives, the want of action, and consequently of interest. Looked at Browning's alterations of the last scene . . . —found them quite bad—mere feeble rant—neither power, nor nature, nor healthful fancy—very unworthy of Browning. I felt certainly convinced that the play must be utterly condemned.

London, April 26th.—Thought in my bed some time on *Strafford*—how I could make the most of every line. I am deeply anxious, though despairing, for Browning's sake, and shall not lose effect from not labouring for it. Told Forster my conviction about the fate of the play, which I look upon, despite all that can be done, as inevitable. Forster related to me the substance of Browning's preface and dedication, which appear very good.

April 27th.—Went to the rehearsal . . . , with which I took much pains and the general effect of which I improved considerably . . .

Browning amused me much by his confidence in the success of the play;[1] he looked at the acting and movement of a subject in which he had a deep interest—ensure that same *interest* in the audience, and I will ensure its success—but the question is: will the audience be kindled to such an interest? I grieve to think that my experience will not allow me to say yes. Gave the evening to the perusal and study of *Strafford*.

April 28th.—Thought over some scenes of *Strafford* before I rose, and went out very soon to the rehearsal of it. There is no chance in my opinion for the play but in the acting,[2] which by possibility might carry it to the end without disapprobation; but that the curtain can fall without considerable opposition, I cannot venture to anticipate under the most advantageous circumstances. In all the historical plays of Shakspeare, the great poet has only introduced such events as act on the individuals concerned, and of which they are themselves a part; the persons are all in direct relation to each other, and the facts are present to the audience. But in Browning's play we have a long scene of passion—upon what? A plan destroyed, by whom or for what we know not, and a parliament dissolved, which merely seems to inconvenience *Strafford* in his arrangements. There is a sad want of judgment and tact in the whole composition. Would it were over! It must fail—and it grieves me to think that *I am so placed.* Browning will efface its memory by the production of *Sordello*; but it will strike me hard, I fear . . . Forster introduced me to young Mr. Longman . . . , who consulted with me upon the publication, and yielded to my reasons for delaying it until Monday afternoon.

The next day, equipped with the wig which he was to wear, he went to the theatre for a rehearsal, and was 'disposed to think [it] might *pass muster*—not more—if it were equally and respectably acted, but Mr. Dale in the King must ensure its utter failure. Browning was incensed at Mr. Dale's unhappy attempts—*it is too bad.*' On the 30th he repeated to Forster his

[1] 'At the rehearsals', Helen Faucit was to record many years later, 'when Mr. Browning was introduced to those ladies and gentlemen whom he did not know, his demeanour was so kind, considerate, and courteous, so grateful for the attention shown to his wishes, that he won directly the warm interest of all engaged in the play. So it was that although many doubtful forecasts were made in the green-room as to the ultimate attraction of a play so entirely turning on politics, yet all were determined to do their very best to insure its success': letter to Anne (Thackeray) Ritchie, dated 30 April 1891, in the latter's *Records of Tennyson, Ruskin and Browning* (2nd ed., 1893), pp. 224–5.

[2] 'that is, his own performance', Browning commented in 1888, '—the other actors, with the notable exception of Vandenhoff and Miss Helen Faucit, being incompetent. The theatre was in a bad way, about to close, and the Manager economized accordingly'. See *Letters*, p. 296–7, for his notes on Macready's Diary.

conviction that *Strafford* '*must fail*—if, by some happy chance, not at once to-morrow, yet still at best it will only stagger out a lingering existence of a few nights and then die out—and for ever'.

On the great day, May the first, Macready was 'gratified with the extreme delight Browning testified at the rehearsal of [his] part, which he said was to him a full recompense for having written the play, inasmuch as he had seen his utmost hopes of character perfectly embodied. He was quite in raptures'—Macready adds—'I warning him that I did not anticipate success. Parted with Browning with wishes of good fortune to him. Read Strafford in bed, and acted it as well as I could under the nervous sensations which I experienced.' Earlier in the day Browning had sent Fox 'the first book of the first bundle', his attempts to procure a printed copy before that having proved fruitless. '*Pray* look over it', he added, '—the alterations tonight will be considerable. The complexion of the piece is, I grieve to say, "perfect gallows" just now—our *king*, Mr. Dale, being . . . but you'll see him, and, I fear, not much applaud'.[1] We know from a letter of Miss Flower's that Browning 'seem[ed] a good deal annoyed at the go of things behind the scenes, and declare[d] he will never write a play again, as long as he lives. You have no idea of the ignorance and obstinacy of the whole set, with here and there an exception; think of his having to write out the meaning of the word *impeachment*, as some of them thought it meant *poaching*.'[2]

Mrs. Orr tells us that on the first night 'the fate of *Strafford* hung in the balance; it was saved by Macready and Miss Helen Faucit'.[3] This gifted young actress, whom Browning had been particularly anxious to have in his play, considered Macready's Strafford 'a fine performance', commenting that 'The character fitted in with his restless, nervous, changeable, impetuous, and emphatic style', and saying that he 'looked the

[1] *Life*, p. 84.
[2] Ibid., p. 85. The playbill advertising the first performance (repr. in *Browning Insitute Studies*, ed. W. S. Peterson, vol. 3, New York, 1975, p. 21) throws vivid light on the theatrical conditions of the time. It mentions that 'an entirely New Farce, entitled The MODERN ORPHEUS' will be performed after *Strafford*, and that the evening will 'conclude with the popular Drama entitled The TWO PAGES OF FREDERICK THE GREAT'. Browning later stated that 'the play had to be reduced by at least one third of its dialogue' on account of the incompetence of most of the actors: *Letters*, p. 297.
[3] p. 85.

very man as we knew him in Vandyck's famous picture'.[1] As
for her own performance as Lady Carlisle, Browning told
Gosse that she 'threw such tenderness and passion into the part
. . . as surpassed all that she had previously displayed of
histrionic power'.[2] So far from sharing his view that the production was skimped,[3] she later wrote that 'The play was
mounted in all matters with great care', remembering with
pleasure her own gown, 'made from a Vandyck picture', and
praising 'the thought bestowed even upon the kind of fur with
which [it] was trimmed'.

According to Griffin and Minchin the theatre was full and
the performance successful, the fall of the curtain being followed by calls for Macready (whose benefit it was), Vandenhoff, and Miss Faucit, and by cries of 'Author', 'Author'
which had to be silenced by the assurance 'that the author was
not in the house',[4] and it is clear that his friends had turned up
in force.[5] What Helen Faucit later remembered most clearly,
however, was that she 'went home very sad; for although the
play was considered a success, yet, somehow, even my small
experience seemed to tell me it would not be a very long life,
and that perhaps kind Mr. Browning would think we had not
done our best for him'.[6] Browning told Gosse that the play
'was well received on the first night, and on the second night
was applauded with enthusiasm by a crowded house',[7] and it
may have been of the second night that he was thinking
(therefore) when he wrote, in the preface to *Pippa Passes*: 'Two
or three years ago I wrote a Play, about which the chief matter
I much care to recollect at present is, that a Pit-full of good-
natured people applauded it'. The comments of William Bell
Scott, which seem to relate to the first night, give a very
different account of the matter. He heard of the play from
Leigh Hunt, and his 'admiration for *Paracelsus* was so great'
that he 'determined to go and to applaud, without rhyme or
reason; and so I did, in the front of the pit. From the first scene
it became plain that applause was not the order. The speakers

[1] op. cit., p. 225.   [2] *Personalia*, p. 45.   [3] *Personalia*, pp. 44–5.
[4] P. 109. If Browning was not in fact present, it was presumably after the second
performance that he took his father into Macready's dressing-room to shake hands
with him.
[5] Joe Dowson, for example, recalled 'being *one* of the "clappers"': Maynard, p. 107.
[6] loc. cit., p. 226.   [7] *Personalia*, pp. 45–6.

had every one of them orations to deliver, and no action of any kind to perform. The scene changed, another door opened, and another half-dozen gentlemen entered as long-winded as the last. Still I kept applauding, with some few others, till the howling was too overpowering, and the disturbance so considerable that for a few minutes I lost my hat. The truth was that the talk was too much the same, and too much in quantity; it was of no use continuing to hope something would turn up to surprise the house'.[1]

When Macready looked at the press notices, however, he 'was gratified to find [them] lenient and even kind to Browning'. He noted that even 'the "brutal and ruffianly"' *Times* 'observed that I "acquitted myself exceedingly well"'.[2] Two days later he was pleased to find a critic in the *Morning Herald* describing the play as the 'best that had been produced for many years', and the 'very kind and judicious criticism' contributed to the *Examiner* by John Forster afforded him much satisfaction. It is unlikely that he would have dissented from Forster's view that 'Mr. Vandenhoff was particularly nauseous with his whining, drawling, and slouching in Pym' or from his further comments that Webster 'whimpered in somewhat too juvenile a fashion through Young Vane' and that 'Some one should have stepped from the pit and thrust Mr. Dale from the stage'.[3] It was clear that Browning's friends had rallied round, and Macready himself gave him excellent advice when he told him (after the first performance) that 'the play was a grand escape, and that he ought to regard it only as such, a mere step to that fame which his talents must procure him'.

Browning refused to see it in that light. On Tuesday the 9th Macready wrote in his Diary:

Called on Forster, who informed me how much he had been hurt by Browning's expressions of discontent at his criticism, which I myself think only too indulgent for such a play as *Strafford*. After all that has been done for Browning with the painful apprehension of failure before us, it is not pleasing to read in his note, "Let . . . write any future tragedies"! Now, really, this is too bad—without *great assis-*

[1] *Autobiographical Notes of the Life of William Bell Scott*, ed. W. Minto (2 vols., 1892), i. 124–5.
[2] *Diaries*, i. 392.
[3] 7 May 1837 (p. 294). Litzinger and Smalley give a brief extract.

tance this tragedy could never have been put in a condition to be proposed for representation—without great assistance it never could have been put upon the stage—nor without great assistance could it ever have been carried through its "perilous" experiment. It is very unreasonable and indeed *ungrateful* in him to write thus.

The fourth performance, that evening, is said to have been greeted with 'fervid applause' by 'an admirably filled house',[1] and the play-bill announced that as the 'New Tragedy of STRAFFORD' continued 'to be received with the same marks of approbation as attended its first representation' it would be repeated 'on Thursday next'. 'Vandenhoff suddenly withdrew', however, as Browning told Gosse, 'and though Elton volunteered to take his place, the financial condition of the theatre, in spite of the undiminished popularity of the piece, put an end to its representation'.[2]

To the end of his life Browning maintained that *Strafford* owed its short run to unfavourable circumstances, and he told Gosse that 'There was every expectation that the tragedy would have no less favorable a "run" than [Talfourd's] *Ion* had enjoyed'. Macready was a better judge, however, and he must have been relieved to drop the play, having honourably done so much to help it. It is not surprising that he was angry when, on the 18th, Browning 'again evinced an irritable impatience about the representation', and when, four days later, he received another letter from Browning about his play:

as if I had done nothing for him—having worn down my spirits and strength as I have done—he now asks me to study a speech at the end of the second act, and an entire scene which I am to restore in the fourth act.[3] Such a selfish, absurd, and useless imposition to lay on me could scarcely have entered into any one's imagination. I was at first disgusted by the sickly and fretful over-estimate of his work and was angry; but reflected that he did not know what he required me to do, and had forgotten what I have done; "so let him pass, a blessing on his head!" I shall not do it.

Two years were to pass before Browning came to Macready again 'to learn . . . whether, if he wrote a really good play, it would have a secure chance of acceptance'.[4]

[1] Griffin and Minchin, p. 110.   [2] op. cit., p. 46.   [3] Cf. p. 10 above.
[4] *Strafford* was revived by the Browning Society at the Strand Theatre on 21 December 1886. Browning's letter to Furnivall, dated 13 December (*Trumpeter*, pp.

It is not difficult to identify most of the books which Browning and Forster 'turned over . . . together', as they are named in the footnotes to the Life, and it is probable that most of them were used in the composition of the play. Since the author of the Life states that 'The collection of documents known by the title of the "Strafford Papers", seems to me to contain within itself every material necessary to the illustration of the public and private character of this statesman',[1] and that it will therefore be his principal authority, it is not surprising to find Browning making extensive use of these volumes. Among the more important of the other books which he probably consulted were Clarendon's *History of the Rebellion*, the *Biographia Britannica*, John MacDiarmid's *Lives of British Statesmen* (1807), the *Memorials of the English Affairs* (1682) of Bulstrode Whitelocke, John Rushworth's *Historical Collections . . . from . . . 1618 to 1648; with Lord Strafford's Trial* (8 vols., 1659–82), and Robert Baillie's *Letters and Journals* (2 vols., Edinburgh 1775). James Wellwood's *Memoirs of the most material Transactions in England . . . preceding the Revolution in 1688* gave Browning the material from which he built up his account of the close friendship between Wentworth and Pym.

While it is understandable that Macready should have feared that the play was 'too historical' for his purposes, anyone who notices which of the events may be precisely dated will see that, by omitting all that is irrelevant to his dramatic purpose, Browning has given the impression that the events succeeded each other more swiftly than they did. Between Acts I and II Charles must be understood to have summoned the Short Parliament, and in II. i we hear of its dissolution; while between Acts II and III there occur the rout of the English forces at Newburn, the armistice at Ripon, and the summoning of the Long Parliament, so that the impeachment of Strafford is imminent.

It is interesting that two of the great historians of the seventeenth century have commented on the play. S. R. Gardiner

---

140–1), makes it evident that he still believed that the play had been let down by its original production. Cf. *Interrogating the Oracle*, by W. S. Peterson (Athens, Ohio, 1969), pp. 41 ff.

[1] *Robert Browning's Prose Life of Strafford*, p. 18. The work in question is *The Earl of Strafforde's Letters and Dispatches, with an Essay towards his Life by Sir George Radcliffe* (ed. William Knowler, 2 vols., 1739).

went so far as to state that Browning 'decisively abandoned all
attempt to be historically accurate. Only here and there does
anything in the course of the drama take place as it could have
taken place at the actual Court of Charles I. Not merely are
there frequent minor inaccuracies, but the very roots of the
situation are untrue to fact. The real Strafford was far from
opposing the war with the Scots at the time when the Short
Parliament was summoned. Pym never had such a friendship
for Strafford as he is represented as having, and to anyone who
knows anything of the habits of Charles, the idea of Pym or his
friends entering into colloquies with Strafford, and even bursting in unannounced into Charles's presence, is . . . simply
ludicrous'.[1] After such a verdict it is surprising to find him
stating that 'every time that I read the play, I feel more certain
that Mr. Browning has seized the real Strafford'.[2]

Sir Charles Firth, a historian who was more at home than
Gardiner with imaginative literature, was struck by the contrast between the Life (which he regarded as the work of
Browning) and the play. 'One might almost say that in the
first Strafford was represented as he appeared to his opponents, and in the second as he appeared to himself; or that,
having painted Strafford as he was, Browning painted him
again as he wished to be . . . as if the play were written to
supplement and correct the biography. Each contains a part of
the truth'.[3] He points out, irrefutably, that 'Strafford is judged
too much by the standards of 1832, and too little by the
standards of 1632'.

From the historian's point of view 'The main interest of
Strafford's career is political', and the interest of politics 'is
mainly indirect',[4] but Browning personalizes everything, as is
immediately evident when we consider the role assigned to
Lady Carlisle. Browning hardly overstates when he describes
her as 'purely imaginary': historically she was no 'child' nor
even a 'girl',[5] but a middle-aged woman who had become a
widow after a marriage lasting almost twenty years. We can
understand Helen Faucit's surprise that Browning wanted her

---

[1] *Strafford, with notes and preface by Emily H. Hickey . . ., and an Introduction by Samuel R. Gardiner* (1884), p. xi.
[2] Ibid., p. xiii.   [3] *Prose Life*, pp. xv–xvi.   [4] Hickey, p. xi.
[5] Strafford uses both words in the play, more than once.

to play the part of 'a woman versed in all the political struggles and intrigues of the times', as well as her astonishment that, 'depending so absolutely as he did upon her . . . , he [Strafford] should only have, in the early part, a common expression of gratitude to give her [Lady Carlisle] in return'. In the play as acted her love for Strafford is that of a young woman for a middle-aged man who appears prematurely old, whereas historically there were only a few years between the two of them; while Sir Tobie Matthew (whom Browning particularly mentions as influencing his interpretation of her character) wrote that 'She cannot love in earnest . . . Naturally she hath no passion at all':[1] a far cry from the woman whom Helen Faucit had to play. And this is only the most striking of Browning's departures from history. The friendship between Strafford and Pym, and the story of their meeting at Greenwich, rest on a slender foundation, as he probably realized; while, as H. B. George pointed out, 'it is unnecessarily departing from historical truth to make Pym force the Bill of Attainder against Strafford on a reluctant House of Commons. Pym was at first altogether against the Bill . . . , and only yielded reluctantly to the pressure of the more extreme members of the party'.[2]

As a dramatic poet, Browning was attracted by the challenge of attempting to understand and re-create this subtle-minded man whose views were so different from his own[3] but who yet resembled himself in being 'amazingly fond' of the poetry of John Donne.[4] Himself the most loyal of men, he decided to make Strafford's loyalty to a weak and ungrateful King the clue to his character. He came to see in him a figure analogous to Paracelsus and Sordello, a man with the elements of greatness in him who was yet destined to be remembered as a failure.[5]

---

[1] Quoted in DNB, in Firth's article on Lucy Hay, Countess of Carlisle.

[2] *Browning's Strafford*, ed. H. B. George (1908), p. xx.

[3] See his reference to 'my republicanism', quoted on p. 330 n below. It should be remembered, too, that his mother had been brought up in Dundee and baptised into the Church of Scotland.

[4] *Prose Life*, p. 188. For his love of Donne see also pp. 196–7 n and 205–6.

[5] Browning will have known the brief fragments of Shelley's unfinished drama, *Charles the First*, printed on pp. 237–48 of the *Posthumous Poems* of 1824. The characters include the King and Queen, Laud, Wentworth, Hampden, Pym, and the younger Vane.

We have consulted the notes to Emily Hickey's ed. throughout, citing them as

The passages quoted above from Macready's *Diaries* make it evident that *Strafford* was revised a great deal before its performance, and that the text printed on the day of the first performance was much longer than that used by the actors. Since no manuscript of the play seems to survive we are concerned with the printed edition of 1837 and its successors.

As an old man, Browning told Gosse that whereas *Paracelsus* had been printed at his father's expense, '*Strafford* was taken by Longmans, and brought out, at their expense, as a little volume,—not, like most of the tragedies of the day, in dark-gray paper covers, with a white label'. [1] It was published on 1 May, the day of the first performance. Although it is well-printed, the text contains a few minor misprints, such as 'bitter' for 'bitterer' at v ii. 278.

Although the press notices were by no means unfavourable, *Strafford* 'was as great a financial failure as *Paracelsus*'[2] and Browning did not reprint it in *1849*. He revised the play thoroughly for the collected edition of 1863.[3] He cut out many of the abundant stage-directions of 1837: some of these read oddly—for example 'rising passionately' at IV. ii. 89—but others usefully indicate movement, direction, or tone. Browning made allusions to the state of King Charles *less* comprehensible by removing the instruction '*The* KING *falls:* HOLLIS *raises him.*' from v. ii. 215. He also changed some of the entrances and exits—again, presumably, simplifying for a 'reading' edition, but perhaps with some loss of dramatic effect in a scene such as Act IV. iii.

Browning, however, must have realized that drastic pruning was needed, and most of his other cuts were judicious. Speeches formerly divided among three or four characters were re-assigned to one speaker, over-liberal expression marks were reduced, frenetic repetitions moderated, and some of the more absurd rant either cut out or re-written with

'EHH'. In 1884 Browning wrote to her: 'nothing can be better than your Notes—and, with a real wish to be of use, I read them carefully that I might detect never so tiny a fault . . .': *New Letters*, p. 297. In her preface she expressed 'very warm thanks to Mr. Browning . . . for his explanation of three or four passages'.
  [1] *Personalia*, p. 46.   [2] Ibid.
  [3] For an account of revisions made by Browning in 1862 in a copy of *Strafford* now in the Berg Collection in New York Public Library, see Appendix B. Our emendation of 'even' to 'ever' at I.ii.33 is supported by an alteration in this copy.

greater restraint. (How, one wonders, had Macready delivered the line 'But 'tis so awkward—dying in a hurry!' in the last scene? (v. ii. 178a)). Altogether Browning altered about two-thirds of the lines in the play. He added twenty lines, mostly in the first Act, including a dignified speech by Hampden (I. i. 235–252); but he cut out over a hundred lines. He seems to have aimed at compression, dramatic impact, and sober dignity. Strafford's curse, and his appeals to Pym at the end, were drastically cut, and the last words of the play were Pym's, not Strafford's. Evidently Browning came to feel he had been too ruthless here, for eighteen lines of the last scene were restored, in a revised version, in 1868.

Typographically, the 1863 edition is substantially accurate. The full-stop after 'Indeed' (II. ii. 175) seems indefensible, and we have restored the reading of 1837; but 'Nor' for 'Not' (IV. iii. 57) is perhaps acceptable: Browning, at any rate, ignored Miss Hickey's restoration of 'Not' in her editions of 1882 and 1884.

As usual, the 1865 edition contains a fair number of misprints, a few genuine revisions, and a handful of readings which may be either one or the other: 'old Vane' at I. ii. 36 and 'Bishops' war' at II. i. 90 look like revisions, whereas 'make' at IV. ii. 138 and 'Annie' at V. ii. 48 are probably misprints. We have emended at III. i. 31, where 1865's omission of 'may' spoils the metre, but have accepted as possible revisions the 1865 versions of I. ii. 280, II. ii. 263 and IV. ii. 29, and other minor alterations.

The more obvious errors of 1863 and 1865 were corrected in 1868, when Browning prepared the text carefully for the six-volume collected edition. Apart from his restoration of eighteen lines in the last scene, he made about thirty verbal changes. Most of these were single-word alterations, designed apparently to improve the style or euphony. 'They lie' for 'They'll lie' (II. ii. 283) may be a misprint, but is in keeping with 'they seek' for 'they'll seek' at III. ii. 48; 'a shame' for 'shame' (V. ii. 226) is a questionable revision. Browning also gave careful attention to the punctuation, removing more dashes and exclamation marks, and rearranging commas to produce, on the whole, a more deliberate, thoughtful effect. In the absence of proofs, it is difficult to tell whether he was responsible also for the fairly consistent changes of italic to roman type, as at I. ii. 118, II. ii. 82, and of capitals to lower-case letters (I. i. 33, 37, 189, etc.) Both of these are characteristic of the 1868 edition as a whole, but they are also in keeping with Browning's revision of *Strafford*. The few misprints in *1868* were mostly corrected in later editions. Our text, like Miss Hickey's, restores the readings of *1863,1865* at V. ii. 114 and 243.

Various corrected reprints of *1868* appeared in subsequent years. That of 1879, for example, has about a dozen punctuation changes, and corrects the misprint 'make' at IV. ii. 138. It also has 'Brooke' for 'Broke' at III. ii. 166, and 'fellow's' for 'fellows'' at III. iii. 77, but it fails to correct 'Hast' at III. ii. 57, and has a rather dubious 'revision' at III. ii. 197—'to seize these' for 'to seize the'—which has survived into all later editions. *1879*, or a similar reprint, is also the source of the misprint 'crouch.' at I. i. 88.

In December 1882 Miss Emily Hickey first produced an edition of the play, with the 'permission of the Author and Publishers' for the use of the North London Collegiate School for Girls, 'who mean to act it', as the inscription on the cover of the British Library copy says. Browning thanked her on 18 December 1882 for the 'pretty dress' she had given his play —'just the appropriate one, I think, for your purpose—which I wish, with all my heart, it may serve in any degree.'[1] She must have used a reprint such as that of 1879 as her copy-text, but may also have consulted the edition of 1863, with which her punctuation occasionally coincides. She removed a few obvious errors, and made a number of sensible improvements in punctuation. (Examples of these appear as isolated readings of '*1882,1884*' in our notes.) The interest of the edition lies in the fact that it served as a basis for the more important one of 1884, and that its existence helps to explain Browning's letter of March 24th, 1883. Miss Hickey had evidently asked leave to make an annotated edition, and Browning replied, 'You are quite welcome to edit and annotate *Strafford* as you propose. If there is any fresh printing to take place, you will kindly treat with the Publisher—as before'.[2]

---

[1] *New Letters*, p. 281.
[2] Ibid., p. 284. (The editors of the *New Letters* were not aware of the 1882 printing.)

In the preface to her revised and annotated edition of 1884 Miss Hickey wrote: 'The text of this edition has been revised by Mr. Browning. There are a good many changes in the punctuation, and a few verbal alterations.' Browning's letters show that he was indeed actively concerned in the production: he wrote to Miss Hickey from Venice on 30 November 1883, 'I return the "Proofs," corrected as far as possible— having, besides altering errors, changed a word or two, so as to strengthen the verse a little.'[1] On 19 December he wrote from Hatfield House, commenting on lines 56 and 204 in the first scene, 'I suppose we may preferably read "The Rights we claimed"—retaining the capital letter, to show the particular claim: and, at page 7., one might change "Bill" to simply "prayer." '[2] Thus the 1884 edition incorporated changes made in 1882, and added a number of useful and authoritative emendations.

When Browning was correcting his poems for the 1888 edition, he borrowed Miss Hickey's copy of the 1884 text to remind himself of the changes he had made. He wrote to her on 25 October 1887, 'Thank you exceedingly for the *Strafford*—which I had fancied might contain more important corrections than proves to be the case. I will return the copy to you—fortunately in person . . .' In fact Browning adopted only about a dozen of the punctuation revisions newly introduced in 1884, and only three of the verbal emendations: 'Right' at I. i. 202, 'right . . . sanctions' at I. i. 232, and 'fault too' at V. ii. 311. He chose to ignore about a hundred of the *1884* revisions—understandably, perhaps, in matters of punctuation; but it is surprising that he did not use at least some of the substantive emendations at I. i. 56, 204, 260; I. ii. 192; III. ii. 75; IV. iii. 32, 51; and V. ii. 40, 144, 168, and 191.

The edition of 1888, then, hardly departs significantly from that of 1868, though Browning, like Miss Hickey, probably used a late corrected reprint of that edition. He made a few independent changes of punctuation—mainly rearrangements of commas and the removal of yet more exclamation-marks—and some half-dozen unimportant verbal changes (for example, the replacing of 'That' by 'Which' on three

---

[1] *New Letters*, p. 291.   [2] Ibid., p. 294, text corrected from MS.

occasions.) Possibly his proof-reading was hasty, for the 1888 *Strafford* is rather carelessly printed. We have corrected about 25 minor misprints, by restoring the readings of earlier editions, or of the Dykes Campbell copy of *1888*. In the latter Browning made 11 corrections, introduced two upper-case initials for 'time', and slightly altered the phrasing of three passages (I. ii. 232–3, II. ii. 206, and IV. i. 44). The last of these ('And they dare' instead of 'And they mean') had been a revision in the 1884 edition.

The edition of 1889 incorporated all but four of the Dykes Campbell corrections, but failed to correct most of the other errors. Our text is based on that of 1888, emended by reference to the Dykes Campbell copy or to previous editions. We record but do not incorporate the revisions peculiar to *1884*, since the 1888 edition, however imperfect, has Browning's final authority. In our recording of variants we have aimed to include all substantive changes, but have been more selective than usual in our recording of accidentals. The large number of different editions and the nature of the revision of the first edition have produced many variants of minimal significance; we have not, therefore, recorded such variants as the habitual replacement of a series of dots in *1837* by a dash in *1863*.

STRAFFORD;

A TRAGEDY.

DEDICATED, IN ALL AFFECTIONATE
ADMIRATION,
TO
WILLIAM C. MACREADY.

LONDON: *April* 23, 1837.

MACREADY: in 1837 'Esq.' followed the name, as did the words 'by His Most Grateful and Devoted Friend, R. B.' The wording was changed in *1863* in consequence of the estrangement of the two men occasioned by the production of *A Blot in the 'Scutcheon*. 23 April is St. George's day and the traditional day of Shakespeare's birth. The word 'LONDON' was added in *1868*.

PERSONS.

CHARLES I.

Earl of HOLLAND.

Lord SAVILE.

Sir HENRY VANE.

WENTWORTH, Viscount WENTWORTH, Earl of STRAFFORD.

JOHN PYM.

JOHN HAMPDEN.

The younger VANE.

DENZIL HOLLIS.

BENJAMIN RUDYARD.

NATHANIEL FIENNES.

Earl of LOUDON.

MAXWELL, *Usher of the Black Rod.*

BALFOUR, *Constable of the Tower.*

A Puritan.

Queen HENRIETTA.

LUCY PERCY, Countess of Carlisle.

Presbyterians, Scots Commissioners, Adherents of Strafford, Secretaries, Officers of the Court, &c. Two of Strafford's children.

STRAFFORD.

ACT I.

SCENE I.—*A House near Whitehall.* HAMPDEN, HOLLIS, *the* younger VANE, RUDYARD, FIENNES *and many of the Presbyterian Party:* LOUDON *and other Scots Commissioners.*

s.d. *1837* HAMPDEN, ... *Commissioners: some seated, some standing beside a table strewn over with papers, &c.* 1 *1837* here . . .|RUDYARD. And he is here!

s.d. HAMPDEN Having been imprisoned for refusing to pay the forced loan of 1626, he became prominent in Charles's third parliament. He was a close associate of Sir John Eliot. In 1635 he resisted the ship-money writ. In Forster's biography of Hampden in the 3rd vol. of his *Eminent British Statesmen* 'the wonderful influence of his character' is emphasized, and the fact that Pym was 'the dearest and most intimate of his friends'. HOLLIS opposed Buckingham's foreign policy. When the King ordered the Speaker to adjourn the Commons on 2 March 1629, Hollis held him in his chair; and at the end of the sitting he recited and put to the House Eliot's resolutions against innovation in religion and arbitrary taxation. For seven or eight years he lived in banishment. 'The earl of Strafford had married his sister: so, though in the parliament he was one of the hottest men of the party, yet when that matter was before them, he always withdrew': *Life*, p. 401 (p. 267 in the edition of 1892; subsequent references are given to both editions, in this way), quoting Burnet. The younger VANE was a religious enthusiast who adopted decidedly puritan views. In 1632 he returned from the embassy in Vienna, going to New England in 1635 and being Governor of Massachusetts, 1636–7. At this time he was Treasurer of the Navy. Forster's vol. iv has a biography of him. RUDYARD was a minor man of letters who had associated with Ben Jonson. Originally a supporter of the King, he came to see 1628 as 'the crisis of Parliaments', since 'If we persevere, the king to draw one way, the parliament another, the Commonwealth must sink in the midst'. He strongly opposed the King's claim to the right of arrest without showing cause. FIENNES was on the threshold of his parliamentary career at this time: he was to make a famous speech against episcopacy in the Long Parliament. LOUDON (John Campbell, first Earl) had his patent for an English earldom stopped by the King in 1633 because of his strong opposition to episcopacy. In 1637–8 he took a leading part in organising the Covenant, and in 1639 he was a leader of the armed resurrection in Scotland. EHH points out that 'The party to which Pym and others belonged was not, at this time, a *Presbyterian party*. It was opposed to Charles politically, and to Laud ecclesiastically. It had strongly resented recent ceremonials in which Laud had taken a most prominent part. If any member of it could at this time have been called a Presbyterian, it would have been Fiennes'.

The action of the play begins in November 1639, and ends in May 1641. As EHH points out, Browning followed the same authorities as those used in the *Life*, 'hence the date of November instead of September'.

Vane. I say, if he be here—
Rudyard.   (And he is here!)—
Hollis. For England's sake let every man be
    still
Nor speak of him, so much as say his name,
Till Pym rejoin us! Rudyard! Henry Vane!
One rash conclusion may decide our course   5
And with it England's fate—think—England's
    fate!
Hampden, for England's sake they should be
    still!
    Vane. You say so, Hollis? Well, I must be
    still.
It is indeed too bitter that one man,
Any one man's mere presence, should suspend   10
England's combined endeavour: little need
To name him!
    Rudyard.   For you are his brother, Hollis!
    Hampden. Shame on you, Rudyard! time to
    tell him that,
When he forgets the Mother of us all.
    Rudyard. Do I forget her?
    Hampden.   You talk idle hate   15
Against her foe: is that so strange a thing?
Is hating Wentworth all the help she needs?

4,5 *1837* Rudyard—Vane—remember|One   *8 {Reading of DC and
1889}   *1837* well, I must be still! *1863,1865* Well, I must be still! *1888* {some
copies} Well, I must be still   9–12 *1837* It is . . . . that one man—|Any one
man . . .|RUDYARD. You are his brother, Hollis! *1863–82* It is . . . . that one
man,|Any one man's mere presence should suspend|England's combined
endeavour: little need|To name him!|*Rud.* For you are his brother, Hollis!
1888 {as text, except that some copies have 'I is'}   10,11 {Not in *1837*}

---

4 *Pym*: he had attained prominence in 1621, being one of the managers of
Buckingham's impeachment in 1626. He supported the Petition of Right two
years later, and took part in the final attack on Buckingham. In 1629 he
opposed the imposition of tonnage and poundage, but took no part in the
disturbance which marked the end of the session and therefore was not one of
those imprisoned. In the Short Parliament he would speak at length on grievances, and oppose supplies. He is the subject of a biography in vol. iii of
Forster's *Eminent British Statesmen.* The seventh of the *Parleyings with Certain
People of Importance in their Day* (1887)—that with Charles Avison—concludes
with the words and music of a song in honour of Pym, strong evidence of
Browning's lifelong admiration for him.
14 *the Mother of us all*: England.

A Puritan. The Philistine strode, cursing as he
    went:
But David—five smooth pebbles from the
    brook
Within his scrip . . .   20
    Rudyard.   Be you as still as David!
    Fiennes. Here's Rudyard not ashamed to wag a
    tongue
Stiff with ten years' disuse of Parliaments;
Why, when the last sat, Wentworth sat with us!
    Rudyard. Let 's hope for news of them now he
    returns—
He that was safe in Ireland, as we thought!   25
—But I 'll abide Pym's coming.
    Vane   Now, by Heaven,
They may be cool who can, silent who will—
Some have a gift that way! Wentworth is here,
Here, and the King 's safe closeted with him
Ere this. And when I think on all that 's past   30
Since that man left us, how his single arm
Rolled the advancing good of England back
And set the woeful past up in its place,

24 *1837* returns: 25 {Not in *1837*}   *26 {Reading of *1884* and DC}
1837–82,1889 I'll abide . . . . Heaven *1888* I'll bide . . . . Heaven   *27
{Reading of *1863–84*} *1837* They may be cool that can, silent that
can, *1888,1889* Then may be cool who can, silent who will— {'They' pencil-
led in margin of DC}   28–9 *1837* way: Wentworth is here—|
Here—and   30 *1837* this! and   31 *1837* us— *1882,1884* us;   32 *1837*
Roll'd back the good of England, roll'd it back   33 *1837* Past up in its
place . . . *1863,1865* Past up in its place,—

18 *The Philistine*: 'And he took his staff in his hand, and chose him five
smooth stones out of the brook, and put them in a shepherd's bag which he
had, even in a scrip; and his sling was in his hand: and he drew near to the
Philistine . . . And the Philistine cursed David by his gods': 1 Samuel 17:40, 43.
Browning reproduces the Biblical idioms and allusions characteristic of many
of the puritan party.
22 *ten years' disuse*: Charles dissolved Parliament on 10 March 1629, as a result
of the dispute about tonnage and poundage, Eliot and others being imprisoned.
Parliament was next summoned on 13 April 1640.
23 *sat with us!*: during Charles's third Parliament, in March 1628, Wentworth
spoke strongly against grievances. 'Whether we shall look upon the king or his
people, it did never more behove this great physician, the parliament, to effect a
true consent amongst the parties than now . . . both . . . [are] innocent, yet
both are injured; both to be cured': *Life*, p. 222 (p. 54). For the charge that
Wentworth became a 'renegade' see I. i. 89 n.
25 *safe in Ireland*: Wentworth came to England to assist the King, on the
latter's order and assurance of his safety, in September 1639.

Exalting Dagon where the Ark should be,—
How that man has made firm the fickle King   35
(Hampden, I will speak out!)—in aught he
    feared
To venture on before; taught tyranny
Her dismal trade, the use of all her tools,
To ply the scourge yet screw the gag so close
That strangled agony bleeds mute to death;   40
How he turns Ireland to a private stage
For training infant villanies, new ways
Of wringing treasure out of tears and blood,
Unheard oppressions nourished in the dark
To try how much man's nature can endure   45
—If he dies under it, what harm? if not,
Why, one more trick is added to the rest
Worth a king's knowing, and what Ireland bears
England may learn to bear:—how all this while
That man has set himself to one dear task,   50
The bringing Charles to relish more and more
Power, power without law, power and blood
    too
—Can I be still?

34 *1837* A PURITAN. Exalting . . . . be!| VANE. . . . How that *1863,1865* Exalt-
ing . . . . be—|How that   36 *1837*—Hampden, I will speak out!—   37
1837–65 Tyranny   *40 {Reading of DC and *1889*.}   *1837* death: *1863–88*
death—   43 *1837* tears and gore,   45 *1837* Man's   46–9 *1837* if not
. . .| FIENNES. Why, one more trick is added to the rest| Worth a King's know-
ing—| RUDYARD.—And what Ireland bears| England may learn to bear.| VANE.
. . . How all this while   *1863,1865* as *1888* except 'bear:'   *1882,1884* as *1888*
except 'King's'   52–3 *1837* Power . . .| RUDYARD. Power without law
. . .| FIENNES. Power and blood too . .| VANE. . . . Can I be still?   *1863,1865* as
1888 except 'too—'   *1868–84* as *1888* except 'too,'

34 *Dagon*: 'When the Philistines took the ark of God, they brought it into the
house of Dagon, and set it by Dagon': 1 Samuel 5:2.
    39 *To ply the scourge*: cf. *Sordello* vi. 770: 'Kings of the gag and flesh-hook,
screw and whip'.
    41 *Ireland*: on 12 January 1632 Wentworth had been appointed Lord Deputy
of Ireland. The *Life* gives a highly unfavourable account of his Irish policy, on
which he particularly prided himself: 'When England herself . . . began to
groan under oppressions, Ireland felt them still more heavily, and was flung
back with a greater shock. The arbitrary decrees of Charles's privy council,
military exactions, and martial law, were strangling the liberties of Ireland *in
their very birth*': *Life*, p. 261 (p. 99). Cf. Firth's Introduction, pp. xxxii–iii.
    52 *power without law*: 'God be praised', Wentworth wrote to the King from
Dublin on 9 September 1639, 'no King can be more absolute than your Majesty

Hampden.   For that you should be still.
Vane.   Oh Hampden, then and now! The year
   he left us,
The People in full Parliament could wrest   55
The Bill of Rights from the reluctant King;
And now, he 'll find in an obscure small room
A stealthy gathering of great-hearted men
That take up England's cause: England is here!
Hampden. And who despairs of England?   60
 Rudyard.   That do I,
If Wentworth comes to rule her. I am sick
To think her wretched masters, Hamilton,
The muckworm Cottington, the maniac Laud,

---

54 *1837* Oh, ... us   *1863,1865* Oh, ... us,   *1884* Oh . . . . us.   55 *1837*
The People by its Parliament   56 *1837* The Bill of Rights from . . .
King: *1884* The rights we claimed from . . . . King;   57 *1837*
now,—   59 *1837* England is—here!   60–1 *1837* That do I | If Wentworth
is to

---

is amongst us : *Strafforde's Letters and Dispatches*, ii. 387. 'He had certainly
entered Ireland with one paramount object', observes the author of the *Life*:
'—that of making his master "the most absolute prince in Christendom", in so
far as regarded that "conquered country."' (p. 297 (142)). On Wentworth's
'despotic genius' see also pp. 307 and 411 (pp. 155 and 278).

54 *The year he left us*: 1628.

56 *The Bill of Rights*: an error for the Petition of Right, passed in the
Parliament of 1628, as Miss Hickey obviously pointed out. 'I suppose we may
preferably read "The Rights we claimed"', Browning wrote on 19 December
1883, '—returning [retaining] the capital letter, to show the particular claim:
and, at page 7. [l. 204], one might change "Bill" to simply "prayer"': *New
Letters*, p. 294. (Miss Harriet McLoone of the Huntington Library kindly
confirms that 'retaining' is what Browning wrote.) Miss Hickey emended
accordingly, but Browning failed to make the corrections in 1888. The correct
phrase is used in l. 202. When Charles gave his assent to the Petition, on 7 June
1628, he acknowledged that a King could not levy taxes without the consent of
Parliament or imprison any man without reason shown.

57 *an obscure small room*: 'Historically, in Pym's house': EHH.

62 *Hamilton*: the King's 'favourite scheme was to deliver up the three
divisions of the kingdom to the superintendence of three favourite ministers,
reserving to himself a general and not inactive control over all. Laud was the
minister for England, and the affairs of Scotland were in the hands of the
marquess of Hamilton. Ireland, accepted by Wentworth, completed the proposed plan': *Life*, p. 260 (p. 98). 'Wentworth, Laud, and Hamilton. . . . formed a
secret council—a "cabinet council," as they were then enviously named by the
other courtiers—a "junto," as the people reproachfully called them': ibid., p.
366 (p. 225).

63 *Cottington*: Francis, Lord Cottington, a close associate of Wentworth who
in July 1638 became a member of the committee for Scots affairs. He was
chancellor of the exchequer, and supported the idea of war with Scotland,
arguing that in such a situation moneys might be raised without the agreement
of parliament. Clarendon states that although he was 'much less hated' than
Wentworth or Laud he was 'as odious as any to the great reformers': *History of*

May yet be longed-for back again. I say,
I do despair.   65
    Vane.   And, Rudyard, I 'll say this—
Which all true men say after me, not loud
But solemnly and as you 'd say a prayer!
This King, who treads our England underfoot,
Has just so much . . . it may be fear or craft,
As bids him pause at each fresh outrage; friends,   70
He needs some sterner hand to grasp his own,
Some voice to ask, "Why shrink? Am I not by?"
Now, one whom England loved for serving her,
Found in his heart to say, "I know where best
"The iron heel shall bruise her, for she leans   75
"Upon me when you trample." Witness, you!
So Wentworth heartened Charles, so England
    fell.
But inasmuch as life is hard to take
From England . . .
    Many Voices. Go on, Vane! 'T is well said,
      Vane!
    Vane. —Who has not so forgotten
      Runnymead!—   80
    Voices. 'T is well and bravely spoken, Vane!
      Go on!
    Vane. —There are some little signs of late she
      knows

---

66 *1837* And, *(turning to the rest)* all true men say after me! not loud—   67
1837 prayer: 68 *1837* This Charles, who . . . . under foot,   69 *1837–65*
much—it . . . . craft—   72 *1837–65* shrink?—am   73 *1837*—A man that
England   77{Not in *1837*.} *1863,1865* Charles, and England   80 *1837* . . .
Who has . . . . Runnymead . . .   *1882,1884* Who has . . . . Runnymead!—

---

the Rebellion, ed. W. Dunn Macray (6 vols., 1888), Book ii, para. 102. All
quotations are from this edition, by Book and paragraph.
   63 *Laud*: William Laud became predominant in the Church of England on
the accession of Charles in 1625. He supported the King in his struggles with
the Commons, and was appointed Archbishop of Canterbury in 1633. It was
his policy to impose compulsory uniformity of action on the part of church-
men. His interference with the Scottish Church was disastrous. 'Of all the
suggesters of the infamous counsels of Charles, Laud and Wentworth were the
most sincere . . . Their friendship, in consequence, notwithstanding Wentworth's immense superiority in point of intellect, continued tolerably firm and
steady': *Life*, p. 313 (p. 162).
   75 *heel shall bruise*: cf. Genesis 3:15   82 *she*: England.

The ground no place for her. She glances round,
Wentworth has dropped the hand, is gone his
    way
On other service: what if she arise?   85
No! the King beckons, and beside him stands
The same bad man once more, with the same
    smile
And the same gesture. Now shall England
    crouch,
Or catch at us and rise?
   Voices.   The Renegade!
Haman! Ahithophel!   90
   Hampden.   Gentlemen of the North,

---

83 *1837* for her! no place for her! *1863,1865* for her! She glances round,   84–5 {Not in *1837*.}   86 *1837* When the King beckons— *87–90 {Reading of *1863–68,1889*} *1837* smile,| And the same savage gesture! Now let England| Make proof of us.| VOICES. Strike him—the Renegade—|Haman—Ahithophel—|HAMPDEN. *(To the Scots.)* Gentlemen of the North, *1879–88* as *1889* except 'crouch.' {Comma inked in over full-stop in DC.}

---

89 *The Renegade!*: it was inevitable that Wentworth should have been widely regarded as a renegade. There is an interesting rebuttal of the charge in the *Life*, in a passage which (as Gardner observes in his introduction to Miss Hickey's edition, p. ix) 'rises far above Mr. Forster's ordinary level', no doubt because it was written by Browning: 'In one word, what it is desired to impress upon the reader, before the delineation of Wentworth in his after years, is this—*that he was consistent to himself throughout.* I have always considered that much good wrath is thrown away upon what is usually called "apostacy". In the majority of cases, if the circumstances are thoroughly examined, it will be found that there has been "no such thing." . . . those who carry their researches into the moral nature of mankind, cannot do better than impress upon their minds, at the outset, that in the regions they explore, they are to expect no monsters . . . Infinitely and distinctly various as appear the shifting hues of our common nature when subjected to the prism of CIRCUMSTANCE, each ray into which it is broken is no less in itself a primitive colour, susceptible, indeed, of vast modification, but incapable of further division. Indolence, however, in its delight for broad classifications, finds its account in overlooking this; and among the results, none is more conspicuous than the long list of apostates with which history furnishes us': *Life*, pp. 228–9 (pp. 60–1). Browning's authorship of the passage is confirmed by the immediate mention of 'Ezzelin', an obvious reminiscence of his reading for *Sordello*. It is curious that the future author of 'The Lost Leader' should have written in this manner.

90 *Haman*: having been promoted by Ahasuerus, 'and set . . . above all the princes that were with him', Haman treacherously 'sought to destroy all the Jews that were throughout the whole kingdom': Esther 3, 1,6. In the end he was hanged.

  Ahithophel: 'And Ahithophel was the king's counsellor': 1 Chronicles 27:33. Cf. 2 Samuel 17:7, 15. Dryden's *Absalom and Achitophel* epitomizes the notion of Ahithophel as an evil counsellor.

It was not thus the night your claims were
    urged,
And we pronounced the League and Covenant,
The cause of Scotland, England's cause as well:
Vane there, sat motionless the whole night
    through.
  Vane. Hampden!   95
  Fiennes.   Stay, Vane!
  Loudon.   Be just and patient, Vane!
  Vane. Mind how you counsel patience,
    Loudon! you
Have still a Parliament, and this your League
To back it; you are free in Scotland still:
While we are brothers, hope 's for England yet.
But know you wherefore Wentworth comes? to
    quench   100
This last of hopes? that he brings war with him?
Know you the man's self? what he dares?
  Loudon   We know,
All know—'t is nothing new.
  Vane.   And what 's new,
    then,
In calling for his life? Why, Pym himself—
You must have heard—ere Wentworth dropped
    our cause   105

---

91 *1863,1865* thus,   92 *1837–65* Covenant   93 *1837* Of Scotland to be England's cause as well! *1863,1865* The cause of Scotland, England's cause as well!   95 *1837* Be patient, gallant Vane!   97 *1837* and a brave League   98 *1837* still—   99,99a,100 *1837* While we are brothers (as these hands are knit| So let our hearts be!)—hope's for England yet!| But know you why this Wentworth comes? to quench   101–3 *1837* This faintest hope? that he brings war with him?| Know you this Wentworth? What he dares?| LOUDON. Dear Vane,| We know—'tis nothing new . . .| 105 *1837* Wentworth left our cause

    92 *the League and Covenant*: the Covenant was a declaration of adherence to Presbyterianism drawn up and signed in Scotland in 1638 as a protest against the King's attempt to impose the English liturgy. In 1643 the Scots and the Parliamentary leaders agreed to introduce the Covenant into England: this was termed 'the Solemn League and Covenant'. Here and at I. ii. 190–1 the title is incorrectly given to the original Covenant.
    96 *Loudon*: John Campbell, first Earl of Loudoun, took a prominent part in the renewal of the Covenant in 1638. On 18 June 1639 he was one of the Scots commissioners at the short-lived pacification of Berwick.
    101 *war*: war against Scotland.

He would see Pym first; there were many
   more
Strong on the people's side and friends of his,
Eliot that's dead, Rudyard and Hampden here,
But for these Wentworth cared not; only, Pym
He would see—Pym and he were sworn, 't is
   said,   110
To live and die together; so, they met
At Greenwich. Wentworth, you are sure, was
   long,
Specious enough, the devil's argument
Lost nothing on his lips; he 'd have Pym own
A patriot could not play a purer part   115
Than follow in his track; they two combined

---

107 *1837* People's side and friends of his,—   109–10 *1837* But Wentworth
cared not for them; only, Pym|He . . . . sworn, they say,   111 *1837*
together—so   112 *1837* Greenwich: 114 *1837* nothing in his   115
1837 A Patriot could not do a purer thing

---

106 *He would see Pym first*: Firth has an important passage on the tradition of
the early friendship between Wentworth and Pym in his introduction to the
Life. Pointing out that it 'supplies one of the leading motives of Browning's
play, and is also referred to in this biography', he continues: 'In the year 1700,
Dr. James Welwood, one of the physicians of William III., published a volume
entitled *Memoirs of the most material transactions in England for the last hundred years
preceding the Revolution of 1688*. It consists of historical anecdotes and traditions,
but does contain a certain amount of fact and a few documents. Speaking of
Strafford, Welwood tells the following story (p. 47). "There had been a long
and intimate friendship betwixt Mr. Pym and him, and they had gone hand in
hand in everything in the House of Commons. But when Sir Thomas Wentworth was upon making his peace with the Court, he sent to Pym to meet him
alone at Greenwich; where he began in a set speech to sound Mr. Pym about
the dangers they were like to run by the courses they were in; and what
advantages they might have if they would but listen to some offers which
would probably be made them from the Court. Pym understanding his speech
stopped him short with this expression: 'You need not use all this art to tell me
you have a mind to leave us; but remember what I tell you, you are going to be
undone. But remember, that though you leave us now I will never leave you
while your head is upon your shoulders.' " The incident is not very probable
. . . Welwood . . . certainly exaggerates their political agreement and perhaps
their personal intimacy also': pp. lxii–iii.
   108 *Eliot that's dead*: the presence of Sir John Eliot, the great Parliamentarian,
is felt throughout the play. His *Life* precedes that of Strafford in the second
volume of Forster's *Eminent British Statesmen*. 'He did not survive to be an actor
in the scene during the most *obvious* part of the great contest', Forster writes in
the preface; 'and posterity has been so much occupied with those who did, that
they are startled when they have leisure to look back, and see these older and
not less noble shapes of its commencement,—these less bodily, yet hardly less
visible, demi-gods,—who were its first inspiring minds. Eliot was the greatest
actor in the outbreak of the Revolution, though it became ultimately the more
memorable part of his lot to think and to suffer'. He died in the Tower in 1632.

Might put down England. Well, Pym heard him
    out;
One glance—you know Pym's eye—one word
    was all:
"You leave us, Wentworth! while your head is
    on,
"I'll not leave you." 120
    Hampden.   Has he left Wentworth,
    then?
Has England lost him? Will you let him speak,
Or put your crude surmises in his mouth?
Away with this! Will you have Pym or Vane?
    Voices. Wait Pym's arrival! Pym shall speak.
    Hampden.   Meanwhile
Let Loudon read the Parliament's report 125
From Edinburgh: our last hope, as Vane says,
Is in the stand it makes. Loudon!
    Vane.   No, no!
Silent I can be: not indifferent!
    Hampden. Then each keep silence, praying
    God to spare
His anger, cast not England quite away 130
In this her visitation!
    A Puritan.   Seven years long
The Midianite drove Israel into dens
And caves. Till God sent forth a mighty man,
              PYM *enters.*
Even Gideon!

---

    117 *1837* Could put . . . . out—   119 *1837* Wentworth: while . . . .
on   120 *1837* Has Pym left   123 *1837* this! (*To the rest.*) Will you   124
1837 shall speak!   127 *1837* VANE. (*As* LOUDON *is about to read*)—No—
no—   129–31 *1837* praying God a space| That he will not cast England quite
away| In this her visitation! (*All assume a posture of reverence.*)   134 *1837* Even
Gideon! (*All start up.*)| PYM. Wentworth's come: he has not reached

---

118 *Pym's eye*: cf. II. ii. 138.
131 *Seven years long*: 'And the children of Israel did evil in the sight of the
LORD: and the LORD delivered them into the hand of Midian seven years. And
the hand of Midian prevailed against Israel: and because of the Midianites the
children of Israel made them the dens which are in the mountains, and caves,
and strong holds': Judges 6:1–2. In verses 11–12 we read of Gideon, who is to
be their saviour, a 'mighty man of valour'.

Pym.   Wentworth 's come: nor sickness, care,

The ravaged body nor the ruined soul,   135

More than the winds and waves that beat his ship,

Could keep him from the King. He has not reached

Whitehall: they 've hurried up a Council there

To lose no time and find him work enough.

Where 's Loudon? your Scots' Parliament . . .   140

Loudon.   Holds firm:

We were about to read reports.

Pym.   The King

Has just dissolved your Parliament.

Loudon and other Scots.   Great God!

An oath-breaker! Stand by us, England, then!

Pym. The King's too sanguine; doubtless Wentworth 's here;

But still some little form might be kept up.   145

Hampden. Now speak, Vane! Rudyard, you had much to say!

Hollis. The rumour 's false, then . . .

Pym.   Ay, the Court gives out

135–7 {Not in *1837*.}   140 *1837* Parliament . . . |LOUDON. Is firm: 141
1837 reports . . .   142 *1837* OTHER OF THE SCOTS.   146–7 *1837* HOLLIS.
Now . . . . say!| HAMPDEN. The rumour's false, then . . .

134 *Wentworth's come*: 'He had arranged everything for his departure [from
Ireland], when one of his paroxysms of illness seized him. He wrestled with it
desperately, and set sail . . . He rallied, . . . and appeared in London in
November, 1639': *Life*, p. 366 (p. 225). Cf EHH note at the beginning of the
play.

142 *your Parliament*: 'Wentworth's share in Scottish affairs began in the
autumn of 1639, when, after some fighting in Scotland, generally unfavourable
to the royal cause, Charles had patched up a peace with the rebels. The Scottish
Parliament making demands which the king refused, he prorogued it, and
another war became inevitable': George, p. x. Charles is called an 'oath-
breaker' because when the General Assembly, which met in 1639 in accordance
with the Treaty of Berwick, abolished episcopacy, the King declared the
session at an end.

147 *the Court gives out*: 'Charles had written to Wentworth in these terms: "I
have . . . too much to desire your counsel and attendance for some time, which
I think not fit to express by letter, more than this—the Scots' Covenant begins
to spread too far. Yet, for all this, I will not have you take notice that I have sent
for you, but pretend some other occasion of business': EHH.

His own concerns have brought him back: I
    know
'T is the King calls him. Wentworth supersedes
The tribe of Cottingtons and Hamiltons   150
Whose part is played; there 's talk enough, by
    this,—
Merciful talk, the King thinks: time is now
To turn the record's last and bloody leaf
Which, chronicling a nation's great despair,
Tells they were long rebellious, and their lord   155
Indulgent, till, all kind expedients tried,
He drew the sword on them and reigned in
    peace.
Laud's laying his religion on the Scots
Was the last gentle entry: the new page
Shall run, the King thinks, "Wentworth thrust it
    down   160
"At the sword's point."
    A Puritan.   I 'll do your bidding,
    Pym,
England's and God's—one blow!
    Pym.   A goodly
    thing—
We all say, friends, it is a goodly thing
To right that England. Heaven grows dark
    above:
Let's snatch one moment ere the thunder fall,   165
To say how well the English spirit comes out
Beneath it! All have done their best, indeed,

149 *1837* 'Tis Charles recalls him: he's to supersede   *1863–82* as *1888* except
'him:'   154 *1837* That, chronicling a Nation's   *1863–84* That, chronicling a
nation's   155 *1837* Lord   159 *1837* entry:—   162–4 *1837* England's
and your's . . one blow!|PYM. A glorious thing—|We all say, friends, it is a
glorious thing|To right that England! Heaven grows dark above,—   *1863,65*
as *1888* except 'England!'   165 *1837* thunder fall   *1882* thunderfall,

149 *Wentworth supersedes*: on 22 September Wentworth informally became
the King's chief counsellor.
157 *He drew the sword on them*: 'The nature of the measures to be taken against
the Scots was variously and earnestly discussed, and Wentworth, considering
the extremity of affairs, declared at once for war': *Life*, p. 366 (p. 225).
158 *Laud's laying his religion on the Scots*: Laud's interference in the religious
affairs of Scotland was to lead to his downfall.
164 *To right*: 'To do justice to; . . . to relieve from wrong': Johnson.

From lion Eliot, that grand Englishman,
To the least here: and who, the least one here,
When she is saved (for her redemption dawns   170
Dimly, most dimly, but it dawns—it dawns)
Who 'd give at any price his hope away
Of being named along with the Great Men?
We would not—no, we would not give that up!
    Hampden. And one name shall be dearer than
      all names.   175
When children, yet unborn, are taught that name
After their fathers',—taught what matchless
    man . . .
    Pym . . . . Saved England? What if
      Wentworth's should be still
That name?
    Rudyard and others. We have just said it, Pym!
      His death
Saves her! We said it—there 's no way beside!   180
I 'll do God's bidding, Pym! They struck down
    Joab
And purged the land.
    Vane.   No villanous
    striking-down!
    Rudyard. No, a calm vengeance: let the whole
      land rise
And shout for it. No Feltons!
    Pym.   Rudyard, no!
England rejects all Feltons; most of all   185

---

170 *1837* When She is saved (and her redemption dawns *1863* as *1888* except
'dawns,'   171 *1837* dawns—it dawns)—   174 *1837* One would not . . no,
one would   175 *1837* names: 177 *1837* taught one matchless   180,181
1837 Saves her!|FIENNES. We said that! There's no way beside!|A PURITAN. I'll do
your bidding, Pym!   183 *1837* No—a calm   184 *1837* Rudyard, no!

181 *Joab*: Solomon had the treacherous Joab killed in the tabernacle, in just
vengeance for his murders: 'Their blood shall therefore return upon the head of
Joab, and upon the head of his seed for ever: but upon David, and upon his seed,
and upon his house, and upon his throne, shall there be peace for ever from the
LORD': I Kings 2. 33.

184 *No Feltons!*: John Felton murdered the Duke of Buckingham in 1628,
believing this to be for the public good. 'Secret congratulations passed, within
a few days after this event, between Wentworth and Weston' *Life*, p. 246 (p.
81). For Weston see note to I. ii. 96.

Since Wentworth . . . Hampden, say the trust
    again
Of England in her servants—but I 'll think
You know me, all of you. Then, I believe,
Spite of the past, Wentworth rejoins you,
    friends!
    Vane and others. Wentworth? Apostate! Judas!
    Double-dyed   190
A traitor! Is it Pym, indeed . . .
    Pym.   . . . Who says
Vane never knew that Wentworth, loved that
    man,
Was used to stroll with him, arm locked in arm,
Along the streets to see the people pass,
And read in every island-countenance   195
Fresh argument for God against the King,—
Never sat down, say, in the very house
Where Eliot's brow grew broad with noble
    thoughts,
(You 've joined us, Hampden—Hollis, you as
    well,)
And then left talking over Gracchus' death . . .   200
    Vane. To frame, we know it well, the choicest
    clause
In the Petition of Right: he framed such clause

186–7 *1837* say the praise again | That England will award me . . . *1884* as
1888 except 'servants!—'   189 *1837*—Spite of the past,— *1863,1865* Spite
of the Past,   190 *1837* RUDYARD *and others.* Wentworth! apostate . . . | VANE.
Wentworth, double-dyed *1863,1865 Vane and others.* Wentworth? apostate!
Judas! double-dyed   192 *1837* Wentworth—loved that Wentworth—| Felt
glad to stroll with him, arm lock'd in arm,   194 *1837* People pass *1863–82*
people pass   197 *1837* sate down . . . say,   199 *1837* Hampden,   201
1837 . . To frame, we know it Pym, the   202 *1837* Rights: which Wentworth
framed *1863–82* Rights: he framed such clause

190 *Apostate!*: cf. 89 n, above, and IV. ii. 120 n., below. Pym termed Wentworth 'the grand Apostate of the Commonwealth'.
200 *Gracchus' death*: 'Both the Gracchi, Tiberius and Caius . . . were prominent as "people's men", and both died the death of martyrs for the people's
cause. Tiberius the elder, who seems to be the one alluded to here, was *tribune*
of the people . . . in the year B.C. 133 . . . Caius became tribune in 123 B.C., and
carried out his brother's reforms with others still more sweeping. He fell in the
year 121 B.C.': EHH.
201 *the choicest clause*: probably that against arbitrary imprisonment. For the
'Petition of Right' see note to l. 56, above.
202 *he framed*: the speech which Wentworth made to Charles's third Parlia-

One month before he took at the King's hand
His Northern Presidency, which that Bill
Denounced.   205
    Pym   Too true! Never more, never more
Walked we together! Most alone I went.
I have had friends—all here are fast my
    friends—
But I shall never quite forget that friend.
And yet it could not but be real in him!
You, Vane,—you, Rudyard, have no right to
    trust   210
To Wentworth: but can no one hope with me?
Hampden, will Wentworth dare shed English
    blood
Like water?
    Hampden. Ireland is Aceldama.

203 *1837* A month   204 *1884* which that Prayer   205,205a–b *1837*
Denounced . . . . .|RUDYARD. And infamy along with it!|A PURITAN. For
whoso putteth his right-hand to the plough|And turneth back . . .|PYM. Never
more, never more   206 *1837* went;   208 *1837* friend!   209 *1837* (*After a
pause*) And yet   210 *1837* You Vane, you Rudyard,   *1863–68* You,
Vane,—you Rudyard,   211–13 *1837* That Wentworth . . . O will no one
hope with me?|—Vane—think you Wentworth will shed English blood|Like
water?|A PURITAN. Ireland is Aceldama!

ment in 1628 (on 22 March) contained the substance of most of the future
Petition of Right and was in a sense responsible for the addition of the
complaint about imprisonment without due cause. 'To frame' in l.201 must
also refer to Wentworth.
    203 *One month before*: a slight exaggeration.
    204 *His Northern Presidency*: Wentworth became president of the Council of
the North on 25 December 1628. The account given here accelerates the course
of events. The author of the *Life*, unfairly, writes as follows: 'almost before the
burning words [of his speech on the Petition] . . . had cooled from off the lips
of the speaker, a transfer of his services to the court was decided on! . . . On the
14th of July sir Thomas Wentworth was created Baron Wentworth, and called
to the privy council. It is clear, however, that *at the same time* he had stipulated to
be made a viscount, and lord president of the North, but this apparently could
not be done, till the death of Buckingham had removed a still lingering
obstacle': *Life*, pp. 225–6 (p. 58).
    that Bill: cf. 56 n., and textual note above.
    211 *can no one hope*: 'In a memorable passage, the historian May has described
the general conversation and conjecture which had prepared for his approach.
Some, he says, remembering his early exertions in the cause of the people,
fondly imagined that he had hitherto been subservient to the court, only to
ingratiate himself thoroughly with the king, and that he would now employ
his ascendancy to wean his majesty from arbitrary counsels. Others, who
knew his character more profoundly, had different thoughts, and secretly
cherished their own most active energies': *Life*, p. 366 (p. 225).
    213 *Aceldama*: 'that field is called . . . Aceldama, that is to say, The field of
blood': Acts 1:19.

Pym. Will he turn Scotland to a hunting-
    ground
To please the King, now that he knows the
    King?   215
The People or the King? and that King, Charles!
  Hampden. Pym, all here know you: you'll not
    set your heart
On any baseless dream. But say one deed
Of Wentworth's since he left us . . . [*Shouting
    without.*
Vane.   There! he
    comes,
And they shout for him! Wentworth 's at
    Whitehall,   220
The King embracing him, now, as we speak,
And he, to be his match in courtesies,
Taking the whole war's risk upon himself,
Now, while you tell us here how changed he is!
Hear you?   225
  Pym.   And yet if 't is a dream, no more,
That Wentworth chose their side, and brought
    the King
To love it as though Laud had loved it first,
And the Queen after;—that he led their cause
Calm to success, and kept it spotless through,
So that our very eyes could look upon   230

216–216a *1837* The People or the King? The People, Hampden,| Or the King
. . . and that King—Charles! Will no one hope?   216 *1884* as *1888* except
'King—Charles!'   217 *1837* Pym, we do know you: you'll not set your
heart|On any baseless thing: but   219 *1837–84* Of Wentworth's,   219
1837 VANE. Pym, he comes   220 *1837* him!—Wentworth!—he's with
Charles—   221 *1837* The king embracing him—now—as we speak
. .   223 *1837* himself!—   224 *1837* Now— while . . . . is—   225 *1837*
Do you hear, Pym? The People shout for him!   225a–f {Six lines in *1837*,
omitted in later editions:} FIENNES. We'll not go back, now! Hollis has no
brother—|Vane has no father . . .|VANE. Pym should have no friend!|Stand
you firm, Pym! Eliot's gone, Wentworth's lost,|We have but you, and stand
you very firm!|Truth is eternal, come below what will,|But. . I know not. . if
you should fail . . O God!|O God!|PYM (*apart and in thought*). And yet if 'tis a
dream, no more,   228 *1837* after—that

---

218 *But say*: suppose there were even one thing you could mention . . .
225 *And yet*: Pym is thinking aloud, as the s.d. to the first edition makes
explicit.
226 *their side*: that of the People.

The travail of our souls, and close content
That violence, which something mars even right
Which sanctions it, had taken off no grace
From its serene regard. Only a dream!
   Hampden. We meet here to accomplish certain
      good   235
By obvious means, and keep tradition up
Of free assemblages, else obsolete,
In this poor chamber: nor without effect
Has friend met friend to counsel and confirm,
As, listening to the beats of England's heart,   240
We spoke its wants to Scotland's prompt reply
By these her delegates. Remains alone
That word grow deed, as with God's help it
      shall—
But with the devil's hindrance, who doubts too?
Looked we or no that tyranny should turn   245
Her engines of oppression to their use?
Whereof, suppose the worst be Wentworth
      here—
Shall we break off the tactics which succeed
In drawing out our formidablest foe,
Let bickering and disunion take their place?   250
Or count his presence as our conquest's proof,
And keep the old arms at their steady play?
Proceed to England's work! Fiennes, read the
      list!
   Fiennes. Ship-money is refused or fiercely paid
In every county, save the northern parts   255

   231 *1837* soul, and close *1863–82* souls and close *1884* souls; and
close,   232–3 *1837* even Right|That sanctions it, *1868,1882* even rights|˙
Which sanction it,   235–52 {Not in *1837*.}   253–5 *1837* HAMPDEN. Pro-
ceed to England's work: who reads the list?|A VOICE. "Ship-money . . . .
northern ones

   231 *The travail*: 'He shall see of the travail of his soul, and shall be satisfied':
Isaiah 53:11.
   and close: so that our eyes could close content in the knowledge that violence
had in no way diminished the beauty of what is right. EHH inserted a comma
after 'close' in an attempt to clarify the passage.
   232 *something*: to some extent.   234 *regard*: appearance.
   241 *to Scotland's prompt reply*: and found that Scotland replied promptly.
   254 *Ship-money*: the tax levied by Charles, ostensibly for the maintenance of
the navy. 'That famous tax had recently been levied. The same success waited
upon Wentworth's present measures in respect to it, as the capacity and energy

Where Wentworth's influence . . .   [*Shouting.*
Vane.   I, in England's name,
Declare her work, this way, at end! Till now,
Up to this moment, peaceful strife was best.
We English had free leave to think; till now,
We had a shadow of a Parliament   260
In Scotland. But all 's changed: they change the
          first,
They try brute-force for law, they, first of all . . .
Voices. Good! Talk enough! The old true
          hearts with Vane!
Vane. Till we crush Wentworth for her,
          there's no act
Serves England!
Voices.   Vane for England!   265
Pym.   Pym should be
Something to England. I seek Wentworth,
          friends.

SCENE II.—*Whitehall.*

LADY CARLISLE *and* WENTWORTH.

Wentworth. And the King?
Lady Carlisle.   Wentworth, lean on
          me! Sit then!

256 *1837* Where Wentworth's influence" . . . (*Renewed shouting.*)| VANE (*passionately striking the table*). I, in England's name   257 *1837* till now—   258 *1837* moment—peaceful strife was well!   260 *1837* We had a shadow of a Parliament: *1884* We had the shadow of a Parliament   261–6 *1837* 'Twas well: but all is changed: they threaten us:|They'll try brute-force for law—here—in our land!|MANY VOICES. True hearts with Vane! The old true hearts with Vane!|VANE. Till we crush Wentworth for her, there's no act|Serves England!|VOICES. Vane for England! PYM. (*As he passes slowly before them*) Pym should be|Something to England! I seek Wentworth, friends!

1 *1837* CARLISLE. Dear Wentworth, lean on me; sit then;   *1863,1865* as *1888* except 'sit then,—'

which animated all he did almost invariably commanded. In every other county, murmurs, threats, and curses, accompanied the payment,—in Yorkshire, during Wentworth's presence, silence': *Life*, p. 347 (pp. 202–3.)

s.d. LADY CARLISLE: for Browning's statement that 'My Carlisle . . . is purely imaginary', see Appendix A, below. The historical Countess was praised and addressed by Carew, Herrick, Suckling, Waller and Davenant. She was famous for her beauty and her intelligence, and had great influence with the Queen.

I 'll tell you all; this horrible fatigue
Will kill you.
    Wentworth. No;—or, Lucy, just your arm;
I 'll not sit till I 've cleared this up with him:
After that, rest. The King?   5
    Lady Carlisle.   Confides in you.
    Wentworth. Why? or, why now?—They have
      kind throats, the knaves!
Shout for me—they!
    Lady Carlisle.   You come so strangely
      soon:
Yet we took measures to keep off the crowd—
Did they shout for you?
    Wentworth.   Wherefore should they
      not?
Does the King take such measures for himself?   10
Beside, there 's such a dearth of malcontents,
You say!
    Lady Carlisle. I said but few dared carp at you.
    Wentworth. At me? at us, I hope! The King and
      I!
He 's surely not disposed to let me bear
The fame away from him of these late deeds   15
In Ireland? I am yet his instrument
Be it for well or ill? He trusts me, too!
    Lady Carlisle. The King, dear Wentworth,
      purposes, I said,
To grant you, in the face of all the Court . . .
    Wentworth. All the Court! Evermore the Court
      about us!   20

---

3 *1837–68* No; or—Lucy,   6–8 *1837* Why? why now?|—They have kind throats, the people!|Shout for me . . . they!—poor fellows.|CARLISLE. Did they shout?|—We took all measures to keep off the crowd—   *1884* as *1888* except 'crowd.'   12 *1837* You say?|CARLISLE. I said . . . . you . . .   *13 {Reading of *1863–84*.}   *1837* At me? at us, Carlisle! The King and I!   *1888,1889* At me? at us, I hope! The King and I   15 *1837* Away the fame from him   17 *1837* ill?|He trusts me then?   18 *1837* purposes, I know

15 *The fame away from him*: there is strong dramatic irony throughout this passage.
19 *To grant you*: this places the scene just before 12 January 1640: cf. ll. 153 and 240, below.

Savile and Holland, Hamilton and Vane
About us,—then the King will grant me—what?
That he for once put these aside and say—
"Tell me your whole mind, Wentworth!"
    Lady Carlisle.   You
    professed
You would be calm.   25
    Wentworth.   Lucy, and I am calm!
How else shall I do all I come to do,
Broken, as you may see, body and mind,
How shall I serve the King? Time wastes
    meanwhile,
You have not told me half. His footstep! No.
Quick, then, before I meet him,—I am calm—   30
Why does the King distrust me?
    Lady Carlisle.   He does not
Distrust you.
    Wentworth. Lucy, you can help me; you
Have ever seemed to care for me: one word!
Is it the Queen?
    Lady Carlisle. No, not the Queen: the party

    22-3 *1837* grant me . . . . Lady,|Will the King leave these—leave all
these—and say   24-5 *1837* CARLISLE. But you said|You would be
calm.   26 *1884* come to do,—   27 *1837*—Broken, as . . . . mind—   29
1837 half . . .   30 *1837* —But now, before I meet him,—(I am
calm)—   32 *1837* help me , . you   *33 { Editors' emendation, based on
Berg copy}. *1837* even . . . . for me: help me!   *1863–89* even . . . . for me: one
word!   34 *1837* No—not the Queen—

---

    21 *Savile*: Thomas Savile, first Viscount Savile in the peerage of Ireland,
second Baron Savile of Pontefract and first Earl of Sussex in the peerage of
England, was Wentworth's 'especial enemy': *Life*, p. 377 (p. 237). He took a
prominent part in drawing up a treaty with the Scots. 'He was a man of an
ambitious and restless nature, of parts and wit enough, but in his disposition
and inclination so false that he could never be believed or depended upon. His
particular malice to the earl of Strafford, which he had sucked in with his milk,
. . . had engaged him with all persons who were willing, and like to be able, to
do him mischieve': Clarendon, vi. 393.
    27 *Broken*: Clarendon describes Wentworth, when he joined the army near
Durham, as 'bringing with him a body much broken with his late sickness . . .,
and a mind and temper confessing the dregs of it': quoted in *Life*, p. 376 (p.
237).
    34 *Is it the Queen?*: the youngest daughter of Henri IV and Marie de Médicis,
Henrietta Maria was married by proxy and came to England in 1625. During
the lifetime of Buckingham she was on indifferent terms with her husband. At
first she abstained from politics, but she was a focus of attraction to politicians
and poets alike. She thwarted Laud's proclamation against Catholic recusants

That poisons the Queen's ear, Savile and
    Holland.   35
  Wentworth. I know, I know: old Vane, too,
    he 's one too?
Go on—and he 's made Secretary. Well?
Or leave them out and go straight to the
    charge—
The charge!
  Lady Carlisle. Oh, there 's no charge, no
    precise charge;
Only they sneer, make light of—one may say,   40
Nibble at what you do.
  Wentworth.   I know! but Lucy,
I reckoned on you from the first!—Go on!
—Was sure could I once see this gentle friend
When I arrived, she 'd throw an hour away
To help her . . . what am I?   45

35 *1837* ear,—Savile—and Holland . . .   36 *1837* I know—I know—and
Vane, too, *1863* I know, I know: and Vane, too,   37 *1837* Secretary
—Well?   *38 {Reading of DC and *1889*} *1837* —Or leave . . . . straight to
the charge! *1863–84* Or leave . . . . straight to the charge; *1888* Or leave
. . . . straight to the charge   39 *1837* charge—no precise charge— 41,41a,42
1837 know: but Lucy,|Go on, dear Lucy—Oh I need you so!|I reckoned   43
1837 . . Was sure . . . . gentle girl *1882,1884* as *1888* except 'Was'   45 *1837*
To help her weary friend . . .

in 1636, and obtained money from the Catholics for the Scottish war. She tried
to save Strafford.

  35 *Holland*: 'But Charles had now the queen's influence in many respects
upon him, and the queen was not displeased to hear of the sinking fortunes of
Wentworth. Lord Holland, her favourite counsellor, was even heard to insinu-
ate that the lord deputy was subject to occasional touches of madness': *Life*, p.
352 (p. 208). A little later the *Life* informs us that 'Intrigues of the most
disgraceful character, carried on by Holland, Hamilton, and Vane, and assisted
every way by the queen, united with his sickness to break him down': p. 376 (p.
237).

  36 *old Vane*: Clarendon tells us that 'Sir Henry Vane had not far to look back
to the time that the earl had with great earnestness opposed his being made
Secretary and prevailed for above a month's delay; . . . after which, or about
the same time, . . . being to be made earl of Strafford, he would needs in that
patent have a new creation of a barony, and was made baron of Raby, a house
belonging to sir H. Vane, and an honour he made account should belong to
him too; which was an act of the most unnecessary provocation (though he
contemned the man with marvellous scorn) that I have known, and I believe
was the loss of his head': ii. 101.

  41 *Nibble*: 'Laud writes:—"I have of late heard some muttering about it in
court, but can meet with nothing to fasten on: only it makes me doubt some
body hath been nibbling [carping] about it."—See Strafford Papers, vol. ii. p.
127': *Life*, p. 354 n. (p. 211 n.).

  45 *what am I?*: whereas the author of the *Life* states that 'the famous countess,

Lady Carlisle.   You thought of me,
Dear Wentworth?
  Wentworth.   But go on! The party here!
  Lady Carlisle. They do not think your Irish
      government
Of that surpassing value . . .
  Wentworth.   The one thing
Of value! The one service that the crown
May count on! All that keeps these very Vanes   50
In power, to vex me—not that they do vex,
Only it might vex some to hear that service
Decried, the sole support that 's left the King!
  Lady Carlisle. So the Archbishop says.
  Wentworth.   Ah? well, perhaps
The only hand held up in my defence   55
May be old Laud's! These Hollands then, these
      Saviles
Nibble? They nibble?—that 's the very word!
  Lady Carlisle. Your profit in the Customs,
      Bristol says,

46,47 *1837* . . But go on! The People here . . .| CARLISLE. They . . . . Govern-
ment *1863–84* as *1888* except 'Government'   50 *1837* very things   51
1837 to vex me . . not that they do vex me,   53 *1837* Decried—   55 *1837* in
its defence   58, *1837* Bristol says, . . .

had secretly become his mistress' (p. 277 n.: p. 118 n.), all that is evident in the
play is that she loves him. Helen Faucit later confessed that 'The only interest
she awoke in me was due to her silent love for Strafford and devotion to his
cause; and I wondered why, depending so absolutely as he did upon her
sympathy, her intelligence, her complete self-abnegation, he should only have,
in the early part, a common expression of gratitude to give her in return. This
made the treatment of Lucy's character . . . all the more difficult in the
necessity it imposed upon me of letting her feeling be seen by the audience,
without its being perceptible to Strafford': *Records of Tennyson, Ruskin and
Browning*, by Anne Ritchie, 2nd ed., 1893, p. 224.

  46 *The party here!*: cf. ll. 34–5, and textual note above.

  47 *your Irish government*: Strafford particularly prided himself on his conduct
of affairs in Ireland. In May 1636 he had 'so delighted the king with his account
of the various measures by which he had consolidated the government of
Ireland, that he was entreated by his majesty to repeat the details "at a very full
council"': *Life*, p. 344 (p. 199).

  50 *All that keeps*: he means that it is only his management of affairs in Ireland
that keeps Vane and the others in power.

  58 *Your profit*: he acknowledged to Laud that his own share in the customs
had proved greater 'than ever I dreamt of'. 'When Laud read this passage to
Charles, the king observed, impatiently, "but he doth not tell you how much,"
and plainly intimated that he grudged the minister his share of profit': *Life*, p.
354 (p. 211).

  Bristol: John Digby, first Earl of Bristol, returned from political seclusion in

Exceeds the due proportion: while the tax . . .
   Wentworth. Enough! 'tis too unworthy,—I am
     not   60
So patient as I thought. What 's Pym about?
   Lady Carlisle. Pym?
   Wentworth.   Pym and the People.
   Lady Carlisle.   Oh, the Faction!
Extinct—of no account: there 'll never be
Another Parliament.
   Wentworth.   Tell Savile that!
You may know—(ay, you do—the creatures
     here   65
Never forget!) that in my earliest life
I was not . . . much that I am now! The King
May take my word on points concerning Pym
Before Lord Savile's, Lucy, or if not,
I bid them ruin their wise selves, not me,   70
These Vanes and Hollands! I'll not be their tool
Who might be Pym's friend yet.
                         But there's the King!
Where is he?
   Lady Carlisle. Just apprised that you arrive.
   Wentworth. And why not here to meet me? I
     was told
He sent for me, nay, longed for me.   75
   Lady Carlisle.   Because,—
He is now . . . I think a Council 's sitting now

---

59 {Not in *1837.*}   61 *1837–84* thought!   62 *1882* Lady Car.
Pym!   63 *1837* account—   67 *1837* I was not . . . not what I am   70
1837 Girl, they shall ruin their vile selves,   71 *1837* Hollands—I'll not be
their tool—   *72 {Reading of *1863–1884,* DC and *1889.*}   *1837* Pym would
receive me yet!|—But then the King!—   *1888* Who might be Pym's friend
yet.|But there's the King   73,73a–75 *1837* I'll bear it all. The King—where
is he, Girl?|CARLISLE. He is apprised that you are here: be calm!|WENTWORTH.
And why not meet me now? Ere now? You said|He sent for me . . he longed
for me!|CARLISLE. Because. .   *1863,1865* as *1888* except 'longed for me!' in l. 75.

1639 when the peers were summoned to take part in the expedition against the
Scots. After the dissolution of the Short Parliament in 1640 he took a very
prominent part in the Great Council at York, being practically accepted as its
leader.
   62 *the Faction!*: cf. ll. 232–3 below.
   76 *a Council's sitting*: a meeting of the Privy Council.

About this Scots affair.

   Wentworth.   A Council sits?
They have not taken a decided course
Without me in the matter?

     Lady Carlisle.   I should say . . .

   Wentworth. The war? They cannot have agreed
     to that?   80
Not the Scots' war?—without consulting me—
Me, that am here to show how rash it is,
How easy to dispense with?—Ah, you too
Against me! well,—the King may take his time.
—Forget it, Lucy! Cares make peevish: mine   85
Weigh me (but 't is a secret) to my grave.

     Lady Carlisle. For life or death I am your own,
     dear friend!   [*Goes out.*

   Wentworth. Heartless! but all are heartless here.
     Go now,
Forsake the People!

             I did not forsake
The People: they shall know it, when the King   90
Will trust me!—who trusts all beside at once,
While I have not spoke Vane and Savile fair,
And am not trusted: have but saved the throne:
Have not picked up the Queen's glove prettily,

---

77 *1837* affair . . .   79 *1837* in this matter?   82 *1837* Me—that   84,85
1837 well,—the King may find me here.|(*As* CARLISLE *is going.*)|—Forget it,
Lucy: 87,87a–d,88 *1837* friend!|(*Aside.*) I could not tell him . . . sick too!. .
And the King|Shall love him! Wentworth here, who can withstand|His
look?—And he did really think of me?|O 'twas well done to spare him all the
pain! (*Exit.*)|WENTWORTH. Heartless! . . . but   89 *1837* people!|—I did
1863–84 People!—I did   90 *1837* know it . . .   *1863–84* know it—
91–2 *1837* once|While I . . .   93 *1837–65* Throne:

---

80 *The war?*: cf. II. ii. 108 ff.: as Gardiner points out in the introduction to
EHH's edition (p. xi), 'The real Strafford was far from opposing the war with
the Scots at the time when the Short Parliament was summoned'.

88 *Go now*: 'Like the French *allez donc!* an ironical encouragement addressed
by Strafford, in bitterness, to himself': EHH, following a note from Browning
(*Checklist*, 83:182).

89 *Forsake The People!*: it was Wentworth's conviction that the interests of
the King and People were ultimately the same.

94 *the Queen's glove*: 'It ought to be stated, to Wentworth's honour, that,
though he much desired to have stood well with her majesty, he declined to
purchase her favour by acts inconsistent with his own public schemes . . . The
king himself appears to have made it a personal request of Wentworth, that he

And am not trusted. But he 'll see me now.   95
Weston is dead: the Queen 's half English
   now—
More English: one decisive word will brush
These insects from . . . the step I know so well!
The King! But now, to tell him . . . no—to ask
What 's in me he distrusts:—or, best begin   100
By proving that this frightful Scots affair
Is just what I foretold. So much to say,
And the flesh fails, now, and the time is come,
And one false step no way to be repaired.
You were avenged, Pym, could you look on me.   105
                 PYM *enters.*
   Wentworth. I little thought of you just then.
   Pym.   No? I
Think always of you, Wentworth.
   Wentworth.   The old voice!
I wait the King, sir.
   Pym.   True—you look so pale!
A Council sits within; when that breaks up
He 'll see you.   110
   Wentworth. Sir, I thank you.
   Pym.   Oh, thank Laud!

95–100 *1837* trusted!|But he'll see me now:|And Weston's dead—and the
Queen's English now—|More English—oh, one earnest word will
brush|These reptiles from . . . *(footsteps within.)*|The step I know so well!|'Tis
Charles!—But now—to tell him . . no—to ask him|What's in me to dis-
trust:—or, best begin   102–3 *1837* foretold: I'll say, "my liege" . . . .|And I
feel sick, now! and the time is come—   *1863*,65 as *1888* except 'now!'   104
1837 be repaired . . . .   *1863–84* be repaired!   105 *1837* were revenged, Pym,
. . . . me!   *1863*,*1865* were avenged, Pym, ... me!   107 *1837* WENTWORTH.
(Aside.) The old voice!   108 *1837* pale:

should carry himself "with all duty and respect to her majesty" ': *Life*, p. 358 n.
(pp. 215–16 n.).
   96 *Weston is dead*: 'The lord treasurer Weston alone, the old propitiator of the
king's regards to the quondam supporter of the petition of rights, but now
bitterly jealous of Wentworth's friendship with Laud, scarcely cared to conceal
his animosity. A fatal attack of illness, however, at this time removed Weston':
Life, p. 325 (pp. 176–7). Weston died in 1635. In the *Life*, p. 325 n. (p. 177 n.) a
letter of Wentworth's is quoted in which he tells the Earl of Newcastle that 'by
his death it is not altogether improbable, that I am delivered of the heaviest
adversary I ever had'.
   half English: revised from *1837*. Henrietta Maria was the sister of Louis XIII
of France.
   98 *These insects*: 'He was possessed with a rooted aversion, from the first, to
the court flies that buzzed around the monarch': *Life*, p. 227 (p. 60).

You know when Laud once gets on Church
    affairs
The case is desperate: he 'll not be long
To-day: he only means to prove, to-day,
We English all are mad to have a hand
In butchering the Scots for serving God   115
After their fathers' fashion: only that!
    Wentworth. Sir, keep your jests for those who
    relish them!
(Does he enjoy their confidence?) 'T is kind
To tell me what the Council does.
    Pym.   You grudge
That I should know it had resolved on war   120
Before you came? no need: you shall have all
The credit, trust me!
    Wentworth.   Have the Council dared—
They have not dared . . . that is—I know you
    not.
Farewell, sir: times are changed.
    Pym.   —Since we two met
At Greenwich? Yes: poor patriots though we be,   125
You cut a figure, makes some slight return
For your exploits in Ireland! Changed indeed,
Could our friend Eliot look from out his grave!
Ah Wentworth, one thing for acquaintance' sake,
Just to decide a question; have you, now,   130
Felt your old self since you forsook us?
    Wentworth.   Sir!
    Pym. Spare me the gesture! you misapprehend.

---

116 *1837* only that.   118 *1837* (*Aside.*) Does *he* enjoy their confidence? (*To
P.*) 'Tis kind *1863,65* as *1888* except '*he*' 121 *1837* no need— *1882,84* No
need: 122 *1837* trust me.|WENTWORTH. Have they, Pym . . . not
dared— *1863,65* as *1888* except '*me.*'   123 *1837* you not—   124 *1837*
Farewell—the times 125 *1837* Yes—poor 126 *1837* You shall see something here, some   129 *1837* Ah, Wentworth, ... acquaintance-
sake; *1863,1865,1884* as *1888* except '*Ah,*' *1882* Ah, Wentworth, . . . acquain-
tance sake,   131–3 *1837* Really felt well since you forsook us?|WENTWORTH.
Pym—|You're insolent!|PYM. Oh, you misapprehend!|Don't think I . . . .
me: *1863–1884* as *1888* except '*misapprehend!*'

---

114 *are mad*: madly eager (spoken ironically).
122 *The credit*: cf. II. ii. 109 ff.
125 *At Greenwich*: see I. i. 106 n. above.
126 *a figure, makes*: a figure which makes.

Think not I mean the advantage is with me.
I was about to say that, for my part,
I never quite held up my head since then—   135
Was quite myself since then: for first, you see
I lost all credit after that event
With those who recollect how sure I was
Wentworth would outdo Eliot on our side.
Forgive me: Savile, old Vane, Holland here,   140
Eschew plain-speaking: 't is a trick I keep.
    Wentworth. How, when, where, Savile, Vane,
       and Holland speak,
Plainly or otherwise, would have my scorn,
All of my scorn, sir . . .
    Pym.   . . . Did not my poor thoughts
Claim somewhat?   145
    Wentworth.   Keep your thoughts! believe the
       King
Mistrusts me for their prattle, all these Vanes
And Saviles! make your mind up, o' God's love,
That I am discontented with the King!
    Pym. Why, you may be: I should be, that I
       know,
Were I like you.   150
    Wentworth.   Like me?
    Pym.   I care not much
For titles: our friend Eliot died no lord,
Hampden 's no lord, and Savile is a lord;
But you care, since you sold your soul for one.
I can't think, therefore, your soul's purchaser
Did well to laugh you to such utter scorn   155
When you twice prayed so humbly for its price,

---

135 *1837* I've never . . . . then,—   *1863,1865* I never . . . . then,—   136
1837 Been quite . . . . see,   *1863–84* Was quite . . . . see,   140–1 *1837* WENT-
WORTH. By Heaven . . .| PYM. Forgive me: Savile, Vane, and Holland| Eschew
plain-speaking: 'tis a trick I have.   142 *1837* where,—Savile, Vane, and
Holland speak,—   *1863–84* where, Savile, Vane and Holland speak,   143
1837 otherwise,—   144 *1837* My perfect scorn, Sir . . .   146 *1837* their
speaking, all   147 *1837* up, all of you,   *1865* up, o' God's love   149 *1837*
be—I should   154,156 *1837* therefore, Charles did well to laugh| When you
twice prayed so humbly for an Earldom. {155,157,158 not in *1837*.}

---

153 *But you care:* having twice asked for an earldom earlier, only to be

The thirty silver pieces . . . I should say,
The Earldom you expected, still expect,
And may. Your letters were the movingest!
Console yourself: I 've borne him prayers just
    now   160
From Scotland not to be oppressed by Laud,
Words moving in their way: he 'll pay, be
    sure,
As much attention as to those you sent.
    Wentworth. False, sir! Who showed them you?
      Suppose it so,
The King did very well . . . nay, I was glad   165
When it was shown me: I refused, the first!
John Pym, you were my friend—forbear me
    once!
    Pym. Oh, Wentworth, ancient brother of my
    soul,
That all should come to this!
    Wentworth.   Leave me!
    Pym.   My friend,
Why should I leave you?   170
    Wentworth.   To tell Rudyard this,
And Hampden this!
    Pym.   Whose faces once were bright
At my approach, now sad with doubt and
    fear,
Because I hope in you—yes, Wentworth, you
Who never mean to ruin England—you

---

159 *1837* WENTWORTH. Pym . . . . | PYM. And your letters were the moving-
est!   160 *1865* born him   161–2 *1837* opprest by Laud—|And mov-
ing   164 *1837* False! a lie, Sir!|. . Who told you, Pym?|—But then
1863,*1865* False, sir!—Who showed them you? suppose it so,   166–7
1837 When it was shewn me why;—I first refused it!|. . . Pym, you
were once my friend—don't speak to me!   172 *1837* approach . .
1863,*1865* approach—   173 *1837* in you—Wentworth—in you

---

refused, Wentworth was created Earl of Strafford on 12 January 1640 (cf. l. 240,
below). 'The lord deputy was created earl of Strafford and baron of Raby,
adorned with the garter, and invested with the title of lord-lieutenant, or
lieutenant-general, of Ireland': *Life*, p. 367 (p. 226).
   157 *The thirty silver pieces*: the price Judas Iscariot accepted for betraying
Christ: Matthew 26:15.
   164 *them*: Wentworth's pleading letters to the King.

Who shake off, with God's help, an obscene
      dream   175
In this Ezekiel chamber, where it crept
Upon you first, and wake, yourself, your true
And proper self, our Leader, England's Chief,
And Hampden's friend!
                            This is the proudest day!
Come, Wentworth! Do not even see the King!   180
The rough old room will seem itself again!
We 'll both go in together: you 've not seen
Hampden so long; come: and there 's Fiennes:
      you 'll have
To know young Vane. This is the proudest day!
[*The* KING *enters.* WENTWORTH *lets fall* PYM'S
      hand.
      Charles. Arrived, my lord?—This gentleman,
      we know   185
Was your old friend.
                            The Scots shall be informed
What we determine for their happiness.
                                  [PYM *goes out.*
You have made haste, my lord.
      Wentworth.   Sir, I am come . . .
      Charles. To see an old familiar—nay, 't is well;
Aid us with his experience: this Scots' League   190
And Covenant spreads too far, and we have
      proofs

175–9 *1837* Who shake, with God's great help, this frightful dream| Away,
now, in this Palace, where it crept| Upon you first, and are yourself—your
good| And noble self—our Leader—our dear Chief—| Hampden's own
friend—   *1863,65* as *1888* except 'yourself—'   *1882,1884* as *1888* except
'chief,'   182–4 *1837* together—you've not seen| Hampden so long—
come—and there's Vane—I know| You'll love young Vane!   186 *1837*
friend:| (*To* PYM) The Scots   187 *1837* happiness. (*Exit* PYM.)   188 *1837*
Sire. . . I am come. . .   189 { Not in *1837.*}   190 *1837* To aid us with your
counsel: this   *1882,1884* as *1888* except 'experience;'

176 *this Ezekiel chamber*: 'So I went in and saw; and behold every form of
creeping things, and abominable beasts, and all the idols of the house of Israel,
pourtrayed upon the wall round about . . . Then said he unto me, Son of man,
hast thou seen what the ancients of the house of Israel do in the dark, every man
in the chambers of his imagery?' Ezekiel 8:10, 12.
181 *The rough old room*: cf. I. i. 57 n.
190–1 *League | And Covenant*: cf. I. i. 92 n. For the intrigue with France, see
Clarendon, ii. 55.

That they intrigue with France: the Faction too,
Whereof your friend there is the head and front,
Abets them,—as he boasted, very like.
 Wentworth. Sir, trust me! but for this once,
  trust me, sir!   195
 Charles. What can you mean?
 Wentworth.   That you should trust me, sir!
Oh—not for my sake! but 't is sad, so sad
That for distrusting me, you suffer—you
Whom I would die to serve: sir, do you think
That I would die to serve you?   200
 Charles.   But rise, Wentworth!
 Wentworth. What shall convince you? What
  does Savile do
To prove him . . . Ah, one can't tear out one's
  heart
And show it, how sincere a thing it is!
 Charles. Have I not trusted you?
 Wentworth.   Say aught but that!
There is my comfort, mark you: all will be 205
So different when you trust me—as you shall!
It has not been your fault,—I was away,
Mistook, maligned, how was the King to know?
I am here, now—he means to trust me, now—
All will go on so well!   210
 Charles.   Be sure I do—
I've heard that I should trust you: as you came,
Your friend, the Countess, told me . . .
 Wentworth.   No,—hear nothing—
Be told nothing about me!—you 're not told

  192 *1837* That they intrigue . . . . Faction, too . . . *1863,82* That they
intrigue . . . . Faction, too, *1884* Their chiefs intrigue . . . . Faction,
too, 193–4 {Not in *1837*.} 195 *1837* WENTWORTH (*Kneels.*) Sire, ...
Sire! 196 *1837* trust me! now! 199 *1837* Sire, 202 *1837* To . . . Ah,
one can't tear out one's heart—one's heart— 205 *1837* It is my 206 *1837*
me . . as 208 *1837* Maligned—away—and how were you to know? 209
1837 now—you mean 210 *1837* sure I will— 211–12 *1837* came | Even
Carlisle was telling me . . . . 213 *1837* me! you're

 192 *the Faction*: see l. 232, below.
 193 *the head and front*: *Othello* I. iii. 80.

Your right-hand serves you, or your children
    love you!
    Charles. You love me, Wentworth: rise!   215
    Wentworth.   I can speak now.
I have no right to hide the truth. 'T is I
Can save you: only I. Sir, what must be?
    Charles. Since Laud's assured (the minutes are
    within)
—Loath as I am to spill my subjects' blood . . .
    Wentworth. That is, he 'll have a war: what 's
    done is done!   220
    Charles. They have intrigued with France;
    that's clear to Laud.
    Wentworth. Has Laud suggested any way to
    meet
The war's expense?
    Charles.   He 'd not decide so far
Until you joined us.
    Wentworth.   Most considerate!
He 's certain they intrigue with France, these
    Scots?   225
The People would be with us.
    Charles.   Pym should
    know.
    Wentworth. The People for us—were the
    People for us!
Sir, a great thought comes to reward your trust:
Summon a Parliament! in Ireland first,
Then, here.   230
    Charles. In truth?
    Wentworth.   That saves us! that puts off

---

215 *1837* You love me . . only rise!   217 *1837* you; only I. Sire, what is
done! *1863* you; only I. Sir, what must be?   218 *1837* assured . . . the
minutes are within . .   219 *1837* Loath   223 *1837* expence?| CHARLES. He'd
not decide on that   225 *1837* You're certain   226,227 *1837* (*Aside.*) The
People . . . . us!| CHARLES. Very sure.| WENTWORTH. (The People for us . . were
the People for us!)   228 *1837* Sire, ... trust! *1882,1884* Sir, ...
trust;   229–30 *1837* first,| And then in England.| CHARLES. Madness!| WENT-
WORTH. (*Aside.*) That puts off *1882,84* as *1888* except 'Then'

---

220 *what's done is done!*: cf. *Macbeth*, III. ii. 12.
229 *Summon a Parliament!*: 'He proposed a loan . . . and pledged himself to

The war, gives time to right their grievances—
To talk with Pym. I know the Faction,—Laud
So styles it,—tutors Scotland: all their plans
Suppose no Parliament: in calling one
You take them by surprise. Produce the proofs   235
Of Scotland's treason; then bid England help:
Even Pym will not refuse.
  Charles.   You would begin
With Ireland?
  Wentworth. Take no care for that: that 's sure
To prosper.
  Charles. You shall rule me. You were best
Return at once: but take this ere you go!   240
Now, do I trust you? You 're an Earl: my Friend
Of Friends: yes, while . . . You hear me not!
  Wentworth. Say it all o'er again—but once
   again:
The first was for the music: once again!
  Charles. Strafford, my friend, there may have
   been reports,   245
Vain rumours. Henceforth touching Strafford is
To touch the apple of my sight: why gaze
So earnestly?
  Wentworth. I am grown young again,

---

231 *1837* The war— gives time to learn their *232 {Reading of DC and
1889.}* *1837* with Pym—(*To* CHARLES). I know the faction, as *1863–88* with
Pym. I know the Faction, as *233 {Reading of DC and *1889*} *1837* They
style it, . .|CHARLES . . . Tutors Scotland!|WENTWORTH. All their plans
1863–88 Laud styles it, tutors Scotland: all their plans 236 *1837* treason;
bid them help you, then! 237 *1837* refuse! 239 *1837* me: you 240
1837 go! (*Giving a paper.*) 241,242 *1837* my Friend| Of Friends: yes, Straf-
ford, while . . . *1882,1884* my friend| Of friends: yes, while . . . 243 *1837*
once again— 244 *1837–84* music— 245–6 *1837* Strafford, my brave
friend, there were wild reports—| Vain rumours . .

bring over a large subsidy from Ireland if the king would call a parliament
there. Encouraged by this assurance, it was resolved to call a parliament in
England also': *Life*, p. 366 (pp. 225–6).
 240 *Return at once: but take this ere you go!*: return to Ireland, as Wentworth did
in March. As the s.d. to *1837* makes clear, the King hands Wentworth the patent
of his earldom. Historically, he became Baron of Raby and Earl of Strafford on
12 January 1640, and landed in Ireland on 18 March.
 247 *the apple of my sight*: 'he that toucheth you toucheth the apple of his eye':
Zechariah 2:8.

And foolish. What was it we spoke of?
    Charles.   Ireland,
The Parliament,—   250
    Wentworth.   I may go when I will?
—Now?
    Charles. Are you tired so soon of us?
    Wentworth.   My King!
But you will not so utterly abhor
A Parliament? I 'd serve you any way.
    Charles. You said just now this was the only
        way.
    Wentworth. Sir, I will serve you.   255
    Charles.   Strafford, spare yourself:
You are so sick, they tell me.
    Wentworth.   'T is my soul
That 's well and prospers now.
                     This Parliament—
We 'll summon it, the English one—I 'll care
For everything. You shall not need them much.
    Charles. If they prove restive . . .   260
    Wentworth.   I shall be with you.
    Charles. Ere they assemble?
    Wentworth.   I will come, or else
Deposit this infirm humanity
I' the dust. My whole heart stays with you, my
        King!
       [*As* WENTWORTH *goes out, the* QUEEN *enters.*
    Charles. That man must love me.
    Queen.   Is it over then?

---

249 *1837* foolish! . . what   251 *1837* of me?|WENTWORTH. My King
. . . .   252 *1837* so very much dislike   253 *1837* A Parliament? . . . .
way! *1865* A parliament? . . . . way, *1868* A parliament? . . . . way.   255
1837 Sire, ... you!|. . . . spare yourself— *1863–84* Sir, ... you!|. . . . spare
yourself—   256 *1837* tell me, . . .   257 *1837* well and happy, now! *1863*
well and prospers, now! *1865* well and prospers now!   259 *1837* every
thing: You . . . . much!   260 *1837* with you!   263 *1837* dust! . . . .
King!|(*As* STRAFFORD *goes*   264 *1837–65* love me!

---

261 *I will come*: 'I shall chearfully venture this crazed Vessel of mine, and
either by God's help wait upon your Majesty before that Parliament begin, or
else deposite this infirm Humanity of mine in the Dust', he wrote to the King
from Dublin on Good Friday 1640: *Letters and Dispatches*, ii. 403.

Why, he looks yellower than ever! Well,   265
At least we shall not hear eternally
Of service—services: he's paid at least.
   Charles. Not done with: he engages to
     surpass
All yet performed in Ireland.
   Queen.   I had thought
Nothing beyond was ever to be done.   270
The war, Charles—will he raise supplies
     enough?
   Charles. We 've hit on an expedient; he . . .
     that is,
I have advised . . . we have decided on
The calling—in Ireland—of a Parliament.
   Queen. O truly! You agree to that? Is that   275
The first fruit of his counsel? But I guessed
As much.
   Charles. This is too idle, Henriette!
I should know best. He will strain every nerve,
And once a precedent established . . .
   Queen.   Notice
How sure he is of a long term of favour!   280
He'll see the next, and the next after that;
No end to Parliaments!
   Charles.   Well, it is done.
He talks it smoothly, doubtless. If, indeed,
The Commons here . . .
   Queen.   Here! you will summon them
Here? Would I were in France again to see   285
A King!

   267 *1837* Of his vast services: he's paid at last.   276–7 *1837* Is this|The
first   278–9 *1837* Henrietta!|I should know best: 280 *1837,1863* term of
favours!   282 *1837* done: 283 *1837* doubtless: if,

   283 *He talks it smoothly*: '"He talks it smoothly" means, "speciously, plausibly", the half sneer in "talks it" shows that already the value of the advice is
diminishing in his [the King's] eyes, or, as he apprehends it may, in those of the
Queen': Browning to Miss Hickey, in a letter of 8 December 1883 known only
from a quotation in a bookseller's catalogue (*Checklist*, 83:182, with the non-
sensical 'Greek' corrected to 'Queen'). Cf. Otway, *Venice Preserved*, II. iii. 135:
'You talk this well, sir'.

Charles. But, Henriette . . .
Queen.   Oh, the Scots see clear!
Why should they bear your rule?
Charles.   But listen, sweet!
Queen. Let Wentworth listen—you confide in
    him!
Charles. I do not, love,—I do not so confide!
The Parliament shall never trouble us   290
. . . Nay, hear me! I have schemes, such
    schemes: we 'll buy
The leaders off: without that, Wentworth's
    counsel
Had ne'er prevailed on me. Perhaps I call it
To have excuse for breaking it for ever,
And whose will then the blame be? See you not?   295
Come, dearest!—look, the little fairy, now,
That cannot reach my shoulder! Dearest, come!

286 *1837* But Henrietta . . .|QUEEN. O the Scots|Do well to spurn your rule!|CHARLES. But, listen, Sweet . . . *1863,1865* But Henriette . . .|*Queen.* Oh, the Scots see clear!|Why should they bear your rule?|*Cha.* But listen, Sweet! 288 *1837* Let Strafford listen— 289 *1837* Love—I do not so confide . . *1863* Love—I do not so confide! *1865* Love,—I do not so confide! 291 *1837* such schemes—we'll 292 *1837* that, Strafford's counsel 294 *1837* it—for ever— 296 *1837–65* Dearest!— *1882,1884* fairy 297 *1837* come!|(*Exeunt.*)|END OF THE FIRST ACT.

ACT II.

SCENE I.—(As in Act I. Scene I.)

The same Party enters.

Rudyard. Twelve subsidies!
Vane.   Oh Rudyard, do not laugh
At least!
   Rudyard. True: Strafford called the
      Parliament—
'T is he should laugh!
   A Puritan.   Out of the serpent's root
Comes forth a cockatrice.
   Fiennes.   —A stinging one,
If that 's the Parliament: twelve subsidies!   5
A stinging one! but, brother, where 's your word
For Strafford's other nest-egg, the Scots' war?
   The Puritan. His fruit shall be a fiery flying
      serpent.
   Fiennes. Shall be? It chips the shell, man; peeps
      abroad.
Twelve subsidies!—Why, how now, Vane?   10

s.d. *1837 The same Party enters confusedly; among the first, the younger* VANE *and*
RUDYARD.   3 *1837* A PURITAN (*entering*).—Out   4 *1837* FIENNES (*enter-*
ing).—A stinging one,   9 *1837* shell, man; peeps abroad: *1884* shell,
man,—peeps abroad.   10 *1837* now Vane?|RUDYARD. Hush, Fiennes!

---

   1 *Twelve subsidies!*: 'A subsidy was originally a grant made by Parliament to
the King "upon need and necessity". In the time of Charles I. the usage of the
word is ordinarily limited to a tax . . . Each subsidy at this time produced about
£70,000': EHH. On 3 May Strafford urged the King not to insist on the whole
twelve subsidies which he had originally demanded.
   2 *Strafford called the Parliament*: on 22 September 1639 Strafford became the
King's chief counsellor, and advised him to summon Parliament. The result
was the Short Parliament of April–May 1640. It has come into session between
Acts I and II.
   3 *the serpent's root*: 'Rejoice not thou, whole Palestina, because the rod of him
that smote thee is broken: for out of the serpent's root shall come forth a
cockatrice, and his fruit shall be a fiery flying serpent': Isaiah 14:29.

Rudyard.   Peace, Fiennes!
Fiennes. Ah?—But he was not more a dupe
    than I,
Or you, or any here, the day that Pym
Returned with the good news. Look up, friend
    Vane!
We all believed that Strafford meant us well
In summoning the Parliament.   15
                    HAMPDEN *enters.*
Vane.   Now, Hampden,
Clear me! I would have leave to sleep again:
I 'd look the People in the face again:
Clear me from having, from the first, hoped,
    dreamed
Better of Strafford!
Hampden.   You may grow one day
A steadfast light to England, Henry Vane!   20
    Rudyard. Meantime, by flashes I make shift to
    see.
Strafford revived our Parliaments; before,
War was but talked of; there 's an army, now:
Still, we 've a Parliament! Poor Ireland bears
Another wrench (she dies the hardest death!)—   25
Why, speak of it in Parliament! and lo,
'T is spoken, so console yourselves!
Fiennes.   The jest!
We clamoured, I suppose, thus long, to win
The privilege of laying on our backs
A sorer burden than the King dares lay!   30

13 *1837* up, dear Vane!   15 *1837* Parliament . . .|(HAMPDEN *enters.*)|VANE
(*starting up*). Now, Hampden,   *1865* as *1888* except 'Now'   16 *1837* sleep
again! *1863,1865* sleep again;   17 *1837* face again!   *19 {Reading of
1863–84, DC, *89*} *1837* Better of Strafford! Fool!|HAMPDEN. You'll grow one
day *1888* Better of Strafford|*Hampden.* You may grow one day   *20
{Reading of *1863–84*} *1837* England, Vane!|RUDYARD. Ay, Fiennes, *1888,89*
England Henry Vane!   *21 {Reading of DC} *1863–82,88,89* flashes I make
shift to see {Not in *1837*.}   *1884* flashes, I make shift to see.   24 *1837*
Parliament. Poor   25 *1837–65* death!)   26 *1837* Why . . . speak . . . . and,
lo,   *1863,65* Why, speak . . . . and, lo,   27 *1837* spoken!—and console
yourselves. *1863,1865* spoken! so console yourselves.   29–30 *1837* laying
on ourselves|A sorer burthen

24–5 *Poor Ireland bears | Another wrench*: Strafford obtained a grant of four
subsidies from the Irish Parliament at this time.

Rudyard. Mark now: we meet at length,
　　complaints pour in
From every county, all the land cries out
On loans and levies, curses ship-money,
Calls vengeance on the Star Chamber; we lend
An ear. "Ay, lend them all the ears you have!"　　　35
Puts in the King; "my subjects, as you find,
"Are fretful, and conceive great things of you.
"Just listen to them, friends; you 'll sanction me
"The measures they most wince at, make them
　　yours,
"Instead of mine, I know: and, to begin,　　　40
"They say my levies pinch them,—raise me
　　straight
"Twelve subsidies!"
　　Fiennes.　　　　　All England cannot furnish
Twelve subsidies!
　　Hollis.　　　　　But Strafford, just returned
From Ireland—what has he to do with that?
How could he speak his mind? He left before　　　45
The Parliament assembled. Pym, who knows
Strafford . . .
　　Rudyard. Would I were sure we know
　　ourselves!
What is for good, what, bad—who friend, who
　　foe!
　　Hollis. Do you count Parliaments no gain?
　　Rudyard.　　　　　　　　　A gain?
While the King's creatures overbalance us?　　　50

31 *1837* length:　　32 *1837* county:　　35 *1837* An ear: "ay, lend . . . .
have,"　　37 *1837* you:　　42 *1837* FIENNES *and others.* All　　46,46a *1837* The
Parliament assembled: Rudyard, friends,│He could not speak his mind! and
Pym, who knows　　48 *1882,1884* what bad,—

34 *Star Chamber*: this hated Court was used ruthlessly by the King and Laud,
as for example in the cruel punishments meted out to Prynne and John
Lilburne.
34–5 *lend / An ear*: cf. *Julius Caesar*, III. ii. 73.
35 *you*: i.e. the members of Parliament. Whereas the King hated the very
word 'parliament', Strafford 'saw, from what had occurred in the council, in
what consideration the mere name was held there; and he saw, moreover,
abroad among the nation, a feeling in favour of it, which might, by a bold
movement, be even wrested to the purpose of tyranny, but could never, with
any safety to that cause, be altogether avoided': *Life*, p. 297 (p. 142).

—There's going on, beside, among ourselves
A quiet, slow, but most effectual course
Of buying over, sapping, leavening
The lump till all is leaven. Glanville 's gone.
I 'll put a case; had not the Court declared   55
That no sum short of just twelve subsidies
Will be accepted by the King—our House,
I say, would have consented to that offer
To let us buy off ship-money!
   Hollis.   Most like,
If, say, six subsidies will buy it off,   60
The House . . .
   Rudyard. Will grant them! Hampden, do you
      hear?
Congratulate with me! the King 's the king,
And gains his point at last—our own assent
To that detested tax! All 's over, then!
There 's no more taking refuge in this room,   65
Protesting, "Let the King do what he will,
"We, England, are no party to our shame:
"Our day will come!" Congratulate with me!
             PYM *enters.*
Vane. Pym, Strafford called this Parliament,
    you say,
But we 'll not have our Parliaments like those   70
In Ireland, Pym!
   Rudyard.   Let him stand forth, your friend!

53–5 *1837* Of buying over, sapping, . . A PURITAN . . . Leavening|The lump
till all is leaven.|A VOICE. Glanville 's gone,|RUDYARD. I'll put a case;   57–9
1837 our House|Would have consented to that wretched offer|To . . . . Ship-
money?   60 *1837* If . . . say six subsidies,   62–3 *1837* Oh, I congratulate
you that the King|Has gained his point at last . .   *64 {Reading of
1868–84.}   *1837* tax! all's over   *1863,1865* tax! all's over,   *1888,1889* tax? All's
over,   65–6 *1837* room|And saying. "Let   67 *1837* shame,—   69 *1837*
Parliament, 'tis like—   71 *1837* forth, that Strafford!

---

53 *sapping*: undermining.
53 *leavening*: 'A little leaven leaveneth the whole lump': Galatians 5:9.
54 *Glanville's gone*: i.e. over to the King's side. According to Clarendon, Sir
John Glanville, Speaker of the Short Parliament, urged Parliament to grant the
twelve subsidies and so 'reconcile him [the King] to Parliaments for ever': ii.
73. Hampden opposed this.
56 *no sum short*: see note to II. ii. 76 ff.
62 *Congratulate*: 'To rejoice in participation': Johnson.
70–1 *like those / In Ireland*: 'By Sir Edward Poyning's bill, a Parliament could

One doubtful act hides far too many sins;
It can be stretched no more, and, to my mind,
Begins to drop from those it covered.
    Other Voices.   Good!
Let him avow himself! No fitter time!   75
We wait thus long for you.
    Rudyard.   Perhaps, too long!
Since nothing but the madness of the Court,
In thus unmasking its designs at once,
Has saved us from betraying England. Stay—
This Parliament is Strafford's: let us vote   80
Our list of grievances too black by far
To suffer talk of subsidies: or best,
That ship-money 's disposed of long ago
By England: any vote that 's broad enough:
And then let Strafford, for the love of it,   85
Support his Parliament!
    Vane.   And vote as well
No war to be with Scotland! Hear you, Pym?
We 'll vote, no war! No part nor lot in it
For England!
    Many Voices. Vote, no war! Stop the new
      levies!
No Bishops' war! At once! When next we meet!   90
    Pym. Much more when next we meet!
      Friends, which of you
Since first the course of Strafford was in doubt,
Has fallen the most away in soul from me?
    Vane. I sat apart, even now, under God's eye,

---

73 *1837* more—and,   74–5 *1837* it covers.|OTHER VOICES. Pym,|
Let   77 *1837* Court   78,79 *1837* once|Had saved   82 *1837* best—
87 *1837–65* No war's to be   90 *1837* No Bishop's War!   *1863* No Bishop's
war!   91 *1837* meet!|—Friends,   *94 {Reading of *1863–84*}   *1837* I sate
apart, even now,   *1888,1889* I sat apart, even now

---

not be summoned more than once a year in Ireland, nor could it be summoned
even then unless the Bills to be proposed to it had been approved by the English
Privy Council': EHH.
    72 *doubtful*: ambiguous.
    73 *It can be stretched no more*: the image of a covering cloak is suggested. Cf.
Sordello, iii. 710.
    90 *No Bishops' war!*: the first Bishops' War (so called because of Laud's
determination to foist episcopacy on the Scottish Church) was in 1639, the
second the following year.

Pondering the words that should denounce you,
    Pym,   95
In presence of us all, as one at league
With England's enemy.
  Pym.   You are a good
And gallant spirit, Henry. Take my hand
And say you pardon me for all the pain
Till now! Strafford is wholly ours.   100
  Many Voices.   Sure? sure?
  Pym. Most sure: for Charles dissolves the
    Parliament
While I speak here.
          —And I must speak, friends, now!
Strafford is ours. The King detects the change,
Casts Strafford off for ever, and resumes
His ancient path: no Parliament for us,   105
No Strafford for the King!
             Come, all of you,
To bid the King farewell, predict success
To his Scots' expedition, and receive
Strafford, our comrade now. The next will be
Indeed a Parliament!   110
  Vane.   Forgive me, Pym!
  Voices. This looks like truth: Strafford can
    have, indeed,
No choice.
  Pym.   Friends, follow me! He 's with the
    King.
Come, Hampden, and come, Rudyard, and
    come, Vane!

---

98 *1837* Henry!   100 *1837* MANY VOICES. 'Tis sure?   101 *1837*
sure—for   102 *1837* here!. . . (*Great emotion in the assembly.*)|. . And   103
1837 ours!   105 *1837* us—   106 *1837* Come all of you   108 *1837*
Scots   109 *1837* now!   *111 {Reading of *1863–84*} *1837* truth—Strafford
can have, indeed,   *1888,1889* truth: Strafford can have, indeed   112 *1837* No
choice!|. . . . King: *113 {Reading of *1863–84*.}   *1837* Come Hampden,
and come Rudyard, and come Vane —   *1888,1889* Come, Hampden, and
come, Rudyard, and come, Vane

---

101 *dissolves the Parliament*: the King dissolved the Short Parliament on 5
May 1640.
   105–6 *no Parliament . . . / No Strafford*: since the King will not allow us a
Parliament, Strafford will not support him.

This is no sullen day for England, sirs!
Strafford shall tell you!   115
    Voices.   To Whitehall then!
    Come!

SCENE II.—*Whitehall.*

CHARLES *and* STRAFFORD.

Charles. Strafford!
Strafford.   Is it a dream? my papers,
    here—
Thus, as I left them, all the plans you found
So happy—(look! the track you pressed my
    hand
For pointing out)—and in this very room,
Over these very plans, you tell me, sir,   5
With the same face, too—tell me just one thing
That ruins them! How 's this? What may this
    mean?
Sir, who has done this?
    Charles.   Strafford, who but I?
You bade me put the rest away: indeed
You are alone.   10
    Strafford.   Alone, and like to be!
No fear, when some unworthy scheme grows
    ripe,

---

115 *1837* Come!|(*Exeunt omnes.*)

s.d. *1837* CHARLES *seated,* STRAFFORD *standing beside a table covered with maps,
&c.*   1 *1837* CHARLES. Strafford . . .   2 *1837* Thus—as I left them—   4
1837 out!)—and . . . . room   5 *1837* me, Sire,   8 *1837* Sire, who
. . . .|CHARLES. Strafford, none but I!   9 *1838* away—   10 *1837*
alone!|STRAFFORD. Alone—   11 *1837–65* scheme's grown ripe,

Strafford: this was Macready's first entrance, and (according to Browning's
own account, as told to Gosse) it was a striking one: 'at last Macready appeared,
in the second scene of the second act, in more than his wonted majesty,
crossing and recrossing the stage like one of Vandyke's courtly personages
come to life again': *Personalia,* p. 45.
10 *alone*: without rival as the King's chief adviser.

Of those, who hatched it, leaving me to loose
The mischief on the world! Laud hatches war,
Falls to his prayers, and leaves the rest to me,
And I 'm alone.   15
    Charles.   At least, you knew as much
When first you undertook the war.
    Strafford.   My liege,
Was this the way? I said, since Laud would lap
A little blood, 't were best to hurry over
The loathsome business, not to be whole months
At slaughter—one blow, only one, then, peace,   20
Save for the dreams. I said, to please you both
I 'd lead an Irish army to the West,
While in the South an English . . . but you look
As though you had not told me fifty times
'T was a brave plan! My army is all raised,   25
I am prepared to join it . . .
    Charles.   Hear me, Strafford!
    Strafford. . . . When, for some little thing, my
        whole design
Is set aside—(where is the wretched paper?)
I am to lead—(ay, here it is)—to lead
The English army: why? Northumberland   30
That I appointed, chooses to be sick—
Is frightened: and, meanwhile, who answers for
The Irish Parliament? or army, either?
Is this my plan?
    Charles.   So disrespectful, sir?
    Strafford. My liege, do not believe it! I am
        yours,   35
Yours ever: 't is too late to think about:

    12 *1837* Of those who hatched it leaving you to loose   *1884* Of those who
hatched it, leaving me to loose   14–15 *1837* to me—|And I'm alone!   17
1837 Is this   18–20 *1837* o'er|The loathsome business—not. . . .|At slaugh-
ter—one blow—only one—then, peace—   21 *1837* dreams!   23 *1837*
South the English. . . . .   25 *1837* My Army is all raised—   30 *1837* This
English Army: 33–34a *1837* or Army, either?|Is this my plan? I say, is this
my plan?|CHARLES. You are disrespectful, Sir!|STRAFFORD. Do not
believe—   35–6 *1837* I am yours—|Yours ever—'tis . . . . about—

    29–30 *I am to lead . . . / The English army*: 'an army, to the command of which

To the death, yours. Elsewhere, this untoward
    step
Shall pass for mine; the world shall think it
    mine.
But here! But here! I am so seldom here,
Seldom with you, my King! I, soon to rush   40
Alone upon a giant in the dark!
    Charles. My Strafford!
    Strafford [*examines papers awhile*]. "Seize the
    passes of the Tyne!"
But, sir, you see—see all I say is true?
My plan was sure to prosper, so, no cause
To ask the Parliament for help; whereas   45
We need them frightfully.
    Charles.   Need the Parliament?
    Strafford. Now, for God's sake, sir, not one
    error more!
We can afford no error; we draw, now,
Upon our last resource: the Parliament
Must help us!   50
    Charles.   I've undone you, Strafford!
    Strafford.   Nay—
Nay—why despond, sir, 't is not come to that!
I have not hurt you? Sir, what have I said
To hurt you? I unsay it! Don't despond!
Sir, do you turn from me?

37–8 *1837* yours! Elsewhere, ...|Shall pass for mine—the . . . .
mine—   39 *1837* But, here! But, here! . . . . here!   *1863–79* But, here! But,
here! . . . . here,   40–3 *1837* I—soon to rush|Alone—upon a Giant—in the
dark!|CHARLES. My Strafford!|STRAFFORD. (*Seats himself at the table; examines
papers awhile; then, breaking off*)| . . "Seize the passes of the Tyne" . . .|But
don't you see—see all I say is true?   *1863–68* as *1888* except 'Tyne'!'   44
1837 prosper,—so,   46–7 *1837* them—frightfully . . .|CHARLES. Need this
Parliament?|STRAFFORD.—Now, for God's sake, mind—not   48 *1837*
error—   49 *1837* resource—this Parliament   51 *1837* Nay—don't
despond—Sire—'tis *1863* 'Nay—why despond, sir? 't is   52 *1837*
Sire—what   53 *1837* you? I'll unsay   54 *1837* Sire, do

Northumberland had been appointed, was marched against the Scots. Severe
illness, however, held Northumberland to his bed, and the king resolved to
appoint Strafford in his place': *Life*, p. 375 (p. 236). Sir Algernon Percy, 10th
Earl of Northumberland (1602–88), was the brother of Lady Carlisle.
    41 *a giant in the dark!*: 'For I seem, dying, as one going in the dark / To fight a
giant': *Pauline*, 1026–7.

Charles.   My friend of friends!
Strafford. We'll make a shift. Leave me the
    Parliament!   55
Help they us ne'er so little and I'll make
Sufficient out of it. We'll speak them fair.
They're sitting, that's one great thing; that half
    gives
Their sanction to us; that's much: don't
    despond!
Why, let them keep their money, at the worst!   60
The reputation of the People's help
Is all we want: we'll make shift yet!
    Charles.   Good Strafford!
    Strafford. But meantime, let the sum be ne'er
        so small
They offer, we'll accept it: any sum—
For the look of it: the least grant tells the Scots   65
The Parliament is ours—their staunch ally
Turned ours: that told, there's half the blow to
    strike!
What will the grant be? What does Glanville
    think?
    Charles. Alas!
    Strafford.   My liege?
    Charles.   Strafford!
    Strafford.   But answer me!
Have they . . . O surely not refused us half?   70
Half the twelve subsidies? We never looked
For all of them. How many do they give?
    Charles. You have not heard . . .
    Strafford.   (What has he done?)—Heard
        what?

55 *1837* shift!   56–8 *1837* They help us ne'er so little but I'll make| A vast
deal out of it. We'll speak them fair:| They're sitting: that's one great
thing: 59 *1837* us: 62 *1837* CHARLES. Dear Strafford!   66,67 *1837* ours
. . their staunch ally| Is ours: that told, there's scarce a blow   69 *1837*
CHARLES. Alas . . .| STRAFFORD. My liege?| CHARLES. Strafford . . .   70,71
1837 us all?| All the twelve   72 *1837*–65 all of them!

55 *make a shift*: find some expedient, manage somehow.
67 *there's half the blow to strike!*: only half as hard a blow will be required!

But speak at once, sir, this grows terrible!

[*The* KING *continuing silent.*

You have dissolved them!—I 'll not leave this
   man.   75

   Charles. 'T was old Vane's ill-judged
   vehemence.

   Strafford.   Old Vane?

   Charles. He told them, just about to vote the
   half,

That nothing short of all twelve subsidies
Would serve our turn, or be accepted.

   Strafford.   Vane!

Vane! Who, sir, promised me, that very Vane . . .   80
O God, to have it gone, quite gone from me,
The one last hope—I that despair, my hope—
That I should reach his heart one day, and cure
All bitterness one day, be proud again
And young again, care for the sunshine too,   85
And never think of Eliot any more,—
God, and to toil for this, go far for this,
Get nearer, and still nearer, reach this heart
And find Vane there!

        [*Suddenly taking up a paper, and continuing
             with a forced calmness.*

                 Northumberland is sick:
Well, then, I take the army: Wilmot leads   90

74 *1837* Sire—this   76–8 *1837* 'Twas Vane—his ill-judged vehemence that
. . .|STRAFFORD. Vane?|CHARLES. He told them, as they were about to vote|The
half, that nothing short of all the twelve| *1865* as *1888* except 'them
just'   *79 {Reading of *1837–1884, 1889*}   *1888* accepted {corrected in
DC}   80 *1837* Vane! and you promised me that very Vane . . .   *1863–84* as
1888 except 'me'   81 *1837* from me   82 *1837–65* despair, *my*
hope—   85 *1882* sunshine, too, *1884* sunshine, too.   88 *1837*
heart—   90 *1837* Well then, I take the Army: *1863* Well then, I take the
army:

76 *old Vane's . . . vehemence*: 'it was generally believed that the question had
been put and carried in the affirmative, . . . if sir H. Vane, the Secretary, had not
stood up and said, "That . . . the putting and carrying that question could be of
no use; for . . . if they should pass a vote for the giving the King a supply, if it
were not in the proportion and manner proposed in his majesty's message it
would not be accepted by him"': Clarendon, ii. 75.
   80 *Who*: Charles, as is clear in *1837*.   83 *his heart*: the King's.
   90 *Wilmot*: Clarendon describes him as an officer 'of name and reputation,
and of good esteem in the Court with all those who were incensed against the
earl of Strafford, towards whom [he was] very indevoted': ii. 111.

The horse, and he, with Conway, must secure
The passes of the Tyne: Ormond supplies
My place in Ireland. Here, we 'll try the City:
If they refuse a loan—debase the coin
And seize the bullion! we 've no other choice.   95
Herbert . . .
         And this while I am here! with you!
And there are hosts such, hosts like Vane! I go,
And, I once gone, they 'll close around you, sir,
When the least pique, pettiest mistrust, is sure
To ruin me—and you along with me!   100
Do you see that? And you along with me!
—Sir, you 'll not ever listen to these men,
And I away, fighting your battle? Sir,
If they—if She—charge me, no matter how—
Say you, "At any time when he returns   105
"His head is mine!" Don't stop me there! You
    know
My head is yours, but never stop me there!
    Charles. Too shameful, Strafford! You advised
    the war,
And . . .
    Strafford. I! I! that was never spoken with
Till it was entered on! That loathe the war!   110
That say it is the maddest, wickedest . . .

---

91 *1837–65* The Horse, and he with Conway   96 *1837* Herbert . . .|(*Fling-
ing down the paper.*) And   97 *1837* go,—   98 *1837* Sire, {This is the usual
form in *1837*; not included in the notes henceforth.}   104–5 *1837* me—no
matter what—|You say, "At   106 *1837* mine."   107 *1837* yours . . only,
don't stop

    91 *Conway*: Viscount Conway was to be routed by the Scots at Newburn, on
28 August 1640. Cf. III. ii. 152 (and III. ii. 59).
    92 *Ormond*: 'Dispatches were sent into Ireland to quicken the preparations
there, which the earl had left in a great forwardness under the care of the earl of
Ormond, his lieutenant-general': Clarendon, ii. 82.
    94 *debase the coin*: on 11 July 1640 Strafford supported a scheme for the
debasement of the coinage.
    96 *Herbert*: Sir Edward Herbert, Solicitor-General from 25 January 1639/40,
knighted a year later.
    106 *there!*: in Ireland.
    108 *You advised the war*: unfair. The *Life* quotes from a letter Strafford had
written to the King: 'If the war were with a foreign enemy, I should like well to
have the first blow; *but being with your majesty's own natural, howbeit rebellious
subjects, it seems to me a tender point to draw blood first*; for till it come to that, all
hope is not lost of reconciliation': p. 358 (p. 216).

Do you know, sir, I think within my heart,
That you would say I did advise the war;
And if, through your own weakness, or what 's
          worse,
These Scots, with God to help them, drive me
          back,   115
You will not step between the raging People
And me, to say . . .
                    I knew it! from the first
I knew it! Never was so cold a heart!
Remember that I said it—that I never
Believed you for a moment!   120
                    —And, you loved me?
You thought your perfidy profoundly hid
Because I could not share the whisperings
With Vane, with Savile? What, the face was
          masked?
I had the heart to see, sir! Face of flesh,
But heart of stone—of smooth cold frightful
          stone!   125
Ay, call them! Shall I call for you? The Scots
Goaded to madness? Or the English—Pym—
Shall I call Pym, your subject? Oh, you think
I 'll leave them in the dark about it all?
They shall not know you? Hampden, Pym shall
          not?   130

112 *1837* know, Charles, I think,   *1863–68* know, sir, I think,   114 *1837*
And if, thro' your own weakness, falsehood, Charles,   *1882,1884* as *1888*
except 'if'   115 *1837* back . . .   117 *1837* knew you! from   118 *1837* I
knew you! Never   122 *1837* share your whisperings   123 *1837* With
Vane? With Savile? But your hideous heart—   *1863,1865* With Vane? With
Savile? What, the face was masked?   124,125 *1837* I had your heart to see,
Charles! Oh, to have|A heart of stone—of smooth, cold, frightful
stone!   *1863,1865* as *1888* except 'smooth, cold,'   130 *1837* Pym shall
not . . . .

112 *Do you know, sir*: note the deletion of the historically absurd 'Charles' of
1837.
113 *you would say*: it is characteristic of you to say.
120 *you loved me?*: the *Life* quotes Cottington's assurance to Strafford, '"you
are his mistress, and must be cherished and courted by none but himself". So
early did the king deem it expedient to exhibit, that peculiar sense of his
minister's service. When the minister had bound himself up inextricably with
the royal cause, it was thought to be less expedient!': p. 249 (p. 85).
124 *the heart*: Charles's heart, as *1837* makes evident.

PYM, HAMPDEN, VANE, *etc., enter.*
[*Dropping on his knee.*] Thus favoured with your
    gracious countenance
What shall a rebel League avail against
Your servant, utterly and ever yours?
So, gentlemen, the King 's not even left
The privilege of bidding me farewell   135
Who haste to save the People—that you style
Your People—from the mercies of the Scots
And France their friend?
    [*To* CHARLES.]   Pym's grave grey eyes
    are fixed
Upon you, sir!
              Your pleasure, gentlemen?
Hampden. The King dissolved us—'t is the
    King we seek   140
And not Lord Strafford.
    Strafford.   —Strafford, guilty too
Of counselling the measure. [*To* CHARLES.]
    (Hush . . . you know—
You have forgotten—sir, I counselled it)
A heinous matter, truly! But the King
Will yet see cause to thank me for a course   145
Which now, perchance . . . (Sir, tell them so!)—
    he blames.
Well, choose some fitter time to make your
    charge:
I shall be with the Scots, you understand?
Then yelp at me!
            Meanwhile, your Majesty
Binds me, by this fresh token of your trust . . .   150

---

134 *1837* (*To the rest*) So, Gentlemen,   139 *1837* Sire! (*To the rest*) Your
pleasure, Gentlemen?   142 *1837* measure: (*To* CHARLES) (Hush . . you know
. .   143 *1837* forgotten . . Sire, I counselled it!)   144 *1837*—(*Aloud*) A
heinous   147 *1837* charge—   148 *1837* Scots—you understand?—

---

138 *Pym's grave grey eyes*: 'All sorts of alterations were made in the text',
Gosse wrote of the original production; 'where the poet spoke of "grave grey
eyes", the manager corrected it in rehearsal to "black eyes" ': quoted in Hickey,
p. iv. See Gosse, p. 45.

[*Under the pretence of an earnest farewell,* STRAFFORD
conducts CHARLES *to the door, in such a manner
as to hide his agitation from the rest: as the King
disappears, they turn as by one impulse to* PYM,
*who has not changed his original posture
of surprise.*

Hampden. Leave we this arrogant strong
    wicked man!
Vane and others. Hence, Pym! Come out of this
    unworthy place
To our old room again! He 's gone.
[STRAFFORD, *just about to follow the* KING, *looks
    back.*
Pym.   Not gone!
[*To* STRAFFORD.] Keep tryst! the old
    appointment's made anew:
Forget not we shall meet again!   155
Strafford.   So be it!
And if an army follows me?
Vane.   His friends
Will entertain your army!
Pym.   I 'll not say
You have misreckoned, Strafford: time shows.
                                Perish
Body and spirit! Fool to feign a doubt,
Pretend the scrupulous and nice reserve   160
Of one whose prowess shall achieve the feat!
What share have I in it? Do I affect

---

150 (s.d.) *1837 the rest:* VANE *and others gazing at them: as the King* *1882,1884* as
1888 except 'rest;'   152 *1837* Dear Pym! . . . . place *1882,1884* Hence, Pym!
. . . . place!   153 *1837* again! Come, dearest Pym! | (*Strafford just* . . . .
back.)   155 *1837* STRAFFORD. Be it so!   158 *1837* time will . . . . | Perish
1863 time shows. Perish, *1865* time shows. Perish   159 *1837* doubt—
161 *1837* prowess is to do the feat! *1863,1865* prowess should achieve the
feat!   162 *1837–65* it? Shall I

154 *Keep tryst!*: 'We have Pym and Strafford as the two antagonists: before,
Pym believed that Strafford might be England's saviour; now, silently, he
accepts the dread office of being the destroyer of England's foe': EHH. Cf. 165
and 276–7, below, as well as III. iii. 97 and V. ii. 301 ff.
159 *Fool to feign a doubt*: Pym reflects that he need not pretend uncertainty
about the outcome, as it is fate rather than his own prowess which determines
it.

To see no dismal sign above your head
When God suspends his ruinous thunder there?
Strafford is doomed. Touch him no one of you!   165
         [PYM, HAMPDEN, *etc., go out.*
  Strafford. Pym, we shall meet again!
        Lady CARLISLE *enters.*
                 You here, child?
  Lady Carlisle. Hush—
I know it all: hush, Strafford!
  Strafford.   Ah? you know?
Well. I shall make a sorry soldier, Lucy!
All knights begin their enterprise, we read,
Under the best of auspices; 't is morn,   170
The Lady girds his sword upon the Youth
(He 's always very young)—the trumpets sound,
Cups pledge him, and, why, the King blesses
    him—
You need not turn a page of the romance
To learn the Dreadful Giant's fate. Indeed   175
We 've the fair Lady here; but she apart,—
A poor man, rarely having handled lance,
And rather old, weary, and far from sure
His Squires are not the Giant's friends. All 's
    one:
Let us go forth!   180
  Lady Carlisle. Go forth?
  Strafford.   What matters it?
We shall die gloriously—as the book says.
  Lady Carlisle. To Scotland? Not to Scotland?

---

165 *1837* doomed!—Touch . . . . you!|(*Exeunt* PYM, HAMPDEN, *&c.*)   166
1837 Pym we shall meet again!| (*Enter* CARLISLE.) You here, girl? *1884* as *1888*
except 'again.'   167–168 *1837* I know it all—hush, dearest Strafford!| STRAF-
FORD. Ah?| Well.   169 *1837* All Knights . . . . enterprise, you know,   170
1837 auspices; 'tis morn— *1884* auspices: 't is morn,   171 *1837*
Youth—   172 *1837* sound—   173 *1837* him, and . . . and . . . the
King   174 *1837,1863* Romance   *175 *1837* fate! Indeed *1863–89* fate.
Indeed.   177 *1837* man, never having   179 *1837* friends: well— well—

---

163 *dismal*: ominous.
166 *child?*: historically, Lady Carlisle was about 40 at this time, some six
years younger than Strafford.
181 *the book*: i.e. another stereotype, that with a tragic hero. Cf. *The
Agamemnon of Æschylus transcribed by Robert Browning,* 1328: 'But gloriously to
die—for man is grace, sure!'

Strafford.   Am I sick
Like your good brother, brave Northumberland?
Beside, these walls seem falling on me.
    Lady Carlisle.   Strafford,
The wind that saps these walls can undermine   185
Your camp in Scotland, too. Whence creeps the
     wind?
Have you no eyes except for Pym? Look here!
A breed of silken creatures lurk and thrive
In your contempt. You 'll vanquish Pym? Old
     Vane
Can vanquish you. And Vane you think to fly?   190
Rush on the Scots! Do nobly! Vane's slight sneer
Shall test success, adjust the praise, suggest
The faint result: Vane's sneer shall reach you
     there.
—You do not listen!
    Strafford.   Oh,—I give that up!
There 's fate in it: I give all here quite up.   195
Care not what old Vane does or Holland does
Against me! 'T is so idle to withstand!
In no case tell me what they do!
    Lady Carlisle.   But, Strafford . . .
    Strafford. I want a little strife, beside; real strife;
This petty palace-warfare does me harm: 200
I shall feel better, fairly out of it.
    Lady Carlisle. Why do you smile?
    Strafford.   I got to fear them, child!
I could have torn his throat at first, old Vane's,
As he leered at me on his stealthy way

184 *1837* Beside the walls seem falling on me!   189 *1837* contempt; you'll
vanquish Pym? Friend, Vane   190 *1837* you! And . . . . fly?—   *1863, 1865*
you! And . . . . fly?   192 *1837* success—adjust the praise—   193 *1837*
there!   194 *1837* Oh . . I give that up—   *1863,1865* Oh,—I give that
up;   195 *1837* it—I give   196 *1837* what Vane does or what Holland
does   197 *1837* withstand them—   *1863* withstand —   199 *1837*
beside—real strife: *1884* beside; real strife.   200 *1837–84* petty,   202
1837 them, girl!   203 *1837* first, that Vane,

188–9 *lurk and thrive* / *In your contempt*: 'by "thriving in your contempt" I
meant simply "while you despise them, and for all that, they thrive and are
powerful to do you harm"', Browning wrote to Miss Hickey: *New Letters*, p.
297.
     200 *palace-warfare*: cf. note to I. ii. 98, above.

To the Queen's closet. Lord, one loses heart!   205
I often found it on my lips to say
"Do not traduce me to her!"
    Lady Carlisle.   But the King . . .
    Strafford. The King stood there, 't is not so
      long ago,
—There; and the whisper, Lucy, "Be my friend
"Of friends!"—My King! I would have . . .   210
    Lady Carlisle.   . . . Died for him?
    Strafford. Sworn him true, Lucy: I can die for
      him.
    Lady Carlisle. But go not, Strafford! But you
      must renounce
This project on the Scots! Die, wherefore die?
Charles never loved you.
    Strafford.   And he never will.
He 's not of those who care the more for men   215
That they 're unfortunate.
    Lady Carlisle.   Then wherefore die
For such a master?
    Strafford.   You that told me first
How good he was—when I must leave true
      friends
To find a truer friend!—that drew me here
From Ireland,—"I had but to show myself   220
"And Charles would spurn Vane, Savile and the
      rest"—
You, child, to ask me this?
    Lady Carlisle.   (If he have set
His heart abidingly on Charles!)
                      Then, friend,

---

205 *1837* closet, Lucy—but of late   *206 {Reading of DC and *1889*.}
1837–68,1888 found it in my heart to say   *1882,1884* found it in my heart to
say,   207 *1837* "Vane—don't traduce   209 *1837* —There,   211, 211a,
212 *1837* . . Sworn . . . . I will die for him.|CARLISLE. (*Aside.*) What can he
mean? You'd say he loved him still! (*To* STRAFFORD.) But go not, Strafford!
. . .   213 *1837,1863* Die! wherefore   214 *1837* you!|STRAFFORD. And he
will not, now: 215–16 *1837* more for you|That you're unfortu-
nate.   222 *1837* You, girl, to ask me that?|CARLISLE. (*Aside.*) If he have
set   223 *1837* Charles!|(*To* STRAFFORD.) Dear friend

211 *Sworn him true*: a harder thing than to die for him.

I shall not see you any more.
   Strafford.   Yes, Lucy.
There 's one man here I have to meet.   225
   Lady Carlisle.   (The King!
What way to save him from the King?
                    My soul—
That lent from its own store the charmed
    disguise
Which clothes the King—he shall behold my
    soul!)
Strafford,—I shall speak best if you 'll not gaze
Upon me: I had never thought, indeed,   230
To speak, but you would perish too, so sure!
Could you but know what 't is to bear, my
    friend,
One image stamped within you, turning blank
The else imperial brilliance of your mind,—
A weakness, but most precious,—like a flaw   235
I' the diamond, which should shape forth some
    sweet face
Yet to create, and meanwhile treasured there
Lest nature lose her gracious thought for ever!
   Strafford. When could it be? no! Yet . . . was it
    the day

224 *1837* any more!|STRAFFORD. Yes, girl— *1863,65* any more!|*Straf.* Yes, Lucy. 225 *1837* here that I shall meet!|CARLISLE. (*Aside.*) The King!— 226 *1837* My soul . . 228 *1837* That clothes the King . . he . . . . soul! *1863–84* That clothes the King—he . . . . . soul!) 229,231 *1837* (*To* STRAFFORD.) Strafford . . . (I shall speak best if you'll not gaze| Upon me.) . . . You would perish, too! So sure! . . . *1863* as *1888* except 'perish, too! So' 230 {Not in *1837*} 232–3 *1837* bear, my Strafford,|One Image 236 *1837* diamond 238 *1837* Lest Nature . . . . ever! . . . *1863,65* Lest Nature . . . . ever! 239 *1837* be? . . . no! . . yet . . was

226 *My soul*: 'What Lady Carlisle means is, perhaps, something like this: "I expressed to Strafford the love I bore him myself as borne to him by Charles; when he loved the King, he was loving a being such as I had represented Charles to be, not such as he really was"': EHH.

235 *like a flaw*: 'The flaw in the diamond may take the shape of some sweet face, which nature means to create some day. But however beautiful this may be in itself, it is a flaw in the diamond, which ought to be absolutely clear. This image which you think to be Charles, this "sweet face" which is not his—for you have never seen the King as he is, and this portrait in your soul is of some one who has never lived;—this image is but a flaw in the diamond, your mind, turning blank its else imperial brilliance': EHH, who comments, justly: 'She does not see that Strafford *knows the King*, and loves him still'.

We waited in the anteroom, till Holland   240
Should leave the presence-chamber?
   Lady Carlisle.   What?
   Strafford.   —That I
Described to you my love for Charles?
   Lady Carlisle.   (Ah, no—
One must not lure him from a love like that!
Oh, let him love the King and die! 'T is past.
I shall not serve him worse for that one brief   245
And passionate hope, silent for ever now!)
And you are really bound for Scotland then?
I wish you well: you must be very sure
Of the King's faith, for Pym and all his crew
Will not be idle—setting Vane aside!   250
   Strafford. If Pym is busy,—you may write of
     Pym.
   Lady Carlisle. What need, since there 's your
     King to take your part?
He may endure Vane's counsel; but for Pym—
Think you he 'll suffer Pym to . . .
   Strafford.   Child, your hair
Is glossier than the Queen's!   255
   Lady Carlisle.   Is that to ask
A curl of me?
   Strafford.   Scotland——the weary way!
   Lady Carlisle. Stay, let me fasten it.
                 —A rival's, Strafford?
   Strafford [*showing the George*]. He hung it there:
     twine yours around it, child!
   Lady Carlisle. No—no—another time—I trifle
     so!

242 *1837* (*Aside.*) Ah, no—   244 *1837* 'Tis past . . . .   246 *1837* hope . .
silent for ever now!   247 *1837* (*To* STRAFFORD.) And . . . . Scotland,
then?   *1863,1882,1884* And. . . . Scotland, then?   252 *1837* What need when
there's your king   254 *1837* STRAFFORD. Girl, your hair   258 *1837* around
it, girl!

256 *the weary way!*: what a long way it is!
  258 s.d. *showing the George*: the mounted figure of Saint George slaying the
dragon, the badge of the Order of the Garter, given to Strafford by Lady
Carlisle's successful 'rival', the King. As it happens, this corresponds to a
favourite image of Browning's own: that of Perseus winning Andromeda by
slaying a monster.

And there 's a masque on foot. Farewell. The
    Court   260
Is dull; do something to enliven us
In Scotland: we expect it at your hands.
    Strafford. I shall not fail in Scotland.
    Lady Carlisle.   Prosper—if
You 'll think of me sometimes!
    Strafford.   How think of him
And not of you? of you, the lingering streak   265
(A golden one) in my good fortune's eve.
    Lady Carlisle. Strafford . . . Well, when the eve
    has its last streak
The night has its first star.   [*She goes out.*
    Strafford.   That voice of hers—
You 'd think she had a heart sometimes! His
    voice
Is soft too.   270
            Only God can save him now.
Be Thou about his bed, about his path!
His path! Where 's England's path? Diverging
    wide,
And not to join again the track my foot
Must follow—whither? All that forlorn way
Among the tombs! Far—far—till . . . What, they
    do   275
Then join again, these paths? For, huge in the
    dusk,
There 's—Pym to face!
            Why then, I have a foe
To close with, and a fight to fight at last
Worthy my soul! What, do they beard the
    King,
And shall the King want Strafford at his need?   280

260 *1837* foot: farewell: 263 *1837,1863* not fall in   265 *1837* of
you—the   266 *1837* eve?   268 *1837* star! (*Exit.*)|STRAFFORD. That . . . .
hers . . .   271 *1837* path! . . .   272 *1863* wide   274 *1837* way—   277
1837 Why then I have a Foe   279 *1837* That's worth my soul! What—do they
beard the King—   280 *1837* his need—

275 *Among the tombs!*: cf. Mark 5:5.
276 *huge in the dusk*: cf. note to l. 41 above.   280 *want*: lack.

Am I not here?
                    Not in the market-place,
Pressed on by the rough artisans, so proud
To catch a glance from Wentworth! They lie
    down
Hungry yet smile "Why, it must end some day:
"Is he not watching for our sake?" Not there!   285
But in Whitehall, the whited sepulchre,
The . . .
                    Curse nothing to-night! Only one name
They 'll curse in all those streets to-night. Whose
    fault?
Did I make kings? set up, the first, a man
To represent the multitude, receive   290
All love in right of them—supplant them so,
Until you love the man and not the king——
The man with the mild voice and mournful eyes
Which send me forth.
                    —To breast the bloody sea
That sweeps before me: with one star for guide.   295
Night has its first, supreme, forsaken star.

281,281a *1837* My King—at his great need? Am I not here?|. . . . Not in the
common blessed market-place| 283 *1837–65* Wentworth! They'll lie
down   284 *1837* Hungry and say "Why, ... day—   *1863* Hungry and
smile "Why, ... day—   285 *1837* sake?"|—Not there!   286,287 *1837*
But in Whitehall—the whited sepulchre—|The . . .|(*At the Window, and look-
ing on London.*)|Curse   288 *1837* streets to-night!   289 *1837* kings—set
up, the first,   *1882,1884* kings? set up the first,   291,292 *1863* supplanting
them|Until   294–6 *1837* That send me forth . . .|To breast the bloody
sea|That sweeps before me—with one star to guide—|Night has its first
supreme forsaken star!|(*Exit.*)|END OF THE SECOND ACT.

---

281 *Not in the market-place*: *1837* emphasizes Strafford's hatred of Whitehall
and the Court intrigues, to which nevertheless he believes his duty calls him. 'I
am now working for the King, not for the people': EHH.
    286 *the whited sepulchre*: 'Woe unto you, scribes and Pharisees, hypocrites! for
ye are like unto whited sepulchres, which indeed appear beautiful outward, but
are within full of dead men's bones, and of all uncleanness': Matthew 23:27.
    287 *one name*: that of the King.
    289 *Did I make kings?*: '"But, above all, divide not between the interests of
the king and his people, as if there were one being of the king, and another
being of his people"': *Life*, p. 307 (p. 155).
    295 *one star*: his passionate loyalty to the King.

ACT III.

Scene I.—*Opposite Westminster Hall.*

Sir Henry Vane, Lord Savile, Lord Holland
and others of the Court.

> *Sir H. Vane.* The Commons thrust you out?
> *Savile.*   And what kept you
> From sharing their civility?
> *Sir H. Vane.*   Kept me?
> Fresh news from Scotland, sir! worse than the
>   last,
> If that may be. All 's up with Strafford there:
> Nothing to bar the mad Scots marching hither   5
> Next Lord's-day morning. That detained me, sir!
> Well now, before they thrust you out,—go
>   on,—
> Their Speaker—did the fellow Lenthal say
> All we set down for him?
> *Holland.*   Not a word missed.

4 *1837* may be! all's . . . . there!   *1863,1865* may be! All's . . . . there: 5
1837 Nothing's to bar   6 *1837* The next fine morning!   7 *1837* out, go
on,   8 *1837* speaker . . . did the fellow Lenthall   *1863,1865* Speaker—did the
fellow Lenthall   9 *1837* missed!

---

1 *The Commons thrust you out?*: between the Acts the King's forces under
Conway have been routed at Newburn, and have been obliged to retire to
Durham, where Strafford has joined them. On the advice of the Council of
Peers (then assembled at York), but against that of Strafford, the King has
opened negotiations with the Scots. The armistice of Ripon was to prove
ruinous for the King, who was driven to summon the Long Parliament. It
opened its proceedings by impeaching Strafford.

6 *Next Lord's-day morning*: 'Observe the sneer in *Lord's-day*': EHH.

8 *the fellow Lenthal*: William Lenthall 'was pitched upon by the King, and
with very great difficulty rather prevailed with than persuaded to accept the
charge' of Speaker, as Clarendon tells us. 'And no doubt a worse could not
have been deputed of all that profession who were then returned; for he was a
man of a very narrow timorous nature, and of no experience or conversation in
the affairs of the kingdom, beyond what the very drudgery in his profession
. . . engaged him in': Clarendon iii. 2.

Ere he began, we entered, Savile, I   10
And Bristol and some more, with hope to breed
A wholesome awe in the new Parliament.
But such a gang of graceless ruffians, Vane,
As glared at us!
   Vane. So many?
   Savile.   Not a bench
Without its complement of burly knaves;   15
Your hopeful son among them: Hampden leant
Upon his shoulder—think of that!
   Vane.   I'd think
On Lenthal's speech, if I could get at it.
Urged he, I ask, how grateful they should prove
For this unlooked-for summons from the King?   20
   Holland. Just as we drilled him.
   Vane.   That the Scots will march
On London?
   Holland.   All, and made so much of it,
A dozen subsidies at least seemed sure
To follow, when . . .
   Vane.   Well?
   Holland.   'T is a strange thing, now!
I 've a vague memory of a sort of sound,   25
A voice, a kind of vast unnatural voice—
Pym, sir, was speaking! Savile, help me out:

---

11 *1837* more, in hopes to   12 *1837* Parliament—   13 *1837* Vane!   14 *1837* They glared at us . . . .   15,16 *1837* burley knaves—| Your son, there, Vane, among them—   18 *1837* Lenthall's . . . . at it . . .   *1863,1865* Lenthall's . . . . at it.   19 *1837* He said, I hope, how grateful they should be   21 *1837* him . . .   22 *1837* of it   24 *1837–82* thing now!   25 *1837* sound—   26 *1837* A voice—a kind of vast,   *1863,1865* A voice, a kind of vast,   27 *1837* Pym, Sir, was . . . . out,—

---

11 *Bristol*: see note to I. ii. 58.

12 *the new Parliament*: the Long Parliament first met on 3 November 1640.

13 *But such a gang*: 'There was observed a marvellous elated countenance in most of the members of Parliament before they met together in the house; the same men who six months before were observed to be of very moderate tempers . . . talked now in another dialect both of things and persons': Clarendon, iii. 3.

26 *A voice*: in his *Life of Pym* Forster comments on 'a certain grave and subdued style and manner' which characterised Pym's speech, 'as though he spoke—and doubtless he did speak—with the thorough knowledge that, as the present parliament had been called by the king, the next was to be forced into existence by the people': p. 89.

What was it all?
   Savile.   Something about "a matter"—
No,—"work for England."
   Holland.   "England's great revenge"
He talked of.   30
   Savile.   How should I get used to Pym
More than yourselves?
   Holland.   However that may be,
'T was something with which we had nought to
   do,
For we were "strangers" and 't was "England's
   work"—
(All this while looking us straight in the face)
In other words, our presence might be spared.   35
So, in the twinkling of an eye, before
I settled to my mind what ugly brute
Was likest Pym just then, they yelled us out,
Locked the doors after us, and here are we.
   Vane. Eliot's old method . . .   40
   Savile.   Prithee, Vane, a truce
To Eliot and his times, and the great Duke,
And how to manage Parliaments! 'T was you
Advised the Queen to summon this: why,
     Strafford
(To do him justice) would not hear of it.
   Vane. Say rather, you have done the best of
   turns   45
To Strafford: he 's at York, we all know why.

28,29 *1837* "a matter" . . .|No . . "a work *1863,1865* "a mat-
ter"—|No,—"a work   30 *1837* I be used   *31 {Reading of *1837* and
1863.} *1865–89* However that be,   35 *1837* spared: 39–40 *1837* are
we!|VANE. Old Eliot's method . . .|SAVILE. Ah, now, Vane,   43–4 *1837*
this—why Strafford|To do him justice would not hear of it!   45–6 *1837*
Say, rather, you . . . .|To Strafford—he's at York—we all know why!

---

29 *"work for England"*: 'he had only laid that scheme before them that *they
might see how much work they had to do to satisfy their country*': *Life of Pym*, p. 88.
   40 *Eliot's old method*: in 1629 the Speaker, commanded by the King, attempted to leave his chair and so dissolve the House, but 'Denzil Hollis and
Valentine dragged him back . . . he was held down in the chair, and Hollis
swore he should sit still, till it pleased them to rise': *Life of Eliot*, p. 98. This
followed Eliot's reading of his remonstrance.
   41 *the great Duke*: Buckingham, the favourite of Charles in his early years and
therefore a man of unrivalled power and influence.

I would you had not set the Scots on Strafford
Till Strafford put down Pym for us, my lord!
   Savile. Was it I altered Strafford's plans? did
      I . . .
               A Messenger *enters.*
   Messenger. The Queen, my lords—she sends
      me: follow me   50
At once; 't is very urgent! she requires
Your counsel: something perilous and strange
Occasions her command.
   Savile.   We follow, friend!
Now, Vane;—your Parliament will plague us all!
   Vane. No Strafford here beside!   55
   Savile.   If you dare hint
I had a hand in his betrayal, sir . . .
   Holland. Nay, find a fitter time for quarrels—
      Pym
Will overmatch the best of you; and, think,
The Queen!
   Vane.   Come on, then: understand, I loathe
Strafford as much as any—but his use!   60
To keep off Pym, to screen a friend or two,
I would we had reserved him yet awhile.

SCENE II.—*Whitehall.*

The QUEEN *and* Lady CARLISLE.

   Queen. It cannot be.
   Lady Carlisle.   It is so.
   Queen.   Why, the House

48 *1837* Till he had put   49 *1837* I? did I alter . . . . did I . . .|(*Enter a*
MESSENGER.)   50 *1837* lords . . she sends me . .   51, 52 *1837* At once . . 'tis
very urgent . . she would have|Your counsel . .   54 *1837* Now Vane
. .   59–61 *1837* Come on then (*as they go out.*) . . . understand, I loathe|Straf-
ford as much as any—but he serves|So well to keep off Pym—to screen us
all! *1863* as *1888* except 'Pym—to . . . . two!' *1865* as *1888* except 'Pym—to
. . . . two'   62 *1837* awhile!

 1 *1837* be!|CARLISLE. It is so.|QUEEN. Why

Have hardly met.
    Lady Carlisle.   They met for that.
    Queen.   No, no!
Meet to impeach Lord Strafford? 'T is a jest.
    Lady Carlisle. A bitter one.
    Queen.   Consider! 'T is the House
We summoned so reluctantly, which nothing   5
But the disastrous issue of the war
Persuaded us to summon. They 'll wreak all
Their spite on us, no doubt; but the old way
Is to begin by talk of grievances:
They have their grievances to busy them.   10
    Lady Carlisle. Pym has begun his speech.
    Queen.   Where 's Vane?—That is,
Pym will impeach Lord Strafford if he leaves
His Presidency; he 's at York, we know,
Since the Scots beat him: why should he leave
    York?
    Lady Carlisle. Because the King sent for him.   15
    Queen.   Ah—but if
The King did send for him, he let him know
We had been forced to call a Parliament—
A step which Strafford, now I come to think,
Was vehement against.
    Lady Carlisle.   The policy
Escaped him, of first striking Parliaments   20

---

   2 *1837* met!|CARLISLE. They met for that.|QUEEN. No—no—   3 *1837*
Strafford! 'Tis a jest.   *1884* Strafford! 'Tis a jest.   5 *1837* reluctantly—   7
1837 summon; they'll   9 *1837* grievances!   10 *1837* them!   11 *1837*
Vane?. . That is   13 *1837* Presidency—he's at York, you know,   14 *1837*
him—why   15 *1837* King sends for him.|QUEEN. Ah . . . but if   19,20
1837 against . . .|CARLISLE. The policy|Escaped him

---

   9 *grievances*: opposite III. iii old editions of Clarendon have the side-note,
'Mr *Pym* begins the debate of Grievances'.
   13 *His Presidency*: see note to I. i. 204.
   14 *Why should he leave York?*: when in York he heard that a parliament had
been summoned, 'Strafford saw at once the extent of his danger . . . He prayed
of the king to be allowed to retire to his government in Ireland, or to some
other place . . . and not deliver himself into the hands of his enraged enemies.
Charles refused. He still reposed on the enormous value of his minister's genius
. . . At the same time he pledged himself by a solemn promise, that, "while
there was a king in England, not a hair of Strafford's head should be touched by
the parliament!" The earl arrived in London': *Life*, p. 378 (p. 239). Strafford

To earth, then setting them upon their feet
And giving them a sword: but this is idle.
Did the King send for Strafford? He will come.
    Queen. And what am I to do?
    Lady Carlisle.   What do? Fail, madam!
Be ruined for his sake! what matters how,   25
So it but stand on record that you made
An effort, only one?
    Queen.   The King away
At Theobald's!
    Lady Carlisle. Send for him at once: he must
Dissolve the House.
    Queen.   Wait till Vane finds the truth
Of the report: then . . .   30
    Lady Carlisle.   —It will matter little
What the King does. Strafford that lends his arm
And breaks his heart for you!
            Sir H. V*ANE enters.*
    Vane.   The Commons, madam,
Are sitting with closed doors. A huge debate,
No lack of noise; but nothing, I should guess,
Concerning Strafford: Pym has certainly   35
Not spoken yet.
    Queen [*to* Lady CARLISLE]. You hear?
    Lady Carlisle.   I do not hear
That the King 's sent for!
    Vane.   Savile will be able
To tell you more.

    22 *1837* idle!   27 *1837* An effort—only one?|QUEEN. The King's away
1863,1865 An effort, only one?|*Queen.* The King's away   28 *1837* At
Theobald's.| . . . . once—   *1863,1865* At Theobald's .| . . . . once: 30–2
1837 report—then . .|CARLISLE. . . it will matter little|What the king does.
Strafford that serves you all—|That's fighting for you now!|(*Enter* SIR H.
VANE.) *1863,1865* as *1888* except 'arm,'   33–4 *1837* doors—a huge
debate—|No lack of noise—

    wrote to Radcliffe that he was setting out for London 'with more dangers
beset, I believe, than ever any man went with out of Yorkshire'. Whitaker, *Life
of Radcliffe* (1740), p. 218.
    28 *At Theobald's!*: James VI and I exchanged Hatfield for this mansion in
Hertfordshire, the property of the Cecils. It was a favourite residence of
Charles.

HOLLAND *enters.*

Queen.   The last news, Holland?
Holland.   Pym
Is raging like a fire. The whole House means
To follow him together to Whitehall   40
And force the King to give up Strafford.
    Queen.   Strafford?
    Holland. If they content themselves with
        Strafford! Laud
Is talked of, Cottington and Windebank too.
Pym has not left out one of them—I would
You heard Pym raging!   45
    Queen.   Vane, go find the King!
Tell the King, Vane, the People follow Pym
To brave us at Whitehall!
                    SAVILE *enters.*
    Savile.   Not to Whitehall—
'T is to the Lords they go: they seek redress
On Strafford from his peers—the legal way,
They call it.   50
    Queen.   (Wait, Vane!)
                          But the adage gives
Long life to threatened men. Strafford can save
Himself so readily: at York, remember,
In his own county: what has he to fear?
The Commons only mean to frighten him

---

39 *1837* Is raving like a fiend! The   43 *1837–68* Windebank too,   45 *1837*
Pym raving!|QUEEN. Vane, find out the King!   *1882,1884* as *1888* except 'rag-
ing.'   48 *1837* go—they'll seek   *1863,1865* go: they'll seek   50 *1837* it
. . .|QUEEN. (Wait, Vane!)|SAVILE. . . But   51 *1837* men!   53 *1837–68*
county,

42–3 *Laud . . . Cottington and Windebank*: Laud was accused of high treason,
and about the same time Sir Francis Windebank 'was accused of many transactions on the behalf of the Papists': Clarendon, iii. 16. As a close colleague of
Strafford's, Cottington was called to account.
    47 *brave*: defy, confront.
    48 *to the Lords*: 'he was scarce entered into the house of peers', writes
Clarendon, as quoted in the *Life*, 'when the message from the house of
commons was called in, and when Mr. Pym at the bar, and in the name of all
the commons of England, impeached Thomas, earl of Strafford . . . of high
treason!' (p. 378 (p. 240)).
    50 *the adage*: 'Threatened men live long': (Sir Gurney) *Benham's Book of
Quotations*, revised edition, n.d., p. 906.

From leaving York. Surely, he will not come.   55
   Queen. Lucy, he will not come!
   Lady Carlisle.   Once more, the King
Has sent for Strafford. He will come.
    Vane.   Oh doubtless!
And bring destruction with him: that 's his way.
What but his coming spoilt all Conway's plan?
The King must take his counsel, choose his
    friends,   60
Be wholly ruled by him! What 's the result?
The North that was to rise, Ireland to help,—
What came of it? In my poor mind, a fright
Is no prodigious punishment.
   Lady Carlisle.   A fright?
Pym will fail worse than Strafford if he thinks   65
To frighten him. [*To the* QUEEN.] You will not
    save him then?
   Savile. When something like a charge is made,
    the King
Will best know how to save him: and 't is clear,
While Strafford suffers nothing by the matter,
The King may reap advantage: this in question,   70
No dinning you with ship-money complaints!
   Queen [*to* Lady CARLISLE]. If we dissolve them,
    who will pay the army?
Protect us from the insolent Scots?
   Lady Carlisle.   In truth,
I know not, madam. Strafford's fate concerns
Me little: you desired to learn what course   75

55–6 *1837* From leaving York.| QUEEN. Surely he will not come!| Carlisle, he
will not come!   57 *1837* Has sent for Strafford—He will come.| VANE. O
doubtless; *1863,1865* as *1888* except 'Oh,' *1868,1879* as *1888* except 'Hast
sent'   62 *1837* rise—Ireland to help—   63 *1837* mind   66 *1837,1863*
save him,   68–9 *1837* clear| That, while he suffers   70 *1837* King will
reap   74–5 *1837* Madam: Strafford's fate concerns| Me little: *1884* madam.
Strafford's fate concerns me| But little:

59 *Conway's plan*: Lord Conway had been routed at Newburn: see II. ii. 91,
above.

70 *this in question*: while the Commons are preoccupied with Strafford the
King and Queen will not be troubled by the usual complaints about ship-
money.

Would save him: I obey you.
   Vane.   Notice, too,
There can 't be fairer ground for taking full
Revenge—(Strafford 's revengeful)—than he 'll
    have
Against his old friend Pym.
   Queen.   Why, he shall claim
Vengeance on Pym!   80
   Vane.   And Strafford, who is he
To 'scape unscathed amid the accidents
That harass all beside? I, for my part,
Should look for something of discomfiture
Had the King trusted me so thoroughly
And been so paid for it.   85
   Holland.   He 'll keep at York:
All will blow over: he 'll return no worse,
Humbled a little, thankful for a place
Under as good a man. Oh, we 'll dispense
With seeing Strafford for a month or two!
             STRAFFORD *enters.*
   Queen. You here!   90
   Strafford.   The King sends for me, madam.
   Queen.   Sir,
The King . . .
   Strafford.   An urgent matter that imports the
    King!
[*To* Lady CARLISLE.] Why, Lucy, what 's in
    agitation now,
That all this muttering and shrugging, see,
Begins at me? They do not speak!
   Lady Carlisle.   'T is welcome!
For we are proud of you—happy and proud   95

   79 *1837* Against this very Pym.   86–7 *1837* worse—|Humbled a
little—   88 *1837* man—   .*90 {Reading of *1863–84,* DC and *1889.*}
1837 Madam.|QUEEN. Sir . . .   *1888* madam,|*Queen.* Sir,   91 *1837* imports
the King . . .   *1863,1865* imports the King.   92 *1837–65* agitation now
94–5 *1837* Oh welcome!|. . And we are proud of you . . . all very proud

   78 *(Strafford's revengeful)*: as shown by the terrible revenge he took on Lord
Mountnorris and Sir David Foulis: *Life,* pp. 338, 250 (pp. 192 ff., 86 ff.).

To have you with us, Strafford! You were
    staunch
At Durham: you did well there! Had you not
Been stayed, you might have . . . . we said, even
    now,
Our hope 's in you!
    Vane [*to* Lady CARLISLE]. The Queen would
    speak with you.
    Strafford. Will one of you, his servants here,   100
    vouchsafe
To signify my presence to the King?
    Savile. An urgent matter?
    Strafford.   None that touches you,
Lord Savile! Say, it were some treacherous
Sly pitiful intriguing with the Scots—
You would go free, at least! (They half divine   105
My purpose!) Madam, shall I see the King?
The service I would render, much concerns
His welfare.
    Queen.   But his Majesty, my lord,
May not be here, may . . .
    Strafford.   Its importance, then,
Must plead excuse for this withdrawal, madam,   110
And for the grief it gives Lord Savile here.
    Queen [*who has been conversing with* VANE *and*
        HOLLAND]. The King will see you, sir!
[*To* Lady CARLISLE.]   Mark me: Pym's worst
Is done by now: he has impeached the Earl,

---

96 *1837* Strafford . . you were brave *1863,1865* Strafford! you were
staunch   97 *1837* Durham . . You did well there . .   99–100 *1837* Our
last, last hope's in you!|VANE. (*To* CARLISLE.) The Queen would speak|A word
with you!|STRAFFORD. (*To* VANE.) Will one of you vouchsafe   105,106 *1837*
least! (*Aside.*) They half divine|My purpose! (*To the* QUEEN.) Madam,   110
1837 Madam—   112 *1837* Sir.   *1863* sir.   *1865* sir,   113 *1837* now—he

97 *at Durham*: see note to III. i. 1, above. Cf. *Life*, p. 376 (p. 237).
    104 *Sly pitiful intriguing*: Clarendon writes of Savile's 'bitter hatred to the earl
of Strafford, and as passionate hope of the Presidentship of the North', describing him as 'a person of so ill a fame that many desired not to mingle with him.
For, besides his no reputation, they began now to know that he had long held
correspondence with the Scots before their coming in, and invited them to
enter the kingdom with an army': Clarendon, ii. 107.

Or found the Earl too strong for him, by now.
Let us not seem instructed! We should work   115
No good to Strafford, but deform ourselves
With shame in the world's eye. [*To* STRAFFORD.]
    His Majesty
Has much to say with you.
    Strafford.   Time fleeting, too!
[*To* Lady CARLISLE.] No means of getting them
    away? And She—
What does she whisper? Does she know my
    purpose?   120
What does she think of it? Get them away!
    Queen [*to* Lady CARLISLE]. He comes to baffle
      Pym—he thinks the danger
Far off: tell him no word of it! a time
For help will come; we 'll not be wanting then.
Keep him in play, Lucy—you, self-possessed   125
And calm! [*To* STRAFFORD.] To spare your
    lordship some delay
I will myself acquaint the King. [*To* Lady
    CARLISLE.] Beware!
    [*The* QUEEN, VANE, HOLLAND, *and* SAVILE *go
    out.*
    Strafford. She knows it?
    Lady Carlisle.   Tell me, Strafford!
    Strafford.   Afterward!
This moment 's the great moment of all time.
She knows my purpose?   130
    Lady Carlisle.   Thoroughly: just now

114 *1837* him, by now;   117 *1837* eye!   118 *1837* STRAFFORD. (*Aside.*)
Time   119,120 *1837* away, Carlisle?| What   123 *1837* Far off—tell him no
word of it—   124 *1837* come—we'll not be wanting, then!   125 *1837*
play, Carlisle—you,   127 s.d. *1837* (*Exeunt* QUEEN, VANE, HOLLAND *and*
SAVILE.)   128 *1837* me, Strafford . . . .   129 *1837* The moment's . . . .
time!   130 *1837* Thoroughly—

130 *Thoroughly*: 'Lady Carlisle thinks Strafford's "purpose" is "to baffle
Pym" . . . When he says, "The whole of the scheme", he means, "What is my
scheme? Do you really know it?" Lady Carlisle thinks he means, "What is the
scheme against me? Do they connive at Pym's procedure?" When she says,
"The whole is known", she means that the Queen and the Lords are acquainted
with Pym's doings. Strafford and Lady Carlisle are at cross-purposes, until
Strafford (l. 160) begins to speak of the ante-room's being filled with his
adherents, and goes on (l. 164) to explain': EHH.

She bade me hide it from you.
   Strafford.   Quick, dear child,
The whole o' the scheme?
   Lady Carlisle.   (Ah, he would learn if they
Connive at Pym's procedure! Could they but
Have once apprised the King! But there's no
    time
For falsehood, now.) Strafford, the whole is
    known.   135
   Strafford. Known and approved?
   Lady Carlisle.   Hardly discountenanced.
   Strafford. And the King—say, the King
    consents as well?
   Lady Carlisle. The King 's not yet informed,
    but will not dare
To interpose.
   Strafford.   What need to wait him, then?
He 'll sanction it! I stayed, child, tell him, long!   140
It vexed me to the soul—this waiting here.
You know him, there's no counting on the
    King.
Tell him I waited long!
   Lady Carlisle.   (What can he mean?
Rejoice at the King's hollowness?)
   Strafford.   I knew
They would be glad of it,—all over once,   145
I knew they would be glad: but he 'd contrive,
The Queen and he, to mar, by helping it,
An angel's making.
   Lady Carlisle.   (Is he mad?) Dear Strafford,

---

131 *1837* dear girl . .|The whole grand scheme?|CARLISLE. (*Aside*.)
Ah,   135 *1837* now. (*To* STRAFFORD.) Strafford,   137–8 *1837* And the
king—say the king consents as well!|CARLISLE. the king's   140 *1837* stayed,
girl tell him, long! *1882,1884* stayed, child, tell him, long;   141 *1837*
here—   142 *1837* him—there's . . . . king!   143 *1837* CARLISLE. (*Aside*.)
What   144 *1837* king's hollowness?   146 *1837* glad . . . but   148 *1837*
making!|CARLISLE. (*Aside*.) Is he mad? (*To* STRAFFORD.) Dear Strafford,

145 *all over once*: once it was all over.
147–8 *to mar . . . / An angel's making*: 'to make or mar' is proverbial: cf.
Othello v. i. 4: 'It makes us or it mars us'.

You were not wont to look so happy.
   Strafford.   Sweet,
I tried obedience thoroughly. I took   150
The King's wild plan: of course, ere I could reach
My army, Conway ruined it. I drew
The wrecks together, raised all heaven and earth,
And would have fought the Scots: the King at
    once
Made truce with them. Then, Lucy, then, dear
    child,   155
God put it in my mind to love, serve, die
For Charles, but never to obey him more!
While he endured their insolence at Ripon
I fell on them at Durham. But you 'll tell
The King I waited? All the anteroom   160
Is filled with my adherents.
   Lady Carlisle.   Strafford— Strafford,
What daring act is this you hint?
   Strafford.   No, no!
'T is here, not daring if you knew! all here!
         [*Drawing papers from his breast.*
Full proof, see, ample proof—does the Queen
    know

---

149 *1837* happy.|STRAFFORD. Girl,   150 *1837* thoroughly: 151 *1837*
king's wild plan . . .   152 *1837* army—Conway ruined it: 154,155 *1837*
Scots—the King at once|. . . . them: then, Lucy, then, dear girl,   157 *1837*
Charles— 158,159 *1837* Rippon|I fell on them at Durham!|. . . But   161
1837 Strafford—Strafford   162 *1837* No—No!   *163 {Reading of
1863–84}   *1837* 'Tis here—not daring if you knew!—   *1888,1889* 'T is here,
not daring if you knew?   164 *1837* Full proof—see—ample

---

151 *The King's wild plan*: when he went to command the King's troops in
Scotland.

155 *Made truce*: 'Still he was making desperate efforts to strengthen and
animate his army, when suddenly he found that a treaty with the Scots had
actually commenced . . . Ultimately, these negotiations were placed in the
hands of sixteen peers, every one of whom were his personal opponents': *Life*,
pp. 376–7 (pp. 237–8).

159 *I fell on them at Durham*: 'thwarted and exasperated on all sides, he
resolved to furnish one more proof (it was destined to be the last!) of the
possibility of recovering the royal authority, but a great and vigorous exertion.
During the negotiations no actual cessation of arms had been agreed to by the
Scots, and he therefore secretly despatched a party of horse . . . to attack them
in their quarters. A large body of the enemy were defeated by this manœuvre,
all their officers taken prisoners, the army inspirited, and the spirits of Strafford
himself restored': *Life*, pp. 377–8 (p. 239).

164 *Full proof*: 'Clarendon says: "It was believed by some (upon what

I have such damning proof? Bedford and Essex,   165
Brooke, Warwick, Savile (did you notice Savile?
The simper that I spoilt?), Saye, Mandeville—
Sold to the Scots, body and soul, by Pym!
   Lady Carlisle. Great heaven!
   Strafford.   From Savile and his lords, to Pym
And his losels, crushed!—Pym shall not ward the
   blow   170
Nor Savile creep aside from it! The Crew
And the Cabal—I crush them!
   Lady Carlisle.   And you go—
Strafford,—and now you go?—
   Strafford.   —About no work
In the background, I promise you! I go
Straight to the House of Lords to claim these
   knaves.   175
Mainwaring!
   Lady Carlisle. Stay—stay, Strafford!
   Strafford.   She 'll return,
The Queen—some little project of her own!
No time to lose: the King takes fright perhaps.
   Lady Carlisle. Pym's strong, remember!
   Strafford.   Very strong, as fits
The Faction's head—with no offence to
   Hampden,   180
Vane, Rudyard and my loving Hollis: one
And all they lodge within the Tower to-night

166 *1837–68* Broke, Warwick,   167 *1837* spoilt?) Say,   *1863–84* spoilt?)
Saye,   169–171 *1837* to Pym—|I crush them, girl—Pym shall not ward the
blow|Nor Savile crawl aside from it! The Court| 173 *1837* now you go?
. . .|Strafford. About   175 *1837* these men.   176 *1837* return—   177
1837 own—   178 *1837* lose—the King . . . . perhaps—   179,180 *1837*
strong—as fits|The Faction's Head . .   181 *1837* Hollis—

ground was never clear enough) that he made haste then to accuse the Lord
Say, and some others, of having induced the Scots to invade the kingdom".
There is no doubt about the matter on far better evidence than Clarendon's:
EHH.
  170 *losels*: worthless fellows.
  171–2 *The Crew* / *And the Cabal*: cf. *1837*. Probably revised because 'Cabal'
sounds more appropriate for the Court conspirators. Cf. 'the Faction,—Laud /
So styles it' at I. ii. 232–3 (and I. ii. 62).

In just equality. Bryan! Mainwaring!

    [*Many of his* Adherents *enter.*

The Peers debate just now (a lucky chance)
On the Scots' war; my visit 's opportune.   185
When all is over, Bryan, you proceed
To Ireland: these dispatches, mark me, Bryan,
Are for the Deputy, and these for Ormond:
We want the army here—my army, raised
At such a cost, that should have done such good, 190
And was inactive all the time! no matter,
We 'll find a use for it. Willis . . . or, no—you!
You, friend, make haste to York: bear this, at
  once . . .
Or,—better stay for form's sake, see yourself
The news you carry. You remain with me   195
To execute the Parliament's command,
Mainwaring! Help to seize these lesser knaves,
Take care there 's no escaping at backdoors:
I 'll not have one escape, mind me—not one!
I seem revengeful, Lucy? Did you know   200
What these men dare!

  Lady Carlisle.   It is so much they dare!

  Strafford. I proved that long ago; my turn is
  now.

Keep sharp watch, Goring, on the citizens!
Observe who harbours any of the brood

---

*183 {Reading of *1837–84*.} *1888,1889* Brian! 185 *1837* Scots war—my
visit's opportune: 186 *1837* Bryan, you'll proceed 188,189 *1837*
Ormond—|We'll want the Army here—my Army, raised 191 *1837* mat-
ter— 192 *1837* Willis . . . no—You! *1863* Willis . . . or, no—
You! 193 *1837* York— 194 *1837* sake— 197 *1837* Mainwaring—
help to seize the lesser knaves: *1863,1865* Mainwaring! help to seize the lesser
knaves; *1868* Mainwaring! Help to seize the lesser knaves, 198,199 *1837*
backdoors!|To not have one escape— 202 *1837–63* is now! *1865–68* is
now 203 *1837–65* citizens;

183 *Bryan!*: unidentified.
188 *the Deputy*: Christopher Wandesford succeeded Strafford in this post in
April 1640.
Ormond: see note on II. ii. 92.
192 *Willis*: Sir Richard Willis was to become governor of Newark, and to be
dismissed by the King in 1645.
203 *Goring*: 'This Colonel Goring would have taken the lead in a plan,
formed when Strafford was in the Tower, to bring the army up to London, but
the other officers refused to submit to his command': EHH.

That scramble off: be sure they smart for it!   205
Our coffers are but lean.
                       And you, child, too,
Shall have your task; deliver this to Laud.
Laud will not be the slowest in my praise:
"Thorough" he 'll cry!—Foolish, to be so glad!
This life is gay and glowing, after all: 210
'T is worth while, Lucy, having foes like mine
Just for the bliss of crushing them. To-day
Is worth the living for.
    Lady Carlisle.   That reddening brow!
You seem . . .
    Strafford.   Well—do I not? I would be well—
I could not but be well on such a day!   215
And, this day ended, 't is of slight import
How long the ravaged frame subjects the soul
In Strafford.
    Lady Carlisle. Noble Strafford!
    Strafford.   No farewell!
I 'll see you anon, to-morrow—the first thing.
—If She should come to stay me!   220
    Lady Carlisle.   Go—'t is nothing—
Only my heart that swells: it has been thus
Ere now: go, Strafford!
    Strafford.   To-night, then, let it be.
I must see Him: you, the next after Him.
I 'll tell you how Pym looked. Follow me,
    friends!
You, gentlemen, shall see a sight this hour   225

206–7 *1837* And you, girl, too,|Shall have your task—deliver this to
Laud—   208 *1837* praise!   209 *1837* "Thorough" he'll say!|—Fool-
ish, *1863,1865* "Thorough" he'll say!—Foolish,   210 *1837* This sort of life
is vivid, after all!   212 *1837* For the dear bliss of crushing them!   213 *1837*
for!|. . . . brow! *1882,1884* for.|. . . . brow?   218 *1837* In Straf-
ford!   219 *1837* you, girl, to-morrow—the first thing!   220 *1837* —If
she   221 *1837* swells—   222 *1837* Ere now—go, Strafford!|STRAFFORD
. . . . . be!   223 *1837* Him . . . I'll see you after Him . .

209 *"Thorough"*: 'His own government was to be, according to the watch-
word frequently found in his correspondence with Laud, "thorough"—that is
to say, founded on a complete disregard of private interests, with a view to the
establishment, for the good of the whole community, of the royal power as the
embodiment of the state': DNB, lx, 273b. Cf. *Life*, p. 314 (p. 163).

To talk of all your lives. Close after me!
"My friend of friends!"
                    [STRAFFORD *and the rest go out.*
 Lady Carlisle.   The King—ever the King!
No thought of one beside, whose little word
Unveils the King to him—one word from me,
Which yet I do not breathe!   230
                    Ah, have I spared
Strafford a pang, and shall I seek reward
Beyond that memory? Surely too, some way
He is the better for my love. No, no—
He would not look so joyous—I 'll believe
His very eye would never sparkle thus,   235
Had I not prayed for him this long, long while.

SCENE III.—*The Antechamber of the House of Lords.*

Many of the Presbyterian Party. The Adherents *of*
 STRAFFORD, *etc.*

 A Group of Presbyterians.—1. I tell you he
  struck Maxwell: Maxwell sought
To stay the Earl: he struck him and passed on.
 2. Fear as you may, keep a good countenance
Before these rufflers.
 3.   Strafford here the first,
With the great army at his back!
 4.   No doubt.   5

---

 227 s.d. *1837* (*Exeunt* STRAFFORD, *&c.*) 229 *1837* from me— 233 *1837*
love . . . No, no 236 *1837* while!

 1 *1837* struck Maxwell— 4 *1837* these ruffians!| . . . . first— 5 *1837*
doubt!

 227 *"My friend of friends"*: Strafford proudly remembers Charles so terming
him: see II. ii. 54.
 229 *Unveils*: could reveal.

 1 *Maxwell*: the gentleman usher of the Black Rod, who took Strafford into
custody. Strafford did not strike him: this is mere gossip.
 4 *rufflers*: swaggering fellows.

I would Pym had made haste: that 's Bryan,
     hush—
The gallant pointing.
     Strafford's Followers. — 1. Mark these worthies,
          now!
     2. A goodly gathering! "Where the carcass is
"There shall the eagles"—what 's the rest?
     3.   For eagles
Say crows.   10
     A Presbyterian. Stand back, sirs!
     One of Strafford's Followers.   Are we in
          Geneva?
     A Presbyterian. No, nor in Ireland; we have
          leave to breathe.
     One of Strafford's Followers. Truly? Behold how
          privileged we be
That serve "King Pym"! There 's Some-one at
     Whitehall
Who skulks obscure; but Pym struts . . .
     The Presbyterian.   Nearer.
     A Follower of Strafford.   Higher,
We look to see him. [*To his* Companions.]
          I'm to have St. John   15
In charge; was he among the knaves just now

---

6 *1837* haste . . . that's *1884* haste. That's   7 *1837* The fellow pointing.   9 *1837* eagles" . . what's   11 *1837* No—nor in Ireland, *1863,1865*
No—nor in Ireland;   12–15 *1837* Really? Behold how grand a thing it is| To
serve "King Pym"! There's some one at Whitehall| That lives obscure, but
Pym lives . . .| *The* PRESBYTERIAN. Nearer!| *A Follower of* STRAFFORD.
Higher| We look to see him! *1863,1865* as *1888* except 'To serve'

---

8 *"Where the carcass is*: 'For wheresoever the carcase is, there will the eagles be
gathered together': Matthew 24:28.
10 *Geneva*: 'Calvin's code of ecclesiastical and moral discipline had been
established at Geneva in 1541. The sharpest vigilance was exercised over the
words and actions of young and old by a tribunal composed of clergy and laity,
and extremely severe penalties were enforced for divergence of opinion as well
as for offences against morals': EHH.
13 *"King Pym"*: 'A nickname given to Pym by the royalists a little later on':
EHH.
     Some-one: capitalized after *1837* to make it clear that the King is intended.
14 *Higher*: i.e. hanged.
15 *St. John*: Oliver St. John had been an active supporter of the Puritan party
in the Short and Long Parliaments, and had great influence with Pym. Charles
made him Solicitor-General in 1641, for tactical reasons. He defended Strafford's attainder before the Lords. Cf. Clarendon, ii. 93.

That followed Pym within there?
    Another.   The gaunt man
Talking with Rudyard. Did the Earl expect
Pym at his heels so fast? I like it not.
               MAXWELL *enters.*
    Another. Why, man, they rush into the net!
    Here 's Maxwell—   20
Ha, Maxwell? How the brethren flock around
The fellow! Do you feel the Earl's hand yet
Upon your shoulder, Maxwell?
    Maxwell.   Gentlemen,
Stand back! a great thing passes here.
    A Follower of Strafford. [*To another.*] The Earl
Is at his work! [*To* M.] Say, Maxwell, what great
    thing!   25
Speak out! [*To a* Presbyterian.] Friend, I 've a
    kindness for you! Friend,
I 've seen you with St. John: O stockishness!
Wear such a ruff, and never call to mind
St. John's head in a charger? How, the plague,
Not laugh?   30
    Another. Say, Maxwell, what great thing!
    Another.   Nay, wait:
The jest will be to wait.
    First.   And who 's to bear
These demure hypocrites? You 'd swear they
    came . . .
Came . . . just as we come!
       [*A* Puritan *enters hastily and without observing*
           STRAFFORD's Followers.
    The Puritan.   How goes on the work?
Has Pym . . .
    A Follower of Strafford. The secret 's out at last.
    Aha,

21 *1837* Maxwell?—How   26 *1837* Friends, I've. . . . Friends,   27 *1837*
St. John . . .   29 *1837* charger?|What—the plague—   30 *1837* Say Max-
well, what it is!|*Another.* Hush—wait—   31 *1837* to wait—   32 *1837*
These quiet hypocrites?   34 *1837* last—

27 *stockishness*: stupidity. OED has no other example.
29 *St. John's head*: Matthew 14:8–11.

The carrion 's scented! Welcome, crow the first!   35
Gorge merrily, you with the blinking eye!
"King Pym has fallen!"

The Puritan.   Pym?

A Strafford.   Pym!

A Presbyterian.   Only Pym?

Many of Strafford's Followers. No, brother, not
     Pym only; Vane as well,
Rudyard as well, Hampden, St. John as well!

A Presbyterian. My mind misgives: can it be
     true?   40

Another.   Lost! Lost!

A Strafford. Say we true, Maxwell?

The Puritan.   Pride before destruction,
A haughty spirit goeth before a fall.

Many of Strafford's Followers. Ah now! The very
     thing! A word in season!
A golden apple in a silver picture,
To greet Pym as he passes!   45

               [*The doors at the back begin to open,*
                       noise and light issuing.

Maxwell.   Stand back, all!

Many of the Presbyterians. I hold with Pym!
And I!

Strafford's Followers.   Now for the text!
He comes! Quick!

The Puritan.   How hath the oppressor ceased!

---

36 *1837* merrily   38–40 *1837* No, brother—not Pym only—Vane as
well—|Rudyard as well—Hampden—Saint John as well—|*A* PRESBYTERIAN.
My mind misgives . .   42 *1837* a fall!   44–5 *1837* picture|To greet Pym
has he passes!|(*The folding-doors*   46 *1837* I'll die with Pym! And I!| . . . .
text—   47 *1837* The PURITAN. (*With uplifted arms.*) How hath the Oppressor
ceased!

41 *Pride before destruction*: 'Pride goeth before destruction, and an haughty
spirit before a fall': Proverbs 16:18.

43 *A word in season!*: Isaiah 50:4. Cf. Proverbs 15:23.

44 *A golden apple*: 'A word fitly spoken is like apples of gold in pictures of
silver': Proverbs 25:11. In his *Life of Pym*, p. 43, Forster follows the *Parliamentary History* in making Pym quote these words, as he urged the granting of the
five subsidies.

46 *the text*: 'That on which a comment is written': Johnson.

47 *How hath the oppressor*: 'How hath the oppressor ceased! . . . The LORD
hath broken the staff of the wicked; and the sceptre of the rulers. He who smote

The Lord hath broken the staff of the wicked!
The sceptre of the rulers, he who smote
The people in wrath with a continual stroke,   50
That ruled the nations in his anger—he
Is persecuted and none hindereth!
[*The doors open, and* STRAFFORD *issues in the greatest*
    disorder, and amid cries from within of "Void the
                                            House!"
  Strafford. Impeach me! Pym! I never struck, I
    think,
The felon on that calm insulting mouth
When it proclaimed—Pym's mouth proclaimed
    me . . . God!   55
Was it a word, only a word that held
The outrageous blood back on my heart—which
    beats!
Which beats! Some one word—"Traitor," did he
    say,
Bending that eye, brimful of bitter fire,
Upon me?   60
  Maxwell. In the Commons' name, their servant
Demands Lord Strafford's sword.
  Strafford.   What did you say?
  Maxwell. The Commons bid me ask your
    lordship's sword.
  Strafford. Let us go forth: follow me,
    gentlemen!

48 *1837* wicked: 49 *1837* Rulers—he who smote|The People . . . .
stroke—   51 *1837* anger . . . He   53 s.d. *1837* (*At the beginning of this
speech, the doors open, and* STRAFFORD *in the greatest disorder, and amid cries from
within of* "Void the House," *staggers out. When he reaches the front of the Stage,
silence.*) *1863–82* as *1888* except 'House." *1884* as *1888* except "form within
. . . . House.' 60 *1837* MAXWELL. (*Advancing.*) In   63 *1837* STRAFFORD (*suddenly recovering, and looking round, draws it, and turns to his followers*). Let us go
forth—follow me, gentlemen—

the people in wrath with a continual stroke, he that ruled the nations in anger, is
persecuted, and none hindereth': Isaiah 14:4–6.
    53 *"Void the House!"*: 'Strafford had entered the house, we learn from one
who observed him, with his usual impetuous step—"with speed," says Baillie,
"he comes to the house; . . . but at once many bid him void the house': *Life*, p. 379
(p. 240).
    61 *Lord Strafford's sword*: '"In the outer room, James Maxwell required him,
as prisoner, to deliver his sword. When he had got it, he cries, with a loud voice,

Draw your swords too: cut any down that bar
  us.
On the King's service! Maxwell, clear the way!   65
  [*The* Presbyterians *prepare to dispute his passage.*
  Strafford. I stay: the King himself shall see me
    here.
Your tablets, fellow!
[*To* MAINWARING.]   Give that to the King!
Yes, Maxwell, for the next half-hour, let be!
Nay, you shall take my sword!
                    [MAXWELL *advances to take it.*
                        Or, no—not that!
Their blood, perhaps, may wipe out all thus far,   70
All up to that—not that! Why, friend, you see
When the King lays your head beneath my foot
It will not pay for that. Go, all of you!
  Maxwell. I dare, my lord, to disobey: none stir!
  Strafford. This gentle Maxwell!—Do not touch
    him, Bryan!   75
[*To the* Presbyterians.] Whichever cur of you will
    carry this
Escapes his fellow's fate. None saves his life?
None?
              [*Cries from within of* "STRAFFORD!"
      Slingsby, I 've loved you at least: make
  haste!

64 *1837* too—cut . . . . us?   65,65a,66,66a,67 *1837 his passage.*)|STRAF-
FORD. Ha—true! . . . That is, you mistake me, utterly—|I will stay—the King
himself shall see me—here—|Here—I will stay, Mainwaring!—First of
all,|(*To* MAXWELL.) Your tablets, fellow! (*He writes on them.*)|(*To* MAIN-
WARING.) Give that to the King!   68,68a *1837* half-hour, I will . . .|I will
remain your prisoner, I will!| 69 *1837 take it.*)|No—no—not that!   70
1837 far—   71 *1863–68* you see,   72 *1837* lays his head   73 *1837* for
that!   74 *1837* I grieve, my lord, to disobey: none stir.   76,77,77a *1837*
carry this|I'll save him from the fate of all the rest—|I'll have him made a
Peer—I'll . . . none will go?   *1863–68* as *1888* except 'fellows' fate.' in line
77.   78 *1837 of* "STRAFFORD."|(*To his* FOLLOWERS.) Slingsby, I've loved you
at least—my friend,   *1863–84* as *1888* except '"STRAFFORD."'

for his man to carry my lord-lieutenant's sword. This done, he makes through
a number of people to his coach, all gazing, no man capping to him, before
whom that morning the greatest in England would have stood uncovered"':
Baillie, quoted in *Life,* p. 379 (pp. 240–1).
  78 *Slingsby*: Strafford's secretary, Guilford Slingsby. Rushworth prints a
letter from Strafford to Slingsby (*Trial,* p. 774) written immediately after the
Bill of Attainder.

Stab me! I have not time to tell you why.
You then, my Bryan! Mainwaring, you then!   80
Is it because I spoke so hastily
At Allerton? The King had vexed me.
[*To the* Presbyterians.]   You!
—Not even you? If I live over this,
The King is sure to have your heads, you know!
But what if I can't live this minute through?   85
Pym, who is there with his pursuing smile!
                    [*Louder cries of* "STRAFFORD!"
The King! I troubled him, stood in the way
Of his negotiations, was the one
Great obstacle to peace, the Enemy
Of Scotland: and he sent for me, from York,   90
My safety guaranteed—having prepared
A Parliament—I see! And at Whitehall
The Queen was whispering with Vane—I see
The trap!   [*Tearing off the George.*
          I tread a gewgaw underfoot,
And cast a memory from me. One stroke, now!   95

79,80 *1837* tell you why . . . | You then, dear Bryan! You Mainwaring, then!
81 *1837* . . . Ah, that's because   82,82a *1837* At Allerton—the King had
vexed me . . . | (*To the* PRESBYTERIANS.) You | Miscreants—you then—that I'll
exterminate!   83,84,84a–c *1837* over it | The King . . . . heads—you
know | I'm not afraid of that—you understand | That if I chose to wait—made
up my mind | To live this minute | he would do me right! | 85,85a,86 *1837*
minute through? | If nothing can repay that minute? Pym | With his pursuing
smile—Pym to be there! | (*Louder cries of* "STRAFFORD.") | *1863–84* {as *1888*
except "STRAFFORD."}   89,90 *1837* peace—the Enemy | Of Scotland—and he
sent for me—from York—   92 *1837* A Parliament!   94,94a–d *1837* The
trap! I curse the King! I wish Pym well! | Wish all his brave friends well! Say, all
along | Strafford was with them—all along, at heart, | I hated Charles and
wished them well! And say | (*tearing off the George and dashing it down*) | That as I
tread this gew-gaw under foot,   95—end of scene. *1837* I cast his memory
from me! One stroke, now! | (*His own adherents disarm him. Renewed cries of*
"STRAF- FORD.") | I'll not go . . . they shall drag me by the hair! | *Changing
suddenly to calm.*) England! I see her arm in this! I yield. | Why—'tis the fairest
triumph! Why desire | To cheat them? I would never stoop to that— | Be mean
enough for that! Let all have end! | Don't repine, Slingsby . . have they not a
right? | They claim me—hearken—lead me to them, Bryan! | No—I myself
should offer up myself. | Pray you now . . . Pym awaits me . . . pray you
now! | (*Putting aside those who attempt to support him,* STRAFFORD | *reaches the
doors—they open wide.* HAMPDEN, &c. *and a crowd discovered; and at the bar,* PYM
standing apart. As STRAFFORD *kneels the scene shuts.*) | END OF THE THIRD
ACT.   *1863–84* {substantially as *1888*.   *1863,1865* have 'Thy arm' in line 96.}

---

82 *at Allerton*: Northallerton in Yorkshire.
91 *My safety guaranteed*: see note to III. ii. 14, above.

[*His own* Adherents *disarm him. Renewed cries of*
    "STRAFFORD!"
England! I see thy arm in this and yield.
Pray you now—Pym awaits me—pray you
    now!   .
[STRAFFORD *reaches the doors: they open wide.* HAMP-
    DEN *and a crowd discovered, and, at the bar,* PYM
    standing apart. As STRAFFORD *kneels, the scene
    shuts.*

ACT IV.

SCENE I.—*Whitehall*.

The KING, *the* QUEEN, HOLLIS, Lady CARLISLE.
(VANE, HOLLAND, SAVILE, *in the background*.)

Lady Carlisle. Answer them, Hollis, for his
    sake! One word!
Charles. [*To* HOLLIS.] You stand, silent and
    cold, as though I were
Deceiving you—my friend, my playfellow
Of other times. What wonder after all?
Just so, I dreamed my People loved me.   5
    Hollis.   Sir,
It is yourself that you deceive, not me.
You 'll quit me comforted, your mind made up
That, since you 've talked thus much and grieved
    thus much,
All you can do for Strafford has been done.
    Queen. If you kill Strafford—(come, we grant
        you leave,
Suppose)—   10
    Hollis.   I may withdraw, sir?
    Lady Carlisle.   Hear them out!

---

  1 *1837* sake!—   4 *1837* times!   5 *1837* Just so . . . . me!|HOLLIS.
Sire,   6 *1837* not me!   7 *1837* comforted—   10,11 *1837* Strafford . . .
come, we grant you leave,|Suppose . . .|HOLLIS. I may withdraw, Sire?

  7 *comforted*: 'When the bill of attainder was passed, the king sent for him
[Hollis], to know what he could do to save the earl of Strafford. Hollis
answered that, if the king pleased, since the execution of the law was in him, he
might legally grant him a reprieve, which must be good in law;—but he would
not advise it': *Life*, pp. 401–2 (p. 267), quoting a note 'taken from the lips of
Hollis himself'. Hollis believed that Strafford might have been saved if he had
begged for 'a short respite, to settle his affairs', and the King and his party had
played their cards differently.
  11 *I may withdraw, sir?*: cf. note to I. i. initial s.d., above.

'T is the last chance for Strafford! Hear them out!
   Hollis. "If we kill Strafford"—on the
      eighteenth day
Of Strafford's trial—"We!"
   Charles.   Pym, my good Hollis—
Pym, I should say!   15
   Hollis.   Ah, true—sir, pardon me!
You witness our proceedings every day;
But the screened gallery, I might have guessed,
Admits of such a partial glimpse at us,
Pym takes up all the room, shuts out the view.
Still, on my honour, sir, the rest of the place   20
Is not unoccupied. The Commons sit
—That 's England; Ireland sends, and Scotland
      too,
Their representatives; the Peers that judge
Are easily distinguished; one remarks
The People here and there: but the close curtain   25
Must hide so much!
   Queen.   Acquaint your insolent crew,
This day the curtain shall be dashed aside!
It served a purpose.
   Hollis.   Think! This very day?
Ere Strafford rises to defend himself?
   Charles. I will defend him, sir!—sanction the
      past   30
This day: it ever was my purpose. Rage

---

*12{Reading of *1837–84*} *1888, 1889* T is   14 *1837* trial—*We!*   *1863,1865*
trial—*"We!"*   16 *1837* day,   18 *1837* us—   19 *1837* view!   21 *1837*
unoccupied: the   25 *1837* there . . . *1882,1884* there;   28 *1837* purpose!   30 *1837* Sir! sanction the past—   *1863,1865* sir!—sanction the
Past   *1884* sir! sanction the past   31 *1837* day—it ever was my purpose!

---

13 *on the eighteenth day*: the trial opened on 22 March 1641, which would
make this 8 April.

17 *the screened gallery*: the *Life* describes the King and his court in a cabinet or
gallery, with trellis work (p. 382 (p. 244)), having earlier described him as 'a
timid auditor, listening unobserved through his screening curtains' (p. 380 (p.
241)). According to Baillie, the King 'brake down the screens with his own
hands': ibid., p. 382 n. (p. 244 n.). Cf. l. 27.

22 *England; Ireland . . . Scotland*: 'Three kingdoms, by their representatives,
were present, and for fifteen days, the period of the duration of the trial, "it was
daily", says Baillie, "the most glorious assembly the isle could afford" ': *Life*, p.
387 (p. 250). Cf. 53n, below.

At me, not Strafford!
 Lady Carlisle. Nobly!—will he not
Do nobly?
 Hollis. Sir, you will do honestly;
And, for that deed, I too would be a king.
  Charles. Only, to do this now!—"deaf" (in
   your style)
"To subjects' prayers,"—I must oppose them
   now!
It seems their will the trial should proceed,—
So palpably their will!
  Hollis.   You peril much,
But it were no bright moment save for that.
Strafford, your prime support, the sole roof-tree 40
Which props this quaking House of Privilege,
(Floods come, winds beat, and see—the
   treacherous sand!)
Doubtless, if the mere putting forth an arm
Could save him, you 'd save Strafford.
  Charles.   And they dare
Consummate calmly this great wrong! No hope? 45

32,32a *1837* At me, not Strafford! Oh I shall be paid|By Strafford's
look!|CARLISLE. (*To* HOLLIS.) Nobly! Oh will he not 34 *1837* that look, I too
would be a king! 35,35a,36 *1837* CHARLES (*after a pause*). Only, to do this
now—just when they seek|To make me out a tyrant—one that's deaf|To
subjects' prayers,—shall I oppose them now? *1863–84* as *1888* except 'them
now.' 37 *1837* Trial should proceed . . . *1863* Trial should pro-
ceed,— 38 *1837* 'Tis palpably their will!|HOLLIS. You'll lose your
throne: 39 *1837* for that! 41 *1837–84* That props 43 *1837* Doubtless 44 *1837* Strafford! *44–5 {Reading of *1884*, DC and *1889*.} *1837–65*
And they mean|Calmly to consummate this wrong! *1868,1882,1888* And they

33 *you will do honestly*: 'Holles tried to arrange that, on the king making
important concessions in other matters, the death penalty should not be
insisted on in the Bill of Attainder, but was unsuccessful. Beyond this, there is
no historical foundation for his views and conduct as given in this scene, and in
the last act': George, pp. 88–9.
 35 *Only, to do this now!*: *1837* helps to make the meaning clear.
 38 *peril*: endanger. Note the revisions from *1837*.
 41 *House of Privilege*: 'It was not the trial of an individual, but the solemn
arbitration of an issue between the two great antagonist principles, liberty and
despotism': *Life*, p. 381 (p. 243).
 42 (*Floods come*: 'And every one that heareth these sayings of mine, and doeth
them not, shall be likened unto a foolish man, which built his house upon the
sand: And the rain descended, and the floods came, and the winds blew, and
beat upon that house; and it fell: and great was the fall of it': Matthew 7:26–7.
 45 *Consummate*: stressed on the second syllable, as in Johnson and elsewhere
in Browning.

This ineffaceable wrong! No pity then?
  Hollis. No plague in store for perfidy?
    —Farewell!
You called me, sir—[*To* Lady CARLISLE.] you,
    lady, bade me come
To save the Earl: I came, thank God for it,
To learn how far such perfidy can go!   50
You, sir, concert with me on saving him
Who have just ruined Strafford!
  Charles.   I?—and how?
  Hollis. Eighteen days long he throws, one after
    one,
Pym's charges back: a blind moth-eaten law!
—He 'll break from it at last: and whom to
    thank?   55
The mouse that gnawed the lion's net for him

---

mean|Consummate calmly this great wrong!   48–9 *1837* You summoned
me . . . (*To* CARLISLE.) You, Lady, bade me come . . . . Earl! *1863* as *1888*
except 'CARLISLE]' *1865–68* as *1888* except 'CARLISLE,]'   51 *1837* . . . You
dare to talk with me of saving him   52 *1837* CHARLES. I?|HOLLIS. See,
now!   54 *1837* Our charges   55 *1837* from us at last! And   56–8 *1837*
Mouse . . . . Lion's . . . . Mouse, ... Lion

    47 *No plague*: no doubt spoken aside.
    53 *Eighteen days*: cf. IV. i. 13 above, and IV. ii. 41 below. Miss Hickey must
have been worried about the chronology, since Browning wrote to her, on 8
December 1883: 'I shall be glad if you substitute "fifteen" for "eighteen",
supposing this last was an error: I tried to be right at the time': *Checklist*, 83:182.
She may have been thinking of the statement in the *Life* (p. 387: p. 250) that
'fifteen days [was] the period of the duration of the trial', a statement which
conflicts with other statements there. In any case, she made no alteration.
    54 *a blind moth-eaten law!*: 'It is now 240 years since any man was touched for
this alleged crime, to this height, before myself. Let us not awaken these
sleeping lions to our destructions, by taking up a few musty records, that have
lain by the walls so many ages, forgotten or neglected': Strafford's own words,
quoted in *Life*, p. 395 (p. 259).
    56 *The mouse*: the fable of 'The *Lion* and the *Mouse*' tells how a lion was about
to kill a mouse which had awakened him when 'the little Suppliant implored
his Mercy in a very moving Manner' with the result that the lion released him.
'Not long after, traversing the Forest in Pursuit of his Prey, he chanced to run
into the Toils of the Hunters; from whence, not able to disengage himself, he
set up a most hideous and loud Roar. The Mouse, hearing the Voice, and
knowing it to be the Lion's, immediately repaired to the Place, and bid him fear
nothing, for that he was his Friend. Then straight he fell to work, and, with his
little sharp Teeth, gnawing asunder the Knots and Fastenings of the Toils, set
the Royal Brute at Liberty'. 'The Application' explains that 'This Fable gives us
to understand, that there is no Person in the World so little, but even the
greatest may, at some Time or other, stand in Need of his Assistance; and
consequently that it is good to use Clemency, where there is any Room for it,
towards those who fall within our Power': *Fables of Æsop and others: translated*

Got a good friend,—but he, the other mouse,
That looked on while the lion freed himself——
Fared he so well, does any fable say?
    Charles. What can you mean?   60
    Hollis.   Pym never could have proved
Strafford's design of bringing up the troops
To force this kingdom to obedience: Vane—
Your servant, not our friend, has proved it.
    Charles.   Vane?
    Hollis. This day. Did Vane deliver up or no
Those notes which, furnished by his son to Pym,   65
Seal Strafford's fate?
    Charles.   Sir, as I live, I know
Nothing that Vane has done! What treason next?
I wash my hands of it. Vane, speak the truth!
Ask Vane himself!
    Hollis.   I will not speak to Vane,
Who speak to Pym and Hampden every day.   70
    Queen. Speak to Vane's master then! What
      gain to him
Were Strafford's death?
    Hollis.   Ha? Strafford cannot turn

---

63 *1837* Your servant, Vane . . .|QUEEN. Well, Sir?|HOLLIS. . . Has proved
it.|CHARLES. Vane? *1884* Your servant, not our friend—has proved it.|*Cha.*
Vane?   64 *1837* day!   66 *1837* Have sealed . . .|CHARLES. Speak Vane! As I
shall live, I know   68 *1837* of it!   69 *1837* —Ask Vane himself!|HOLLIS. I
. . . . Vane   *1863,1865* Ask Vane himself!|*Hollis*. I . . . . Vane   70 *1837*
day!   71 *1837* then! Why should he wish|For Strafford's death?|HOLLIS.
Why? Strafford cannot turn

. . . *With Instructive Applications; and a print before each fable*, by Samuel Croxall
(16th ed., 1798). Mrs. Orr tells us that Browning's mother 'used to read
Croxall's Fables to his little sister and him': *Life*, p. 26.
   65 *Those notes*: 'on the morning of the 10th of April, before the opening of
that day's trial, Pym entered the house of commons and announced a communication respecting the earl of Strafford, of vital importance. The members
were ordered to remain in their places, and the doors of the house were locked.
Pym and the young sir Harry Vane then rose, and produced a paper containing
"a copy of notes taken at a junto of the privy council for the Scots affairs, about
the 5th of May last". These were notes made by sir Henry Vane the elder, and
Clarendon says, that he placed them in the hands of Pym out of hatred to
Strafford. With much more appearance and likelihood of truth, however,
Whitelocke states that the elder Vane, being absent from London, . . . sent the
key of his study to his son, and that the latter . . . found this paper, and was
ultimately induced by Pym to allow its production against Strafford': *Life*, p.
393 (pp. 256–7).
   68 *I wash my hands of it*: like Pontius Pilate: cf. Matthew 27:24.

As you, sir, sit there—bid you forth, demand
If every hateful act were not set down
In his commission?—whether you contrived   75
Or no, that all the violence should seem
His work, the gentle ways—your own,—his
    part,
To counteract the King's kind impulses—
While . . . but you know what he could say! And
    then
He might produce,—mark, sir!—a certain charge   80
To set the King's express command aside,
If need were, and be blameless. He might add . . .
    Charles. Enough!
    Hollis. —Who bade him break the Parliament,
Find some pretence for setting up sword-law!
    Queen. Retire!   85
    Charles.   Once more, whatever Vane dared
    do,
I know not: he is rash, a fool—I know
Nothing of Vane!
    Hollis.   Well—I believe you. Sir,
Believe me, in return, that . . .
[*Turning to* Lady CARLISLE.] Gentle lady,
The few words I would say, the stones might
    hear
Sooner than these,—I rather speak to you,   90

73 *1837* As you sit there—bid you come forth and say   77 *1837* your own,
as if *1863,1865* your own, his part   78 *1837* He counteracted your kind
impulses   80 *1837* Would he produce, mark you, a certain charge *1863,1865*
He might produce,—mark sir,—a certain charge   81 *1837* To set your own
express commands aside,   82 *1837* blameless! He'd say, then
. . . . *1863,1865* blameless! He might add . . .   83 *1837* CHARLES.
Hold!|HOLLIS. . . . . Say who bade him break the Parliament,—   84 *1837*
Find out some pretext to set up sword-law . . .   *1863–84* Find some pretext for
setting up sword-law!   85–6 *1837* QUEEN. Retire, Sir!|CHARLES. Vane—once
more—what Vane dares do|I know not . . . he is rash . . . a fool . . . I
know   87 *1837* you; Sire   89,90 *1837* say the stones might hear|Sooner
than these . . . I'll say them all to you,

80 *a certain charge*: 'Not even content with these vast and extraordinary
powers and precautions, lord Wentworth engaged for another condition—the
most potent and remarkable of all—that he was to consider them changeable
on the spot whenever the advancement of his majesty's affairs required': *Life*,
p. 272 (p. 112).
  84 *sword-law*: *Paradise Lost*, xi. 672.

You, with the heart! The question, trust me,
    takes
Another shape, to-day: not, if the King
Or England shall succumb,—but, who shall pay
The forfeit, Strafford or his master. Sir,
You loved me once: think on my warning now!   95
                         [*Goes out.*

    Charles. On you and on your warning both!—
    Carlisle!
That paper!
    Queen.   But consider!
    Charles.   Give it me!
There, signed—will that content you? Do not
    speak!
You have betrayed me, Vane! See! any day,
According to the tenor of that paper,   100
He bids your brother bring the army up,
Strafford shall head it and take full revenge.
Seek Strafford! Let him have the same, before
He rises to defend himself!
    Queen.   In truth?
That your shrewd Hollis should have worked a
    change   105
Like this! You, late reluctant . . .
    Charles.   Say, Carlisle,
Your brother Percy brings the army up,
Falls on the Parliament——(I 'll think of you,
My Hollis!) say, we plotted long—'t is mine,

92 *1837* to-day: 'tis not if Charles   93 *1837* but which shall   94 *1837*
Master: Sire,   95 *1837* once . . . think . . . . now!|(*Exit.*)   98 *1837*
There—signed—will that content you?—   99 *1837* Vane!—See—any
day   100 *1837* (According to the tenour of that paper)   102–3 *1837*
revenge!|Seek Strafford! Let him have it, look, before   105–6 *1837* Clever of
Hollis, now, to work a change|Like this! You were reluctant . . .|CHARLES. Say,
Carlisle   107 *1837* Army up—   108–9 *1837* you|My Hollis!)—say we
plotted long . . . 'tis *mine,*

---

101 *He bids your brother:* 'The Earl of Northumberland. There was a plot
formed, originally by Sir John Suckling, to bring the army up to London,
overawe the Parliament, and render the King absolute. This was to be combined with the escape of Strafford from the Tower': EHH. Cf. Clarendon iii.
181 ff. George rightly comments that 'Nothing . . . happened at all closely
resembling what appears in this scene. The exigencies of dramatic construction
are responsible for this way of representing it, which makes the king appear
more selfish than he really was'.

The scheme is mine, remember! Say, I cursed   110
Vane's folly in your hearing! If the Earl
Does rise to do us shame, the fault shall lie
With you, Carlisle!
 Lady Carlisle. Nay, fear not me! but still
That 's a bright moment, sir, you throw away.
Tear down the veil and save him!   115
 Queen.   Go, Carlisle!
 Lady Carlisle. (I shall see Strafford—speak to
  him: my heart
Must never beat so, then! And if I tell
The truth? What 's gained by falsehood? There
  they stand
Whose trade it is, whose life it is! How vain
To gild such rottenness! Strafford shall know,   120
Thoroughly know them!)
 Queen. Trust to me! [*To* CARLISLE.] Carlisle,
You seem inclined, alone of all the Court,
To serve poor Strafford: this bold plan of yours
Merits much praise, and yet . . .
 Lady Carlisle.   Time presses, madam.
 Queen. Yet—may it not be something
  premature?   125
Strafford defends himself to-day—reserves
Some wondrous effort, one may well suppose!
 Lady Carlisle. Ay, Hollis hints as much.
 Charles.   Why linger then?
Haste with the scheme—my scheme: I shall be
  there
To watch his look. Tell him I watch his look!   130
 Queen. Stay, we 'll precede you!
 Lady Carlisle.   At your pleasure.

110 *1837* Say 111 *1837* If that man 114 *1837* Sire, you throw away
. . . 115 *1837* Oh, draw the veil 116 *1837* CARLISLE (*aside, and going*). I
shall 119 *1837* it is—whose 121 *1837* THE QUEEN (*as she leaves the* KING,
&c.*) Trust 127,127a,128 *1837* effort . . one may well suppose—|He'll say
some overwhelming fact, Carlisle!|CARLISLE. Aye, 129 *1837* my
scheme—I 130 *1837* look! Tell

126 *Strafford defends himself to-day*: he began to speak in his own defence on 13
April.

Charles.   Say—
Say, Vane is hardly ever at Whitehall!
I shall be there, remember!
   Lady Carlisle.   Doubt me not.
   Charles. On our return, Carlisle, we wait you
    here!
   Lady Carlisle. I'll bring his answer. Sir, I
    follow you.   135
(Prove the King faithless, and I take away
All Strafford cares to live for: let it be——
'T is the King's scheme!
            My Strafford, I can save,
Nay, I have saved you, yet am scarce content,
Because my poor name will not cross your mind.   140
Strafford, how much I am unworthy you!)

Scene II.—*A Passage adjoining Westminster Hall.*

Many Groups of Spectators *of the Trial.* Officers
of the Court, etc.

   1st *Spectator.* More crowd than ever! Not
    know Hampden, man?
That 's he, by Pym, Pym that is speaking now.
No, truly, if you look so high you 'll see
Little enough of either!
   2nd *Spectator.*   Stay: Pym's arm
Points like a prophet's rod.   5
   3rd *Spectator.*   Ay, ay, we 've heard
Some pretty speaking: yet the Earl escapes.

131,132 *1837* Say . . .|Say . . Vane   133 *1837* not!   135,135a–137 *1837*
answer; Sire, I follow you. (*Exeunt* K. &c.)|Ah . . . but he would be very sad to
find| The King so faithless, and I take away| All that he cares to live for: let it
go—   138 *1837* can save . . .   139 *1837* I *have* saved you—yet am   *1863* I
have saved you, yet am   *1865* I have saved you, yet I am   140 *1837* mind
. . .   141 *1837* you!|(*Exit.*)

   s.d. *1837 Many* . . . . *Trial* (*which is visible from the back of the Stage*)—
Officers 1 *1837* ever! . . . Not   2 *1837* he—by Pym—Pym that is speaking
now!   3 *1837* truly—   4 *1837* SECOND SPECTATOR. Hush . . Pym's   5
1837 rod!|. . . . Ay—ay—   6 *1837* speaking . . yet the Earl escapes!

4th Spectator. I fear it: just a foolish word or
   two
About his children—and we see, forsooth,
Not England's foe in Strafford, but the man
Who, sick, half-blind . . .   10
   2nd Spectator.   What's that Pym's saying now
Which makes the curtains flutter? look! A hand
Clutches them. Ah! The King's hand!
   5th Spectator.   I had thought
Pym was not near so tall. What said he, friend?
   2nd Spectator. "Nor is this way a novel way of
   blood,"
And the Earl turns as if to . . . look! look!   15
   Many Spectators.   There!
What ails him? no—he rallies, see—goes on,
And Strafford smiles. Strange!
   An Officer.   Haselrig!
   Many Spectators.   Friend? Friend?
   The Officer. Lost, utterly lost: just when we
   looked for Pym
To make a stand against the ill effects
Of the Earl's speech! Is Haselrig without?   20
Pym's message is to him.

---

8 *1837* children . . . and they see,   9 *1837* Foe in Strafford—but the
Man   11 *1837* That makes the curtains flutter . .   12 *1837* them . .   13
1837 tall!   14 *1837* blood" . . .   15 *1837* MANY SPECTATORS. Heaven—|
What ails him . . no—he rallies . . see—goes on| And Strafford smiles.
Strange!|(*Enter a* PURITAN.)|THE PURITAN. Haselrig   *1863–84* as *1888* except
'on'   18 *1837* THE PURITAN. Lost—utterly lost . . just   *1863,1865* as *1888*
except 'lost! just'   21 *1837* to him! (*Exit.*

---

8 *his children*: "'My lords, I have troubled you longer than I should have
done, were it not for the interest of those dear pledges a saint in Heaven hath left
me". At this word (says the reporter) he stopped awhile, letting fall some tears
to her memory': *Life*, p. 395 (pp. 259–60), quoting Whitelocke's *Memorials*.
  11 *Which makes the curtains flutter?*: cf. note to l. 17, above.
  14 *"Nor is this way*: "'Neither will this", Pym contended . . . with a terrible
earnestness, "be a new way of blood. There are marks enough to trace this law
to the very original of this kingdom"': *Life*, p. 398 (p. 263).
  16 *What ails him?*: 'At this moment, it is said, Strafford had been closely and
earnestly watching Pym, when the latter, suddenly turning, met the fixed and
wasted features of his early associate. A rush of other feelings crowding into
that look, for a moment dispossessed him': *Life*, p. 398 (p. 263). Cf. ll. 189 ff.
  17 *Haselrig!*: 'Sir Arthur Hazlerigg's name is prominently connected with
the proposal to bring in a Bill of Attainder against Strafford. Hazlerigg was one
of the five members whom Charles tried to impeach in 1642': EHH.

3rd Spectator.   Now, said I true?
Will the Earl leave them yet at fault or no?
    1st Spectator. Never believe it, man! These
        notes of Vane's
Ruin the Earl.
    5th Spectator. A brave end: not a whit
Less firm, less Pym all over. Then, the trial   25
Is closed. No—Strafford means to speak
        again?
    An Officer. Stand back, there!
    5th Spectator.   Why, the Earl is
        coming hither!
Before the court breaks up! His brother, look,—
You 'd say he 'd deprecated some fierce act
In Strafford's mind just now.   30
    An Officer.   Stand back, I say!
    2nd Spectator. Who 's the veiled woman that he
    .   talks with?
    Many Spectators. Hush—
The Earl! the Earl!
    [*Enter* STRAFFORD, SLINGSBY, *and other* Secretaries,
        HOLLIS, Lady CARLISLE, MAXWELL, BALFOUR,
        etc. STRAFFORD *converses with* Lady CARLISLE.
    Hollis.   So near the end! Be patient—Return!
    Strafford [*to his* Secretaries]. Here—anywhere
        —or, 't is freshest here!
To spend one's April here, the blossom-
        month:
Set it down here! [*They arrange a table, papers, etc.*   35
                So, Pym can quail, can cower
Because I glance at him, yet more 's to do?
What's to be answered, Slingsby? Let us end!

      24 *1837* Earl!|. . . . end . .   25 *1837* less . . . Pym all over! Then the
Trial   *1863* less Pym all over. Then, the Trial   26 *1837* Is closed . . . no . .
Strafford means to speak again!   29 *1837,1863* he deprecated   30 *1837*
now!   33 *1837* or—'tis freshest here . .   34 *1837* here—the blossom-
month!)   *1863,1865,1884* here, the blossom-month!   35,36 *1837* What, Pym
to quail, to sink|Becauce I glance at him, yet . . .|Well, to end—

22 *at fault*: off the scent (in hunting): cf. l. 49, below.
28 *His brother*: Hollis.

[*To* Lady CARLISLE.] Child, I refuse his offer;
    whatsoe'er
It be! Too late! Tell me no word of him!
'T is something, Hollis, I assure you that—   40
To stand, sick as you are, some eighteen days
Fighting for life and fame against a pack
Of very curs, that lie through thick and thin,
Eat flesh and bread by wholesale, and can't say
"Strafford" if it would take my life!   45
    Lady Carlisle.   Be moved!
Glance at the paper!
    Strafford.   Already at my heels!
Pym's faulting bloodhounds scent the track
    again.
Peace, child! Now, Slingsby!
    [Messengers *from* LANE *and other of* STRAFFORD'S
      Counsel *within the Hall are coming and going
      during the Scene.*
    Strafford [*setting himself to write and dictate*]. I
    shall beat you, Hollis!
Do you know that? In spite of St. John's tricks,
In spite of Pym—your Pym who shrank from
    me!   50
Eliot would have contrived it otherwise.
[*To a* Messenger.] In truth? This slip, tell Lane,
    contains as much
As I can call to mind about the matter.

---

   38 *1837* (*To* CARLISLE.) Girl, I refuse   40 *1837* (*To* HOLLIS.)
'Tis   45,45a,46 *1837* Be kind|This once! Glance at the paper . . if you
will|But glance at it. . .|STRAFFORD. Already   47 *1837* again!   *48 {Read-
ing of *1863–82*.}   *1837* Peace, girl! Now, Slingsby!|. . . . Hollis!   {*1884* as *1863*
except "Hollis:"}   *1888,1889* Peace, child! Now, Slingsby|. . . . Hollis!
49,50 *1837* of all your tricks—|In spite of Pym! Your Pym that shrank
51 *1837* otherwise!

   41 *sick as you are*: 'His face was dashed with paleness, and his body stooped
with its own infirmities even more than with its master's cares:' *Life*, p. 388 (p.
251).
   44 *Eat flesh and bread*: 'Much noise and confusion prevailed at all times
through the hall': ibid.
   44–5 *and can't say* / *"Strafford"*: i.e. they refuse to give me my title.
   46 *Glance at the paper!*: cf. IV. i. 99 ff.
   52 *Lane*: 'Mr. Lane, who argued the matter of law for the earl': Clarendon,
iii. 123.

Eliot would have disdained . . .
[*Calling after the* Messenger.] And Radcliffe, say,
The only person who could answer Pym,   55
Is safe in prison, just for that.
                           Well, well!
It had not been recorded in that case,
I baffled you.
[*To* Lady CARLISLE.] Nay, child, why look so
    grieved?˙
All 's gained without the King! You saw Pym
    quail?
What shall I do when they acquit me, think you,   60
But tranquilly resume my task as though
Nothing had intervened since I proposed
To call that traitor to account! Such tricks,
Trust me, shall not be played a second time,
Not even against Laud, with his grey hair—   65
Your good work, Hollis! Peace! To make
    amends,
You, Lucy, shall be here when I impeach
Pym and his fellows.
    Hollis.   Wherefore not protest
Against our whole proceeding, long ago?
Why feel indignant now? Why stand this while   70
Enduring patiently?
    Strafford.   Child, I 'll tell you—
You, and not Pym—you, the slight graceful girl
Tall for a flowering lily, and not Hollis—
Why I stood patient! I was fool enough

54 *1837* (*To* HOLLIS.) Eliot . . . . say—   55 *1837* answer Pym—   56
1837 that!|(*Continuing to* HOLLIS). Well—well—   58 *1837* you!|(*To*
CARLISLE.) Nay, girl, why   60 *1837* . . . What shall   64 *1837*
time—   65 *1837* Even against old Laud, with his grey hair . . .   *1863,1865*
Say, even against Laud, with his grey hair—   66 *1837* Hollis!—And to make
amends   *1863,1865* Hollis! Peace! to make amends   67 *1837*–65 be there
when   68 *1837* fellows!   69 *1837* proceeding   71,72 *1837* patiently
. . .|STRAFFORD.(*To* CARLISLE.) Girl, I'll tell you—|You—and not Pym
. .   73 *1837* lily—and not Charles . . .

54 *Radcliffe*: 'the person on whose evidence Strafford mainly relied in the
proof of his answers, sir George Radcliffe, had, by a master-stroke of Pym's,
been incapacitated suddenly by a charge of treason against himself': *Life*, p. 389
(p. 253).
65 *Laud*: now in the Tower, having been impeached.

To see the will of England in Pym's will;   75
To fear, myself had wronged her, and to wait
Her judgment: when, behold, in place of it . . .
[*To a* Messenger *who whispers.*] Tell Lane to
    answer no such question! Law,—
I grapple with their law! I 'm here to try
My actions by their standard, not my own!   80
Their law allowed that levy: what 's the rest
To Pym, or Lane, any but God and me?
    Lady Carlisle. The King 's so weak! Secure
    this chance! 'T was Vane,
Never forget, who furnished Pym the notes . . .
    Strafford. Fit,—very fit, those precious notes
    of Vane,   85
To close the Trial worthily! I feared
Some spice of nobleness might linger yet
And spoil the character of all the past.
Vane eased me . . . and I will go back and say
As much—to Pym, to England! Follow me!   90
I have a word to say! There, my defence
Is done!
        Stay! why be proud? Why care to own
My gladness, my surprise?—Nay, not surprise!
Wherefore insist upon the little pride
Of doing all myself, and sparing him   95
The pain? Child, say the triumph is my King's!
When Pym grew pale, and trembled, and sank
    down,

75 *1837* Pym's will—   *1863,1865* Pym's will,   76 *1837* To dream that I had wronged her—   *1884* To fear myself had wronged her,   77 *1837–65* Her judgment,—when, behold,   *1884* Her judgment: when, behold   78–9 *1837* Law . . .|I grapple with their Law!   81–82a,83,84 *1837* Law allowed that levy. . . what's the rest|To Pym, or Lane, or any but myself?|CARLISLE. Then cast not thus your only chance away—|The King's so weak . . secure this chance! 'Twas Vane|—Vane, recollect, who   85 *1837* Fit . . very fit . .   88 *1837* To spoil . . . . all the past!   *1863,1865* And spoil . . . . all the Past.   89,90 *1837* It pleased me . . and (*rising passionately*) I will go back and say|As much—to them—to   91 *1837* There!   92 *1837* (*To* CARLISLE.) Stay . . why be   93–4 *1837* My gladness—my surprise? . . no—not surprise!|Oh, why insist   96 *1837* pain? Girl, say   97 *1837* down—

75 *To see the will of England*: cf. III. iii. 96–7.
78 *Law*: see note to l. 52 above.

One image was before me: could I fail?
Child, care not for the past, so indistinct,
Obscure—there 's nothing to forgive in it   100
'T is so forgotten! From this day begins
A new life, founded on a new belief
In Charles.
    Hollis.   In Charles? Rather believe in Pym!
And here he comes in proof! Appeal to Pym!
Say how unfair . . .   105
    Strafford.   To Pym? I would say nothing!
I would not look upon Pym's face again.
    Lady Carlisle. Stay, let me have to think I
      pressed your hand!
               [STRAFFORD *and his friends go out.*

          Enter HAMPDEN *and* VANE.
Vane. O Hampden, save the great misguided
    man!
Plead Strafford's cause with Pym! I have
    remarked
He moved no muscle when we all declaimed   110
Against him: you had but to breathe—he turned
Those kind calm eyes upon you.
    [*Enter* PYM, *the* Solicitor-General ST. JOHN, *the*
      Managers *of the Trial*, FIENNES, RUDYARD, *etc.*
    Rudyard.   Horrible!
Till now all hearts were with you: I withdraw
For one. Too horrible! But we mistake
Your purpose, Pym: you cannot snatch away   115

---

    98 *1837* His image was before me . . .   99 *1837* Girl, care not for the
past—so indistinct—   *1863,1865* Child, care not for the Past, so indis-
tinct,   103 *1837* In Charles . . .|HOLLIS. Pym comes . . tell Pym it is
unfair!   *1863–68* as *1888* except 'Rather,'   104 *1837* Appeal to Pym! Hamp-
den—and Vane! see, Strafford!   106–7 *1837* again!|CARLISLE. Stay . . let
. . . . hand!| (*Exeunt* STRAFFORD &c.)   108 *1837–65* save that great   109
1837 Pym—   110–11 *1837* all spoke loud|Against him . . .   112,112a
1837 Those kind, large eyes upon you—kind to all|But Strafford . . whom I
murder!|(*Enter* PYM (*conversing with the Solicitor-General*, St. JOHN), *the Man-
agers* . . . .|RUDYARD. Horrible!   *1863,1865* as *1888* except 'kind,'   *1884* as *1888*
except 'Those cold calm'   113,114 *1837* you . . . I withdraw|For one! Too
horrible! Oh we mistake   115 *1837* Pym . .

---

  107 *let me have to think*: let me have the memory of having pressed your hand.

The last spar from the drowning man.
   Fiennes.   He talks
With St. John of it—see, how quietly!
[*To other* Presbyterians.] You 'll join us?
     Strafford may deserve the worst:
But this new course is monstrous. Vane, take
    heart!
This Bill of his Attainder shall not have   120
One true man's hand to it.
   Vane.   Consider, Pym!
Confront your Bill, your own Bill: what is it?
You cannot catch the Earl on any charge,—
No man will say the law has hold of him
On any charge; and therefore you resolve   125
To take the general sense on his desert,
As though no law existed, and we met
To found one. You refer to Parliament
To speak its thought upon the abortive mass
Of half-borne-out assertions, dubious hints   130
Hereafter to be cleared, distortions—ay,
And wild inventions. Every man is saved

---

116 *1837* man!   117 *1837* see   118 *1837* us? Mind, we own he merits
death—   119 *1837* monstrous!   121 *1837* to it!|VANE. But hear me,
Pym!|Confront your Bill . . your own Bill . . what is it?   123 *1837* charge
. .   124 *1837* Law   125 *1837* charge . .   126 *1837* desert,—   127 *1837*
Law   128 *1837* To found one!—You refer to every man   129 *1837* To
speak his thought upon this hideous mass   *1863,1865* To speak its thought
upon this hideous mass   130 *1837* assertions—   131 *1837* cleared—distortions—aye,

---

120 *This Bill of his Attainder*: 'A Bill of Attainder differs from an Impeachment by being a legislative act, to which the consent of Crown, Lords, and
Commons, is necessary, whereas, in an Impeachment the House of Commons
prosecutes, and the House of Lords judges': EHH. 'Meanwhile, before this
opinion was taken [that of the Lords, who found against Strafford], the
Commons had changed their course, and introduced a bill of attainder. This
has been sorely reproached to them, and one or two of the men who had acted
with them up to this point now receded. Lord Digby was the principal of these.
"Truly, sir," he said, on the discussion of the bill, "I am still the same in my
opinions . . . I believe him to be still that grand apostate to the commonwealth,
who must not expect to be pardoned in this world . . . And yet, . . . my hand
must not be to that dispatch. I protest, as my conscience stands informed, I had
rather it were off!" ': *Life*, pp. 398–9 (pp. 263–4). In his preface Firth comments
that while 'In the play the significance of the change [from Impeachment to
Attainder] is very well brought out in the speeches attributed to Vane and
Pym, Act IV. scene ii. ll. 125–137, 170–183', it is not adequately dealt with in
the *Life* (p. xlvi and n.).

The task of fixing any single charge
On Strafford: he has but to see in him
The enemy of England.   135
    Pym.   A right scruple!
I have heard some called England's enemy
With less consideration.
    Vane.   Pity me!
Indeed you made me think I was your friend!
I who have murdered Strafford, how remove
That memory from me?   140
    Pym.   I absolve you, Vane.
Take you no care for aught that you have done!
    Vane. John Hampden, not this Bill! Reject this
      Bill!
He staggers through the ordeal: let him go,
Strew no fresh fire before him! Plead for us!
When Strafford spoke, your eyes were thick with
      tears!   145
    Hampden. England speaks louder: who are we,
      to play
The generous pardoner at her expense,
Magnanimously waive advantages,
And, if he conquer us, applaud his skill?
    Vane. He was your friend.   150
    Pym.   I have heard that before.

---

    134 *1837* but too see   135 *1837* The Enemy of England . . . | PYM. A right
scruple! *1884* The enemy of England. | *Pym.* A right scruple. {*1882* has 'scru-
ple:'}   136 *1837* Enemy   137,137a,b *1837* Pity me! | Me—brought so
low—who hoped to do so much | For England—her true servant—Pym, your
friend . . . | 138 *1865–68* you make me   139,139a *1837* But I have mur-
dered Strafford . . I have been | The instrument of this! who shall
remove   140 *1837* Vane! 142 *1837* Dear Hampden,   143 *1837* thro' the
ordeal . . . let him go!   144,144a,b,145,145a,146 *1837* us | With Pym . . what
God is he, to have no heart | Like ours, yet make us love him? | RUDYARD.
Hampden, plead | For us! When Strafford spoke your eyes were thick | With
tears . . save him, dear Hampden! | HAMPDEN. England speaks | Louder than
Strafford! Who are we, to play   147 *1837* expense—   148,149 *1837*
advantages— | And if he conquer us . . . .   150 *1837* VANE. (*To* PYM) He . . . .
friend!

---

    139 *I who have murdered Strafford*: proleptic, as in Keats, *Isabella*, 209: 'So the
two brothers and their murdered man'. Cf. IV. ii. 113 (*1837*), above.
    143 *the ordeal*: 'A trial by fire or water, by which the person accused appealed
to heaven; by walking blindfold over hot bars of iron . . .': Johnson.

Fiennes. And England trusts you.

Hampden.   Shame be his, who turns
The opportunity of serving her
She trusts him with, to his own mean account—
Who would look nobly frank at her expense!

   Fiennes. I never thought it could have come to
    this.   155

   Pym. But I have made myself familiar, Fiennes,
With this one thought—have walked, and sat,
    and slept,
This thought before me. I have done such things,
Being the chosen man that should destroy
The traitor. You have taken up this thought   160
To play with, for a gentle stimulant,
To give a dignity to idler life
By the dim prospect of emprise to come,
But ever with the softening, sure belief,
That all would end some strange way right at
    last.   165

   Fiennes. Had we made out some weightier
    charge!

   Pym.   You say
That these are petty charges: can we come
To the real charge at all? There he is safe
In tyranny's stronghold. Apostasy
Is not a crime, treachery not a crime: 170
The cheek burns, the blood tingles, when you
    speak
The words, but where 's the power to take
    revenge

---

151 *1837* But England trusts you . . .   155 *1837* this!   156 *1837* PYM
(*turning from* St. JOHN). But   157 *1837* With that one   158 *1837* That
thought before me!   160 *1837* This Strafford! You have taken up that
thought   161 *1837* with—for a gentle stimulant—   163 *1837* of this deed
to come . . .   165 *1837* would come some . . . . last!   166 *1837* charge
. . .   167 *1837* charges! Can   168 *1837* safe!   169 *1837* strong
hold!   170 *1837* crime —Treachery not a crime!   171,172 *1837* you
name|Their names, but

---

159 *Being the chosen man*: 'I have exalted one chosen out of the people': Psalms
89:19. Cf. *Life*, p. 380 (p. 242): 'Pym [was] no longer the mouth-piece of a
faction . . ., but recognised as the chosen champion of the people of England,
"the delegated voice of God"'.

Upon them? We must make occasion
　serve,—
The oversight shall pay for the main sin
That mocks us.
　Rudyard.　　But this unexampled course,　　　175
This Bill!
　Pym.　By this, we roll the clouds away
Of precedent and custom, and at once
Bid the great beacon-light God sets in all,
The conscience of each bosom, shine upon
The guilt of Strafford: each man lay his hand　　180
Upon his breast, and judge!
　Vane.　　　　　　　　I only see
Strafford, nor pass his corpse for all beyond!
　Rudyard and others. Forgive him! He would join
　us, now he finds
What the King counts reward! The pardon, too,
Should be your own. Yourself should bear to　　185
　Strafford
The pardon of the Commons.
　Pym.　　　　　　　Meet him? Strafford?
Have we to meet once more, then? Be it so!
And yet—the prophecy seemed half fulfilled

---

173 *1837* serve:　　174 *1837* The Oversight, pay for the Giant Sin *1863,1865*
The oversight here, pay for the main sin　　175 *1837* us!|RUDYARD. But . . . .
course—　　176 *1837* This Bill . . . .　　177,178 *1837* Of Precedent and Cus-
tom, and at once|Bid the great light which God has set in all,　　180 *1837–65*
each shall lay　　181,181a–c *1837* breast, and say if this one man|Deserve to
die, or no, by those he sought|First to undo.|FIENNES. You, Vane—you answer
him!|VANE. Pym, you see farthest . . . I can only see　　*1863,1865* as *1888* except
'judge.'　　182, 182a *1837* Strafford . . . I'd not pass over that pale corse|For all
beyond!|RUDYARD *and others.* Pym, you would look so great!　　183 *1837*
us!　　184 *1837* How false the King has been! The pardon, too,　　186 *1837*
Commons!|PYM (*starting*). Meet　　188 *1884* yet the

---

174 *The oversight*: 'By the "oversight which pays for the main sin" I meant
"failing to punish what are the main faults, we must ava ourselves of any
occasion to punish what is in reality or by comparison a mere oversight:" they
failed, you know, to convict Strafford of direct legal crime, and brought in
their special Bill of Attainder in consequence': Browning to Miss Hickey,
Checklist, 83: 182.
　175 *this unexampled course*: cf. IV. i. 54 n., above.
　176 *roll the clouds away*: '"My lords", Pym said, ". . . we charge him with
nothing but what the 'law' in every man's breast condemns, the light of nature,
the light of reason, the rules of common society"': EHH.

When, at the Trial, as he gazed, my youth,
Our friendship, divers thoughts came back at   190
    once
And left me, for a time . . . 'T is very sad!
To-morrow we discuss the points of law
With Lane—to-morrow?
    Vane.   Not before to-morrow—
So, time enough! I knew you would relent!
    Pym. The next day, Haselrig, you introduce   195
The Bill of his Attainder. Pray for me!

SCENE III.—*Whitehall.*

The KING.

    Charles. My loyal servant! To defend himself
Thus irresistibly,—withholding aught
That seemed to implicate us!
                            We have done
Less gallantly by Strafford. Well, the future
Must recompense the past.   5
                            She tarries long.
I understand you, Strafford, now!
                            The scheme—
Carlisle's mad scheme—he 'll sanction it, I fear,
For love of me. 'T was too precipitate:
Before the army 's fairly on its march,

189 *1837* trial, as he gazed—my youth   190 *1837* friendship—all old
thoughts   191 *1837* time . . . .|VANE (*aside to* RUDYARD). Moved, is he
not?   193,194 *1837* With Lane . . to-morrow!|VANE. Time enough, dear
Pym!|See, he relents! I knew he would relent!   195 *1837* Haselrig,
you   196 *1837* Attainder. (*After a pause.*) Pray

1,1a,b *1837* CHARLES. Strafford, you are a Prince! Not to reward
you|—Nothing does that—but only for a whim!|My noble servant!—To
defend himself *1863,1865* as *1888* except 'servant!—'   2 *1837* irresistibly
. .   4 *1837* Strafford! Well, the future *1863,1865* Strafford. Well, the
Future   5 *1837* past.|She tarries long! *1863,1865* Past.|She tarries
long.   8 *1837* me!

192 *the points of law*: see note to l. 52, above.

He 'll be at large: no matter.   10
                              Well, Carlisle?
                         Enter PYM.
  Pym. Fear me not, sir:—my mission is to save,
This time.
  Charles. To break thus on me! Unannounced!
  Pym. It is of Strafford I would speak.
  Charles.   No more
Of Strafford! I have heard too much from you.
  Pym. I spoke, sir, for the People; will you hear   15
A word upon my own account?
  Charles.   Of Strafford?
(So turns the tide already? Have we tamed
The insolent brawler?—Strafford's eloquence
Is swift in its effect.) Lord Strafford, sir,
Has spoken for himself.   20
  Pym.   Sufficiently.
I would apprise you of the novel course
The People take: the Trial fails.
  Charles.   Yes, yes:
We are aware, sir: for your part in it
Means shall be found to thank you.
  Pym.   Pray you, read
This schedule! I would learn from your own
        mouth   25
—(It is a matter much concerning me)—
Whether, if two Estates of us concede

----

10 *1837* matter . .   11 *1837* Sire . . .   12 *1837* This time!| CHARLES. To
. . . . me!—Unannounced . . .   14 *1837* you!   15 *1837* Sire, for the People: *1863,1865* sir, for the People: 17 *1837* (*Aside.*) So, turns *1863,1865*
(So, turns   18–19 *1837* Strafford's brave defence| Is swift in its effect! (*To*
PYM.) Lord Strafford, Sir,   20 *1837* himself!   *22 {Reading of
1868–84} *1837* The people take: the Trial fails, . . .| CHARLES. Yes—
yes— *1863,1865* The People take: the Trial fails.| *Cha.* Yes—yes—{*1865* has
'trial'} *1888,1889* The People take: the Trial fails.| *Charles.* Yes, yes   25
1837 schedule! (*as the* KING *reads it*) I would   27 *1837* of England shall concede

----

12 *To break thus on me*: 'the idea of Pym . . . bursting in unannounced',
Gardiner comments (EHH, p. xi), '. . . is, from the historical point of view,
simply ludicrous'.
  25 *This schedule!*: a list of the offences for which he wished a bill of attainder
to be brought in.
  27 *two Estates*: i.e. the Lords and the Commons.

The death of Strafford, on the grounds set forth
Within that parchment, you, sir, can resolve
To grant your own consent to it. This Bill   30
Is framed by me. If you determine, sir,
That England's manifested will should guide
Your judgment, ere another week such will
Shall manifest itself. If not,—I cast
Aside the measure.   35
    Charles.   You can hinder, then,
The introduction of this Bill?
    Pym.   I can.
    Charles. He is my friend, sir: I have wronged
      him: mark you,
Had I not wronged him, this might be. You
      think
Because you hate the Earl . . . (turn not away,
We know you hate him)—no one else could love   40
Strafford: but he has saved me, some affirm.
Think of his pride! And do you know one
      strange,
One frightful thing? We all have used the man
As though a drudge of ours, with not a source
Of happy thoughts except in us; and yet   45
Strafford has wife and children, household cares,
Just as if we had never been. Ah sir,
You are moved, even you, a solitary man
Wed to your cause—to England if you will!

---

30 *1837* your full consent to it. That Bill   31 *1837* me: if you determine,
Sire,   32 *1837* will shall guide *1884* will may guide   33 *1837* week that
will   35 *1837* . . You can   36 *1837* of that Bill?   38 *1837* him—this
might be!—You think *1882,1884* him, this might be. You think,   39 *1837*
away—   41, 42, 42a *1837* Strafford . . . but he has saved me—many
times—|Think what he has endured . . proud too . . you feel|What he
endured!—And, do you *1863,1865* as *1888* except 'And, do'   43–4 *1837*
used that man|As though he had been ours . .   45–6 *1837* us . . and
yet|Strafford has children, and a home as well,   47 *1837* been! . . Ah
Sir, *1863,1882,1884* been. Ah, sir,   48 *1837* moved—you—   49
1882,1884 England,

---

48 *a solitary man:* Pym's wife died in 1620, leaving him 'with five young
children . . .; and he did not marry again': Forster, *Life of Pym*, p. 6. Forster
emphasizes, however, that public affairs never led him to deprive his children
of his 'affectionate care. . ., observed upon by many of those who were about
him'.

Pym. Yes—think, my soul—to England! Draw
    not back!   50
Charles. Prevent that Bill, sir! All your course
    seems fair
Till now. Why, in the end, 't is I should sign
The warrant for his death! You have said much
I ponder on; I never meant, indeed,
Strafford should serve me any more. I take   55
The Commons' counsel; but this Bill is yours—
Nor worthy of its leader: care not, sir,
For that, however! I will quite forget
You named it to me. You are satisfied?
    Pym. Listen to me, sir! Eliot laid his hand,   60
Wasted and white, upon my forehead once;
Wentworth—he 's gone now!—has talked on,
    whole nights,
And I beside him; Hampden loves me: sir,
How can I breathe and not wish England well,
And her King well?
    Charles.   I thank you, sir, who leave   65
That King his servant. Thanks, sir!
    Pym.   Let me speak!
—Who may not speak again; whose spirit yearns
For a cool night after this weary day:
—Who would not have my soul turn sicker yet
In a new task, more fatal, more august,   70
More full of England's utter weal or woe.

---

51 *1837* Prevent that Bill, Sir . . Oh, your course was fair *1884* Prevent this
Bill, sir! All your course seems fair   52 *1837* now!   54 *1837* That I shall
ponder on; I never meant   55 *1837* more: 57 *1837* Not worthy of its
leader . . care not, Sir, *1882* Not . . . . leader: care not, sir, *1884* Not . . . .
leader; care not, sir,   59 *1837* me!   *61 {Reading of *1837–65,1882,
1884*},*1868,1888,1889* white   64 *1837* well—   65–6 *1837* Sir! You leave|
That King his servant! Thanks, Sir!|Pʏм. Let me speak   67 *1837* again!
68 *1837* day!   69 *1837* my heart turn   71 *1837* woe . . .

54–5 *I never meant . . . .*: 'I do think my lord Strafford is not fit hereafter to
serve me or the commonwealth in any place of trust, no, not so much as that of
a constable': *Life*, p. 400 (p. 265), quoting the King's address to the Lords when
the Bill of Attainder had been passed. Cf. *Life*, p. 389 (p. 252). Cf. V. ii. 65–6,
below.

62 *he's gone now!*: the old Wentworth, the friend of the People as well as of the
King, Wentworth as distinct from the Earl of Strafford.

I thought, sir, could I find myself with you,
After this trial, alone, as man to man—
I might say something, warn you, pray you,
    save—
Mark me, King Charles, save——you!   75
But God must do it. Yet I warn you, sir—
(With Strafford's faded eyes yet full on me)
As you would have no deeper question moved
—"How long the Many must endure the One,"
Assure me, sir, if England give assent   80
To Strafford's death, you will not interfere!
Or——
    Charles. God forsakes me. I am in a net
And cannot move. Let all be as you say!
              Enter Lady CARLISLE.
    Lady Carlisle. He loves you—looking beautiful
    with joy
Because you sent me! he would spare you all   85
The pain! he never dreamed you would forsake
Your servant in the evil day—nay, see
Your scheme returned! That generous heart of
    his!
He needs it not—or, needing it, disdains
A course that might endanger you—you, sir,   90
Whom Strafford from his inmost soul . . .
    [*Seeing* PYM.]   Well met!
No fear for Strafford! All that 's true and brave
On your own side shall help us: we are now

72 *1837* Sire, could. . . . you—   73 *1837* Trial—alone—   *1863,1884* Trial,
alone,   74 *1837* something—warn you—pray you—save you—   79
1837 Many shall endure the One" . . . *1884* Many must endure the
One—"   80 *1837* Sire, if England shall assent   82 *1837* me—I am in a net
. . *1863,1865* me. I am in a net.   83 *1837* I cannot move!   91,92 *1837*
(*Seeing* PYM.) No fear—|No fear for Strafford! all   93 *1837* us!

73 *as man to man*: cf. Shelley, *The Cenci*, III. i. 284.
75 *Mark me*: a short line, for particular emphasis.
79 *"How long the Many*: cf. Byron, *The Corsair*, i. 187–8: 'Such hath it
been—shall be—beneath the Sun / The many still must labour for the one!'
88 *Your scheme returned!*: cf. IV. i. 110, 129, 138, and IV. iii. 6–7. One of
Strafford's last actions was to release the King 'from his pledged word' that no
harm should come to him: *Life*, pp. 400–1 (p. 266).

Stronger than ever.

Ha—what, sir, is this?

All is not well! What parchment have you there?   95

    Pym. Sir, much is saved us both.

    Lady Carlisle.   This Bill! Your lip

Whitens—you could not read one line to me

Your voice would falter so!

    Pym.   No recreant yet!

The great word went from England to my soul,

And I arose. The end is very near.   100

    Lady Carlisle. I am to save him! All have shrunk
        beside;

'T is only I am left. Heaven will make strong

The hand now as the heart. Then let both die!

---

94 *1837* ever!|Ha—what, Sire,   95 *1837* you there?|(CHARLES *drops it, and exit.*)   96,96a,b *1837*. PYM. Sire, much is saved us both: farewell!|CARLISLE. Stay—stay—|This cursed measure—you'll not dare—you mean|To frighten Charles! This Bill—look—|(*As* PYM *reads it.*)|Why, your lip   98,98a *1837* Your voice would falter so! It shakes you now—|And will you dare . . .|PYM. No recreant yet to her!   100 *1837* arose! . . . . near! (*Exit.*)   101 *1837* I save him! All have shrunk from him beside—   *1863,1865* as *1888* except 'beside—'   *1884* as *1888* except 'besides;'   102 *1837–65* left!   103 *1837* The hand as the true heart! Then let me die! (*Exit.*)|END OF THE FOURTH ACT.

ACT V.

SCENE I.—*Whitehall*.

HOLLIS, Lady CARLISLE.

Hollis. Tell the King then! Come in with me!
Lady Carlisle.   Not so!
He must not hear till it succeeds.
    Hollis.   Succeed?
No dream was half so vain—you 'd rescue
    Strafford
And outwit Pym! I cannot tell you . . . lady,
The block pursues me, and the hideous show.   5
To-day . . . is it to-day? And all the while
He 's sure of the King's pardon. Think, I have
To tell this man he is to die. The King
May rend his hair, for me! I 'll not see Strafford!
    Lady Carlisle. Only, if I succeed, remember
    ——Charles   10
Has saved him. He would hardly value life
Unless his gift. My staunch friends wait. Go in—
You must go in to Charles!
    Hollis.   And all beside
Left Strafford long ago. The King has signed
The warrant for his death! the Queen was sick   15
Of the eternal subject. For the Court,—
The Trial was amusing in its way,

1 *1837,1863,1884* King, then!   2 *1837* 'till it succeeds!|HOLLIS. Vain!
Vain!   3 *1837* you'll rescue   4 *1837* you . . . girl,   5 *1837* me—all the
hideous show . .   *1863* me, and the hideous show   7 *1837* pardon . .
think,   8 *1837* die!|The King   11 *1837* saved him!   12 *1837*
wait!   14 *1837* ago—the   15 *1837* death . . the   *1863–68* death: the
1882,1884 death! The   16 *1837* subject!   17 *1837* Trial . . . . way *1865*
trial . . . . way,

6 *To-day*: Strafford was executed on 12 May.

Only too much of it: the Earl withdrew
In time. But you, fragile, alone, so young
Amid rude mercenaries—you devise   20
A plan to save him! Even though it fails,
What shall reward you?
   Lady Carlisle.   I may go, you think,
To France with him? And you reward me,
    friend,
Who lived with Strafford even from his youth
Before he set his heart on state-affairs   25
And they bent down that noble brow of his.
I have learned somewhat of his latter life,
And all the future I shall know: but, Hollis,
I ought to make his youth my own as well.
Tell me,——when he is saved!   30
   Hollis.   My gentle friend,
He should know all and love you, but 't is vain!
   Lady Carlisle. Love? no—too late now! Let
    him love the King!
'T is the King's scheme! I have your word,
    remember!
We'll keep the old delusion up. But, quick!
Quick! Each of us has work to do, beside!   35
Go to the King! I hope—Hollis—I hope!
Say nothing of my scheme! Hush, while we
    speak

18 *1837* Only too much of it . .   *1884* Only, too much of it: 19 *1837* In
time! But you—fragile—alone—so young!   *1863–84* In time. But you,
fragile, alone, so young,   20 *1837* you devised   23 *1837* friend!   26
1837 of his—   28 *1837* know—   29 *1837* well!   30 *1837* Tell me—
when he is saved!|HOLLIS. My gentle girl   31 *1837* all—should love
you—   32 *1837* CARLISLE. No—no—too late   33 *1837* word
—remember!—   34 *1837* up! But, hush!   *1882,1884* up. But quick!   35 *1837*
Hush! Each . . . . do, beside!   *1882* Quick! Each . . . . do, beside   *1884* Quick!
Each . . . . do, beside.

21 *A plan*: as George points out, Browning compresses the historical facts:
'Two schemes had been formed for saving Strafford, one for an ordinary
escape, which had apparently gone no further than having a ship ready in the
Thames in case it should be wanted, and one for introducing soldiers into the
Tower on a flimsy pretext which did not deceive Balfour, who was in charge of
the fortress': loc. cit., p. xvii.
26 *that noble brow*: 'Habitual pain had increased the dark hue and deep
contractions of a brow, formed and used to "threaten and command" . . . He
alludes to this sportively in a letter . . . "*This bent and ill favoured brow of mine
was never prosperous in the favour of ladies*"': *Life*, p. 284 (p. 127).

Think where he is! Now for my gallant friends!
 Hollis. Where he is? Calling wildly upon
    Charles,
Guessing his fate, pacing the prison-floor.   40
Let the King tell him! I 'll not look on Strafford.

SCENE II.—*The Tower.*

STRAFFORD *sitting with his* Children. *They sing.*

    O bell' andare
    Per barca in mare,
    Verso la sera
    Di Primavera!
William. The boat 's in the broad moonlight
    all this while—   5
    Verso la sera
    Di Primavera!
And the boat shoots from underneath the moon

38 *1837* Think where He is! . . . . friends!|(*Exit.*)   39 *1837* Where He is!
. . . . Charles—   40 *1837* fate—pacing the prison-floor . . .   41 *1837* on
Strafford!|(*Exit.*)
    Scene ii.   5 *1837* (The . . . . while)   7 *1837* Primavera.

s.d. Strafford's love for his children is emphasized in the *Life*. Historically,
they were in Ireland at this time.
    1 *O bell' andare*: see note to Preface to *1837*, p. 501 below. 'When the play was
rehearsing, Mr. Browning gave Macready a *lilt* which he had composed for the
children's song in Act v. His object was just to give the children a thing
children would croon; but the two little professed singers, Master and Miss
Walker, preferred something that should exhibit their powers more effectually, and a regular *song* was substituted, scarcely, it will be thought, to the
improvement of the play. By kind permission I print the original music.'

(EHH, pp. iv–v).

Into the shadowy distance; only still
You hear the dipping oar—   10
   Verso la sera,
And faint, and fainter, and then all 's quite gone,
Music and light and all, like a lost star.
  Anne. But you should sleep, father: you were
   to sleep.
  Strafford. I do sleep, Anne; or if not—you
   must know   15
There 's such a thing as . . .
  William.   You 're too tired to sleep?
  Strafford. It will come by-and-by and all day
   long,
In that old quiet house I told you of:
We sleep safe there.
  Anne.   Why not in Ireland?
  Strafford.   No!
Too many dreams!—That song 's for Venice,
  William: 20
You know how Venice looks upon the map—
Isles that the mainland hardly can let go?
  William. You 've been to Venice, father?
  Strafford.   I was young, then.
  William. A city with no King; that 's why I
   like
Even a song that comes from Venice.   25
  Strafford.   William!
  William. Oh, I know why! Anne, do you love
   the King?
But I 'll see Venice for myself one day.

---

9 *1837* distance—only still   *1884* distance; only, still   10 *1837* You hear
the dipping oar,|. . . . *sera* . . .   *1865* Your hear the dipping oar—|. . . .
sera,   11 *1837* And faint—and fainter—   14 *1837* to sleep!   15 *1837*
sleep, dearest; or if not—you know   *1884* sleep, Anne; or if not—you must
know,   19 *1837* We'll sleep . . . .| |Ah!   20 *1882,1884* Venice, Wil-
liam.   *23 {Reading of *1865–84*}   *1837,1863* young then.   *1888,1889*
young, then   25 *1837* from Venice!

18 *that old quite house:* Wentworth: see l. 72, below.
20 *Venice:* after his early marriage at the age of eighteen, Wentworth had
travelled on the Continent, no doubt visiting Venice, which was noted for its
republican government.

Strafford. See many lands, boy—England last
   of all,—
That way you 'll love her best.
   William.   Why do men say
You sought to ruin her then?   30
   Strafford.   Ah,—they say that.
   William. Why?
   Strafford.   I suppose they must have words
   to say,
As you to sing.
   Anne.   But they make songs beside:
Last night I heard one, in the street beneath,
That called you . . . Oh, the names!
   William.   Don't mind her, father!
They soon left off when I cried out to them.   35
   Strafford. We shall so soon be out of it, my
   boy!
'T is not worth while: who heeds a foolish song?
   William. Why, not the King.
   Strafford.   Well: it has been the fate
Of better; and yet,—wherefore not feel sure
That Time, who in the twilight comes to mend   40
All the fantastic day's caprice, consign
To the low ground once more the ignoble Term,

---

30 *1837* her, then!|STRAFFORD. Ah . . . *1863–84* her, then?|*Straf.*
Ah,—   31 *1837* to say.   32 *1882,1884* songs beside!   34 *1837* That
named you . . .   35 *1837* I called out to them!   38 *1837* King!   39 *1837*
Of better men, and yet . . . . why not feel sure   *40 {Reading of *1837,1863*,
DC, 89} *1865–82,88* That time, who in   *1884* That time, which in   41 *1837*
Day's caprice—   42 *1837* Unto the ground

---

42 *the ignoble Term:* 'In Mr. Browning's own words, "Suppose the enemies
of a man to have thrown down the image and replaced it by a mere *Term,* and
you have what I put into Strafford's head". "Putting the Genius on the pedestal
usurped by the *Term* means—or tries to mean—substituting eventually, the
true notion of Strafford's endeavour and performance in the world, for what he
conceives to be the ignoble and distorted conception of these by his contemporary judges"': EHH. Miss Hickey obviously found the passage puzzling, as
she says that she is 'specially indebted to [Browning] for most of the note': p.
vii. The word 'Term' is common in art criticism, for a representation of the
god Terminus, often phallic: 'an ignoble one, with ignoble attributes', as Miss
Hickey puts it. In 'The Bishop Orders his Tomb' the speaker would like a
'Term' as part of the decoration is his monument (line 108). See also *The Ring
and the Book,* v. 304, and 'Æschylus' Soliloquy', 9–11 (*New Poems,* 1914, p. 62).
The notion of a man's 'Genius on his Orb' is a further reminder of Browning's

And raise the Genius on his orb again,—
That Time will do me right?
   Anne.   (Shall we sing, William?
He does not look thus when we sing.)
   Strafford.   For Ireland,   45
Something is done: too little, but enough
To show what might have been.
   William.   (I have no heart
To sing now! Anne, how very sad he looks!
Oh, I so hate the King for all he says!)
   Strafford. Forsook them! What, the common
      songs will run   50
That I forsook the People? Nothing more?
Ay, Fame, the busy scribe, will pause, no doubt,
Turning a deaf ear to her thousand slaves
Noisy to be enrolled,—will register
The curious glosses, subtle notices,   55
Ingenious clearings-up one fain would see
Beside that plain inscription of The Name—
The Patriot Pym, or the Apostate Strafford!
[*The* Children *resume their song timidly, but break*
   off.

       Enter HOLLIS *and an* Attendant.
   Strafford. No,—Hollis? in good time!—Who is
      he?
   Hollis.   One
That must be present.   60
   Strafford.   Ah—I understand.

   43 *1837* again—   *44 {Reading of *1837,1863,DC,1889*}   *1865–88* That
time will   45 *1837* Ireland,—   46 *1837* done . .   47 *1837*
been:—   48 *1865* Annie, how   49 *1837* Oh . . . . King for *1884* Oh,
. . . . King, for   52   *1837* . . . Aye, Fame, the scribe, will pause awhile, no
doubt,   55 *1837* All curious   59 *1837* No . . .   60 *1837* understand—

familiarity with iconography, from the early days when he pored over
Quarles's *Emblems.*
   44 *Time will do me right?*: cf. *Paracelsus* v. 899 ff.
   William: Strafford's eldest son: cf. l. 104.
   51 *That I forsook the People?*: cf. I. ii. 89–90.
   55 *curious glosses*: ingenious commentaries.

They will not let me see poor Laud alone.
How politic! They 'd use me by degrees
To solitude: and, just as you came in,
I was solicitous what life to lead
When Strafford 's "not so much as Constable   65
"In the King's service." Is there any means
To keep oneself awake? What would you do
After this bustle, Hollis, in my place?
 Hollis. Strafford!
 Strafford.   Observe, not but that Pym and
  you
Will find me news enough—news I shall hear   70
Under a quince-tree by a fish-pond side
At Wentworth. Garrard must be re-engaged
My newsman. Or, a better project now—
What if when all 's consummated, and the Saints
Reign, and the Senate's work goes
  swimmingly,—   75
What if I venture up, some day, unseen,
To saunter through the Town, notice how Pym,
Your Tribune, likes Whitehall, drop quietly
Into a tavern, hear a point discussed,
As, whether Strafford's name were John or
  James—   80
And be myself appealed to—I, who shall

 61 *1837* alone! 63 *1837–82* and just as you came in 67 *1837–84* one's
self 69 *1837* Strafford . . . 72–3 *1837* At Wentworth. Or, a better project now—{Parts of ll. 72, 73 not in *1837*} 73 *1884* now! 74 *1837* What if
when all is over, and *1884* What if, when all's consummated, and 75 *1837*
the Senate goes on swimmingly,— 76 *1837* unseen— 77 *1837*
Town— 78 *1837* The Tribune, likes Whitehall— 79 *1837* tavern—hear
. . . . discussed— 80 *1837* John or Richard—

 61 *poor Laud*: 'Laud, old and feeble, staggered to the window of his cell as
Strafford passed on the following morning, and, as he lifted his hands to
bestow the blessing his lips were unable to utter, fell back and fainted in the
arms of his attendant': *Life*, p. 408 (p. 275).
 65 *"not so much as Constable*: see IV. iii. 54–5 above.
 72 *Garrard*: in 1633 Wentworth had 'instructed a gossiping person, a hired
retainer of his own, the rev. Mr. Garrard, to furnish him, in monthly packets of
news, with all the private scandal and rumours and secret affairs of the court,
and of London generally': *Life*, p. 290 (p. 134).
 74 *consummated*: stressed on the second syllable, as at IV. i. 45.

Myself have near forgotten!
 Hollis.   I would speak . . .
 Strafford. Then you shall speak,—not now. I
  want just now,
To hear the sound of my own tongue. This
  place
Is full of ghosts.
 Hollis. Nay, you must hear me, Strafford! 85
 Strafford. Oh, readily! Only, one rare thing
  more,—
The minister! Who will advise the King,
Turn his Sejanus, Richelieu and what not,
And yet have health—children, for aught I
  know—
My patient pair of traitors! Ah,—but, William— 90
Does not his cheek grow thin?
 William.   'T is you look thin,
Father!
 Strafford. A scamper o'er the breezy wolds
Sets all to-rights.
 Hollis. You cannot sure forget
A prison-roof is o'er you, Strafford?
 Strafford.   No,
Why, no. I would not touch on that, the first. 95
I left you that. Well, Hollis? Say at once,
The King can find no time to set me free!
A mask at Theobald's?
 Hollis.   Hold: no such affair

---

 83 *1837* not now: I want, just *1863,1865* not now: I want just *1884* not now.
I want, just 85–6 *1837* ghosts!| HOLLIS. Will you not hear me, Straf-
ford?| STRAFFORD. Oh, readily! . . . Only, one droll thing more,— *1868,1882*
as *1888* except 'Only' 88 {Not in *1837.*} 89 *1837,1884* I know! 90
1837 —My. . . . Ah. . but, 93 *1837* to-rights! 96 *1837* Hollis?|. . . . Say
at once 97 *1837* The King could find 98 *1837* A mask at
Theobald's?| HOLLIS. Hush . . . no *1884* A masque at Theobald's? *Hol.*
Hold: no

 88 *Sejanus*: the favourite of the emperor Tiberius, as Richelieu was the
trusted minister of Louis XIII. Strafford is now thinking of what will happen if
the King continues to reign, but he himself is removed.
 90 *My patient pair of traitors!*: his children.
 98 *Theobald's*: see note to III. ii. 28.

Detains him.

   Strafford. True: what needs so great a matter?
The Queen's lip may be sore. Well: when he
    pleases,—   100
Only, I want the air: it vexes flesh
To be pent up so long.

   Hollis.   The King—I bear
His message, Strafford: pray you, let me speak!

   Strafford. Go, William! Anne, try o'er your
    song again!

                     [*The* Children *retire.*

They shall be loyal, friend, at all events.   105
I know your message: you have nothing new
To tell me: from the first I guessed as much.
I know, instead of coming here himself,
Leading me forth in public by the hand,
The King prefers to leave the door ajar   110
As though I were escaping—bids me trudge
While the mob gapes upon some show prepared
On the other side of the river! Give at once
His order of release! I've heard, as well,
Of certain poor manœuvres to avoid   115
The granting pardon at his proper risk;
First, he must prattle somewhat to the Lords,
Must talk a trifle with the Commons first,
Be grieved I should abuse his confidence,
And far from blaming them, and . . . Where's
    the order?   120

   Hollis. Spare me!

   Strafford.   Why, he 'd not have me steal
    away?

---

100 *1837* sore!—   101 *1837* vexes one   102 *1837* long!|HOLLIS. The
King . . .   103 *1837* Strafford . . .   108 *1837* coming here at
once—   *1863,1865* coming here himself   109 *1837* forth before them by the
hand,—   110–11 *1837* I know the King will leave the door ajar| As though I
were escaping . . . let me fly   113,113a,b *1837* river!|HOLLIS (*to his Compan-
ion*). Tell him all;|I knew my throat would thicken thus . . Speak, you!|
STRAFFORD. 'Tis all one—I forgive him. Let me have   *114 {Reading of
1863,65,82,84}* 1837 The order of release!|. . . I've heard, as well,   *1868,88,89*
His order of release! I've heard, as well   115 *1837–65* poor manoeuvrings
to   117 *1837* Lords—   118 *1837* first—   121 *1837* Why . . . . he'd

116 *proper:* own.

With an old doublet and a steeple hat
Like Prynne's? Be smuggled into France,
    perhaps?
Hollis, 't is for my children! 'T was for them
I first consented to stand day by day   125
And give your Puritans the best of words,
Be patient, speak when called upon, observe
Their rules, and not return them prompt their
    lie!
What 's in that boy of mine that he should prove
Son to a prison-breaker? I shall stay   130
And he 'll stay with me. Charles should know as
    much,
He too has children!
[*Turning to* HOLLIS's Companion.] Sir, you feel
    for me!
No need to hide that face! Though it have looked
Upon me from the judgment-seat . . . I know
Strangely, that somewhere it has looked on
    me . . .   135
Your coming has my pardon, nay, my thanks:
For there is one who comes not.
    Hollis.   Whom forgive,
As one to die!
    Strafford.   True, all die, and all need

---

122 *1837* —With   125 *1837* I e'er consented   126 *1837* And give those
Puritans the best of words—   127 *1837* patient—speak when called upon—
128,128a *1837* Their rules,—and not give all of them the lie!|HOLLIS. No
—Strafford . . no escape . . no . . dearest Strafford!   129 *1837* should
be   131 *1837–65* much— *1882* much *1884* much: 132 *1837* HOLLIS's
companion.) Ah, you   136 *1837* Still there is One who does not come
—there's One *1863–68* as *1888* except 'thanks.'   137,137a *1837* That shut
out Heaven from me . . .|HOLLIS. Think on it then!|On Heaven . . and calmly
. . as one . . as one to die! *1863,1865* as *1888* except 'One who'   138 *1837*
STRAFFORD. Die? True, friend, all must die, and all must need

---

122 *a steeple hat*: OED's first example of the word is from 1629. Anthony
Wood mentions that when Prynne studied he would 'put on a long quilted Cap
which came an Inch over his Eyes, serving as an *Umbrella* to defend them from
too much light': *Athenæ Oxonienses* (2nd ed., 2 vols., 1721), ii. 439. William
Prynne, the author of *Histrio-mastix*, is described by Clarendon as 'a person of
great industry' characterized by 'rudeness and arrogancy' who 'had contracted
a proud and venomous dislike against the discipline of the Church of England,
and so by degrees (as the progress is very natural) an equal irreverence to the
government of the State': iii. 59.

Forgiveness: I forgive him from my soul.
  Hollis. 'T is a world's wonder: Strafford, you
    must die!   140
  Strafford. Sir, if your errand is to set me free
This heartless jest mars much. Ha! Tears in
    truth?
We 'll end this! See this paper, warm—feel
    —warm
With lying next my heart! Whose hand is there?
Whose promise? Read, and loud for God to hear!   145
"Strafford shall take no hurt"—read it, I say!
"In person, honour, nor estate"—
  Hollis.   The King . . .
  Strafford. I could unking him by a breath! You
    sit
Where Loudon sat, who came to prophesy
The certain end, and offer me Pym's grace   150
If I 'd renounce the King: and I stood firm
On the King's faith. The King who lives . . .
  Hollis.   To sign
The warrant for your death.
  Strafford   "Put not your trust

139,139a,b *1837* from my soul.|HOLLIS. Be constant, now . . . be grand and
brave . . be now|Just as when . . . Oh, I cannot stay for words . . .   140 *1837*
'Tis a world's wonder . . but . . but . . you must die!   142,142a *1837* This
heartless jest will . .|Hollis—you turn white,|And your lip shivers!—What if
. . .|Oh, we'll end,   *1865* as *1888* except 'truth'   143 *1837* paper—warm . .
feel . . warm   144 *1884* hand is plain?   145 *1837* Read! Read loud! For God
to hear!   147 *1837* estate" . . . .   *1884* estate."   149 *1837* Where Loudon
sate . . Loudon, who came to tell   150–2 *1837* Pym's pardon|If I'd forsake
the King—and I stood firm|On my King's faith! The King who lived . . .

146 "*Strafford shall take no hurt*": the *Life* quotes a letter from the King to
Strafford in prison which contains an explicit promise: 'I cannot satisfy myself
in honour or conscience, without assuring you (now in the midst of your
troubles) that upon the word of a king you shall not suffer in life, honour, or
fortune. This is but justice, and therefore a very mean reward from a master to
so faithful and able a servant': *Life*, p. 389 (p. 252).
  148 *unking*: 'common in 17c': OED.
  149 *Loudon*: cf. note to I. i. 95. In March 1640 he was committed to the
Tower, but was released after some months. He took part in the battle of
Newburn, and was one of the Scots commissioners at Ripon. In pursuance of
the policy of reconciliation he was appointed lord chancellor of Scotland on 30
September 1641.
  153 "*Put not your trust*: 'He asked if the king had indeed assented to the bill.
Secretary Carleton answered in the affirmative, and Strafford, laying his hand

"In princes, neither in the sons of men,
"In whom is no salvation!"   155
   Hollis.   Trust in God!
The scaffold is prepared: they wait for you:
He has consented. Cast the earth behind!
   Charles. You would not see me, Strafford, at
     your foot!
It was wrung from me! Only, curse me not!
   Hollis [*to* STRAFFORD]. As you hope grace and
     pardon in your need,   160
Be merciful to this most wretched man.
                      [*Voices from within.*

        Verso la sera
        Di Primavera.

   Strafford. You 'll be good to those children, sir?
     I know
You 'll not believe her, even should the Queen   165
Think they take after one they rarely saw.
I had intended that my son should live
A stranger to these matters: but you are
So utterly deprived of friends! He too
Must serve you—will you not be good to him?   170

155,155a *1837* salvation!" On that King—|Upon his head . . .|CHARLES. O
Hollis, he will curse me! *1863,1865* salvation!"|*Hol.* Trust in God.   156
1837 prepared—they wait for you— *1884* prepared: they wait for
you;   157–9,159a,b,c,160 *1837* He has consented . . .|CHARLES. No,
no—stay first—Strafford!|You would not see me perish at your foot . . .|It
was wrung from me! Only curse me not!|The Queen had cruel eyes! And Vane
declared . .|And I believed I could have rescued you . .|Strafford—they
threaten me! and . . well, speak now,|And let me die!—|HOLLIS. (*To* STRAF-
FORD.) As you hope grace from God, *1863–84* as *1888* except 'Only
curse'   161 *1837–68, 1884* man! *1879* man *1882* man.   164 *1837* STRAF-
FORD (*after a pause*). You'll. . . . Sire?   166 *1837* they never saw!   168 *1837*
matters . . . but you are *1884* matters: but you stand

---

on his heart, and raising his eyes to heaven, uttered the memorable
words,—"Put not your trust in princes, nor in the sons of men, for in them
there is no salvation'": *Life* p. 406 (p. 272). Cf. Psalm 146:3. Firth points out
that the anecdote first appears in Sanderson's *Life and Reign of Charles I* in 1658
(*Life*, p. lii).
  168 *A stranger to these matters*: in his final letter to his eldest son Strafford
wrote: 'Be sure to avoid as much as you can to enquire after those that have
been sharp in their judgments towards me, and I charge you never to suffer
thought of revenge to enter your heart': *Life*, p. 407 (p. 273).
  170 *will you not be good to him?*: 'The king I trust will deal graciously with
you', he wrote in the same letter: ibid.

Or, stay, sir, do not promise—do not swear!
You, Hollis—do the best you can for me!
I 've not a soul to trust to: Wandesford 's dead,
And you 've got Radcliffe safe, Laud's turn comes
    next:
I 've found small time of late for my affairs,   175
But I trust any of you, Pym himself—
No one could hurt them: there 's an infant, too.
These tedious cares! Your Majesty could spare
    them.
Nay—pardon me, my King! I had forgotten
Your education, trials, much temptation,   180
Some weakness: there escaped a peevish word—
'T is gone: I bless you at the last. You know
All 's between you and me: what has the world
To do with it? Farewell!
    Charles [*at the door*]. Balfour! Balfour!
        Enter BALFOUR.
The Parliament!—go to them: I grant all   185
Demands. Their sittings shall be permanent:
Tell them to keep their money if they will:
I 'll come to them for every coat I wear

---

171 *1837* Stay—Sire—stay—do not promise—   172 *1837* And, Hollis—   *1884* You, Hollis,   173 *1837* dead—   174 *1837* safe—and Laud is here . .   *1884* safe, Laud's turn comes next.   175–6 *1837* I've had small . . . . affairs—|But I'll trust any of you . . .   177 *1837–82* infant, too— 178,178a *1837* . . . These . . . . spare them—|But 'tis so awkward—dying in a hurry! *1863–84* These . . . . spare them!   179 *1837* . . . Nay—Pardon   180 *1837* trials, and temptations   181 *1837* And weakness . . I have said a peevish word—   *1884* as *1888* except 'word:'   182–3 *1837* But, mind I bless you at the last! You know|'Tis between you and me . . .   *1884* as *1888* except 'know,'   184,184a,b *1837* Balfour! Balfour!|. . . What, die? Strafford to die? This Strafford here?|Balfour! . . Nay Strafford, do not speak . . Balfour!   185–6 *1837* The Parliament . . . go to them—I grant all|Demands! Their . . . . permanent—   187 *1837* will . . . *1884* will;

173 *Wandesford's dead*: Christopher Wandesford, lord deputy of Ireland from the time of Strafford's departure in 1640. The difficulties of his office, and the news of Strafford's fall, were held responsible for his death of a fever on 3 December 1640.
174 *Radcliffe*: see note on IV. ii. 54.
Laud's turn: Laud was beheaded in 1645.
177 *an infant*: in his final speech he sent his blessing 'to my eldest son, and to Ann, and Arabella, not forgetting my little infant, that knows neither good nor evil, and cannot speak for itself': *Life*, p. 410 (pp. 276–7).
184 *Balfour!* Sir William Balfour was lieutenant of the Tower.

And every crust I eat: only I choose
To pardon Strafford. As the Queen shall   190
    choose!
—You never heard the People howl for blood,
Beside!
    Balfour. Your Majesty may hear them now:
The walls can hardly keep their murmurs out:
Please you retire!
    Charles.   Take all the troops, Balfour!
    Balfour. There are some hundred thousand of   195
    the crowd.
    Charles. Come with me, Strafford! You 'll not
    fear, at least!
    Strafford. Balfour, say nothing to the world of
    this!
I charge you, as a dying man, forget
You gazed upon this agony of one . . .
Of one . . . or if . . . why you may say, Balfour,   200
The King was sorry: 't is no shame in him:
Yes, you may say he even wept, Balfour,
And that I walked the lighter to the block
Because of it. I shall walk lightly, sir!
Earth fades, heaven breaks on me: I shall stand   205
    next
Before God's throne: the moment 's close at
    hand

189 *1837* eat, only I choose   *1884* eat: only, I choose   190,190a,b *1837* To
pardon Strafford—Strafford—my brave friend!|BALFOUR (*aside*). Is he mad,
Hollis?|CHARLES. Strafford, now, to die!| . . But the Queen . . . ah, the
Queen!—make haste, Balfour! *1884* To pardon Strafford:—as the Queen
shall choose!   191 *1837*—You never . . . . people   *1884*—She never . . . .
People   *195 {Reading of *1837–84*} *1888,1889* crowd   196 *1837* fear
them friend!   201 *1837* sorry—very—'tis no shame! *1884* sorry: 't is no
shame in him;   202 *1837* wept, Balfour,—   204,204a *1837* lightly,
Sire!|—For I shall save you . . save you at the last!   205 *1837* Heaven dawns
on me . . I shall wake next *1863,1865* Heaven breaks on me: I shall stand
next   *1884* heaven breaks on me:—I shall stand next   206 *1884* throne. The

192 *may hear them now*: 'A furious mob of upwards of 6,000 people, variously
armed, thronged round Westminster Hall, clamoured for Strafford's blood,
and placarded the names of those members of the Commons who . . . had
voted against the attainder, as Straffordians, and betrayers of their country':
Forster's *Life of Pym*, p. 183, quoted in EHH.

When man the first, last time, has leave to lay
His whole heart bare before its Maker, leave
To clear up the long error of a life
And choose one happiness for evermore.   210
With all mortality about me, Charles,
The sudden wreck, the dregs of violent death—
What if, despite the opening angel-song,
There penetrate one prayer for you? Be saved
Through me! Bear witness, no one could prevent   215
My death! Lead on! ere he awake—best, now!
All must be ready: did you say, Balfour,
The crowd began to murmur? They 'll be kept
Too late for sermon at St. Antholin's!
Now! But tread softly—children are at play   220
In the next room. Precede! I follow—
    Enter Lady CARLISLE, *with many* Attendants.
    Lady Carlisle.   Me!
Follow me, Strafford, and be saved! The King?
[*To the* KING.] Well—as you ordered, they are
    ranged without,
The convoy . . . [*seeing the* KING's *state.*]
[*To* STRAFFORD.] You know all, then! Why, I
    thought
It looked best that the King should save
    you,—Charles   225

---

207 *1837–65* When Man the first, last time,   *1884* When man,—the first,
last time,—   208 *1837* Maker—   *1868,1882* maker,   212–14, 214a–
216   *1837* wreck—the dregs—the violent death . . .|I'll pray for you! Thro'all
the Angel-song| Shall penetrate one weak and quivering prayer—|I'll say how
good you are . . inwardly good| And pure . . (*The* KING *falls:* HOLLIS *raises him.*)
Be witness, he could not prevent| My death! I'll go—ere he awakes—go
now!   217 *1837* ready—   218 *1837* murmur?—   220 *1837*
Now—but   *1863–68* Now! but   221,221a,b *1837* In the next
room—Ah, just my children—Hollis!|—Or . . . no—support the King! (*a
door is unbarred.*) Hark . . they are here!| Stay Hollis!—Go Balfour! I'll follow
. . . . .|CARLISLE (*entering with many Attendants*). Me!| 222 *1837* saved!
. . . . .   223 *1837* ordered . . They are ranged without . .   224 *1837* all
then!   225 *1837* It looked so well that Charles should save you—Charles
1863–82 as *1888* except 'you,'

---

216 *ere he awake*: the King has swooned: cf. line 251, and *1837*.
219 *St. Antholin's*: 'Government had appropriated the Church of St. Antholin's to the use of the Scotch Commission. Alexander Henderson preached
there to crowded audiences': EHH.

Alone; 't is a shame that you should owe me
    aught.
Or no, not shame! Strafford, you 'll not feel
    shame
At being saved by me?
    Hollis.   All true! Oh Strafford,
She saves you! all her deed! this lady's deed!
And is the boat in readiness? You, friend,   230
Are Billingsley, no doubt. Speak to her,
    Strafford!
See how she trembles, waiting for your voice!
The world 's to learn its bravest story yet.
    Lady Carlisle. Talk afterward! Long nights in
    France enough,
To sit beneath the vines and talk of home.   235
    Strafford. You love me, child? Ah, Strafford
    can be loved
As well as Vane! I could escape, then?
    Lady Carlisle.   Haste!
Advance the torches, Bryan!
    Strafford.   I will die.
They call me proud: but England had no right,
When she encountered me—her strength to
    mine—   240
To find the chosen foe a craven. Girl,
I fought her to the utterance, I fell,

---

226 *1837* Alone . . 'tis shame that you should owe it me—   *1863,1865* Alone;
't is shame that you should owe me aught.   227 *1837* Me . . no, not
shame! *1863* Or, no, not shame!   229 *1837* her deed . . this girl's own
deed   230 *1837* —And . . . . readiness? . . .   231 *1837–68,84* doubt! *1882*
doubt?   232 *1837* trembles . .   233 *1837–84* yet!   234 *1837*
enough   235 *1837,1863* home!   236 *1837* me, girl! . . . . Ah, *1863* me,
child! Ah,   237 *1837* Haste . .   238 *1837* die!   239 *1837* proud . . but
. . . . right   241 *1837* craven!   242 *1837* utterance—I fell—

231 *Billingsley*: 'Balfour was desired by the King to receive Captain Billingsley and 100 men into the Tower, to effect Strafford's escape': ibid.

237 *As well as Vane*: at last Strafford realizes that she loves him, as the King
loves Vane.

238 *Bryan!*: unidentified: cf. iii. ii. 183.

242 *to the utterance*: Fr. *à outrance*, to the bitter end. Cf. *Macbeth* iii. i. 70–1:
'Come, Fate, into the list, / And champion me to th' utterance!'

I am hers now, and I will die. Beside,
The lookers-on! Eliot is all about
This place, with his most uncomplaining brow.   245
   Lady Carlisle. Strafford!
   Strafford. I think if you could know how much
I love you, you would be repaid, my friend!
   Lady Carlisle. Then, for my sake!
   Strafford.   Even for your sweet sake,
I stay.
   Hollis. For *their* sake!
   Strafford.   To bequeath a stain?
Leave me! Girl, humour me and let me die!   250
   Lady Carlisle. Bid him escape—wake, King!
     Bid him escape!
   Strafford. True, I will go! Die, and forsake the
     King?
I 'll not draw back from the last service.
   Lady Carlisle. Strafford!
   Strafford. And, after all, what is disgrace to me?
Let us come, child! That it should end this way!   255
Lead then! but I feel strangely: it was not
To end this way.
   Lady Carlisle. Lean—lean on me!
   Strafford.   My King!
Oh, had he trusted me—his friend of friends!
   Lady Carlisle. I can support him, Hollis!
   Strafford.   Not this way!

---

*243 {Reading of *1863,1865,82,84.*} *1837* hers now .. and I will die!
Beside   *1868,1888,1889* her's now, and I will die. Beside,   245 *1837* place
with .... brow! *1863,1865* place with .... brow.   247 *1837* my
girl!   248 *1837* sweet sake ..   249 *1837* STRAFFORD. I bequeath a stain
. . .   250,250a *1837* let me die!|HOLLIS. No way to draw him hence—Car-
lisle—no way? *1868* as *1888* except 'die?'   251 *1837* CARLISLE (*suddenly to*
CHARLES). Bid him escape .. wake, King!   252 *1837* STRAFFORD. (*Looks
earnestly at him.*) Yes, I will go!   255 *1837* come, girl! ... That ....
way! *1865,1868* come, child! That .... way *1882* come, child! That ....
way,   256*1837* Lead then... but I feel strangely... *1884* Lead, then! but I
feel strangely: 258 *1837* Friend of friends— *1863,1865* friend of
friends!— *1884* "friend of friends!"   258a *1837* Had he but trusted
me!|CARLISLE. Leave not the king—   259 *1837* STRAFFORD. (*Starting as they
approach the door at the back.*) Not this way;

---

244 *The lookers-on!*: cf. *Childe Roland*, last stanza.

This gate—I dreamed of it, this very gate.   260
    Lady Carlisle. It opens on the river: our good
    boat
Is moored below, our friends are there.
    Strafford.   The same:
Only with something ominous and dark,
Fatal, inevitable.
    Lady Carlisle. Strafford! Strafford!
    Strafford. Not by this gate! I feel what will be   265
    there!
I dreamed of it, I tell you: touch it not!
    Lady Carlisle. To save the King,—Strafford, to
    save the King!
    [*As* STRAFFORD *opens the door,* PYM *is discovered*
    with HAMPDEN, VANE, *etc.* STRAFFORD *falls*
    back; PYM *follows slowly and confronts him.*
    Pym. Have I done well? Speak, England!
    Whose sole sake
I still have laboured for, with disregard
To my own heart,—for whom my youth was
    made   270
Barren, my manhood waste, to offer up
Her sacrifice—this friend, this Wentworth
    here—
Who walked in youth with me, loved me, it may
    be,
And whom, for his forsaking England's cause,

---

260 *1837* This gate . . . I dreamed of it . . . this very gate! *1882,1884* This gate—I dreamed of it—this very gate.   261 *1837* river—   262 *1837* below—our friends are there!|STRAFFORD. The same!   *1863* below, our friends are there.|*Strafford.* The same.   264 *1837* inevitable . . .   265 *1837* gate. . I feel it will   266 *1837* you . .   267 s.d. *1837 back to the front of the stage:* PYM *follows* *1863–84 back:* PYM *follows*   268 *1837* Whose great sake   271 *1837* Barren, my future dark, to *1863,1865* Barren, my Future waste, to   272 *1837–65* this man, this   273 *1837* That walked in youth with me—loved me

---

267 s.d. 'The last scene must have been very exciting and touching', Helen Faucit wrote many years later. 'Lucy believes that by her means Strafford's escape is certain; but when the water-gates open, with the boat ready to receive him, Pym steps out of it! This effect was most powerful. It was a dreadful moment. My heart seemed to cease to beat. I sank on my knees, burying my head in my bosom, and stopping my ears with my hands while the death-bell tolled for Strafford': Anne Ritchie, loc. cit., pp. 225–6.

I hunted by all means (trusting that she   275
Would sanctify all means) even to the block
Which waits for him. And saying this, I feel
No bitterer pang than first I felt, the hour
I swore that Wentworth might leave us, but I
Would never leave him: I do leave him now.   280
I render up my charge (be witness, God!)
To England who imposed it. I have done
Her bidding—poorly, wrongly,—it may be,
With ill effects—for I am weak, a man:
Still, I have done my best, my human best,   285
Not faltering for a moment. It is done.
And this said, if I say . . . yes, I will say
I never loved but one man—David not
More Jonathan! Even thus, I love him now:
And look for my chief portion in that world   290
Where great hearts led astray are turned again,
(Soon it may be, and, certes, will be soon:
My mission over, I shall not live long,)—
Ay, here I know I talk—I dare and must,
Of England, and her great reward, as all   295
I look for there; but in my inmost heart,
Believe, I think of stealing quite away
To walk once more with Wentworth—my
        youth's friend
Purged from all error, gloriously renewed,
And Eliot shall not blame us. Then indeed . . .   300

---

276 *1837* to the grave   277 *1837* That yawns for him. And saying
this, *1884* as *1888* except 'And,'   278 *1837* No bitter pang   279 *1837*
us,—   280 *1837* now!   282 *1837* imposed it!   283 *1837* may be   284
1837 I am but a man . . . . .   285 *1837* my very best,   286 *1837* moment! I
have done!   287 *1837* (*After a pause.*) | And that said, I will say . . .   *1884* And
this said, if I say . . ,   288 *1837* but this man—   289 *1884* thus   291 *1884*
again,—   292 *1837* be . . and . . yes . . it will   293 *1837*
long!)—   *1863,1865* long.)—   294 *1837* . . . Aye here I know I talk—and I
will talk   295 *1837* England—and her great reward—   296-7 *1837*
heart|Believe   298 *1837* Wentworth—with my friend   300 *1837* us!

278–9 *the hour / I swore*: see note to I. i. 106.
288–9 *David . . . Jonathan*: 'the soul of Jonathan was knit with the soul of
David, and Jonathan loved him as his own soul': 1 Samuel 18:1.
293 *I shall not live long*: he died in 1643.

This is no meeting, Wentworth! Tears increase
Too hot. A thin mist—is it blood?—enwraps
The face I loved once. Then, the meeting be!
   Strafford. I have loved England too; we 'll meet
     then, Pym.
As well die now! Youth is the only time   305
To think and to decide on a great course:
Manhood with action follows; but 't is dreary,
To have to alter our whole life in age—
The time past, the strength gone! As well die
     now.
When we meet, Pym, I 'd be set right—not now!   310
Best die. Then if there 's any fault, fault too
Dies, smothered up. Poor grey old little Laud
May dream his dream out, of a perfect Church,
In some blind corner. And there 's no one left.
I trust the King now wholly to you, Pym!   315
And yet, I know not: I shall not be there:
Friends fail—if he have any. And he 's weak,
And loves the Queen, and . . . Oh, my fate is
     nothing—
Nothing! But not that awful head—not that!
   Pym. If England shall declare such will to
     me . . .   320

<hr/>

301–2 *1837* (This . . . . Tears rise up|Too hot . .   303,303a loved so!)
Then, shall the meeting be!|Then—then—then—I may kiss that hand, I
know!   304 *1837* STRAFFORD. (*Walks calmly up to* PYM *and offers his hand.*) I
. . . . then, Pym! *1863,1865* I . . . then, Pym! *1868,1882* I . . . . then,
Pym;   305 *1837* As well to die! Youth is the time—our youth,   307 *1837*
Age with its action . . . . dreary *1863,1865* Manhood with action . . . .
dreary   308 *1837* alter one's whole   310,310a *1837* not now!|I'd die as I
have lived . . too late to change!   311,312,312a,b,c *1837* any fault, it will|Be
smothered up: much best! You'll be too busy|With your hereafter, you will
have achieved|Too many triumphs to be always dwelling|Upon my downfall,
Pym? Poor little Laud   *1863–82* as *1888* except 'fault, it too'   313 *1837,63,65*
out of a perfect Church   314 *1837* corner? And there's no one left . . .|(*He
glances on the* KING.)   316,316a *1837* And yet . . I know not! What if with this
weakness . . .|And I shall not be there . . . And he'll betray *1863,1865* And
yet, I know not! I shall not be there!   317 *1837* His friends—if he has any . . .
And he's false . .   *1863,1865* as *1888* except 'any!'   319 *1837* head . .   320
1837 Pym, save the King! Pym, save him! Stay—you shall . . . {line 320 not in
1863,1865.}

<hr/>

304 *I have loved England too*; on the scaffold Strafford 'declared the innocence
of his intentions . . . and said that the prosperity of his country was his fondest
wish': *Life*, p. 409 (p. 276).

Strafford. Pym, you help England! I, that am to
    die,
What I must see! 't is here—all here! My God,
Let me but gasp out, in one word of fire,
How thou wilt plague him, satiating hell!
What? England that you help, become through
    you   325
A green and putrefying charnel, left
Our children . . . some of us have children,
    Pym—
Some who, without that, still must ever wear
A darkened brow, an over-serious look,
And never properly be young! No word?   330
What if I curse you? Send a strong curse forth
Clothed from my heart, lapped round with horror
    till
She 's fit with her white face to walk the world
Scaring kind natures from your cause and you—
Then to sit down with you at the board-head,   335
The gathering for prayer . . . O speak, but speak!
. . . Creep up, and quietly follow each one home,
You, you, you, be a nestling care for each
To sleep with,—hardly moaning in his dreams,
She gnaws so quietly,—till, lo he starts,   340

---

321 *1837* For you love England! I, that am dying, think   322 *1837* see . . 'tis
here . . all here! My God! *1863* see! 't is here—all here! My God!   324
1837–65 How Thou . . . . Hell!   325 *1837* you love—our land—become
1884 you help, become through you,   330,330a–d *1837* be young . . . |No
word!| You will not say a word—to me—to Him!| (*Turning to*
CHARLES.)| Speak to him . . . as you spoke to me . . . that day!| Nay, I will let
you pray to him, my King—| Pray to him! He will kiss your feet, I
know!   331 *1837* strong Curse {lines 331–342 not in *1863*,
1865.}   332,333 *1837* horror, till| She's fit, with her white face,   335 *1837*
with you,   336 *1837* prayer . . . . | VANE. O speak, Pym! Speak!   337 *1837*
STRAFFORD. . . . Creep . . . . home—   338 *1837* You—you—you—be a
nestling Care   339 *1837* with, hardly . . . . dreams . . .   340 *1837* quietly
. . . until he starts—

322 *What I must see!* cf. *Paracelsus* i. 765–70 and v. 507–9.
327 *some of us have children*: cf. note to IV. iii. 48.
332 *lapped round with horror*: cf. *Macbeth*, I. ii. 55: 'Bellona's bridegroom,
lapp'd in proof'.
335 *at the board-head*: cf. *Macbeth*, III. iv. where Banquo's ghost appals the
murderer of King Duncan.

Gets off with half a heart eaten away!
Oh, shall you 'scape with less if she 's my child?
You will not say a word—to me—to Him?
 Pym. If England shall declare such will to
  me . . .
 Strafford. No, not for England now, not for
  Heaven now,—   345
See, Pym, for my sake, mine who kneel to you!
There, I will thank you for the death, my friend!
This is the meeting: let me love you well!
 Pym. England,—I am thine own! Dost thou
  exact
That service? I obey thee to the end.   350
 Strafford. O God, I shall die first—I shall die
  first!

341,342 *1837* away . . .|Oh you shall 'scape with less, if she's my child! 343,343a *1837* VANE (*to* PYM). We never thought of this . . . surely not dreamed| Of this. . it never can . . . could come to this! 344 *1837* PYM (*after a pause*). If England should declare her will to me . . . {lines 344–348 not in *1863,1865*.} 345,346 *1837* No—not for England, now—not for Heaven, now . . .|See, Pym—for me! My sake! I kneel to you! 347 *1837* There. . I will thank you for the death . . . my friend, 348,348a,b,349 *1837* This is the meeting . . . you will send me proud| To my chill grave! Dear Pym—I'll love you well!| Save him for me, and let me love you well!| PYM. England—I am 350 *1837* end! 351 *1837* STRAFFORD (*as he totters out*). O God, I shall die first—I shall die first!| CURTAIN FALLS.| THE END. *1884* Straf. O God, I shall die first! I shall die first! {line 351 not in *1863,65*.}

351 *I shall die first*: i.e. without having to witness the death of the King.
 Macready suggested that the children's voices should be heard after Strafford's death (cf. p. 8 above). There is no s.d. about this.

INTRODUCTION TO 'SORDELLO'

There were many singular incidents attending my work on that subject.[1]

Soon after the publication of *Pauline* Browning tired of the plan for a series of compositions supposedly by different writers and destroyed some works inspired by it, including a second Part of that poem. Instead he turned to what he was later to call 'a genuine work of my own',[2] *Sordello*, the composition of which was soon to be interrupted by that of *Paracelsus*. In a letter dated 5 December 1834 Browning reveals that the summer of that year had been an important time: 'as for Sordello', he wrote to Ripert-Monclar, 'I *this day* began to look over my labours of the summer—I had some idea of sending them both into the world together, but do not expect to be able to lick the latter into shape before a month or two—I have changed my conception, & 'tis as bad as beginning all over again'. Of the close connection between the two poems, particularly in their origin, there is clear evidence. 'I did mean to make a companion to *Paracelsus*', Browning wrote to Edward Dowden years later, 'and remember while employed on it, telling Leigh Hunt so'.[3] The reference to 'other productions which may follow in a more popular, and perhaps less difficult form' in the preface to *Paracelsus* clearly includes *Sordello*, similarly described in a letter to Fox dated 16 April 1835 as 'another affair on hand, rather of a more popular nature, I conceive, but not so decisive and explicit on a point or two'.[4] When Browning sent Ripert-Monclar his advance copy of *Paracelsus* on 30 July, he asked him for his criticisms, 'as the effect of this production will have an influence on its successors'.

---

[1] Browning to Elizabeth Barrett, 21 December 1845: Kintner, i. 336.
[2] Letter dated 9 August 1837. I am indebted to Professor Richard L. Purdy for access to this and other unpublished letters to Ripert-Monclar, and for permission to quote from several of them.
[3] *Letters*, p. 92.
[4] *Life*, p. 66. There appears to be no evidence for DeVane's assumption that the reference to *Sordello* in the preface to *Paracelsus* 'may . . . safely be assumed to have been written just before publication in August, 1835, though he dated it March 15, the date of the completion of the poem': p. 77.

We may assume that work on *Sordello* began again in the spring of 1835. A year later Browning believed that he was nearing the end. 'I am now engaged in a work which is nearly done', he wrote to Macready on 28 May: 'I allow myself a month to complete it: from the first of July I shall be free'.[1] In the event, however, he decided to lay the poem aside in order to write his play, as the preface to *Strafford* informs us: 'I had for some time been engaged in a Poem of a very different nature, when induced to make the present attempt; and am not without apprehension that my eagerness to freshen a jaded mind by diverting it to the healthy natures of a grand epoch, may have operated unfavourably on the represented play'. Since *Strafford* occupied Browning for far longer than he had anticipated (from late July or early August 1836 to 1 May 1837), *Sordello* suffered another serious interruption. The announcement at the end of *Strafford*—'Nearly ready, SORDELLO, in Six Books. By the Author of "Paracelsus"'—was clearly optimistic, though it may be taken as an expression of his determination to complete the poem as fast as he could.

Any possibility of such an achievement was destroyed by a singular stroke of ill fortune. On 22 July the *Athenæum* noticed the publication of two volumes of *Plays and Poems* by Mrs Busk, containing a long poem entitled 'Sordello', and asked the obvious question: 'Is this founded upon the same subject as that chosen by the author of "Paracelsus" for his announced poem?'[2] We may imagine with what feelings Browning read Mrs. Busk's introductory note:

The once renowned Mantuan Troubadour, SORDELLO, probably owes the faint glimmering of celebrity that he may still enjoy, to the distinction with which he is treated by Dante, to the embrace of fraternity bestowed upon him by Virgil in the *Purgatorio*. It may, therefore, be advisable to preface the poem bearing his name by an assurance that none of the adventures here ascribed to the Poet-hero are imaginary, at least of recent imagining. Sordello's prowess and high fame in arms, as well as in the *gai science*,[3] his chivalrous duel of emulation, not enmity, with an Apulian champion, the competition of kings and princes for the honour of possessing him at their several courts, his connexion of vassalage or service with the powerful

---

[1] *New Letters*, p. 12.   [2] Page 537, column c.
[3] A phrase used by the troubadours for the Art of Poetry.

Lombard despots, the Signori da Romano, and the mutual attach-
ment that existed betwixt him and their sister Cuniza, are all
recorded by divers early Italian writers, as Rolandino, Nostradamus,
Benvenuto da Imola, Bartolommeo Platina, and others, whose
somewhat contradictory statements Tiraboschi has collected, compared, and examined. It was the striking discrepancy between Sordello's career, according to these accounts, and the lives of poets of
more recent date, together with the impressive illustration of the
ephemeral nature of literary fame exhibited in our general and utter
ignorance of the history and writings of a poet once so celebrated,—for great must the celebrity have been which could give
birth to such romance as is here versified—that awoke the desire to
sketch his adventures, fictitious or real, as a picture of what a
Troubadour was, or, in early times, was supposed to be.

The only deviations from historic or traditionary truth in the
following Tale will be found in the representing Mantua as part of
Ezzelino's patrimonial dominions, and the conduct of the loves of
Sordello and Cuniza . . .

In the present Poem the conduct of the lovers has been purified
from actual guilt . . . we may surely be allowed to hope that a private
but lawful union sanctified the early loves of Sordello and Cuniza.

Mrs Busk's poem is a romantic narrative in six cantos of
predominantly tetrameter lines in the manner which Scott had
rendered popular, but while its humble merit gave Browning
nothing to fear it was clear that he could not complete his own
poem on the lines which he had planned. The whole thing had
to be reconsidered.

If the idea of abandoning the poem even crossed his mind, it
did so only to be rejected. In a letter to Fanny Haworth,
probably written 'about the first of August, 1837',[1] he wrote
that he was 'going to begin the finishing Sordello', and in the
letter to Ripert-Monclar written on 9 August Browning told
him that he hoped to be able to publish 'my first poem' in a few
months' time: he added that it had been his principal occupa-
tion for two years and was now being revised for the last time.
Our next evidence comes from the diary of Harriet Martineau.
On 23 December she wrote: 'Browning called. "Sordello"

---

[1] The letter is undated, and Mrs. Orr (p 95) says that it 'may have been written at any
period of this or the ensuing year', i.e. 1838 or 1839. We follow DeVane's conjecture (p.
79), largely because this letter could well have been written about the same time as the
letter to Ripert-Monclar.

will soon be done now. Denies himself preface and notes. He must choose between being historian or poet. Cannot split the interest. I advised him to let the poem tell its own tale'.[1] It is clear that he was having difficulties with his work, however, for on 11 April 1838 she records that he 'is just departing for Venice to get a view of the localities of Sordello', adding: 'He is right'. Two days later, on Good Friday, he wrote to John Robertson: 'I sail this morning for Venice—intending to finish my poem among the scenes it describes'.[2]

After the voyage to Trieste, which took nearly seven weeks, he went at once to Venice, where he spent more than half of the month during which he remained in Italy. The headnotes to Book III[3] make it clear that Venice had a powerful imaginative effect on Browning. There 'the poet may pause and breathe, . . . watching his own life . . ., because it is pleasant to be young'. Immediately, however, 'suffering humanity' makes its appearance, 'which instigates to tasks like this, and doubtlessly compensates them, as those who desist should remember': a clear admonition. From Venice, as he told Fanny Haworth, he went 'thro' Treviso and Bassano to the mountains, delicious Asolo, all my places and castles, you will see. Then to Vicenza, Padua and Venice again. Then to Verona, Trent, Inspruck (the Tyrol) Munich, "Wurzburg in Franconia"! Frankfort and Mayence,—down the Rhine to Cologne, thence to Aix-la-Chapelle, Liège, and Antwerp—then home'.[4] Griffin and Minchin rightly comment that while 'not one of these places except Verona has anything whatever to do with Sordello . . . they have everything to do with the historical background, with Verci and his *History of the Ecelini Family*'.[5]

Everything points to the importance of Venice, which Browning reached on 1 June. The next day he wrote 'To-day Venezia, June 2 1838' on a piece of paper or parchment which appears to contain a number of cryptic references to the composition of *Sordello*.[6] Since he later destroyed the letters which

---

[1] *Harriet Martineau's Autobiography, with Memorials by Maria Weston Chapman* (2nd ed., 3 vols., 1877), iii. 207. The next quotation is from p. 219.
[2] *Life*, p. 88.   [3] See pp. 326 ff., below.   [4] *Letters*, p. 3.
[5] Griffin and Minchin, p. 96. They should also have excepted Vicenza.
[6] I am grateful to Professor John Grube for drawing my attention to the description of this document in Moncure D. Conway's *Autobiography* (2 vols., Boston 1904), ii. 18 ff. See Appendix D below.

he had written to his parents 'by way of minute daily journal',[1] our principal record of his Italian sojourn, apart from the poem itself and this problematic series of jottings, is the letter to Fanny Haworth already quoted. It is clear that while he did not fulfil his plan of completing the poem 'among the scenes it describes', the journey confirmed him in his determination to complete it. 'You will see Sordello in a trice, if the fagging-fit holds. I did not write six lines while absent (except a scene in a play, jotted down as we sailed thro' the Straits of Gibraltar) —but I did hammer out some four, two of which are addressed to you, two to the Queen . . the whole to go in Book 3—perhaps. I called you, "Eyebright"—meaning a simple and sad sort of translation of "Euphrasia" into my own language: folks would know who Euphrasia, or Fanny was'.[2] 'I shall be off again as soon as my book is out—whenever that will be', he wrote later in the same letter: 'This sort of thing gets intolerable and I had better have done'. In a later letter to the same friend he revealed that he had been tempted to abandon the poem, but only momentarily (as it would seem): 'as I stopped my task awhile, left off my versewriting one sunny June day with a notion of not taking to it again in a hurry, the sad disheveled form[3] . . . renewed me, gave me fresh spirit, made me after finishing Book 3d commence Book 4th'.[4]

Browning's announcement to Macready on 26 May 1839 that the poem was finished[5] had clearly been premature. When it was completed, as Dante Gabriel Rossetti was later informed, the poet's sister Sarianna, 'performed the singular female feat of copying Sordello for him'. He adds that she remembered it all, 'and even *Squarcialupe, Zin the Horrid*, and the *sad dishevelled ghost*', commenting that 'some of its eccentricities may possibly be referred' to errors in her transcription.[6] About 1864 Moncure D. Conway saw what he took to

---

[1] *Francis Turner Palgrave: His Journals and Memories of his Life*, by G. F. Palgrave (1899), p. 202.

[2] *Letters*, p. 2. Cf. note to iii. 968, below. We do not know to which 'play' he is referring. The lines 'to the Queen' must have been omitted. Victoria had succeeded on 20 June 1837: she was crowned on 28 June 1838, while Browning was abroad.

[3] *Sordello*, iii. 696 ff., 969 ff.

[4] *New Letters*, p. 18, tentatively dated May 1840.

[5] *The Diaries of Macready*, ii. 4.

[6] *Letters of Dante Gabriel Rossetti to William Allingham 1854–1870*, ed. G. Birkbeck Hill (1897), p. 161, dated 8 January 1856. The allusions in the poem occur at ii. 118 (and ii. 783, v. 1014), iii. 817 and iii. 696 respectively.

be the manuscript in a 'wrapper',[1] but no manuscript is now known to exist. The poem may have been shown to one or two friends in manuscript or proof: in 1850 John Westland Marston (to whom Browning had presented a copy of *Paracelsus*) told Rossetti that 'Browning, before publishing *Sordello*, sent it him to read, saying that this time the public should not accuse him at any rate of being unintelligible (!!)'.[2] The date 'Feb. 23, 1840' and the Greek abbreviation apparently expressing relief[3] may well refer to the completion of proof-reading. In any event an advertisement in the *Times* for Saturday 29 February announced that the poem would be available 'In a few days, price 6s.6d. boards'.[4] On 7 March Browning inscribed one copy to his mother and another to Alfred Domett: both copies survive, and we have drawn on both in our notes. Many copies contain an advertisement stating that *Pippa Passes*, *King Victor and King Charles* and *Mansoor the Hierophant* are 'Nearly Ready'.[5]

The disastrous reception of the poem is well known. The most that Browning could claim for it was that it had been 'praised by the units, cursed by the tens, and unmeddled with by the hundreds!'[6] According to the Sotheby catalogue of the

[1] Cf. p. 160, above.

[2] 'Browning's system of composition', the account continues, 'is to write down on a slate in prose what he wants to say, and then to turn it into verse, striving after the greatest amount of condensation possible; thus, if an exclamation will suggest his meaning, he substitutes this for a whole sentence': *The P. R. B. Journal*, ed. W. E. Fredeman (1975), p. 58 (26 February 1850). Mrs. Orr tells us that 'The poem was written under the dread of diffuseness which had just then taken possession of Mr. Browning's mind': *Handbook*, p. 35. Earlier in the same work, on p. 11, Mrs. Orr states that Browning was coming to the conclusion that 'he had failed to be intelligible' in *Paracelsus* 'because he had been too concise, when an extract from a letter of Miss Caroline Fox was forwarded to him by the lady to whom it had been addressed. The writer stated that John Sterling had tried to read the poem and been repelled by its *verbosity*; and she ended with this question: "*doth he know that Wordsworth will devote a fortnight or more to the discovery of the single word that is the one fit for his sonnet?*"'. According to Mrs. Orr, Browning gave this criticism more weight than it deserved; 'and often, he tells us, during the period immediately following, he contented himself with two words where he would rather have used ten'. Marston's annotated copy of *Paracelsus* is now in the library of Balliol College, Oxford.

[3] Cf. pp. 529–30, below.

[4] The advertisement is disingenuous, as it also mentions, as 'Just published, price 6s. boards, Paracelsus; a Poem'.

[5] The obvious hypothesis that the earliest copies lacked this announcement seems to be ruled out by a remark in a letter to Fanny Haworth already referred to: 'You don't know, it seems, that I have announced Three Dramas—I see—the fly-leaf was left out of your copy': *New Letters*, p. 19. *Mansoor the Hierophant* was renamed *The Return of the Druses*.

[6] To Macready, letter conjecturally dated 'August 23, 1840': *New Letters*, p. 23. Macready's presentation copy remained unopened.

Browning Collections, Browning's account with Moxon in 1855 revealed that 'of an edition of 500 copies, only 157 had been sold, while 86 had been given away to reviewers and friends since the publication of the poem'.[1]

Sordello as published differed greatly from the poem which Browning had originally intended to write. His 'conception' had changed by December 1834, and it was to change again, more than once. We know so little of the composition of the poem, however, that DeVane's statement that 'there were four distinct periods of composition'[2] must be treated with reserve, while his further assertion that 'four different *Sordellos* were written' goes well beyond the evidence. There appears to be no justification for his claim that Browning 'temporarily laid *Sordello* aside' when he completed *Paracelsus*, or for his statement that it was probably during the second phase of composition 'that the verse . . . became rhymed couplets, instead of blank verse'. The latter conjecture sorts oddly with DeVane's claim (in itself a strange one) that Mrs Busk's poem 'was so much upon the same subject as to be in the same manner' as Browning's *Sordello*, in its (hypothetical) second form. As her poem is largely in rhymed couplets (predominantly tetrameters rather than pentameters, admittedly), he would have been more likely to change from rhymed verse to blank verse, had he wished to be different. In fact we have no reason to suppose that his *Sordello* was ever in blank verse: DeVane seems to introduce the notion simply to help to account for the unusual versification of the poem as we have it.

We know that the notion of writing 'in a more popular, and perhaps less difficult form' antedated the publication of *Paracelsus*, and that may mean that the use of a third-person narrator, 'if not the worst, Yet not the best expedient' (i. 12–13) was also part of the original plan. If not, the reception of *Paracelsus* probably suggested it. There can be no doubt that the writing of that poem modified the conception of *Sordello*, and DeVane may be right in his conjecture that (to some extent, at least) *Paracelsus* 'usurped the ideas which Browning had intended to use in *Sordello*' (although the example which

---

[1] Note to Lot 174, on p. 39.   [2] Pp. 72 ff.

he cites is unconvincing). The idea of writing a popular type of poem is likely to have faded on the publication of Mrs Busk's commonplace production, and the same event seems to have led to the decision to strengthen the historical element.

The introduction of Taurello Salinguerra, probably soon after Browning's visit to Italy, may have been the most important alteration in the plot. There is no historical evidence to suggest that he ever met Sordello, but the fact that he married a sister of Cunizza's no doubt suggested his introduction. Browning uses him for his own purposes, not only in relation to his plot but also as an opportunity of contrasting two psychological types, extrovert and introvert, man of action and man of thought.

The fact that Mrs Busk had written about Sordello proves that Browning's choice of a protagonist was slightly less eccentric on this occasion than when he decided to make Paracelsus the subject of a long poem. His sister had been studying Italian since 1828, and Maynard plausibly conjectures that Browning himself began with the same master in the autumn of 1829.[1] To study Italian is to study Dante, and while Browning may first have heard of Sordello from his father he is virtually certain to have come on him in a footnote to Cary's translation of the *Divina Commedia*.[2] The note on *Purgatorio* vi. 75 is as follows:

The history of Sordello's life is wrapt in the obscurity of romance. That he distinguished himself by his skill in Provençal poetry is certain; and many feats of military prowess have been attributed to him. It is probable that he was born towards the end of the twelfth,

---

[1] *Browning's Youth*, p. 304.

[2] I quote from the influential 'Second Edition Corrected' published in three volumes in 1819. The very strong *a priori* assumption that Browning would know this book is supported by verbal parallels in *Sordello*: see, e.g., notes to i. 67, 290, 905. DeVane strangely suggests that Browning first heard of Sordello from a textbook produced by his Italian teacher, Angelo Cerutti: 'it is probable, I think, that Browning's attention was first attracted to the poet Sordello by Angelo Cerutti's edition of Daniello Bartoli's *De' Simboli trasportati al morale*, published in London in 1830' (p. 74). While it is true that Browning (or his father) is listed among the subscribers, and while Mrs. Orr tells us, in her *Handbook* (p. 346 n.), that Browning 'had, as a young man, so great an admiration' for the book 'that when he travelled he always carried it with him', it is not true (as DeVane states) that 'Bartoli had expatiated at length upon Sordello (Book I, Ch.XI)'. Browning's copy of the work is now in Balliol. It is not divided into Books and Chapters, and while it contains numerous quotations from Dante the only reference to his description of Sordello occurs on pp. 170–1, with a quotation of *Purgatorio* vii. 28–31.

and died about the middle of the succeeding century. Tiraboschi, who terms him the most illustrious of all the Provençal poets of his age, has taken much pains to sift all the notices he could collect relating to him, and has particularly exposed the fabulous narrative which Platina has introduced on this subject in his history of Mantua. Honourable mention of his name is made by our Poet in the Treatise de Vulg. Eloq. lib. i. cap. 15. where it is said that, remarkable as he was for eloquence, he deserted the vernacular language of his own country, not only in his poems, but in every other kind of writing.

In a note to *Paradiso* ix. 32 Cary provides information about Cunizza, the Palma of Browning's poem:

The adventures of Cunizza, overcome by the influence of her star, are related by the chronicler Rolandino of Padua, lib. i. cap. 3. in Muratori. Rer. It. Script. tom. viii. p. 173. She eloped from her first husband, Richard of St. Boniface, in the company of Sordello, (see Purg. canto vi. and vii.) with whom she is supposed to have cohabited before her marriage . . .

Before he consulted Tiraboschi and the earlier authorities here cited it is virtually certain that Browning turned to the *Biographie Universelle*, the voluminous compilation which was 'at hand' when he wrote *Paracelsus* and which he quoted in his notes to that poem. Here is a translation of the article on Sordello:

SORDELLO, troubadour of the thirteenth century, is named by only one of the historians or chroniclers of his time, that is by Rolandino, who does not introduce him in a very honourable connection. Rolandino describes how the sister of Ezzelino da Romano, called Cunizza, married the Count Richard de Saint-Boniface, and was carried off from her husband by a certain Sordellus, who was *de ipsius familiâ*. These last words do not seem at all clear to Tiraboschi, first because one cannot be sure whether they signify relationship or fealty, and further because they leave it uncertain whether it was to the house of the Ezzelini or to that of Saint-Boniface that Sordello belonged. After having passed some time with Cunizza, at this lady's father's house, the abductor was finally chased away: that is all that Rolandino tells us of him.[1] But Dante meets Sordello at the entrance to Purgatory (canto vi), in the place where those are to be found who delayed their penitence and above all those who died violent deaths: 'O Mantuan', cries this suffering soul, addressing Virgil, 'I am Sor-

---

[1] *Script. rer. italic. collect. Muratori*, t. VIII, p. 173.

dello, born in the same territory as you': *o Mantovano io son Sordello, della tua terra*. We must conclude from this that this troubadour was born in Mantuan territory; and we can also deduce from it, though with less certainty, that he did not die in a peaceable manner. Dante attributes to him, further, the appearance and regard of a lion; which, according to certain commentators, signifies noble extraction or high rank. The Latin Treatise which Dante wrote on the colloquial tongue contains some lines relating to Sordello. In them we read that he excelled in every sort of poetry and that he contributed to establishing the Italian language by happy and sagacious borrowings from the dialects of Cremona, Brescia and Verona, cities neighbouring on his native Mantua. In another place in the same Treatise Dante mentions a Mantuan Goito, the author of several good songs in each stanza of which he left one line unrhymed, *scompagnato*, which he termed 'the key'. Crescimbeni and Quadrio believed that this name Goito referred to a poet distinct from Sordello; but according to Tiraboschi it refers to the same man, and in fact, as we shall soon see, he does seem to have come from Goito in Mantua. After Rolandino and Dante the earliest writer to have spoken of Sordello is Benvenuto da Imola, who wrote a commentary on Dante in the fourteenth century and who added to the passage we have quoted from the sixth canto of the *Purgatorio* a historical note in these terms: 'Sordello was a citizen of Mantua, a famous and able warrior, and a courtier' (for this seems the appropriate translation here of the word *curialis*). The commentator adds, although without positive affirmation, that this noble knight lived in the time of Ezzelin da Romano, whose sister Cunizza conceived so ardent a love for him that on several occasions she ordered him to come to her by a secret way. On hearing of this intrigue Ezzelino disguised himself one evening as a servant and took Sordello by surprise: he asked his forgiveness, and promised not to return there any more. But, says Benvenuto, it was the cursed Cunizza who inveigled him into a repetition of his first offence: *Tamen Cunitia maledicta traxit eum in primum fallum*: by his natural disposition he was virtuous, serious and of excellent morals. Nonetheless he fled, to escape from the resentment of the lady's brother; but he was taken and assassinated by emissaries of Ezzelino. Sordello had composed a book entitled *Thesaurus thesaurorum*, says Benvenuto further, although he declares that he had never seen this work. At almost the same time as this commentator was writing in this way what he had learned of the life of Sordello, Biographical Accounts of the Troubadours were being written in the Provençal language, and in them it was stated that Sordello had been born in Mantua, the son of a poor knight called El

Cort, and had written songs and sirventes early in his life: that he had
been attracted to the court of the Count of Saint-Boniface and had
there become the lover of the wife of this lord and had carried her off
and been received with her by her brothers, who were then at odds
with the Count: that from there he went to Provence, where his gifts
secured him such brilliant success that he was given a castle and made
an honourable marriage. Such had been the historical notices relating
to this poet when, at the beginning of the fifteenth century, Aliprando wrote a fabulous Chronicle in Italian verse about Milan in
which he speaks of Sordello at much greater length. Perhaps he
borrowed these details from an older collection of stories: what is
certain is that they passed from this Chronicle into the History of
Mantua written by Platina, where they are to be found translated
into Latin prose.[1] According to these accounts, Sordello was born in
1189, in the bosom of the family of the Visconti, which originated in
Goito. Already in his youth he commenced a literary career with a
book entitled *Treasure*. The career of arms opened to him when he
had reached his twenty-fifth year, and in it he distinguished himself
by his courage, his address, and by the nobility and grace of his
demeanour, although he was only of middle stature. He accepted a
number of challenges, emerged victorious from all his encounters,
and despatched the adversaries whom he had overcome to inform
the king of France of his great exploits. Attracted by this prince, he
was dreaming of crossing the Alps when (yielding to the solicitations
of Ezzelino) he made up his mind to establish himself in Verona. For
a long time he there resisted the prayers, the tears and the swoonings
of Beatrice, Ezzelino's sister, who pursued him (disguised as a man)
as far as Mantua, where he had fled to be rid of her. Yet in the end he
married her; but a few days after the wedding, remembering
promises which he had made to King Louis, he hastened into France,
passed four months between Troyes and the Court, and attracted
admiration there by his gallant behaviour, his valour, and his gifts as
a poet. Having received from the king the dignity of knight, a gift of
three thousand francs, and a golden sparrow-hawk, he returned to
Italy. All the cities received him ceremoniously as the greatest warrior of the century: the Mantuans came to meet him. He left them to
go to Padua to recover his wife, and when he returned with her they
celebrated his return by eight days of festivities. He was then forty
years old, and consequently this must have been in 1229. Platina goes
on to describe how Ezzelino came to lay siege to the city of Mantua,
in 1250, and kept it in a state of siege until 1253: how Sordello saved

---

[1] Muratori, *Scrip. rer.ital.*, t. XX, p. 680.

it, and then assisted the Milanese in their battle against Ezzelino: and finally how this tyrant received a wound from which he died. What happened to Sordello after this event? How much longer did he live? There is nothing about this in Platina's book, or in Aliprando's poem. Tiraboschi submitted their account to an examination which such a tissue of fictions could not sustain. This story mentions a Roger, King of Apulia, between 1197 and 1250, a time when this part of Italy had no other sovereign but the Emperor Frederick II. Before he was thirty years old, and therefore before 1219, Sordello is called to France by a king called Louis, although [in fact] Philippe-Auguste was still on the throne. No other historian gives Ezzelino a sister of the name of Beatrice: no other makes the siege of Mantua begin before 1256 or Ezzelino die before 1259. The lives of several troubadours have been filled with anachronisms and lies in this way; and these poets have themselves contributed to this by sometimes making themselves the heroes of chivalric and gallant adventures which they invented. It is possible that Sordello, in poems which we no longer possess, had attributed to himself some of the adventures which Aliprando and Platina recount at great length and of which we have given only a brief idea. Nostradamus does not repeat them, although he inserted a great many fables in his Lives of the Provençal Poets, published in the sixteenth century. He limits himself to saying that Sordello was a Mantuan, that at the age of fifteen he entered the service of Bérenger, Count of Provence, that his poems were preferred to those of Folquet de Marseille, Perceval Doria and other Genoese or Tuscan troubadours, that he composed excellent songs on philosophical subjects and not on love—which will be contradicted by details which we shall set out in a moment—that he translated into Provençal the Body of laws, and wrote, in the same language, a Treatise entitled *Lou progrès et avansament dels reys d'Aragon en la contat de Provenza*: that among his poems one is celebrated in which, in the course of a funeral elegy on Blacas, he censured all the princes of Christendom: that this production dates from the year 1281: and that he died about this same time. That is what Nostradamus extracts from the accounts written by the Monk of the îles d'Or, by Hugues de Saint-Césaire, by the Monk of Montemaïor, and by Pierre de Castelnuovo. Duverdier's article on Sordello is a mere translation of that of Nostradamus. Alessandro Zilioli's Memoirs of the Italian Poets have not been printed, but they are preserved in manuscript and it seems that, so far as Sordello is concerned, he reproduces in them some of the fables of Platina. It is from these different sources that Crescimbeni and Quadrio have drawn, without a sufficiently critical and orderly method, what they

have said about this troubadour. Millot divides all the facts into two
sets: the one set seems to him probable, namely that consisting of
those which are connected with the original account of Rolandino:
whereas he dismisses as fabulous or irrelevant those retailed by the
historians of Mantua. These questions were considered by the Count
Giambattista d'Arco in an academic dissertation which had been
communicated to Tiraboschi before it was printed.[1] It is in the work
of this last[2] that we find the best documentation on the life of
Sordello: what it amounts to is that, to all appearances, this poet was
born in Goito, a small town in Mantuan territory, that in the course
of the last twenty years of the twelfth century he carried off the wife
of his patron, the Count of Saint-Boniface, and that at some time, but
not at the age of fifteen, he stayed for a considerable time in Provence. Tiraboschi rejects everything further, except that he believes
that Sordello belonged to a noble family: that he was a warrior,
although without ever having performed the functions of captain-
general or podestà of Mantua attributed to him by some authors: and
that in the end he died a violent death, at an unknown time (it is hard
to believe that it could have been in 1281, since he would in that case
have been a centenarian or a nonagenarian). We believe that the most
plausible conclusions are still those which Millot stated, although
he abstained to excess from discussion, a failure with which Tiraboschi reproaches him. Ginguené did not examine the circumstances of Sordello's life, either; and M. Raynouard limited himself
to transcribing some lines from a Roman chronicle,[3] distinguishing
him (perhaps erroneously) from the lover of Cunizza, a Sordel of
Goi, of whom he quotes seven lines, without saying anything about
his identity. Ultimately it is the writings of Sordello which it would
be most important to know. None of his poems in the Italian language, nor of the prose works signalised as having been written by him
in the course of this article, have been published: we only know his
poems in Provençal. Of them at least thirty-four are preserved, half of
which (or very nearly half) consist of very gallant songs, whatever
Nostradamus said of them. M. Raynouard has printed two of them,[4]

---

[1] This dissertation, printed at Cremona in 1783 (8°, 150 pp.), is entitled *Sordello*, and
has the epigraph *Post fata resurgam*, but is without the author's name on the title-page.
At the end of it one finds an inferior map of the environs of Goïto. [Browning came on
a copy of this 'quite at the end' of his work on *Sordello*, as he told Elizabeth Barrett in
1845: Kintner i. 336 and note.] The Comte d'Arco, according to the authority of a
certain Richard de Modigliana, credits Sordello with having thrice translated Caesar's
Commentaries, and twice the History of Quintus Curtius, and with having presented
the Council of Mantua with some ideas on defence.
[2] *Storia della letter. ital.*, 2° Modena, IV., p. 373–90.
[3] *Choix des poés. des Troub.*, V, p. 444–5.   [4] Ibid., t. III, p. 441–4.

which had been translated by Millot. One has as refrain: *Aylas! E que me fan miey huels*, etc., (*Alas! what use are my eyes to me, if they do not see her whom I desire!*)—it is a composition in a very pure taste: the second falls back rather on the commonplaces of this genre. Millot cites a third of them, in which the poet boasts of his conquests and his infidelities; and we may consider as a fragment of a fourth the couplet which M. Raynouard attributes to Sordel of Goi. Three of the pieces by our poet belong to the genre of Tensons, that is to say dialogues or controversies. In the one the problem is whether a lover should die or resign himself to living, after having lost his beloved. In another, whether honour should be sacrificed to love, or the glory of knightly combats should be preferred to love. The bad faith of princes is the subject of the third: it has a political character, which is to be found again in an Epistle in which Sordello begs his lord, the Count of Provence, not to take him to the Crusade (of 1248). The troubadour cannot make up his mind to cross the sea: he wishes, he says, to reach eternal life as late as possible: this piece would not give an elevated idea of his courage. The other poems of his which are known are sirventes or satires: several of them are against the troubadour Pierre Vidal: in them violent threats are joined to insults which become merely gross when one translates them. Four other sirventes by Sordello relate to the moral and political history of his century and from every point of view deserve more attention. Such is that of which M. Raynouard has published the text, pages 329 and 330 of Volume VI of his Collection. Elsewhere the poet censures the princes who, under the pretence of extinguishing the Albigensian heresy, had leagued together to enrich themselves with the spoils of Raimond VI, Count of Toulouse. The Satire in which the princes are exhorted no longer to allow themselves to be insulted or robbed of their states appeared in the year 1228, since the pardon which Raimond VII has just obtained is mentioned in it. Of all the poems of Sordello the most highly esteemed is his lament on the death of Blacas (see this name, IV, 546): it is also a satire. In it the rulers are invited to share among them the heart of this brave man: 'The Emperor shall be the first to eat of it, in order that he may recover the territories which the Milanese have taken from him. The noble King of France shall eat of it, to regain Castille; but if his mother knows, he will not eat; for he is too afraid to displease her, etc.' We believe, with Millot, that this King of France is Louis IX, and that this satiric lament was written between the years 1226 and 1236, not in 1281, as Nostradamus and others have supposed. For the rest, this piece, the finest of the songs which we have mentioned, and some remarkable touches in the other fragments, assure for Sordello an eminent position among the poets of the thirteenth century who wrote in the Provençal language.[1]

We may safely assume that Browning went on to read Tiraboschi's account of Sordello, the importance of which is so clearly indicated by both Cary and Daunou. It was most readily available in the handy little volumes edited by T. J. Mathias and published in London in 1803. Here Browning will have found Sordello set in his place in the development of Italian poetry, and the traditions relating to his life subjected to a close analysis. As Daunou (quite rightly) draws heavily on Tiraboschi, Browning will have found in the latter more detailed support for the same distrust of Platina's *History of Mantua* (shown to derive largely from Aliprandi), the same insistence on the importance of Rolandino (the only writer before Dante to have mentioned Sordello), the same reference to Benvenuto da Imola, a distinct dubiety about the 'cavalleresche avventure'[2] attributed to Sordello, and above all an emphasis on the unreliability of most of the traditions about him:

But let us first reflect here to what extent there is agreement between the various writers whose views we have reported so far. Nostradamus makes Sordello the son of a poor father: Platina says that he sprang from a wealthy and noble family, that of the viscounts of Goito. According to Nostradamus Sordello went to Provence at the age of fifteen and there is no indication that he returned again to Italy. In the account given in the Vatican codex Sordello did not go into Provence until he had had a number of amorous adventures. According to this same codex Sordello fell in love with the sister of Ezzelino, the wife of the Count of S. Bonifacio: in the opinion of Platina that same sister fell in love with Sordello, while she was still unmarried. According to the Vatican codex Ezzelino's sister was torn from her husband by force and brought back to the house, with Sordello, by her brothers; in the opinion of Platina she fled back to Sordello, and did not seek marriage. According to the Vatican codex Sordello married a lady of Provence: according to Platina he became the husband of Beatrice. In the Vatican codex, finally, Sordello went off, after his adventures with the Ezzelino family, to be a poet in

---

[1] *Biographie Universelle* xliii (1825) pp. 131–5. The author was Pierre-Claude-François Daunou.
[2] *Storia della Poesia Italiana* (3 vols. in 4), i. 65.

Provence: Platina has him go to Paris to fight a duel. Of those accounts, so disparate, which are we to follow?[1]

In almost thirty pages devoted to Sordello Tiraboschi provides just the sort of detailed background which Browning must have desired, and precisely the sort of conflicting evidence which left him in full measure a poet's liberty to choose, to reject, and to invent.

Such freedom suited him admirably. His Sordello seems to be born (following most authorities) about 1189, although at i. 569–70 he is said to have been 'Born . . . With the new century'. He is brought up at Goito, in Mantuan territory, and the tradition that he was the son of a poor knight called El Cort plays a prominent part in the poem. He is very far from being the Don Juan suggested by certain of his poems, but rather the sort of man described by Benvenuto da Imola, a lover of solitude who is serious and of excellent character.[2] It seems that he becomes the lover of Palma ('*Cunizza*, as he [Dante] called her!': v. 995), a sister of Ecelin (the future Tyrant) who is contracted (but not here married) to Count Richard. He is a poet noted for his tensons and sirventes, and he writes an elegy (on Eglamor, however, not on Blacas). He wins fame at Court (not at the court of the King of France, but at Palma's Love Court in Mantua). He is portrayed as contemptuous of Pierre Vidal (ii. 714 ff.), the rival with whom Sordello is said to have engaged in poetic contests. Tiraboschi's discussion of the place of Sordello in the history of Italian poetry (and therefore in relation to Dante) seems to lie behind that at v. 109 ff. He does not live to be old, as in the biographical accounts, nor does he meet a violent death. At the end of his poem (indeed) Browning states that the historians have given a false account of his protagonist:

> The Chroniclers of Mantua tired their pen
> Telling how *Sordello Prince Visconti* saved
> Mantua, and elsewhere notably behaved—
> Who thus, by fortune ordering events,
> Passed with posterity, to all intents,
> For just the god he never could become.
> As Knight, Bard, Gallant, men were never dumb
> In praise of him.   (vi. 822–9)

[1] Ibid., 59–60.   [2] Tiraboschi, i. 68 ff.

The uncertainty about his parentage is central to the poem.

Before he read Tiraboschi's *Storia* (necessarily in Italian) Browning is almost certain to have read Sismondi's *Historical View of the Literature of the South of Europe*, translated by Thomas Roscoe, with additional notes, in four volumes in 1823. It seems likely that this will have led him to consult (at least) the *Histoire Littéraire des Troubadours* by the Abbé Millot (3 vols., 1774), a work based on the researches of Lacurne de Sainte-Palaye; and by a fortunate chance we know that his father gave him a copy of a book called *The Literary History of the Troubadours . . . Collected and Abridged* from this larger work by Mrs Dobson, the biographer of Petrarch.[1] That he also consulted François Raynouard's great collection, the *Choix de Poésies Originales des Troubadours* (eventually 7 vols., 1816–43) seems likely, as it too is mentioned by Sismondi; but evidence is lacking.

Wherever we look we come on Sismondi, a passionate lover of liberty and an 'austere republican'[2] whose political views must have made a great appeal to Browning. It has been well said that 'what Grote was to do for Greece, Sismondi accomplished for the Italian Republics by bringing them before the

[1] See a letter by D. C. Joseph in the *TLS* for 3 April 1953. The book is said to be inscribed 'Robert Browning from his Father. March 2nd, 1838', and to contain 'a handwritten index of 14 of the 69 Troubadours', and a few brief notes. The present whereabouts of this volume, which had passed into the possession of Arthur J. Whyte (?Whyte) by February 1890, is unknown. The abridgement was first published in 1779, but Browning's copy was of the edition of 1807. For 'a rough draft' of a proposed version of the story of Sordello by Robert Browning Senior, see Griffin and Minchin, pp. 98 ff.

[2] *History and Historians in the Nineteenth Century*, by G. P. Gooch (1913), p. 167, followed by a quotation from p. 166. Sismondi was descended from a family of Ghibellins who had been expelled from Italy in the sixteenth century and had fled from France to Geneva on the revocation of the Edict of Nantes. When the Revolution broke upon Switzerland, he moved to Tuscany. His *Histoire* appeared in 16 vols. between 1807 and 1818. He enthusiastically admired the Lombard League, as Gooch remarks, but also appreciated the greatness of Barbarossa. His 'rigid Puritanism' (ibid. p. 168) will have appealed to Browning, while the lack of true historical imagination in his work—what Gooch terms its 'lack of relativity' (p. 167)—will not have troubled him. He contributed many articles to the *Biographie Universelle*. John Grube has performed a service by pointing out that Mrs Busk 'laid out the ideological foundation for her poem in a review-article' in *Blackwood's* for October 1832. There 'she maintains that the early democracies of northern Italy were an unfortunate development, and relates what she regards as that triumph of the "mob" to the agitation surrounding the unfortunate Reform Bill of 1832'. She concludes her attack on Sismondi by prophesying that civil war will break out in England as a result of the Reform Act. See '*Sordello*, Browning's Christian Epic', in *English Studies in Canada*, iv. (Winter, 1978), pp. 413–29.

mind of cultured Europe'. One has only to turn the pages of the first volumes of his *Histoire des Républiques Italiennes du Moyen Âge* to find there most of the historical background of the poem. It seems certain that Browning knew the first two volumes (at least) in the full French version, but even the headings in the 'Analytical and Chronological Table' at the beginning of the one-volume English abridgement of 1832 emphasize the relevance of the work: 'Importance of the Study of the Italian Republics; the Science of governing Men for their Advantage began with them . . . The instructive Part of History begins with the Fusion of the Conquerors with the conquered for the good of all'. Near the beginning of his book Sismondi deals with Barbarossa, the Lombard League, and the Peace of Constance, while he is continually concerned with the progress of the cities towards independence and with the struggles between the Guelfs and Ghibellins. He emphasizes the historical significance of Ezzelin III, 'the Tyrant'. He teaches that no state can be great without liberty: 'The duty of every ruler and every citizen before God and man is to introduce the guarantee of liberty into the constitution, whatsoever it be. Through it and it alone will men be truly men'.[1] His interpretation of Italian history made it appear highly relevant to nineteenth-century readers concerned with the progress of mankind. When Browning decided to increase the historical element in *Sordello*, therefore, he found in Sismondi ample material with which to portray the development of mankind as the background to the development of a soul.

According to Mrs Orr, who no doubt had it from Browning himself, he 'prepared himself for writing "Sordello" by studying all the chronicles of that period of Italian history which the British Museum supplied'.[2] There is no need to question her statement elsewhere that he 'studied no less than thirty works',[3] so long as we realize that his study was that of a poet rather than that of a minute scholar. Most of the chronicles had been assembled in one of the great collections of European history, the *Rerum Italicarum Scriptores* edited by Ludovico Antonio Muratori and published in Milan in 25 volumes between 1723 and 1751. The most important volume

---

[1] Quoted by Gooch, p. 165.   [2] *Handbook*, p. 32.   [3] *Life*, p. 99.

for Browning was viii (1726), which includes the *Historia de rebus gestis Eccelini de Romano* of Gerardo Maurisio, the *De Factis in Marchia Tarvisina* of Rolandino of Padua, the anonymous *Chronica parva Ferrariensis*, and the *Chronicon de rebus gestis in Lombardia* of the 'Monachus Patavinus'. Browning also knew Platina's *Historia di Mantua*, which he probably found (with other material) in Muratori's vol. xx. He seems also to have looked into Pietro Gerardo's *Vita et gesti d'Ezzelino Terzo da Romano* (Venice, 1552) and the *Historia de principi di Este* (Ferrara, 1570) of G. B. Pigna. An important source was clearly Giambatista Verci's *Storia degli Ecelini* (3 vols., Bassano 1779), and Griffin and Minchin are probably right in their suggestion that Browning studied it in the early months of 1838, before he visited Italy.[1]

In spite of all this reading, however, the poem is profoundly unhistorical, and while Browning uses the names of actual personages his principal characters have little or nothing in common with their originals. While he insists that she is the woman whom Dante (and history) called Cunizza, and terms her 'passion's votaress', his Palma is a strange recreation of a woman so celebrated for her 'folli amori',[2] a woman who had five husbands—if indeed (as Verci takes leave to doubt) all these men really were husbands—a celebrated beauty who was so free of her favours that commentators on Dante have been puzzled to account for her presence in Paradise. Whereas Cunizza was married to Count Richard, and bore him a son, Palma is merely engaged to marry him; but although he has avoided the slur of adultery by this alteration Browning leaves any sexual relationship between Palma and Sordello remarkably inexplicit.[3]

Taurello Salinguerra in the poem has hardly any resem-

---

[1] Cf. p. 160, above. While the appearance of Mrs Busk's poem may have been the principal reason for the increased emphasis on the historical element in *Sordello*, there were others, notably Browning's immersion in the conflict between King and Parliament as he worked on *Strafford*.

[2] Verci i. 114.

[3] 'The "intrigue" between him and Palma', observes Mrs Orr in her *Handbook* (p. 31), '. . . appears in due time as a poetical affinity, strongest on her side . . .' We note that whereas Dante places Cunizza in the Heaven of Venus, among the 'Spiriti Amanti' (*Paradiso* ix. 32), Browning has her under the influence of 'Fomalhaut' (iii. 430).

blance to his historical counterpart, while the preface to *Alastor* throws more light on Sordello himself than anything in Muratori.[1] Like Shelley's poet, Browning's is 'a youth of uncorrupted feelings . . . led forth by an imagination inflamed and purified through familiarity with all that is excellent and majestic, to the contemplation of the universe'. 'The magnificence and beauty of the external world sinks profoundly into the frame of [Sordello's] conceptions', as into that of Shelley's protagonist. When he 'thirsts for intercourse with an intelligence similar to' his own Sordello is fortunate enough to encounter Palma, but he too is at home only with 'objects . . . infinite and unmeasured', and his essentially 'self-centred' nature brings him to 'an untimely grave' when he rejects the power offered him by Taurello. Like Paracelsus, Sordello is (in Shelley's phrase) one of the 'luminaries of the world', a luminary destined (like the poet in *Alastor*) to 'sudden darkness and extinction'. The manner of his death comes as no surprise to a reader of Shelley.

A passage in one of the letters to Elizabeth Barrett emphasizes the element of Browning himself in Sordello's character: it is that in which he confesses to a 'folly . . ., which I shall never wholly get rid of, of desiring to do nothing when I cannot do all'.[2] Sordello's perplexity about the relationship between poet and audience, particularly prominent in Book II, expresses a perplexity of Browning's own, while his commitment to the service of mankind through writing difficult poetry which is likely to be unpopular with critics, who will stigmatize it as mere metaphysics, is similarly close to Browning's own concerns. There is a highly personal element in his portrayal of Sordello as a Moses who can point the way to the Promised Land, even if he cannot reach it himself. Sordello's consideration of the relative importance of poet and man of action may also reflect a pre-occupation of Browning's own, and it is tempting to speculate on a biographical origin for his

---

[1] So far from being a great warrior, he is of poor physique and has hair which is prematurely faded, as Taurello notes (e.g. at v. 360–2).

[2] Kintner i. 53–4. Cf., too, Sordello's habit of coming, 'constant as eve', to sit by one or other of the Caryatides which support the mysterious font with Browning's comment on his own visits to the Dulwich Gallery, as a young man: 'I have sate before one, some *one* of those pictures I had predetermined to see—, a good hour and then gone away': Kintner i. 509.

encounter with the 'sad dishevelled ghost' in Book III (696 ff., 969 ff.). While the critique of the romantic solitary may owe its origin to that in *Alastor*, it is possible that the critical presentation of Sordello became more pronounced as the poem developed, as if Browning had been laying to heart Mill's comments on *Pauline*, and his charge of 'intense and morbid self-consciousness'.[1]

Such criticism is part of the element of reflection and commentary in the poem, an element which is at least as important as the narrative, and it is obvious that any attempt to distinguish between Browning and the 'narrator' is unlikely to prove fruitful. At ii. 296 'My own month came', a comment which simply refers to the month of Browning's birth.[2] In the latter part of Book III, indeed, Sordello is forgotten as Browning himself bursts into the poem.

When we consider the 'plot', such as it is, we find that *Sordello* owes something to the tradition of the historical romance. As we read the description of Sordello's early life in Book I, following him through the 'maze of corridors' by

Dusk winding-stairs, dim galleries,

and so to the 'maple-panelled room' and the mysterious vault, we are inevitably reminded of Mrs. Radcliffe and her followers. To readers of their books the fact that the northern side of the castle 'Lay under a mysterious interdict' is in no way surprising. *The Mysterious Interdict* would serve as a suitable title for one of the 'horrid novels' published by the Minerva Press.[3]

Scott is the presiding genius of this territory, and Edward Waverley is one of the romantic protagonists of whom we are fleetingly reminded. 'As living in this ideal world became daily more delectable to our hero', we read at the end of ch. iv of *Waverley*, 'interruption was disagreeable in proportion'. He loved 'to "chew the cud of sweet and bitter fancy,"' and, like a child among his toys, culled and arranged, from the splendid yet useless imagery and emblems with which his imagination

---

[1] It would be interesting to know when the lines bidding Shelley to 'come not near' (i. 60 ff.) were written. DeVane conjectures that this passage 'was originally . . . an invocation to the Sun-treader for aid': p. 73.

[2] As Elizabeth Barrett realized: 'Nor think that I shall forget how tomorrow is the seventh of May . . your month as you call it somewhere . . in Sordello, I believe . . so that I knew before, you had a birthday there': Kintner, ii. 683.

[3] It is appropriate that echoes of *The Eve of St. Agnes* are noticeable at this point.

was stored, visions as brilliant and as fading as those of an evening sky'. Some of the dangers of his indulging in 'that . . . sorcery, by which past or imaginary events are presented in action, as it were, to the eye of the muser' are described in the following chapter. Scott comments that 'the reader may perhaps anticipate . . . an imitation of the romance of Cervantes', but stresses that he is not concerned with 'such total perversion of intellect . . ., but [with] that more common aberration from sound judgment, which apprehends occurrences . . . in their reality, but communicates to them a tincture of its own romantic tone and colouring'. It is a striking fact that 'Pentapolin / Named o' the Naked Arm' is mentioned at the very beginning of *Sordello*, while the first of the headnotes added in 1863 describes the poem as 'A Quixotic attempt'.

Sordello's appearance and triumph at Palma's Court of Love are highly reminiscent of Scott, and the way in which a totally inexperienced young man soon finds himself in a position of the greatest historical importance is in the manner of Scott but carried to the *n*th degree. Instead of the conflict between Jacobite and Hanoverian, or Cavalier and Roundhead, it is the opposition between Guelf and Ghibellin which provides the background to Browning's excursion into history, and it is even harder to understand why Palma should regard Sordello as the destined leader of the House of Romano than why Edward Waverley and the protagonist of *The Abbot* should soon find themselves prominently involved in historical events of such great importance.

Those who read the summaries of the six Books in the present edition may well be reminded of E. M. Forster's mocking summary of *The Antiquary* in *Aspects of the Novel*. The sequence of events is hard to disentangle. No adequate explanation is provided of the strange mutual recognition of Sordello and his father, or of the latter's sudden decision to hand over his power. We never learn why, as a boy, Sordello had been in the habit of visiting the mysterious font in the castle at Goito, who the Caryatides who support it are intended to represent, or why he should wish to assist them in their penance.[1] The end of the story is huddled up, much in

---

[1] He does not know that his mother is buried beneath the font. It is tempting to suppose that we have here a loose end due to revision, but that is mere conjecture.

Scott's manner: Sordello dies as abruptly as Eglamor, and with as little apparent reason.

Such resemblances to Scott are of course superficial. Browning's 'stress [lies] on the incidents in the development of a soul'—and beyond that he is concerned with no less a theme than the development of mankind, and the role played by exceptional individuals in that development. *Sordello* is as truly an emanation of the spirit of the early Victorian Age as the lectures *On Heroes, Hero-worship, and the Heroic in History* which Carlyle was to deliver only a few weeks later. In Book V an attempt is made to account for human progress in terms of a somewhat confused dialectic between Strength and Knowledge, while the fact that the subject of the poem embraces much more than the life of its protagonist becomes particularly explicit in Book VI.

It is significant that the only considerable character who is portrayed (so far as he is portrayed) more or less as history presents him is Ecelin the Tyrant. Browning may first have met him in *The Cenci*, where (at II. ii. 48 ff.) he is described as one of 'The memorable torturers of this land' (Italy), or in 'Lines written among the Euganean Hills', where we hear how 'Death and Sin, / Played at dice for Ezzelin'; and he will have come on Ariosto's description of him as 'a most atrocious tyrant, . . . reputed the very son of Satan', a monster to be compared with Nero, Caligula and Attila the Hun, one of those whom 'God inflicted upon us, to plague and torment us'.[1]

When we remember the monstrosities perpetrated by this evil man, of whom Jacob Burckhardt was soon to write that 'as a political type he was a figure of no less importance for the future than his imperial protector Frederick',[2] we are in a position to appreciate the momentous consequences of Sor-

---

[1] *Orlando Furioso* (trans. G. Waldman, 1974), iii. 33 and xvii. 3.

[2] *The Civilization of the Renaissance* (trans. S. G. C. Middlemore, 1878, Phaidon Press ed., 1944), p. 3. Burckhardt writes that 'Here for the first time the attempt was openly made to found a throne by wholesale murder and endless barbarities, by the adoption . . . of any means with a view to nothing but the end pursued. None of his successors, not even Cesare Borgia, rivalled the colossal guilt of Ezzelino; but the example once set was not forgotten, and his fall led to no return of justice among the nations, and served as no warning to future transgressors'. In 'The Hundred Old Tales', as Burckhardt reminds us, 'Ezzelino . . . became the centre of a whole literature from the chronicle of eye-witnesses to the half-mythical tragedy of later poets'. The original edition of Burckhardt's book appeared in 1860.

dello's failure when he rejects the power offered him by Taurello.

That Sordello is a failure is made evident again and again. As early as i. 585–6 we hear of 'The leprosy' of his spirit: at iii. 982 he is described as 'a god's germ, doomed to remain a germ': while in Book VI we hear of his fatal flaw, 'his strange disbelief that aught / Was ever to be done' (758–9). Tradition falsely portrays him as 'just the god he never could become':

> while what he should have been,
> Could be, and was not—the one step too mean
> For him to take,—we suffer at this day
> Because of.   (829–32)

Browning immediately refers to Ecelin's appearance at this point in history, so reminding us of one of the 'brilliant fictions' about Sordello recorded by Sismondi, the story that 'he had fought this monster, with glory to himself'.[1] The manner in which Dante introduces him in the *Purgatorio* suggests a great but unrealized power for good.[2] In Browning's poem his life may be regarded as no more than 'A sorry farce' (vi. 850), because he was one (to adapt *Paracelsus* i. 142–3) who had

> Abandoned the sole end for which he lived,
> Rejected God's great commission, and so died!

Yet that is perhaps too straightforward a reading of so complicated a poem, and it is best to leave the last word with Browning himself, writing to Elizabeth Barrett:

---

[1] 'The age of Sordello was that of the most brilliant chivalric virtues, and the most atrocious crimes. He lived in the midst of heroes and monsters. The imagination of the people was still haunted by the recollection of the ferocious Ezzelino, tyrant of Verona, with whom Sordello is said to have had a contest . . . He united, according to popular report, the most brilliant military exploits to the most distinguished poetical genius.': *Historical View*, i. 132.

[2] Cf. the comment of a recent writer on this passage: 'The figure of Sordello, who appears in *Purgatorio* vi and guides Dante and Vergil to the valley of the princes, has long puzzled critics, since his stature in the *Comedy* seems greater than his historical achievements warrant. He is noted chiefly for a *planh* with political overtones, the lament for Blacatz. Of the *Comedy*'s lyric poets, the other known especially for political poetry is Bertran de Born, among the "sowers of scandal and of schism" in *Inferno* xxviii. By comparing Dante's treatment of these two "political poets", we see that they are used within the poem in a way that necessarily transcends their historical identities: they have become emblematic, respectively, of good and bad uses to which poets can put their verse in the service of the state': Teodolinda Barolini, 'Bertran de Born and Sordello: the Poetry of Politics in Dante's Comedy': PMLA 94 (May 1979), pp. 395–405. I quote the writer's own summary, from p. 381.

yesterday I was reading the "Purgatorio" and the first speech of the group of which Sordello makes one[1] struck me with a new significance, as well describing the man and his purpose and fate in my own poem—see; one of the burthened, contorted souls tells Virgil & Dante—

> Noi fummo già tutti per forza morti,
> E *peccatori infin' all' ultim' ora:*
> Quivi—*lume del ciel ne fece accorti;*
> Si *chè, pentendo e perdonando, fora*
> Di *vita uscimmo a Dio pacificati*
> Che *del disio di se veder n'accora.*

Which is just my Sordello's story . . could I '*do*' if off hand, I wonder—

> And sinners were we to the extreme hour;
> *Then*, light from heaven fell, making us aware,
> So that, repenting us and pardoned, out
> Of life we passed to God, at peace with Him
> Who fills the heart with yearning Him to see.[2]

The Text

As mentioned above, no manuscript survives, but there is a proof copy of the first edition (1840), which formerly belonged to the Browning Society of Boston, in Boston Public Library.[3] 'Many of these proofs are Browning's own', someone has written on the first page. 'I know not whether they have a higher value therefore': the date 'Mar. 13, 1905' is added in a different hand. The copy contains several distinct kinds of markings: notes made by or for the printer, proof-corrections giving the readings of the first edition, and marginal comments in a hand similar to that of the first inscription quoted above. Publishing or printing-house marks are found throughout the copy. They include instructions to add the running-titles (which are lacking in the first gathering), initials at the end of most gatherings, and corrections of technical printing errors such as turned letters. Proof-corrections which are recognizably Browning's, on the other hand, do not occur

---

[1] The group of those who died (by violence) before they could repent.

[2] Kintner, i. 336, quoting *Purgatorio* v. 52–7.

[3] The pages of the first gathering (B), probably representing an early state of proof, have been re-bound in the wrong order, and they end at i. 362, whereas gathering C begins with i. 373.

in all gatherings: C to E, G, H, and K have no obviously
authorial corrections, but the remaining gatherings contain
interesting revisions. Browning made several changes in the
original wording in, for example, lines i. 219, ii. 733–56, iii.
628, v. 596, v. 664, and vi. 530–886. Gatherings I (iii.
625–1018) and R (vi. 593 to the end) have an exceptionally
large number of alterations. Browning also drew attention to
unusual words such as 'chequed' at vi. 365, and answered
emphatically *'All right'* when the printer queried the connection between pages 208 and 209 (before v. 877). Most of his
revisions were stylistic: on four occasions, for example, he
replaced 'to be' by a more distinctive phrase in the nine lines vi.
837–45. In one instance, his 'revision' obscured the meaning of
a line which had originally been clear: ii. 844 had read,
'Whence blunders which untruths must cure—'.

The marginal comments which are not in Browning's hand
are confined to gatherings B to E (i.e., from the beginning to ii.
492). They are especially numerous in Book I, and consist
mainly of explanatory notes by a highly perceptive commentator, who also criticizes occasionally: *'radiant chance'*, he
remarks at i. 521, 'with all submission has not much meaning'.
It seems likely that the same commentator was responsible for
the many underlinings, and for the inverted commas and other
punctuation marks which are inserted into the text without
corresponding marginal corrections. Such markings occur in
abundance in gatherings B to E, and more sparsely in
gathering F, but not beyond that; i.e., their placing coincides
approximately with the presence of marginal notes by the
commentator. Some, but not all, of the inverted commas
correspond to those added in 1863. Other marks seem to be an
attempt to interpret the lines: for example line i. 125 is divided
by comma-like marks: 'That quick, with prey enough, her
hunger blunts,' and the word 'quickly' is written in the margin
as a gloss on the underlined 'quick'. Markings at i. 129 indicate
a rearrangement of words in prose-order, shifting the rhyming word to mid-line. It seems clear that such markings,
though often intelligently made, have no authority as revisions. We have therefore recorded in our textual notes (as
'*1840 proof*') all revisions by Browning, but only a selection of
the more interesting textual insertions made by the commen-

tator. Our explanatory notes aim to include all marginal
comments by Browning and all of significance by the commentator.

When *Sordello* was published on 7 March 1840 Browning
gave copies to his mother and to his friend Domett. The
Ashley copy now in the British Library is that presented to
'Alfred Domett Esq with RB's best regards'. 'Pray accept the
book, and do not reject me', Browning wrote. 'However, I
hope you will like it a little.'[1] Domett soon replied, in a letter
containing 'blame as well as praise' which gratified Browning
and elicited a frank and revealing reply: 'The one point that
wants correcting is where you surmise that I am "difficult on
system". No, really—the fact is I live by myself, write with no
better company, and forget that the "lovers" you mention are
part and parcel of that self, and their choosing to comprehend
my comprehensions but an indifferent testimony to their
value'. Opposite the half-title of his copy Domett wrote 23
lines of his own composition, a translation in English *terza
rima* of *Purgatorio* vi. 58–78. (The Italian is copied out opposite
the title-page). Browning refers to this in a letter dated 22 May
1842. 'With this I send you your "Sordello". I suppose (am
sure indeed) that the translation from Dante . . . is your own'.[2]
The copy contains evidence of Domett's struggle to understand the poem, and also of Browning's willingness to help, as
it is here that we first find the headlines (to p. 21: 'How a Poet's
soul comes into play') which were to be completed and printed
in 1863. There are numerous annotations by Domett,[3] and
some suggested alterations in punctuation. There is only one
note in Book II, and none in the first half of Book V, or after
p. 239 (vi. 596–end). Occasionally Domett provides an internal
cross-reference to another part of the poem. Examples of his
comments are 'matchless from page 16' on p. 21 (opposite i.
478), a description of i. 531 ff. as 'an eloquent but not overclear
amplification of Byron's lines . . .', with a quotation from
memory from *Childe Harold*, praise of iii. 319 ff. as 'ingenious',
with the qualification that the passage is *'expressed* in far too
abstract a manner', the impatient comment 'What the devil is

---

[1] *Browning and Domett*, pp. 27–8 and 28–9.
[2] *Browning and Domett*, p. 37.
[3] We give these in our explanatory notes, but ignore the vertical lines of approbation which Domett scored against many passages.

the *proper* life to us?' on p. 113 (referring to iii. 625–6), and the query 'is *labouring*?' with the complaint that 'These little carelessnesses make his style so obscure' at the foot of p. 131, (with reference to iv. 40). On p. 41 there is a particularly tantalizing note, 'is not this the attitude of the girl in a picture in the Louvre?'—this with reference to the description of Palma at i. 948 ff. On p. 158 Domett underlines 'He' (iv. 690), writing 'Who?' Browning replies laconically '(S².)', so showing that a conjecture of Domett's, just below, was correct. On p. 213 (v. 977) Domett wrongly guesses 'Salinguerra(?)', and Browning replies, '(no—Young Ecelin)'. Domett's last note, on p. 239 (vi. 547 ff.) is: 'beautiful, but query if true', with a large question-mark beside it.

There is a most interesting reference to this copy in Domett's Diary. In March 1872 he wrote:

Browning I saw had not lost the good humoured patience with which he would listen to friendly criticism of any of his works. I have proof of this in a copy of the original edition of *Sordello* which he sent me when it appeared. The poem is undoubtedly somewhat obscure, though curiously enough, much more so in the mere 'objective' (so to speak) incidents of the story, than in its 'subjective' phases, that is, in the narration of the hero's varying moods of mind or the philosophical reflections of the poet. Accordingly I had scribbled in pencil on the book, two or three impatient remarks such as "Who says this?", "What does this mean?" &c. Some time after, Browning asked me to let him see my copy of the poem, which I lent him. He returned it with 2 or 3 pencil notes of his own answering my questions. But I was amused many years afterwards, in New Zealand, on the appearance of a 2nd edition of *Sordello*, to find he had altered I think all the passages I had hinted objection to, or questioned the meaning of. One instance is curious. Speaking of a picture of the Madonna by Guidone . . . . the poet says:

> a painful birth must be
> Matured ere San Eufemia's sacristy
> Or transept gather fruits of one great gaze
> At the noon-sun: look you! An orange haze—
> The same blue stripe round that—and i' the midst,
> Thy spectral whiteness, mother-maid, who didst
> Pursue the dizzy painter!

I had written carelessly in pencil on the margin, 'Rather the *moon*, from the description.'[1]

Another revision may be an indirect response to a query by Domett, who had been puzzled by the phrase 'By his sole agency' (iv. 1025). Browning's note explained that the agency was 'S.', i.e. Sordello's, but he evidently decided to remove the phrase altogether in revision.[2]

On 31 July 1844 Browning wrote to Domett: 'I have not opened the book . . . since I returned your copy—and all of it is clean gone'.[3] His interest soon revived, however, largely because he found in Elizabeth Barrett such a keen and perceptive critic. On 9 September of the following year she wrote:

I have been thinking much of your 'Sordello' since you spoke of it—& even, I *had* thought much of it before you spoke of it yesterday,—feeling that it might be thrown out into the light by your hand, and greatly justify the additional effort. It is like a noble picture with its face to the wall just now—or at least, in the shadow. And so worthy as it is of you in all ways! —individual all through: you have *made* even the darkness of it! And such a work as it might become if you chose . . if you put your will to it—!—What I meant to say yesterday was not that it wanted more additional verses than the 'ten per cent' you spoke of . . though it does perhaps . . so much as that (to my mind) it wants drawing together & fortifying in the connections & associations . . which hang as loosely every here & there, as those in a dream, & confound the reader who persists in thinking himself awake.[4]

In October she referred to 'the new avatar of "Sordello" . . ., which you taught me to look for'. 'I mean to set about that reconsidering "Sordello", he replied in December: '—it has always been rather on my mind'. There follows the passage

[1] *The Diary of Alfred Domett 1872–1885*, ed. E. A. Horsman (1953), pp. 48–9 (with misprints corrected). In fact Browning did not by any means alter 'all the passages' Domett had objected to.

[2] Some notes in the Domett copy are later than 1842. At i. 446, for example, 'southward' is underlined and '(eastward 65)'—the reading of *1865*, as of *1863* and all later editions—appears in the margin. At i. 291–2 'Edition 1865' is quoted in the margin. On p. 126, (referring to iii. 968) there is a reference to 'Handbook p. 41'. This refers to the first edition of Mrs Orr's *Handbook* (1885): the note explaining that '"Eyebright" . . . refers to one of Mr. Browning's oldest friends' is on p. 41 in that edition, but on p. 42 by the 2nd edition of 1886. As Domett did not die until 1887, these notes are probably by him, and not by T. J. Wise, whose book-plate adorns the volume.

[3] *Browning and Domett*, p. 105.

[4] Kintner i. 186–7, followed by 238, 336 and 342.

quoted above on p. 181. 'An excellent solemn chiming, the passage from Dante makes with your Sordello', she replied, 'and the Sordello *deserves* the labour which it needs, to make it appear the great work it is. I think that the principle of association is too subtly in movement throughout it—so that *while* you are going straight forward you go at the same time round & round, until the progress involved in the motion is lost sight of by the lookers on'.

Almost ten years later, when Browning was awaiting the publication of *Men and Women*, Elizabeth persuaded him to begin the task of remoulding *Sordello*. Early in 1856, when they were together in Paris and she was hard at work on *Aurora Leigh*, Browning was, for a few weeks, 'much occupied with "Sordello"', as she wrote to Mrs Jameson on 28 February.[1] It seems likely that the copy of the first edition now at Syracuse University, NY, was the one Browning used at this time. He had originally presented it to his mother on the day of publication, as his inscription, 'S.A.B. March 7ʰ 1840', shows, and he may well have regained it after his mother's death in 1849.[2] The extensive annotations cannot be precisely dated, but their nature is in keeping with a date in the 1850s: they include wide-ranging, ambitious, but inconclusive commentary, frequent references to 'mesmerism', and anticipations of revisions made in 1863 and of at least one poem published in 1864.

A striking feature of this copy is the presence of caret marks in the margin of pp. 4–12 (numbered 5 to 22), 13 (numbers altered to 32 and 33), 14 (34, 35), 17 (36), 18 (37), 20 (39, apparently altered), 21 (40), 22 (41, 42), 24 (43, 44), 25 (45–7), 27 (48), 29 (49), 30 (50, 51), and 31 (52).[3] There are several caret marks without numbers in the remainder of Book I and in Books II and III, and a few in Books IV–VI. It must be assumed that the numbers refer to a list of intended insertions designed to clarify and otherwise improve the text. Many of the caret marks are accompanied by (or placed just before)

[1] *Letters of Elizabeth Barrett Browning*, ii. 228. See p. 192, n. 3, below.
[2] A late note on a preliminary leaf stating that the book was a presentation 'from Browning to his sister' is erroneous, as the middle initial makes clear.
[3] All in Book I. The insertions were to be made in the middle of l. 73, between 100/101, 126/7, 308/9, 312/3, 373/4, 504/5, 548/9, 566/7, 612/3, and 704/5; and to replace ll. 77, 87, 103–5, 110–14, 137, part of 151, 153, 165–7, 173, 187, 188, 209–12, 222–3, 227–8, 249, 276–9, 283–5, 297–8, 405, 461, 483, 496, 553, 569, 583, 663, 693, 709. Lines 281, 290, 291 and 465 are also enclosed by brackets.

round brackets inserted into the text, perhaps indicating that the words so enclosed are to be replaced by new material.

There are also numerous marginal alterations to the text, most and perhaps all of them in Browning's hand. Those corresponding to revisions in later editions occur mainly in Book I: this copy has 14 of the 65 verbal revisions made in that Book in *1863*. Few consist of more than one word. Most of them are in ink, in neat handwriting (unlike the scribbled pencil comments which begin on p. 20 at l. 458). The neatly-written emendations do not continue after the last numbered caret mark (52): it is probable that Browning's formal revision, as distinct from his tentative suggestions, ended at that point, i. 709. The change of 'noon-sun' to 'moon' at l. 580 shows that the copy was annotated after Browning had seen Domett's criticisms. Some of the revisions have slight but significant variations from the 1863 text (for example in the meaning of the word 'only' at i. 614). From Book II onwards revisions (as distinct from comments) are sparse: Book II has only four substantive revisions used in 1863, and Book III only two.

Other marginal notes indicate revisions which were never in fact introduced: at i. 117, for example, 'the Ecelin;' is deleted in favour of 'Romano: just', i. 215 is altered to 'From out a multitudinous chokeweed grown', at i. 254 'the Lombard Chief' is revised to 'the stuttering Chief', making it clear that the man referred to is 'Ecelino il Balbo' (the Stutterer). At i. 566 ('Thrusting in time eternity's concern') the suggested capitalisation of 'time' and 'eternity's' would have been helpful to the reader. The revision to 'Those minions found him!' at i. 643 would have removed the ambiguity of 'Confessed those minions!' We have recorded in our textual notes most of the annotations which seem intended as revisions (the test being whether they are metrically acceptable) but which are not in fact introduced in later editions.

In our explanatory notes we have recorded most of the other annotations. Some, such as 'Oh, this morn drew out many among them' (after 'Sordello' at ii. 13), are presumably hints to be versified later. Opposite ii. 69 ff. Browning wrote 'Describe the song of Elys, Mesmeric song—at the beginning   How it operated at first', and below this: '(The way was to challenge anyone to go beyond *that*)'. The word 'mesmeric' occurs several times, apparently referring to some notion of 'animal magnetism' (cf. Elizabeth's letter of 28 February 1856, where 'Pen' is said to be 'learning everything by magnetism'[1]), or some paranormal or almost paranormal gift. On p. 45, apparently in connection with lines ii. 27 ff., we have 'otter' in the margin, 'golden swarm of insects' a little lower, and 'sleek wet black & lithe as a leech—' at the bottom of the page, the last a striking anticipation of 'Caliban upon Setebos', 46. Two further notes foreshadow the same passage: on p. 84, opposite lines ii. 955–964, Browning has written, 'There was the Badger feeding with his slant white wedge eye by moonlight', and on p. 89 a caret mark between lines iii. 42 and 43 is accompanied by the words 'oak warts' (cf. 'Caliban', 48–51.) It seems unlikely that Browning would have made such notes after the publication of 'Caliban upon Setebos'.

A number of the annotations are clarifications which need not indicate intended revisions, but probably all do. At i. 965 there is a caret mark in the middle of the line, and in the margin: 'The soul endures but the body *changes*—even if for the better': the caret suggests that Browning contemplated an addition, but we cannot be certain. The note at the end of Book I—'Troubadours to the Ghibs what singers & priests are to the Guelfs as instruments'—may indicate a suggested addition, but need not. At the foot of p. 24 (after i. 561) the note again seems explanatory, and need not imply revision. The same is true of the note at v. 93.

In the end Browning was dissatisfied with this projected recasting of *Sordello*, but he may still have been thinking of it in 1858. He wrote to William Michael Rossetti on 28 December of that year, in connection with the latter's proposed 'Exposition of *Sordello*': 'use what you will, do what you will—of course with exactly the same freedom and assurance of not being misunderstood . . . Your quotations will not interfere with my own additions because they *are* purely additions, accretions, innestations, merely explanatory—I change *nothing*, but interpolate; and those who don't want more

---

[1] *Letters of Elizabeth Barret Browning*, ii. 227 (in the same letter as the reference to work continuing on *Sordello*).

than they have already will be able to stick to *that* and welcome . . ."[1]

Browning eventually reprinted *Sordello* in *The Poetical Works* of 1863, 23 years after its first appearance. In the dedication which was now added, he mentions that he 'lately gave time and pains to turn my work into what the many might,—instead of what the few must,—like', adding: 'but after all, I imagined another thing at first, and therefore leave as I find it'. '*Sordello* is corrected *throughout*', he wrote to Moncure Conway; 'not altered at all, but really elucidated, I hope, by a host of little attentions to the reader: the "headlines," or running commentary at the top of the page, is added for the first time'.[2] Reviewing the new edition, Conway commented that although the poem had not been altered 'materially, . . . yet the mere changes of punctuation and the introduction of "he said" or "she said" before the quotation marks which once bewildered the reader, have removed a host of difficulties'.[3] It was no doubt because he had once considered a comprehensive rewriting of the poem that Browning often minimized the changes introduced in 1863. In 1886, for example, he wrote to Furnivall as follows:

I don't understand what Mrs Dall can mean by saying that "Sordello" has been "re-written": I did certainly at one time intend to rewrite much of it,—but changed my mind,—and the edition which I reprinted was the same in all respects as its predecessor—only with an elucidatory heading to each page, and some few alterations, presumably for the better, in the text—such as occur in most of my works: I cannot remember a single instance of any importance that is "rewritten"—and I only suppose that Mrs Dall has taken project for performance, and set down as "done" what was for a while intended to be done.[4]

[1] *Ruskin: Rossetti: PreRaphaelitism*, ed. W. M. Rossetti (1899), 217–19. The word 'innestations', not in OED, probably derives from It. 'innestare', to graft. Rossetti's summary of *Sordello* seemed to William Bell Scott 'nearly as obscure as the poem itself'. (*Autobiographical Notes of the Life of William Bell Scott*, ed. W. Minto, 2 vols., 1892, ii. 57–8.)

[2] *New Letters*, 157. It is remarkable that the 'running commentary', retained in 1865 and 1868, seems not to have been restored until 1970, when it was printed in the margin of the Oxford Standard Authors edition of the *Poetical Works 1833–1864*, ed. Ian Jack, and among the textual notes in vol. ii of the Ohio edition, ed. John Berkey and Roma A. King, Jr.

[3] 'Robert Browning', in the *Victoria Magazine*, ii (February 1864), p. 301 (as quoted in *New Letters*, 158 n.).

[4] *Trumpeter*, p. 134.

The revision had been rather more extensive than he suggested. He expanded the poem from 5,897 lines to 5,981,[1] split up many of the long sentences, introduced further paragraph divisions, rewrote some of the most obscure phrases, removed some of the ambiguities, and (not the least of his 'little attentions to the reader') introduced fuller punctuation, notably hundreds of sets of inverted commas, totally absent in *1840*. Although, as our explanatory notes occasionally mention, a few of the revisions lead to new confusions, *1863* is on the whole an improvement on *1840*, and the 'running commentary' provides an invaluable series of stepping-stones. We have sometimes preferred the readings of *1863* to those of *1888–9* because the former seems to have been proof-read with greater care. On the other hand, 'couch' (i. 599) and 'Conjecture' (v. 435) are almost certainly errors, so we have restored *1840* in these places. At iii. 440 'he waned' may be an authorial revision, but it is inconsistent with the following lines, so that *1840* is preferable.

The 'Fourth Edition' of 1865 has a few slight alterations which may be revisions, ('retain' for 'retained' at ii. 988, 'Than' for 'To' at iv. 254). It eliminates a number of capitals (which had often been helpful[2]), probably on Browning's own authority. Some new errors are introduced, however, on one of which Browning commented in a letter to Edward Dowden: 'I fear there are more blunders than those you so kindly pointed out', he wrote on 13 December 1867. 'Somebody told me a week ago there was an expression "blooming carroch" which he felt difficulty in understanding! Such printer's-perversity as this I shall rectify by myself, but, should any slip of my very own seem discovered in the course of your reading, I shall regard the mention of it as one more favour . . .'[3] Browning did 'rectify' this and several other misprints in later editions, but some escaped his notice. We have restored the readings of *1863* at v. 396, v, 748, and vi. 360. Book V seems particularly faulty in *1865*: we should perhaps have emended the readings which derive from it at lines 179 and 838.

Browning prepared *Sordello* for the edition of 1868 with

---

[1] DeVane is misleading on the number of lines in *1840*. Browning did not expand either of the first two books, and he added only four lines to Book VI.

[2] For example in lines i. 843, iv. 310, v. 323, v. 500 and v. 515.

[3] *Letters*, p. 124. See i. 317 n.

considerable care. Using *1865* as copy, he revised the punctuation throughout, making it heavier and more precise; for
example, he frequently substituted colons for semi-colons,
and semi-colons for commas. He continued the process of
assisting the reader by using more parentheses and inverted
commas, and by introducing further paragraph divisions. As
in *1865*, he reduced the number of capitalized abstract nouns.
He also made some sixty substantive changes, most of them of
one or two words only. The aim was usually to clarify, to
increase accuracy, or (on occasion) to improve the metre.
Books III and VI contain more revisions of every kind than the
four other books. While *1868* must be treated with respect,
as a text which received careful attention from its author,
it fails to correct some of the errors introduced in *1865*. It
is possible that some of its readings are not true revisions:
'nature' for 'natures' at i. 703, for example, and the curious and
metrically clumsy inversion of 'Reflecting, Demonstrating' at
ii. 996.

'Yes, the new Edition promises to be successful', he wrote
to George Barrett twenty years later, of the collected edition of
1888, '. . . I do my part and correct what little I can,—but there
will be no material change anywhere'.[1] *Sordello* is 'corrected'
more frequently in this edition than in *1868*, particularly in
Book II. Browning was at pains to polish his style as well as to
clarify his meaning. Sometimes whole lines are changed, so
long as the rhyming word can remain (*Pauline* and *Paracelsus*,
being in blank verse, had been much easier to revise). A new
style of punctuation is introduced in Book I: in some ways this
reverses the trend of previous revisions, since dashes and
exclamation marks are now added, whereas earlier they had
been removed. Similar revisions also occur in the remainder of
the poem.

While the 1888 edition is by no means perfect, it is the
obvious choice for copy-text: Browning himself praised the
accuracy of the printing:[2] it contains such revisions as he found

---

[1] *Letters of the Brownings to George Barrett*, ed. P. Landis and R. E. Freeman (Urbana, Illinois, 1958), 313.
[2] On 27 February 1888 he wrote to George Smith: 'When I received the Proofs of the 1st vol. on Friday evening, I made sure of returning them next day—so accurately are they printed'; but then he looked into 'that unlucky *Pauline*', and decided to improve it (see Vol. I, p. 16 above): *Life*, p. 380.

practicable: and most of the more obvious errors of previous editions are now removed. When he marked the Dykes Campbell copy in preparation for the reprint of 1889 he found little to correct (one example, however, is 'throng' for 'thong' at v. 959, a mistake deriving from *1865.*) Of these last corrections, the only one which we have not incorporated is the colon at iv. 707, where we agree with Morse Peckham[1] that a comma (the reading of *1868*) is preferable. Otherwise we have emended only where the punctuation of *1888* is so misleading as to hinder understanding, or when it seems certain that simple misprints escaped Browning's notice. Several of these, as we have shown, had become embedded in the text in earlier editions. Substantive errors introduced in *1888* are 'Not' for 'Nor' (i. 761), 'Turned' for 'Tuned' (ii. 768), 'induce' for 'induced' (iii. 366), 'loathy' for 'loathly' (iv. 23), 'than' for 'that' (iv. 62), 'though' for 'through' (iv. 813) and 'Giver' for 'Give' (vi. 417, corrected in some later printings). It is possible that 'he' for 'be' is a misprint at iii. 574, but it may equally be a revision of a clumsy passive construction, so we have allowed it to stand. Almost a century ago, Mrs Sutherland Orr mentioned 'misprints, and errors in punctuation which will be easily corrected in a later edition, but which mar the present one'[2] as being among the features which rendered *Sordello* so perplexing that it 'is the one of Mr. Browning's works which still remains to be read'. We hope to have done something to render the poem a little more intelligible.[3]

---

[1] *Sordello: a Marginally Emended Edition*, ed. Morse Peckham (Troy, New York, 1977), p. xviii.

[2] *Handbook* (1st ed., 1885), p. 34. In later editions the statement occurs on p. 35 (with 'including' for 'and').

[3] For further details about Browning's attempt to revise *Sordello*, see Ian Jack, 'Browning on *Sordello* and *Men and Women*: Unpublished Letters to James T. Fields', *Huntington Library Quarterly* 45, no. 3 (Summer 1982), 185–99.

SORDELLO

TO J. MILSAND, OF DIJON.

DEAR FRIEND,—Let the next poem be introduced by your name, therefore remembered along with one of the deepest of my affections, and so repay all trouble it ever cost me. I wrote it twenty-five years ago for only a few, counting even in these on somewhat more care about its subject than they really had. My own faults of expression were many; but with care for a man or book such would be surmounted, and without it what avails the faultlessness of either? I blame nobody, least of all myself, who did my best then and since; for I lately gave time and pains to turn my work into what the many might,— instead of what the few must,—like: but after all, I imagined another thing at first, and therefore leave as I find it. The historical decoration was purposely of no more importance than a background requires; and my stress lay on the incidents in the development of a soul: little else is worth study. I, at least, always thought so—you, with many known and unknown to me, think so—others may one day think so; and whether my attempt remain for them or not, I trust, though away and past it, to continue ever yours,

R. B.

London: *June* 9, 1863.

The dedication first appeared in *1863*, the words 'therefore remembered . . . affections' being added in *1868*. Browning met Joseph Milsand, a member of a prominent Dijon family, in Paris in 1851. A strong Anglophile, Milsand wrote two remarkable articles on Browning's poetry in the *Revue des deux mondes* for 15 August 1851 and the *Revue contemporaine* for 15 September 1856. 'I never knew or shall know his like among men', Browning wrote in 1870 (*Dearest Isa*, p. 344). Milsand died in 1886: the following year Browning dedicated the *Parleyings* to his memory.

   We have slightly adjusted the position of some of Browning's elucidatory headings in our text of the poem, since they no longer have to appear at the tops of pages, as in *1863–8*.

BOOK THE FIRST.

Who will, may hear Sordello's story told:
His story? Who believes me shall behold
The man, pursue his fortunes to the end,
Like me: for as the friendless-people's friend *A Quixotic*
5 Spied from his hill-top once, despite the din *attempt.*
And dust of multitudes, Pentapolin
Named o' the Naked Arm, I single out
Sordello, compassed murkily about
With ravage of six long sad hundred years.
Only believe me. Ye believe?

                               Appears
Verona . . . Never,—I should warn you first,—
Of my own choice had this, if not the worst
Yet not the best expedient, served to tell
A story I could body forth so well
By making speak, myself kept out of view,
The very man as he was wont to do,
And leaving you to say the rest for him: *Why the poet*
Since, though I might be proud to see the dim *himself addresses*
Abysmal past divide its hateful surge,
Letting of all men this one man emerge
Because it pleased me, yet, that moment past,

---

4 *1840* Like me; for as the friendless people's friend   9 *1840* years: 11
1840–1868 Never, I should warn you first,   13 *1840 proof* best expedient, >
best, expedient   *17 {Reading of *1840*.}   *1863–1889* him.

---

4 *friend*: 'Don Quixote, named rightly thus, not for his madness, but for
his good will': *1840 proof*. In *Don Quixote*, Part I, ch. xviii, he and Sancho
Panza see a great cloud of dust raised by two flocks of sheep. The Don
insists that they are caused by opposing armies, one of them led by 'the
King of the Garamantes, Pentapoline of the naked arme, so called, because
he still entereth in battayle, with his right arme naked': trans. Thomas Shel-
ton (repr. 1896, with introductions by J. Fitzmaurice-Kelley), p. 153. By
1863, when he added the first few elucidatory headings, Browning seems to
have come to accept the common view that his attempt had been 'Quixotic'
in the usual sense.

18 *Since*: I should have preferred the method of the monologue because,
proud as I might have been of my power to call this man up from the past, I
would have delighted to become an auditor like you, my readers, no more in
the secret than you are. Cf. v. 599–601 below.

19 *surge*: cf. *The Ring and the Book* ix. 906: 'Such spells subdue the surge'.

I should delight in watching first to last
His progress as you watch it, not a whit
More in the secret than yourselves who sit
Fresh-chapleted to listen. But it seems   25
Your setters-forth of unexampled themes,
Makers of quite new men, producing them,
Would best chalk broadly on each vesture's hem
The wearer's quality; or take their stand,
Motley on back and pointing-pole in hand,   30
Beside him. So, for once I face ye, friends,
Summoned together from the world's four ends,
Dropped down from heaven or cast up from hell,
To hear the story I propose to tell.
Confess now, poets know the dragnet's trick,   3
Catching the dead, if fate denies the quick,
And shaming her; 't is not for fate to choose
Silence or song because she can refuse
Real eyes to glisten more, real hearts to ache
Less oft, real brows turn smoother for our sake: 4
I have experienced something of her spite;
But there 's a realm wherein she has no right
And I have many lovers. Say, but few
Friends fate accords me? Here they are: now
        view
The host I muster! Many a lighted face

---

25 *1840* to listen: but   28 *1840* Had best . . . . hem   *1863–68* Would best
. . . . hem,   29 *1840* The wearer's quality, or take his stand   31 *1840*
Beside them; so for once   35 *1840 proof* Confest > Confess   *SB* {rejected}
Confess now, you behold my dragnet's trick,   43 *1840* lovers: say but few

25 *Fresh-chapleted*: like the audience at a Greek play. Cf. *Pippa Passes*, ii. 59.
        But it seems: a reference to the reception of *Paracelsus*: see lines 36 and 41.
30 *pointing-pole*: as at some crude dramatic entertainment. At 72 the poet refers to his 'puppets' and at v. 612 to 'the platform's side'. In 'Browning's *Sordello*: The Art of the Makers-see' (PMLA lxxx, 1965, 554–61) Daniel Stempel has suggested the influence of the Victorian diorama.
37 *'t is not for fate*: 'It is not for Fate to determine our activity because she can determine the results thereof': *1840 proof*. The poet plays with the fancy of circumventing fate by writing for an audience summoned from the realms of the dead. Cf. i. 747–8, where the youthful Sordello wonders how to 'contrive A crowd'.
39 *Real eyes to glisten*: cf. *Pauline*, 535.
45 *Many a lighted face*: 'old authors': *Domett*. Cf. *King Victor and King*

Foul with no vestige of the grave's disgrace;   *his audience—few*
What else should tempt them back to taste our   *living—many dead.*
   air
Except to see how their successors fare?
My audience! and they sit, each ghostly man
50 Striving to look as living as he can,
Brother by breathing brother; thou art set,
Clear-witted critic, by . . . but I 'll not fret
A wondrous soul of them, nor move death's
   spleen
Who loves not to unlock them. Friends! I mean
55 The living in good earnest—ye elect
Chiefly for love—suppose not I reject
Judicious praise, who contrary shall peep,
Some fit occasion, forth, for fear ye sleep,
To glean your bland approvals. Then, appear,
60 Verona! stay—thou, spirit, come not near
Now—not this time desert thy cloudy place
To scare me, thus employed, with that pure face!
I need not fear this audience, I make free
With them, but then this is no place for thee!
65 The thunder-phrase of the Athenian, grown
Up out of memories of Marathon,
Would echo like his own sword's griding screech
Braying a Persian shield,—the silver speech

---

49 *1840* My audience: 61 *1840* Now—nor this

Charles, Second Year . . . King Charles, Part I, 191: 'Lighted like life but silent as the grave'.
   46 *disgrace*: disfigurement.
   55 *ye elect*: you who are the elect mainly because of love. Cf. *Paracelsus* i. 632. And cf. Browning to Domett, p. 183, above.
   57 *contrary*: on the contrary, as at *Paracelsus* i. 749.
   59 *bland*: 'soft; mild; gentle': Johnson.
   60 *thou, spirit*: Shelley. 'He apostrophiseth the spirit of a dead Poet': *1840 proof*.
   61 *cloudy*: because Shelley is 'a star to men': *Pauline* 171.
   65 *the Athenian*: Aeschylus, who fought against the Persians at Marathon. In *The Frogs* of Aristophanes (line 814) the chorus describes Aeschylus as ἐριβρεμέτας, 'loud-thundering'.
   67 *griding*: piercing, wounding. Cf. 'The griding force of Guiscard's Norman steel': *The Vision . . . of Dante Alighieri*, trans. Cary, *Hell* xxviii.12. A number of verbal resemblances suggest that Browning used Cary as well as the Italian text of the *Commedia*. 'Griding' naturally suggests a harsh sound, as in Shelley's *Prometheus Unbound* III. i. 47–8.
   68 *Braying*: destroying.

Of Sidney's self, the starry paladin,
Turn intense as a trumpet sounding in   70
The knights to tilt,—wert thou to hear! What
     heart
Have I to play my puppets, bear my part
Before these worthies?
                                           Lo, the past is hurled

Shelley departing,   In twain: up-thrust, out-staggering on the world,
Verona appears.   Subsiding into shape, a darkness rears   75
Its outline, kindles at the core, appears
Verona. 'T is six hundred years and more
Since an event. The Second Friedrich wore
The purple, and the Third Honorius filled
The holy chair. That autumn eve was stilled: 80
A last remains of sunset dimly burned
O'er the far forests, like a torch-flame turned
By the wind back upon its bearer's hand
In one long flare of crimson; as a brand,
The woods beneath lay black. A single eye   85
From all Verona cared for the soft sky.
But, gathering in its ancient market-place,
Talked group with restless group; and not a face

71 *1840 proof* what heart>What heart   *1840* tilt—wert thou to hear! What
hear   73 *1840 proof* past>Past   *1840–65* Past   74 *1889* {some copies}
world.   86 *1840* sky:

69 *paladin*: knightly hero. Sir Philip Sidney was often associated with
stars, partly because of the title of his sonnet-sequence, *Astrophil and Stella*
(star-lover and star).
70 *intense*: the verse even of Æschylus and Sidney would sound unmusi-
cal to Shelley's ears.
sounding in: summoning.
73 *Lo*: 'What was it for? And, lo': SB. Immediately before these words
there is a caret with the number 5, apparently indicating an insertion to be
made from a list of additions. See Introduction, p. 186 above.
the past: cf. *Pauline* 290.
74 *up-thrust*: the chroniclers whom Browning read as he worked on the
poem mention an earthquake which occurred in 1222: see, e.g., Rolandino,
II. iii, 'De tempore Terræmotus': Muratori viii. 185. OED particularly
associates the noun 'up-thrust' with volcanic action.
78 *The Second Friedrich*: Friedrich II (1194–1250) was crowned Emperor in
1220. Honorius III was Pope 1216–27. The action of the poem begins in
1224: see note on line 102.
85 *A single eye*: 'There was but one eye in Verona alive to that evening's
beauty': *1840 proof*. No doubt Sordello's.
88 *not a face*: 'News of Azzo & Boniface's (Guelfs) having been trapped by
Salinguerra . . .': Domett.

But wrath made livid, for among them were
90   Death's staunch purveyors, such as have in care
To feast him. Fear had long since taken root
In every breast, and now these crushed its fruit,
The ripe hate, like a wine: to note the way
It worked while each grew drunk! Men grave
    and grey
95   Stood, with shut eyelids, rocking to and fro,
Letting the silent luxury trickle slow
About the hollows where a heart should be;
But the young gulped with a delirious glee
Some foretaste of their first debauch in blood
100 At the fierce news: for, be it understood,
Envoys apprised Verona that her prince
Count Richard of Saint Boniface, joined since
A year with Azzo, Este's Lord, to thrust   *How her Guelfs*
Taurello Salinguerra, prime in trust   *are discomfited.*
105 With Ecelin Romano, from his seat

90 *Death's staunch purveyors*: 'love's purveyors': Cary, *Hell*, v. 134.
102 *Count Richard*: 'In the year of our Lord 1224 the young Lord Azzo and
Richard Count of Saint Boniface besieged Salinguerra in Ferrara, with the
support of the Veronese and Mantuans. But since he was a clever and astute
man, he persuaded the Count to enter Ferrara under the pretext of an agreement: capturing him and all who had entered with him, Salinguerra freed
Ferrara from the siege. But after a reasonable time an agreement was reached
and the Count was freed from bondage': *Monachi Patavini Chronicon de rebus
gestis in Lombardia praecipuè & Marchia Tarvisina*, in Muratori viii. 671. Rolandino gives a similar account, mentioning that Count Richard did not realize
that 'a wolf was concealed in lamb's clothing', and saying that the siege was
abandoned and the whole army withdrawn: Muratori viii. 185–6. The same
volume of Muratori contains a Life of Richard of uncertain authorship.
103 *Azzo*: Azzo VII, whose doings are chronicled by the various writers in
Muratori viii. In his *Storia degli Ecelini* (3 vols., Bassano, 1779), Giambatista
Verci describes the renewal of 'la famosa fazione de' Guelfi e de' Gibellini' (i.
91). He mentions that the leader of the Ghibellin party in the 'Marca Tri-
vigiana' was Ecelino II, who was opposed to 'la linea degli Estensi Italiani',
which was 'sempre aderente alla parte de' Guelfi: di modo che la fazione Guelfa
in questi paesi fu in alcuni tempi denominata *la parte de' Marchesi*': i. 92. Modern
historians point out that it is an anachronism to use the terms 'Guelf' and
'Ghibellin' in relation to north-eastern Italy at this time: they spread slowly
from Tuscany about the middle of the 13th century.
104 *Taurello Salinguerra*: Verci tells us that Taurello (whose name W. M.
Rossetti translated as 'Bullock Sally-in-war' or 'Dash-into-fight': Berdoe, p.
538) 'was a powerful personage, and head of the Ghibellin faction in those
parts. To gain a just notion of his greatness it is enough to reflect that he was
powerful enough, on several occasions, to drive away the marquises of Este
from Ferrara, and finally to make himself absolute master of that same city':
Storia, i. 113.
105 *Ecelin Romano*: as there were several generations of Ezzelini their con-

Ferrara,—over zealous in the feat
And stumbling on a peril unaware,
Was captive, trammelled in his proper snare,
They phrase it, taken by his own intrigue.
Immediate succour from the Lombard League   110
Of fifteen cities that affect the Pope,
For Azzo, therefore, and his fellow-hope
Of the Guelf cause, a glory overcast!
Men's faces, late agape, are now aghast.
"Prone is the purple pavis; Este makes   115
"Mirth for the devil when he undertakes
"To play the Ecelin; as if it cost
"Merely your pushing-by to gain a post
"Like his! The patron tells ye, once for all,
"There be sound reasons that preferment fall   120
"On our beloved" . . .
                    "Duke o' the Rood, why not?"

108 *1840* "trammelled . . . . snare,"   109 *1840* "taken . . . .
intrigue:"   112 *1840* For Azzo therefore and his fellow—hope   114 *1840*
agape, are now aghast: *1865* agape, now are aghast.   115 *1840* Prone . . . .
pavice;   117 *SB* the Ecelin; as>Romano: just as   121 *1840* On our
beloved . . .|Duke . . . . not?

temporary nicknames are used throughout these notes. This was 'The Monk'.
Cf. notes to ll. 254 and 457, below.
  108 *Was captive*: 'The envoys are from Taurello, as the tone of their language
makes plain. The "immediate succour" would be the voluntary and spontane-
ous response of the Veronese, who were members of the Lombard League.
The envoys' speech stops at "intrigue"': Whyte.
  trammelled: cf. Keats, *Lamia*, ii. 52: 'How to entangle, trammel up and snare'.
  110 *the Lombard League*: on 2 March 1226 representatives of Milan, Bologna,
Piacenza, Verona, Brescia, Faenza, Mantua, Vercelli, Lodi, Bergamo, Turin,
Alessandria, Vicenza, Padua, and Treviso renewed the old Lombard League for
twenty-five years. 'So arose', as Sismondi comments, 'a new power, well
calculated to cause the Emperor disquiet'.
  111 *affect*: love, adhere to.
  112 *For Azzo*: 'Must needs be had': *1840 proof*.
  115 *the purple pavis*: 'Pavisses were a species of large shields covering the
whole person': Scott, *Ivanhoe*, ch. xxviii (note). The arms of the Este party had
a silver eagle on an azure ground. The speaker is a Ghibellin: a Guelf replies at
121.
  116 *Mirth for the devil*: 'Azzo attempts to match Eccelin makes mirth for the
devil': *Domett*.
  117 *To play the Ecelin*: 'To assume Ecelin's *rôle*': *1840 proof*. *SB* alters to read:
'To play Romano: just'.
  119 *The patron*: this must be the Emperor, as Duff concludes.
  121 *Duke o' the Rood*: probably an oath. It may refer to Azzo, on the other
hand, although the Estes were not dukes at this time.

Shouted an Estian, "grudge ye such a lot?
"The hill-cat boasts some cunning of her own,
"Some stealthy trick to better beasts unknown,
125 "That quick with prey enough her hunger blunts,
"And feeds her fat while gaunt the lion hunts."
   "Taurello," quoth an envoy, "as in wane
"Dwelt at Ferrara. Like an osprey fain
"To fly but forced the earth his couch to make
130 "Far inland, till his friend the tempest wake,
"Waits he the Kaiser's coming; and as yet
"That fast friend sleeps, and he too sleeps: but let
"Only the billow freshen, and he snuffs
"The aroused hurricane ere it enroughs
135 "The sea it means to cross because of him.
"Sinketh the breeze? His hope-sick eye grows   *Why they entreat*
   dim;   *the Lombard*
"Creep closer on the creature! Every day   *League,*
"Strengthens the Pontiff; Ecelin, they say,
"Dozes now at Oliero, with dry lips

---

122 *1840* grudge ye *SB* ye>we   126 *1840* hunts.   127 *1840* **q**
Taurello, quoth an envoy, as in wane   135 *1840* of him: 139 *1840* Dozes
at Oliero,   *SB* Dozes at [his] Oliero,

---

123 *The hill-cat*: Ecelin: see lines 239 and 261 ff.
125 *quick*: 'quickly': *1840 proof.*
126 *the lion*: Azzo: see line 292.
127 *'Taurello'*: 'Here follows the narrative of that device alluded to above, which entrapped Count Richard': *1840 proof.* The unidentified 'envoy' continues speaking to 187.
128 *an osprey*: a large bird which frequents the shore of sea and lake. In fact it does not like stormy weather: T. P. Harrison, 'Birds in the Poetry of Browning', *RES* n.s. vii (1956), 404.
132–3 *let Only the billow freshen*: if the sea grows a little rougher Taurello jumps to the conclusion that a hurricane is about to storm across the sea to help him.
134 *ere it enroughs*: 'ere it wrinkle the sea which it will cross only for the sake of its friend': *1840 proof.* Cf. Donne, 'Infinitati Sacrum . . . The Progresse of the Soule', 52–3: 'In vaine this sea shall enlarge, or enrough / It selfe'.
139 *Dozes . . . at Oliero*: 'He also founded a church at Oliero, with a Benedictine monastery, to which he later withdrew at the time when he resolved to lead a monastic life': Verci i. 90. At i. 94 Verci explains that Oliero 'is a village about six miles above Bassano beyond the Brenta in Vicentine territory'. Ecelin, who became known as 'The Monk' although he did not in fact become a monk (cf. ii. 879), is here portrayed as calculating how many of his ancestors he will have to depose, when he reaches Hell, in order to become Satan's viceroy there, as he has been the Emperor's viceroy on earth. Cf. Shelley, 'Lines Written among the Euganean Hills', 236 ff., in which Death and Sin play at dice for the soul of Ezzelin III (the Tyrant): Death wins, but promises Sin 'that he would petition for / Her to be made Vice-Emperor'.

"Telling upon his perished finger-tips 140
"How many ancestors are to depose
"Ere he be Satan's Viceroy when the doze
"Deposits him in hell. So, Guelfs rebuilt
"Their houses; not a drop of blood was spilt
"When Cino Bocchimpane chanced to meet 145
"Buccio Virtù—God's wafer, and the street
"Is narrow! Tutti Santi, think, a-swarm
"With Ghibellins, and yet he took no harm!
"This could not last. Off Salinguerra went
"To Padua, Podestà, 'with pure intent,' 150
"Said he, 'my presence, judged the single bar
"'To permanent tranquillity, may jar
"'No longer'—so! his back is fairly turned?
"The pair of goodly palaces are burned,
"The gardens ravaged, and our Guelfs laugh,
　　　drunk 155
"A week with joy. The next, their laughter sunk
"In sobs of blood, for they found, some strange
　　　way,

143 *1840* hell; so　　145 *1840 proof* lino>Cino　　146 *1840* Virtù; *1840
proof* wafer,>wafer! {No marginal confirmation of alterations in proof, lines
146–151, except 'Padua,'}　　147 *1840 proof* narrow! Tutti Santi—>nar-
row!—Tutti Santi!—　　148 *1840* harm.　　150 *1840 proof* To Padua:
Podestà,>To Padua, "Podestà,"　　150–1 *1840* with pure intent,| Said he, my
presence, *1840 proof* "my presence,　　153 *1840* No longer—so!　　155–7
1840 The gardens ravaged, and your Guelf is drunk| A week with joy; the next,
his laughter sunk| In sobs of blood, for he found, some strange way,　　*SB* your
Guelf is drunk>our Guelfs were drunk

145 *Cino Bocchimpane*: like Buccio Virtù, an imaginary character, but Whyte
notes (p. 186 n.) 'In the list of leading families at Ferrara in the *Chronica Parva*
[*Ferrariensis*] occurs, "In Parochia Sancti Vitalis Buchinpanes habentur" . . .
Note Browning's accuracy. San Vitale was in the south-east corner of Ferrara,
next to the San Pietro quarter, where was Taurello's palace'. The reference,
which Whyte does not supply, is to Muratori viii. 480. I have corrected his text.
146 *God's wafer*: 'Ostia di Dio', still in use as a strong oath.
147 *Tutti Santi*: either an imaginary street or square, or an oath.
150 *To Padua, Podestà*: according to the *Chronica Parva* it was to Mantua that
he went. During his absence 'The citizens of the opposite faction, thinking the
time ripe for them to expel their opponents, took up arms, and having taken
the city by storm obliged the opposing party to flee into Salinguerra's castle.
On hearing of this, Salinguerra hastened to Ferrara with an armed band of his
friends . . . Gathering his forces he expelled his enemies from the city':
Muratori viii. 482. The 'podestà' was the chief magistrate of a diocese, and was
an outsider whose tenure of office was limited. Sismondi gives a critical
account of the office: *Histoires des Républiques Italiennes du Moyen Âge* (16 vols.,
Paris 1809–18) ii. 106–7. Domett notes: 'Salinguerra affects to retire—goes to
Padua Guelfs & Azzo enter his town Ferrara he surprizes them'.

"Old Salinguerra back again—I say,
"Old Salinguerra in the town once more
160 "Uprooting, overturning, flame before,   *in their changed*
"Blood fetlock-high beneath him. Azzo fled;   *fortune at Ferrara:*
"Who 'scaped the carnage followed; then the
          dead
"Were pushed aside from Salinguerra's throne,
"He ruled once more Ferrara, all alone,
165 "Till Azzo, stunned awhile, revived, would
          pounce
"Coupled with Boniface, like lynx and ounce,
"On the gorged bird. The burghers ground their
          teeth
"To see troop after troop encamp beneath
"I' the standing corn thick o'er the scanty patch
170 "It took so many patient months to snatch
"Out of the marsh; while just within their walls
"Men fed on men. At length Taurello calls
"A parley: 'let the Count wind up the war!'
"Richard, light-hearted as a plunging star,
175 "Agrees to enter for the kindest ends
"Ferrara, flanked with fifty chosen friends,
"No horse-boy more, for fear your timid sort
"Should fly Ferrara at the bare report.
"Quietly through the town they rode, jog-jog;
180 "'Ten, twenty, thirty,—curse the catalogue

---

158 *1840* again; I say   161 *1840* him;   164 *1863–8* alone.   165 *1840*
proof Still Azzo,>Till Azzo,   169 *1840 proof* thick on>thick o'er   172
1840 Astute Taurello   173 *1840* let. . . . war!   *1840 proof* war.>war!   177
1840 more   180 *1840* Ten, twenty, thirty . . . curse

161 *fetlock-high*: cf. *Henry V*, IV. vii. 76: 'fetlock deep in gore'.
162 *Who*: those who.
166 *ounce*: 'The ounce . . . is much less than the panther': Goldsmith, *Natural History* (1776) iii. 255.
167 *the gorged bird*: 'Salinguerra the osprey': *1840 proof*. Cf. iii. 262.
171 *Out of the marsh*: the author of the *Chronica Parva* mentions that what became the diocese of Ferrara had in former times been sparsely inhabited 'because for the most part those regions were surrounded by swampy ground': Muratori viii. 474.
173 *A parley*: see note to l. 102 above.
176 *fifty chosen friends*: 'con circa cinquanta caualli': Pietro Gerardo, *Vita et Gesti d'Ezzelino Terzo da Romano* (Venice, 1552), p. 18 [a].

"'Of burnt Guelf houses! Strange, Taurello
  shows
"'Not the least sign of life'—whereat arose
"A general growl: 'How? With his victors by?
"'I and my Veronese? My troops and I?
"'Receive us, was your word?' So jogged they
  on,   185
"Nor laughed their host too openly: once gone
"Into the trap!—"
                        Six hundred years ago!

for the times grow Such the time's aspect and peculiar woe
stormy again.   (Yourselves may spell it yet in chronicles,
                      Albeit the worm, our busy brother, drills   190
                      His sprawling path through letters anciently
                      Made fine and large to suit some abbot's eye)
                      When the new Hohenstauffen dropped the mask,
                      Flung John of Brienne's favour from his casque,
                      Forswore crusading, had no mind to leave   195
                      Saint Peter's proxy leisure to retrieve
                      Losses to Otho and to Barbaross,
                      Or make the Alps less easy to recross;
                      And, thus confirming Pope Honorius' fear,

181 *1840* Strange   182 *1840* life—   183 *1840* How?   184 *SB* troops>
friends   185 *1840* word?   187 *1840* trap . . .   *1863,1865* trap!—   193
SB the new>Friedrich   199 *1840* And

186 *once gone*: it would be time enough for Taurello to laugh when they were
all securely in his trap.
193 *the new Hohenstauffen*: 'Friedrich': *SB*. Friedrich II was the son of
Emperor Heinrich VI and grandson of Friedrich I ('Barbarossa').
193 *dropped the mask*: 'The Emperor has given up pretence of crusading & the
Pope excommunicate[s] him & the Guelfs & Ghibel go to war': Domett.
194 *John of Brienne*: according to the *Biographie Universelle*, he united all the
qualities of a 'vrai chevalier français'. He first set out for the Holy Land in 1209.
In 1222 he 'made his appearance at the assembly at Ferentino, which had as its
objective a new crusade. The Pope advised John of Brienne to give Frederick II
his daughter Yolante in marriage in order to interest him in the fate of the
kingdom of Jerusalem. John of Brienne consented, and Frederick married the
princess Yolante, previously taking the title of king of Jerusalem, which
belonged to his father-in-law; and did not leave for Palestine. From then
onwards the West was troubled by the quarrels of the Pope and of Frederick'.
For the 'favour' see 871 ff., below.
196 *Saint Peter's proxy*: the Popes were accused of taking advantage of the
absence of temporal rulers on crusades. Otto IV (1174–1218) had been
excommunicated: in 1211 he had been deposed in favour of Friedrich II.
198 *the Alps*: the Alps were of great importance to the Emperors, who
wished to dominate Italy.

200 Was excommunicate that very year.
"The triple-bearded Teuton come to life!"
Groaned the Great League; and, arming for the
    strife,
Wide Lombardy, on tiptoe to begin,
Took up, as it was Guelf or Ghibellin,
Its cry: what cry?

205   "The Emperor to come!"   *The Ghibellins'*
His crowd of feudatories, all and some,   *wish: the Guelfs'*
That leapt down with a crash of swords, spears,   *wish.*
    shields,
One fighter on his fellow, to our fields,
Scattered anon, took station here and there,
210 And carried it, till now, with little care—
Cannot but cry for him; how else rebut
Us longer?—cliffs, an earthquake suffered jut

---

201 *1840 proof* life,>life! *1840* The . . . . life!   203 *1840 proof* Lom-
bardy>Lombardy,   205 *1840* Its cry; what cry?|The Emperor to come!
SB what cry?>Cry these— *1863–8* Its cry; what cry?|"The Emperor to
come!" 206 *1840* some   212 *1840* longer? Cliffs *1863–8* longer? Cliffs,

---

200 *excommunicate*: in fact Friedrich was first excommunicated in 1227, by
Gregory IX.
201 *triple-bearded*: there was a popular belief that Barbarossa would return
and come to the aid of Germany when his beard had grown three times round a
table in a castle in Thuringia at which he was still sitting with his knights. The
Lombard League feared that Friedrich II might be Barbarossa over again.
204 *as it was*: according to whether it was.
205 *"The Emperor*: the cry of the Ghibellins.
210 *carried it*: prevailed.
212 *cliffs*: 'These feudatories are like rocks which an earthquake has uplifted
in the mid-sea; but now conceive a certain choke-weed tangled round them;
how shall they free themselves of this but by another earthquake. But what a
wreck the sun shall then shine on; that sun which has blazed so kindly on the
weed that it has grown carpet-like, and thereon borne a new growth. We
people are the weed, therefore the sunlike Pope, rather than the earthquake
Emperor': *1840 proof*. In this complicated metaphor, which continues to 233,
the cliffs stand for the Ghibellins and the 'chokeweed' for the Guelfs. The
'earthquake' refers to the Emperor's invasion of Lombardy. Only a second
great invasion like that which brought the Ghibellins into existence (argues the
speaker, who is a Guelf) can save the Imperial cause. Then Lombardy would
become a wreck. To think that all the good done by the Papal sun should be
undone in such a manner! Beneath that sun a network of fibres is growing
which will eventually become the cause of the People. Domett writes: 'The
Church overgrowing the Feudal powers &c (?) chieftains—the Church's
strength being embodied in & by the people'. The lines may have been
suggested by a passage in Byron's Diary dated 9 January 1821: 'It is not one
man, nor a million, but the *spirit* of liberty which must be spread. The waves
which dash upon the shore are, one by one, broken, but yet the *ocean* conquers,

In the mid-sea, each domineering crest
Which nought save such another throe can wrest
From out (conceive) a certain chokeweed grown   215
Since o'er the waters, twine and tangle thrown
Too thick, too fast accumulating round,
Too sure to over-riot and confound
Ere long each brilliant islet with itself
Unless a second shock save shoal and shelf,   220
Whirling the sea-drift wide: alas, the bruised
And sullen wreck! Sunlight to be diffused
For that!—sunlight, 'neath which, a scum at first,
The million fibres of our chokeweed nurst
Dispread themselves, mantling the troubled main,   225
And, shattered by those rocks, took hold again,
So kindly blazed it—that same blaze to brood
O'er every cluster of the multitude
Still hazarding new clasps, ties, filaments,
An emulous exchange of pulses, vents   230
Of nature into nature; till some growth
Unfancied yet, exuberantly clothe
A surface solid now, continuous, one:
"The Pope, for us the People, who begun
"The People, carries on the People thus,   235
"To keep that Kaiser off and dwell with us!"
See you?
          Or say, Two Principles that live

213 *1863–8* crest,   214 *1840–68* Nothing save such another   215 *SB* (conceive) a certain>a multitudinous   219   *1840 proof* little islet>brilliant islet   223 *1840–68* For that! Sunlight,   232 *1840* yet   234–6 *1840* The Pope, ... us!   237 *SB* Or say,>Next say,

nevertheless. It overwhelms the Armada, it wears the rock, and, if the *Nep-tunians* are to be believed, it has not only destroyed, but made a world. In like manner, whatever the sacrifice of individuals, the great cause will gather strength, sweep down what is rugged, and fertilise (for *sea-weed* is *manure*) what is cultivable.' Moore gives the passage under the year 1821.

215 (*conceive*): 'use your fancy for my metaphor': *1840 proof.*
    chokeweed: not used in the botanical sense, but for some kind of seaweed.

226 *shattered by those rocks*: 'broken by the sea-bursts against the rocks': *1840 proof.*

234 "*The Pope*: '"The Emperor" is the first cry "The Pope" the other': *1840 proof.*

237 *Two Principles*: we first hear of the 'Representative' of the Ghibellins and then of that of the Guelfs (291).

Each fitly by its Representative.
"Hill-cat"—who called him so?—the gracefullest
240 　Adventurer, the ambiguous stranger-guest
Of Lombardy (sleek but that ruffling fur,
Those talons to their sheath!) whose velvet purr
Soothes jealous neighbours when a Saxon scout
—Arpo or Yoland, is it?—one without　　　　*How Ecelo's house*
245 　A country or a name, presumes to couch　　　　*grew head of those,*
Beside their noblest; until men avouch
That, of all Houses in the Trevisan,
Conrad descries no fitter, rear or van,
Than Ecelo! They laughed as they enrolled
250 　That name at Milan on the page of gold,
Godego's lord,—Ramon, Marostica,
Cartiglion, Bassano, Loria,
And every sheep-cote on the Suabian's fief!
No laughter when his son, "the Lombard Chief"

---

238 *1840* Representative:　　239–40 *1840* Hill-cat . . . who called him so,
our gracefullest|Adventurer?　　244 *1840* . . . Arpo or Yoland, is it?
one　　247 *1840* That of all Houses in the Trivisan　　250–1 *1840* of gold|For
Godego, Ramon,　　254 *1840* the Lombard Chief　*SB* Lombard>stuttering

---

239 *"Hill-cat"*: cf. l. 123 above. If anyone before Browning called the original
Ecelin by this name, the allusion has not been found. The origin of the Romano
family is discussed at length in the introduction to Verci's *Storia*. The first
Ecelin probably came to Italy in 1036, in the train of the Emperor Konrad. This
'prowler', a Saxon with only one horse (cf. iii. 449–51) who swiftly acquired
lands and power, is traced by Verci to one Ecelo, 'son of Arpo'. The words
'Arpo or Yoland, is it?' echo Verci's suggestion that 'the father of Ecelo was
called Arpone, and never Alberico da Olanda': i. xxxiv.
241 *sleek but*: i.e. do not let it be evident that you are dangerous.
244 *Arpo or Yoland, is it?*: the question suggests the disdain of the Lombards
for the obscure origins of the Ezzelini. *SB* emends to 'Arpon'.
245 *to couch*: to lie with, marry.
247 *the Trevisan*: the Trevisan March was the name given to the north-east
part of the Lombard plain. 'It extended, roughly speaking, from the Adige on
the west to the Piave on the east, and the principal cities were Verona, Vicenza,
Padua and Treviso. Venice . . . was never included': A. M. Allan, *A History of
Verona* (1910), 18 n.
248 *Conrad*: Konrad II (*c.* 990–1039), Emperor from 1017.
250 *Milan*: stressed on the first syllable throughout the poem.
the page of gold: the register of the principal landowners. In a letter Browning
later referred to 'the Golden Book of the old Republic' of Venice: *Letters of the
Brownings to George Barrett*, ed. P. Landis (Urbana, Illinois, 1958), p. 322. The
names of all the fiefs here named may be found in Verci: see the index in vol. iii,
and cf. v. 681 n., below.
253 *the Suabian*: Konrad II.
254 *"the Lombard Chief"*: Verci tells us that Barbarossa 'descended . . . Italy
by the valley of the Trent in the month of October 1154 with a very large

Forsooth, as Barbarossa's path was bent   255
To Italy along the Vale of Trent,
Welcomed him at Roncaglia! Sadness now—
The hamlets nested on the Tyrol's brow,
The Asolan and Euganean hills,
The Rhetian and the Julian, sadness fills   260
Them all, for Ecelin vouchsafes to stay
Among and care about them; day by day
Choosing this pinnacle, the other spot,
A castle building to defend a cot,
A cot built for a castle to defend,   265
Nothing but castles, castles, nor an end
To boasts how mountain ridge may join with
          ridge
By sunken gallery and soaring bridge.
He takes, in brief, a figure that beseems
The griesliest nightmare of the Church's dreams,   270
—A Signory firm-rooted, unestranged
From its old interests, and nowise changed
By its new neighbourhood: perchance the vaunt
Of Otho, "my own Este shall supplant
"Your Este," come to pass. The sire led in   275

---

257 *1840 proof* now,> now—   261 *1840* Them all that Ecelin   268 *1840*
bridge—{Full-stop inserted after dash in Domett copy.}   270 *1868* grisli-
est   271 *1840* A Signory

---

army': i. 204. At Roncaglia a great Diet was attended by almost all the leaders
of the Italian cities. Verci refers to an old MS which stated that 'Ecelino il
Balbo' (the Stutterer) also attended to pay court to the Emperor. Some chroniclers make the Stutterer the son of Ecelo, some the grandson.

259 *Asolan*: stressed on the first syllable, as is normal. These mountains are
part of the range which divides Germany from Italy.

264 *A castle building*: see T. S. Van Cleve, *The Emperor Frederick II of
Hohenstauffen* (1972), 140–2.

269 *beseems*: matches, seems to realize.

270 *griesliest*: 'grieslie' is a Spenserian spelling. Cf. *The Ring and the Book* viii.
1723 and xi. 1124, and 'Apollo and the Fates', 256.

271 *Signory*: lordship, dominion.

274 *"my own Este*: 'Otho IV. was distantly connected with the house of Este
. . . Thus the house of Este was represented on the Ghibelline side by the
Emperor (or his nominée Ecelin) and on the Guelf side by the present Marquis
Azzo VII. Thus if the Imperial cause triumphed through the rise of the Romano
family, the Guelf Este might be said to be supplanted by the Ghibelline Este':
Whyte.

275 *The sire*: Ecelin the Stutterer, whose son Ecelin the Monk had two sons,
Ecelin (later the Tyrant) and Alberico, and six daughters, including Palma and

A son as cruel; and this Ecelin
Had sons, in turn, and daughters sly and tall
And curling and compliant; but for all
Romano (so they styled him) throve, that neck
280　　Of his so pinched and white, that hungry cheek
Proved 't was some fiend, not him, the
　　　　man's-flesh went
To feed: whereas Romano's instrument,
Famous Taurello Salinguerra, sole
I' the world, a tree whose boughs were slipt the
　　　　bole
285　　Successively, why should not he shed blood
To further a design? Men understood
Living was pleasant to him as he wore
His careless surcoat, glanced some missive o'er,
Propped on his truncheon in the public way,
290　　While his lord lifted writhen hands to pray,
Lost at Oliero's convent.
　　　　　　　　　　　　Hill-cats, face
Our Azzo, our Guelf Lion! Why disgrace　　　*as Azzo Lord of*
A worthiness conspicuous near and far　　　　*Este heads these.*
(Atii at Rome while free and consular,

279 *1840* they style him) thrives,　　281 *1840* Prove 'tis some fiend, not him,
men's flesh is meant　*1865* Proved 'twas some fiend, not him, the man's flesh
wen　284 *1840* are slipt　285 *1840* why shall　289 *1840* way.　290–1
1840 Ecelin lifts two writhen hands to pray|At Oliero's convent now: so,
place　292 *1840* For Azzo, Lion of the . . . why disgrace　*1863,1865* With
Azzo, our Guelf Lion!—nor disgrace　*1868* Our Azzo, our Guelf-Lion! Why
disgrace

Cunizza (see note to line 941). Of his four wives two, Agnes D'Este and
Adelaide, are mentioned in the poem.
　282 *whereas*: both men were cruel, the one because he was hardly natural, the
other because he had no family to care for. At iv. 849–54 'cold-blooded men'
are described as 'The careless tribe'.
　284 *slipt the bole*: the members of his family had died and left him, as the
boughs of a tree wither and fall away.
　289 *truncheon*: 'A staff of command': Johnson. Cf. Scott, *Lord of the Isles*, VI.
xiii. 16: 'Truncheon or leading staff he lacks', and also *Pippa Passes* ii. 51 and
Colombe's Birthday, iii. 108.
　290 *writhen*: twisted, distorted. Cf. Cary, Hell, xiv. 44 (= Italian 'torto').
　290 *to pray*: 'retires to a convent & Azzo hopes to succeed to his power':
Domett.
　291 *Hill-cats*: supporters of Ecelin. Cf. ll. 123 and 239.
　292 *Why disgrace*: i.e. there is no need to disgrace. The speaker is still a Guelf.
　294 *(Atii at Rome*: Whyte rightly refers us to G. B. Pigna's *Historia de Principi
di Este* (Ferrara, 1570). On p. 2 Pigna tells us that 'Questa gente Atia è quella

Este at Padua who repulsed the Hun)   295
By trumpeting the Church's princely son?
—Styled Patron of Rovigo's Polesine,
Ancona's march, Ferrara's . . . ask, in fine,
Our chronicles, commenced when some old
        monk   300
Found it intolerable to be sunk
(Vexed to the quick by his revolting cell)
Quite out of summer while alive and well:
Ended when by his mat the Prior stood,
'Mid busy promptings of the brotherhood,
Striving to coax from his decrepit brains   305
The reason Father Porphyry took pains
To blot those ten lines out which used to stand
First on their charter drawn by Hildebrand.
        The same night wears. Verona's rule of yore
Was vested in a certain Twenty-four;   310
Count Richard's And while within his palace these debate
palace at Verona. Concerning Richard and Ferrara's fate,
Glide we by clapping doors, with sudden glare
Of cressets vented on the dark, nor care
For aught that 's seen or heard until we shut   315
The smother in, the lights, all noises but

295 *1840* Padua to repulse   296 *1840–65* son   297 *1840–65* Styled Patron   299 *1840* Your chronicles,   306 *1865* The season Father

donde . . . derivano i Principi di Este'; while on p. 4 he writes: 'Reggendo
adunque gli Atij buona parte della provincia Veneta: & dimorando in Este, per
essere costume, che gli Imperatori nelle Colonie constituivano un Magistrato,
che per l'ordinario era di quattro principali della terra: & vi creavano un capo
chiamato Decurione; Caio Attio figliuolo di Caio, da cui per filo perpetuo
discende il sangue di Este, fu Decurione'. Later in the *Historia* Pigna describes
the prowess of the House of Este during the Hunnish invasion under Attila.
  297 *Rovigo's Polesine*: 'polesine' means delta. Rovigo, north-west of Ferrara,
was for long usually in the power of the Este family.
  298 *march*: territory.   306 *Father Porphyry*: imaginary.
  307 *To blot those ten lines out*: perhaps (we are to imagine) because Hildebrand
(cf. iii. 273 n.) was so severe.
  309 *The same night*: 'The night described in pp. 4–5': *1840 proof*, referring to
lines 80 ff. 'Council at Verona debating in Boniface's palace there con. him &
Azzo': Domett.
  310 *Twenty-four*: twenty-four of the thirty-two Consuls formed a tribunal
for civil actions.
  312 *Richard*: see 102 n.
  313 *clapping doors*: cf. Leigh Hunt, *The Story of Rimini*, i. 41: 'Callings, and
clapping doors . . .'; and Byron, *Lara*, i. 261.
  314 *cressets*: torches.   316 *smother*: smoke.

The carroch's booming: safe at last! Why strange
Such a recess should lurk behind a range
Of banquet-rooms? Your finger—thus—you
    push
320 A spring, and the wall opens, would you rush
Upon the banqueters, select your prey,
Waiting (the slaughter-weapons in the way,
Strewing this very bench) with sharpened ear
A preconcerted signal to appear;
325 Or if you simply crouch with beating heart,
Bearing in some voluptuous pageant part
To startle them. Nor mutes nor masquers now;
Nor any . . . does that one man sleep whose
    brow
The dying lamp-flame sinks and rises o'er?
330 What woman stood beside him? not the more   *Of the couple found*
Is he unfastened from the earnest eyes   *therein,*

---

317 *1840* booming;   *1865* blooming: 319 *1889* {some copies} banquet
rooms?   322 *1840–65* Waiting, the   323 *1840–65* bench,

---

317 *The carroch's booming*: Sismondi (i. 394) describes the carroccio as 'a
four-wheeled chariot drawn by four pairs of oxen. It was painted in red; the
oxen which drew it were covered, down to their hoofs, with red coverings; a
mast, also of red, rose from the middle of the chariot to a very great height, and
was topped by a golden globe. Below it, between two white sails, there floated
the standard of the commune. Lower down again, towards the middle of the
mast, a figure of Christ, his arms extended on the Cross, seemed to bless the
army'. A folding plate in Muratori illustrates the 'Carrocium Patavinum' and
the 'Carrocium Cremonense' and makes it clear (as does a long footnote on the
accompanying text of the *Historiae Mantuanae*) that the various carrocci differed in detail. The carroccio had great symbolical significance, acting as a
rallying-point in war and as a focus of communal pride and loyalty. Musicians
would travel on it, services often being held on and around it. The 'booming'
was caused by a large bell on the mast. The carroccio is the subject of Diss. xxvi
in Muratori's *Antiquitates*, vol. ii. For a good recent description and illustration
see Daniel Waley, *Italian City-Republics* (2nd ed., 1978), pp. 81–2 and plate.
'Somebody told me a week ago', Browning wrote to Edward Dowden
when he was revising his poems for the 1868 edition, 'there was an expression
"blooming carroch" which he felt difficulty in understanding!' *Letters*, p. 124.
Cf. textual note above.
318 *Such a recess*: 'a recess behind the banquet rooms for murder or masques':
Domett.
322 *slaughter-weapons*: the word occurs in Scott, *The Heart of Mid-Lothian*, ch.
x.
324 *A preconcerted signal*: Domett wrote 'how dimly expressed' beneath this
line, at the bottom of p. 14.
330 *What woman*: the scene is more fully described at iii. 273 ff.
331 *he*: 'Sordello & Palma': Domett.
   unfastened: cf. the anonymous 1655 translation of Charles Sorel's *Vraie*

Because that arras fell between! Her wise
And lulling words are yet about the room,
Her presence wholly poured upon the gloom
Down even to her vesture's creeping stir.   335
And so reclines he, saturate with her,
Until an outcry from the square beneath
Pierces the charm: he springs up, glad to breathe
Above the cunning element, and shakes
The stupor off as (look you) morning breaks   340
On the gay dress, and, near concealed by it,
The lean frame like a half-burnt taper, lit
Erst at some marriage-feast, then laid away
Till the Armenian bridegroom's dying day,
In his wool wedding-robe.
                   For he—for he,   345
Gate-vein of this heart's blood of Lombardy,
(If I should falter now)—for he is thine!
one belongs to   Sordello, thy forerunner, Florentine!
Dante; his   A herald-star I know thou didst absorb
birthplace.

---

335 *1840* stir: *338 {Reading of *1840–65*}   *1868–89* breathe,   345
1840 wedding-robe; for he—for he—   *1863,1865* wedding-robe. For he—for
he, {No paragraph division in *1840–65*}   *346 {Editors' emendation} *1840*
"Gate-vein of this hearts' blood of Lombardy"   *1863–89* Gate-vein of this
hearts' blood of Lombardy,   347 *1840 proof* now)>now)—

histoire comique de Francion, ii. 29, as cited in OED: 'as soon as I could unfasten
my self from my Mistresse'.
335 *creeping stir*: cf. Keats, *The Eve of St. Agnes*, 230.
339 *the cunning element*: the atmosphere by which he has been surrounded.
341 *the gay dress*: that of Court minstrel, as we learn later.
near: nearly.
342 *a half-burnt taper*: confirmation of this Armenian custom has so far eluded
the editors.
346 *Gate-vein*: in *1840* the line is placed in inverted commas, apparently for
emphasis. The term is anatomical: cf. Bacon, *The Historie of the Raigne of King
Henry The Seventh* (1622), p. 161: 'beeing a King that loued Wealth and
Treasure, hee could not indure to haue *Trade* sicke, nor any Obstruction to
continue in the *Gate-vaine*, which disperseth that bloud'. Cf. iii. 556, below
(and see *Pauline*, 189). In his *French Revolution* (1837) Carlyle had described the
members of the National Convention as the 'Heart' of France and their
movements as 'fiery venous–arterial circulation' which is 'the function of that
Heart': Centenary ed., iv. 70: cf. i (*Sartor Resartus*), 195.
348 *Florentine!*: the poet addresses Dante, whose presence is felt throughout.
'Dante first mentions Sordello in Canto 6 of the *Purgatory*. See Sismondi, Lit. of
South. vol. I. p. 103, Roscoe's transl.': *1840 proof*. The reference should be to p.
131. See Introduction, p. 173 above.

350   Relentless into the consummate orb
       That scared it from its right to roll along
       A sempiternal path with dance and song
       Fulfilling its allotted period,
       Serenest of the progeny of God—
355   Who yet resigns it not! His darling stoops
       With no quenched lights, desponds with no
           blank troops
       Of disenfranchised brilliances, for, blent
       Utterly with thee, its shy element
       Like thine upburneth prosperous and clear.
360   Still, what if I approach the august sphere
       Named now with only one name, disentwine
       That under-current soft and argentine
       From its fierce mate in the majestic mass
       Leavened as the sea whose fire was mixt with
           glass
365   In John's transcendent vision,—launch once more
       That lustre? Dante, pacer of the shore
       Where glutted hell disgorgeth filthiest gloom,
       Unbitten by its whirring sulphur-spume—
       Or whence the grieved and obscure waters slope
370   Into a darkness quieted by hope;

354 *1840* God   *1863,1865* God!   355 *1840* not; his *1863* not; His   359
1840 clear: *1868* clear,   363–72 {not in Boston copy of *1840 proof*}   365
1840 vision,   370 *1840* hope—

351 *That scared it*: i.e. but for Dante, Sordello would be better remembered.
it: 'Sordello': Domett. Cf. Charles Herbert, *Italy and Italian Literature* (1835),
p. 66: 'The bard of Hell, and Purgatory, and Paradise, . . . was the first to arise
like a sun, dispelling the mists of the dark ages, rivalling, and even extinguishing by his appearance, all preceding lights'.
352 *dance and song*: cf. Keats, 'Ode to a Nightingale', 14.
355 *His darling*: the historical Sordello could hardly be so described.
358 *element*: part (of the brightness). Perhaps influenced by *Othello* III. iii.
467–8.
359 *Like thine upburneth*: Sordello's light burns on, as part of the great blaze of
Dante's fame.
362 *argentine*: Sordello's silver has blended with Dante's gold, as glass is
blended with fire in Revelation 15:2: 'And I saw as it were a sea of glass mingled
with fire'.
366 *That lustre*: cf. Cary, *Paradise*, v. 126 ff., where Dante is unable to identify
Justinian, a 'lustre, that with greeting kind / Erewhile had hail'd me', because
he is assigned to the planet Mercury and 'is oftenest hidden by that luminary'
(Cary's footnote).
the shore: probably that of the Stygian lake: Cary, *Hell*, vii.
368 *Unbitten*: Dante is not wounded by the sulphur.
369 *Or whence*: from Purgatory.

Plucker of amaranths grown beneath God's eye
In gracious twilights where his chosen lie,—
I would do this! If I should falter now!
    In Mantua territory half is slough,
Half pine-tree forest; maples, scarlet oaks   375
Breed o'er the river-beds; even Mincio chokes
With sand the summer through: but 't is morass
In winter up to Mantua walls. There was,
Some thirty years before this evening's coil,
One spot reclaimed from the surrounding spoil,   380
Goito; just a castle built amid
A few low mountains; firs and larches hid
Their main defiles, and rings of vineyard bound
The rest. Some captured creature in a pound,
Whose artless wonder quite precludes distress,   385
Secure beside in its own loveliness,
So peered with airy head, below, above,
The castle at its toils, the lapwings love
To glean among at grape-time. Pass within.
A maze of corridors contrived for sin,   390
Dusk winding-stairs, dim galleries got past,

372 *1840* his Chosen lie, *1863,1865* His chosen lie, *1868* his chosen
lie,   373 *1840* if I should falter now— *1863,1865* if I should falter
now!   375 *1840–68* scarlet-oaks   379 *1840* (Some . . . . coil)   384 *1840*
rest: some   389 *1840* within:

372 *gracious twilights*: Whyte states that 'Hell, Purgatory, and Paradise are
successively indicated', but (as Duff had earlier remarked) this describes the
Earthly Paradise at the summit of the Mount of Purgatory rather than Paradise
itself. Dante makes no mention of the amaranth, the immortal flower of
Paradise: cf. Fowler's note to *Paradise Lost* iii. 353 ff., in *The Poems of John
Milton*, ed. John Carey and Alastair Fowler (1968).
    374 *In Mantua territory*: 'His youth at Goito—a castle of Ecelins—where his
last wife Adelaide lives': Domett. We now hear of Sordello's boyhood.
    376 *Mincio*: for this river in summer see Cary, *Hell*, xx. 74–80.
    379 *coil*: trouble. Cf. Cary, *Hell*, vii. 64.
    380 *spoil*: unserviceable ground.
    381 *Goito*: the traditional birthplace of Sordello, a village about ten miles
north-west of Mantua.
    384 *Some captured creature*: the strange comparison of the castle to a captured
bird or animal is characteristic of Browning. The 'rings of vineyard' become
'toils' or nets for the capture of game.
    388 *the lapwings*: Harrison indignantly comments that grapes are 'strange
food for this insectivorous plover of field and shore' (loc. cit., p. 405), but it is
no doubt the insects available 'at grape-time' on which they feed.
    389 *Pass within*: a characteristic stage-direction. Cf. 405–6, 505, 587.
    390 *A maze of corridors*: the castle at Goito is reminiscent of Mrs. Radcliffe and
her imitators.

You gain the inmost chambers, gain at last
A maple-panelled room: that haze which seems
Floating about the panel, if there gleams
A sunbeam over it, will turn to gold
And in light-graven characters unfold
The Arab's wisdom everywhere; what shade
Marred them a moment, those slim pillars made,
Cut like a company of palms to prop
The roof, each kissing top entwined with top,
Leaning together; in the carver's mind
Some knot of bacchanals, flushed cheek
      combined
With straining forehead, shoulders purpled, hair
Diffused between, who in a goat-skin bear
A vintage; graceful sister-palms! But quick
To the main wonder, now. A vault, see; thick
Black shade about the ceiling, though fine slits
Across the buttress suffer light by fits
Upon a marvel in the midst. Nay, stoop—
A dullish grey-streaked cumbrous font, a group
Round it,—each side of it, where'er one sees,—
Upholds it; shrinking Caryatides
Of just-tinged marble like Eve's lilied flesh
Beneath her maker's finger when the fresh
First pulse of life shot brightening the snow.

*A vault inside the
castle at Goito,*

395
400
405
410
415

---

405 *1840* sister-palms: but   409 *1840* midst: nay,   411–12 *1840–63*
Round it, each side of it, where'er one sees,|Upholds it—   415 *1840*
snow: *SB* [cold] snow:

---

397 *The Arab's wisdom*: 'The historian Rolandino notes that Adelaide was a
perfect mistress of Astrology, that she comprehended the ways of the stars and
the other movements of the heavens, and was able to predict the future': Verci
i. 88. For the passage in Rolandino see Muratori viii. 173. Literary historians all
stress the importance of Arabic as an influence on mediaeval learning and
poetry: see, e.g., ch. iv of P.-L. Ginguené's *Histoire Littéraire d'Italie* (Paris
1811).
   what shade: such shade as momentarily fell on the written characters was that
of the pillars of the tall room.
   399 *a company of palms*: there may be a reminiscence of *Lamia*, ii. 125 ff. here.
With 'A vintage' (405) cf. *Endymion*, iv. 200.
   412 *Caryatides*: female figures supporting the font. The scansion requires five
syllables, as in Latin. The uncertain number of the figures suggests that
Browning had no specific original in mind for this highly 'neo-classical' piece
of statuary. At iv. 144–8 we find it is made of Messina marble.

*and what Sordello
would see there.*

The font's edge burthens every shoulder, so
They muse upon the ground, eyelids half closed;
Some, with meek arms behind their backs
    disposed,
Some, crossed above their bosoms, some, to veil
Their eyes, some, propping chin and cheek so
    pale,   420
Some, hanging slack an utter helpless length
Dead as a buried vestal whose whole strength
Goes when the grate above shuts heavily.
So dwell these noiseless girls, patient to see,
Like priestesses because of sin impure   425
Penanced for ever, who resigned endure,
Having that once drunk sweetness to the dregs.
And every eve, Sordello's visit begs
Pardon for them: constant as eve he came
To sit beside each in her turn, the same   430
As one of them, a certain space: and awe
Made a great indistinctness till he saw
Sunset slant cheerful through the buttress-chinks,
Gold seven times globed; surely our maiden
    shrinks
And a smile stirs her as if one faint grain   435
Her load were lightened, one shade less the stain
Obscured her forehead, yet one more bead slipt
From off the rosary whereby the crypt

---

419 *SB* [held] to veil   421 *SB* an utter helpless>and dead a long
white   422 *SB* vestal>vestal's   423 *1840* heavily;   427 *1840* dregs;

---

419 *crossed*: cf. *The Eve of St. Agnes*, 35–6: 'upon their heads the cornice rests,
/ With hair blown black, and wings put cross-wise on their breasts'.

422 *a buried vestal*: Roman priestesses were obliged to remain virgins for
thirty years. 'Such . . . as proved incontinent were punished in the most
rigorous manner. Numa ordered them to be stoned, but Tarquin the elder dug
a large hole under the earth, where a bed was placed with a little bread, wine,
water, and oil, and a lighted lamp, and the guilty vestal was . . . compelled to
descend into the subterraneous cavity, which was immediately shut, and she
was left to die through hunger': J. Lemprière, *A Classical Dictionary*, 5th ed.,
1804.

424 *patient to see*: patient in their appearance.

434 *globed*: purified. When gold is refined by fire, in the process called
cupelling or cupellation, it forms into globules.

our maiden: the one we are concerned with, the one Sordello is sitting beside
on this occasion.

Keeps count of the contritions of its charge?
440　Then with a step more light, a heart more large,
He may depart, leave her and every one
To linger out the penance in mute stone.
Ah, but Sordello? 'T is the tale I mean
To tell you.
　　　　　In this castle may be seen,　　　　*His boyhood in the*
445　On the hill tops, or underneath the vines,　　*domain of Ecelin.*
Or eastward by the mound of firs and pines
That shuts out Mantua, still in loneliness,
A slender boy in a loose page's dress,
Sordello: do but look on him awhile
450　Watching ('t is autumn) with an earnest smile
The noisy flock of thievish birds at work
Among the yellowing vineyards; see him lurk
('T is winter with its sullenest of storms)
Beside that arras-length of broidered forms,
455　On tiptoe, lifting in both hands a light
Which makes yon warrior's visage flutter bright
—Ecelo, dismal father of the brood,
And Ecelin, close to the girl he wooed,
Auria, and their Child, with all his wives
460　From Agnes to the Tuscan that survives,
Lady of the castle, Adelaide. His face
—Look, now he turns away! Yourselves shall
　　trace

444 *1840–65* {No paragraph division.}　446 *1840* Or southward　454 *1889* arras length {some copies}　459 *1840*—Auria,　460 *1840 proof* survives>survives,　461 *1840* Adelaide: his

442 *mute stone*: cf. Keats, *The Eve of St. Agnes*, 16: 'dumb orat'ries'.

446 *eastward:* 'south' underlined in *SB*, and 'east' written above. Domett underlines 'southward' and has '(eastward 65)' in the margin, no doubt a later emendation from *1865*.

457 *Ecelo, dismal father:* 'dismal' in the original sense of the word, 'unpropitious, of evil omen'. Cf. *Strafford*, II. ii. 163. The genealogy in Verci (i. 198) makes Arpone the father of Ecelo, the grandfather of Alberico, and the great-grandfather of 'Ecelino Balbo', the Stutterer. Like Rolandino, Browning omits Alberico and so makes the Stutterer the son of Ecelo. It is of interest that *SB* has 'stuttering' above 'wooed'. The Stutterer married Auria da Baone (according to Verci), by whom he had two sons, Ecelin the Monk and Giovanni, and two daughters, Cunizza and Gisla. The Monk married (1) Agnese, daughter of Azzo VI of Este, (2) Speronella, (3) Cecilia, and (4) Adelaide [or Adeleita], sister of the Counts of Mangona, a leading Tuscan family.

(The delicate nostril swerving wide and fine,
A sharp and restless lip, so well combine
With that calm brow) a soul fit to receive   465
Delight at every sense; you can believe
Sordello foremost in the regal class
Nature has broadly severed from her mass
Of men, and framed for pleasure, as she frames
Some happy lands, that have luxurious names,   470
For loose fertility; a footfall there
Suffices to upturn to the warm air
Half-germinating spices; mere decay
Produces richer life; and day by day
New pollen on the lily-petal grows,   475
And still more labyrinthine buds the rose.

How a poet's soul
comes into play.

You recognise at once the finer dress
Of flesh that amply lets in loveliness
At eye and ear, while round the rest is furled
(As though she would not trust them with her
    world)   480
A veil that shows a sky not near so blue,
And lets but half the sun look fervid through.
How can such love?—like souls on each
    full-fraught
Discovery brooding, blind at first to aught
Beyond its beauty, till exceeding love   485
Becomes an aching weight; and, to remove
A curse that haunts such natures—to preclude
Their finding out themselves can work no good

---

475 *SB* New pollen {'pollen' underlined; 'powder' written in the margin.}   482 *1840* through: 483 *1840* love like

467 *the regal class*: cf. *Paracelsus* v. 412. Sordello, who is probably turning from the tapestry-portraits of the Ecelini family in contempt, is a natural king among men. For a comparison with the poet in *Alastor* see p. 176 above. At ll. 523 ff., below, we hear of another exceptional class of men.
477–8 *the finer dress / Of flesh*: i.e. even in bodily appearance such men are exceptional.
478 *loveliness*: opposite this word Domett wrote: 'matchless from page 16', i.e. from l. 349.
479 *the rest*: other, ordinary, men.
483 *How can such love*: 'How can such men love like those souls who brood &c.': *1840 proof.*
487 *A curse*: as in *Alastor*(which means 'Avenging Spirit').
488 *themselves*: 'that they themselves': *1840 proof.*

To what they love nor make it very blest
By their endeavour,—they are fain invest
The lifeless thing with life from their own soul,
Availing it to purpose, to control,
To dwell distinct and have peculiar joy
And separate interests that may employ
That beauty fitly, for its proper sake.
Nor rest they here; fresh births of beauty wake
Fresh homage, every grade of love is past,
With every mode of loveliness: then cast
Inferior idols off their borrowed crown
Before a coming glory. Up and down
Runs arrowy fire, while earthly forms combine
To throb the secret forth; a touch divine—
And the scaled eyeball owns the mystic rod;
Visibly through his garden walketh God.
        So fare they. Now revert. One character

490 *1840* endeavour, 491 *1840* soul   495 *1840* sake;   500 *1840* glory:
up   505 *1840* So fare they—Now revert: one character *1863,1865* So fare
they. Now revert. One character {No paragraph division in *1840–65*}

490 *they are fain invest*: they are obliged to imagine that the lifeless thing is
alive, endowing it with purpose and control over itself so that it may have an
existence and interests of its own appropriate to the enjoyment of its own
beauty.
491 *The lifeless thing*: see ll. 638 ff.
492 *Availing it*: availing themselves of it for their own purposes. Cf. 735 ff.
496 *fresh births of beauty*: cf. *Endymion*, i. 298 and iv. 506.
499 *Inferior idols*: the love of such a soul moves swiftly from one object of
admiration to another.
501 *arrowy fire*: cf. Ezekiel 1:1, 13–14: '. . . the heavens were opened, and I
saw visions of God . . . As for the likeness of the living creatures, their
appearance was like burning coals of fire . . .; it went up and down among the
living creatures; and the fire was bright, and out of the fire went forth
lightning'. Cf. l. 999, below.
502 *a touch divine*: cf. *Endymion*, i. 298: 'a touch ethereal'.
503 *the scaled eyeball*: the eyeball from which the scales have fallen. OED cites
'An Epigrame to the Reader' by 'H.C.' in the *Works* of Richard Greenham
(1601, and reprs.), ll. 15–16: 'From whose hie top thy scaled eyes may see, / A
glorious light that shall enlighten thee'.
504 *walketh God*: 'And they heard the voice of the LORD God walking in the
garden': Genesis 3:8.
505 *One character*: one characteristic marks such men, the desire to lose
themselves in the objects of their admiration, 'something not themselves'. In a
sense they find no home of their own, and 'forego their just inheritance', but
perhaps they are happy so. There is also another class of lovers of beauty (523–)
which is much more self-centred: such men believe that every quality of beauty
which they encounter corresponds to something already revealed to their own

Denotes them through the progress and the
    stir,—
A need to blend with each external charm,
Bury themselves, the whole heart wide and
    warm,—
In something not themselves; they would belong
To what they worship—stronger and more
    strong   510
Thus prodigally fed—which gathers shape
And feature, soon imprisons past escape
The votary framed to love and to submit
Nor ask, as passionate he kneels to it,
Whence grew the idol's empery. So runs   515
A legend; light had birth ere moons and suns,
Flowing through space a river and alone,
Till chaos burst and blank the spheres were
    strown
Hither and thither, foundering and blind:
When into each of them rushed light—to find   520
Itself no place, foiled of its radiant chance.
Let such forego their just inheritance!

---

506 *1840* stir;   507 *1868* eternal charm,   508 *1840–65* warm,   511
1840 fed—that gathers   514 *1863,1865* as passionately

souls. It is not their fault (they reason) that the quality of 'being fair, or good, or
wise, or strong' has merely remained dormant within their natures. Such
natures are content to admire their own Will, and to live in their own minds.
They 'laugh . . . at envious fate', reflecting complacently that they are not
limited by the paltry limitations of actual life, and so can 'soar to heaven's
complexest essence'.
    509 *In something*: 'some worship external things of beauty thinking it in
them. Others are conscious 'tis in themselves—& give the homage to their
own souls': Domett. *1840 proof*: 'they would belong to what they worship,
which prodigally fed by that very worship grows strong and stronger thereon
then gathers, &c.'
    511 *which*: the *1840* reading, 'that', is underlined in the Domett copy, 'this'
being added in the margin and then deleted in favour of 'which'. *SB* has 'that'
scored out and 'which' written in.
    516 *A legend*: no specific legend has been traced. According to Genesis 1:3,
14–18 God created light before he created the heavenly bodies, and in *Paradise
Lost* (particularly vii. 243 ff.) we hear of light travelling 'through the airy
gloom' before the sun had been created. Dante describes the river of light in
Paradiso, xxx. Cf. Fowler's notes on *PL*, iii. 1, vii. 243, and vii. 361, in Carey
and Fowler (cf. 372 n., above).
    521 *radiant chance*: '*radiant chance*, with all submission, has not much mean-
ing': *1840 proof*.
    522 *Let such forego*: as light, according to the legend, illuminates the universe

For there 's a class that eagerly looks, too,
On beauty, but, unlike the gentler crew,
525   Proclaims each new revealment born a twin
With a distinctest consciousness within,
Referring still the quality, now first
Revealed, to their own soul—its instinct nursed
In silence, now remembered better, shown
530   More thoroughly, but not the less their own;
A dream come true; the special exercise
Of any special function that implies
The being fair, or good, or wise, or strong,
Dormant within their nature all along—
535   Whose fault? So, homage, other souls direct
Without, turns inward. "How should this deject
"Thee, soul?" they murmur; "wherefore
      strength be quelled

---

526 *1840–68* within   528 *1840* soul;   535 *1840* So homage   *1868* So homage,   536 *1840* inward; how *1863,1865* inward; "How   537 *1840* Thee, soul? they murmur; wherefore

yet has no proper home, so such loving natures are destined to find no resting-place.

529 *remembered better*: a reference to the Platonic doctrine of ἀνάμνησις, which maintains that the soul recognizes Ideas as if it remembered them.

533 *or strong*: 'an eloquent but not overclear amplification of Byron's lines—Alas 'twas not in them—'twas in thy power / To double even the beauty of a flower—& the lines preceding': Domett. The passage is *Don Juan*, I. ccxiv. 7–8, where the poet laments that 'never more on me / The freshness of the heart can fall like dew, / Which out of all the lovely things we see / Extracts emotions beautiful and new . . . / Alas! 'twas not in them, but in thy power / To double even the sweetness of a flower'.

535 *Whose fault?*: such men believe that it is not their fault that the extraordinary powers which they believe themselves to possess have remained 'Dormant'. Duff offers the following paraphrase of 535–48: 'Whose fault is it if the conception is never wrought out by themselves—if they do not find their own expression for it? There is no fault at all: far from blaming themselves, they do themselves homage. "How should the failure to act out such conceptions deject thee, my soul?" they murmur. "Why should the power of thine inward life be quenched simply because, fit opportunities for the proper revelation of these conceptions being withheld, thou lackest the means of outward expression that belong to common men, who, indeed, are cumbered by their means of expression, which are far too great for anything there is in them to express,—who have not a mind like thine, which existence itself, with all its wealth, cannot satisfy and cannot surprise, since thou hast already dreamed the fairest it can show? Laugh thou at envious fate, which denies thee sufficient temporal powers to reveal thy soul—thou who dost boldly soar from the conception of the nature of the lowest form of individual life, too slenderly endowed to feel its earthly limitations, to the conception of heaven's complexest essence, and art able to realise in thine imagination all existences in the universe, however grand they be"'.

"Because, its trivial accidents withheld,
"Organs are missed that clog the world, inert,
"Wanting a will, to quicken and exert,   540
"Like thine—existence cannot satiate,
"Cannot surprise? Laugh thou at envious fate,
"Who, from earth's simplest combination stampt
"With individuality—uncrampt
"By living its faint elemental life,   545
"Dost soar to heaven's complexest essence, rife
"With grandeurs, unaffronted to the last,

How poets class at   "Equal to being all!"
length—for
honour,   In truth? Thou hast
Life, then—wilt challenge life for us: our race
Is vindicated so, obtains its place   550
In thy ascent, the first of us; whom we
May follow, to the meanest, finally,
With our more bounded wills?
                                      Ah, but to find

---

542 *1840* surprise: laugh thou   *1863,1865* surprise? laugh thou   546 *1868*
complext essence,   548 *1840* Equal to being all.   549 *1840* us: thy race

---

538 *trivial accidents*: such vain idealists consider merely trivial the 'organs'
which in fact make it possible for great human powers to come into play.

541 *Like thine—*: like thine which. At the top of the page (p. 24) Domett
writes: 'Instead of living in external objects of adoration, knows that their
beauty springs from itself, so turns inward & seeks still higher & higher
existence'.

548 *In truth?*: the comment of a choric voice.

553 *Ah, but to find*: The choric commentator continues by asking rhetorically
what happens if this sort of mind is weakened by disdaining action in the world
because the possibilities are too limiting for it—or ('yet worse') insists on
attempting to display its own 'mastery' completely, as would only be appropriate in a world of Eternity. 'Enervate' is stressed on the second syllable, as
commonly in the seventeenth and eighteenth centuries. 'Emprize', enterprise,
endeavour.

Answering a question from Edward Dowden, Browning agreed that Sordello exemplifies the second class 'as "enervated" and modified by the impulse
to "thrust in time eternity's concern"—*that*, or nothing . . . the rest of the
poem is an example of the same': *Letters*, p. 92. Dowden's essay, reprinted in his
Transcripts and Studies (2nd edn., 1896) gives a lucid account of the matter. Of
Sordello's class he writes: 'These are not the worshipping spirits; they are
characterised not by a predominance of love but of *will*; they would subdue all
things to themselves; their claims on life are boundless, and they compel life
(unless failure overtake them) to yield up to their sublime self-assertion untried
forms of beauty, goodness, knowledge, power; and thus they vindicate the
rights of humanity, thus they raise the standard of the general demands on life
and the gifts of life, so that we all, to the meanest of us, may in the end follow
them with our more bounded wills' (p. 483). It is interesting that the next

A certain mood enervate such a mind,
555 Counsel it slumber in the solitude
Thus reached nor, stooping, task for mankind's
    good
Its nature just as life and time accord
"—Too narrow an arena to reward
"Emprize—the world's occasion worthless since
560 "Not absolutely fitted to evince
"Its mastery!" Or if yet worse befall,
And a desire possess it to put all
That nature forth, forcing our straitened sphere
Contain it,—to display completely here
565 The mastery another life should learn,   *or shame—which*
Thrusting in time eternity's concern,—   *may the gods avert*
So that Sordello. . . .
                  Fool, who spied the mark
Of leprosy upon him, violet-dark
Already as he loiters? Born just now,
570 With the new century, beside the glow
And efflorescence out of barbarism;

---

558 *1840* (Too narrow   561 *1840* Its mastery)   564 *1840* Contain
it;   566 *1840* concern, *SB* time eternity's>Time Eternity's   567
1840–65 Fool, {No paragraph division.}   569 *1840* now—   570 *1840*
century—

---

sentence in Browning's letter is this: 'I did mean to make a companion to
Paracelsus, and remember while employed on it, telling Leigh Hunt so'.

557 *as life and time accord*: *SB* expands to: 'as Life and Time accord . . . They
appearing too narrow an arena to reward Emprize—& the world's occasion
appearing worthless', etc. At the foot of the page it comments: 'The others
born merely to love *must* love—these, born to put in evidence their power to be
loved, *may* refuse to do that'.

563 *our straitened sphere*: cf. *Paracelsus*, i. 792 ff.

567 *So that Sordello . . . .*: the poet checks himself when he is on the point of
telling Sordello's story prematurely. In his boyhood no one noticed the warning signs.

567–8 *the mark / Of leprosy*: cf. *Paracelsus*, i. 614, where Festus points out 'a
plague-spot' in Paracelsus: see the same poem, too, at iii. 759 and iv. 140.

570 *the new century*: Sordello is often said to have been born *c.* 1200, but
Browning generally seems to accept 1189, following the *Biographie Universelle*
and most earlier authorities. He is a child during the disturbance in Vicenza in
1194, and thirty when Count Richard is captured at Ferrara in 1224. There is an
element of approximation: cf. iv. 418.

571 *efflorescence*: a reference to the view that the thirteenth century saw the
end of the Dark Ages and the prologue to the Renaissance. 'It was in those
times', Verci comments (i. 53), 'that the peoples began to shake off the
servitude which had kept them in subjection until then, and began to make the
arts and commerce flourish'. The 'abysm' is probably the sacking of Constan-

Witness a Greek or two from the abysm
That stray through Florence-town with studious
    air,
Calming the chisel of that Pisan pair:
If Nicolo should carve a Christus yet!   575
While at Siena is Guidone set,
Forehead on hand; a painful birth must be
Matured ere Saint Eufemia's sacristy
Or transept gather fruits of one great gaze
At the moon: look you! The same orange haze,—   580
The same blue stripe round that—and, in the
    midst,
Thy spectral whiteness, Mother-maid, who didst
Pursue the dizzy painter!
                                   Woe, then, worth
Any officious babble letting forth
The leprosy confirmed and ruinous   585

---

574 *1840* pair . . .   578 *1840* ere San Eufemio's   580 *1840* At the noon-
sun: look you! An orange haze—   581 *1840–68* i' the midst,   582 *1840*
mother-maid,   583 *1840* Woe then worth

---

tinople by the Crusaders in 1204, an event which had a momentous effect in
disseminating new models for the arts.

574 *that Pisan pair*: Luigi Lanzi tells us that it was the Tuscans, and 'more
especially . . . the people of Pisa', who 'taught artists how to shake off the
trammels of the modern Greeks, and to adopt the ancients for their models',
which probably explains 'Calming the chisel'. In the same passage Lanzi states
that 'Niccola Pisano was the first who discovered and pursued the true path':
The History of Painting in Italy, translated by Thomas Roscoe (6 vols., 1828), i.
4–5. The other Pisan is probably Andrea Pisano, Niccola's associate, whose
work in Florence is immediately mentioned by Lanzi (i. 6). Crucifixions by
Niccola are in Pisa baptistery and Siena cathedral.

576 *Guidone*: Guido or Guidone, whose known work dates from twenty
years later. 'Siena', Lanzi writes, 'at this period, could boast her Guido, who
painted from the year 1221, but not entirely in the manner of the Greeks, as we
shall find under the Sienese school': i. 14. Elsewhere (i. 378) he observes: 'The
series of painters known by name commences with Guido, or Guidone, . . .
[who] flourished before Cimabue . . . The writers of Siena have declaimed
against Vasari and Baldinucci for omitting this artist'. Lanzi particularly praises
'his picture of the Virgin now hung up in the Malevolti chapel in the church of
S. Domenico . . . [whose] countenance . . . is lovely, and participates not in the
stern aspect that is characteristic of the [modern] Greeks': (i. 379), a painting
reproduced by Bernard Berenson in *Italian Pictures of the Renaissance* (*Central
. . . and North Italian Schools*, 3 vols. (1968), ii. plate 21). There is no 'Saint
Eufemia's' church in Siena.

580 *At the moon*: revised from *1840*. To keep the metre right Browning
changes 'An orange haze' to 'The same orange haze'. Cf. Introduction, pp.
184–5 above. The revision from 'i' the midst' was also suggested by Domett,
but not made until 1888.

583 *Woe . . . worth*: a curse upon!: as in Scott, *The Lady of the Lake*, I. ix. 15.

To spirit lodged in a contracted house!
Go back to the beginning, rather; blend
It gently with Sordello's life; the end
Is piteous, you may see, but much between

590 Pleasant enough. Meantime, some pyx to screen
The full-grown pest, some lid to shut upon
The goblin! So they found at Babylon,
(Colleagues, mad Lucius and sage Antonine)
Sacking the city, by Apollo's shrine,

595 In rummaging among the rarities,
A certain coffer; he who made the prize
Opened it greedily; and out there curled
Just such another plague, for half the world
Was stung. Crawl in then, hag, and crouch
      asquat,

600 Keeping that blotchy bosom thick in spot
Until your time is ripe! The coffer-lid
Is fastened, and the coffer safely hid

from Sordello, now in childhood.

---

589 *1840* you shall see,   590 *1840* enough; meantime   592 *1840* As
they   593 *1840* (Colleagues   594 *SB* in{written above 'by'}   *1840*
shrine   595–6 *1840* Its pride, in rummaging the rarities,| A cabinet; be sure,
who   *599 {Reading of *1840*.}   *1863–89* and couch asquat,   602 *1840* Is
fastened

---

586 *a contracted house*: the body which housed Sordello's soul.
587 *Go back*: 'His disease of soul grew up gradually. Talk not of it yet':
Domett.
588 *It*: the fatal weakness symbolised as leprosy.
588–9 *the end / Is piteous*: cf. *Richard III*, IV. iv. 74: 'his piteous and unpitied
end'. Browning was profoundly influenced by this play: see Vol. I, p. 3.
590 *pyx*: box. OED cites only two examples of the non-religious use of the
word, both from dictionaries.
592 *at Babylon*: at Seleucia, in fact, as Duff pointed out. The reference is to
Ammianus Marcellinus XXIII. vii: 'which [city] being by the captaines of
[Lucius] *Verus Cæsar* sore shaken and brought to ruine . . . the image of *Apollo
Chomeus* being displaced, unshrined, and brought to Rome, the Prelats bestowed in the temple of *Apollo Palatinus*. And the voice goeth, That after this
very same image was thus caried away, and the citie burnt, the souldiors in
rifling and ransacking the temple, met with a narrow hole; which when they
had layed open, therein to find some precious treasure, out of a certaine
sanctuarie, shut up sometimes by the privie counsellors of the Chaldæans,
sprung forth that originall disease and corruption, which having once conceived the force of an incurable maladie, in the daies of the same *Verus* and
Marcus Antoninus, from the very bounds of Persia unto Rhene and Gaule,
infected all places with contagion, and bred much mortalitie': *The Roman
Historie*, trans. Philemon Holland (1609), p. 230. Babylon is mentioned in the
previous sentence.

Under the Loxian's choicest gifts of gold.
   Who will may hear Sordello's story told,
And how he never could remember when   605
He dwelt not at Goito. Calmly, then,
About this secret lodge of Adelaide's
Glided his youth away; beyond the glades
On the fir-forest border, and the rim
Of the low range of mountain, was for him   610
No other world: but this appeared his own
To wander through at pleasure and alone.
The castle too seemed empty; far and wide
Might he disport; only the northern side
Lay under a mysterious interdict—   615
Slight, just enough remembered to restrict
His roaming to the corridors, the vault
Where those font-bearers expiate their fault,
The maple-chamber, and the little nooks
And nests, and breezy parapet that looks   620
Over the woods to Mantua: there he strolled.
Some foreign women-servants, very old,
Tended and crept about him—all his clue
To the world's business and embroiled ado
Distant a dozen hill-tops at the most.   625
   And first a simple sense of life engrossed
Sordello in his drowsy Paradise;

The delights of his The day's adventures for the day suffice—
childish fancy,   Its constant tribute of perceptions strange,
With sleep and stir in healthy interchange,   630
Suffice, and leave him for the next at ease
Like the great palmer-worm that strips the trees,

---

604 *1840* Who will {No paragraph division.}   606 *1840* Goito; calmly
then   *SB* He dwelt {'was' written in the margin.}   609 *1840–65* fir-
forest's border,   611 *1840* but that appeared   614 *1840* disport unless
the *SB* disport unless>disport; only,   *626 {Reading of *1863–68*}
1840,1888,1889 {No paragraph division.}

603 *the Loxian*: Apollo.
604 *Who will*: cf. line 1. 'Sordello's infancy': Domett.
610 *was*: there was.
615 *a mysterious interdict*: cf. 660–3: explained at ii. 957–8.
   632 *palmer-worm*: the term, which occurs in the Geneva Bible (Joel i. 4), has
been used for various caterpillars which wander, like palmers or pilgrims.

Eats the life out of every luscious plant,
And, when September finds them sere or scant,
635   Puts forth two wondrous winglets, alters quite,
And hies him after unforeseen delight.
So fed Sordello, not a shard dissheathed;
As ever, round each new discovery, wreathed
Luxuriantly the fancies infantine
640   His admiration, bent on making fine
Its novel friend at any risk, would fling
In gay profusion forth: a ficklest king,
Confessed those minions!—eager to dispense
So much from his own stock of thought and
sense
645   As might enable each to stand alone
And serve him for a fellow; with his own,
Joining the qualities that just before
Had graced some older favourite. Thus they
wore
A fluctuating halo, yesterday
650   Set flicker and to-morrow filched away,—   *which could blow*
Those upland objects each of separate name,   *out a great bubble,*
Each with an aspect never twice the same,
Waxing and waning as the new-born host
Of fancies, like a single night's hoar-frost,
655   Gave to familiar things a face grotesque;
Only, preserving through the mad burlesque
A grave regard. Conceive! the orpine patch

---

636 *1840* delight;   637 *1840–68* disheathed;   638 *1840* As ever . . . .
discovery   642 *1840* king   643 *1840–1865* minions! Eager   *SB* Confessed those minions!>Those minions found him!   648 *1840* favourite: so
they   650 *1840* away;   657 *1840* regard: conceive; the orpine patch
1863,1865 regard. Conceive! the orpine-patch

637 *not a shard dissheathed*: no sign of his wings was yet to be seen, no
fragment or tiny part of them. Cf. *Cymbeline*, III. iii. 20.
642 *a ficklest king*: such objects, rendered unrecognizable by the working of
Sordello's fancy, were in the power of a very changeable master. Cf. *Pauline*
474 ff. and *Paracelsus*, ii. 340.
649 *A fluctuating halo*: cf. *Pauline*, 320: 'All halo-girt with fancies of my own'.
657 *regard*: expression.
Conceive!: just think!—he would imagine that the patch of orpine was
connected with Ecelin climbing the northern stair in the forbidden part of the
castle, on that day when the archers had come past! (Orpine is a herbaceous
plant often grown in cottage gardens.)

Blossoming earliest on the log-house thatch
The day those archers wound along the vines—
Related to the Chief that left their lines   66c
To climb with clinking step the northern stair
Up to the solitary chambers where
Sordello never came. Thus thrall reached thrall;
He o'er-festooning every interval,
As the adventurous spider, making light   66;
Of distance, shoots her threads from depth to
    height,
From barbican to battlement: so flung
Fantasies forth and in their centre swung
Our architect,—the breezy morning fresh
Above, and merry,—all his waving mesh   67
Laughing with lucid dew-drops rainbow-edged.
    This world of ours by tacit pact is pledged
To laying such a spangled fabric low
Whether by gradual brush or gallant blow.
But its abundant will was baulked here: doubt   6'
Rose tardily in one so fenced about

being secure awhile From most that nurtures judgment,—care and
from intrusion.   pain:

658 *1840* on our log-house-thatch   *1863–68* on the log-house-thatch   660
SB Related to the Chief> Relates to Ecelin   669 *1840* architect: 670 *1840*
merry;   672 *1840–65* This {No paragraph division}   674 *1840*
blow: 675 *1840* balked   677 *1840–68* judgment,

   663 *Thus thrall reached thrall*: thus one captive of his fancy was connected with
another. Alternatively, the first 'thrall' may refer to Sordello himself: cf. iv.
255.
   665 *As the adventurous spider*: cf. the opening of Shelley's 'Letter to Maria
Gisborne':
      The spider spreads her webs, whether she be
      In poet's tower, cellar, or barn, or tree;
      The silk-worm in the dark green mulberry leaves
      His winding sheet and cradle ever weaves;
      So I . . .
In *An Essay on Shelley* Browning states that Shelley 'throws, from his poet's
station between both [Power and Love in the absolute and Beauty and Good in
the concrete], swifter, subtler, and more numerous films for the connexion of
each with each, than have been thrown by any modern artificer of whom I have
knowledge': third para. from the end. Cf. a letter to the Revd. V. D. Davis, 30
December 1881: 'A film or two, even so slight as the above, may sufficiently
support a tolerably big spider-web of a story—where there is ability and good
will enough to look most at the main fabric in the middle'. This unpublished
letter, which refers to 'How they Brought the Good News', was quoted in part
in *TLS*, 8 February 1952, p. 109.

Judgment, that dull expedient we are fain,
Less favoured, to adopt betimes and force
680 Stead us, diverted from our natural course
Of joys—contrive some yet amid the dearth,
Vary and render them, it may be, worth
Most we forego. Suppose Sordello hence
Selfish enough, without a moral sense
685 However feeble; what informed the boy
Others desired a portion in his joy?
Or say a ruthful chance broke woof and warp—
A heron's nest beat down by March winds sharp,
A fawn breathless beneath the precipice,
690 A bird with unsoiled breast and unfilmed eyes
Warm in the brake—could these undo the trance
Lapping Sordello? Not a circumstance
That makes for you, friend Naddo! Eat fern-seed
And peer beside us and report indeed
If (your word) "genius" dawned with throes and
695   stings
And the whole fiery catalogue, while springs,
Summers, and winters quietly came and went.
        Time put at length that period to content
By right the world should have imposed: bereft
700 Of its good offices, Sordello, left

678 *SB* we are>those are   680 *SB* Stead us, diverted from our>Stead
them, diverted from their   681 *1840* joys,   *1863,1865* joys,—   683 *1840*
forego: suppose   *SB* Most   we>Most they   690 *1840–68* and filmless
eyes   695 *1840* Genius   697 *1840* Summers and . . . . went,   *1863–8*
Summers and . . . . went.   *698 {Editors' emendation}   *1840* Putting at
length . . . . content {No   paragraph division.}   *1863–89* Time put at
length. . . . content,

678 *we*: unlike Sordello.   680 *Stead*: suffice.
681 *contrive*: an infinitive.   683 *hence*: as a result of his upbringing.
687 *a ruthful chance*: suppose some pitiful accident tore down the fabric of his
usual serene existence.
693 *friend Naddo!*: the first appearance of a subsidiary character with an
important role. He is a commonplace jongleur (ii. 117) whose criticism irks
Sordello: the sort of critic from whose attentions Browning himself suffered
throughout his life: cf. '"Transcendentalism": A Poem in Twelve Books', in
Men and Women. Here we see that Naddo subscribes to the romantic notion that
a genius must have had an unhappy childhood.
Eat fern-seed: before the fern's method of reproduction was known its seed
was supposed to have the property of conferring invisibility. Cf. *I Henry IV*, ii.
i. 83–4: 'we have the receipt of fern-seed, we walk invisible'.
698 *put . . . content*: the end to his content which . . .

To study his companions, managed rip
Their fringe off, learn the true relationship,
Core with its crust, their nature with his own:
Amid his wild-wood sights he lived alone.
As if the poppy felt with him! Though he   705
Partook the poppy's red effrontery
Till Autumn spoiled their fleering quite with rain,
And, turbanless, a coarse brown rattling crane
Lay bare. That 's gone: yet why renounce, for
    that,
His disenchanted tributaries—flat   710
Perhaps, but scarce so utterly forlorn,
Their simple presence might not well be borne
Whose parley was a transport once: recall
The poppy's gifts, it flaunts you, after all,
A poppy:—why distrust the evidence   715
Of each soon satisfied and healthy sense?

But it comes; and   The new-born judgment answered, "little boots
new-born judgment   "Beholding other creatures' attributes
"And having none!" or, say that it sufficed,
"Yet, could one but possess, oneself," (enticed   720
Judgment) "some special office!" Nought beside

703 *1840* their natures with his own; *1863,1865* their natures with his
own: 704 *1840* alone: 707 *1840* Autumn spoils   709 *1840* Protrudes:
that's gone! *1863,1865* Lay bare. That's gone!   712 *1840* presence may
not   715 *1840–65* poppy: why   717 *1840* Judgment answered: little
1863,1865 judgment answered: "little   719 *1840* none: or say   720 *1840*
Yet, ... oneself,   721 *1840* some special office!

  701 *his companions*: inanimate objects, such as the poppies, which his imagination had endowed with fanciful qualities.
  708 *crane*: 'skull?', *1840 proof*, a correct conjecture. Domett was also puzzled:
he deletes the 'r' of 'crane' and puts an 'o' in the opposite margin.
  709 *yet why renounce*: even though he now saw natural objects as they really
were, and no longer imagined them his subjects (as if enchanted), or beings
with whom he could converse, were they not still satisfying to his senses?
  710 *his disenchanted tributaries*: the natural objects which he had fancied his
subjects but which are now released from the enchantment.
  712 *Their simple presence*: i.e. it was something that such things as poppies
remained to him, although he no longer fancied himself in communication
with them.
  713–14 *recall | The poppy's gifts*: take away the imaginary qualities with
which your fancy has endowed the poppy.
  714 *it flaunts you*: a type of locution familiar in Shakespeare. Cf. 'He pluckt
me ope his doublet': *Julius Caesar* I. ii. 264.
  after all: after these words Domett wrote 'Conscious of *himself*', apparently
misunderstanding the passage.
  721 *office*: function.

Serves you? "Well then, be somehow justified
"For this ignoble wish to circumscribe
"And concentrate, rather than swell, the tribe
725 "Of actual pleasures: what, now, from without
"Effects it?—proves, despite a lurking doubt,
"Mere sympathy sufficient, trouble spared?
"That, tasting joys by proxy thus, you fared
"The better for them?" Thus much craved his
    soul.
730 Alas, from the beginning love is whole
And true; if sure of nought beside, most sure
Of its own truth at least; nor may endure
A crowd to see its face, that cannot know
How hot the pulses throb its heart below:
735 While its own helplessness and utter want
Of means to worthily be ministrant
To what it worships, do but fan the more
Its flame, exalt the idol far before
Itself as it would have it ever be.
740 Souls like Sordello, on the contrary,
Coerced and put to shame, retaining will,

722 *1840* Well   727 *1840* spared;   728 *1840* —He tasted joys by proxy,
clearly fared   *1863* That tasting joys by proxy thus, you fared   *729 {Read-
ing of *1863*,*1865*,*1889*}   *1840* The better for them; thus . . . . soul.   *1868–88*
"The better for them?" Thus . . . . soul, {Comma corrected in Dykes Campbell copy.}   730 *1840* Love   *734 {Reading of *1889*}   *1840* below;
1863–88 below. {Full-stop altered to colon in Dykes Campbell copy.}
739 *1840* would ever have it be;   741 *1840* Will,

722 *"Well then*: Sordello is debating with himself. His 'new-born judgment'
asks how he can justify his apparently ignoble desire to concentrate pleasures,
rather than increasing their number. Outside himself, what is there that gives
him this wish and persuades him (in spite of lurking doubts) that 'mere
sympathy' is sufficient and that he need take no action? What proves that he is
any the better for the delights which he enjoys only in imagination?
729 *craved his soul*: normally the world would quickly have put an end to
Sordello's solitary communion with nature, but even in his case time performed that office. He realized how absurd many of his fancies had been. He
realized that his soul craved for love.
738 *exalt the idol*: it is characteristic of love to idolize its object and suppose it
greatly superior to itself, as it wishes it always to remain.
740 *on the contrary*: cf. the difference between the two classes of lovers of
beauty at ll. 467 ff. and ll. 523 ff. Unlike members of the 'gentler class', men like
Sordello are unabashed: they retain a strong Will (so capitalized in *1840*) and are
not easily daunted, but they are anxious to gain the recognition of others, 'a
crowd'. Shallow critics put this down to vanity.

Care little, take mysterious comfort still,
But look forth tremblingly to ascertain
If others judge their claims not urged in vain,
decides that And say for them their stifled thoughts aloud.   745
he needs So, they must ever live before a crowd:
sympathizers. —"Vanity," Naddo tells you.

                           Whence contrive
A crowd, now? From these women just alive,
That archer-troop? Forth glided—not alone
Each painted warrior, every girl of stone,   750
Nor Adelaide (bent double o'er a scroll,
One maiden at her knees, that eve, his soul
Shook as he stumbled through the arras'd glooms
On them, for, 'mid quaint robes and weird
    perfumes,
Started the meagre Tuscan up,—her eyes,   755
The maiden's, also, bluer with surprise)
—But the entire out-world: whatever, scraps
And snatches, song and story, dreams perhaps,
Conceited the world's offices, and he
Had hitherto transferred to flower or tree,   760
Nor counted a befitting heritage

---

744 *1840* vain   745 *1840* —Will say . . . . aloud;   746 *1840* So
they   747 *1840* Vanity,   748 *1840* now? These brave women   751 *1840*
—Nor Adelaide bent   752 *1840* eve   755 *1840* up (her eyes   757 *1840*
whatever   760 *1840* Transferred to the first comer, flower   *761 {Read-
ing of *1840–68*}   *1888,1889* Not counted

748 *these women*: the 'foreign women-servants, very old' of l. 622 and the
archers of l. 659. But he also enlists other auditors such as the warriors on the
tapestries, the Caryatides, Adelaide and the girl he had seen with her, and 'the
entire out-world'. The only earlier instance of this last word in OED is in
Henry More's poem, 'Resolution'. Two copies of More's scarce and obscure
Philosophicall Poems (1647) are listed in *Browning Collections*, p. 118, though we
do not know when Browning acquired them. The word has neo-Platonic
overtones: cf. 'out-soul' at iii. 317, 320. Cf. v. 43 n., below.
753 *arras 'd glooms*: 'glooms' occurs nine times in Keats, 'arras' once, memorably, in *The Eve of St. Agnes*, 358. OED has no example of 'arras'd' between
Chapman and D. G. Rossetti, who no doubt took it from here.
759 *Conceited*: gave a conception of. *SB* expands 'he / Transferred' to 'he
hitherto had transferred'. All the qualities or characteristics Sordello had
gained any conception of from his limited experience, his reading and his
dreams, and which he had previously fancifully associated with natural objects,
now presented themselves to his mind individually, so giving him a highly
schematized notion of human life.
761 *Nor counted*: 'nor was it enough to dower every individual flower & tree

Each, of its own right, singly to engage
Some man, no other,—such now dared to stand
Alone. Strength, wisdom, grace on every hand
765 Soon disengaged themselves, and he discerned
A sort of human life: at least, was turned
A stream of lifelike figures through his brain.
Lord, liegeman, valvassor and suzerain,
Ere he could choose, surrounded him; a stuff
770 To work his pleasure on; there, sure enough: *He therefore*
But as for gazing, what shall fix that gaze?   *creates such a*
Are they to simply testify the ways   *company;*
He who convoked them sends his soul along
With the cloud's thunder or a dove's
      brood-song?
—While they live each his life, boast each his
775   own
Peculiar dower of bliss, stand each alone
In some one point where something dearest
      loved
Is easiest gained—far worthier to be proved
Than aught he envies in the forest-wights!
780 No simple and self-evident delights,

---

763 *1840* Some Man, no other; such availed to stand   764 *1840* Alone:
strength,   ·765 *1840* themselves;   767 *1840* brain   768 *1840* —Lord,
Liegeman, Valvassor and Suzerain,   775 *1840* While they live each its life,
boast each its own

---

with the attributes of one individual Man, & with those of no other—but these
flowers & trees would stand alone [?]': Domett.
   763 *such availed to stand* (*1840*): *SB* adds a comma, and 'now', at the end of the
line.
   767 *A stream*: as in a magic lantern, or a diorama: see 30 n., above.
   768 *valvassor and suzerain*: the former is 'a feudal tenant ranking immediately
below a baron' (OED), the latter a feudal overlord.
   769–70 *a stuff / To work his pleasure on*: by providing him with subject-
matter. The question 'what shall fix that gaze?' probably means 'what was to
draw his particular attention?' and not (as Duff supposes) 'how is he to fix the
gaze of all upon himself?' Are such creatures simply to testify to his profound
sympathy with the world of external nature? Is each of them merely to embody
some one of his own sources of bliss?—something much more profound than
the qualities with which (for example) he had endowed the poppy?
   774 *a dove's brood-song*: cf. the last line of 'A Forest Thought': 'And the
brood-song of the cushat-dove!' (Vol. I, p. 543).
   777 *In some one point*: cf. Charlotte Brontë, *Villette*, ch. iv: 'my feelings . . .
had their object; which, in its single self, was dear to me, as, to the majority of
men and women, are all the unnumbered points on which they dissipate their
regard'.

But mixed desires of unimagined range,
Contrasts or combinations, new and strange,
Irksome perhaps, yet plainly recognized
By this, the sudden company—loves prized
By those who are to prize his own amount   785
Of loves. Once care because such make account,
Allow that foreign recognitions stamp
The current value, and his crowd shall vamp
Him counterfeits enough; and so their print
Be on the piece, 't is gold, attests the mint,   790
And "good," pronounce they whom his new
        appeal
Is made to: if their casual print conceal—
This arbitrary good of theirs o'ergloss
What he has lived without, nor felt the loss—
Qualities strange, ungainly, wearisome,   795

each of which,
leading its own
life,

—What matter? So must speech expand the
        dumb
Part-sigh, part-smile with which Sordello, late
Whom no poor woodland-sights could satiate,
Betakes himself to study hungrily
Just what the puppets his crude phantasy   80c
Supposes notablest,—popes, kings, priests,
        knights,—
May please to promulgate for appetites;
Accepting all their artificial joys
Not as he views them, but as he employs

787 *1840–68* Allow a foreign recognition stamp   788 *1840* and your
crowd   789 *1840* You counterfeits   791 *1840* And good, ... whom my
new   794 *1840* What I have lived . . . . felt my loss— *1863–68* What he
have lived . . . . felt the loss—   798 *1840–68* No foolish woodland-
sights   801 *1840–68* notablest, ... knights,

784 *the sudden company*: the audience he has swiftly summoned for himself,
which is to appreciate the beings he has created.
786 *Once care*: once he takes into account the opinions of such an audience, he
will find that base coin suffices.
796 *What matter?*: what does it matter if they are content with counterfeit, the
value of which depends on ignoring his deeper and much less attainable
aspirations? Such (at least) is the best way I can put into words the wry
reflections of Sordello, no longer satisfied and more than satisfied with his
loved woodland-sights, as he tried eagerly to understand the desires of men
such as his raw imagination considered most important in this world. (He did
not share their own estimate of their 'artificial joys', but accepted them merely
for his own dramatic purposes.)

805 Each shape to estimate the other's stock
 Of attributes, whereon—a marshalled flock
 Of authorized enjoyments—he may spend
 Himself, be men, now, as he used to blend
 With tree and flower—nay more entirely, else
810 'T were mockery: for instance, "How excels
 "My life that chieftain's?" (who apprised the
  youth
 Ecelin, here, becomes this month, in truth,
 Imperial Vicar?) "Turns he in his tent
 "Remissly? Be it so—my head is bent
815 "Deliciously amid my girls to sleep.
 "What if he stalks the Trentine-pass? Yon steep *has qualities*
 "I climbed an hour ago with little toil: *impossible to a*
 "We are alike there. But can I, too, foil *boy,*
 "The Guelf's paid stabber, carelessly afford
820 "Saint Mark's a spectacle, the sleight o' the
  sword
 "Baffling the treason in a moment?" Here
 No rescue! Poppy he is none, but peer

806 *1840–68* attributes, that on a 807 *1840–68* enjoyments 808 *1840*
Men, 810 *1840* how *1863–68* "how 811 *1840* Chieftain's? 812 *1840*
month 813 *1840* Turns 815 *1840* sleep: 817 *1840–65* toil— 818
1840 there: 819 *1840,1863* Guelfs' 820 *1840* St. Mark's 821 *1840*
Baffling their project in a moment? *1863,1865* Baffling their project in a
moment?"

807 *authorized*: because acceptable (as he imagines) to his audience.
808 *be men*: he now wishes to be a dramatic poet, no longer one who is
concerned only with trees and flowers.
810 *"How excels*: how does the life of the mighty Ecelin (the Monk) excel my
own? he wonders, with youthful arrogance. According to the *Biographie
Universelle* ('Romano') Ecelin became the Emperor's 'vicaire impérial' in or
about 1209. 'Ecelin accompanied Otho IV to Rome, and received from him, on
his return, the government of Vicenza, as imperial vicar'. Sismondi, the author
of this article, gives 4 October 1209 as the date of Otho's coronation in his
Histoire, ii. 525. Cf. note to line 570.
814 *Remissly*: negligently, in a carefree manner.
815 *my girls*: the Caryatides.
816 *the Trentine-pass*: the Ghibellins were obliged to keep open their com-
munications with Germany.
819 *The Guelf's paid stabber*: Sismondi describes how, in 1209, Ecelin declared
in Otho's presence that while they were walking together in Saint Mark's
Square Azzo VI had had him attacked by assassins: *Histoire* ii. 330–1. Maurisius
has an account of the attack in his *Historia*, in Muratori viii. 19.
821–2 *Here / No rescue!*: even he cannot imagine himself Ecelin's equal in this,
as he cannot handle a sword or bow like that great powerful man. He therefore
returns to the realm of the imagination. After 826 (at the foot of p. 35) Domett

To Ecelin, assuredly: his hand,
Fashioned no otherwise, should wield a brand
With Ecelin's success—try, now! He soon   825
Was satisfied, returned as to the moon
From earth; left each abortive boy's-attempt
For feats, from failure happily exempt,
In fancy at his beck. "One day I will
"Accomplish it! Are they not older still   830
"—Not grown-up men and women? 'T is beside
"Only a dream; and though I must abide
"With dreams now, I may find a thorough vent
"For all myself, acquire an instrument
"For acting what these people act; my soul   835
"Hunting a body out may gain its whole
"Desire some day!" How else express chagrin
And resignation, show the hope steal in
With which he let sink from an aching wrist

so, only to be The rough-hewn ash-bow? Straight, a gold shaft
appropriated in   hissed   840
fancy,
Into the Syrian air, struck Malek down
Superbly! "Crosses to the breach! God's Town
"Is gained him back!" Why bend rough
          ash-bows more?
     Thus lives he: if not careless as before,
Comforted: for one may anticipate,   845
Rehearse the future, be prepared when fate

829 *1840* One   836 *1840* out, obtain its   *1863* out, may gain its   837
1840 day!   840 *1840* ash bow, and a gold   *1863* ash bow? straight, a gold
1865 ash-bow? straight, a gold   842 *1840* Crosses   843 *1840* Was gained
Him back!   *1863* Is gained Him back!"   844 *1840* So lives   846 *1840*
future;   *1863* Future,

comments: 'the growth of the habit of satisfying himself with *imaginary*
pleasures & triumphs—& waking up with them for the unattainable real is well
imagined'.
     834 *acquire an instrument*: acquire a body which will serve my soul.
     840 *ash-bow*: the boy's bow which he actually possessed, in contrast to the
fine bow he dreamed of owning.
     841 *Malek*: a generic name for a Moorish or Saracen chief. Cf. vi. 130: 'Makes
havoc soon with Malek and his Moors'. Sordello is imagining himself a hero
on a Crusade.
     842 *Crosses*: wearers of the Cross, fighting to capture Jerusalem. Sismondi
habitually calls the crusaders 'les croisés'. Roscoe has 'all the Crosses' in his
translation of Sismondi's *Dè la littérature du Midi de l'Europe* (London, 3 vols.,
1823), i. 149.

Shall have prepared in turn real men whose
    names
Startle, real places of enormous fames,
Este abroad and Ecelin at home
850   To worship him,—Mantua, Verona, Rome
To witness it. Who grudges time so spent?
Rather test qualities to heart's content—
Summon them, thrice selected, near and far—
Compress the starriest into one star,
And grasp the whole at once!
855   The pageant thinned
Accordingly; from rank to rank, like wind
His spirit passed to winnow and divide;
Back fell the simpler phantasms; every side
The strong clave to the wise; with either classed
860   The beauteous; so, till two or three amassed
Mankind's beseemingnesses, and reduced
Themselves eventually,—graces loosed,
Strengths lavished,—all to heighten up One
    Shape
Whose potency no creature should escape.
865   Can it be Friedrich of the bowmen's talk?
Surely that grape-juice, bubbling at the stalk,
Is some grey scorching Saracenic wine
The Kaiser quaffs with the Miramoline—
Those swarthy hazel-clusters, seamed and
    chapped,

849,850 *1840* Estes abroad and Ecelins at home|To worship him, Mantuas,
Veronas, Rome   854 *1840* star   855 *1840* So grasp . . . . once! The
pageant's thinned {No paragraph division.}   862 *1840–68* eventually,   863 *1840–68* And lavished strengths, to   864 *1840* escape:

---

847 *real men*: in the future (as he fancies) he will be admired by real men of
fame, as distinct from the imaginary audience he has had to be content with so
far.

849 *Este*: see note to l. 103.   853 *Summon them*: cf. l. 32.
thrice: rigorously winnowed.   854 *starriest*: most glorious.
861 *Mankind's beseemingnesses*: all the qualities that become a man.
866 *that grape-juice*: he imagines that the grape-juice which is before him is a
rare wine: 'the stalk' is that of a glass. The 'grey scorching Saracenic wine' is
not likely to be identified.
868 *Miramoline*: 'not the name of a person, but a title, *quasi, Soldan*. The
Arabs call it Emir-Almoumini, *the Emperor of the Faithful*': W. J. Mickle, *The
Lusiad of Camoëns* (3rd edn., 2 vols., 1798), i. p. 116 n.
869 *hazel-clusters*: he imagines that the nuts he sees are dates from a bough

Or filberts russet-sheathed and velvet-capped,   870
Are dates plucked from the bough John Brienne
     sent
To keep in mind his sluggish armament
Of Canaan:—Friedrich's, all the pomp and
     fierce

and practised on
till the real come.

Demeanour! But harsh sounds and sights
     transpierce
So rarely the serene cloud where he dwells   875
Whose looks enjoin, whose lightest words are
     spells
On the obdurate! That right arm indeed
Has thunder for its slave; but where 's the need
Of thunder if the stricken multitude
Hearkens, arrested in its angriest mood,   880
While songs go up exulting, then dispread,
Dispart, disperse, lingering overhead
Like an escape of angels? 'T is the tune,
Nor much unlike the words his women croon
Smilingly, colourless and faint-designed   885
Each, as a worn-out queen's face some remind
Of her extreme youth's love-tales. "Eglamor

---

873 *1840* Canaan . . . *1863,1865* Canaan.—   877 *1840* Upon the obdurate; that arm   884 *1840–68* words the women   887 *1840* Eglamor

(apparently unhistorical) John of Brienne had sent Friedrich to remind him of
his promise to go on a crusade. Cf. l. 194.
   873–4 *the pomp and fierce / Demeanour!*: 'In imagination Emperor': Domett.
   876 *enjoin*: he thinks of himself as having a commanding eye.
   877 *Upon the obdurate (1840)*: *SB* has 'Up' deleted and a line to indicate the
pronunciation 'obdúrate', which is Johnson's.
   877 *That right arm*: 'Friedrich's': *SB*.
   881 *While songs go up*: he need not emulate the military might of the
Emperor, if his poetry is even more powerful. 'Dispread' and 'dispart' both
occur in *The Faerie Queene* and in Thomson's *Seasons*: the former is also used at
i. 225, iii. 593 and vi. 186, the latter at ii. 177 and iii. 594 (and *Paracelsus*, ii. 538).
Cf. note to iii. 593–5, below. *SB* has 'by the lute' between 880 and 881.
   885 *faint-designed*: i.e. faded.
   887 *Eglamor*: now first mentioned: prominent in Book II. As a youth,
Sordello derives his notion of poetry from the songs of this popular poet, as
sung by the women-servants. As is natural, he begins by imitating Eglamor's
songs. Browning may conceivably have found the name in the essay 'On the
Ancient Metrical Romances' which Thomas Percy included in his *Reliques of
Ancient English Poetry*, where we hear of a poem, '*Eglamour of Artas* (or *Artoys*)':
2nd edn. (1767), vol. iii. p. xxviii.

"Made that!" Half minstrel and half emperor,
What but ill objects vexed him? Such he slew.
890 The kinder sort were easy to subdue
By those ambrosial glances, dulcet tones;
And these a gracious hand advanced to thrones
Beneath him. Wherefore twist and torture this,
Striving to name afresh the antique bliss,
895 Instead of saying, neither less nor more,
He had discovered, as our world before,
Apollo? That shall be the name; nor bid
Me rag by rag expose how patchwork hid
The youth—what thefts of every clime and day
900 Contributed to purfle the array
He climbed with (June at deep) some close
    ravine
'Mid clatter of its million pebbles sheen,
Over which, singing soft, the runnel slipped
Elate with rains: into whose streamlet dipped
He foot, yet trod, you thought, with unwet
905   sock—
Though really on the stubs of living rock

He means to be perfect—say, Apollo:

888 *1840* Made that!   889 *1840* Who but   899 *1840* The man—
what   901 *1840* He climbs with (June's   *902 {Reading of *1840–68*}
1888,1889 Mid   903 *1840* Over which singing soft the runnel slipt
1863,1865 Over which, singing soft, the runnel slipt   904 *1840–65*
dipt   906 *1840 proof* rook>rock

---

888 *Half minstrel*: he imagines himself half a poet and half an emperor, a
beneficent world-dictator.
897 *Apollo*: the type of perfection, to which he now absurdly aspires. 'His
great dexterity in the management of the bow is celebrated; and in every part of
the world he received homage as the president of the Muses, the oracle of poets
and musicians, and the patron of every liberal and ingenious profession in arts
and science': Lemprière. As Mrs Orr comments, Sordello craves for 'that
magnitude of poetic existence, which means all love and all knowledge, as all
beauty and all power in itself': *Handbook*, p. 33. Domett: 'then adds poetry &
becomes Apollo—careering with the sun'. At iii. 50–1 Sordello no longer
imagines himself Apollo.
898 *how patchwork hid*: how he contrived to patch himself up with borrowings from every country and age to make him seem (at least to himself) a very
Apollo.
900 *to purfle*: to decorate with an ornamental border.
901 *(June at deep)*: in the depth of June.
904 *Elate*: swollen (Latin 'elatus').
905 *with unwet sock*: he trod so joyously that you would have thought he was
not even getting his feet wet, although in fact he was walking on the rock made
jagged by the water ages before. Cf. Cary, *Hell*, ix. 80: 'Who passed with
unwet feet the Stygian sound'.

Ages ago it crenelled; vines for roof,
Lindens for wall; before him, aye aloof,
Flittered in the cool some azure damsel-fly,
Born of the simmering quiet, there to die.   910
Emerging whence, Apollo still, he spied
Mighty descents of forest; multiplied
Tuft on tuft, here, the frolic myrtle-trees,
There gendered the grave maple stocks at ease.
And, proud of its observer, straight the wood   915
Tried old surprises on him; black it stood
A sudden barrier ('twas a cloud passed o'er)
So dead and dense, the tiniest brute no more
Must pass; yet presently (the cloud dispatched)
Each clump, behold, was glistering detached   920
A shrub, oak-boles shrunk into ilex-stems!
Yet could not he denounce the stratagems
He saw thro', till, hours thence, aloft would hang
White summer-lightnings; as it sank and sprang
To measure, that whole palpitating breast   925
Of heaven, 't was Apollo, nature prest
At eve to worship.
                              Time stole: by degrees

---

910 *1840* Child of . . . . die: *SB* Child>Born . . . . die: [; i' the simmering green]   914 *1840* ease;   915 *1840–65* strait   *1840* proof {'gh' inserted, but cancelled.}   920 *1840* clump, forsooth, was   925 *1840* In measure,

909 *damsel-fly*: 'the slender dragon-fly . . . and kindred species, called in French *demoiselle*': OED, which refers to Thomas Moore, *Lalla Rookh*, 'Paradise and the Peri' 407–8: 'The beautiful blue damsel-flies, / That flutter'd round the jasmine stems'. Moore has a note on the word, from the traveller Sonnini. Cf. Domett's reference to Moore's poem, in a comment on *Paracelsus*, iv. 536 given above.
910 *the simmering quiet*: a phrase admired by Elizabeth Barrett: 'your "*simmering* quiet" in Sordello, which brings the summer air into the room as sure as you read it': Kintner i. 130.
913 *frolic*: because they sway so gaily in the wind: cf. Milton, 'L'Allegro', 18: 'The frolic wind that breathes the spring'.
914 *gendered*: reproduced themselves.
916 *old surprises*: they had been familiar to him in his boyhood.
921 *oak-boles*: deliberately or inadvertently, a false antithesis is suggested, as 'ilex' here seems to be used in the sense of the holm-oak. The contrast of long vowels and short vowels enhances the apparent antithesis.
922 *Yet could not he denounce*: although he saw through these tricks of nature, he could not proclaim them as such until summer-lightning lit up the whole scene; and then, as the heavens palpitated, he fancied that the aim was to bring people to worship himself, Apollo.

The Pythons perish off; his votaries
Sink to respectful distance; songs redeem   *and Apollo*
Their pains, but briefer; their dismissals seem   *must one day find*
Emphatic; only girls are very slow   *Daphne.*
To disappear—his Delians! Some that glow
O' the instant, more with earlier loves to wrench
Away, reserves to quell, disdains to quench;
Alike in one material circumstance—
All soon or late adore Apollo! Glance
The bevy through, divine Apollo's choice,
His Daphne! "We secure Count Richard's voice
"In Este's counsels, good for Este's ends
"As our Taurello," say his faded friends,
"By granting him our Palma!"—the sole child,

930

935

940

928 *1840* perished off;   929 *1840* Sunk to   932 *1840* disappear: 938
1840 A Daphne! We   939 *1840* counsels, one for   940 *1840*
Taurello,   941 *1840* By . . . . Palma! The   *1863* "By . . . Palma!"—The
1865 "By . . . . Palma!" the

928 *The Pythons*: as he grew older his imaginary enemies died off. Cf.
Lemprière: 'As soon as he was born, Apollo destroyed with arrows the serpent
Python, which Juno had sent to persecute Latona' (Apollo's mother). Cf. 'The
Two Poets of Croisic', 966–7.
930 *but briefer*: he takes less trouble to write songs to please his admirers.
932 *his Delians*: the priestesses of Delos, the reputed birth-place of Apollo,
who worshipped him.
938 *Count Richard's voice*: according to the old women the plan is to win a
friend at Azzo's court by giving Count Richard Palma as his wife. Duff takes
'good for Este's ends / As our Taurello' to be ironical (since he hated the House
of Este); but the meaning may be that Richard is as important to Azzo as
Taurello is to Ecelin.
940 *his faded friends*: the 'sleepy women' of 945, who are gossiping idly. *SB*
adds: 'that were the one prize fit to buy such a happiness [?for] us. They must
keep him in expectation [?no] longer'.
941 *By granting him our Palma!*: the woman who is to love Sordello has
already appeared, anonymously, at 752. Historically, it was Cunizza with
whom Sordello absconded, and he took her from her husband Richard of St.
Boniface. Browning prefers the name of a sister or half-sister of hers, perhaps
because it is more harmonious: he comments on the change of name at v.
993–5. By the fourth and last of his wives, Adelaide, Ecelin the Monk had four
daughters, Palma 'Novella' (at i. 196 Verci states that the first Palma is said to
have been the child of Ecelin's first wife, Agnese), Imia or Emilia, Sofia, and
Cunizza. Cunizza becomes Browning's Palma, and he makes her the daughter
of Agnese. Cunizza was born 'about 1198' (Verci i. 115).
   The historical Cunizza was a remarkable person, 'one of the most celebrated
women of her century', as Verci remarks: i. 114. 'Dante places her in Paradise',
he continues, 'and in his ninth canto makes her predict some calamities which
are to befall the Trevisan March. He there sets her in the sphere of Venus, with
the precise intention of indicating that she was much given to the follies of love.
And in fact the amorous adventures which are related of this lady by historians,
and in particular by Rolandino, are something quite exceptional'. Verci discusses why Dante should have placed so amorous a woman in Paradise. He

They mean, of Agnes Este who beguiled
Ecelin, years before this Adelaide
Wedded and turned him wicked: "but the maid
"Rejects his suit," those sleepy women boast.   945
She, scorning all beside, deserves the most
Sordello: so, conspicuous in his world
Of dreams sat Palma. How the tresses curled
Into a sumptuous swell of gold and wound
About her like a glory! even the ground   950
Was bright as with spilt sunbeams; breathe not,
          breathe
Not!—poised, see, one leg doubled underneath,
Its small foot buried in the dimpling snow,
Rests, but the other, listlessly below,
O'er the couch-side swings feeling for cool air,   955
The vein-streaks swollen a richer violet where
The languid blood lies heavily; yet calm
On her slight prop, each flat and outspread palm,
As but suspended in the act to rise
By consciousness of beauty, whence her eyes   960
Turn with so frank a triumph, for she meets
Apollo's gaze in the pine glooms.

But when will this   Time fleets:
dream turn truth?
That 's worst! Because the pre-appointed age

---

944 *1840* wicked; but   945 *1840* suit,   947 *1840* so conspicuous   950
1840 glory,   951 *1840* with shed sunbeams; (breathe   952 *1840*
Not)—   956 *1840–65* swoln   957 *1840* and calm   *SB* and>
queenly   962 *1840* fleets

records that she had five husbands, 'if indeed all of them should be given such a
name'. Cf. Introduction, p. 165 above.
945 *"Rejects his suit*: this is the rumour that the women have heard. In the
poem Palma is betrothed to Richard (at Padua, it seems, a betrothal to be
confirmed at Verona: iii. 236–7, 507–8), but not yet married to him. Historically they were married, at a splendid wedding ceremony in 1221: the marriage
was short-lived, but she bore her husband a son.
950 *a glory*: a halo, as in *Paracelsus*, i. 417 and *The Eve of St. Agnes*, 222: 'And
on her hair a glory, like a saint'.
953 *the dimpling snow*: of her thigh. Cf. l. 415, above.
955 *swings*: 'is not this the attitude of the girl in a picture in the Louvre?':
Domett. If so, numerous enquiries have failed to identify it.
962 *Apollo's gaze*: because Sordello is dreaming that he is Apollo, and she his
Daphne: Cf. *Pauline*, 321–2.
Time fleets: before these words *SB* adds: 'each is happy up to this: only,'.

Approaches. Fate is tardy with the stage
965   And crowd she promised. Lean he grows and
        pale,
Though restlessly at rest. Hardly avail
Fancies to soothe him. Time steals, yet alone
He tarries here! The earnest smile is gone.
How long this might continue matters not;
970   —For ever, possibly; since to the spot
None come: our lingering Taurello quits
Mantua at last, and light our lady flits
Back to her place disburthened of a care.
Strange—to be constant here if he is there!
975   Is it distrust? Oh, never! for they both
Goad Ecelin alike, Romano's growth
Is daily manifest, with Azzo dumb
And Richard wavering: let but Friedrich come,
Find matter for the minstrelsy's report

965 *1840* She all but promised.   970 *1840* For   971 *1840* come: for
lingering   976 *1840–65* alike—   977 *1840* So daily manifest that Azzo's
dumb *1863,1865* as *1840*, except 'manifest,' *1868* Is daily manifest, and
Azzo's dumb   978 *1840* And Richard wavers . . . let . . . . come! *1863,1865*
And Richard wavers: let . . . . come! *1868* And Richard wavers: let . . . .
come,   979 *1840* —Find . . . . report *1863,1865* —Find . . . . report, *1868*
Find . . . . report!

964–5 *the stage | And crowd*: cf. 746 ff.
965 *Lean*: 'The soul endures but the body *changes*—even if for the better': *SB*.
973 *Back to her place*: 'in the world': *SB*. Adelaide returns to Mantua as soon
as Taurello leaves it. She is always 'here' in Goito when he is 'there' in Mantua.
The reason becomes evident at ii. 339 ff.
975 *Is it distrust?*: 'Is it that she does not wish to meet him in Mantua? The
lines following represent the general popular opinion, though there were not
lacking reports of Taurello's inclination to break away (Bk. II., l. 351.)': Duff.
Cf. ii. 342 n.
976 *Goad Ecelin alike*: Taurello and Adelaide are both strong supporters of
the House of Romano against the Guelfs as represented by Azzo and Count
Richard. If only the Emperor Friedrich will come, accompanied by
troubadours to celebrate his exploits, the day will be won! Cf. Ernst Kantorowicz, *Frederick the Second*, trans. E. O. Lorimer (1931), p. 105: 'the country
was seething with excitement, and people were just waiting in momentary
quiet to see which of the parties in upper Italy Frederick would elect to join. A
reputation for extraordinary vigour, courage and shrewdness had preceded the
King, spread during the recent years by the songs of the troubadours, as they
travelled from court to court of the north Italian nobility'.
Romano's growth: 'now that Taurello goads his soul . . .': *SB*.
979 *the minstrelsy's report*: cf. Sismondi, *Literature of the South*, i. 202: 'the
Provençal poetry, taking its rise in the eleventh century, and spreading
throughout the south of France, and over a portion of Spain and Italy, was the
delight of every court, animated all the festivals, and was familiar to all classes

—Lured from the Isle and its young Kaiser's
   court   980
To sing us a Messina morning up,
And, double rillet of a drinking cup,
Sparkle along to ease the land of drouth,
Northward to Provence that, and thus far south
The other! What a method to apprise   985
Neighbours of births, espousals, obsequies,
Which in their very tongue the Troubadour

---

980 *1840–65* Lured   981 *1840* up;   982 *1840* Who, double rillets   985
1840 proof apprize>apprise   *1840* other: what   *1863–68* other. What   986
1840–68 obsequies!

---

of the people'. Later Sismondi writes: 'All the north of Italy received with
eagerness the lessons of the Troubadours. Azzo VII. of Este, invited them to
the court of Ferrara': p. 231. He adds that 'The crusade against the Albigenses
. . . entirely put an end to the influence of the Provençals':
  980 *the Isle*: Sicily.
  981 *To sing . . . up*: perhaps 'to sing us an aubade in the manner they
practised in Messina'. Cf. such phrases as 'to sing down the sun' and 'sing in the
May'. At ii. 785 we have 'To sing us out . . . a mere romance'.
  982 *double rillet*: their songs will flow in two directions.
  987 *in their very tongue*: in Chapter iii of his *Historical View* Sismondi writes of
the diffusion of the Romance language, and describes how 'Thousands of poets
flourished, almost contemporaneously, in this new language' (p. 78), and how
'the birth of the Romance language in Gaul, preceded that of the Italian [and]
was divided into two principal dialects: the Romance-Provençal, spoken in all
the provinces to the south of the Loire . . and the Romance-Wallon, . . . to the
north of the Loire' (p. 84). He mentions that 'the Romance-Provençal, in the
kingdom of Arles, completely displaced the Latin' (p. 85). The last entries in
the chronological table at the end of vol. ii of his *Histoire des Républiques
Italiennes* are also relevant: 'Beginnings of Italian poetry in Sicily: the Provençal
language, cultivated at this time in Lombardy: Italian troubadours who wrote
in Provençal: Sordello of Mantua, the most celebrated of them all'. In Chapter
xv of this book Sismondi writes: 'The creation of Italian poetry, then, was in
some sort the work of the Kings of Sicily and their subjects: this advantage
which they had over the Italian republics must certainly be attributed in part to
the love of pleasure and of luxury which is only too common with poets, and
which has almost always led them to prefer the luxury and flattery of courts to
republican severity and equality' (p. 494). Here too he emphasizes the importance of Azzo VII, particularly naming Ugo Catola and Sordello as having
'gained a great reputation in the Lombard republics through their Provençal
songs': pp. 496–7. 'Sordello of Mantua', he writes, 'is enveloped in a mysterious obscurity: the writers of the following century speak of him with a
profound sentiment of respect, without giving us any information about his
life: those who came later made of him a generous warrior, a valiant defender
of his country: and some a Prince of Mantua. The nobility of his birth and his
marriage (or perhaps his love-affair) with a sister of Ecelin of Romano are
attested to us by contemporaries of his: his violent death is obscurely intimated
by the great Florentine poet; and the only titles to immortality which remain to
him today are the role which Dante makes him play and (above all) the manner
in which he depicts him when, ready to enter with Virgil the precinct of
Purgatory, he sees him some distance off': p. 497.

Records! and his performance makes a tour,
For Trouveres bear the miracle about,
990　Explain its cunning to the vulgar rout,
Until the Formidable House is famed
Over the country—as Taurello aimed,
Who introduced, although the rest adopt,
The novelty. Such games, her absence stopped,
995　Begin afresh now Adelaide, recluse
No longer, in the light of day pursues
Her plans at Mantua: whence an accident
Which, breaking on Sordello's mixed content,
Opened, like any flash that cures the blind,　　*For the time is*
1000　The veritable business of mankind.　　*ripe, and he ready.*

---

988 *1840–68* Records;　　994 *1840* Their games her absence stopped　*1865*
Such games her absence stopped,　　997 *1840* Mantua—　　*998 {Reading
of *1863–68*}　　*1840* That breaking . . . . content　　*1888,1889* Which, breaking
. . . content

---

988 *makes a tour*: travels far and wide. Cf. Carlyle, *The French Revolution*, Vol.
II, Bk. i, ch. v, para. 6: 'The Jacobins are buried; but their work . . . continues
"making the tour of the world"'.

989 *Trouveres*: Sismondi distinguishes the 'Trouveurs' from the
Troubadours by defining the former as 'the poets of the country to the north of
the Loire': *Literature of the South*, i. 11: cf. pp. 265 ff., and 310. In this poem,
however, a Trouvère is inferior to a Troubadour, almost as a Jongleur is: he is a
minstrel who sings songs written by a Troubadour: cf. ii. 82, ii. 186, iii. 222.

991 *the Formidable House*: that of Hohenstaufen. Members of this House
reigned from 1138 to 1250, but for the period 1198–1218.

993 *Who introduced*: cf. 987 n. Browning chooses to make Taurello the man
who promoted the poetry of the Troubadours, unhistorically.

997 *at Mantua*: *SB* adds: 'and elsewhere'.

998 *mixed content*: he is 'restlessly at rest' (966).

1000 *The veritable business*: at the foot of page 43, at the end of the Book, *SB*
has: 'Troubadours to the Ghibs what singers [?] & priests are to the Guelfs as
instruments.'

BOOK THE SECOND.

THE woods were long austere with snow: at last
Pink leaflets budded on the beech, and fast
Larches, scattered through pine-trees solitudes,
Brightened, "as in the slumbrous heart o' the
    woods
"Our buried year, a witch, grew young again   5
"To placid incantations, and that stain
"About were from her cauldron, green smoke
    blent
"With those black pines"—so Eglamor gave vent
To a chance fancy. Whence a just rebuke
From his companion; brother Naddo shook   10
The solemnest of brows: "Beware," he said,
"Of setting up conceits in nature's stead!"

This bubble of
fancy,
Forth wandered our Sordello. Nought so sure
As that to-day's adventure will secure
Palma, the visioned lady—only pass   15
O'er yon damp mound and its exhausted grass,
Under that brake where sundawn feeds the stalks
Of withered fern with gold, into those walks
Of pine and take her! Buoyantly he went.
Again his stooping forehead was besprent   20
With dew-drops from the skirting ferns. Then
    wide
Opened the great morass, shot every side

9 *1840* fancy: whence   11 *1840* brows; Beware, *1863–68* brows;
"Beware,"   12 *1840* Nature's stead!   15 *1840* the forest-lady—

2–3 *fast / Larches*: larches bud early.   8 *Eglamor*: see i. 887 n.
10 *Naddo*: see i. 693 n.
13 ∧ *Forth wandered*: 'Oh, this morn drew out many, among them': *SB*.
15 *visioned*: a word used by Shelley, e.g. in *Queen Mab*, ix. 179: 'visioned
bliss'.
17 *sundawn*: as in *Paracelsus* i. 104. After this line, at the foot of the page (44),
SB has: 'After the struggle to hold out [? through winter]'.
20 *besprent*: cf. Milton, *Comus*, 541: 'knot-grass dew-besprent'.
22 *shot*: variegated: cf. 'shot silk'.

With flashing water through and through;
    a-shine,
Thick-steaming, all-alive. Whose shape divine,
25   Quivered i' the farthest rainbow-vapour, glanced
Athwart the flying herons? He advanced,
But warily; though Mincio leaped no more,
Each foot-fall burst up in the marish-floor
A diamond jet: and if he stopped to pick
30   Rose-lichen, or molest the leeches quick,
And circling blood-worms, minnow, newt or
    loach,
A sudden pond would silently encroach
This way and that. On Palma passed. The verge
Of a new wood was gained. She will emerge
Flushed, now, and panting,—crowds to
35   see,—will own
She loves him—Boniface to hear, to groan,
To leave his suit! One screen of pine-trees still
Opposes: but—the startling spectacle—
Mantua, this time! Under the walls—a crowd
40   Indeed, real men and women, gay and loud
Round a pavilion. How he stood!

                    In truth   *when greatest and*
No prophecy had come to pass: his youth   *brightest, bursts.*
In its prime now—and where was homage
    poured
Upon Sordello?—born to be adored,
45   And suddenly discovered weak, scarce made

---

24 *1840,1863* divine   29 *1840* if you stopped   35 *1840* panting; crowds
to see;   40 *1840* Indeed—real men and women—

28 *the marish-floor*: *SB* has 'otter—' in the margin, and at the foot of the page
(45): 'sleek wet black & lithe as a leech—', a striking anticipation of 'Caliban
upon Setebos', 46. Cf. 954 n., below.
30 *leeches quick*: 'golden swarm of insects': *SB*.
31 *blood-worms*: OED defines blood-worm as 'The scarlet larva of a genus of
crane-flies . . . found in rain-water cisterns and pools'. For Browning's interest
in small creatures see *Paracelsus*, i. 39 n.
33 *Palma passed*: in Sordello's imagination.
36 *Boniface*: see notes to i. 102 and i. 941. Sordello dreams that Count Richard
will make way for him, finding that it is Sordello whom Palma loves.
41 *How he stood!*: 'His dream had swelled up to the Real, & burst': *SB*.
42 *No prophecy*: cf. i. 963 ff. So far the homage of which he has dreamed has
been paid him by no one.

To cope with any, cast into the shade
By this and this. Yet something seemed to prick
And tingle in his blood; a sleight—a trick—
And much would be explained. It went for
     nought—
The best of their endowments were ill bought   50
With his identity: nay, the conceit,
That this day's roving led to Palma's feet
Was not so vain—list! The word, "Palma!" Steal
Aside, and die, Sordello; this is real,
And this—abjure!
                         What next? The curtains see   55
Dividing! She is there; and presently
He will be there—the proper You, at length—
In your own cherished dress of grace and
     strength:
Most like, the very Boniface!
                              Not so.
It was a showy man advanced; but though   60
A glad cry welcomed him, then every sound
Sank and the crowd disposed themselves around,
—"This is not he," Sordello felt; while, "Place
"For the best Troubadour of Boniface!"
At a court of love, Hollaed the Jongleurs,—"Eglamor, whose lay   65
a minstrel sings.   "Concludes his patron's Court of Love to-day!"

---

51 *1840* conceit   52 *1840* This present roving leads to   53 *1840* vain . . .
list! The word, Palma?   55 *1840–65* curtains, see,   59 *1840* Most like the
very Boniface . . .   63 *1840* —This is not he,   64 *1840* Boniface,"   65
1840 Jongleurs, "Eglamor   66 *1840* to-day."

---

48 *a sleight*: if he could only get the knack of it, it would prove the clue to a
great deal. But in any case he would rather remain himself.
51 *the conceit*: the notion.
53–5 *Steal . . . abjure!*: the comment of the narrator, who knows that
Sordello is ill equipped to deal with reality.
57 *the proper You*: such a hero as Sordello had dreamed of becoming . . .
Probably this will be Boniface himself!
65 *the Jongleurs*: 'The Jongleurs . . . were a set of men, who went about
singing or reciting the compositions of the Troubadours, and who sometimes
aspired at the rewards and honours of both professions': *The Literary History of
the Troubadours . . . Collected and Abridged from the French of Mr. De Saint-Pelaie*,
by Mrs Susanna Dobson (1779), p. [v]. Cf. p. 173, above.
66 *Court of Love*: 'When the haughty baron invited to his court the neighbouring lords and the knights his vassals, three days were devoted to jousts and
tourneys . . . The lady of the castle, surrounded by youthful beauties, . . then,

Obsequious Naddo strung the master's lute
With the new lute-string, "Elys," named to suit
The song: he stealthily at watch, the while,
70   Biting his lip to keep down a great smile
Of pride: then up he struck. Sordello's brain
Swam; for he knew a sometime deed again;
So, could supply each foolish gap and chasm
The minstrel left in his enthusiasm,
75   Mistaking its true version—was the tale
Not of Apollo? Only, what avail
Luring her down, that Elys an he pleased,
If the man dared no further? Has he ceased?
And, lo, the people's frank applause half done,
80   Sordello was beside him, had begun
(Spite of indignant twitchings from his friend
The Trouvere) the true lay with the true end,   *Sordello, before*
Taking the other's names and time and place   *Palma, conquers*
                                                    him,

---

67 *1840* strung his master's   68 *1840* Elys,   *78 {Reading of
1863–68} *1840* man dares no further? Has he ceased? *1888,1889* man dared no
further? Has he ceased

in her turn, opened her . . . Court of Love . . . A new career was opened to
those who dared the combat, not of arms but of verse, and the name of *Tenson*,
which was given to these dramatic skirmishes, in fact signified a contest':
Sismondi, *Historical View*, i. 136–7. At the end of the line *SB* has: 'For this was
&c'.
    67 *the master's lute*: modern scholars doubt whether troubadours accom-
panied themselves, and point out that in any case it could not have been with a
lute. Poets of the early nineteenth century had no such doubts, however: see,
e.g., *The Troubadour*, by L[etitia] E[lizabeth] L[andon] (1825), p. 12.
    68 *"Elys"*: the name of the lady whom Eglamor is praising. When Dowden
asked Browning about this passage, he replied: '"Elys," then, is merely the
ideal subject, with such a name, of Eglamor's poem—and referred to in the
other places as his type of perfection, realised according to his [limited] faculty
(El lys—the Lily)': *Letters*, p. 92. For the other references see ii. 77, 139, 151; iii.
107; and v. 245, 257 and 905. The name Elys, variously spelled, occurs in
several of the poems of the Troubadours, with particular reference to Elis,
Countess of Flanders. The notion of a lute-string with a name is strange.
    71 *he struck*: *SB* has an interesting note: 'Describe the song of Elys, Mesmeric
song—at the beginning. How it operated at first'. Below this *SB* has: '(The
way was to challenge anyone to go beyond *that*)'.
    72 *he knew*: he recognised something he already knew, the story of Apollo
and Daphne: cf. lines 129 ff.
    76 *what avail*: what point was there in singing about such perfection ('Elys',
as Eglamor was pleased to term it) if he was so timid in his attempt?
    82 *the true lay with the true end*: Browning may have read how Wolfram von
Eschenbach implies, at the end of *Parzival*, that Chrétien de Troyes had told the
story wrongly, but that he himself has told it aright (with the aid of Kyot of
Provence, who had it from the Arabic).

For his. On flew the song, a giddy race,
After the flying story; word made leap   85
Out word, rhyme—rhyme; the lay could barely
    keep
Pace with the action visibly rushing past:
Both ended. Back fell Naddo more aghast
Than some Egyptian from the harassed bull
That wheeled abrupt and, bellowing, fronted full 90
His plague, who spied a scarab 'neath the tongue,
And found 't was Apis' flank his hasty prong
Insulted. But the people—but the cries,
The crowding round, and proffering the prize!
receives the prize,   —For he had gained some prize. He seemed to
and ruminates.   shrink   95
Into a sleepy cloud, just at whose brink
One sight withheld him. There sat Adelaide,
Silent; but at her knees the very maid
Of the North Chamber, her red lips as rich,
The same pure fleecy hair; one weft of which,   100
Golden and great, quite touched his cheek as o'er
She leant, speaking some six words and no more.
He answered something, anything; and she
Unbound a scarf and laid it heavily
Upon him, her neck's warmth and all. Again   10

---

89 *1840* Than your Egyptian   90 *1840* That wheels . . . . fronts full   91
1840 who spies a scarab 'neath his tongue,   *1863,1865* who spied a scarab 'neath
his tongue,   92 *1840* And finds 'twas   94 *1840* And crowding   95
1840–65 (For he had gained some prize)—He   97 *1840* him; there   100
1840 one curl of   102 *1840* more;   105 *1840* all; again

---

88 *more aghast*: brackets from here to the word 'Insulted' at 93 might help the
reader. Apis, as Lemprière records, was 'a god of the Egyptians, worshipped
under the form of an ox'. One of the distinguishing marks by which a
particular ox was chosen for worship was 'a knot under the tongue like a
beetle'. Here, as 'some Egyptian' is tormenting a bull (cf. 1016 below), he
suddenly recognises that it is Apis. The strange choice of simile may have been
influenced by the fact that Apollo was sometimes believed to have been the
father of another Apis, 'one of the ancient kings of Peloponnesus'. Cf.
Herodotus iii. 28, Pliny viii. 71, and Shelley, 'The Witch of Atlas', 627–8.
    98 *the very maid*: cf. i. 752. She is Palma: ii. 51 ff.
    105 *her neck's warmth*: cf. Madeline's 'warmed jewels' in *The Eve of St. Agnes*,
228. In 1875 Domett mentioned to Browning 'the absurdity of the praise
Swinburne . . . had bestowed on the idea in Rossetti's *Blessed Damozel*, of the
Damozel's arm resting on the Bar of Heaven and "making it warm!"—a fancy

Moved the arrested magic; in his brain
Noises grew, and a light that turned to glare,
And greater glare, until the intense flare
Engulfed him, shut the whole scene from his
     sense.
110 And when he woke 't was many a furlong
     thence,
At home; the sun shining his ruddy wont;
The customary birds'-chirp; but his front
Was crowned—was crowned! Her scented scarf
     around
His neck! Whose gorgeous vesture heaps the
     ground?
115 A prize? He turned, and peeringly on him
Brooded the women-faces, kind and dim,
Ready to talk—"The Jongleurs in a troop
"Had brought him back, Naddo and
     Squarcialupe
"And Tagliafer; how strange! a childhood spent
120 "In taking, well for him, so brave a bent!
"Since Eglamor," they heard, "was dead with
     spite,
"And Palma chose him for her minstrel."

                                        Light

---

109 *1840* sense,   117 *1840* talk. The   *1863–68* talk.—"The   120 *1840*
Assuming, well   121 *1840* Since Eglamor, they heard, was   122 *1840*
minstrel.

---

after all originally and infinitely better given in *Sordello* . . . Browning said he
was afraid I was going to quiz the notion . . .': *Diary*, pp. 164–5.
  112 *The customary birds'-chirp*: *SB* indicates an addition here: 'round the patch
of cress in the castle-chink'.
  front: forehead, as at 939.
  114 *vesture*: as well as a crown, he has been awarded garments proper to
Palma's minstrel.
  118 *Squarcialupe*: an imaginary jongleur: cf. 1. 783 below, and v. 1014 and n.
Browning had probably come on the name as he worked on *Paracelsus*, on the
title-page of *De Cometis Dissertationes Novae Clariss. Virorum Thom. Erasti,
Andr. Dudithij, Marc. Squarcialupi, Symon. Grynaei* ('Ex officina Leonardi
Ostenij', 1580).
  119 *Tagliafer*: another imaginary jongleur, perhaps named after the minstrel
who sang at the battle of Hastings. Whyte (p. 8) mentions that the name occurs
in Verci, in another connection.
  120 *so brave a bent*: he has developed in such a splendid manner. Cf. iii. 358
('Palma's bent'), v. 686, and *Paracelsus*, iii. 597. 'Now, that would exactly do. a
minstrel was . . . . a fantastic king of men': *SB*.
  121 *with spite*: he was dead, but not with spite: see 242 ff.

How had he been superior to Eglamor?

Sordello rose—to think, now; hitherto
He had perceived. Sure, a discovery grew
Out of it all! Best live from first to last   125
The transport o'er again. A week he passed,
Sucking the sweet out of each circumstance,
From the bard's outbreak to the luscious trance
Bounding his own achievement. Strange! A man
Recounted an adventure, but began   130
Imperfectly; his own task was to fill
The frame-work up, sing well what he sung ill,
Supply the necessary points, set loose
As many incidents of little use
—More imbecile the other, not to see   135
Their relative importance clear as he!
But, for a special pleasure in the act
Of singing—had he ever turned, in fact,
From Elys, to sing Elys?—from each fit
Of rapture to contrive a song of it?   140
True, this snatch or the other seemed to wind
Into a treasure, helped himself to find
A beauty in himself; for, see, he soared
By means of that mere snatch, to many a hoard
Of fancies; as some falling cone bears soft   145
The eye along the fir-tree-spire, aloft
To a dove's nest. Then, how divine the cause
Why such performance should exact applause
From men, if they had fancies too? Did fate
Decree they found a beauty separate   150

---

130 *1840* Recounted that adventure, and began   132 *1840,1863* sang ill,   137 *1840* But   145 *1840* bears oft   148 *1840* Such a performance should exact   *1863–68* Such a performance might exact   149 *1840* From men if they have fancies too? Can Fate   *1863–68* From men, if they had fancies too? Could fate   150 *1840* they find a

---

127 *each circumstance*: 'The triumph was good for *him*—but why had it been [illegible] by them?': *SB*.
129 *Strange!*: 'he summed it up on a bank [illegible]': *SB*.
133 *set loose*: drop.
137 *But, for a special pleasure*: '(apart from his getting the triumph)': *SB*. Sordello had sung well on a subject about which Eglamor had sung indifferently, but had he ever given his mind to the art of creating a song?
145–6 *bears soft | The eye*: leads our eye upwards until we see a dove's nest high up in the fir tree.

In the poor snatch itself?—"Take Elys, there,
"—'Her head that 's sharp and perfect like a pear,
"'So close and smooth are laid the few fine locks
"'Coloured like honey oozed from topmost
        rocks
"'Sun-blanched the livelong summer'—if they
155   heard
"Just those two rhymes, assented at my word,
"And loved them as I love them who have run
"These fingers through those pale locks, let the
        sun
"Into the white cool skin—who first could
        clutch,
160   "Then praise—I needs must be a god to such.
"Or what if some, above themselves, and yet
"Beneath me, like their Eglamor, have set
"An impress on our gift? So, men believe
"And worship what they know not, nor receive
"Delight from. Have they fancies—slow,
165   perchance,
"Not at their beck, which indistinctly glance
"Until, by song, each floating part be linked
"To each, and all grow palpable, distinct?"
He pondered this.   *This is answered*
                Meanwhile, sounds low and drear   *by Eglamor*
170   Stole on him, and a noise of footsteps, near   *himself:*

151 *1840* itself . . . our Elys, there,   152 *1840* ("Her   155 *1840* summer")—   158 *1840* those fine locks,   159 *1840* skin . . . nay, thus I
clutch   160 *1840* "Those locks!— I needs must be a God   *1863* Then
praise—I needs must be a God   161 *1840–68* Or if some few, above   163
1840 So men   168 *1840* distinct?

151 *In the poor snatch itself?*: as distinct from the beauty inherent in the subject.
151–68 *"Take Elys*: Sordello meditates. The quotation is from an imaginary
poem, the 'Goito lay', quoted again at vi. 867–9.
157 *who have run*: in imagination.
163 *An impress*: a stamp of value. Mediocre poets like Eglamor have rendered
poetry popular, so that ordinary men regard poetry as a great thing, although
they neither understand it nor derive delight from it.
164 *worship what they know not*: cf. John 4:22: 'Ye worship ye know not
what'.
165 *Have they fancies*: do they in fact possess imaginations (however sluggish) which gleam fitfully until a poet brings them into focus, and they see
distinctly? 'Or is the mesmeric effect I can command, mine peculiarly?': *SB*.
169 *pondered this*: 'not knowing yet what it was—mesmerism': *SB*.

And nearer, while the underwood was pushed
Aside, the larches grazed, the dead leaves crushed
At the approach of men. The wind seemed laid;
Only, the trees shrunk slightly and a shade
Came o'er the sky although 't was midday yet: 175
You saw each half-shut downcast floweret
Flutter—"a Roman bride, when they 'd dispart
"Her unbound tresses with the Sabine dart,
"Holding that famous rape in memory still,
"Felt creep into her curls the iron chill,   180
"And looked thus," Eglamor would say—indeed
'T is Eglamor, no other, these precede
Home hither in the woods. "'T were surely
   sweet
"Far from the scene of one's forlorn defeat
"To sleep!" judged Naddo, who in person led   185
Jongleurs and Trouveres, chanting at their head,
A scanty company; for, sooth to say,
Our beaten Troubadour had seen his day.
Old worshippers were something shamed, old
   friends
Nigh weary; still the death proposed amends.   190
"Let us but get them safely through my song
"And home again!" quoth Naddo.

one who belonged
to what he loved,
                                        All along,
This man (they rest the bier upon the sand)
—This calm corpse with the loose flowers in his
   hand,

171 *1840–68* nearer, and the   176 *1840* downcast violet   177 *1840* —a
Roman bride, when they dispart   181 *1840* thus,   183 *1840* 'Twere
185 *1840* To sleep! thought Naddo,   188 *1840* day: 190 *1840*
amends: 191 *1840* Let   192 *1840* again,   194 *1840* in its hand,

178 *the Sabine dart*: 'It was another Ceremony at *Rome*, Festus says, to comb
the Hair of the Bride, and divide the Locks with the Point of a Spear, which
they call'd *hasta caelibaris*, and which had been dipped in the Blood of a
Gladiator': *Antiquity Explained, by Father Montfaucon*, trans. David Humph-
reys, iii. (1722), p. 139. Cf. Ovid, *Fasti*, ii. 559–60. 'Sabine' alludes to the
chastity of the bride: when the Romans violated the Sabine women, the
Sabines took arms against them. This far-fetched conceit is characteristic of
Eglamor.
186 *Jongleurs and Trouveres*: see i. 989 n., above.
191 *my song*: Naddo had written a 'luckless' ode on Eglamor: l. 276.

195
Eglamor, lived Sordello's opposite.
For him indeed was Naddo's notion right,
And verse a temple-worship vague and vast,
A ceremony that withdrew the last
Opposing bolt, looped back the lingering veil
200
Which hid the holy place: should one so frail
Stand there without such effort? or repine
If much was blank, uncertain at the shrine
He knelt before, till, soothed by many a rite,
The power responded, and some sound or sight
205
Grew up, his own forever, to be fixed,
In rhyme, the beautiful, forever!—mixed
With his own life, unloosed when he should
     please,
Having it safe at hand, ready to ease
All pain, remove all trouble; every time
210
He loosed that fancy from its bonds of rhyme,
(Like Perseus when he loosed his naked love)
Faltering; so distinct and far above
Himself, these fancies! He, no genius rare,
Transfiguring in fire or wave or air
215
At will, but a poor gnome that, cloistered up

195 *1840* opposite: 197 *1840* Verse   200 *1840–65* place—   202
1840–68 That much was   204 *1840–65* Power   205 *1840* forever! to be
fixed   *1863–1868* forever, to be fixed   206 *1840* forever; mixed   *1863,1865*
forever! mixed   211 *1840–65* Like . . . . love,   215 *1840* up,

195 *Sordello's opposite*: Eglamor seems to belong to the first of the two classes
of lovers of beauty distinguished in Book I, 'the gentler crew' (524) who are
content to lose themselves in what they worship. He accepts the common-
sense view that a great deal of 'effort' is required in the writing of poetry. He
relies on rhyme, indeed, and his imagination falters without it. 'No genius rare'
(213), he is less than his poems, while Sordello is greater than his (iii. 615 ff., 636
ff.). He is rather like a magician who can work one particular trick. He revels in
being a poet. Opposite 195 *SB* comments: 'Born in a city, a cultivated poet'. He
is a mere ministrant in 'a temple-worship vague and vast'.
    211 *Like Perseus*: cf. *Pauline* 656 n.
    214 *Transfiguring*: '"changing *himself* into all the shapes of fire or wave or
air"': *1840 proof*: intransitive for the reflexive, as OED notes.
    215 *a poor gnome*: Eglamor is a dwarf compared to Sordello. This odd image
probably derives from Browning's reading of *Paracelsus*: OED refers to
Bitiskius's edition of his *Works* (the 'good edition' cited by Browning), ii. 391,
for the word 'gnome'. Pagel remarks that while gnomes are 'physically . . . like
man and even reason and work like man, . . . unlike man they are not endowed
with an immortal soul': op. cit., p. 62. The 'agate cup' etc. are treasures which a
gnome uses for his own purposes: the agate was believed to possess medicinal
value, while topaz (an emblem of fidelity) is said by Reginald Scot to have the

In some rock-chamber with his agate cup,
His topaz rod, his seed-pearl, in these few
And their arrangement finds enough to do
For his best art. Then, how he loved that art!
The calling marking him a man apart   220
From men—one not to care, take counsel for
Cold hearts, comfortless faces—(Eglamor
Was neediest of his tribe)—since verse, the gift,
Was his, and men, the whole of them, must shift
Without it, e'en content themselves with wealth   225
And pomp and power, snatching a life by stealth.

*loving his art and
rewarded by it,*

So, Eglamor was not without his pride!
The sorriest bat which cowers throughout
    noontide
While other birds are jocund, has one time
When moon and stars are blinded, and the prime   230
Of earth is his to claim, nor find a peer;
And Eglamor was noblest poet here—
He well knew, 'mid those April woods he cast
Conceits upon in plenty as he passed,
That Naddo might suppose him not to think   235
Entirely on the coming triumph: wink
At the one weakness! 'T was a fervid child,
That song of his; no brother of the guild
Had e'er conceived its like. The rest you know,
The exaltation and the overthrow: 240
Our poet lost his purpose, lost his rank,

222 *1840* faces (Eglamor   223 *1840* tribe)   227 *1840* So   228 *1840–68*
through noontide   231 *1840* is its to claim,   232 *1840* here,   *1863*
here   233 *1840* He knew, among the April woods   *1863–68* He knew that,
'mid the April woods,   238 *1840,1863* his—

power of healing lunacy. The words 'Fire or wave or air' (214) refer to
salamanders, nymphs, and sylphs, the respective inhabitants of these three
elements, as gnomes are of the earth. Unlike man, each species of these
creatures can live only in the element to which it belongs.

219 *how he loved that art!*: in a sense Eglamor exemplifies the commonplace
stereotype of the poet as a man indifferent to the ordinary concerns of mankind.

222 *comfortless*: giving no comfort, as in *Titus Andronicus* III. i. 251.

229 *other birds*: cf. *Christmas-Eve*, 992–5, where the bat is again contrasted
with 'other birds'.

234 *Conceits . . . in plenty*: for examples see ii. 4–9, ii. 177 ff., and vi. 1–5.
as he passed: 'Going to the great Love Court that morning': SB.

236 *wink*: let us overlook . . .! Cf. ll. 69–71 above.

His life—to that it came. Yet envy sank
Within him, as he heard Sordello out,
And, for the first time, shouted—tried to shout
245 Like others, not from any zeal to show
Pleasure that way: the common sort did so,
What else was Eglamor? who, bending down
As they, placed his beneath Sordello's crown,
Printed a kiss on his successor's hand,
250 Left one great tear on it, then joined his band
—In time; for some were watching at the door:
Who knows what envy may effect? "Give o'er,
"Nor charm his lips, nor craze him!" (here one
    spied
And disengaged the withered crown)—"Beside
"His crown? How prompt and clear those verses
255   rang
"To answer yours! nay, sing them!" And he
    sang
Them calmly. Home he went; friends used to
    wait
His coming, zealous to congratulate;
But, to a man—so quickly runs report—
260 Could do no less than leave him, and escort
His rival. That eve, then, bred many a thought:
What must his future life be? was he brought
So low, who stood so lofty this Spring morn?
At length he said, "Best sleep now with my
    scorn,

247 *1840–68* And what was   248 *1840–68* The same, placed   251 *1840*
door—   252 *1840* Give   253 *1840* him!   254 *1840 proof* crown),—
Beside >crown)—Beside   *1840* —Beside   255 *1840,1863* crown! . . . .
rung   *1865,1868* crown? . . . . rung   256 *1840* nay sing them! And he
sung   *1863–68* nay, sing them!" And he sung   258 *1840* anxious to congratulate,   *1863,1865* zealous to congratulate,   259 *1840–68* man, so quickly
runs report,   261 *1840* thought   262 *1840* be: 263 *1840–68* who was
so   264 *1840* Best

242 *envy sank*: cf. l. 121 above.   247 ∧ *was Eglamor?*: 'now': *SB*.
253 *charm his lips*: Eglamor is bidden not to curse Sordello, or to make him
mad. Cf. 'charm the tongue', described in OED as 'formerly a very common
phrase' meaning to silence.
261 *many a thought*: 'First he thought, shall I beat him? But all his excellencies
came from study of others—dead, [illegible] He foresaw a new spirit—un-
approachable yet—& that his own age was over—': *SB*.

ending with what
had possessed him.

"And by to-morrow I devise some plain   265
"Expedient!" So, he slept, nor woke again.
They found as much, those friends, when they
     returned
O'erflowing with the marvels they had learned
About Sordello's paradise, his roves
Among the hills and vales and plains and groves,   270
Wherein, no doubt, this lay was roughly cast,
Polished by slow degrees, completed last
To Eglamor's discomfiture and death.
     Such form the chanters now, and, out of breath,
They lay the beaten man in his abode,   275
Naddo reciting that same luckless ode,
Doleful to hear. Sordello could explore
By means of it, however, one step more
In joy; and, mastering the round at length,
Learnt how to live in weakness as in strength,   280
When from his covert forth he stood, addressed
Eglamor, bade the tender ferns invest,
Primæval pines o'ercanopy his couch,
And, most of all, his fame—(shall I avouch
Eglamor heard it, dead though he might look,   285
And laughed as from his brow Sordello took
The crown, and laid on the bard's breast, and
     said

266 *1840* Expedient! So he slept,   270 *1840–68* and valleys, plains   277
1840 hear: 287 *1840* laid it on his breast, and said,   *1863,1865* laid it on his
breast, and said

269 *roves*: rambles, as in Edward Young, *Night Thoughts*, ix. 673. Cf. iii. 877
below: 'one rove'.
271 *no doubt*: this supposition was, of course, erroneous.
274 *Such*: '(his friends)': *1840 proof*.
276 *that same luckless ode*: probably not the lay of Eglamor's which Sordello
had outdone, as Whyte supposes, but a poor 'song' by Naddo; cf. l. 191 above.
277 *could explore*: listening to Naddo's inferior ode enabled Sordello to learn
one more thing: 'mastering the round' probably means 'completely understanding this stage in life'.
281 *addressed*: 'The best piece of Sordel's was an elegy on Blacas', as Mrs
Dobson remarks (op. cit., p. 263), but this is of course an imaginary elegy.
286 *from his brow*: '"his own"': *1840 proof*, which also has '"Eglamor's"' to
explain 'his breast'. Sordello pays the dead poet a compliment by saying that
the crown which he himself has won becomes more valuable as a result of
resting for a moment on the breast of the dead man. The omission of 'it' (287)
after *1840*, designed to remove ambiguity, is infelicitous.

It was a crown, now, fit for poet's head?)
—Continue. Nor the prayer quite fruitless fell.
290　A plant they have, yielding a three-leaved bell
Which whitens at the heart ere noon, and ails
Till evening; evening gives it to her gales
To clear away with such forgotten things
As are an eyesore to the morn: this brings
295　Him to their mind, and bears his very name.
　　So much for Eglamor. My own month came; *Eglamor done*
'T was a sunrise of blossoming and May. *with, Sordello*
Beneath a flowering laurel thicket lay *begins.*
Sordello; each new sprinkle of white stars
300　That smell fainter of wine than Massic jars
Dug up at Baiæ, when the south wind shed
The ripest, made him happier; filleted
And robed the same, only a lute beside
Lay on the turf. Before him far and wide
305　The country stretched: Goito slept behind
—The castle and its covert, which confined
Him with his hopes and fears; so fain of old
To leave the story of his birth untold.
At intervals, 'spite the fantastic glow
310　Of his Apollo-life, a certain low
And wretched whisper, winding through the
　　　bliss,
Admonished, no such fortune could be his,
All was quite false and sure to fade one day:

---

289 *1840* fell;　　306 *1840* covert

---

290 *A plant*: almost certainly an imaginary plant. Birrell glosses it as 'St. Bruno's lily, the *Anthericum Liliastrum*', but that has six petals. Browning may be remembering the mythological origins ascribed to the different species of flower in Ovid's *Fasti*, v. 223 ff., and adding a flower of his own invention. Cf. *Pauline*, 711 ff.
296 *My own month*: '"The month I myself most delight in"': *1840 proof*. It was also the month in which he had been born: 'Nor think that I shall forget how tomorrow is the seventh of May . . your month as you call it . . in *Sordello*, I believe': Elizabeth Barrett, 6 May 1846: Kintner ii. 683.
300 *Massic jars*: Massicus was a mountain in Campania famous for its wine, Baiæ a pleasure-resort near Naples.
302 *The ripest*: beneath this line, at the foot of p. 56, *SB* has 'A cloud of birds,—The shrike & eft—'.
　filleted: wearing a head-band.　　303 *the same*: as before.
307 *so fain*: so content.
310 *his Apollo-life*: the brilliant Apollo-like life he had imagined for himself.

The closelier drew he round him his array
Of brilliance to expel the truth. But when   315
A reason for his difference from men
Surprised him at the grave, he took no rest
While aught of that old life, superbly dressed
Down to its meanest incident, remained
A mystery: alas, they soon explained   320
Away Apollo! and the tale amounts

Who he really
was, and why at
Goito.

To this: when at Vicenza both her counts
Banished the Vivaresi kith and kin,
Those Maltraversi hung on Ecelin,
Reviled him as he followed; he for spite   325
Must fire their quarter, though that self-same
    night
Among the flames young Ecelin was born
Of Adelaide, there too, and barely torn
From the roused populace hard on the rear,
By a poor archer when his chieftain's fear   33
Grew high; into the thick Elcorte leapt,
Saved her, and died; no creature left except
His child to thank. And when the full escape
Was known—how men impaled from chine to
    nape

---

320 *1840,1863* mystery—   325 *1840* Reviling as   331 *1840* Was high;

316*A* ∧ reason: 'quite other': *SB*, which adds, in the margin: 'The mesmeric one'.
317 *at the grave*: see 277 ff.
318 *While aught of that old life*: 'now become unnecessary': *SB*.
321 *the tale*: Sismondi (*Histoire*, ii. 290) describes how, in 1194, one of Ecelin's enemies having been named podestà of Vicenza, Ecelin 'was exiled from that city with his whole family and the whole faction designated by the name of Vivario. Before submitting to this sentence, he set about defending himself by setting fire to the nearest buildings; a great part of the city was burnt in this disturbance. These were the first scenes of violent bloodshed which occurred before the eyes of the newly-born son of the Lord of Romano, the ferocious Ecelin'. The podestà was Giacomo de' Bernardi of Bologna, as we know from the fuller account in Verci i. 285–7.
322 *Vicenza*: 'E^n & S^a had been established there—': *SB*.
both her counts: 'Guelfs': *SB*.   323 *the Vivaresi*: 'Ghibellins': *SB*.
325 *as he followed* ∧ : 'the Vivaresi': *SB*.
331 *Elcorte*: '"the archer"': *1840 proof*. As the *Biographie Universelle* records, some believed Sordello to have been the son of 'a poor knight called El Cort'. As Holmes comments, 'Thus did Browning fuse the account of the flight at Vicenza and the suggestion' that Sordello was Elcorte's son'. (p. 481).

335   Unlucky Prata, all to pieces spurned
      Bishop Pistore's concubines, and burned
      Taurello's entire household, flesh and fell,
      Missing the sweeter prey—such courage well
      Might claim reward. The orphan, ever since,
340   Sordello, had been nurtured by his prince
      Within a blind retreat where Adelaide—
      (For, once this notable discovery made,
      The past at every point was understood)
      —Might harbour easily when times were
         rude,
345   When Azzo schemed for Palma, to retrieve
      That pledge of Agnes Este—loth to leave
      Mantua unguarded with a vigilant eye,
      While there Taurello bode ambiguously—
      He who could have no motive now to moil
350   For his own fortunes since their utter spoil—
      As it were worth while yet (went the report)

---

341 *1840* Adelaide   344–7 *1840* Can harbour easily when times are
rude,|When Este schemes for Palma—would retrieve|That pledge, when
Mantua is not fit to leave|Longer unguarded with a vigilant eye, {*1863,1865*
have 'loath' in line 346; otherwise as *1888*}   348 *1840* Taurello bides there so
ambiguously   *1863,1865* Taurello biding there ambiguously—   349 *1840*
(He who can have   350 *1840* spoil)   351 *1840* (goes the report)

---

335 *Prata*: apparently a fictitious incident. The da Prata family had various
dealings with the Ecelini, as recorded in the index in the third volume of Verci.

335 *spurned*: kicked, the first meaning of the verb in Johnson.

336 *Bishop Pistore*: Maurisius (in Muratori viii. 11) mentions that the Bishop
of Vicenza, 'Pistor of honoured memory', left the city with Ecelin; as does
Verci. Neither says anything of concubines.

337 *flesh and fell*: flesh and skin, wholly: cf. *King Lear*, v. iii. 24.

338 *the sweeter prey*: probably the infant Ecelin. *SB* has an arrow apparently
indicating an intended insertion between 336 and 337, with the words 'his son'
(or '*his* son').

341 *blind*: 'Unseen; out of the publick view; private': Johnson.

342 *this notable discovery*: ironical, for reasons which become apparent later.
'The tale', as Sordello hears it, is that he has been brought up (on Ecelin's
orders) in Goito, where Adelaide would lie low when times were
difficult—namely when Azzo was scheming to get back Palma and to marry
her to his ally Count Richard. She is a 'pledge of Agnes Este' because she is
Ecelin's only child by his first wife, Agnes.

344 *are rude* (*1840*): 'say some': *SB*.

346 *when Mantua is not fit to leave* (*1840*): 'say [? others]': *SB*.

loth to leave: although she was (or was said to be) unwilling . . .

349 *to moil*: to work.

349–50 *He who . . . spoil*: 'which comes in so conveniently for us': *SB*.

To disengage himself from her. In short,
Apollo vanished; a mean youth, just named
His lady's minstrel, was to be proclaimed
He, so little,   —How shall I phrase it?—Monarch of the   355
would fain be so   World!
much:
For, on the day when that array was furled
Forever, and in place of one a slave
To longings, wild indeed, but longings save
In dreams as wild, suppressed—one daring not
Assume the mastery such dreams allot,   360
Until a magical equipment, strength,
Grace, wisdom, decked him too,—he chose at
     length,
Content with unproved wits and failing frame,
In virtue of his simple will, to claim
That mastery, no less—to do his best   365
With means so limited, and let the rest
Go by,—the seal was set: never again
Sordello could in his own sight remain
One of the many, one with hopes and cares
And interests nowise distinct from theirs,   370
Only peculiar in a thriveless store
Of fancies, which were fancies and no more;

352 *1840* from us. In short,   355 *1840* it? Monarch of the World.   356
1840 But on the morning that   *1863–68* For, on the morning that   362 *1840*
length   363 *1840* (Content . . . . frame)   364 *1840* Will,

352 *from her*: 'from us' (*1840*) emphasizes that the report is that of Adelaide's
supporters.
352 *In short*: before these words *SB* has: 'He is young, & his careless
disinterested good-nature is not a sufficient [?pledge]'.
353 *Apollo vanished*: to the right of this line *SB* has 'recapitulation'. The truth
(or what he takes to be the truth) about his birth now being revealed, Sordello
comes down to earth with a bump. Yet he retains his wild ambitions.
354 *to be proclaimed*: '(. . in virtue of mesmeric—)': *SB*.
356 *on the day*: on the very day when the splendour appropriate to Apollo had
to be renounced for ever and when, instead of being a slave to wild longings
which he suppressed except in his dreams (not daring to stand forth as Apollo
until he was in every respect fitted for the role), he decided that he would claim
an equally splendid role as he was, without proving his abilities and in spite of
his feeble physique, merely by virtue of his Will. He would do all that he could
with his means, limited as they were. So the seal was set . . . The syntax is loose
and confusing, but such seems to be the meaning. 'Array' means splendour,
with a suggestion of the singing robes of a great poet: cf. *Paracelsus*, i. 526 and
Sordello, i. 900 and ii. 314. The capitalization of 'Will' (364) in 1840 helps the
reader.
371 *thriveless*: see *Paracelsus*, i. 256 and note.

Never again for him and for the crowd
A common law was challenged and allowed
375   If calmly reasoned of, howe'er denied
By a mad impulse nothing justified
Short of Apollo's presence. The divorce
Is clear: why needs Sordello square his course
By any known example? Men no more   *leaves the dream*
380   Compete with him than tree and flower before.   *he may be*
                                                        something,
Himself, inactive, yet is greater far
Than such as act, each stooping to his star,
Acquiring thence his function; he has gained
The same result with meaner mortals trained
385   To strength or beauty, moulded to express
Each the idea that rules him; since no less
He comprehends that function, but can still
Embrace the others, take of might his fill
With Richard as of grace with Palma, mix
390   Their qualities, or for a moment fix
On one; abiding free meantime, uncramped
By any partial organ, never stamped
Strong, and to strength turning all energies—
Wise, and restricted to becoming wise—
395   That is, he loves not, nor possesses One   *for the fact that he*
Idea that, star-like over, lures him on   *can do nothing,*
To its exclusive purpose. "Fortunate!

---

377 *1840* presence: 380 *1840–68* before;   388 *1840* Might   389 *1840*
Grace   393 *1840* Strong, so to Strength   394 *1840* becoming
Wise—   397 *1840* Fortunate

---

374 *A common law*: he regarded himself as a hero or superman: 'challenged',
invoked, permitted to be invoked.

376 *impulse* ∧ *nothing*: '"which"': *1840 proof*.

377 *divorce*: separation.   380 *tree and flower before*: see i. 704 ff.

382 *each stooping to his star*: Sordello vaingloriously believes himself greater
than even the most gifted of ordinary men, each of whom has to follow his
own destiny, 'the idea that rules him'. Whyte comments (p. 88) that 'Sordello is
the realization of the Hegelian dictum that Thought is Being': at least he
believes that he is. For Browning's emphatic denial of any reading of Hegel, see
Vol. I, p. 43 n., above.

384 *with*: as.   392 *organ*: instrument.

395–7 *That is . . . purpose*: bracketed in *1840 proof*, which anticipates *1863* in
opening inverted commas at 'Fortunate' (but forgets to close them in 415), and
has the comment: 'Sordello loquitur'. Sordello's reflections are (of course)
misguided.

"This flesh of mine ne'er strove to emulate
"A soul so various—took no casual mould
"Of the first fancy and, contracted, cold,   400
"Clogged her forever—soul averse to change
"As flesh: whereas flesh leaves soul free to
     range,
"Remains itself a blank, cast into shade,
"Encumbers little, if it cannot aid.
"So, range, free soul!—who, by
     self-consciousness,   405
"The last drop of all beauty dost express—
"The grace of seeing grace, a quintessence
"For thee: while for the world, that can
     dispense
"Wonder on men who, themselves, wonder—
     make
"A shift to love at second-hand, and take   410
"For idols those who do but idolize,

---

400 *1840* and contracted, cold   401 *1840–68* Lay clogged forever thence,
averse to change   402 *1840* As that. Whereas it left her free to range,   *1863–8*
As that: whereas it left her free to range,   405 *1840* So, range, my soul! Who
by self-consciousness   *1863–8* So, range, my soul!—who, by self-
consciousness,   408 *1840–68* thee: but for   409 *1840* men, themselves that
wonder—   411 *1840–68* Those for its idols who but idolize,

399 *A soul so various*: the context suggests a conscious or subconscious
reminiscence of Dryden's 'Zimri' (*Absalom and Achitophel*, 545).
   no casual mould: if his flesh had taken its form from his first fancy, and had
then contracted in its mould as a metal does when it cools, it would have
clogged his soul and have made it as unwilling to change as his flesh itself. As it
is, however, his flesh has left his soul free—merely at the expense of taking no
particular form.
402 *free to range*: 'to mesmerize—': *SB*.
404 *Encumbers little*: 'lucky dog': Domett.
405 *self-consciousness*: by being aware of its own (infinite) range and potential-
ity. Cf. *Pauline* 269–70 and note. As Sordello's ruminations become wilder and
wilder, Browning seems to be remembering and perhaps acknowledging
Mill's comment that the author of *Pauline* was 'possessed with a more intense
and morbid self-consciousness than I ever knew in any sane human being'
(Vol. I, pp. 11–12 above). Here, at least, there is no doubt that the 'self-
consciousness' is dramatized. Cf. l. 429.
408–9 *that can dispense | Wonder*: the world (i.e. ordinary people) are impres-
sed by people who are themselves impressed, idolize men who themselves are
given to idolizing: Sordello regards himself as above all this.
411 *idolize,*: the comma, in all editions, makes it clear that the verb is
intransitive.

"Themselves,—the world that counts men
    strong or wise,
"Who, themselves, court strength, wisdom,—it
    shall bow
"Surely in unexampled worship now,
"Discerning me!"—

415   (Dear monarch, I beseech,
Notice how lamentably wide a breach
Is here: discovering this, discover too
What our poor world has possibly to do
With it! As pigmy natures as you please—
420 So much the better for you; take your ease,
Look on, and laugh; style yourself God alone;
Strangle some day with a cross olive-stone!
All that is right enough: but why want us
To know that you yourself know thus and thus?)
425 "The world shall bow to me conceiving all
"Man's life, who see its blisses, great and small,
"Afar—not tasting any; no machine
"To exercise my utmost will is mine:

412–13 *1840* Themselves,—that loves the soul as strong, as wise,| Whose
love is Strength, is Wisdom,—such shall bow   *1863–8* Themselves,—world
that loves souls as strong or wise,| Who, themselves, love strength, wis-
dom,—it shall bow   415 *1840* me!—   417 *1840–65* here!   422 *1840*
olive-stone;   *1863–8* olive-stone: 424 *1840* thus and thus?   425 *1840*
Nay finish—)| —Bow to me   426 *1865* sees   428 *1840* mine,

---

412 *that counts*: the revision is not altogether happy, although it removes the
ambiguity of 'souls as strong or wise'.

415 *Discerning me!*: '—mesmerism': *SB*.

(Dear monarch: the narrator apostrophizes Sordello in an admonitory
aside: it is as if one aspect of the youthful Browning were now being subjected
to criticism by a more mature Browning, or by Browning as he struggles for
maturity.

416 *a breach*: cf. 'divorce' in line 377.

418 *What*: i.e. how little. *SB* adds: 'in *this* stage'.

422 *Strangle*: '"and strangle yourself"': *1840 proof.*

424–5 between these lines *SB* has: 'except for some good you intend to do
with your power'.

425 "*The world*: Sordello recommences his vainglorious musings, which
continue to line 440.

Nay finish—) / Bow (1840): 1840 proof has '"The people shall"' to be
inserted immediately before 'Bow'
conceiving all: to me, who conceive all.

427 *no machine*: since he lacks a machine to implement the wishes of his
'utmost will' Sordello prefers to remain in the realm of 'mere consciousness'.
Cf. iii. 25 below, and *Paracelsus*, iii. 679 ff.

yet is able to imagine everything,

"Be mine mere consciousness! Let men perceive
"What I could do, a mastery believe,   430
"Asserted and established to the throng
"By their selected evidence of song
"Which now shall prove, whate'er they are, or
     seek
"To be, I am—whose words, not actions speak,
"Who change no standards of perfection, vex   435
"With no strange forms created to perplex,
"But just perform their bidding and no more,
"At their own satiating-point give o'er,
"While each shall love in me the love that leads
"His soul to power's perfection." Song, not
     deeds,   440
(For we get tired) was chosen. Fate would brook
Mankind no other organ; he would look
For not another channel to dispense
His own volition by, receive men's sense
Of its supremacy—would live content,   445
Obstructed else, with merely verse for vent.

---

429 *1840* Therefore mere consciousness for me!—Perceive *1863–8* Be mine mere consciousness! Let them perceive   432 *1840* Song   433 *1840* prove   434 *1840–68* To be, I am—who take no pains to speak,   435 *1840–68* Change no old standards   437 *1840* But mean perform   *1863–8* But will perform   439 *1840* And each   440 *1840* His soul to its perfection. Song, not Deeds,   *1863–8* His soul to its perfection." Song, not deeds,   444 *1840* volition and receive their sense   *1863–8* volition, and receive their sense   445 *1840* Of its existing, but would be content,   *1863–8* Of its existing; but would be content,   446 *1840* vent—

---

429 *for me!—Perceive*: *1840 proof* has '"The people shall"' to be inserted before 'Perceive'.
430 *could do*: the sense would be clearer if 'could' were italicized.
432 *their selected evidence*: people have chosen that poetry should be the means through which Sordello should prove his transcendent ability (because they set such store by it). He will not make any attempt to go beyond their capacities, whether by essaying 'strange forms' or otherwise, but will simply give them what they want and are capable of appreciating.
437 *But mean ∧ perform* (*1840*): '"to"': *1840 proof*.
440 *perfection* (*1840*): *1840 proof* adds closed inverted commas, with the comment 'Sordello ends' in the margin.
441 *(For we get tired)*: the narrator is tired of Sordello's youthful vanity.
441–2 *Fate would brook / Mankind*: after 'brook' *SB* has 'from him to'. 'It was the only method granted to men of receiving his self-revealment': Duff. 'Brook' here means vouchsafe.
444 *volition*: i.e. Will.

Nor should, for instance, strength an outlet seek
And, striving, be admired: nor grace bespeak
Wonder, displayed in gracious attitudes:
Nor wisdom, poured forth, change unseemly
450   moods;
But he would give and take on song's one point: *if the world*
Like some huge throbbing stone that, poised   *esteem this*
a-joint,   *equivalent.*
Sounds, to affect on its basaltic bed,
Must sue in just one accent; tempests shed
455   Thunder, and raves the windstorm: only let
That key by any little noise be set—
The far benighted hunter's halloo pitch
On that, the hungry curlew chance to scritch
Or serpent hiss it, rustling through the rift,
460   However loud, however low—all lift
The groaning monster, stricken to the heart.
    Lo ye, the world's concernment, for its part,
And this, for his, will hardly interfere!
Its businesses in blood and blaze this year

---

447 *1840* Strength   448 *1840* And striving be admired, nor Grace bespeak   *1863,1865* And, striving, be admired, nor grace bespeak   *1868* And,
striving, be admired; nor grace bespeak   450 *1840* Wisdom, ...
moods;   *1863–8* wisdom, ... moods: *451 *1840* Song's one point:
1863–89 song's one point.   453 *1840* Sounds . . . . bed   455 *1840–68* the
landstorm:

451 *song's one point*: he would stake all on poetry.
452 *throbbing stone*: the stone is the object of the clause, 'sounds' the subject.
While rocking stones are a familiar phenomenon, I am assured that no such
stone as this exists, or could exist. Sonnenschein, quoted by Berdoe, states that
'In one of Ossian's poems a description is given of bards walking around a
rocking stone, and by their singing making it move as an oracle of battle', but
the passage has not been found.
    a-joint: 'on a joint or pivot', OED, which cites no earlier example.
457–8 *pitch / On that*: happen to be in that key: 'scritch': screech, shriek.
461 *stricken to the heart*: 'Then shall superstition believe it perceives in that one
wierd [illegible] of sound, capacities of doing all that created things can
do—howling with the lion, cheering with the man—though all that is *put in
evidence* is one mere voice in the midst of the silent world of moor. (a solitary
singing bird, singing for its [?like], is better' *SB*.
462 *Lo ye*: notice that the concerns of the world and those of Sordello (so
expounded) are unlikely to have anything to do with each other.
464 *blood and blaze*: warfare and violence. Cf. iv. 934 and vi. 693. Johnson's
second definition of 'blaze', 'Publication; wide diffusion of report', exem-
plified in *The Ring and the Book*, i. 43–4 ('Across a Square in Florence, crammed
with booths, / Buzzing and blaze, noontide and market-time') is less likely
here. *SB* adds, in the margin, 'Gu. & Gh.'

But wile the hour away—a pastime slight   465
Till he shall step upon the platform: right!
And, now thus much is settled, cast in rough,
Proved feasible, be counselled! thought
        enough,—
Slumber, Sordello! any day will serve:
Were it a less digested plan! how swerve   470
To-morrow? Meanwhile eat these sun-dried
        grapes,
And watch the soaring hawk there! Life escapes
Merrily thus.
                    He thoroughly read o'er
His truchman Naddo's missive six times more,
Praying him visit Mantua and supply   475
A famished world.
                    The evening star was high
When he reached Mantua, but his fame arrived
Before him: friends applauded, foes connived,
And Naddo looked an angel, and the rest
Angels, and all these angels would be blest   480
Supremely by a song—the thrice-renowned
Goito-manufacture. Then he found
(Casting about to satisfy the crowd)
That happy vehicle, so late allowed,
A sore annoyance; 't was the song's effect   485
He cared for, scarce the song itself: reflect!

*He has loved
song's results, not
song;*

---

465 *1840* —But wile   468 *1840* enough,

467 *cast in rough*: sketched out.
468 *be counselled!*: the poet ironically counsels Sordello to stop thinking and
have a sleep. Since he has planned everything so well, surely he cannot
fail—tomorrow! Meanwhile he will be well advised to continue enjoying his
carefree escapist existence.
474 *truchman*: interpreter, go-between.
477 *his fame arrived*: cf. *Absalom and Achitophel*, 731 ff.
484 *That happy vehicle*: in the preface to *Paracelsus* Browning had referred to
the 'facilities placed at an author's disposal by the vehicle he selects'. Cf. l. 602
below, and v. 244 and 653. See, too, a letter to Domett written in 1844: 'I must
write a line or two, with all the old misery which years ago I attributed to one
Sordello . . . the misery I made him feel at "inadequate vehicles" of feeling—of
which this letter-writing always seemed to me the worst': *Browning and
Domett*, p. 105.
484 *so late allowed*: which he had so recently found perfectly tolerable.

In the past life, what might be singing's use?
Just to delight his Delians, whose profuse
Praise, not the toilsome process which procured
That praise, enticed Apollo: dreams abjured,
No overleaping means for ends—take both
For granted or take neither! I am loth
To say the rhymes at last were Eglamor's;
But Naddo, chuckling, bade competitors
Go pine; "the master certes meant to waste
"No effort, cautiously had probed the taste
"He 'd please anon: true bard, in short,—disturb
"His title if they could; nor spur nor curb,
"Fancy nor reason, wanting in him; whence
"The staple of his verses, common sense:
"He built on man's broad nature—gift of gifts,
"That power to build! The world contented
     shifts
"With counterfeits enough, a dreary sort
"Of warriors, statesmen, ere it can extort
"Its poet-soul—that 's, after all, a freak
"(The having eyes to see and tongue to speak)
"With our herd's stupid sterling happiness
"So plainly incompatible that—yes—
"Yes—should a son of his improve the breed

490

495

500

505

488 *his Delians*: see i. 932. In his early life he had sung merely to delight the
girls his imagination had conjured up, as Delians to his Apollo.

490 *dreams abjured*: now that he has a real audience, he can no more take for
granted the means to his end than that end itself. *SB*: 'the one real thing to *do*
must be done'.

493 *the rhymes*: in the literal sense, presumably, and not the poems in their
entirety. Browning may have been remembering Sismondi's account of the
'Tenson': 'One of the two [candidates for poetical honours at a Court of Love]
. . . proposed the subject of the dispute. The other then advancing, and singing
to the same air, answered him in a stanza of the same measure, and very
frequently having the same rhymes': *Historical View*, i. 137. Here, however, the
fact that Sordello finally had recourse to using Eglamor's very rhymes is a sign
of lack of inspiration. We note that the idea of the 'Tenson' lies behind
Sordello's defeat of Eglamor.

498 *nor spur nor curb*: in his own tedious way Naddo is referring to standard
'neo-classical' doctrine: cf. Pope, *An Essay on Criticism*, 82–7.

502 *shifts*: makes do.   506 *eyes to see*: cf. Mark 8:18.
and tongue to speak): 'and soul to——': *SB*.

509 *a son of his*: if he should have a son who turned out a better poet than
himself (says the worldly-wise Naddo) that would be a disaster, for he would

"And turn out poet, he were cursed indeed!"   510
"Well, there 's Goito and its woods anon,
"If the worst happen; best go stoutly on

*so, must effect this
to obtain those.*

"Now!" thought Sordello.
                         Ay, and goes on yet!
You pother with your glossaries to get
A notion of the Troubadour's intent   515
In rondel, tenzon, virlai or sirvent—
Much as you study arras how to twirl
His angelot, plaything of page and girl
Once; but you surely reach, at last,—or, no!
Never quite reach what struck the people so,   520
As from the welter of their time he drew
Its elements successively to view,
Followed all actions backward on their course,
And catching up, unmingled at the source,
Such a strength, such a weakness, added then   525

---

510 *1840* poet he were cursed indeed.   511 *1840 proof* Goit>Goito   *1840*
Well, there's Goito to retire upon   513 *1840* Now!   515 *1840*
intent—   516 *1840 proof* Rondels>Rondels,   *1840* His Rondels, Tenzons,
Virlai or Sirvent—   525 *1840* Strength, such a Weakness,

---

be destined to misery. The verse that Sordello is providing is the best that
people can stomach. Duff takes 'of his' to mean of Naddo's, but the reference to
'improv[ing] the breed' makes it seem more likely that a son of Sordello's is
meant.

513 *yet!*: i.e. his poetry still survives.

514 *glossaries*: the most comprehensive, the *Lexique roman ou dictionnaire de la
langue des Troubadours* of François Raynouard, was appearing at this time (6
vols., 1838–44), as a companion to the same author's *Choix de poésies originales
des Troubadours* (7 vols., 1816–43), which Browning is likely to have consulted.
We know that he owned an abridgment (cf. ii. 65 n., above) of the *Histoire
littéraire des troubadours* published by the Abbé Millot in 3 vols. in 1774, a study
based on the work of Lacurne de Sainte-Palaye: if he used the original he will
have found a useful 'Discours préliminaire' in vol. i.

516 *rondel*: a rondel is a poem of 13 lines with a strict rhyme-scheme, a tenzon
or Tençon a debate between two poets (or a poet and a fictitious character) in
alternate stanzas, a vir(e)lai 'a short poem . . . on two (sometimes three)
rhymes variously arranged' in which two of the lines of the first stanza are
repeated alternately as refrains, and a sirvent (serventois) a lyric, 'very like the
chant royal . . . in form, of serious character, moral, satirical, or political, in
couplets': *The Oxford Companion to French Literature*, ed. Sir Paul Harvey and
J. E. Heseltine (1959).

517 *you study arras*: you study old tapestries to try to make out how the
angelot was played. The word is rare: Johnson defines it as 'A musical instrument somewhat resembling a lute', having no doubt found it in the 2nd ed.
(1678) of *The New World of English Words*, by Edward Phillips.

521 *As from the welter of their time*: '1st verses What *was*—externally, Narrative
Ballads': *SB*.

A touch or two, and turned them into men.
Virtue took form, nor vice refused a shape;
Here heaven opened, there was hell agape,
As Saint this simpered past in sanctity,
530   Sinner the other flared portentous by
A greedy people. Then why stop, surprised
At his success? The scheme was realized
Too suddenly in one respect: a crowd
Praising, eyes quick to see, and lips as loud
535   To speak, delicious homage to receive,
The woman's breath to feel upon his sleeve,
Who said, "But Anafest—why asks he less
"Than Lucio, in your verses? how confess,
"It seemed too much but yestereve!"—the youth,
540   Who bade him earnestly, "Avow the truth!
"You love Bianca, surely, from your song;
"I knew I was unworthy!"—soft or strong,
In poured such tributes ere he had arranged   *He succeeds a*
Ethereal ways to take them, sorted, changed,   *little, but fails*
545   Digested. Courted thus at unawares,   *more;*
In spite of his pretensions and his cares,
He caught himself shamefully hankering
After the obvious petty joys that spring
From true life, fain relinquish pedestal

---

526 *1840* Men.   527 *1840* Vice   528 *1840* Heaven . . . . Hell   529
1840 proof sanctity;>sanctity,   531 *1840* People: then   532 *1840 proof*
By>At   536 *1840* Bianca's breath . . . . sleeve   537 *1840 proof*
said;>said,   539 *1840* yestereve!" The youth   540 *1840* earnestly "avow
the truth,   542 *1840* unworthy!" soft   545 *1840* Digested: courted 548
1840 After your obvious   549 *1840–65* From real life,

---

527 *Virtue took form*: 'The tales of the Troubadours have nothing romantic or
warlike about them. They always relate to allegorical personages, Mercy,
Loyalty, and Modesty, whose duty it is to speak, and not to act . . . the moral
stands perfectly naked': Sismondi, *Historical View*, i. 210.
531 *greedy*: greedy for his songs, with their portrayal of life. Cf. 'Fra Lippo
Lippi', 166 ff.
537–8 *Anafest*: a girl asks Sordello why her lover Anafest (perhaps called
after the first Doge of Venice) is less ardent than 'Lucio' in one of his songs;
while a young man is convinced that Sordello must love the girl whom he
himself loves—so well does Sordello sing of love.
544 *Ethereal ways*: in a sense he succeeded 'Too suddenly' (533), before he was
able to digest all the praise instead of taking it in the ordinary human fashion.
548 *the obvious petty joys*: cf. *Paracelsus* iii. 565 ff.

And condescend with pleasures—one and all   550
To be renounced, no doubt; for, thus to chain
Himself to single joys and so refrain
From tasting their quintessence, frustrates, sure,
His prime design; each joy must he abjure
Even for love of it.

                    He laughed: what sage   555
But perishes if from his magic page
He look because, at the first line, a proof
'T was heard salutes him from the cavern roof?
"On! Give yourself, excluding aught beside,
"To the day's task; compel your slave provide   560
"Its utmost at the soonest; turn the leaf
"Thoroughly conned. These lays of yours, in
      brief—
"Cannot men bear, now, something better?—fly
"A pitch beyond this unreal pageantry
"Of essences? the period sure has ceased   565
"For such: present us with ourselves, at least,
"Not portions of ourselves, mere loves and hates
"Made flesh; wait not!"

                    Awhile the poet waits
However. The first trial was enough:
He left imagining, to try the stuff   570
That held the imaged thing, and, let it writhe
Never so fiercely, scarce allowed a tithe

---

551 *1840 proof* abjured,> renounced, *1840* for thus   553 *1863,1865* frustrated, sure,   559 *1840* On! Give thyself,   560 *1840* thy slave   562 *1840* Thoroughly conned; these lays of thine, in brief—   563 *1840* now, somewhat better?—fly   568 *1840* not!

---

551 *To be renounced*: cf. 381 ff., above.
555 *what sage*: a magician should not look up from his book in triumph the moment his spell begins to work.
559 *"On!*: an interior voice urges Sordello to make swift progress in poetry. It is time for the over-simplified characters and psychology of earlier mediaeval verse to give way to recognizable human beings. We are reminded that Sordello is portrayed as living on the threshold of the Renaissance: see i. 569–71.
560 *your slave*: his art.   565 *essences*: abstractions.
568 *wait not!*: 'Why it is—2ᵈ verses':*SB*, which adds:\'"Philosophy, not Love"?' at the foot of the page (68), perhaps in amplification here.
570 *the stuff*: language, which he tested so rigorously that scarcely a tenth part of what he wrote was allowed to see the light of day.

To reach the light—his Language. How he
   sought
The cause, conceived a cure, and slow
   re-wrought
575 That Language,—welding words into the crude
Mass from the new speech round him, till a rude
Armour was hammered out, in time to be
Approved beyond the Roman panoply
Melted to make it,—boots not. This obtained
580 With some ado, no obstacle remained
To using it; accordingly he took
An action with its actors, quite forsook
Himself to live in each, returned anon
With the result—a creature, and, by one
585 And one, proceeded leisurely to equip
Its limbs in harness of his workmanship.
"Accomplished! Listen, Mantuans!" Fond essay! *tries again, is no*
Piece after piece that armour broke away,   *better satisfied,*
Because perceptions whole, like that he sought
590 To clothe, reject so pure a work of thought

575 *1840* Language, welding   579 *1840* it, boots   585 *1840* And one
proceeded leisurely equip   587 *1840* Accomplished! Listen Mantuans! Fond
essay!   588 *1840* away   589 *1840 proof* Forthwith:>Because

574 *conceived a cure*: cf. Dante, *De Vulgari Eloquentia*, i. xv: 'perhaps those are
not far wrong who assert that the people of Bologna use a more beautiful
speech [than the others], since they receive into their own dialect something
borrowed from their neighbours of Imola, Ferrara, and Modena, just as we
conjecture that all borrow from their neighbours, as Sordello showed with
respect to his own Mantua, which is adjacent to Cremona, Brescia, and
Verona; and he who was so distinguished by his eloquence . . . forsook his
native vulgar tongue'.
   578 *the Roman panoply*: perhaps Latin, but more probably Provençal, which
was called 'roman'. Sismondi states that 'the birth of the Romance language in
Gaul, preceded that of the Italian': *Historical View*, i. 84. 'The union of Provence', he remarks on the following pages, '. . . consolidated the laws, the
language, and the manners of Provence. It was at this period, that . . . the
Romance-Provençal, in the kingdom of Arles, completely displaced the Latin
[becoming] universally spoken, [and being] soon . . . applied to the purposes
of literature'. Browning may be alluding to the fact that no Italian works by
Sordello survive, and suggesting that he attempted such only to fail. Historically, at least, Sordello was not an innovator in writing verse in the vernacular.
Apart from the *De Vulgari Eloquentia* of Dante, the *Vita Nuova* is relevant here,
particularly ch. xxv.
   586 *harness*: referring back to 'Armour' (577).
   587 *Fond essay!*: attempt doomed to failure!
   590 *so pure a work of thought*: language is too abstract to convey the full
complexity of perception and experience.

As language: thought may take perception's place
But hardly co-exist in any case,
Being its mere presentment—of the whole
By parts, the simultaneous and the sole
By the successive and the many. Lacks 595
The crowd perception? painfully it tacks
Thought to thought, which Sordello, needing
 such,
Has rent perception into: its to clutch
And reconstruct—his office to diffuse,
Destroy: as hard, then, to obtain a Muse 600
As to become Apollo. "For the rest,
"E'en if some wondrous vehicle expressed
"The whole dream, what impertinence in me
"So to express it, who myself can be
"The dream! nor, on the other hand, are those 605
"I sing to, over-likely to suppose
"A higher than the highest I present
"Now, which they praise already: be content
"Both parties, rather—they with the old verse,
and declines from
the ideal of song. "And I with the old praise—far go, fare worse!" 610
A few adhering rivets loosed, upsprings
The angel, sparkles off his mail, which rings
Whirled from each delicatest limb it warps;

591 *1840* Thought. . . . Perception's 593–5 *1840* the Whole| By Parts, the Simultaneous and the Sole| By the Successive and the Many. 596 *1840* The crowd perceptions? 597 *1840* Together thoughts Sordello, *598 {emendation suggested by J. C. Maxwell *NQ* vol. 20 (1973), p. 270} *1840–89* it's to clutch 600 *1840* as difficult obtain 601 *1840* In short, as be Apollo. For 608 *1840* Now, and they 609 *1840* rather; 610 *1840* worse! 612 *1840–68* mail, and rings 613 *1840–68* warps,

596 *The crowd*: lacking the perceptive power of Sordello, the crowd has to try to piece together the perceptions which he has been obliged to analyze into words: he has dissected and so murdered, they have to try to put it all together again, from his words.

600 *obtain a Muse*: it was as difficult for him to become a true poet as it would have been to become as perfect as Apollo (the wild ambition of his early youth: see i. 897). Cf. ll. 352 ff., above.

602 *vehicle*: kind of poetry: cf. l. 484 n., above.

603 *what impertinence*: what an irrelevance.

610 *far go*: 'You may go farther and fare worse': proverbial.

611 *rivets loosed*: the new armour thrown off, the 'creature' Sordello has striven to create is released, but is found to have been killed by the weight of the armour. 'Sparkles off', scatters in bright fragments: 'rings', spirals away.

So might Apollo from the sudden corpse
615   Of Hyacinth have cast his luckless quoits.
He set to celebrating the exploits
Of Montfort o'er the Mountainers.
                                        Then came
The world's revenge: their pleasure, now his aim
Merely,—what was it? "Not to play the fool
620   "So much as learn our lesson in your school!"
Replied the world. He found that, every time
He gained applause by any ballad-rhyme,
His auditory recognized no jot
As he intended, and, mistaking not
625   Him for his meanest hero, ne'er was dunce
Sufficient to believe him—all, at once.
His will . . . conceive it caring for his will!
—Mantuans, the main of them, admiring still
How a mere singer, ugly, stunted, weak,
630   Had Montfort at completely (so to speak)
His fingers' ends; while past the praise-tide swept
To Montfort, either's share distinctly kept:

614 *1840–68* As might   615 *1840 proof* quoits,>quoits.   618 *1840*
pleasure   619 *1840* Merely—what was it? Not   620 *1840* school,   621
1840 world: he found that   622 *1840* any given rhyme   626 *1840 proof*
him. All at once>him—All at once. {as in *1840*}   627 *1840* His Will . . .
conceive it caring for his Will!   631 *1840 proof* on>past

615 *Hyacinth*: Apollo and Zephyrus were rivals for the love of the beautiful
young Hyacinthus. Zephyrus 'resolved to punish his rival. As Apollo . . . once
played at quoit with his pupil, Zephyrus blew the quoit, as soon as it was
thrown by Apollo, upon the head of Hyacinthus, and he was killed with the
blow': Lemprière.
    615 *his luckless quoits*: 'The idea [illegible] untouched, for the old song': *SB*.
    617 *Montfort*: the father of the Simon de Montfort celebrated in English
history. Sismondi gives an account of the Albigenses in ch. xiii of his *Histoire*
(vol. ii), while ch. vi of his *Historical View* deals with 'The War against the
Albigenses [and] The Last Provençal Poets . . .' He and his contemporaries
believed (unlike modern historians) that 'The Crusade against the Albigenses
. . . entirely put an end to the influence of the Provençals' and that 'The country
which had given birth to so many elegant poets, was now only a scene of
carnage and torture': *Historical View*, i. 231. By taking such a subject to
celebrate, Sordello is betraying his higher aspirations for poetry—ineffectually, since his poems aroused admiration for such 'heroes', not for the poet who
wrote of them. Cf. 865 n., below. Scott refers to 'the heresy of the moun-
taineers' (Albigenses) in *The Betrothed*, ch. v.
    621 *Replied the world*: 'worship & contempt going together': *SB*.
    626 *all, at once*: all his heroes rolled into one.
    628 *admiring*: wondering.

The true meed for true merit!—his abates
Into a sort he most repudiates,
And on them angrily he turns. Who were   635

*What is the
world's recognition
worth?*

The Mantuans, after all, that he should care
About their recognition, ay or no?
In spite of the convention months ago,
(Why blink the truth?) was not he forced to help
This same ungrateful audience, every whelp   640
Of Naddo's litter, make them pass for peers
With the bright band of old Goito years,
As erst he toiled for flower or tree? Why, there
Sat Palma! Adelaide's funereal hair
Ennobled the next corner. Ay, he strewed   645
A fairy dust upon that multitude,
Although he feigned to take them by themselves;
His giants dignified those puny elves,
Sublimed their faint applause. In short, he found
Himself still footing a delusive round,   650
Remote as ever from the self-display
He meant to compass, hampered every way
By what he hoped assistance. Wherefore then
Continue, make believe to find in men
A use he found not?

                         Weeks, months, years went by   655

*How, poet no
longer in unity
with man,*

And lo, Sordello vanished utterly,

---

633 *1840* merit—His   639 *1840* truth)   642 *1840* of those Goito   644
1840 proof Palma;>Palma!   1840 Sate Palma!   645 *1840 proof* corner;
Aye,>corner. Ay,   655 *1840–68* by;

634 *a sort*: merely the praise granted to a successful rhymer.
638 *In spite of the convention*: the reference is presumably to the 'Court of
Love' (66) and its acknowledgement of his excellence as a poet. Was he not
obliged (nonetheless) to make these very ordinary people (veritable Naddos) as
wonderful to his own mind as he had made the imaginary beings of his youth
and (earlier) such natural objects as flowers and trees? Accordingly he transformed the people surrounding him until some ordinary girl seemed to turn
into Palma, some ordinary woman into Adelaide, with her jet-black hair.
'Sublimed': rendered sublime.
650 *footing a delusive round*: he was dancing round in circles, deceiving himself
and as far as ever from the display of his own character and genius to which he
had aspired. Cf. Browning to Elizabeth Barrett, 11 February 1845: 'what I have
printed gives *no* knowledge of me—it evidences abilities of various kinds, if
you will . . .: but I never have begun, even, what I hope I was born to begin and
end,—"R. B. a poem"': Kintner i. 17.

Sundered in twain; each spectral part at strife
With each; one jarred against another life;
The Poet thwarting hopelessly the Man—
660 Who, fooled no longer, free in fancy ran
Here, there: let slip no opportunities
As pitiful, forsooth, beside the prize
To drop on him some no-time and acquit
His constant faith (the Poet-half's to wit)
665 That waiving any compromise between
No joy and all joy kept the hunger keen
Beyond most methods—of incurring scoff
From the Man-portion—not to be put off
With self-reflectings by the Poet's scheme,
Though ne'er so bright. Who sauntered forth in
670   dream,
Dressed any how, nor waited mystic frames,
Immeasurable gifts, astounding claims,
But just his sorry self?—who yet might be
Sorrier for aught he in reality

---

659 *1840–68* Man   662 *1840* Forsooth, as pitiful beside   *664 {Reading
of *1840*}   *1863–89* to wit—   *1840 proof* Poet's-half>Poet-half's   *667 *1840*
proof methods,>methods—{as in *1840*}   *1863–89* methods)—   668
1840–65 Man-portion not   670 *1840* bright; which sauntered   *1863,1865*
bright; that sauntered   *1868* bright;—that sauntered   673 *1840* self; *1863–8*
self—

657 *Sundered in twain*: an obscure passage, rendered more obscure by revision. The meaning seems to be that the real Sordello disappeared, splitting into
two insubstantial and conflicting personages, Poet and Man. The Man was no
longer taken in by the grandiose notions of the Poet, but fancied himself
running hither and thither and not rejecting the ordinary human joys which the
Poet insisted on abjuring because of his belief that rejecting all compromise
was more effective than most methods—'methods of *what?*', the Man inter-
jects: 'simply of becoming ridiculous!' And so the Man dreamed of wandering
out, dressed carelessly, not waiting for inspired moods and the rest. Such were
the dreams of the two parts of Sordello. The result in fact was pitiful: the Poet,
playing with the notion of great verse—verse which would develop his own
soul most wonderfully and win for him universal acclaim—simply prevented
the Man from doing anything. Cf. *Paracelsus*, iv. 240 ff.
  663 *some no-time*: this year, next year, some time, never.
  668 *From the Man-portion—not to be put off*: it is tempting to substitute a
comma for the dash.
  670 *in dream*: unlike Paracelsus, Sordello does not follow the course desired
by his Man-part. The phrase is used again at iii. 704.
  671 *frames*: frames of mind, moods. OED mentions that the phrase 'Frames
and feelings' was 'often used in religious literature of the 18th and 19th c. as a
disparaging term for emotional states as a criterion of the reality of spiritual
life'. Cf. v. 572.

Achieved, so pinioned Man's the Poet-part,   675
Fondling, in turn of fancy, verse; the Art
Developing his soul a thousand ways—
Potent, by its assistance, to amaze
The multitude with majesties, convince
Each sort of nature that the nature's prince   680
Accosted it. Language, the makeshift, grew
Into a bravest of expedients, too;
Apollo, seemed it now, perverse had thrown
Quiver and bow away, the lyre alone
Sufficed. While, out of dream, his day's work
went   685
To tune a crazy tenzon or sirvent—
So hampered him the Man-part, thrust to judge
Between the bard and the bard's audience, grudge
A minute's toil that missed its due reward!
But the complete Sordello, Man and Bard,   690
John's cloud-girt angel, this foot on the land,
That on the sea, with, open in his hand,
A bitter-sweeting of a book—was gone.
Then, if internal struggles to be one,

*the whole visible
Sordello goes
wrong*

675 *1840* pinioned that the   *1863–8* pinioned That the   676 *1840*
Verse;   677 *1840* ways;   680 *1840* nature that same nature's   *1863–8*
nature, that same nature's   681 *1840* it: language,   685 *1840* Sufficed:
while,   694 *1840–65* And if . . . . one   *1868* Then, if . . . . one

681 *Language, the makeshift*: language, which had in reality proved inadequate, now seemed to his Poet-half something quite splendid.
683 *perverse*: Probably ironical.|Sordello now contented himself with one of
Apollo's gifts, rejecting the others! Hood suggests an echo of Horace, *Odes*, II.
x. 18–20.
685 *out of dream*: in reality he was merely writing conventional verses of the
sort his audience desired, since his Man-part insisted that there was no point in
his writing anything that did not win him popularity.
687 *thrust*: thrust between, interposed.
691 *John's cloud-girt angel*: 'And I saw another mighty angel come down from
heaven, clothed with a cloud . . . And he had in his hand a little book open: and
he set his right foot upon the sea, and his left foot on the earth': Revelation
10:1–2. The angel told John to eat the book: 'it shall make thy belly bitter, but it
shall be in thy mouth sweet as honey . . . And he said unto me, Thou must
prophesy again before many peoples, and nations, and tongues, and kings':
10:9, 11. The meaning is that Sordello, unlike John, failed to be true to his
vocation. *SB* has a note: 'Land of sense & emotion sea of thought & fancy'.
693 *A bitter-sweeting*: cf. *Romeo and Juliet*, II. iv. 77: 'Thy wit is a very bitter
sweeting'.
694 *Then, if internal struggles*: it became even more impossible for him, as he

695 Which frittered him incessantly piecemeal,
Referred, ne'er so obliquely, to the real
Intruding Mantuans! ever with some call
To action while he pondered, once for all,
Which looked the easier effort—to pursue
This course, still leap o'er paltry joys, yearn
700   through
The present ill-appreciated stage
Of self-revealment, and compel the age
Know him—or else, forswearing bard-craft,
    wake
From out his lethargy and nobly shake
705 Off timid habits of denial, mix
With men, enjoy like men. Ere he could fix
On aught, in rushed the Mantuans; much they
    cared
For his perplexity! Thus unprepared,   *with those too hard*
The obvious if not only shelter lay   *for half of him,*
710 In deeds, the dull conventions of his day
Prescribed the like of him: why not be glad
'T is settled Palma's minstrel, good or bad,
Submits to this and that established rule?
Let Vidal change, or any other fool,

---

695 *1840* That frittered . . . . piece-meal, *1863–8* That frittered . . . .
piecemeal,   697 *1840–68* Mantuans! intruding ever   703 *1840–68*
him;   706 *1840* men: ere

was continually worn away by the struggle to achieve personal unity, if he
allowed the real Mantuans (however indirectly) to affect the issue. They
always wanted him to take some action, while he was trying to make up his
mind, once for all, whether to continue on his course of abjuring ordinary
pleasures as paltry and putting up with neglect in the short term until the age
was obliged to recognize his genius (such were the prompting of his Poet-part)
or to give up poetry and live as a man among men (as his Man-part urged him
to do).

710 *In deeds,*: in deeds which.

714 *Vidal*: 'Peter Vidal might justly be called the Don Quixotte of the
Troubadours. . . . His behaviour . . . was full of extravagance, and led [people]
to consider him as an agreeable fool . . . On the death of his Lord . . . he gave
unheard-of proofs of affliction; he dressed himself in the deepest mourning, cut
off the ears and tails of his horses, and his own hair, let his beard and his nails
grow to an immoderate length, and required all his servants to do the same':
Literary History of the Troubadours (see 65 n., above), pp. 325, 333. There are
accounts of Vidal (whom Sordello attacked violently in several satirical poems)
in the *Biographie Universelle* and in Sismondi's *Historical View*.

His murrey-coloured robe for filamot,   715
And crop his hair; too skin-deep, is it not,
Such vigour? Then, a sorrow to the heart,
His talk! Whatever topics they might start
Had to be groped for in his consciousness
Straight, and as straight delivered them by guess.   720
Only obliged to ask himself, "What was,"
A speedy answer followed; but, alas,
One of God's large ones, tardy to condense
Itself into a period; answers whence
A tangle of conclusions must be stripped   725
At any risk ere, trim to pattern clipped,
They matched rare specimens the Mantuan flock
Regaled him with, each talker from his stock
Of sorted-o'er opinions, every stage,
Juicy in youth or desiccate with age,   730
Fruits like the fig-tree's, rathe-ripe, rotten-rich,
Sweet-sour, all tastes to take: a practice which
He too had not impossibly attained,
Once either of those fancy-flights restrained;
(For, at conjecture how might words appear   735

715 *1840* philamot   *1863,1865* philamot,   716 *1840 proof* cross> crop *1840*
so skin-deep,   720 *1840* Strait, and as strait . . . . guess: 727 *1840* the
Mantua flock   731 *1840 proof* rather ripe,> rathe-ripe,   735 *1840 proof*
now>how   *1840* For, at . . . . how the words   *1863,1865* For, at . . . how
might words

715 *murrey-coloured . . . filamot*: mulberry, purple-red . . . drab, the colour of
a dead leaf.
716 *skin-deep*: defending his timidity in his own mind, Sordello argues that
obvious eccentrics like Vidal are superficial.
717 *Such vigour*: 'Vidal is so little [? nearer] Apollo': *SB*.
718 *His talk!*: his conversation was lamentably inept. A profound introvert,
when he had to answer a question immediately (as the Mantuans expected) he
responded at random. If, on the other hand, he wondered about something on
his own account ('Only obliged to ask himself'), he soon found an
answer—but a long and complicated one, very different from the facile clichés
of the Mantuans. *SB* has 'intermediate life' opposite 'His talk'.
724 *a period*: a sentence.   731 *rathe-ripe*: prematurely ripe.
734 *those fancy-flights*: 'to the real & ideal': *SB*.
735 *(For, at conjecture*: for, as he could only speculate about how his words
would seem to others . . . he missed his opportunity, when he returned and
tried to seize it. Duff paraphrases: 'while he was wondering what words would
convey to others, who were toying with conventional ideas, and not with vital
inward ones like his . . .'

To others, playing there what happened here,
And occupied abroad by what he spurned
At home, 't was slipped, the occasion he returned
To seize:) he 'd strike that lyre adroitly—speech,
Would but a twenty-cubit plectre reach;
A clever hand, consummate instrument,
Were both brought close; each excellency went
For nothing, else. The question Naddo asked,
Had just a lifetime moderately tasked
To answer, Naddo's fashion. More disgust
And more: why move his soul, since move it
    must
At minute's notice or as good it failed
To move at all? The end was, he retailed
Some ready-made opinion, put to use
This quip, that maxim, ventured reproduce
Gestures and tones—at any folly caught
Serving to finish with, nor too much sought
If false or true 't was spoken; praise and blame
Of what he said grew pretty nigh the same
—Meantime awards to meantime acts: his soul,
Unequal to the compassing a whole,
Saw, in a tenth part, less and less to strive
About. And as for men in turn . . . contrive

*of whom he is also
too contemptuous.*

736 *1840* what passes here,   738 *1840* slipt *1863,1865* slipt,   739 *1840–65*
seize: 742 *1840* close!   743 *1840 proof* else—That>else. The *1840*
nothing else. . . . . asked *1863,1865* nothing else. . . . . asked,   745 *1840*
fashion; more   746 *1840* more; *1863,1865* more!   747 *1840* At
minutes' *1863,1865* At a minute's   751 *1840 proof* thing he>folly   754
1840–68 pretty well the   756 *1840* a Whole,   758 *1840* Men

740 *a twenty-cubit plectre*: he would manage to express himself if (and only if)
a plectrum of impossible reach were provided. The 'clever hand' is no use of
itself, any more than a 'consummate instrument' is.

743 *The question Naddo asked*: *SB* expands: 'Any question Naddo asked, for
instance, Would have'.

750 *ventured reproduce*: *SB* has a caret mark between these words, probably to
suggest the insertion of 'to'.

755 *Meantime*: short-lived praise was the fitting reward of short-lived utter-
ances.

758 *And as for men*: just as he worried less and less about the responses he
made, so he found it impossible to take a profound interest in mankind, hating
and loving as was expected of him. So he contented himself with conventional
judgements.

Who could to take eternal interest
In them, so hate the worst, so love the best: 760
Though, in pursuance of his passive plan,
He hailed, decried, the proper way.

                                  As Man

He pleases neither
himself nor them:

So figured he; and how as Poet? Verse
Came only not to a stand-still. The worse,
That his poor piece of daily work to do   765
Was—not sink under any rivals; who
Loudly and long enough, without these qualms,
Tuned, from Bocafoli's stark-naked psalms,
To Plara's sonnets spoilt by toying with,
"As knops that stud some almug to the pith   770
"Prickèd for gum, wry thence, and crinklèd
    worse
"Than pursèd eyelids of a river-horse
"Sunning himself o' the slime when whirrs the
    breese"—
Gad-fly, that is. He might compete with these!
But—but—
            "Observe a pompion-twine afloat;   77$

---

   *760 *1840–68* best! *1888,1889* best: {punctuation mark indistinctly prin-
ted}   762 *1840–65* decried   766 *1840* Was *1863–8* Was,   *768 {Reading
of *1840–68}   *1888,1889* Turned, from   770 *1840 proof* As>"As   771 *1840
proof* crinkled>crinklèd   772 *1840* Than pursed-up eyelids   773 *1840
proof* breeze>breese" *1840* breese" *1863–8* breeze"—   774 *1840* Ha, ha!
Of course he might compete with these   775 *1840* Observe

---

   768 *Tuned*: intransitive, meaning 'played' or 'sang'. The misprint 'Turned'
survives in many modern editions. *SB* has 'others—' in the margin.
   768–9 *Bocafoli . . . Plara*: 'mannerists', as Mrs Orr observes: 'one of the
sensuous school, the other of the pompously pure;' and she adds, enigmatic-
ally, 'imaginary personages, but to whom we may give real names': *Handbook*,
p. 39 n. The name of the former may be made up from Italian 'bocca' (mouth)
and 'folle'. Plara, whose sonnets (as the example illustrates) are fantastically
over-elaborated, reappears at iii. 882 ff.
   770 *knops . . . almug*: OED defines 'knop' as 'The bud of a flower; a compact
or rounded flower-head or seed-vessel'. The almug is an exotic tree referred to
by travellers, and in 1 Kings 10:11–12. A comma after 'almug' would slightly
clarify this deliberately absurd passage.
   771 *wry*: twisted, warped.   772 *river-horse*: hippopotamus.
   773 *breese*: correcting 'breeze' in *1840 proof* Browning writes: 'To the Printer /
Be particular with this word.' Johnson defines 'breese' as 'A stinging fly; the
gadfly'.
   775 *'Observe a pompion-twine*: Sordello is ruminating on the sort of poetry he
would like to write. A pompion is a pumpkin, a plant with long stems trailing

"Pluck me one cup from off the castle-moat!
"Along with cup you raise leaf, stalk and root,
"The entire surface of the pool to boot.
"So could I pluck a cup, put in one song
780 "A single sight, did not my hand, too strong,
"Twitch in the least the root-strings of the
    whole.
"How should externals satisfy my soul?"
"Why that 's precise the error Squarcialupe"
(Hazarded Naddo) "finds; 'the man can't stoop
785 "'To sing us out,' quoth he, 'a mere romance;
"'He'd fain do better than the best, enhance
"'The subjects' rarity, work problems out
"'Therewith.' Now, you 're a bard, a bard past
    doubt,
"And no philosopher; why introduce
790 "Crotchets like these? fine, surely, but no use   *which the best*
"In poetry—which still must be, to strike,   *judges account for.*
"Based upon common sense; there 's nothing
    like
"Appealing to our nature! what beside
"Was your first poetry? No tricks were tried
795 "In that, no hollow thrills, affected throes!
"'The man,' said we, 'tells his own joys and
    woes:

776 *1840* castle-moat—   782 *1840* soul?   783 *1840* Why . . . . Squarcialupe   784 *1840* finds; the   785 *1840* To sing us out, quoth he, a   788
1840 Therewith: now   *1863–8* Therewith:' now,   796 *1840* The man, said
we, tells . . . . woes—   *1863,1865* 'The man,' said we, 'tells . . . . woes—

---

on the ground: here the reference is clearly to a similar plant which grows in
water, no doubt the yellow water-lily (*Nuphar lutea*). If you pick one cup-
shaped flower (he muses), it draws with it from the water leaves, stems and
roots. He himself finds it hard or impossible to write a simple lyric because he
cannot remain satisfied with externals; he wants to put the whole of his
philosophy into each poem (as, we may reflect, Shelley often did). 'Pompion-
plant' and 'pompion-bell' occur again in 'Caliban upon Setebos', 7 and 259.
    783 *Squarcialupe*: a jongleur already mentioned at l. 118 above. Here he
reappears as a commonplace critic. He is mentioned again at v. 1014.
    784 *Hazarded Naddo*: 'who had got familiar now': SB.
    789 *no philosopher*: cf. the view of the speaker in '"Transcendentalism:" A
Poem in Twelve Books', in *Men and Women*. SB has 'Priests, &c', perhaps
indicating a possible amplification here.
    792 *common sense*: cf. l. 500.
    794 *your first poetry*: cf. ll. 80 ff. and ll. 490 ff.

"'We 'll trust him.' Would you have your songs
  endure?
"Build on the human heart!—why, to be sure
"Yours is one sort of heart—but I mean theirs,
"Ours, every one's, the healthy heart one cares   800
"To build on! Central peace, mother of strength,
"That 's father of . . . nay, go yourself that
  length,
"Ask those calm-hearted doers what they do
"When they have got their calm! And is it true,
"Fire rankles at the heart of every globe?   805
"Perhaps. But these are matters one may probe
"Too deeply for poetic purposes:
"Rather select a theory that . . . yes,
"Laugh! what does that prove?—stations you
  midway
"And saves some little o'er-refining. Nay,   810
"That 's rank injustice done me! I restrict
"The poet? Don't I hold the poet picked
"Out of a host of warriors, statesmen . . . did
"I tell you? Very like! As well you hid
"That sense of power, you have! True bards
  believe   815
"All able to achieve what they achieve—
"That is, just nothing—in one point abide
"Profounder simpletons than all beside.
"Oh, ay! The knowledge that you are a bard
"Must constitute your prime, nay sole, reward!"   820
So prattled Naddo, busiest of the tribe

---

797 *1840* him.   804 *1840* Nay, is it true   806 *1840–65* Perhaps!   809
1840 prove? . . .   813 *1840* statesmen—did   816 *1840* Us able   818
1840 beside: 820 *1840* reward!

801 *Central peace*: in expressing his admiration for men of 'healthy heart'
Naddo produces a personification, as if he himself were on the point of taking
off into poetry.
   805 *Fire rankles*: Naddo is anticipating Sordello's reply. Just as intense heat
('fite') is to be found at the centre of the world, so (according to Paracelsus)
'There is something like a fire (energy) within ourselves which continually
consumes our form': Hartmann, loc. cit., p. 196. Cf. *Paracelsus*, v. 653 ff.
   813–14 *did / I tell you?*: he did, at lines 502 ff., above.
   817 *just nothing*: an exasperated aside.

*Their criticisms
give small comfort:*

Of genius-haunters—how shall I describe
What grubs or nips or rubs or rips—your louse
For love, your flea for hate, magnanimous,
825 Malignant, Pappacoda, Tagliafer,
Picking a sustenance from wear and tear
By implements it sedulous employs
To undertake, lay down, mete out, o'er-toise
Sordello? Fifty creepers to elude
830 At once! They settled staunchly; shame ensued:
Behold the monarch of mankind succumb
To the last fool who turned him round his
      thumb,
As Naddo styled it! 'T was not worth oppose
The matter of a moment, gainsay those
835 He aimed at getting rid of; better think
Their thoughts and speak their speech, secure to
      slink
Back expeditiously to his safe place,
And chew the cud—what he and what his race
Were really, each of them. Yet even this
840 Conformity was partial. He would miss
Some point, brought into contact with them ere
Assured in what small segment of the sphere
Of his existence they attended him;
Whence blunders, falsehoods rectified—a grim

844 *1840 proof* blunders which untruths must cure—> blunders—falsehoods
rectify—{The mark before 'falsehoods' is a thick line which may not be
intended as a dash.}   *1840–65* blunders—falsehoods rectify—   *1868* blunders,
falsehoods rectify—

823 *What grubs or nips*: four types of parasite, each of which preys on Sordello
in its own fashion. 'Tagliafer' perhaps suggests It. 'tagliare', to cut or rip (but
cf. l. 119). The four adverbs which accompany the infinitives in 828 suggest
attacks from all sides. Duff explains 'undertake' as 'Take under their management': it can also suggest trapping, seizing upon, 'taking on', &c., with the
further suggestion of the office of the funeral undertaker: 'lay down' may mean
to overthrow or lay low: 'mete out' means to measure: while OED describes
'o'ertoise' as a nonce-word meaning 'To measure out in toises' (French feet).
Sordello is like Gulliver overrun by the Lilliputians.
831 *the monarch of mankind*: as at 355 and 415, above.
838 *And chew the cud*: he found it easier to escape from the 'genius haunters'
by seeming to concur with them, so that he could get away and continue his
meditation on the nature of humanity. But in fact he was never a convincing
conformist, because he never had time to discover where and how far they
were capable of understanding him. His scope was large, theirs small. Innumerable blunders and misunderstandings were the consequence.

List—slur it over! How? If dreams were tried,   845
His will swayed sicklily from side to side,
Nor merely neutralized his waking act

and his own   But tended e'en in fancy to distract
degradation is
complete.   The intermediate will, the choice of means.
He lost the art of dreaming: Mantuan scenes   850
Supplied a baron, say, he sang before,
Handsomely reckless, full to running-o'er
Of gallantries; "abjure the soul, content
"With body, therefore!" Scarcely had he bent
Himself in dream thus low, when matter fast   855
Cried out, he found, for spirit to contrast
And task it duly; by advances slight,
The simple stuff becoming composite,
Count Lori grew Apollo: best recall
His fancy! Then would some rough peasant-Paul,   860
Like those old Ecelin confers with, glance
His gay apparel o'er; that countenance
Gathered his shattered fancies into one,
And, body clean abolished, soul alone
Sufficed the grey Paulician: by and by,   865

849 *1840* means: 850 *1840* Mantua scenes   853 *1840* abjure   854
1840 therefore!   859 *1840–68* Apollo—   863 *1840–68* shattered fancy into

845 *If dreams were tried*: it was no better if he had recourse to his dreams for
inspiration. He could not make up his mind: there was not only conflict
between his dreams and his waking actions: he could not decide what type of
poem to write.

850 *He lost the art of dreaming*: if he stooped to choose an adventurous hero for
his song, having decided to 'abjure the soul' and content himself 'With body',
he found it would not do: his imagination demanded soul or spirit as well as the
merely bodily. Gradually, therefore, the Mantuan baron who was his hero
turned into Apollo. That was no good! If, on the other hand, his attention was
caught by the face of some rough old Paulician of the sort Ecelin had dealings
with—a simple man who was gazing in astonishment at Sordello's minstrel-
dress—and he thought of taking him for a subject (a man supposedly all soul,
with 'body clean abolished'), he was equally frustrated; for he found passions
needed 'To balance the ethereality'.

865 *the grey Paulician*: 'The reformed Christian sect of the Paulicians had
spread, during the seventh century, from Armenia, over all the provinces of the
Greek empire . . . those Paulicians, who had become subjects of the Mussul-
mans, insinuated themselves . . . into the south of France and Italy. In Lan-
guedoc and Lombardy, the name of *Paterins* was given to them, . . . and they
afterwards received the name of Albigenses, from the numbers who inhabited
the diocese of Alby': Sismondi, *Literature of the South*, i. 215–16. Ecelin was
sometimes accused of sympathy with the Paulician heresy, which was most
cruelly persecuted by Simon de Montfort, 'the athlete of Christ'. Cf. 617 n.,
above.

To balance the ethereality,
Passions were needed; foiled he sank again.
  Meanwhile the world rejoiced ('t is time
    explain)
Because a sudden sickness set it free
From Adelaide. Missing the mother-bee,
Her mountain-hive Romano swarmed; at once
A rustle-forth of daughters and of sons
Blackened the valley. "I am sick too, old,
"Half-crazed I think; what good 's the Kaiser's
    gold
"To such an one? God help me! for I catch
"My children's greedy sparkling eyes at watch—
" 'He bears that double breastplate on,' they say,
" 'So many minutes less than yesterday!'
"Beside, Monk Hilary is on his knees
"Now, sworn to kneel and pray till God shall
    please
"Exact a punishment for many things
"You know, and some you never knew; which
    brings
"To memory, Azzo's sister Beatrix

Adelaide's death: what happens on it:

870
875
880

873 *1840* I am   877 *1840–65* He . . . . on,   878 *1840–65* So . . . . yesterday!   879 *1840* Beside

870 *Adelaide*: at i. 944 we have heard that it had been she who had 'turned
[Ecelin] wicked'. Rolandino records that she died about her fiftieth year:
Muratori viii. 173. Palma's account of her death is given later in the poem, at iii.
383 ff.
  871 *Romano*: the Romano family and faction.
  872 *A rustle-forth*: cf. 'The Pied Piper', 197: 'a rustling that seemed like a
bustling'.
  873 *'I am sick*: this is the opening of a letter from Ecelin to Taurello
Salinguerra, as we find at 887–9.
  876 *greedy sparkling eyes*: cf. 'The Bishop Orders his Tomb', 104–5.
  877 *"He bears*: i.e. he is growing weaker every day.
  879 *Monk Hilary*: more probably an imaginary monk than 'Ecelin's monastic
name' (Duff), since Ecelin never in fact became a monk, as Verci explains:
'towards the last years of his life Ecelino was given the nickname of Monk; not
because he had really donned the religious habit, which never occurred . . .; but
because when he was advanced in years and saw the end of his life approaching
he retired to a Benedictine monastery to lead a monastic life: a pious action
which was commonly taken in those centuries by persons of great temporal
importance': *Storia*, i. 75.
  883 *Beatrix*: 'Do let us be Guelfs': *SB*. Maurisius (in Muratori viii. 26) records
that Alberic married Beatrice, Ecelin married Zilia (sister of Count Richard of
Saint Boniface), while Count Richard himself married Cuniza, 'sister of those

"And Richard's Giglia are my Alberic's
"And Ecelin's betrothed; the Count himself   885
"Must get my Palma: Ghibellin and Guelf
"Mean to embrace each other." So began
Romano's missive to his fighting man
Taurello—on the Tuscan's death, away
With Friedrich sworn to sail from Naples' bay   890
Next month for Syria. Never thunder-clap
Out of Vesuvius' throat, like this mishap
Startled him. "That accursed Vicenza! I
"Absent, and she selects this time to die!
"Ho, fellows, for Vicenza!" Half a score   895
Of horses ridden dead, he stood before
Romano in his reeking spurs: too late—
"Boniface urged me, Este could not wait,"
The chieftain stammered; "let me die in peace—
"Forget me! Was it I who craved increase   900
"Of rule? Do you and Friedrich plot your worst
"Against the Father: as you found me first
"So leave me now. Forgive me! Palma, sure,
"Is at Goito still. Retain that lure—
"Only be pacified!"

              The country rung   905
With such a piece of news: on every tongue,

---

884 *1840 proof* Alboric's>Alberic's   887 *1840* other.   888 *1840–65*
fighting-man   889 *1840* Taurello   892 *1840* Vesuvius' mount like
893 *1840* That   895 *1840* for Vicenza!   896 *1840* dead   898 *1840*
Boniface . . . . wait,   899 *1840* let   900 *1840–68* I e'er craved   905 *1840*
pacified!

Lords of Romano'. Verci gives 'Giglia' as an alternative form of 'Zilia': *Storia*, i.
149. For the fact that Browning's Palma derives from Cunizza see i. 941 n.,
above. Cf. v. 993–5.
  889 *on the Tuscan's death*: at the time of Adelaide's death.
  889–90 *away / With Friedrich*: 'on just the opposite quest': *SB*.
  891 *for Syria*: 'and so looking at Lombardy': *SB*, which adds, opposite 892–3:
'Ecelin *alone!*'.
  897 *too late*: Ecelin has already withdrawn from the world and divided his
possessions. Cf. the rather different account of the matter at iv. 660 ff.
  898 *Este*: Azzo.   902 *the Father*: the Pope.
  903 *Forgive me!*: *SB* has 'one has to do such things!', apparently with
reference to these words.
  904 *that lure*: strengthen your hand by keeping Palma for Count Richard to
marry. This repeats the point already made in his letter.
  905 *be pacified*: literally: remain at peace.

How Ecelin's great servant, congeed off,
Had done a long day's service, so, might doff
The green and yellow, and recover breath
910 At Mantua, whither,—since Retrude's death,
(The girlish slip of a Sicilian bride
From Otho's house, he carried to reside
At Mantua till the Ferrarese should pile
A structure worthy her imperial style,
915 The gardens raise, the statues there enshrine,
She never lived to see)—although his line
Was ancient in her archives and she took
A pride in him, that city, nor forsook
Her child when he forsook himself and spent
920 A prowess on Romano surely meant
For his own growth—whither he ne'er resorts

908 *1840* so might   909 *1840* yellow to recover   910 *1840*
whither,   912 *1840* House   *1863,1865* House,   915 *1840* raise, their tenantry enshrine   916 *1840* see)   919 *1840* child though he   921 *1840* own
purposes—he

907 *congeed off*: dismissed. Cf. Carlyle, *The French Revolution*, Vol. II, Book i,
ch. i, para. 4: 'the King's rough answer . . . is congéed and bowed away, in
expressive grins'.
909 *The green and yellow*: the colours of the Ecelini, and of the Ghibellins.
'Tebaldo Cortelerio . . . asserts that the fesses of Ecelino's arms were yellow
and green in colour: which two colours were proper to the Ghibellins': Verci i.
192. Cf. iv. 390, below.
910 *Retrude*: trisyllabic. 'The only source of Salinguerra's marriage to
Retrude which I have been able to find is in Frizzi . . . There is no indication
whatever that Retrude was the daughter of Heinrich and Constance, and
silence on such an important subject implies that this detail was Browning's
addition': Holmes, op. cit., p. 478. The reference is to A. Frizzi's *Memorie di
Ferrara* (5 vols., Ferrara, 1793).
915 *The gardens*: the author of the *Chronica Parva Ferrariensis* tells us that
before 1224 Taurello Salinguerra, 'who had the reputation of being a prudent
and cautious man in worldly affairs, since he owned not merely houses and
mansions, but also orchards, gardens, a vineyard and a meadow in the parish of
St. Salvator, where he lived, constructed there for the protection of his own
property and that of his followers a castle most serviceable in times of
emergency, fortifying it with moats, a rampart, a stockade, and turrets':
Muratori viii. 482.
916 *She never lived to see*: 'because he took her to Vicenza on E[celi]n's
account': *SB*.
917 *Was ancient*: Holmes (p. 473) cites L. Ughi's *Dizionario Storico degli
Uomini Illustri Ferraresi* (2 vols., Ferrara, 1804), ii. 189, on the antiquity of the
family.
919 *forsook himself*: Browning makes Taurello Salinguerra a man whose
nature it is to serve others (in fact the Romano family), to the detriment of his
own fortunes.
921 *whither*: to Mantua.

If wholly satisfied (to trust reports)
With Ecelin. So, forward in a trice
Were shows to greet him. "Take a friend's
and a trouble it   advice,"
occasions Sordello.   Quoth Naddo to Sordello, "nor be rash   925
"Because your rivals (nothing can abash
"Some folks) demur that we pronounced you
     best
"To sound the great man's welcome; 't is a test,
"Remember! Strojavacca looks asquint,
"The rough fat sloven; and there 's plenty hint   930
"Your pinions have received of late a shock—
"Outsoar them, cobswan of the silver flock!
"Sing well!" A signal wonder, song 's no whit
Facilitated.
                    Fast the minutes flit;
Another day, Sordello finds, will bring   935
The soldier, and he cannot choose but sing;
So, a last shift, quits Mantua—slow, alone:
Out of that aching brain, a very stone,
Song must be struck. What occupies that front?
Just how he was more awkward than his wont   940
The night before, when Naddo, who had seen
Taurello on his progress, praised the mien
For dignity no crosses could affect—
Such was a joy, and might not he detect

---

923 *1840* So   924 *1840* Take . . . . advice,   925 *1840* nor   929 *1840*
Remember;   933 *1840* Sing well! A signal wonder   937 *1840* So quits, a
last shift, Mantua—

924 *shows*: such as 'the bull-bait' mentioned in the last line of this Book.
929 *Strojavacca*: as Whyte points out (p. 8), the name occurs in Verci, but in a
context irrelevant to this passage.
932 *cobswan*: 'The head or leading swan': Johnson. Cf. the 'white swan', with
its 'silver pinions', in *Pauline*, 101 ff., and 'the silver speech / Of Sidney's self' at
i. 68–9, above.
933 *A signal wonder*: ironical. No wonder this made it more difficult for
Sordello to compose. *SB* has 'There's a new man—Cry'.
939 *What occupies that front?*: what is going on in his mind?
944 *might not he detect*: 'it occurred to Sordello that Taurello would be pleased
with a song in which such an external joy as this dignified mien should be
proved a hollow thing—that this warrior, who had lost wife and child, and
whose life-work was now threatened by Ecelin's last move, might have a
secret satisfaction if the minstrel cunningly represented that "things are not
what they seem"': Duff. It seems more likely that 'he' is Sordello, and that he

945
A satisfaction if established joys
Were proved imposture? Poetry annoys
Its utmost: wherefore fret? Verses may come
Or keep away! And thus he wandered, dumb
Till evening, when he paused, thoroughly spent,

950
On a blind hill-top: down the gorge he went,
Yielding himself up as to an embrace.
The moon came out; like features of a face,
A querulous fraternity of pines,
Sad blackthorn clumps, leafless and grovelling
        vines

955
Also came out, made gradually up
The picture; 't was Goito's mountain-cup
And castle. He had dropped through one defile
He never dared explore, the Chief erewhile
Had vanished by. Back rushed the dream,
        enwrapped

He chances upon his old environment,

960
Him wholly. 'T was Apollo now they lapped,
Those mountains, not a pettish minstrel meant
To wear his soul away in discontent,
Brooding on fortune's malice. Heart and brain
Swelled; he expanded to himself again,

965
As some thin seedling spice-tree starved and frail,
Pushing between cat's head and ibis' tail

---

951 *1840* embrace;   954 *1840 proof* chumps,> clumps,   960 *1840* lapped   963 *1840* malice; heart   965 *1840* As that thin . . . . frail   966 *1840*
head or ibis'

---

finds himself wishing to show that Taurello was not all that he seemed. That is
why he had been 'awkward' as he listened to Naddo's praise of Taurello.

946 *Poetry annoys*: he had never found the writing of poetry more trouble-
some.

950 *a blind hill-top*: dark, because the moon had not yet come out. Cf. ii. 987
and iii. 127.

954 *grovelling vines*: 'trodden down by the wild cattle', *SB*, which also adds:
'There was the Badger feeding with his slant *white* wedge eye by moonlight', a
striking anticipation of 'Caliban upon Setebos', 48–50.

957 *one defile*: that narrow pass which had been forbidden him as a boy. Why
Taurello Salinguerra used it we hear later.

959 *the dream*: of being Apollo.

965 *As some . . . spice-tree*: Sordello had been unable to flourish in Mantua,
like some spice-tree trying to grow between the decorated stones of an Eastern
courtyard and left there for the pleasure of a sickly princess. Johnson defines
'Soldan' as 'The emperour of the Turks'. After 970 *SB* adds: 'Who said—Let
be'. On the death of the girl the little spice-tree is flung into the outer court,
where it flourishes.

Crusted into the porphyry pavement smooth,
—Suffered remain just as it sprung, to soothe
The Soldan's pining daughter, never yet
Well in her chilly green-glazed minaret,—   970
When rooted up, the sunny day she died,
And flung into the common court beside

*sees but failure in
all done since,*

Its parent tree. Come home, Sordello! Soon
Was he low muttering, beneath the moon,
Of sorrow saved, of quiet evermore,—   975
Since from the purpose, he maintained before,
Only resulted wailing and hot tears.
Ah, the slim castle! dwindled of late years,
But more mysterious; gone to ruin—trails
Of vine through every loop-hole. Nought avails   980
The night as, torch in hand, he must explore
The maple chamber: did I say, its floor
Was made of intersecting cedar beams?
Worn now with gaps so large, there blew cold streams
Of air quite from the dungeon; lay your ear   985
Close and 't is like, one after one, you hear
In the blind darkness water drop. The nests
And nooks retain their long ranged
        vesture-chests
Empty and smelling of the iris root
The Tuscan grated o'er them to recruit   990
Her wasted wits. Palma was gone that day,
Said the remaining women. Last, he lay
Beside the Carian group reserved and still.

968 *1840* sprung   970 *1840* in the chilly . . . . minaret—   975 *1840*
evermore,   976 *1840* How from his purposes maintained before   982
1840 maple chamber—did I say   *1863,1865* maple chamber—did I say,   987
1840 water-drops.   988 *1840,1863* nooks retained their

973 *Come home, Sordello!*: he seems to hear a voice summoning him.
977 *Only resulted*: 'Nothing could come': *SB*.
978 *dwindled*: looking smaller to his adult eyes.
987 *nests*: niches, a sense described in OED as obsolete and rare.
989 *iris root*: iris root was used for its agreeable perfume, and also for
supposed medicinal qualities.
993 *the Carian group*: the marble font at i. 410 ff., above, which is made of
Messina marble (iv. 144 ff.). No doubt Browning calls it a 'Carian group'

The Body, the Machine for Acting Will,
995 Had been at the commencement proved unfit;
That for Demonstrating, Reflecting it,
Mankind—no fitter: was the Will Itself
In fault?
         His forehead pressed the moonlit shelf
Beside the youngest marble maid awhile;
1000 Then, raising it, he thought, with a long smile,
"I shall be king again!" as he withdrew
The envied scarf; into the font he threw
His crown.

and resolves to desist from the like.

         Next day, no poet! "Wherefore?" asked
Taurello, when the dance of Jongleurs, masked
1005 As devils, ended; "don't a song come next?"
The master of the pageant looked perplexed
Till Naddo's whisper came to his relief.
"His Highness knew what poets were: in brief,
"Had not the tetchy race prescriptive right
1010 "To peevishness, caprice? or, call it spite,
"One must receive their nature in its length
"And breadth, expect the weakness with the
     strength!"
—So phrasing, till, his stock of phrases spent,
The easy-natured soldier smiled assent,
1015 Settled his portly person, smoothed his chin,
And nodded that the bull-bait might begin.

---

996 *1840–65* for Reflecting, Demonstrating it,   1001 *1840* I shall be king again!   *1002 *1840* crown.|. . . . Wherefore? *1888,1889* crown|. . . . "Wherefore?"   1005 *1840* As devils ended; don't . . . . next?   1007 *1840* relief;   1008 *1840* His   1012 *1840* strength!   1013 *1840* So   1016 *1840* the bull-chase might

---

because the word Caryatides derives from Caryae, a village in Laconia. The reference is not (as might be supposed) to Caria, on the west coast of Asia Minor.
   994 *the Machine*: cf. 427 n., above.
   995 *at the commencement*: 'at Goito': *SB*.
   997 *Mankind—no fitter*: 'at Mantua': *SB*.
   998 *In fault?*: 'Is the Mesmerism an advantage?': *SB*.
   1001 *"I shall be king again!"*: in a sense Sordello, like Paracelsus, 'aspires' again; but not necessarily for fame as a poet. 'I will live, simply': *SB*.
   1003 *Next day*: SB inserts 'at Mantua' before these words.
   1009 *the tetchy race*: 'genus irritabile vatum': Horace, *Epistolae*, II, ii. 102.
   1013 *phrasing*: prosing away (intransitive).

BOOK THE THIRD.

Nature may
triumph therefore;

AND the font took them: let our laurels lie!
Braid moonfern now with mystic trifoly
Because once more Goito gets, once more,
Sordello to itself! A dream is o'er,
And the suspended life begins anew;   5
Quiet those throbbing temples, then, subdue
That cheek's distortion! Nature's strict embrace,
Putting aside the past, shall soon efface
Its print as well—factitious humours grown
Over the true—loves, hatreds not his own—   10
And turn him pure as some forgotten vest
Woven of painted byssus, silkiest
Tufting the Tyrrhene whelk's pearl-sheeted lip,
Left welter where a trireme let it slip
I' the sea, and vexed a satrap; so the stain   15
O' the world forsakes Sordello, with its pain,
Its pleasure: how the tinct loosening escapes,

---

14 *1840 proof* trirene>trireme   16 *1840* Sordello with its pain   17 *1840*
escapes

1 *them*: the scarf and the crown of laurels. 'Sordello in retirement again':
Domett.
    2 *Braid moonfern*: 'Make some fantastic triumph elsewhere unknown &
unvalued': *SB*. Instead of trying to deserve the laurel awarded by public
acclamation, Sordello turns away towards herbs with allegedly mystical prop-
erties. Moonwort is under the domination of the moon, trifoly is associated
with the Trinity and other mysteries.
    7 *strict embrace*: close embrace, as in Cowper, 'Retirement', 234.
    9 *Its*: i.e. that of the (immediate) past.
    12 *Byssus*: 'The tuft of fine silky filaments by which molluscs of the genus
Pinna and various mussels attach themselves to the surface of rocks'. The word
was also used for 'An exceedingly fine and valuable textile fibre and fabric'
sometimes woven from byssus. OED cites Beck's *Draper's Dictionary*: 'These
filaments have been spun, and made into small articles of apparel'. The word
'of' is to be understood after 'Tufting'.
    12 *silkiest*: 'glossiest': *SB*.
    15 *satrap*: the governor of a province under the ancient Persian monarchy.
    the stain: 'for it was storied [?] o'er with wars & loves & [illegible]': *SB*.
    17 *tinct*: *SB* has a line possibly suggesting revision to 'loosening tinct'. Cf.
Hamlet, III. iv. 90–1: 'And there I see such black and grained spots / As will not
leave their tinct'. Ll. 23 ff. of 'Popularity' suggest Browning may be associating
'Tyrrhene' with 'Tyrian'.

Cloud after cloud! Mantua's familiar shapes
Die, fair and foul die, fading as they flit,
20   Men, women, and the pathos and the wit,
Wise speech and foolish, deeds to smile or sigh
For, good, bad, seemly or ignoble, die.
The last face glances through the eglantines,
The last voice murmurs, 'twixt the blossomed
        vines,
25   Of Men, of that machine supplied by thought
To compass self-perception with, he sought
By forcing half himself—an insane pulse
Of a god's blood, on clay it could convulse,
Never transmute—on human sights and sounds,
30   To watch the other half with; irksome bounds
It ebbs from to its source, a fountain sealed
Forever. Better sure be unrevealed
Than part revealed: Sordello well or ill
Is finished: then what further use of Will,   *for her son, lately*
35   Point in the prime idea not realized,   *alive, dies again,*
An oversight? inordinately prized,
No less, and pampered with enough of each
Delight to prove the whole above its reach.

---

22 *1840* die: 24 *1840–68* murmurs . . . . vines   25 *1840* This May of the
Machine supplied by Thought   26 *1840* Self-perception idly sought   29
1840 sounds   34 *1840* Is finished with: what further use of Will?   35 *1840*
—Point *1863,1865* A point   36 *1840* oversight, inordinately prized

25 *Of Men*: the revision from 'This May of the Machine supplied by
Thought' is revealing. The clue lies in ii. 994–8. Sordello had attempted to
achieve fulfilment by forcing half of himself to participate in human life while
his other half played the observer, which was as mad as it would be for a god to
try to animate mere human clay (cf. *Pauline*, 282–3, 593–4). As a natural result,
his self retreated into itself, feeling it was better to be wholly unrevealed than
revealed only in part. What point was there in his willing any further, since his
'Will itself' had been at fault originally?
    SB has 'Of Man,' or 'Of Men,' in place of 'This May', which is deleted.
    33–4 *Sordello well or ill / Is finished*: 'Browning omits to give us the key to the
whole passage, which is what the "prime idea" was, leaving it to be deduced by
the reader from the previous line. He also omits to say clearly that "his will"
(which is the prime idea) has failed. Expanded, it means that "In the prime idea,
which was to move mankind simply by his Will, he omitted the possibility of
its failing; which was certainly a point not realized, an oversight. He had prized
his will inordinately, and now it has failed, he sees how the very degree of
success which it obtained in isolated cases should have shown him that success
on a large scale was hopeless. His successes were exceptions which should
have proved to him the rule of failure, but did not"': Whyte, pp. 6–7.
    35 *Point*: 'A point' (*1863,1865*) is clearer: an absolute construction.

"To need become all natures, yet retain
"The law of my own nature—to remain   40
"Myself, yet yearn . . . as if that chestnut, think,
"Should yearn for this first larch-bloom crisp and
    pink,
"Or those pale fragrant tears where zephyrs
    stanch
"March wounds along the fretted pine-tree
    branch!
"Will and the means to show will, great and
    small,   45
"Material, spiritual,—abjure them all
"Save any so distinct, they may be left
"To amuse, not tempt become! and, thus bereft,
"Just as I first was fashioned would I be!
"Nor, moon, is it Apollo now, but me   50
"Thou visitest to comfort and befriend!
"Swim thou into my heart, and there an end,
"Since I possess thee!—nay, thus shut mine eyes
"And know, quite know, by this heart's fall and
    rise,
"When thou dost bury thee in clouds, and when   55
"Out-standest: wherefore practise upon men

39 *1840* To need . . . . natures   40 *1840* of one's own   41 *1840* Oneself,
yet yearn . . . aha, that   42 *1840* To yearn   43 *1840* With those . . . .
staunch   45 *1840* show it, great and small   46 *1840* spiritual,   47–49
1840 distinct as to be left| Amuse, not tempt become: and, thus bereft,| Say, just
as I am fashioned   50 *1840,1863* Moon,   51 *1840* befriend;   53 *1840*
thee! nay   54 *1840* by that heart's fall and rise   55 *1840* If thou . . . .
clouds   56 *1840* Men

39 *become all natures*: as he meditates, Sordello here describes Browning's
ideal of the 'dramatic' poet.
41 *as if that chestnut*: such an aspiration is as absurd as it would be for a
chestnut tree to wish to have the characteristics of a larch or the tear-shaped
globules of resin that form on the branches of a pine-tree in early spring. *SB* has
'oak warts' after 'pink,'.
46 *abjure them all*: Sordello is now disposed (foolishly) to withdraw into
himself, and to make no attempt to implement his Will, but for such attempts
as may serve merely to amuse him. He will be again as he was before, in his
early days at Goito. Like Endymion, he addresses the moon, saying that it is no
Apollo whom she will now be comforting, but merely himself. His very
breathing will respond to her. What need has he to have dealings with mankind, to make his responsiveness any clearer?

"To make that plainer to myself?"

Slide here   —*was found and*
is lost.

Over a sweet and solitary year
Wasted; or simply notice change in him—
How eyes, once with exploring bright, grew dim
And satiate with receiving. Some distress
Was caused, too, by a sort of consciousness
Under the imbecility,—nought kept
That down; he slept, but was aware he slept,
So, frustrated: as who brainsick made pact
Erst with the overhanging cataract
To deafen him, yet still distinguished plain
His own blood's measured clicking at his brain.
    To finish. One declining Autumn day—
Few birds about the heaven chill and grey,
No wind that cared trouble the tacit woods—
He sauntered home complacently, their moods
According, his and nature's. Every spark
Of Mantua life was trodden out; so dark
The embers, that the Troubadour, who sung
Hundreds of songs, forgot, its trick his tongue,
Its craft his brain, how either brought to pass
Singing at all; that faculty might class

57 *1840* myself?   60 *1840–68* eyes, bright with exploring once, grew   61 *1840* As satiate   62 *1840* Occasioned, too, a   63 *1840* imbecility;   64,65 *1840* aware he slept|And frustrate so: as   67 *1840* yet may distinguish now   *1863–8* yet still distinguished slow   68 *1840–68* at his brow.   73 *1840–65* Nature's.   75 *1840* embers .... Troubadour   76,77 *1840* songs forgot, its trick the tongue,|Its craft the brain,   78 *1840* Singing so e'er;

58 *a . . . year*: 'The time here must be incorrect', Whyte comments, with a reference to line 517. 'Sordello retired to Goito when Taurello came to Mantua, after hearing of Adelaide's death; Ecelin went into a monastery shortly after the same event, and the rising of the Ferrarese took place within a month, and Sordello is with Palma in the castle at Verona when news of Richard's capture then came'. The reader is unlikely to be troubled. Commenting on the fact that Dante describes Sordello as standing all alone, Benvenuto da Imola remarks that Sordello 'amava la solitudine': Tiraboschi i. 70.
63 *imbecility*: 'Weakness; feebleness of mind or body': Johnson.
64 *he slept*: cf. i. 965–6.
65 *frustrated*: stressed on the first syllable, as in Johnson.
67 *To deafen him*: 'hears *not* the &c.': SB.
76 *its trick his tongue*: an unusual elliptical construction.
78 *that faculty*: the humble gift of writing popular songs now seemed to him as remote as the high mysteries of Apollo.

With any of Apollo's now. The year
Began to find its early promise sere   80
As well. Thus beauty vanishes; thus stone
Outlingers flesh: nature's and his youth gone,
They left the world to you, and wished you joy.
When, stopping his benevolent employ,
A presage shuddered through the welkin; harsh   85
The earth's remonstrance followed. 'T was the
    marsh
Gone of a sudden. Mincio, in its place,
Laughed, a broad water, in next morning's face,
And, where the mists broke up immense and
    white
I' the steady wind, burned like a spilth of light   90
Out of the crashing of a myriad stars.
And here was nature, bound by the same bars

But nature is one   Of fate with him!
thing, man   "No! youth once gone is gone:
another—
"Deeds, let escape, are never to be done.
"Leaf-fall and grass-spring for the year; for us—   95
"Oh forfeit I unalterably thus
"My chance? nor two lives wait me, this to
    spend,

81,82 *1840* vanishes! Your stone|Outlasts your flesh.   87,88 *1840* Mincio
in its place|Laughed a broad water . . . . face   92 *1840–65* Nature,   93
1840 ¶ No: 94 *1840* Deeds let escape . . . . done: *1863–8* Deeds let escape
. . . . done.   95 *1840* year, but us—

---

83 *to you*: so Sordello reflects, a futile employment ironically described as
'benevolent'.
85 *A presage*: lightning, followed by thunder. The third chapter of Rolandino's second Book is devoted to an earthquake which took place in 1222:
Muratori viii, 185. The *Chronicon Veronense* assigns what seems to be the same
earthquake to Christmas 1223: ibid., 623–4.
86 *remonstrance*: manifestation, as well (perhaps) as complaint.
92 *And here was nature*: if the Mincio could be so transformed overnight,
could he himself not change?
93 *'No!*: Sordello's soliloquy continues to line 204. 'Review of his past life':
Domett.
93–4 *gone . . . done*: cf. Carlyle, *The French Revolution*, Vol. II., Book III, ch. i:
'"The gods themselves," sings Pindar, "cannot annihilate the action that is
done." No: this, once done, is done always'.
95 *Leaf-fall and grass-spring*: unrecorded in OED, like many other compound
words in the poem: see too lines 108–9.

"Learning save that? Nature has time, may mend
"Mistake, she knows occasion will recur;
100 "Landslip or seabreach, how affects it her
"With her magnificent resources?—I
  Must perish once and perish utterly.
"Not any strollings now at even-close
"Down the field-path, Sordello! by thorn-rows
105 "Alive with lamp-flies, swimming spots of fire
"And dew, outlining the black cypress' spire
"She waits you at, Elys, who heard you first
"Woo her, the snow-month through, but ere she
  durst
"Answer 't was April. Linden-flower-time-long *having*
110 "Her eyes were on the ground; 't is July, strong *multifarious*
"Now; and because white dust-clouds *sympathies,*
  overwhelm
"The woodside, here or by the village elm
"That holds the moon, she meets you, somewhat
  pale,
"But letting you lift up her coarse flax veil
115 "And whisper (the damp little hand in yours)
"Of love, heart's love, your heart's love that
  endures
"Till death. Tush! No mad mixing with the rout
"Of haggard ribalds wandering about

98,99 *1840* Nature has leisure mend│Mistake, occasion, knows she, will
recur— *1863,1865* Nature has time to mend│Mistake, she knows occasion
will recur— 101 *1840* resources? I 102 *1840–65* utterly! 104 *1840*
Sordello, 108 *1840* Woo her the snow-month—ah, but 109 *1840–65*
April! 116 *1840* Of love—heart's love—

98 *Learning save*: learning how to save.
102 *perish utterly*: cf. *Pauline* 526, 'So, I should not die utterly'.
103 *Not any strollings now*: Sordello reflects on the opportunities he has
missed, 'fragments of a whole ordained to be' (141). He now realizes that they
were rungs of a ladder which he should have ascended, whereas earlier he had
supposed the ladder a mere temptation, an end in itself, and had accordingly
refused to climb it. He should have welcomed the opportunity of ordinary love
('Elys' being Eglamor's 'type of perfection, realised according to his [limited]
faculty': cf. ii. 68 n.), and the more exotic temptations of the Emperor's
'wine-scented island-house', and might even have lived a happy and trium-
phant life like the famous Doge, Dandolo. He fears that he has for ever missed
his chance of all the experiences of life (140). The running summary is helpful.
105 *lamp-flies*: OED defines 'lamp-fly' as '? a glow-worm', with no further
example.
109 *Linden-flower-time-long*: presumably May–June.

"The hot torchlit wine-scented island-house
"Where Friedrich holds his wickedest carouse,   120
"Parading,—to the gay Palermitans,
"Soft Messinese, dusk Saracenic clans
"Nuocera holds,—those tall grave dazzling
    Norse,
"High-cheeked, lank-haired, toothed whiter than
    the morse,
"Queens of the caves of jet stalactites,   125
"He sent his barks to fetch through icy seas,

121 *1840* Parading to   123 *1840* From Nuocera, those   124 *1840* Clear-
cheeked,   125 *1840* Queens of . . . . stalactites   *1865*,*1868* Queen of . . . .
stalactites,

120 *Friedrich*: Friedrich II was a man of great gifts. In the collection of tales
known as the *Novellino* he is described as a 'very noble gentleman' who
attracted to his court at Palermo 'all those people who had excellence; players,
troubadours, and fine story-tellers'. Because of the fame of that court as a
centre for the arts 'all the poets of that day were known collectively as
"Sicilians", though many of them belonged to quite other parts of Italy':
Francesco De Sanctis, *History of Italian Literature*, trans. Joan Redfern (ed. of
1968), i. 3. Here, however, Sordello is influenced by the unfavourable view of
Friedrich favoured by the Guelfs. In the *Istoria Fiorentina* attributed to Ricor-
dano Malespini and certainly known to Browning Friedrich is described as a
most gifted man given to a life of dissolute luxury 'who had many concubines
and minions disguised as Saracens, and abandoned himself to every fleshly
pleasure, leading a sort of Epicurean existence and having no belief in a life
beyond death': Muratori viii. 953. The 'island-house' probably refers to La
Favara, the Castello di Mare Dolce near Palermo, although in fact Friedrich
spent little time in this district after his childhood.
    121 *the gay Palermitans*: 'The court of Palermo, early in the twelfth century,
abounded in riches, and consequently indulged in luxurious habits; and there
the first accents of the Sicilian muse were heard. There, too, at the same period,
the Arabs acquired a degree of influence and credit which they have never
possessed in any other christian court': Sismondi, *Literature of the South*, i. 360.
    123 *Nuocera*: Friedrich planted a colony of Saracens at Nocera Inferiore,
some twenty miles south of Naples: according to Sismondi (*Histoire*, ii. 462)
this accounts for its name, 'Nocera de' Pagani'. Thus there grew up in the heart
of the oldest Christian country near the frontier of the papal *patrimonium* a
genuine Muhammadan town with all its characteristic mosques and minarets
. . . There were always numerous Saracen servants in Frederick's household,
while in the imperial quarters in Lucera, the notorious "harem", the industri-
ous Saracen maidens had to weave and work for their master . . . This Muslim
colony in the middle of a Christian country was a rock of offence to the
Church': *Frederick the Second*, by Ernst Kantorowicz, trans. E. O. Lorimer (ed.
of 1957), pp. 130–1.
    grave dazzling Norse: Dr. Daniel Waley kindly informs us that he knows of
no evidence of Norsemen at the court of Friedrich: 'But he himself was of
Norse descent (through his mother) and of course these Normans who ruled
Sicily in the later eleventh century and the twelfth century were ultimately of
Norse descent'.
    124 *morse*: 'A sea horse': Johnson.
    125 *stalactites*: the scansion requires the Latin pronunciation, with four
syllables.

"The blind night seas without a saving star,
"And here in snowy birdskin robes they are,
"Sordello!—here, mollitious alcoves gilt
130   "Superb as Byzant domes that devils built!
"—Ah, Byzant, there again! no chance to go
"Ever like august cheery Dandolo,
"Worshipping hearts about him for a wall,
"Conducted, blind eyes, hundred years and all,
"Through vanquished Byzant where friends note
135   for him
"What pillar, marble massive, sardius slim,
"'T were fittest he transport to Venice' Square—
"Flattered and promised life to touch them there
"Soon, by those fervid sons of senators!
"No more lifes, deaths, loves, hatreds, peaces,
140   wars!

129 *1840* Sordello, here,   130 *1840* Byzant-domes the devils built   132
1840–68 august pleasant Dandolo,   135 *1840* Byzant to have noted
him   137 *1840* we transport   139 *1840–65* by his fervid sons *SB*
Soon,> Too, {?}   140 *1840–65* wars—

128 *birdskin*: his biographer Einhard has an anecdote of Charlemagne, himself dressed in sheepskin, reproving his courtiers, who had just returned from a Pavian fair at which they had found 'all the wealth of the east', for 'strutting in robes made of pheasant skins and silk; or of the necks, backs and tails of peacocks in their first plumage': Marjorie Rowling, *Everyday Life in Medieval Times* (1973), pp. 13–14.

129 *mollitious*: luxurious. The word occurs in an amorous passage in a letter to Elizabeth Barrett: 'I fancy myself meeting you . . . and sudden turns and visions of half open doors into what Quarles calls "mollitious chambers" . . .': Kintner, i. 404. Although Quarles (the only writer to use the word, according to OED, but for Browning himself) does not seem to have the phrase 'mollitious chambers', he uses 'mollitious' on at least four occasions (as Dr. John Horden has confirmed). It is interesting that 'mollitious rest' occurs in the section of his *Judgement and Mercy* (1646) entitled 'The Lascivious man's Heaven'.

130 *Byzant domes*: Byzantine architecture makes much use of domes. Kantorowicz describes Palermo as exhibiting 'an amazing variety of peoples, religions and customs . . . mosques with their minarets, synagogues with their cupolas . . . cheek by jowl with Norman churches and cathedrals, which again had been adorned by Byzantine masters with gold mosaics, their rafters supported by Greek columns on which Saracen craftsmen had carved in Kufic script the name of Allah': p. 27.

131 *Ah, Byzant*: the mention of Byzantium brings into his mind the famous Enrico Dandolo, Doge of Venice from 1192 to 1205. He was almost blind, and lived to a great age: 97, according to Gibbon. After the sack of Constantinople (Byzantium) in 1204–5 many of its treasures, including the famous bronze horses, were taken to Venice. Shelley uses 'Byzant' for 'Byzantium': 'Prince Athanase', 148. Byron refers to 'blind old Dandolo' in *Childe Harold*, iv. 107, and also mentions him elsewhere.

135 *noted (1840)*: 'felt': *SB*.

he may neither
renounce nor
satisfy;

"Ah, fragments of a whole ordained to be,
"Points in the life I waited! what are ye
"But roundels of a ladder which appeared
"Awhile the very platform it was reared
"To lift me on?—that happiness I find   145
"Proofs of my faith in, even in the blind
"Instinct which bade forego you all unless
"Ye led me past yourselves. Ay, happiness
"Awaited me; the way life should be used
"Was to acquire, and deeds like you conduced   150
"To teach it by a self-revealment, deemed
"Life's very use, so long! Whatever seemed
"Progress to that, was pleasure; aught that stayed
"My reaching it—no pleasure. I have laid
"The ladder down; I climb not; still, aloft   155
"The platform stretches! Blisses strong and soft,
"I dared not entertain, elude me; yet
"Never of what they promised could I get
"A glimpse till now! The common sort, the
        crowd,

141 *1840* Whole ordained to be!   *1863,1865* whole ordained to be!   145
1840 on—that Happiness   148 *1840* yourselves? Ay, Happiness   151 *1840*
self-revealment (deemed   152 *1840* That very use too long).   *1863–8* The
very use, so long!   153 *1840* Pleasure;   154 *1840* Me reaching it—No
Pleasure.   155 *1840* The roundels down; . . . . still

143 *a ladder*: a characteristic image: see, e.g., the French note to *Pauline*, 811,
where each of a sequence of objectives is thought of as forming 'une espèce de
plateau' on a long ascent. Sordello says that he has mistaken the roundels of a
ladder by which he was intended to climb up to a platform for that platform
itself. Cf. 103 n., above.
145 *on*: on to.   148 *happiness*: ', behind *life*,': SB.
149 *the way life should be used*: the proper use of life was there for the
learning, if only I had realized it!
150 *deeds*: the 'Points' or 'roundels' of 142–3. As Duff comments, they 'are
means to an end, yet they combine to form the end'.
151 *a self-revealment*: this has been his aim, but he has failed to see that the
route to it lay through the ordinary experiences of life.
159 *The common sort*: Sordello now believes that he has at last caught a
glimpse of the meaning of life. For ordinary people (he reflects) happiness lies
in enriching their Being from their perceptions—however limited both may
be. That is the process whereby 'The Alien' turns 'Native to the soul / Or
body'. His position is different. He already comprehends the whole world, in
spirit: in that sense he is 'whole'. What he needs is to comprehend the world in a
manner which is not confined to the spirit, to comprehend it through the flesh:
he needs 'a Palma'.

160 "Exist, perceive; with Being are endowed,
"However slight, distinct from what they See,
"However bounded; Happiness must be,
"To feed the first by gleanings from the last,
"Attain its qualities, and slow or fast
"Become what they behold; such
165 　　peace-in-strife,
"By transmutation, is the Use of Life,
"The Alien turning Native to the soul
"Or body—which instructs me; I am whole　　*in the process to*
"There and demand a Palma; had the world　　*which is pleasure,*
170 "Been from my soul to a like distance hurled,
"'T were Happiness to make it one with me:
"Whereas I must, ere I begin to Be,
"Include a world, in flesh, I comprehend
"In spirit now; and this done, what 's to blend
175 "With? Nought is Alien in the world—my Will
"Owns all already; yet can turn it—still
"Less—Native, since my Means to correspond
"With Will are so unworthy, 't was my bond
"To tread the very joys that tantalize
180 "Most now, into a grave, never to rise.
"I die then! Will the rest agree to die?
"Next Age or no? Shall its Sordello try
"Clue after clue, and catch at last the clue
"I miss?—that 's underneath my finger too,
"Twice, thrice a day, perhaps,—some yearning
185 　　traced
"Deeper, some petty consequence embraced

165 *1840* one beholds; such peace-in-strife　　*1863–8* they behold; such peace-in-strife　　166 *1840* By transmutation　　171 *1840–65* with me—　　175–7 *1840* Alien here—my Will|Owns it already; yet can turn it still|Less Native,　　*1863–8* Alien in the world—my Will|Owns all already; yet can turn it still|Less Native,　　178 *1840* unworthy　　179 *1840* very ones that　　180 *1840* Me now . . . . rise—　　184 *1840* I miss,

175 *Nought is Alien*: to him, because he is so different from ordinary men.
178 *my bond*: with himself: cf. 146–8.
180 *never to rise*: 'The Ideal must be of some good': SB.
181 *the rest*: his successors, later luminaries.
183 *Clue after clue*: cf. 'Two in the Campagna', stanzas ii and xii.

"Closer! Why fled I Mantua, then?—
      complained
"So much my Will was fettered, yet remained
"Content within a tether half the range
"I could assign it?—able to exchange   190
"My ignorance (I felt) for knowledge, and
"Idle because I could thus understand—
"Could e'en have penetrated to its core
"Our mortal mystery, yet—fool—forbore,
"Preferred elaborating in the dark   195
"My casual stuff, by any wretched spark
"Born of my predecessors, though one stroke
"Of mine had brought the flame forth! Mantua's
      yoke,
"My minstrel's-trade, was to behold
      mankind,—
"My own concern was just to bring my mind   200
"Behold, just extricate, for my acquist,
"Each object suffered stifle in the mist
"Which hazard, custom, blindness interpose
"Betwixt things and myself."
                                        Whereat he rose.

while renunciation
ensures despair.   The level wind carried above the firs   205
                          Clouds, the irrevocable travellers,

---

187 *1840* Mantua then? Complained   191 *1840* My ignorance, I
felt,   194 *1840–68* mystery, and yet forbore,   199 *1840* mankind,   200
1840 And my own matter—just   *1863–8* My own concernment—just
203–4 *1840* Convention, hazard, blindness could impose|In their relation to
myself. ¶ He rose.   *1863–8* Which hazard, use and blindness could impose|In
their relation to myself." ¶ He rose.

---

187 *Why fled I Mantua?*: he cannot understand why he has run away from his
life in Mantua, where he had complained that his scope was limited yet had of
his own accord limited it still further. He had felt that he could have attained
knowledge, yet had persevered in idleness: instead of penetrating our mortal
mystery, he had foolishly continued writing conventional verse 'in the dark',
prompted by some dim hint from some earlier poet, when he could have struck
flame by his own original effort. Cf. iv. 263 ff., on his 'exceeding error'.
      190 *able to exchange*: cf. Byron, *Manfred*, II. iv. 60–3.
      191 *for knowledge, and*: 'yet': SB.
      198 *Mantua's yoke*: with this contrast between his task as a minstrel and his
own profounder desire, he abandons his rumination for a moment. Cf. l. 928 ff.
below.

Onward.
                    "Pushed thus into a drowsy copse,
"Arms twine about my neck, each eyelid drops
"Under a humid finger; while there fleets,
210 "Outside the screen, a pageant time repeats
"Never again! To be deposed, immured
"Clandestinely—still petted, still assured
"To govern were fatiguing work—the Sight
"Fleeting meanwhile! 'T is noontide: wreak ere
        night
215 "Somehow my will upon it, rather! Slake
"This thirst somehow, the poorest impress take
"That serves! A blasted bud displays you, torn,
"Faint rudiments of the full flower unborn;
"But who divines what glory coats o'erclasp
220 "Of the bulb dormant in the mummy's grasp
"Taurello sent?" . . .
                    "Taurello? Palma sent
"Your Trouvere," (Naddo interposing leant
"Over the lost bard's shoulder)—"and, believe,   *There is yet a way*
"You cannot more reluctantly receive   *of escaping this;*
225 "Than I pronounce her message: we depart
"Together. What avail a poet's heart

---

207 *1840* ¶ Pushed   211 *1840–65* deposed—   214 *1840* 'Tis noontide—   215 *1840* Somehow one's will upon it   219 *1840* what petal
coats   221 *1840* Taurello sent . . . ¶ Taurello?   *1863,1865* Taurello sent"
. . . ¶ "Taurello?   222 *1840* Your Trouvere   223 *1840* shoulder) and
believe   224 *1840* reluctantly conceive   226 *1840* Together: what

---

207 *"Pushed thus*: in horror, he reflects that he is in danger of becoming a
lotus-eater: 'humid finger' recalls 'the damp little hand' of l. 115.
210 *Outside the screen*: perhaps a reminiscence of Plato's allegory of the cave:
The Republic, vii. 514 ff.
214 *ere night*: 'the night cometh, when no man can work': John 9:4.
216 *the poorest impress*: rather than 'opting out' of life he should be content
with 'the poorest impress' that will enable him to serve some purpose.
219 *what glory*: highly ambiguous syntax. Who can guess what glorious
flowering lurks under the layers of the bulb clasped in the hand of the mummy
sent by Taurello?—The Egyptians sometimes placed a lotus on the breast of a
mummy, or a small tray filled with earth and planted with seeds or bulbs,
symbols of immortality.
221 *"Taurello?*: Sordello must have been musing aloud, as Naddo—'Your
Trouvere'—has overheard him. 'Palma sends for him': Domett.
225 *her message*: 'She wants you at Verona where . . .': SB.

"Verona's pomps and gauds? five blades of grass
"Suffice him. News? Why, where your marish
     was,
"On its mud-banks smoke rises after smoke
"I' the valley, like a spout of hell new-broke.   230
"Oh, the world's tidings! small your thanks, I
     guess,
"For them. The father of our Patroness
"Has played Taurello an astounding trick,
"Parts between Ecelin and Alberic
"His wealth and goes into a convent: both   235
"Wed Guelfs: the Count and Palma plighted troth
"A week since at Verona: and they want
"You doubtless to contrive the marriage-chant
"Ere Richard storms Ferrara." Then was told
The tale from the beginning—how, made bold   240
By Salinguerra's absence, Guelfs had burned

---

227 *1840* Verona and her gauds?   229 *1863–8* smoke fast rises   231 *1840*
tidings! little thanks,   *232 {Reading of *1840*}   *1863–89* Patroness,   233
1840 Playing Taurello . . . . trick   237 *1840* and she wants   238 *1840*
marriage-chants   239 *1840* Ere Richard storms Ferrara. {*1840* omits the
rest of this line and lines 240–51 as far as 'at Verona?'}   *1863,1865* Ere Richard
storms Ferrara." Here was told

---

228 *News?*: the worldly Naddo excites Sordello's curiosity and flatters him at
the same time by assuming that a great poet is above curiosity about such
matters.
     229 *smoke rises*: after the earthquake: see iii. 85 n.
     232 *The father of our Patroness*: 'goes on his declining way &': *SB*.
     233 *an astounding trick*: see i. 139 n. Their Patroness is Palma. At i. 90 Verci
describes how Ecelin effected 'the solemn division of all his possessions between his two sons Ecelino and Alberico' in 1223, in the church which he had
founded.
     235–6 *both / Wed Guelfs*: cf. ii. 883 ff. Ecelin married Giglia, sister of Count
Richard, while Alberic married Beatrice d'Este. The projected marriage between Count Richard and Palma would form a third link. Browning departs
from his sources in this matter: historically Count Richard and Cunizza were
married in 1221 or 1222, and 'In the brief period that Cunizza was married to
Count Richard she bore him a baby son, who was the only scion of this most
noble family': Verci i. 122.
     239 *storms Ferrara*: 'Enters with fifty &c': *SB*. indicating the intention to add,
as in *1863* ff.
     240 *The tale*: cf. i. 149 ff. As Duff points out, Naddo does not know that
Count Richard has been captured.
     241 *Guelfs had burned*: 'This, though Naddo of course does not know, was
planned by Salinguerra, to get the Guelfs to compromise themselves and give
him a reason to break off the engagement between Palma and Boniface, and
restore, if possible, the waning fortunes of Romano': Whyte.

And pillaged till he unawares returned
To take revenge: how Azzo and his friend
Were doing their endeavour, how the end
O' the siege was nigh, and how the Count,
245 released
From further care, would with his
  marriage-feast
Inaugurate a new and better rule,
Absorbing thus Romano.
      "Shall I school
"My master," added Naddo, "and suggest
250 "How you may clothe in a poetic vest
"These doings, at Verona? Your response
"To Palma! Wherefore jest? 'Depart at once?' *which he now*
"A good resolve! In truth, I hardly hoped   *takes by obeying*
"So prompt an acquiescence. Have you groped *Palma:*
"Out wisdom in the wilds here?—thoughts may
255 be
"Over-poetical for poetry.
"Pearl-white, you poets liken Palma's neck;
"And yet what spoils an orient like some speck
"Of genuine white, turning its own white grey?
"You take me? Curse the cicala!"
         One more day,
260 One eve—appears Verona! Many a group,
(You mind) instructed of the osprey's swoop

---

245 *1863–8* Of the siege 252 *1840* To Palma? *252 {Reading of
1863–8} *1840* Depart at once? *1888,1889* 'Depart at once? 256 *1840*
poetry? 257 *1840 proof* neck>neck, *1840* Pearl-white you minstrels liken
Palma's neck, 259 *1840* white turning 260 *1840* cicales!¶ One more
day— *1863,1865* cicale!"¶ One more day. *1868* cicala!"¶ One more day.

242 *unawares*: unobserved. 243 *his friend*: Count Richard.
244 *their endeavour*: their utmost.
251 *Your response*: 'Sordello leaves his retirement learning Palma's betrothal':
Domett.
258 *an orient*: a pearl. The only exact parallel in OED is from *Sartor Resartus*, I.
ii. para. I.
260 *Curse the cicala!*: Naddo is irritated by the sound of the crickets.
261 *appears Verona!*: 'The evening with which the poem opens': Domett. Cf.
i. 10–11 and 76–7. The osprey is Taurello Salinguerra, the lynx Count Richard,
and the ounce Azzo. On 'osprey's' Domett notes: 'i.e. Taurello's on Boniface &
Azzo—page 6', referring to i. 127 ff.

On lynx and ounce, was gathering—
     Christendom
Sure to receive, whate'er the end was, from
The evening's purpose cheer or detriment,   265
Since Friedrich only waited some event
Like this, of Ghibellins establishing
Themselves within Ferrara, ere, as King
Of Lombardy, he 'd glad descend there, wage
Old warfare with the Pontiff, disengage   270
His barons from the burghers, and restore
The rule of Charlemagne, broken of yore
By Hildebrand.
                         I' the palace, each by each,
Sordello sat and Palma: little speech
At first in that dim closet, face with face   275
(Despite the tumult in the market-place)

who thereupon
becomes his
associate.
Exchanging quick low laughters: now would
     rush
Word upon word to meet a sudden flush,
A look left off, a shifting lips' surmise—
But for the most part their two histories   280
Ran best thro' the locked fingers and linked arms.
And so the night flew on with its alarms

---

263 *1840 proof* lynx   *1840* l nx   264 *1840* whate'er it might be,   273 *1840*
By Hildebrand. That eve-long each by each   *1863–8* by Hildebrand. ¶ In the
palace, each by each,   276 *1840* Despite . . . . market place   277 *1840*
would gush

---

263 *Christendom*: a reminder of the far-reaching importance of the local
struggle.
267 *of Ghibellins establishing*: '(under Taurello)': Domett.
271 *His barons*: Sismondi (*Histoire*, ii. 313–4) expresses the common view (no
longer accepted by historians) that the city-dwellers usually supported the
Pope, while the country nobility favoured the Emperor.
273 *Hildebrand*: from the days of Charlemagne the Roman Emperors had
represented the summit of earthly authority; but Hildebrand (who was proclaimed Pope, as Gregory VII, in 1073) set himself to separate the civil and
ecclesiastical powers, denying any layman the right to invest ecclesiastics. It is
of interest that in the fourth of his *Lectures on the History of Literature*, delivered
on 11 May 1838 (ed. J. Reay Greene, 1892), 'about all things in the world; the
whole spiritual history of man from the earliest times to the present', Carlyle
gave great prominence to Hildebrand. Although there is no evidence that
Browning was present, he certainly knew Carlyle early in the following year.
Carlyle dealt with the Crusades and the Troubadours in the same lecture.
274 *Sordello sat and Palma*: 'Interview between Sordello & Palma with
whi[ch] the poem opens': Domett.

Till in burst one of Palma's retinue;
"Now, Lady!" gasped he. Then arose the two
285 And leaned into Verona's air, dead-still.
A balcony lay black beneath until
Out, 'mid a gush of torchfire, grey-haired men
Came on it and harangued the people: then
Sea-like that people surging to and fro
290 Shouted, "Hale forth the carroch—trumpets, ho,
"A flourish! Run it in the ancient grooves!
"Back from the bell! Hammer—that whom
     behoves
"May hear the League is up! Peal—learn who
     list,
"Verona means not first of towns break tryst
"To-morrow with the League!"
295   Enough. Now turn—
Over the eastern cypresses: discern!
Is any beacon set a-glimmer?
                                    Rang
The air with shouts that overpowered the clang
Of the incessant carroch, even: "Haste—
300 "The candle 's at the gateway! ere it waste,
"Each soldier stand beside it, armed to march
"With Tiso Sampier through the eastern arch!"
Ferrara's succoured, Palma!

---

284 *1840* Now Lady,   *1868* "Now, lady!"   285 *1840* air dead still.   290
1840 Shouted, Hale   291 *1840–65* run . . . . grooves—   292 *1840–65*
Hammer!   293 *1840–65* Peal!   294 *1840–68* not be the first break
tryst   295 *1840* League.   296 *1840* Eastern cypresses: discern   *1863,1865*
eastern cypresses: discern—   297 *1840* You any   299 *1840* carroch even.
Haste—   301 *1840* Each soldier stands beside, armed fit to march   302
1840 thro' that Eastern arch!

---

288 *Came on it*: the effect is like that of a scene in a play.
290 *the carroch*: cf. note to i. 317. The bell on the carroch is to be rung as loudly
as possible.
293 *the League*: 'The 15 cities that affect the Pope': Domett, quoting i. 111.
300 *The candle*: used as a measure of time.
302 *Tiso Sampier*: Verci (i. 59) gives the name as 'Tiso da Camposampiero'.
Rolandino states at the beginning of his chronicle that the four most famous
Houses of the Marchia Tarvisina were those of Este, de Camino, de Romano,
and 'de Campo Sancti Petri': Muratori viii. 169. Tiso was a close ally of Azzo.
Cf. iv. 614.
303 *Ferrara's succoured, Palma!*: probably Sordello is the speaker. Cf. 561–3.
SB comments, obscurely: 'The old way—& what does it matter to you?

                                        Once again
They sat together; some strange thing in train
To say, so difficult was Palma's place   305
In taking, with a coy fastidious grace
Like the bird's flutter ere it fix and feed.
But when she felt she held her friend indeed
Safe, she threw back her curls, began implant
Her lessons; telling of another want   310

As her own history
will account for,

Goito's quiet nourished than his own;
Palma—to serve him—to be served, alone
Importing; Agnes' milk so neutralized
The blood of Ecelin. Nor be surprised
If, while Sordello fain had captive led   315
Nature, in dream was Palma subjected
To some out-soul, which dawned not though she
        pined
Delaying, till its advent, heart and mind
Their life. "How dared I let expand the force
"Within me, till some out-soul, whose resource   320

---

307 *1840* feed;   312 *1840–68* Palma—to serve, as him—be served,   315
1840 If, while Sordello nature captive led,   316 *1840* In dream was Palma
wholly subjected   *1863,1865* Nature, in dream was Palma wholly subjected   318 *1840* Delaying still (pursued she) heart and mind *1863–8* Delaying till its advent, heart and mind,   319 *1840* To live: how

---

304 *some strange thing*: she was so fastidious about sitting down that it was
evident that she had something remarkable to say. 'Taking' is a second (or
ablative) supine.
310 *another want*: her own. Palma needed to serve someone, as Sordello
needed to be served. 'Palma's story': Domett.
313 *Agnes' milk*: Agnes had been Ecelin's first wife: cf. i. 457 n. It was her
successor, Adelaide, who 'turned him wicked' (i. 944). Browning wishes to
provide Palma with suitable parents. *SB* inserts 'Estes' after 'Agnes''.
314 *Nor be surprised*: do not be surprised that, while Sordello dreamed of
dominating Nature, Palma dreamed of subordinating herself to some power
outside herself which should determine the direction of her life. Meanwhile she
waited, pining for the time when her heart and mind could be allowed to live
fully.
316 *Nature*: opposite this word, which occurs in the previous line in *1840*, *SB*
has 'Relation [? Relating] to Adelaide—influence of things', with a mark
rearranging the words to read 'Sordello captive led nature'.
317 *out-soul*: not otherwise in OED. Cf. Shelley, *Epipsychidion*, 238: 'this soul
out of my soul'. The concept is neo-Platonic. Cf. *Pauline*, 818–19.
318 *Delaying*: 'denying' would provide a more orthodox construction.
319 *'How dared I*: Palma speaks, to line 551. In the margin Domett wrote: 'all
this ingenious [?] but *expressed* in far too *abstract* a manner'. *SB*: 'made prematurely to understand life—& how souls operate on souls—'.

"It grew for, should direct it? Every law
"Of life, its every fitness, every flaw,
"Must One determine whose corporeal shape
"Would be no other than the prime escape
325 "And revelation to me of a Will
"Orb-like o'ershrouded and inscrutable
"Above, save at the point which, I should know,
"Shone that myself, my powers, might overflow
"So far, so much; as now it signified
"Which earthly shape it henceforth chose my
330 　　　guide,
"Whose mortal lip selected to declare
"Its oracles, what fleshly garb would wear
"—The first of intimations, whom to love;　　*—a reverse to, and*
"The next, how love him. Seemed that orb,　　*completion of, his.*
　　above
335 "The castle-covert and the mountain-close,
"Slow in appearing?—if beneath it rose
"Cravings, aversions,—did our green precinct
"Take pride in me, at unawares distinct
"With this or that endowment,—how, repressed
340 "At once, such jetting power shrank to the rest!
"Was I to have a chance touch spoil me, leave
"My spirit thence unfitted to receive

322–3 *1840* Of life, its fitnesses and every flaw,| Must that determine　　327
1840 Above except the point I was to know　　330–1 *1840* chose to guide| Me
by, whose lip　　332 *1840* wear: *1863* wear;　　334 *1840* And that orb
above　　335–7 *1840* mountain-close| Slow in appearing, if beneath it
arose| Cravings, aversions, and our　　*1863–8* mountain-close,| Slow in appear-
ing,—if beneath it rose| Cravings, aversions,—did our　　338 *1840* Took
pride in me　　339 *1840* endowment, how represt, *1863,1865* endowment,—how, represt　　340 *1840* At once . . . . shrunk　*1863–8* At once,
. . . . shrunk

327 *save at the point*: cf. ii. 840–3. Palma's dream of a supreme human being
corresponds to Sordello's notion that other people could only have contact
with him in one 'small segment of the sphere / Of his existence'. One point in
the orb would be visible to her, as an indicator that all her powers should be
directed towards it.
　329 *as now it signified*: as the Will now indicated which man she was to follow.
　331 *selected*: it selected.
　332 *would wear*: it (the shape) would wear.
　337 *Cravings*: if desires and aversions arose in her while she waited—if she
was valued, meanwhile, for some gift of which she was unaware—such
potential was sternly restrained. She was keeping herself for the Coming Man.
　339 *With this or that endowment*: i.e. if she was admired for gifts she had,
without being aware of them.

"The consummating spell?—that spell so near
"Moreover! 'Waits he not the waking year?
"'His almond-blossoms must be honey-ripe   345
"'By this; to welcome him, fresh runnels stripe
"'The thawed ravines; because of him, the wind
"'Walks like a herald. I shall surely find
"'Him now!'
                    "And chief, that earnest April morn
"Of Richard's Love-court, was it time, so worn   350
"And white my cheek, so idly my blood beat,
"Sitting that morn beside the Lady's feet
"And saying as she prompted; till outburst
"One face from all the faces. Not then first
"I knew it; where in maple chamber glooms,   355
"Crowned with what sanguine-heart
      pomegranate blooms,
"Advanced it ever? Men's acknowledgment
"Sanctioned my own: 't was taken, Palma's
      bent,—

344 *1840* Moreover: waits   349 *1840* Him now! ¶ And chief *1863,1865*
Him now! ¶ And chief,   351 *1840* white her cheek, ... her blood   354
1840–68 faces—not   355 *1840* She knew it; . . . . maple-chamber   358
1840 her own: . . . . bent,

  344 '*Waits he not*: her communing with herself.
  349 '*And chief*: in *1840* lines 349–58 are given as indirect speech.
  earnest: important, momentous.
  353 *outburst*: the verb is rare, according to OED, but it is a favourite with
Browning.
  355 *maple chamber glooms*: a reference to her early life with Adelaide: i. 751 ff.
'Advanced' is a strange choice of verb. She had had a growing premonition that
the young man she had seen with eyes blue with surprise (i. 756) was to be the
important man. It is significant that she saw him as crowned with pomegranate, which had powerful connotations for Browning. After much persuasion
from Elizabeth Barrett (*Kintner* i. 239, 553; and cf. 241 and ii. 619), he inserted a
note on the reverse of the title-page of *A Soul's Tragedy* (in the last of the *Bells
and Pomegranates* pamphlets), 'explaining, in reply to inquiries, that I only
meant by that title to indicate an endeavour towards something like an alterna-
tion, or mixture, of music with discoursing, sound with sense, poetry with
thought . . . Giotto placed a pomegranate fruit in the hand of Dante, and
Raffaelle crowned his Theology . . . with blossoms of the same; as if the Bellari
and Vasari would be sure to come after, and explain that it was merely "*simbolo
delle buone opere—il qual Pomo granato fu però usato nelle vesti del Pontefice appresso
gli Ebrei*"'. 'Bellari' should be '[Giovanni Pietro] Bellori': *NQ* ccxv (1970), p.
334.
  357 *Men's acknowledgment*: at the Court of Love, when Sordello had vanquished Eglamor. *SB* comments, cryptically: 'then she remembered speeches
of Ez. fears & reverences of Adel.'
  358 *Palma's bent*: cf. ii. 120 above.

"Sordello,—recognized, accepted.

                     "Dumb

360 "Sat she still scheming. Ecelin would come   *How she ever*
    "Gaunt, scared, 'Cesano baffles me,' he 'd say: *aspired for his*
    "'Better I fought it out, my father's way!   *sake,*
    "'Strangle Ferrara in its drowning flats,
    "'And you and your Taurello yonder!—what 's
365   "'Romano's business there?' An hour's
        concern
    "To cure the froward Chief!—induced return
    "As heartened from those overmeaning eyes,
    "Wound up to persevere,—his enterprise
    "Marked out anew, its exigent of wit
370 "Apportioned,—she at liberty to sit
    "And scheme against the next emergence, I—
    "To covet her Taurello-sprite, made fly
    "Or fold the wing—to con your horoscope
    "For leave command those steely shafts shoot
        ope,
375 "Or straight assuage their blinding eagerness

359–60 *1840* She said.¶And day by day the Tuscan dumb|Sat scheming, scheming; *1863–8* Sordello, accepted.¶And the Tuscan dumb|Sat scheming, scheming;   361 *1840* Gaunt, scared, Cesano baffles me, he'd say: 364 *1840–68* yonder—what's   365 *1840* there?   *366 {Reading of *1863–8*} *1840* Chief! induced return   *1888,1889* Chief!—induce return   367 *1840–68* Much heartened   368 *1840* persevere,   370 *1840* Apportioned, she   372 *1840* To covet what I deemed their sprite,

360 *would come*: '"climb with clinking step" &c': *SB* (referring to l. 661).
361 *Cesano*: probably Celano (as at iv. 525), as John Pettigrew suggested: 'For "Flute" read "Lute"': *The Library*, 5th series, xxxiii (1978), p. 166.
365 *Romano's business*: i.e. our business.
367 *overmeaning*: not in OED, but cf. two of the senses of the prefix 'over-': (a) 'overcoming, putting down, or getting the better of' and (b) 'bringing or gaining over to a party, opinion, etc.' Cf. 'overbearing'. In the *Divine Fancies* of Quarles (1641), Lib. II, no. 33, the Queen of Sheba is 'overdaz'd' by Solomon's 'bright beams' (lines 27–8). For Browning and Quarles see 129 n., above.
369 *exigent*: required amount.
371 *emergence*: '"Taurello would come"': *SB*.
372 *Taurello-sprite*: Palma envies Adelaide her servant Taurello, a sort of spirit that can be commanded to fly on errands or sit awaiting the pleasure of his mistress. He is 'Romano's angel' (433).
374 *those steely shafts*: almost certainly Sordello's eyes. She consults his horoscope to discover whether she is to stimulate him to action or occupy him with the delights of love. At i. 953 we hear of 'the dimpling snow' of Palma's thigh (and cf. i. 415).

"In blank smooth snow. What semblance of
    success
"To any of my plans for making you
"Mine and Romano's? Break the first wall
    through,
"Tread o'er the ruins of the Chief, supplant
"His sons beside, still, vainest were the vaunt: 380
"There, Salinguerra would obstruct me sheer,
"And the insuperable Tuscan, here,
"Stay me! But one wild eve that Lady died
"In her lone chamber: only I beside:
"Taurello far at Naples, and my sire   385
"At Padua, Ecelin away in ire
"With Alberic. She held me thus—a clutch
"To make our spirits as our bodies touch—
"And so began flinging the past up, heaps
"Of uncouth treasure from their sunless sleeps   390
"Within her soul; deeds rose along with dreams,
"Fragments of many miserable schemes,
"Secrets, more secrets, then—no, not the last—
"'Mongst others, like a casual trick o' the past,
"How . . . ay, she told me, gathering up her face,   395
circumstances "All left of it, into one arch-grimace
helping or "To die with . . .
hindering.   "Friend, 't is gone! but not the fear

---

*376 {Editors' emendation}   *1840* To blank smooth snow: what   *1863–8*
To blank smooth snow. What   *1888,1889* In blank smooth snow What   378
1840 Romano's lord? That Chief—her children too—   379,380 {Not in
1840}   383 *1840–65* Stayed me!   387 *1840* Alberic: she   *389 {Reading
of *1840,1868,1889*}   *1863,1865* Past up,   *1888* past up {Dykes Campbell copy
has the comma inked in.}   395 *1840* gathering her face   *1863,1865* gathering
up her face   396 *1840* —That face of hers into   *1863,1865* —All left of it, into

377 *for making you*: 'a purely new plan of her own': *SB*.
379 *the ruins of the Chief*: what is left of the Monk, the first obstacle to her
making Sordello the leader of the House of Romano.
385 *my sire*: the Monk, the 'Ecelin' of the following line being his son, the
future Ecelin the Tyrant. Cf. 517 n.
386 *Ecelin away in ire*: *SB* inserts a comma after 'away' and comments in the
margin: 'all weak & wrong' and below that: 'a protest that it was not owing to
her'.
390 *sunless sleeps*: cf. *Prometheus Unbound* III. iii. 100: 'my sunless sleep'.
393 *no, not the last*: jumbled among all these secrets there was one . . . which
Palma has been on the point of telling Sordello, until she changes her mind.

"Of that fell laughing, heard as now I hear.
"Nor faltered voice, nor seemed her heart grow
   weak
400 "When i' the midst abrupt she ceased to speak
"—Dead, as to serve a purpose, mark!—for in
"Rushed o' the very instant Ecelin
"(How summoned, who divines?)—looking as if
"He understood why Adelaide lay stiff
405 "Already in my arms; for 'Girl, how must
"'I manage Este in the matter thrust
"'Upon me, how unravel your bad coil?—
"'Since' (he declared) ''t is on your brow—a soil
"'Like hers there!' then in the same breath, 'he
   lacked
410 "'No counsel after all, had signed no pact
"'With devils, nor was treason here or there,
"'Goito or Vicenza, his affair:
"'He buried it in Adelaide's deep grave,
"'Would begin life afresh, now,—would not
   slave
415 "'For any Friedrich's nor Taurello's sake!
"'What booted him to meddle or to make
"'In Lombardy?' And afterward I knew
"The meaning of his promise to undo

399 *1840* seemed herself grow weak,   *1863,1865* seemed her heart grow
weak,   401 *1840* mark,   403 *1840* summoned who divines?) looking   404 *1840* Part understood he why his mate lay stiff   405 *1840* arms
for, Girl,   407 *1863–8* arms; for, 'Girl,   407 *1840* unravel their bad coil?   408
1840 Since (he declared) 'tis   409 *1840* Like hers there! then said in a breath he
lacked *1863,1865* Like hers, there!' then in the same breath, 'he lacked   *1868*
"'Like hers, there!' then in the same breath, 'he lacked   413–14 *1840* He'd
bury it . . . . grave| And begin life afresh, nor, either, slave   415 *1840* Fried-
rich's or Taurello's   417 *1840* In Lombardy? 'Twas afterward

398 *fell*: fierce, terrible.
401 *as to serve a purpose*: as if she had chosen her time to die.
402 *Ecelin*: her husband, the Monk.
407 *coil*: confusion, bad business: cf. i. 379. 'Saling. & Ad's': *SB*.
408 *a soil*: a stain or mark he thinks he sees on Palma's forehead, a sign that
she has ambitions for the House of Romano, as Adelaide had had—or perhaps
that she has something of Adelaide's quasi-magical powers.
416 *to meddle or to make*: proverbial. Cf. Shakespeare, *Troilus and Cressida*, I. i.
14, etc.
418 *The meaning*: Ecelin had arranged the marriages of Alberic, Ecelin and
Palma in the hope of bringing the feud between Guelfs and Ghibellins to an
end.

"All she had done—why marriages were made,
"New friendships entered on, old followers paid   420
"With curses for their pains,—new friends'
     amaze
"At height, when, passing out by Gate Saint
     Blaise,
"He stopped short in Vicenza, bent his head
"Over a friar's neck,—'had vowed,' he said,
"'Long since, nigh thirty years, because his wife   425
"'And child were saved there, to bestow his life
"'On God, his gettings on the Church.'
                                        "Exiled
"Within Goito, still one dream beguiled
"My days and nights; 't was found, the orb I
     sought
"To serve, those glimpses came of Fomalhaut,   430

---

421 *1840* In curses for their pains, people's amaze   *422 {Reading of
1889} *1840* when . . . . St. Blaise   *1863–88* when, ... St. Blaise,   424
1840 had vowed,   425 *1840* Long   427 *1840* Church. ¶ Exiled   428 *1840*
still that dream   429 *1840* Her days and nights; 'twas found the orb she
sought

---

422 *Gate Saint Blaise*: the building of the Porta S. Biagio was begun by
Marquis Nicolò III in the fifteenth century, so this may be considered as an
anachronism. See M. A. Guarini, *Compendio historico dell'Origine, Accrescimento
e Prerogative delle Chiese e Luoghi Pii della Città e Diocesi di Ferrara* (Ferrara,
1621), p. 55.
    423 *in Vicenza*: Verci (i. 93–4) opposes the view of certain recent writers,
'relying on the sole authority of the impostor Pietro Gerardo', that Ecelin took
his decision to retire from the world in the castle of Meda, in the territory of
Vicenza. Cf. ll. 517–18 below.
    427 *the Church*: 'so went into the convent, already the Monk—as his Ances-
tors were the Stammerer [&c.]': *SB*.
    429 *the orb*: cf. 334–6, above.
    430 *Fomalhaut*: a significant difference from Dante, who places Cunizza
(Browning's Palma) in the Heaven of Venus, 'The radiant planet, that to love
invites' (Purgatory i. 19). Verci points out (*Storia* i. 114) that Dante does this
'precisely to indicate that she was much given to mad love affairs'. Browning's
heroine is a very different woman, hence (in all probability) the change.
Fomalhaut is 'A star of the first magnitude in the constellation Southern Fish'
(OED), adjacent to Venus. It occurs again in *Ferishtah's Fancies* ('A Bean-
Stripe', line 462). It is possible that Browning remembered Burton's *Anatomy
of Melancholy*, Part II, Section 3, Member 7: 'Cardan comforted himself with
this, "the star Fomalhaut would make him immortal", and that after his
decease his books should be found in ladies' studies. *Dignum laude virum Musa
vetat mori*'. Burton quotes Cardan's words in Latin, 'Stella Fomalhaut immor-
talitatem dabit', but his reference—'Lib. de lib. propriis'—appears to be
erroneous. In astrology Fomalhaut was one of four royal stars.

"No other: but how serve it?—authorize
"You and Romano mingle destinies?

How success at last seemed possible,

"And straight Romano's angel stood beside
"Me who had else been Boniface's bride,
435　"For Salinguerra 't was, with neck low bent,
"And voice lightened to music, (as he meant
"To learn, not teach me,) who withdrew the pall
"From the dead past and straight revived it all,
"Making me see how first Romano waxed,
440　"Wherefore it waned now, why, if I relaxed
"My grasp (even I!) would drop a thing effete,
"Frayed by itself, unequal to complete
"Its course, and counting every step astray
"A gain so much. Romano, every way
"Stable, a Lombard House now—why start

by the intervention of Salinguerra:

445　　　back
"Into the very outset of its track?
"This patching principle which late allied
"Our House with other Houses—what beside
"Concerned the apparition, the first Knight
450　"Who followed Conrad hither in such plight
"His utmost wealth was summed in his one steed?

431-2 *1840* No other: how then serve it?—authorise|Him and
Romano　　434 *1840* Her who　　435 *1840* 'twas, the neck　　436 *1840* The
voice . . . . music as　　437-38 {Not in *1840*}　　*439-40 {Editors' emen-
dation}　　*1840* To learn not teach me how Romano waxed,|Wherefore it
waned, and why if I relaxed　　*1863-89* Making me see how first Romano
waxed, Wherefore he waned now, why, if I relaxed　　441 *1840* grasp (think,
I!)　　443 *1840* The course　　445 *1840* Stable, a House now—why this
starting back　　447 *1840* This recent patching- principle allied　　*1863,1865*
This patching-principle which late allied　　449 *1840* yon grim Knight
451 *1840* was reckoned in his steed?

---

432 *mingle destinies?*: 'Bring the two into a constellation?': *SB.*
433 *Romano's angel*: Taurello.
434 *Boniface's bride*: 'forthwith—': *SB.* Cf. i. 941 n.
440 *it*: underlined in Domett, with 'the orb' written in the margin.
441 *would*: i.e. it would.　　442 *Frayed*: worn out.
445 *Stable*: now that Romano is stable in every way, why should it revert
to its old ways, when it was still insignificant? 'This patching principle', now
wrongly proposed by the Monk (by means of alliances with other Houses),
had been the means rightly adopted by his ancestor, the 'weather-beaten thief'
of unprepossessing appearance who had first come to Lombardy and founded a
family. Cf. i. 239-49.
452 *one steed*: Verci i. 5 quotes Rolandino [Muratori viii. 176] on the fact that
the originator of the House had arrived with Conrad from Germany as a 'miles
ab uno equo'. Cf. i. 239 ff.

"For Ecelo, that prowler, was decreed
"A task, in the beginning hazardous
"To him as ever task can be to us;
"But did the weather-beaten thief despair   455
"When first our crystal cincture of warm air
"That binds the Trevisan,—as its spice-belt
"(Crusaders say) the tract where Jesus dwelt,—
"Furtive he pierced, and Este was to face—
"Despaired Saponian strength of Lombard grace?   460
"Tried he at making surer aught made sure,
"Maturing what already was mature?
"No; his heart prompted Ecelo, 'Confront
"'Este, inspect yourself. What 's nature? Wont.
"'Discard three-parts your nature, and adopt   465
"'The rest as an advantage!' Old strength
     propped
"The man who first grew Podestà among
"The Vicentines, no less than, while there sprung
"His palace up in Padua like a threat,
"Their noblest spied a grace, unnoticed yet   470
"In Conrad's crew. Thus far the object gained,

---

456 *1840* air, *1863–8* air,—   457 *1840* Trivisan as   458 *1840*
dwelt,   460 *1840* Strength . . . . Grace?   461 *1840* Said he for making   463 *1840* Confront   466 *1840* The . . . . advantage! Old
Strength   467 *1840* The earliest of Podestas among   468 *1840–65* The
Vicentines,   470 *1840* Grace unnoticed

---

457 *the Trevisan*: cf. i. 247 n.
460 *Saponian strength*: Berdoe described this as 'the hardest of the Browning
nuts to crack'. In 'A Browning Examination Paper' in his *Browning Cyclopædia*
(2nd ed., 1892) he claimed that this problem had recently been 'probably the
literary riddle of the season' (p. x). He believed that the matter had been settled
by a letter 'from a country correspondent, who said that some years ago Mr.
Browning was asked to explain his dark saying at dinner. He replied that it
referred to the Saponi, a branch of the Eccelini family which settled in Lombardy before Sordello's time'. This should perhaps be treated with reserve.
The text seems to require the general meaning Teuton or Swabian.
464 *inspect yourself*: compare yourself and Este.
What's nature?: 'Use is second nature': Domett.
467 *The man*: Ecelin the Stutterer ('il Balbo'), one of the first to be elected to
the position of podestà, as Verci mentions (i. 231), adding that the chroniclers
Maurisius and Godi agree that he ruled 'with the greatest justice and prudence'.
At i. 65 Verci refers to Ecelin's battlemented palace and tower, with a gate in
the city wall, 'a fact which bore witness to greatness and power'. On the office
of podestà see i. 150 n.
468 *The Vicentines* (*1840*): 'to *their* amazement': SB.
470 *"Their noblest*: 'His own': SB.

"Romano was established—has remained—
"'For are you not Italian, truly peers
"'With Este? *Azzo* better soothes our ears *who remedied ill*
475 "'Than *Alberic*? or is this lion's-crine   *wrought by Ecelin,*
"'From over-mounts' (this yellow hair of mine)
"'So weak a graft on Agnes Este's stock?'
"(Thus went he on with something of a mock)
"'Wherefore recoil, then, from the very fate
480 "'Conceded you, refuse to imitate
"'Your model farther? Este long since left
"'Being mere Este: as a blade its heft,
"'Este required the Pope to further him:
"'And you, the Kaiser—whom your father's
  whim
485 "'Foregoes or, better, never shall forego
"'If Palma dare pursue what Ecelo
"'Commenced, but Ecelin desists from: just *and had a project*
"'As Adelaide of Susa could intrust   *for her own glory,*
"'Her donative,—her Piedmont given the Pope,
490 "'Her Alpine-pass for him to shut or ope

472 *1840* established; 473 *1840* For .... peer *1863–68* For ....
peers 474–5 *1840* With Este? Azzo better soothes it ear|Than
Alberic? *1863–8* With Este? 'Azzo' better soothes our ears|Than 'Alberic?'
476 *1840* over-mount 477 *1840* stock? 479 *1840* Wherefore recoil then
483 *1840* Este requires 484 *1840* Kaiser: 486 *1840* Palma dares
489–90 *1840* Her donative (that's Piedmont to the Pope,|The Alpine-pass

473 *"'For are you not*: the inverted commas become confusing. From 439 to
472 Palma has been telling Sordello the argument put to her by Taurello: lines
473–96 are a direct quotation of his words, so that 'you' (473) means Palma:
'peers', the equals of.
 474–5 *Azzo . . . Alberic?*: is Azzo a more musical name than Alberic?
 475 *lion's-crine*: her yellow hair: cf. ii. 100–1.
 476 *From over-mounts*: It. 'oltramonti', from beyond the Alps. OED cites
only this passage and *Ferishtah's Fancies* ('A Bean-Stripe', 239 [and 243]).
 482 *as a blade*: 'a coarse motive power': SB.
 486–7 *Ecelo . . . Ecelin*: the Monk's father, contrasted with the Monk.
 487 *Ecelin*: 'these boys are too young to put forward—I can put *you* forward.
I will not act for myself in [illegible] lest I be tempted': SB.
 488 *Adelaide of Susa*: cf. iv. 569 ff. In the *Biographie Universelle* Sismondi
wrote that she 'governed Piedmont with wisdom and firmness, and shared
with Mathilda the admiration of her century; but she was more restrained in
her opinions and more moderate in her passions and on several occasions
offered herself as mediatrix between Gregory VII and the Emperor Henry IV'.
Sismondi adds that she was considered one of the founders of the power of the
house of Savoy in Piedmont. Each of her three marriages brought her more
territory, so that 'the marquisate of Suze became in her hands one of the most
important fiefs in Italy'. She conveyed her estates to the Pope in 1110, but the
'donative' entrusted to Matilda appears to be unhistorical.

"'Twixt France and Italy,—to the superb
"'Matilda's perfecting,—so, lest aught curb
"'Our Adelaide's great counter-project for
"'Giving her Trentine to the Emperor
"'With passage here from Germany,—shall you   495
"'Take it,—my slender plodding talent, too!'
"—Urged me Taurello with his half-smile.
                                                "He

"As Patron of the scattered family
"Conveyed me to his Mantua, kept in bruit
"Azzo's alliances and Richard's suit   500
"Until, the Kaiser excommunicate,
"'Nothing remains,' Taurello said, 'but wait
"'Some rash procedure: Palma was the link,
"'As Agnes' child, between us, and they shrink
"'From losing Palma: judge if we advance,   505
"'Your father's method, your inheritance!'
"The day I was betrothed to Boniface
"At Padua by Taurello's self, took place

---

491 *1840* Italy)   492 *1840* Matilda's perfecting,—lest aught disturb   495 *1840* And passage . . . . Germany,   496 *1840* Take it, my . . . .
talent, too—   *497 {Reading of *1863–8*} *1840* Urged . . . . half-
smile. *1888,1889* "—Urged . . . . half-smile   499 *1840* Conveyed her
to   502 *1840* Nothing remains, Taurello said, but wait   505 *1840*
advance   506 *1840* method your inheritance!   507 *1840* That day she
was *1840–68* That day I was

494 *Trentine*: the Trentine Pass.
497 *with his half-smile*: 'I agreed—bade him act': *SB*.
497 *He*: *SB* inserts 'at once' before this word.
499 *his Mantua*: cf. ii. 910 ff.
kept in bruit: saw to it that talk continued about alliances with Azzo of Este
(cf. ii. 883–7) and Richard's suit for my hand.
501 *excommunicate*: in fact Friedrich was first excommunicated in 1227, by
Gregory IX. Pettigrew states that the word 'here obviously means "out-of-
touch" and not "excommunicated"', referring to i. 130–7. But OED provides
virtually no support for such a meaning, and it is more likely that Browning
has modified historical fact, as he so often does. *SB*'s '& ready to break bounds,'
is compatible with the normal meaning of the word; and cf. i. 200.
503 *Some rash procedure*: 'of our enemies': *SB*.
Palma was the link: it is awkward that she should use her own name, in
repeating what Taurello had said to her. Note the revision from 'her' to 'me' in
499: there is perhaps some confusion between direct and indirect speech.
505 *From losing Palma*: 'once promised:' *SB*.
judge if we advance: i.e. your father's proposed method is futile. 'If by
concessions to them we strengthen ourselves': *SB*.
507 *betrothed*: but not married (in the poem, as distinct from historical fact).
SB inserts 'provisionally' before 'betrothed'. Cf. i. 941 n.

"The outrage of the Ferrarese: again,
510 "The day I sought Verona with the train
"Agreed for,—by Taurello's policy
"Convicting Richard of the fault, since we
"Were present to annul or to confirm,—
"Richard, whose patience had outstayed its term,
"Quitted Verona for the siege.
515　　　　　　　　　　　　　　　　"And now
"What glory may engird Sordello's brow
"Through this? A month since at Oliero slunk
"All that was Ecelin into a monk;
"But how could Salinguerra so forget
520 "His liege of thirty years as grudge even yet
"One effort to recover him? He sent
"Forthwith the tidings of this last event
"To Ecelin—declared that he, despite
"The recent folly, recognized his right
525 "To order Salinguerra: 'Should he wring
"'Its uttermost advantage out, or fling
"'This chance away? Or were his sons now
　　　Head
"'O' the House?' Through me Taurello's
　　　missive sped;
"My father's answer will by me return.

which she would change to Sordello's.

---

510 *1840* That day she sought　*1863–8* That day I ,sought　511 *1840*
Agreed for,　512 *1840* since she　513 *1840* Was present . . . .
confirm,　517–18 *1840* For this? A month since Oliero sunk|All Ecelin that
was into a Monk;　520 *1840* thirty summers as grudge yet　522 *1840* of
the Town's event　523 *1840* To Oliero, adding, he, despite　525 *1840* To
order such proceedings: should　527 *1840* This chance away? If not him,
who was Head　528 *1840* Now of the House? Through me that missive
1863–8 Of the House?' Through me Taurello's missive

---

509 *The outrage*: cf. i. 149 ff. In fact the outrage played into Taurello's hands,
as it gave him an excuse for establishing himself in Ferrara.
511–3 *by Taurello's policy . . . confirm*: bracketed in *SB*.
515 *And now*: before these words *SB* has: 'Then the last man[illegible]', and
'all was ready:' after them.
517 *For this?* (*1840*): *SB* changes to 'By this?' and adds: 'opportunity for
Romano?'
522 *this last event*: 'The outrage of the Ferrarese' (509).
527 *his sons*: Ecelin and Alberic.
528 *Taurello's missive*: this is a fictitious letter, but a letter from Taurello to
Ecelin, and the reply, are given in Muratori viii. 186–8, and in Verci iii. 207–8.

"Behold! 'For him,' he writes, 'no more concern   530
"'With strife than, for his children, with fresh
     plots
"'Of Friedrich. Old engagements out he blots
"'For aye: Taurello shall no more subserve,
"'Nor Ecelin impose.' Lest this unnerve
"Taurello at this juncture, slack his grip   535
"Of Richard, suffer the occasion slip,—
"I, in his sons' default (who, mating with
"Este, forsake Romano as the frith
"Its mainsea for that firmland, sea makes head
"Against) I stand, Romano,—in their stead   540
"Assume the station they desert, and give
"Still, as the Kaiser's representative,
"Taurello licence he demands. Midnight—
"Morning—by noon to-morrow, making light
"Of the League's issue, we, in some gay weed   545
"Like yours, disguised together, may precede
"The arbitrators to Ferrara: reach
"Him, let Taurello's noble accents teach
"The rest! Then say if I have misconceived
"Your destiny, too readily believed   550

530–1 *1840* For him, he writes, no more concern| With strife than for his
children with the plots   534 *1840* impose.   535 *1840* Him therefore
at   536 *1840* slip,   539 *1840* the firmland that makes *1863–8* the
firmland, sea makès   540 *1840* Romano; in   546 *1840* Like yours

---

533 *subserve*: OED describes the intransitive use as obsolete and rare, citing
Samson Agonistes, 57: 'Not made to rule, / But to subserve where wisdom bears
command'.
536 *suffer the occasion slip*: 'or, on the other hand, stimulate him to set up on his
own account': *SB*.
537 *who, mating*: *SB* inserts 'having' before 'mating', which it alters to
'mated', and inserts 'inexorably[?]' after 'mated'. *Domett* notes: 'her brothers
join the Guelfs'.
538 *as the frith*: his sons are forsaking the House of Romano as the sea deserts
itself when it invades the land and becomes a firth. Cary uses 'main-sea' in *Hell*,
xx. 47.
540 *I stand, Romano*: Palma's taking on herself the leadership of the House of
Romano is, of course, unhistorical.
543 *he demands*: 'for I know words of might to touch him at his strongest':
SB.
545 *the League's issue*: the gathering of the Lombard League.
some gay weed: she is to be dressed as a minstrel, as he is.
548 *Taurello's noble accents*: i.e. he will explain to you how you are to assume
the leadership of Romano. 'I will not make myself known—but let you speak':
SB.

"The Kaiser's cause your own!"

And Palma's fled.

Though no affirmative disturbs the head,
A dying lamp-flame sinks and rises o'er,
Like the alighted planet Pollux wore,
555 Until, morn breaking, he resolves to be
Gate-vein of this heart's blood of Lombardy,
Soul of this body—to wield this aggregate
Of souls and bodies, and so conquer fate   *Thus then, having*
Though he should live—a centre of disgust   *completed a circle,*
560 Even—apart, core of the outward crust
He vivifies, assimilates. For thus
I bring Sordello to the rapturous
Exclaim at the crowd's cry, because one round
Of life was quite accomplished; and he found
565 Not only that a soul, whate'er its might,
Is insufficient to its own delight,

---

551 *1840* your own.   557 *1840* Soul to their body—have their aggregate   559 *1840* live,   560 *1840* Even,   561 *1863,1865* He vivified,
assimilated. Thus   562 *1840* Bring I Sordello   564 *1840* accomplished
565 *1840* howe'er its might,

---

551 *your own*: 'Go *you* forward!': SB.

552 *no affirmative*: Palma leaves Sordello without awaiting his answer, and in
fact he does not make up his mind until dawn. 'Though': however.

553 *A dying lamp-flame*: cf. i. 329. This is the moment at which we have first
seen Sordello and Palma, before we knew their names. Domett correctly refers
to 'page 15', i.e. i. 329 and the 'lady there described'.

554 *Pollux*: 'all *merciful Kings*, and *Saviours of their Country*, were called
Dioscuri . . . as were *Castor* and *Pollux*': *An Historical Account of the Heathen Gods
and Heroes*, by Dr King, fifth edition, (1731), p. 181. Each was commonly
portrayed with a star over his head. Beneath this line, at the foot of p. 109, SB
has: 'Here is the opportunity for the realisation of the dream'.

556 *Gate-vein*: cf. i. 346.

557 *Soul of this body*: he decides to become the informing soul of Romano, so
'conquer[ing] fate'. Domett writes: 'To lead the Emperor's party in place of
Ecelin (?)', correctly.

to wield: to rule over, OED has no example after 1633.

559 *a centre of disgust*: even if he should be very unpopular.

561 *He vivifies, assimilates*: 'complete *one* function, at least': SB, which has the
further note: 'He would push the people to its *ultimate* development'.

562–3 *the rapturous / Exclaim*: cf. i. 337 ff. It seems that when Sordello heard
the cries of the crowd he himself exclaimed in excitement.

563 *one round*: one phase of Sordello's spiritual Odyssey has been completed.
He has learned that his soul cannot be self-sufficient, and that neither personal
happiness nor any worthwhile achievement can result from acting as if it could.
He has the notion that the true way to serve men would be to cause them to act,
but his belief that *he* has been chosen 'to rescind / The ignominious exile of
mankind' is an immature illusion—as that very phrase, and the word 'Seemed'
in line 585, make explicit.

Both in corporeal organs and in skill
By means of such to body forth its Will—
And, after, insufficient to apprise
Men of that Will, oblige them recognize   57
The Hid by the Revealed—but that,—the last
Nor lightest of the struggles overpast,—
Will, he bade abdicate, which would not void
The throne, might sit there, suffer he enjoyed
Mankind, a varied and divine array   57
Incapable of homage, the first way,
Nor fit to render incidentally
Tribute connived at, taken by the by,
In joys. If thus with warrant to rescind
The ignominious exile of mankind—   58
Whose proper service, ascertained intact
As yet, (to be by him themselves made act,
Not watch Sordello acting each of them)
Was to secure—if the true diadem
Seemed imminent while our Sordello drank   5
The wisdom of that golden Palma,—thank
Verona's Lady in her citadel
Founded by Gaulish Brennus, legends tell:
And truly when she left him, the sun reared

---

571 *1840–68* that,   572 *1840–68* overpast,   573 *1840–68* His Will, bade
abdicate,   574 *1840–68* suffer be enjoyed   575 *1840* The same a varied   579 *1840* In joys: and if, thus warranted rescind   580 *1840* mankind   582 *1840* As yet (by Him to be themselves   586 *1840* Palma,
thank   588 *1840* Brennus legends tell—

---

573 *he bade abdicate*: '(at Goito)': SB.
574 ∧ *might sit there*: 'now': SB.
575 *The same a varied and divine array* (*1840*): SB has 'all' before this line, and
'of human beings of various quality' at the end.
587 *Verona's Lady*: the statue on the top of a fountain at one end of Piazza
delle Erbe, called by the inhabitants 'Madonna Verona'.
588 *Gaulish Brennus*: 'This citie is of that antiquitie, that some do write it was
first founded by the ancient Hetruscans . . . But afterwards in processe of time,
the Gaules that are called Senones, having passed over the Alpes under the
conduct of their Captaine Brennus, came into this part of Italy, and ejected
those Hetruscans . . . So that it was called Verona quasi Brenona, from their
Captaine Brennus': *Coryat's Crudities Hastily gobled up in five Moneths travells*,
by T. Coryat (1611), repr. 1905, ii. 16–17.
589 *when she left him*: when Palma left Sordello enlightenment (the sun)
seemed to dawn on him, like the rising head of the first soldier to scale the
Roman Capitol in 390 BC. The legend that Brennus founded Verona prompts a
reference to his capture of Rome. His troops were on the point of scaling the

590 A head like the first clamberer's who peered
    A-top the Capitol, his face on flame
    With triumph, triumphing till Manlius came.
    Nor slight too much my rhymes—that spring,
        dispread,
    Dispart, disperse, lingering over head
595 Like an escape of angels! Rather say,
    My transcendental platan! mounting gay
    (An archimage so courts a novice-queen)
    With tremulous silvered trunk, whence branches
        sheen
    Laugh out, thick-foliaged next, a-shiver soon
600 With coloured buds, then glowing like the moon
    One mild flame,—last a pause, a burst, and all
    Her ivory limbs are smothered by a fall,
    Bloom-flinders and fruit-sparkles and leaf-dust,
    Ending the weird work prosecuted just
605 For her amusement; he decrepit, stark,
    Dozes; her uncontrolled delight may mark
    Apart—   *the poet may pause*
        Yet not so, surely never so!   *and breathe,*

590 *1840–68* clamberer's that peered   592 *1888,1889* came, {some copies
only, with worn type}   593 *1840* rhymes—"that spring,   595 *1840* angels?"
Rather say   601 *1840* flame, last   *607 {Reading of *1840–68*}   *1888,1889*
never so

walls when Manlius, awakened by the sacred geese, gave the alarm and flung
down 'the first clamberer'.
    593 *Nor slight too much my rhymes*: the reader should neither despise the
youthful Sordello nor the poet who is writing his story.
    593–5 *that spring . . . angels!*: the quotation marks in *1840* draw attention to
the repetition from i. 881 ff. The passage emphasizes that it is often impossible
to distinguish Sordello from the poet who is telling the story.
    596 *My transcendental platan!*: cf. 'Transcendentalism' in *Men and Women*.
Under 'Plane-tree' Johnson quotes Miller's description of this tree and its
flowers, 'consisting of several slender stamina, which are all collected into
spherical little balls and are barren'. In the *Georgics* (ii. 70) Virgil writes of
'steriles platani', explaining (however) that they may be grafted.
    597 *An archimage*: the poet is displaying his powers as a great wizard might,
to impress a young queen. Cf. Shelley, 'Letter to Maria Gisborne', 106 ff: 'And
here like some weird Archimage sit I'. The word 'weird' occurs in line 604.
    601 *One mild flame*: 'when the yellow thins to white, brighter & more bright':
SB.
    a pause, a burst: as in a firework-display. The young queen's limbs are
momentarily covered with fragments of flowers. OED records no other
example of 'bloom-flinders'.
    607 *Yet not so*: he will not abandon the poem, as the old magician, weary and
decrepit, loses interest in his own exhibition.

Only, as good my soul were suffered go
O'er the lagune: forth fare thee, put aside—
Entrance thy synod, as a god may glide   610
Out of the world he fills, and leave it mute
For myriad ages as we men compute,
Returning into it without a break
O' the consciousness! They sleep, and I awake

being really in the
flesh at Venice,

O'er the lagune, being at Venice.

                         Note,   615
In just such songs as Eglamor (say) wrote
With heart and soul and strength, for he
    believed
Himself achieving all to be achieved
By singer—in such songs you find alone
Completeness, judge the song and singer one,   620
And either purpose answered, his in it
Or its in him: while from true works (to wit
Sordello's dream-performances that will
Never be more than dreamed) escapes there still

---

608 *1840* Only as   609 *1840–65* aside   612 *1840* A myriad   614 *1840* I'
the   615 *1840* lagune. ¶ Sordello said once, note   *1863,1865* lagune. ¶ Sordello said once, "Note,   616 *1840* Eglamor, say,   620 *1840* One   621
1840–65 And either's purpose   624 *1840* Be never more than
dream)   *1863–8* Be never more than dreamed)

    608 *my soul*: that of the narrator, hardly to be differentiated from Browning's
own.
    609 *the lagune*: as in line 87 of Shelley's 'Julian and Maddalo; A Conversa-
tion', which is set in Venice.
    610 *Entrance*: lay a spell on the characters of your story, just as a god existing
(as he does) outside our time-scheme, can leave his world silent for a thousand
ages (of human time), returning to it at will. The poet waves his wand, and the
world of his poem goes to sleep for as long as he wishes.
    615 *at Venice*: Browning left England on 13 April 1838, Good Friday, and
reached Venice on 1 June. The following day he made a cryptic note about the
poem: see Appendix D below.
    Note: this passage comments on the abrupt hiatus in the poem. In *1840, 1863*
and *1865* the view expressed is attributed to Sordello, in later editions (perhaps
to obviate the awkwardness occasioned by the parenthesis in 622–4) to the
narrator. It anticipates Ruskin's doctrine of the imperfection of the greatest
works. The reviewer of *Pauline* in the *Monthly Repository* for 1833 had written
that there had never been 'a genuine bard, who was not in himself more poetical
than any of his productions. They are emanations of his essence' (p. 253). Cf.
Browning's own remark, in the *Essay on Chatterton*, that 'ever in Chatterton
did his acquisitions, varied and abundant as they were, do duty so as to seem
but a little out of more in reserve' (p. 132). The word 'looking-off' occurs in
Paracelsus, iii. 647.
    616 ∧ *In*: 'that': *SB*.   617–9 *for he . . . singer*: bracketed in *SB*.

625   Some proof, the singer's proper life was 'neath
The life his song exhibits, this a sheath
To that; a passion and a knowledge far
Transcending these, majestic as they are,
Smouldered; his lay was but an episode
630   In the bard's life: which evidence you owed
To some slight weariness, some looking-off
Or start-away. The childish skit or scoff
In "Charlemagne," (his poem, dreamed divine
In every point except one silly line
635   About the restiff daughters)—what may lurk
In that? "My life commenced before this work,"
(So I interpret the significance
Of the bard's start aside and look askance)
"My life continues after: on I fare
640   "With no more stopping, possibly, no care
"To note the undercurrent, the why and how,
"Where, when, o' the deeper life, as thus just
      now.
"But, silent, shall I cease to live? Alas

---

625 *1840* Some proof the singer's proper life's beneath   628 *1840 proof*
Exceeding>Transcending   629 *1840* Smoulder;   630 *1840* life.
Which   631 *1840* weariness, a looking-off   632 *1840* Or start-away,
the   633 *1840* "Charlemagne," for instance, dreamed   634–5 *1840* one
restive line|(Those daughters!)—what significance may lurk   *1863,1865* one
silly line|About the restiff daughters!)—what may lurk   636 *1840* My . . . .
before that work,   637 {Not in *1840*}   *1863,1865* (Thus I interpret   638
{Not in *1840*}   639 *1840* Continues after it, as on I fare   640 *1840* stop-
ping   641–3 *1840* To jot down (says the bard) the why and how|And where
and when of life as I do now:|But shall I cease to live for that? Alas   642
1863–8 Where, when, of the deeper life, as thus just now.

---

625 *proper life*: Domett comments, in exasperation, 'What the devil is the
proper life to us?'

633 *"Charlemagne"*: an imaginary poem by Sordello.

dreamed divine: it is tempting to emend to 'deemed', but there is no authority.

635 *restiff* stubborn, refractory. It was said that Charlemagne could not bear
the thought of his daughters leaving him.

636 *In that?* ∧ : 'This:' SB.

"My life commenced: the very line which has been thought 'silly' constitutes an}
affirmation that the poet is not wholly concerned with the present poem: he
will continue to live when it has been completed and dismissed from his
attention—and may not even bother to give a hint of the 'undercurrent' of his
'deeper life', as he had done in that line, that 'look askance'.

643 *shall I cease to live?*: he will not cease to have a deeper life, although he will
not speak or write of it. So much the worse for readers who long to read 'the
better lay' in which his profoundest thought will be revealed.

and watching his own life sometimes,

"For you! who sigh, 'When shall it come to pass
"'We read that story? How will he compress   645
"'The future gains, his life's true business,
"'Into the better lay which—that one flout,
"'Howe'er inopportune it be, lets out—
"'Engrosses him already, though professed
"'To meditate with us eternal rest,   650
"'And partnership in all his life has found?'"
'T is but a sailor's promise, weather-bound:
"Strike sail, slip cable, here the bark be moored
"For once, the awning stretched, the poles
          assured!
"Noontide above; except the wave's crisp dash,   655
"Or buzz of colibri, or tortoise' splash,
"The margin 's silent: out with every spoil
"Made in our tracking, coil by mighty coil,
"This serpent of a river to his head
"I' the midst! Admire each treasure, as we spread   660
"The bank, to help us tell our history
"Aright: give ear, endeavour to descry
"The groves of giant rushes, how they grew
"Like demons' endlong tresses we sailed through,
"What mountains yawned, forests to give us vent   665

---

644 *1840* sigh, when   645 *1840* story, when   646 *1840* The future years,
his whole life's business,   647 *1840* Into another lay which that   648 *1840*
out   649 *1840* already while professed   650 *1840* rest?   651–2 {Not in
1840}   651 *1863,1865* found?   653 *1840* Strike sail, slip cable! here the
galley's moored   654 *1840 proof* morning's> awning's *1840* awning's
stretched, ... assured;   661 *1840* The turf to   662 *1840* Aright: give ear
then, gentles, and descry   665 *1840* How mountains

---

650 *To meditate with us*: he has undertaken to remain with us for ever, and to
share with us all his life's discoveries, yet that revealing aside in "Charlemagne" makes it clear that he is already preoccupied with a more profound
poem dealing with 'the deeper life'.
652 *a sailor's promise*: proverbial.
653 *slip cable*: drop anchor. The poet's profession that he will always remain
with his audience is no more to be trusted than the promise of a sailor who
merely awaits a favourable wind.
654 *the poles*: of a tent. Cf. 671.   656 *colibri*: humming-bird.
657 *The margin*: the edge of the water.
658 *Made in our tracking*: the poet is compared to adventurous traders who
have been tracing a serpentine river to its head, in the middle of a continent.
Browning is no doubt remembering the shipping which he must have watched
at Venice.
662 *endeavour to descry*: try to visualize.

"Opened, each doleful side, yet on we went
"Till . . . may that beetle (shake your cap)
    attest
"The springing of a land-wind from the West!"
    —Wherefore? Ah yes, you frolic it to-day!
670 To-morrow, and, the pageant moved away
Down to the poorest tent-pole, we and you
Part company: no other may pursue
Eastward your voyage, be informed what fate
Intends, if triumph or decline await
675 The tempter of the everlasting steppe.
    I muse this on a ruined palace-step
At Venice: why should I break off, nor sit
Longer upon my step, exhaust the fit
England gave birth to? Who 's adorable
680 Enough reclaim a —— no Sordello's Will
Alack!—be queen to me? That Bassanese
Busied among her smoking fruit-boats? These

*because it is
pleasant to be
young,*

668–9 *1840* West!|Wherefore? Ah yes, we frolic it to-day: *1863,1865*
West!'|—'Wherefore? Ah yes, you frolic it to-day!   670 *1840–65* and the
pageant's moved   671 *1840–65* tent-pole: 675 *1863,1865* steppe.'   676
1840 I sung this on an empty palace-step   679 *1840 proof* Whose> Who's

667 *may that beetle*: optative. The sailor hopes that the beetle indicates the
advent of a favourable wind. The poet is in the same situation.
669 *you frolic it*: the speaker, to l. 675, may be one of the friends the sailors
have made during their compulsory halt.
675 *tempter*: attempter, a sense not given in OED. 'Steppe' suggests south-
east Europe or Siberia, but may also be used in relation to other parts of the
world.
676 *I muse this*: possibly revised because (according to what he told Fanny
Haworth) Browning 'did not write six lines while absent (except a scene in a
play . . .)': *Letters*, p. 2. He mentions that he wrote two lines addressed to her
and 'two to the Queen . . the whole to go in Book 3—perhaps'. For the lines to
her, see ll. 968 ff.
678 *the fit*: of musing. Browning is likely to have received mail at Venice.
680 *no Sordello's Will*: a reminder of the importance of Will to Sordello. The
dash no doubt stands for 'Browning'.
681 *be queen to me?*: Sordello is a king among men, but the word 'queen' may
equally have been prompted by the accession of Queen Victoria on 20 June
1837 and her coronation, now imminent (it took place on 28 June 1838). The
two lines addressed to the Queen do not appear, possibly because of Browning's republican sympathies. In any event, his eye is caught by the Italian girls
whom he is watching at their work. Who can reclaim him, and give him
purpose, as Palma did for Sordello? In 1846 he asked Elizabeth Barrett: 'is it not
right you should be my Lady, my Queen?': Kintner, i. 543.
That Bassanese: on leaving Venice Browning went to visit Bassano, which
the Monk had given Alberic when he retired from the world.

Perhaps from our delicious Asolo
Who twinkle, pigeons o'er the portico
Not prettier, bind June lilies into sheaves   685
To deck the bridge-side chapel, dropping leaves
Soiled by their own loose gold-meal? Ah,
    beneath
The cool arch stoops she, brownest cheek! Her
    wreath
Endures a month—a half-month—if I make
A queen of her, continue for her sake   690
Sordello's story? Nay, that Paduan girl
Splashes with barer legs where a live whirl
In the dead black Giudecca proves sea-weed
Drifting has sucked down three, four, all indeed
Save one pale-red striped, pale-blue turbaned
    post   695
For gondolas.

would but suffering   You sad dishevelled ghost
humanity allow!

---

685 *1840* bind late lilies   693 *1840 proof* Gindecca>Giudecca

683 *delicious Asolo*: the phrase occurs in the letter quoted in 676 n. Browning
stayed in Asolo a few weeks before his death, and found it as enchanting as
ever. He told George Barrett that 'properly speaking, it was the first spot of
Italian soil I ever set foot upon—having proceeded to Venice by sea—and
thence here [to Asolo]. It is an ancient city, older than Rome . . . the immense
charm of the surrounding country is indescribable—I have never seen its
like—the Alps on one side, the Asolan mountains all round,—and opposite the
vast Lombard plain . . .': *Letters of the Brownings to George Barrett*, ed. Paul
Landis (Urbana, Illinois, 1958), p. 329. Eight days earlier he had told J. D.
Williams that 'this lovely Asolo' was his 'spot of predilection in the whole
world, I think': 'Letters from Robert Browning to The Rev. J. D. Williams,
1874–1889', ed. Thomas J. Collins, in *Browning Institute Studies*, ed. W. S.
Peterson, vol. 4 (The Browning Institute, 1976), p. 56. See, too, the 'Prologue'
to *Asolando*, published on the day of Browning's death.
687 *gold-meal*: golden-yellow pollen.
693 *Giudecca*: an island in the Venetian lagoon: here the canal of the same
name.
694 *all*: all the poles but one.
696 *dishevelled ghost*: in a letter to Fanny Haworth conjecturally dated May
1840, on a passage she wanted 'cleared up' (obviously the lines addressed to
her, 968 ff.), Browning told her that she should be 'glad' because, 'as I stopped
my task awhile, left off my versewriting one sunny June day with a notion of
not taking to it again in a hurry, the sad disheveled form I had just been talking
of, that plucked and pointed, wherein I put, comprize, typify and figure to
myself Mankind, the whole poor-devildom one sees cuffed and huffed from
morn to midnight, that, so typified, she may come at times and keep my pact in
mind, prick up my republicanism [cf. note to l. 681, above] and remind me of
certain engagements I have entered into with myself about that same, renewed
me, gave me fresh spirit, made me after finishing Book 3d commence Book

That pluck at me and point, are you advised
I breathe? Let stay those girls (e'en her
        disguised
—Jewels i' the locks that love no crownet like
700   Their native field-buds and the green
        wheat-spike,
So fair!—who left this end of June's turmoil,
Shook off, as might a lily its gold soil,
Pomp, save a foolish gem or two, and free
In dream, came join the peasants o'er the sea.)
705   Look they too happy, too tricked out? Confess
There is such niggard stock of happiness
To share, that, do one's uttermost, dear wretch,
One labours ineffectually to stretch
It o'er you so that mother and children, both
710   May equitably flaunt the sumpter-cloth!
Divide the robe yet farther: be content
With seeing just a score pre-eminent

---

699 *1840–68* in the   701 *1840 proof* turmoil>turmoil, *1840* —Who
704 *1840 proof* peasant's>peasants   *1840* Came join the peasants o'er the kissing sea.)   705 *1840* proof two happy,>too happy,   706 *1840* You have so
niggard   708 *1840* ineffectually stretch   709 *1840* mother, children,   711 *1840* No: tear the robe   712 *1840* With seeing some few score

---

4th': *New Letters*, p. 18. Browning had presumably 'stopped' actual writing
before he left England: the reference here is probably to a decision, taken in
June, not to go on with the poem, a decision abandoned at the prompting of the
'dishevelled ghost', no doubt a Venetian beggar or street-walker. Mrs. Orr
calls her 'some frail and suffering woman': *Handbook*, p. 41. Domett wrote
'human nature (?)' opposite 'ghost', and, at the foot of the page, 'as if, his
attention diverted from his story, the figure of mankind, his *subject*, came to
remind him of his story—see page 127', i.e. l. 970 ff.
    698 *Let stay*: never mind those beautiful girls.
    e'en her disguised: perhaps a reference to Fanny Haworth, whom he
imagines escaping 'In dream' from the London Season, where she is decked out
with unnecessary jewels, and coming to join the peasant-girls whom he is
watching. At l. 968 he associates her with a flower, 'Eyebright.'
    704 *In dream*: as at ii. 670.
    705 *Look they too happy?*: the poet apologizes to the beggar, and explains that
there is simply not enough felicity (symbolized by 'the sumpter-cloth') to
enable everyone to have a share. (The word occurs in *The Bride of Lammermoor*,
ch. ix; sumpter-cloths, used to cover pack-horses, were often richly embroi-
dered.)
    706 *There is*: 'You have' (*1840*) probably means the same, while 'dear wretch'
is addressed to the 'sad dishevelled ghost'.
    711 *Divide the robe*: 'if we try to share out further such luxury as is avail-
able—to twenty people (say) . . .' The passage was probably suggested by the
legend that St. Martin once divided his cloak with a naked beggar who begged
alms of him: a favourite subject for religious illustrators.

Through shreds of it, acknowledged happy
    wights,
Engrossing what should furnish all, by rights!
For, these in evidence, you clearlier claim   715
A like garb for the rest,—grace all, the same
As these my peasants. I ask youth and strength
And health for each of you, not more—at
    length
Grown wise, who asked at home that the whole
    race
Might add the spirit's to the body's grace,   720
And all be dizened out as chiefs and bards.
But in this magic weather one discards
Much old requirement. Venice seems a type
Of Life—'twixt blue and blue extends, a stripe,
As Life, the somewhat, hangs 'twixt nought and
    nought: 725
'T is Venice, and 't is Life—as good you sought
To spare me the Piazza's slippery stone
Or keep me to the unchoked canals alone,
As hinder Life the evil with the good
Which make up Living, rightly understood.   730
—which instigates Only, do finish something! Peasants, queens,
to tasks like this, Take them, made happy by whatever means,

---

714 *1840–65* rights—   715–20 {Not in *1840*}   721 *1840 proof* deck
out>dizen *1840* (At home we dizen scholars, chiefs and kings,   722–3 *1840*
weather hardly clings|The old garb gracefully: Venice, a type *1863,1865*
weather one discards|Much old requirement—Venice seems a type   724
1840 Life, *1863–8* Life,—   725 *1863* nought and nought   726 *1840 proof*
life—>Life—   727 *1840 proof* stone>stone, *1840,1863* stone,   728 *1840*
proof alone>alone,   728–30 *1840* Or stay me thrid her cross canals alone,|As
hinder Life what seems the single good|Sole purpose, one thing to be under-
stood {line 730 is added in handwriting in *1840 proof*}   731 *1840* Of
Life)—best, be they Peasants, be they Queens, *1863,1865* Only, do finish
something! Peasants or queens,   732 *1840* Take them, I say, made happy any
means,

---

719 *who asked at home*: whereas he had demanded spiritual grace for everyone
while he was still in England, in Italy he has become wiser and now asks only
for 'youth and strength / And health' for them. He no longer believes that all
men may become 'chiefs and bards'.

729 *As hinder Life*: as to try to interfere with Life, in its mixture of evil and
good.

731 *do finish something!*: the poet addresses himself.

Parade them for the common credit, vouch
That a luckless residue, we send to crouch
In corners out of sight, was just as framed
For happiness, its portion might have claimed
As well, and so, obtaining joy, had stalked
Fastuous as any!—such my project, baulked
Already; I hardly venture to adjust
The first rags, when you find me. To mistrust
Me!—nor unreasonably. You, no doubt,
Have the true knack of tiring suitors out
With those thin lips on tremble, lashless eyes
Inveterately tear-shot: there, be wise,
Mistress of mine, there, there, as if I meant
You insult!—shall your friend (not slave) be
    shent
For speaking home? Beside, care-bit erased
Broken-up beauties ever took my taste

735
740
745

---

734 *1840* A luckless residue   735 *1840 proof* were>was *1840*
sight   736 *1840 proof* their>its   737 *1840* And so, could we concede that
portion, stalked   *1863,1865* As well, and so, obtaining it, had stalked   738
1840 any—   739–41 *1840* Already; hardly venture I adjust| A lappet when I
find you! To mistrust| Me!   741 *1840 proof* Me!—nor unreasonably!> Me!
nor unreasonably.   744 *1840–65* tear-shot—there, be wise *1868* tear-
shot—there, be wise,   746 *1840,1863* insult! Shall   748 *1840 proof*
features>beauties

---

733 *for the common credit*: to the common credit of mankind.

738 *Fastuous*: 'Proud; haughty': Johnson.

739–40 *to adjust | The first rags*: the poet was just beginning to try to make
himself look more approachable to the poor by adjusting his clothing ('A
lappet', *1840*, is 'The part of a head dress that hangs loose', Johnson): cf. 756 ff.
There may be a secondary meaning relating to the kind of poem he is now
writing.

740 *you*: addressed to 'The sad dishevelled ghost'.

743 *lips on tremble, lashless eyes*: OED notes that '*On* was formerly frequent in
connexions in which *a-* is now usual' ('On', 29): 'lashless eyelids' occurs in
Keats, *Lamia*, ii. 288.

746 *your friend*: allow me as your friend, and not your slave (i.e. not your
lover?), to say what I think, without reproach.

shent: reproached.   747 *erased*: damaged.

748 *took my taste*: Browning may possibly be influenced by the tradition of
'deformed and suffering female beauty' mentioned by Mario Praz in *The
Romantic Agony* (trans. A. Davidson, 1933), pp. 36 ff. He could have known the
translation from Claudio Achillini in *Lyric Poems, Made in Imitation of the
Italians* by Philip Ayres (1687), which includes the lines: 'Barefoot and ragged,
with neglected hair, / She whom the heavens at once made poor and fair, / With
humble voice and moving words did stay, / To beg an alms of all who pass'd
that way' ('On a Fair Beggar'). Praz comments that 'what was often, in the
seventeenth-century writers, a mere intellectual pose, became, in the Roman-
tics, a pose of sensibility' (p. 38).

Supremely; and I love you more, far more
Than her I looked should foot Life's
    temple-floor—   750
Years ago, leagues at distance, when and where
A whisper came, "Let others seek!—thy care
"Is found, thy life's provision; if thy race
"Should be thy mistress, and into one face
"The many faces crowd?" Ah, had I, judge,   755
Or no, your secret? Rough apparel—grudge
All ornaments save tag or tassel worn
To hint we are not thoroughly forlorn—
Slouch bonnet, unloop mantle, careless go
Alone (that 's saddest, but it must be so)   760
Through Venice, sing now and now glance aside,
Aught desultory or undignified,—
Then, ravishingest lady, will you pass
Or not each formidable group, the mass
Before the Basilic (that feast gone by,   765
God's great day of the Corpus Domini)

---

*750 {Editors' emendation} *1840* That she I looked . . . . temple-
floor— *1863–89* Than her I looked . . . . temple-floor.   752-3 *1840* came,
Seek others, since thy care|Is found, a life's provision; if thy race   754 *1840*
proof a mistress,>thy mistress,   755 *1840* The . . . . crowd?   760 *1840*
proof Alone, that's . . . . so,>Alone (that's . . . . so)   *1840,1863* sad-
dest   762-3 *1840* undignified,|And, ravishingest   765 *1840*
Basilike   766 *1840* God's day, the great June Corpus Domini)

---

750 *Than her I looked*: than the woman I expected to be my inspiration, long
ago and in another country, until I heard a voice prompting me to make the
whole human race my mistress. Will you not agree, then, that I understand
your secret?
    foot: cf. *The Ring and the Book*, i. 613: 'And all five found and footed it, the
track'.
    756 *Rough apparel*: the poet tells himself to dress in a rough-and-ready
manner, suggesting reforming or revolutionary sympathies, so as not to
discourage beggars like this unfortunate girl. Some imperative verb is perhaps
to be understood before 'Rough'. Cf. Carlyle, *The French Revolution*, Vol. I,
Book V, ch. i, para. 3: 'The omen of the "slouch-hats clapt on" shows the
Commons Deputies to have made up their minds on one thing: that neither
Noblesse nor Clergy shall have precedence of them; hardly even Majesty
itself'. Here 'Slouch' is probably an imperative (= 'Pull down').
    762 *Aught desultory*: do anything (he bids himself) to give yourself a casual
and *dégagé* air.
    765 *the Basilic*: Saint Mark's.
    766 *God's great day*: the Thursday after Trinity Sunday. As the latter fell on 10
June in 1838, the reference is to 14 June. Browning left Venice soon afterwards:
cf. note to l. 615.

And, wistfully foregoing proper men,
Come timid up to me for alms? And then
The luxury to hesitate, feign do
Some unexampled grace!—when, whom but
770   you
Dare I bestow your own upon? And hear
Further before you say, it is to sneer
I call you ravishing; for I regret
Little that she, whose early foot was set
775   Forth as she 'd plant it on a pedestal,
Now, i' the silent city, seems to fall
Toward me—no wreath, only a lip's unrest
To quiet, surcharged eyelids to be pressed
Dry of their tears upon my bosom. Strange
Such sad chance should produce in thee such
780   change,
My love! Warped souls and bodies! yet God
      spoke
Of right-hand, foot and eye—selects our yoke,
Sordello, as your poetship may find!
So, sleep upon my shoulder, child, nor mind
785   Their foolish talk; we 'll manage reinstate
Your old worth; ask moreover, when they prate

*and doubtlessly
compensates them,*

770 *1840* grace, when   772 *1840* Me out before you say   777 *1840*
Towards me—   779 *1840* bosom: strange   781 *1840* warped men, souls,
bodies! *1863,1865* warped souls and bodies!   782 *1840 proof* right
hand>right-hand *1840* right-hand . . . . yoke   783 *1840* Sordello! . . . .
find: 784 *1840* So sleep   786 *1840* The matter; ask

767 *proper men*: men of more dignified appearance.

774 *whose early foot*: earlier in the day (or perhaps in her life) there had been a
spring in her step; but now, in the evening, she seems to be falling towards him.

777 *no wreath*: no laurel wreath for the speaker, only the task of comforting
the unfortunate girl.

778 *surcharged eyelids*: 'The surcharged heart cannot resist . . . unmerited
kindness': Sophia and Harriet Lee, *The Canterbury Tales* (1798), ii. 283.

781–2 *God spoke / Of right-hand*: cf. Mark 9:43–7: 'And if thy hand offend
thee, cut it off . . . And if thy foot offend thee, cut it off . . . And if thine eye
offend thee, pluck it out'. Whereas the corresponding verses in Matthew (5:29
ff.) follow a passage about adultery, in Mark the previous passage describes
Christ's taking 'a child . . . in his arms' (36) and commending children to his
disciples.

784 *child*: the girl who has accosted him. Line 786 suggests that she has lost
her 'good name'.

786 *ask moreover*: the poet gives the woman a lesson in casuistry, to enable her
to answer the Pharisees. First of all she should ask them whether it is not true
that every ne'er-do-well ('losel') retains in himself a notion of his own version

as those who desist
should remember.

Of evil men past hope, "Don't each contrive,
"Despite the evil you abuse, to live?—
"Keeping, each losel, through a maze of lies,
"His own conceit of truth? to which he hies   790
"By obscure windings, tortuous, if you will,
"But to himself not inaccessible;
"He sees truth, and his lies are for the crowd
"Who cannot see; some fancied right allowed
"His vilest wrong, empowered the losel clutch   795
"One pleasure from a multitude of such
"Denied him." Then assert, "All men appear
"To think all better than themselves, by here
"Trusting a crowd they wrong; but really," say,
"All men think all men stupider than they,   800
"Since, save themselves, no other comprehends
"The complicated scheme to make amends
"—Evil, the scheme by which, thro' Ignorance,
"Good labours to exist." A slight advance,—

---

787 *1840* don't each contrive   *1863,1865* "don't each contrive,   788 *1840*
abuse to live?   791 *1840 proof* windings if you will>windings, if you
will,   *1840* By obscure tortuous windings, if   793 *1840* He sees it,   795
1840 proof fool to>fellow   *1840–68* the fellow clutch   796 *1840* from the
multitude   797 *1840* Denied him: then assert, all   *1863,1865* Denied him."
Then assert, "all   799–800 *1840* really, say,|All   804 *1840* Good . . . .
exist. A slight advance

of the truth. He lies to others because he knows that they cannot see his version.
Even in the worst thing he does, he somehow fancies that his action is justified.
Secondly, she should point out that every person seems to think more highly of
others than of himself, since he trusts others although he knows himself to be
untrustworthy. Yet it is only a matter of seeming: in fact they think others
more stupid than themselves, since they believe that no one else understands
'The complicated scheme' by which ignorance makes it necessary for evil to be
done that good may come of it. It may not represent a great advance—merely
to be able to name the disease from which you are dying; but at least it is better
than hinting that one has (oneself) all the answers.

799 *but really," say*: 'As we cannot conscientiously send our readers to the
book itself, and yet feel bound to afford them some evidence of the art with
which the author has concealed his treasures, let him work out the following
problem, and give us its result if he can', wrote the reviewer in the *Athenæum*
for 30 May, 1840 (p. 431c), quoting lines 799–861. After the quotation he
commented: 'If the above specimen be within the compass of the reader's
faculties, then he may refer to the volume, which abounds in such'.

800 *All men*: cf. Young, *Night-Thoughts*, i. 422: 'All men think all men
Mortal, but themselves'.

803 *Evil*: cf. Carlyle, *French Revolution*, Vol. I, Book I, ii. para. 8: 'may we not
again say, that in the huge mass of Evil, as it rolls and swells, there is ever some
Good working imprisoned; working towards deliverance and triumph?'

805 Merely to find the sickness you die through,
And nought beside! but if one can't eschew
One's portion in the common lot, at least
One can avoid an ignorance increased
Tenfold by dealing out hint after hint
810 How nought were like dispensing without stint
The water of life—so easy to dispense
Beside, when one has probed the centre whence
Commotion 's born—could tell you of it all!
"—Meantime, just meditate my madrigal
815 "O' the mugwort that conceals a dewdrop safe!"
What, dullard? we and you in smothery chafe,
Babes, baldheads, stumbled thus far into Zin
The Horrid, getting neither out nor in,
A hungry sun above us, sands that bung
820 Our throats,—each dromedary lolls a tongue,
Each camel churns a sick and frothy chap,
And you, 'twixt tales of Potiphar's mishap,
And sonnets on the earliest ass that spoke,
—Remark, you wonder any one needs choke

---

805 *1840* through   806 *1840* beside: 810 *1840* nought is like   813
1840 all   814 *1840* —Meantime,   815 *1840* safe!   816 *1840 proof* all of
us>we and you 1840 chafe   819 *1840* sands among   820 *1840*
throats,   824 *1840* Remark . . . . choak

810 *How nought were like*: at least we can refrain from extreme forms of the
progressive fallacy that everything may readily be put right.
811 *The water of life*: see 817 n.
814 *my madrigal*: this is the sort of nonsense produced by poetical persons,
who write about such topics as a dewdrop to be found within wormwood.
816 *What, dullard?*: addressed to the writer of the absurd madrigal.
  in smothery chafe: angry and half choked.
817 *Zin*: 'Then came the children of Israel . . . into the desert of Zin . . . And
there was no water for the congregation; and they gathered themselves
together against Moses and against Aaron': Numbers 20:1–2. 'And the LORD
spake unto Moses, saying, 'Take the rod, and gather thou the assembly
together. . ., and speak ye unto the rock before their eyes . . . And Moses lifted
up his hand, and with his rod he smote the rock twice: and the water came out
abundantly, and the congregation drank, and their beasts also. And the LORD
spake unto Moses and Aaron, Because ye believed me not . . ., therefore ye
shall not bring this congregation into the land which I have given them. This is
the water of Meribah': ibid. 7–13. Cf. 27:14. Meribah means 'strife'. The sense
is that we (the human race) are in a situation as desperate as that of the children
of Israel, in the desert of Zin, yet you complacent fools produce reassuring
madrigals, stories on the old theme of Potiphar's wife (Genesis 39) or sonnets
about Balaam's ass (Numbers 22), and express your wonder that anyone
should require any more refreshing 'water of life'.

With founts about! Potsherd him, Gibeonites!   825

Let the poet take
his own part, then,

While awkwardly enough your Moses smites
The rock, though he forego his Promised Land
Thereby, have Satan claim his carcass, and
Figure as Metaphysic Poet . . . ah,
Mark ye the dim first oozings? Meribah!   830
Then, quaffing at the fount my courage gained,
Recall—not that I prompt ye—who
    explained . . .
      "Presumptuous!" interrupts one. You, not I
'T is, brother, marvel at and magnify
Such office: "office," quotha? can we get   835
To the beginning of the office yet?
What do we here? simply experiment
Each on the other's power and its intent
When elsewhere tasked,—if this of mine were
    trucked
For yours to either's good,—we watch construct,   840

---

825 *1840* Gibeonites,   827 *1840* The rock. . . . Land,   *1863,1865* The rock,
. . . . Land,   829 *1840* Dance, forsooth, Metaphysic Poet . . . ah   *1863,1865*
Figure as Metaphysic Poet . . . ah   831 *1840* And quaffing . . . .
gained   833 *1840 proof* Interrupts>interrupts   *1840* Presumptuous! . . . .
You not I {No indentation *1840–68*.}   *834 {Reading of *1863–68*}   *1840*
'Tis, Brother,   *1888,1889* 'T is brother,   835 *1840* Mine office:
office,   839 *1840* tasked,   840 *1840* For thine to either's profit,— watch
construct,

825 *Potsherd him!*: stone him to death! The Gibeonites hanged seven sons and
grandsons of Saul, in revenge for Saul's slaying of the Gibeonites: 2 Samuel 21.
Readers of this poem are exhorted to have no patience with such trivial and
complacent poets.
826 *your Moses*: the poet does not expect to enter the Promised Land himself,
but to be claimed by Satan and reviled by critics as a 'Metaphysic Poet'; yet he
points to the first oozings of water coming from the rock, bids his audience
drink, and hopes they will remember what he has done for them. The term
'metaphysic(al)' had already been applied to Browning and his poetry, not
necessarily as a term of censure. The reviewer of *Pauline* in *The Atlas*, e.g.,
wrote that it is 'metaphysical throughout, or is intended to be so': 14 April 1833
(p. 228), quoted in *Litzinger and Smalley*, p. 36. In 1842 Browning told Domett
that he was going to 'finish a wise metaphysical play (about a great mind and
soul turning to ill)': *Browning and Domett*, p. 36, probably referring to *A Soul's
Tragedy*. Cf. 'Transcendentalism'.
828 *claim his carcass*: Whyte cites Jude 9: 'Michael the archangel, when
contending with the Devil he disputed about the body of Moses'.
835 *Such office*: that of poet.
837 *here*: in this present life, which is a mere rehearsal for the life which is to
come. Cf. *Paracelsus*, iii. 1009–11.
839 *if this of mine were trucked*: whether—for example—it would be to the
advantage of either of us if we exchanged our abilities and aims.

In short, an engine: with a finished one,
What it can do, is all,—nought, how 't is done.
But this of ours yet in probation, dusk
A kernel of strange wheelwork through its
     husk
845 Grows into shape by quarters and by halves;
Remark this tooth's spring, wonder what that
     valve's
Fall bodes, presume each faculty's device,
Make out each other more or less precise—
The scope of the whole engine 's to be proved;
We die: which means to say, the whole 's
850   removed,
Dismounted wheel by wheel, this complex
     gin,—
To be set up anew elsewhere, begin
A task indeed, but with a clearer clime
Than the murk lodgment of our building-time:
855 And then, I grant you, it behoves forget
How 't is done—all that must amuse us yet
So long: and, while you turn upon your heel,   *should any object*
Pray that I be not busy slitting steel   *that he was dull*

---

842 *1840* can do is all, nought how 'tis done;   849 *1840* proved—   851
1840 wheel that complex gin,   *854 {Reading of *1840*}   *1863–68* building-
time.   *1888,1889* building-time: 857 *1840* and while thou turnest on thy
heel

---

841 *an engine*: the human soul is merely under construction in this life, so we
are naturally concerned with the question how it functions. Cf. *Paracelsus*, iii.
679 ff.
843 *dusk*: for 'duskily', in the dark.
847 *presume each faculty's device*: form your conjectures about the devising of
each of our faculties.
849 *The scope*: what remains to be demonstrated is the raison d'être of the
whole contrivance.
851 *gin*: piece of mechanism: Cf. Shelley, 'Letter to Maria Gisborne', 19:
'some machine portentous, or strange gin'.
853 *a clearer clime*: in much better circumstances than in the dark and obscure
dwelling-place of this earth. Cf. Waller, 'Of the Last Verses in the Book',
13–14: 'The soul's dark cottage, battered and decayed, / Lets in new light
through chinks that time has made'.
855 *And then*: when the human soul is set up in the next life we shall rightly
cease to be concerned with how it is put together—a problem that must
perplex ('amuse') us for a long time, meanwhile.
857 *turn upon your heel*: in impatience or contempt.
858 *slitting steel*: 'Slitting' is a term used for cutting iron or steel into rods.

Or shredding brass, camped on some virgin
    shore
Under a cluster of fresh stars, before   860
I name a tithe o' the wheels I trust to do!
    So occupied, then, are we: hitherto,
At present, and a weary while to come,
The office of ourselves,—nor blind nor dumb,
And seeing somewhat of man's state,—has been,   865
For the worst of us, to say they so have seen;
For the better, what it was they saw; the best
Impart the gift of seeing to the rest:
"So that I glance," says such an one, "around,
"And there 's no face but I can read profound   870
"Disclosures in; this stands for hope, that—fear,
"And for a speech, a deed in proof, look here!
"'Stoop, else the strings of blossom, where the
    nuts

859 *1840* brass upon a virgin shore   861 *1840* a tithe the wheels   862
1840–68 {No indentation.}   864 *1840* ourselves . . . . dumb   865 *1840*
state,   866 *1840* The worst   867 *1840* The better, ... best,   869 *1840*
So that I glance, says . . . . around,   873 *1840* Stoop,   *1863,1865* 'Stoop,

860 *Under a cluster of fresh stars*: in another life. In a letter to George Barrett,
after an important anecdote (from Severn) of how Keats 'revolted against
death', E. B. B. wrote: 'There would be no answer to such "divine despairs", if
it were not in the facts in which I deeply believe, that life and work, yes, the sort
of work suitable to the artist-nature, are continued on the outside of this crust
of mortal manhood, & that the man will be permitted to complete himself, if
not *here, there': Letters to George Barrett*, p. 260.
864 *The office*: our task as poets. At our present stage of development we may
be divided into three classes: the duty of the first class is to say that they have
seen, that of the second to describe what they have seen, while the third is able
to endow others with the gift of seeing. These last are 'the Makers-see' (line
928).
869 *"So that I glance*: one of the most gifted class of poets has only to glance
around him to penetrate the characters of the people he observes. Cf. 'Fra
Lippo Lippi', 112 ff.
871 *this stands for hope*: cf. 'Fra Lippo Lippi', 208 ff.
872 *look here!*: I shall now exemplify my gift.
873 *"Stoop*: seeing a young man in prison, for example, such a poet impro-
vises the sort of thoughts which may be passing through his mind. To preserve
his sanity, he may be remembering a country walk he once took with a
beautiful girl called Zanze ('Elys' in *1840*, cf. 107 ff. above). Cf. *Pauline*, 764 ff.
As Browning remained in Venice for more than a fortnight he is most likely to
have visited the notorious Piombi, the prison in the Doges' palace, one of the
sights of the place. For 'rove' cf. ii. 269. Cf. Shelley, *The Revolt of Islam*, 3734–8:
                    and—as some most serene
And lovely spot to a poor maniac's eye,
After long years, some sweet and moving scene
Of youthful hope, returning suddenly,
Quells his long madness—thus man shall remember thee.

875

"'O'erarch, will blind thee! Said I not? She shuts
"'Both eyes this time, so close the hazels meet!
"'Thus, prisoned in the Piombi, I repeat
"'Events one rove occasioned, o'er and o'er,
"'Putting 'twixt me and madness evermore
"'Thy sweet shape, Zanze! Therefore stoop!'
                                          'That's truth!'

880

"(Adjudge you) 'the incarcerated youth
"'Would say that!'
                    "Youth? Plara the bard? Set down
"That Plara spent his youth in a grim town
"Whose cramped ill-featured streets huddled
    about
"The minster for protection, never out

885

"Of its black belfry's shade and its bells' roar.
"The brighter shone the suburb,—all the more
"Ugly and absolute that shade's reproof
"Of any chance escape of joy,—some roof,
"Taller than they, allowed the rest detect,—

890

"Before the sole permitted laugh (suspect
"Who could, 't was meant for laughter, that
    ploughed cheek's
"Repulsive gleam!) when the sun stopped both
    peaks

beside his sprightlier predecessors.

---

874 *1840–65* said I not? she shuts *1868* Said I not? She shut 875 *1840 proof*
meet,>meet! 879 *1840* shape, Elys! therefore stoop— *1863,1865* shape,
Zanze! therefore stoop!' *879–81 {Reading of *1863,1865*} *1840* That's
truth!|(Applaud you) the incarcerated youth|Would say that!¶ Youth? . . . .
set *1868–89* "'That's truth!'|"(Adjudge you) 'the incarcerated youth|
"'Would say that!'¶"Youth? . . . . Set 885–6 *1840* belfry's shadow or
bells' roar:|Brighter the sun illumed the suburbs, more 888 *1840* For any
. . . .joy some roof 889 *1840* they. . . . detect *1863,1865* they, ... detect

---

879 *Zanze*: a common name for a girl. It also occurs in *Pippa Passes* and 'In A
Gondola'.

881 *"Youth?":* when his interlocutor uses the word 'youth' the poet is
reminded of Plara, the writer of over-elaborate sonnets (ii. 769). 'I can
imagine', he says, 'that his background was the opposite of that Vale of Tempe
of which he loved to write'.

887 *that shade's reproof*: the shadow of the minster is fancied to reprove any
gleam of light from the sun reflected on a high roof. The moment of sunset,
when the sun appears like a fiery wedge between the two peaks of the belfry,
seems like a sinister laugh.

888 *escape of joy*: cf. 'escape of angels', i. 883 and iii. 595.

"Of the cleft belfry like a fiery wedge,
"Then sank, a huge flame on its socket edge,
"With leavings on the grey glass oriel-pane   895
"Ghastly some minutes more. No fear of rain—
"The minster minded that! in heaps the dust
"Lay everywhere. This town, the minster's trust,
"Held Plara; who, its denizen, bade hail
"In twiçe twelve sonnets, Tempe's dewy vale.   900
"'Exact the town, the minster and the street!'
"As all mirth triumphs, sadness means defeat:

893 *1840 proof* wedge>wedge,   894 *1840–65* Then sunk, ... socket's
edge,   *1868* "Then sunk, ... socket edge,   895 *1840* Whose leavings   896 *1840* Were ghastly some few minutes more: no rain—   898
1840 Lay every where: that town, the Minster's trust,   *900 {Editors'
emendation.}   *1840* sonnets, Naddo, Tempe's vale.   *1863,1865* sonnets,
Tempe's dewy vale.'   *1868–89* sonnets, Tempe's dewy vale."   *901 {Read-
ing of *1863,1865*}   *1840* Exact . . . . street!   *1868–89* "'Exact . . . .
street!'"   902 *1840* As *1863,1865* 'As

895 *leavings*: i.e. the last gleams.
900 *Tempe's dewy vale*: 'a valley in Thessaly, between mount Olympus at the
north, and Ossa at the south, through which the river Peneus flows into the
Ægean. The poets have described it as the most delightful spot on the earth,
with continually cool shades, and verdant walks': Lemprière.
901 *'Exact the town*: spoken by the same interlocutor as 'That's truth!' above.
902 *As all mirth triumphs*: mirth is a sign of triumph, sadness of failure. Lust
triumphs and is gay, love fails and is sad. Why (then) is Lucio sad? It is his love
that is sad, not Lucio—it is the nature of love to be sad (although a lover may be
gay in hope, just as a lustful man may be sad because the woman he desires has
escaped). What concerns me, in any case, is the mood itself.—The introduction
of Lucio (whether or not he is to be identified with the lover in a poem of
Sordello's mentioned at ii. 538) is puzzling, and the whole passage remains
obscure. Whyte comments as follows: 'Happiness, says Browning, is in reality
a question of moral motive not of circumstance. Mirth or melancholy may be
due to either a good or evil cause. But the man whose heart is right has
happiness, even though outwardly sad and apparently defeated. Retrospec-
tively the passage shows both how the young man in the Piombi could be
happy in his prison and how Plara, shut in the grim town, could write sonnets
on Tempe's vale, and looking forward it suggests how Sordello, though
outwardly a failure, yet, because his heart was right, triumphs even in death'.
This has the merit of relating these lines to the lines about the youth in the
Piombi and about Plara, but it sits rather loosely to the text. Duff offers a
straightforward, précis, introduced by the words 'Now, I will show another
thing.' 'All mirth signifies triumph; all sadness signifies defeat Sometimes
lust triumphs, as you see from its being gay. Sometimes pure love is
triumphed over—fails to attain its object—and is sad. Here I see a sad man,
Lucio. Now, I said a moment ago, "Love is triumphed over and is sad"; but
when I said "Lucio's sad", it did not necessarily follow that he was sad because
a pure love in him had been defeated: his sadness, representing defeat, arises
from the fact that the object of his lust had escaped the snare he laid to catch it.
Another man, hoping for the enjoyment of a pure love, may be as full of joy as
Lucio is of sadness; whereas in Lucio mirth would have signified that he had
succeeded in lust. I speak of the mood—mirth or melancholy—and of what
gives it colour, whether it be a good moral quality or an evil one'.

"Lust triumphs and is gay, Love 's triumphed
  o'er
"And sad: but Lucio 's sad. I said before,
905   "Love 's sad, not Lucio; one who loves may be
"As gay his love has leave to hope, as he
"Downcast that lust's desire escapes the springe:
"'T is of the mood itself I speak, what tinge
"Determines it, else colourless,—or mirth,
910   "Or melancholy, as from heaven or earth.
"'Ay, that 's the variation's gist!'
                             "Indeed?
"Thus far advanced in safety then, proceed!
"And having seen too what I saw, be bold
"And next encounter what I do behold
"(That 's sure) but bid you take on trust!"

915   Attack

The use and purpose of such sights! Alack,   *One ought not*
Not so unwisely does the crowd dispense   *blame but praise*
On Salinguerras praise in preference   *this;*
To the Sordellos: men of action, these!
920   Who, seeing just as little as you please,
Yet turn that little to account,—engage
With, do not gaze at,—carry on, a stage,
The work o' the world, not merely make report
The work existed ere their day! In short,
925   When at some future no–time a brave band

---

904 *1840* sad: I said before   *907 { Editors' emendation}   *1840* Downcast
his lusts' *1863–89* Downcast that lusts'   909 *1840 proof* colourless> colourless, *1840* colourless,   *910 { Editors' emendation} *1840 proof* and
Earth.> or Earth.   *1840* Heaven or Earth. *1863,1865* heaven or earth.'
1868–89 heaven or earth."   911 *1840* Ay, ... gist! Indeed? *1863–8* 'Ay,
. . . . gist!' Indeed? {No line division.}   914 *1840* Enough encounter
915 *1840* (That's sure) but you must take on trust! Attack *1863,1865*
(That's sure) but bid you take on trust! Attack {No line division}
916 *1863–8* sights?   917 *1840* unwisely hastes the   921 *1840* account;
922 *1840* gaze at; carry on a stage   924 *1840* their time—

---

911 *the variation's gist!*: the essential difference.
914 *what I do behold*: i.e. the end of Sordello's story.
915 *Attack*: you are determined to attack poetry? Well then, no wonder the
crowd prefers men of action like Taurello.
925 *When at some future no–time*: when the millenial day comes on which a
brave band of men is able both to see and to act accordingly, then you will
realize that we are both in another world. Meanwhile, those who have the
single gift of being able to make-see have their value, and should be kept up to
their duty.

Sees, using what it sees, then shake my hand
In heaven, my brother! Meanwhile where 's the
    hurt
Of keeping the Makers-see on the alert,
At whose defection mortals stare aghast
As though heaven's bounteous windows were
    slammed fast   930
Incontinent? Whereas all you, beneath,
Should scowl at, bruise their lips and break their
    teeth
Who ply the pullies, for neglecting you:
And therefore have I moulded, made anew
A Man, and give him to be turned and tried,   935
Be angry with or pleased at. On your side,
Have ye times, places, actors of your own?
Try them upon Sordello when full-grown,

at all events, his   And then—ah then! If Hercules first parched
own audience may: His foot in Egypt only to be marched   940
A sacrifice for Jove with pomp to suit,
What chance have I? The demigod was mute

928 *1840* To keep the . . . . alert   931 *1840* you beneath   932 *1840–68*
scowl at, curse them, bruise lips, break   933 *1840* pullies   935 *1840* A
Man, delivered to be   938 *1840* Sordello once full-grown,

930 *heaven's bounteous windows*: 'What even if a ray of light should straggle
over the unsunned hoards of sumless wealth in the Vatican? "If windows were
in heaven, might this thing be"': *Essay on Chatterton*, p. 105. Smalley refers to 2
Kings 7:2: 'Then a lord on whose hand the king leaned answered the man of
God, and said, Behold, if the LORD would make windows in heaven, might this
thing be?' The meaning here is that people are as disconcerted by the failure of
poets to fulfil their duty as if the windows of heaven had been slammed shut.
This failure should not be tolerated: you ordinary people should protest, and
even attack the poets, who should be operating the pulleys that control the
windows [what Keats had called the 'magic casements'].
    935 *turned*: turned round, examined.
    938 *Try them upon Sordello*: I have done my best. Do you have rival stories (or
poems)? Just compare them with this poem, *Sordello*, when it is 'full-grown'!
    939 *If Hercules*: 'When Hercules passed through Egypt, Busiris was king of
the country . . . an intolerable tyrant . . . [who] sacrificed whatever stranger
came into the country upon the altar of Neptune . . . Busiris seized Hercules,
regardless of the name of Jupiter whose son he was, and dragged him to the
place of sacrifice: but Hercules burst his chains; and by the law of retaliation of
which the hero was fond, he slew the tyrant upon his own altar': *The Pantheon:
or Ancient History of the Gods of Greece and Rome*, by Edward Baldwin [William
Godwin], 3rd ed. (1810), p. 224. The poet here warns his readers that he is no
more helpless than Hercules was on that occasion. But (he relents) he will not
turn on them—nor will he tear off his chaplet, which is not that of a destined
victim but is made from the verse addressed to him by Landor.

Till, at the altar, where time out of mind
Such guests became oblations, chaplets twined
945 His forehead long enough, and he began
Slaying the slayers, nor escaped a man.
Take not affront, my gentle audience! whom
No Hercules shall make his hecatomb,
Believe, nor from his brows your chaplet rend—
That 's your kind suffrage, yours, my
950   patron-friend,
Whose great verse blares unintermittent on
Like your own trumpeter at Marathon,—
You who, Platæa and Salamis being scant,
Put up with Ætna for a stimulant—
955 And did well, I acknowledged, as he loomed
Over the midland sea last month, presumed
Long, lay demolished in the blazing West

---

946 *1840 proof* man>man—   *1840* man—   947 *1840 proof* Assure yourselves,>Take not affront,   948 *1840* hecatomb   950 *1840* yours, nay,
yours, my friend   952 *1840* Like any trumpeter at Marathon,   953 *1840*
He'll testify who when Platæas grew scant   *1863–8* You who, Platæas and
Salamis being scant,   954–7 *1840* stimulant! | And well too, I acknowledged,
as it loomed | Over the Midland sea that morn, presumed | All day, demolished
by the   957 *1840 proof* west>West

---

949 *Believe*: believe me.
his brows: the brows of the man who is addressing you (myself, no Hercules).
950 *my patron-friend*: 'Yes, Landor was the Friend, and his praise was prompt,
both private and public—(in his Satire on Satirists)': *Letters*, p. 206, referring to
A Satire on Satirists (1836), l. 67: 'Did *Paracelsus* spring from poet's brain . . .?'
952 *Like your own trumpeter*: in *1840* the sense of the passage is clear. Landor's
verse is like that of a trumpeter at Marathon, as Æschylus will bear witness—Æschylus, who wrote of Platæa (in *The Persae*), and then turned to write
The Women of Ætna (a lost play). Ætna is the 'it' of 955 and 958. The revisions
introduce obscurities which have perplexed all commentators, and may indicate confusion on Browning's part. It may be that lines 952–4 are addressed to
Æschylus—which would explain the tense of 'did well' (955). If 952–4 are
addressed to Landor, and Æschylus is Landor's 'own trumpeter' (cf. i. 65–6),
the meaning must be that Landor, lacking such stimulants (known to
Æschylus) as the battles of Platæa and Salamis, makes the best of Etna. The
tense of 'did well' is then surprising. On any reading it is odd that Etna should
be called 'he' and 'him'.
956 *the midland sea*: the Mediterranean: 'presumed', loomed up presumptuously: cf. *Paradise Lost*, vii. 13: 'Into the heaven of heavens I have presumed'
last month: revised from 'that morn'. Dates had probably become blurred
in Browning's mind by the time of the revision. Griffin and Minchin tell us that
'during a calm on 16 May [1838] Mount Etna was in sight all day': p. 95 n.
Browning probably returned to England in July. Whyte and others associate
the passage with a striking description of a wreck in a letter printed in Mrs.
Orr's *Life* (pp. 90–3: now also available in *Letters*, pp. 1–3); but apart from a

At eve, while towards him tilting cloudlets
  pressed
Like Persian ships at Salamis. Friend, wear
A crest proud as desert while I declare   960
Had I a flawless ruby fit to wring
Tears of its colour from that painted king
Who lost it, I would, for that smile which went
To my heart, fling it in the sea, content,
Wearing your verse in place, an amulet   965
Sovereign against all passion, wear and fret!
My English Eyebright, if you are not glad
That, as I stopped my task awhile, the sad
Dishevelled form, wherein I put mankind
To come at times and keep my pact in mind,   970
Renewed me,—hear no crickets in the hedge,
Nor let a glowworm spot the river's edge
At home, and may the summer showers gush
Without a warning from the missel thrush!
So, to our business, now—the fate of such   975

what if things brighten, who knows?

958 *1840* towards it . . . . prest *1863,1865* towards him . . . . prest   959
1840 ships for Salamis.   962 *1840* A tear its   963 *1840 proof* would
>would,   *1840* To lose, I would, for that one smile   964 *1840* sea con-
tent   966 *1840* Sovereign against low-thoughtedness and fret!   969 *SB*
mankind>Mankind   973 *1840 proof* let>may   975 *1840 proof* Nay, Eyebright,>For, Eyebright,   *1840* For, Eyebright, what I sing's the fate of such

reference to 'the most gorgeous and lavish sunset in the world' little or no
correspondence is apparent.

962 *that painted king*: Berdoe and subsequent commentators refer to Poly-
crates, King of Samos, who threw an emerald ring into the sea to escape the
envy of the gods, only to find it again in a large fish presented to him by a
fisherman (Herodotus, iii. 40 ff.). This is clearly irrelevant, but the story to
which Browning is alluding has not been found.

963 *that smile*: probably a reference to the evening at Talfourd's house after
the first night of *Ion*. Landor was one of those who raised their glasses to 'the
youngest poet of England': *Life*, 82.

967 *My English Eyebright*: 'I called you, "Eyebright"—meaning a simple and
sad sort of translation of "Euphrasia" into my own language: folks would
know who Euphrasia, or Fanny was,—and *I* should not know Ianthe or
Clemanthe': *Letters*, p. 2 (to Euphrasia Fanny Haworth). Cf. the passage from
New Letters, p. 18, quoted in 696 n. above. 'Eyebright' is the English name for
the herb Euphrasia (OED).

969 *Dishevelled form*: l. 696.   *mankind*: capitalised in *SB*.

971 *hear no crickets*: a humorous curse on her. If she is not pleased that he has
gone on with the poem, may she be deprived of the delights of summer!

974 *the missel thrush!*: 'The people of Hampshire and Sussex call the Missel-
bird the storm-cock': Gilbert White, *Natural History of Selborne* (1789), cited in
OED.

975 *our business*: our theme, which is the fate of those (like Sordello) who try

As find our common nature—overmuch
Despised because restricted and unfit
To bear the burthen they impose on it—
Cling when they would discard it; craving
    strength
980 To leap from the allotted world, at length
They do leap,—flounder on without a term,
Each a god's germ, doomed to remain a germ
In unexpanded infancy, unless . . .
But that 's the story—dull enough, confess!
985 There might be fitter subjects to allure;
Still, neither misconceive my portraiture
Nor undervalue its adornments quaint:
What seems a fiend perchance may prove a saint.
Ponder a story ancient pens transmit,   *Whereupon, with*
990 Then say if you condemn me or acquit.   *a story to the*
    John the Beloved, banished Antioch   *point,*
For Patmos, bade collectively his flock
Farewell, but set apart the closing eve

---

976 *1840* nature (overmuch   978 *1840* on it)   981 *1840* 'Tis left—they
floundering without a term   982 *1840* God's germ, but doomed
remain   983 *1840* infancy, assure   984–5 {Not in *1840*}   986 *1840*
Yourself, nor misconceive   987 *1840* quaint!   988 *1840* saint: 991
1840–65 {No paragraph division}

---

to escape from the limits of humanity (which they despise, as it actually is) and
to become gods.
   981 *without a term*: indefinitely.
   986–7 *portraiture . . . adornments quaint*: cf. Dedication.
   988 *What seems a fiend*: however unattractive the portrait Browning has so far
daubed, Sordello may turn out to be a saint in the end.
   991 *John the Beloved*: the ultimate source is the passage in the Apocryphal *Acts
of John* (26 ff.) which describes how Lycomedes, 'who had a friend who was a
skilful painter', caused a likeness of John to be painted without the latter's
knowledge. Coming on the picture unexpectedly, John 'saw the portrait of an
old man crowned with garlands, and lamps and altars set before it. And he
called him and said: "Lycomedes, what meanest thou by this matter of the
portrait? can it be one of thy gods that is painted here? for I see that thou art still
living in heathen fashion"'. After the explanation John, 'who had never at any
time seen his own face said to him: Thou mockest me, child: am I like that in
form, [excelling] thy Lord? how canst thou persuade me that the portrait is like
me? And Lycomedes brought him a mirror': *The Apocryphal New Testament*,
trans. M. R. James (1924), pp. 232–3. Professor Lampe points out that Browning must have come on the story at second-hand, as the passage quoted would
not have been available to him. Professor John Grube pointed out the Apocryphal source of the story in '*Sordello*, Browning's Christian Epic', in *English
Studies in Canada*, IV. 4 (Winter 1978), p. 428 n. 4. 'Antioch' is an error for
Ephesus.

To comfort those his exile most would grieve,
He knew: a touching spectacle, that house   995
In motion to receive him! Xanthus' spouse
You missed, made panther's meat a month since;
    but
Xanthus himself (his nephew 't was, they shut
'Twixt boards and sawed asunder) Polycarp,
Soft Charicle, next year no wheel could warp   1000
To swear by Cæsar's fortune, with the rest
Were ranged; thro' whom the grey disciple
    pressed,
Busily blessing right and left, just stopped
To pat one infant's curls, the hangman cropped
Soon after, reached the portal. On its hinge   1005
The door turns and he enters: what quick twinge
Ruins the smiling mouth, those wide eyes fix
Whereon, why like some spectral candlestick's
Branch the disciple's arms? Dead swooned he,
    woke
Anon, heaved sigh, made shift to gasp,
    heart-broke,   1010
"Get thee behind me, Satan! Have I toiled
"To no more purpose? Is the gospel foiled
"Here too, and o'er my son's, my Xanthus'
    hearth,
"Portrayed with sooty garb and features
    swarth—
"Ah Xanthus, am I to thy roof beguiled   1015

994 *1840* To comfort some his .... grieve   998 *1840* (for 'twas his
nephew shut   999 *1840* and sawn   1005 *1840* portal; on   *1863,1865* portal—on   1006 *1840* enters—what deep twinge   *1863,1865* enters—what
quick twinge   1008 *1840 proof* candlesticks>candlestick's   *1840* Whereon?
How like   1009 *1840* arms!   1011 *1840* Get.... me Satan! have *1863,1865*
"Get .... me, Satan! have   1014 *1840* Pourtrayed   1015 *1840 proof*
Oh>Ah

998 *Xanthus*: an imaginary character, like Charicle.
999 *Polycarp*: Bishop of Smyrna and author of an Epistle to the Philippians.
He was believed to have heard John in his youth. His martyrdom is described at
length in a contemporary account. It is told of him that he was urged 'To swear
by Caesar's fortune' (τύχη).
1001 *To swear by Cæsar's fortune*: 'Thou shalt fear the LORD thy God, and
serve him, and shalt swear by his name': Deuteronomy 6:13.
1008 *Whereon*: interrogative: cf. *1840*.
1011 *Get thee behind me, Satan!* Luke iv. 8.

"To see the—the—the Devil domiciled?"
Whereto sobbed Xanthus, "Father, 't is yourself
"Installed, a limning which our utmost pelf
"Went to procure against to-morrow's loss;
1020   "And that 's no twy-prong, but a pastoral cross,
"You 're painted with!"
                        His puckered brows unfold—
And you shall hear Sordello's story told.   *he takes up the*
                                                    thread of discourse.

1016 *1840* domiciled?   1017 *1840* Father,   1021 *1840* with! The puckered   *1863,1865* with!" His puckered {No line division.}

1020 *twy-prong*: the Devil's two-pronged fork, as in *Ferishtah's Fancies* ('A
Camel-Driver', l. 51). OED has no other example. An instrument of this sort
was used in black magic. Berdoe points out that there is no such thing as 'a
pastoral cross', though there is a pastoral staff. It is conceivable that Browning
is remembering some pictorial representation of a Byzantine bishop, since in
the East the pastoral staff is topped by a cross.
1022 *And you shall hear*: below this line *SB* has: 'He goes on to Ferrara with
Palma Let us precede & await them there'.

BOOK THE FOURTH.

Men suffered much,

MEANTIME Ferrara lay in rueful case;
The lady-city, for whose sole embrace
Her pair of suitors struggled, felt their arms
A brawny mischief to the fragile charms
They tugged for—one discovering that to twist   5
Her tresses twice or thrice about his wrist
Secured a point of vantage—one, how best
He 'd parry that by planting in her breast
His elbow spike—each party too intent
For noticing, howe'er the battle went,   10
The conqueror would but have a corpse to kiss.
"May Boniface be duly damned for this!"
—Howled some old Ghibellin, as up he turned,
From the wet heap of rubbish where they burned
His house, a little skull with dazzling teeth: 15
"A boon, sweet Christ—let Salinguerra seethe
"In hell for ever, Christ, and let myself
"Be there to laugh at him!"—moaned some
     young Guelf
Stumbling upon a shrivelled hand nailed fast
To the charred lintel of the doorway, last   20
His father stood within to bid him speed.
The thoroughfares were overrun with weed
—Docks, quitchgrass, loathly mallows no man
whichever of the   plants.
parties was victor.   The stranger, none of its inhabitants

---

5 *1840* Each tugged for—one discovering to twist   9 *1840* elbow-
spike—both parties *1863,1865* elbow-spike—each party   11 *1840* Its conqueror would have   12 *1840* May . . . . this!   13 *1840* Howled some old
Ghibellin   16 *1840* A boon,   18 *1840* him!   20 *1840* doorway   22
1840 thoroughfares looked overrun   *23 {Reading of *1840–68*} *1888, 1889*
loathy mallows

---

23 *quitchgrass*: a coarse grass regarded as a weed. Browning was to remember
this nightmare landscape when he wrote 'Childe Roland', 55 ff.
loathly: the misprint 'loathy' found its way into OED.
24 *The stranger*: it was all the stranger that.

25   Crept out of doors to taste fresh air again,
     And ask the purpose of a splendid train
     Admitted on a morning; every town
     Of the East League was come by envoy down
     To treat for Richard's ransom: here you saw
30   The Vicentine, here snowy oxen draw
     The Paduan carroch, its vermilion cross
     On its white field. A-tiptoe o'er the fosse
     Looked Legate Montelungo wistfully
     After the flock of steeples he might spy
35   In Este's time, gone (doubts he) long ago
     To mend the ramparts: sure the laggards know
     The Pope 's as good as here! They paced the
          streets
     More soberly. At last, "Taurello greets
     "The League," announced a pursuivant,—"will
          match

---

26 *1840* Or ask . . . . a sumptuous train   *1863,1865* And ask . . . . a sumptuous train   32 *1840* field: a-tiptoe   36 *1840–65* ramparts—   38 *1840*
Taurello   39 *1840* The League, ... will

27 *a morning*: 'that morning': *SB*, which adds: 'The great arm was in
requisition at last, and' before the words 'every town', referring to the Lombard League.
28 *the East League*: the Lombard League: see i. 110 n.
31 *The Paduan carroch*: Verci mentions that 'eight white oxen with purple
coverings drew this machine, which was the mark of a free city'. The device of
the city, displayed on its standard, was 'the vermilion cross on a white field':
Storia, i. 301.
32 *fosse*: moat, trench.
33 *Montelungo*: there is no evidence that the apostolic delegate Gregorio da
Montelungo was present on this occasion. Browning may have remembered
the opening of the article on him in the *Biographie Universelle*: 'cardinal-legate
in Lombardy in the thirteenth century, [he] was the principal opponent of the
Emperor Frederick II, and of the Ghibellins. At the time when Gregory IX was
making every effort to overthrow the power of Frederick II he sent Cardinal
Gregory of Montelungo into Lombardy, the member of the Sacred College
who was most active, most enterprising, and most zealous for the privileges of
the Church'. It was in 1238, however, that Montelungo was sent to Milan and
became influential.
34 *the flock of steeples*: probably suggested, as Whyte pointed out, by a passage
in the *Chronica Parva Ferrariensis*: 'as a boy I heard from my father, as he chatted
by the hearth on a winter's evening, that in his time he had seen thirty-two tall
towers in the city of Ferrara, which he soon saw thrown down and destroyed'.
Muratori viii. 482.
37 ∧ *They paced*: 'Remembering so many old wiles,': *SB*.
39 *announced a pursuivant*: Domett bracketed these words, perhaps prompting the repunctuation.

"Its courtesy, and labours to dispatch   40
"At earliest Tito, Friedrich's Pretor, sent
"On pressing matters from his post at Trent,
"With Mainard Count of Tyrol,—simply waits
"Their going to receive the delegates."
"Tito!" Our delegates exchanged a glance,   45
And, keeping the main way, admired askance
The lazy engines of outlandish birth,
Couched like a king each on its bank of earth—
Arbalist, manganel and catapult;
While stationed by, as waiting a result,   50
Lean silent gangs of mercenaries ceased
Working to watch the strangers. "This, at least,
How Guelfs   "Were better spared; he scarce presumes gainsay
criticize Ghibellin   "The League's decision! Get our friend away
work   "And profit for the future: how else teach   55
"Fools 't is not safe to stray within claw's reach
"Ere Salinguerra's final gasp be blown?
"Those mere convulsive scratches find the bone.
"Who bade him bloody the spent osprey's nare?"
     The carrochs halted in the public square.   60
Pennons of every blazon once a-flaunt,

---

42 *1840* Trent   44 *1840* delegates.   45 *1840* Tito!   52 *1840*
strangers—this,   56–7 *1840* Azzo 'tis not so safe within claw's reach|Till
Salinguerra's   58 *1840* bone   59 *1840*—Who . . . . nare?

---

40 *labours*: 'is *labouring*? these little carelessnesses make his style so obscure—': Domett.
41 *Tito*: Sodigerio di Tito, described by Verci as 'the famous Podestà of
Trent . . . a great friend and partisan of Ecelino': ii. 312.
43 *Mainard*: no doubt the first Count, a supporter of Friedrich who died in
1258.
45 *Tito!*: 'He too tries the great Arm!' *SB.*
47 *outlandish*: foreign.
49 *Arbalist, manganel*: an arbalist is a large crossbow, a manganel a particular
type of catapult. Both words occur in *Ivanhoe*: in *The Betrothed* a 'mangonel' is
defined as 'a military engine for casting stones' and described at work in ch.
viii.
54 *our friend*: Count Richard.
55–7 *how else . . . be blown?*: 'Are we to have a dismal *general* contest again?':
SB.
58 *convulsive scratches*: assuming that Taurello Salinguerra is near his end, the
Guelf speaker warns that he may still be dangerous. Count Richard has been
ill-advised to bloody Taurello's nose. For Taurello as osprey see i. 128. OED
points out that 'nare' is specifically used for the nostril of a hawk.
61 *Pennons*: once flags bearing all the coats of arms were displayed, men
began to chatter, the more freely because those of the House of Romano were

Men prattled, freelier that the crested gaunt
White ostrich with a horse-shoe in her beak
Was missing, and whoever chose might speak
65 "Ecelin" boldly out: so,—"Ecelin
"Needed his wife to swallow half the sin
"And sickens by himself: the devil's whelp,
"He styles his son, dwindles away, no help
"From conserves, your fine triple-curded froth
70 "Of virgin's blood, your Venice viper-broth—
"Eh? Jubilate!"—"Peace! no little word
"You utter here that 's not distinctly heard
"Up at Oliero: he was absent sick
"When we besieged Bassano—who, i' the thick
"O' the work, perceived the progress Azzo
75   made,
"Like Ecelin, through his witch Adelaide?
"She managed it so well that, night by night
"At their bed-foot stood up a soldier-sprite,
"First fresh, pale by-and-by without a wound,
"And, when it came with eyes filmed as in
80   swound,

---

*62 {Reading of *1840–68*} *1888,1889* freelier than the {corrected to 'that' in some copies of *1889*.} 64 *1840* Was missing; whosoever chose *1868* "Was missing, and whoever chose 65 *1840 Ecelin* boldly out: so, Ecelin *1863,1865 Ecelin* boldly out: so,—"Ecelin 71 *1840* Eh? Jubilate! Tush! *1863,1865* Eh? Jubilate! Peace! 73 *1840* At Oliero: 76 *1840* Like Ecelin? . . . . Adelaide 77 *1840* Who managed . . . . that night by night *1863–8* She managed . . . . that, night by night, 80 *1840* And when he came . . . . swound

---

missing: anyone who wished might talk quite openly about Ecelin. An engraving of the 'Stemma Gentilizio degli Ecelini' faces p. 190 of Verci's *Storia*, vol. i. He observes that 'the principal symbol of this family tree is a crested ostrich which holds a horseshoe in its beak'.

65 *so*: before this word, *SB* inserts: 'that's one good thing—only Saling. remains. no better Hand—if the great contest is to begin again.'

66 *Needed his wife*: see i. 943–4.

68 *his son*: 'eldest': *SB*.

70 *viper-broth*: 'The lingering belief in the wonderfully invigorating qualities of "viper-broth" is not yet quite extinct in some places': *Penny Cyclopaedia* xxvi (1843), 349/1, quoted in OED. Its sinister name makes it a suitable medicine (with 'virgin's blood') for the young Ecelin, who was to become one of the most terrible of all tyrants. *SB* has 'Alberic work' in margin.

71 *Jubilate!*: rejoice (at that)!

73 ∧ *at Oliero*: 'I'll wager,': *SB*.

78 *a soldier-sprite*: conjured up by Adelaide. Cf. iii. 372, where Palma describes Taurello as a 'sprite' who obeys Adelaide's bidding.

as unusually energetic
in this case.

"They knew the place was taken."—"Ominous
"That Ghibellins should get what cautelous
"Old Redbeard sought from Azzo's sire to
     wrench
"Vainly; Saint George contrived his town a
     trench
"O' the marshes, an impermeable bar."   85
"—Young Ecelin is meant the tutelar
"Of Padua, rather; veins embrace upon
"His hand like Brenta and Bacchiglion."
What now?—"The founts! God's bread, touch not
     a plank!
"A crawling hell of carrion—every tank   90
"Choke-full!—found out just now to Cino's
     cost—
"The same who gave Taurello up for lost,
"And, making no account of fortune's freaks,
"Refused to budge from Padua then, but sneaks
"Back now with Concorezzi: 'faith! they drag   95
"Their carroch to San Vitale, plant the flag

81 *1840* taken—Ominous *1863,1865* taken. Ominous   82 *1840* Your
Ghibellin   84 *1840* St. George   85 *1840* bar: *1863,1865* bar.   86
1840–65 Young   88 *1840* Bacchiglion . . . *1863,1865* Bacchiglion.   89
1840–65 What now? The founts!   91 *1840* Choke full! found   92 *1840*
Taurello's side for lost,   95 *1840–68* Concorezzi—   96 *1840,1863* San
Vital,

81 "*Ominous*: it is a bad omen that the Ghibellins should now get what crafty
old Barbarossa tried in vain to win from the previous Azzo—in *his* day Saint
George was the patron-saint of Ferrara and provided it with the marshes a
moat which could not be penetrated. Young Ecelin [the future Tyrant], on the
other hand, is intended to be the tutelar spirit of Padua: veins on his hand come
together as the rivers Brenta and Bacchiglione come together at Padua.
82 *That Ghibellins*: revised from 'Your Ghibellin' to 'These Ghibellins' in
SB, in which 'what' is deleted and 'Ferrara which' inserted in its place.
cautelous: 'Wily; cunning; treacherous': Johnson.
84 *Saint George*: the patron saint of Ferrara.
86 *Young Ecelin is*: in *SB* Browning has written 'Old' and 'was' above,
faintly.
88 *Bacchiglion*: *SB* has, below: 'Lord, what a life has this family led us now
happily extinct'.
89 "*The founts!*: cf. *The Revolt of Islam*, 3973 ff. In this passage there may also
be reminiscences of ll. 2398 ff. and 3946 ff. of the same poem.
God's bread: an oath: cf. 'God's wafer', i. 146.
91 *Cino*: see i. 145 n.
95 *Concorezzi*: 'At this time Dominus Robertus de Concorezo of Milan had
been chosen Podestà of Padua': Rolandino, in Muratori viii. 186.
96 *San Vitale*: 'San Vitale was in the south-east corner of Ferrara, next to the
San Pietro quarter, where was Taurello's palace': Whyte.

    "On his own palace, so adroitly razed
    "He knew it not; a sort of Guelf folk gazed
    "And laughed apart; Cino disliked their air—
100 "Must pluck up spirit, show he does not care—
    "Seats himself on the tank's edge—will begin
    "To hum, *za, za, Cavaler Ecelin*—
    "A silence; he gets warmer, clinks to chime,
    "Now both feet plough the ground, deeper each
       time,
105 "At last, *za, za* and up with a fierce kick
    "Comes his own mother's face caught by the
       thick
    "Grey hair about his spur!"
                    Which means, they lift
    The covering, Salinguerra made a shift
    To stretch upon the truth; as well avoid
10   Further disclosures; leave them thus employed.
    Our dropping Autumn morning clears apace,
    And poor Ferrara puts a softened face
    On her misfortunes. Let us scale this tall
    Huge foursquare line of red brick garden-wall
15   Bastioned within by trees of every sort
    On three sides, slender, spreading, long and
       short;
    Each grew as it contrived, the poplar ramped,

---

107 *1840* spur!   108 *1840* The covering Taurello made   113 *1840* On her misfortunes, save one spot—this tall   116 *1840–65* short,   117 *1840* (Each   *1863* —Each

102 *za, za*: when Ecelin arrived unexpectedly in Verona in 1227, Rolandino tells us (Muratori viii, 188), there was a shout, '*ad arma, ad arma, za za Cavaler Ecelin*'. SB comments: 'The war tune which so oft has [remainder illegible]'.

103 *clinks to chime*: rhymes. Cf. *The Two Poets of Croisic*, 620–1: 'Some other poet's clink / "Thetis and Tethys"'.

106 *his own mother's face*: cf. 'Childe Roland', 121 ff.

108 *The covering*: the planks which had been placed over the poisoned tanks, with their hideous contents, are taken as a symbol of Taurello's attempt to cover the truth of what had been happening.

109 ∧ *as well avoid*: 'his situation was or (rather) had been critical': SB.

113 ∧ *save one spot* (*1840*): 'All was ruin—': SB.

114 *garden-wall*: as Holmes points out (p. 479), Browning probably took the hint for this description of Taurello's palaces and garden from the *Chronica Parva Ferrariensis*. Cf. ii. 915 n., above.

The fig-tree reared itself,—but stark and
  cramped,
Made fools of, like tamed lions: whence, on the
  edge,
Running 'twixt trunk and trunk to smooth one
  ledge   12
Of shade, were shrubs inserted, warp and woof,

*How, passing
through the rare
garden,*

Which smothered up that variance. Scale the
  roof
Of solid tops, and o'er the slope you slide
Down to a grassy space level and wide,
Here and there dotted with a tree, but trees   12
Of rarer leaf, each foreigner at ease,
Set by itself: and in the centre spreads,
Borne upon three uneasy leopards' heads,
A laver, broad and shallow, one bright spirt
Of water bubbles in. The walls begirt   1
With trees leave off on either hand; pursue
Your path along a wondrous avenue
Those walls abut on, heaped of gleamy stone,
With aloes leering everywhere, grey-grown
From many a Moorish summer: how they wind   1
Out of the fissures! likelier to bind
The building than those rusted cramps which
  drop
Already in the eating sunshine. Stop,
You fleeting shapes above there! Ah, the pride
Or else despair of the whole country-side!
A range of statues, swarming o'er with wasps,
God, goddess, woman, man, the Greek
  rough-rasps

    118 *1840* itself,)   119 *1840* of; whence upon the very edge,   *1863,1865* of,
like tamed lions; whence, on the·edge,   121 *1840* shade, are shrubs   122
1840 Which smother   128 *1840–65* Born   130 *1840* in: the   133 *1840*
proof on>on,   *1840* The walls   138–9 *1840* Stop|Yon fleeting   140
1840–65 country-side—   142 *1840* man, your Greek

    118 *stark*: rigid,.incapable of movement.   122 *Scale*: cf. i. 389 n.
138 *eating sunshine*: cf. *Paracelsus*, i. 694 and iv. 139.
139 *You fleeting shapes*: the statues, which seem to move: cf. 149.
140 *Or else despair*: according to differing views of art.

In crumbling Naples marble—meant to look
Like those Messina marbles Constance took
Delight in, or Taurello's self conveyed
To Mantua for his mistress, Adelaide.—
A certain font with caryatides
Since cloistered at Goito; only, these
Are up and doing, not abashed, a troop
Able to right themselves—who see you, stoop
Their arms o' the instant after you! Unplucked
By this or that, you pass; for they conduct
To terrace raised on terrace, and, between,
Creatures of brighter mould and braver mien
Than any yet, the choicest of the Isle
No doubt. Here, left a sullen breathing-while,
Up-gathered on himself the Fighter stood
For his last fight, and, wiping treacherous
　　　blood
Out of the eyelids just held ope beneath
Those shading fingers in their iron sheath,
Steadied his strengths amid the buzz and stir
Of the dusk hideous amphitheatre
At the announcement of his over-match
To wind the day's diversion up, dispatch
The pertinacious Gaul: while, limbs one heap,

143 *1840–65* marble!　146 *1840–68* Adelaide,　151 *1840* O' the instant after you their arms! unplucked　*1863–8* {as *1840*, except 'Unplucked'} 152 *1840* that you pass,　*1863,1865* that, you pass,　156 *1840* No doubt; here,　162 *1840* Of a dusk　165 *1840* Their pertinacious friend: while,

---

143 *Naples marble*: for the contrast between good stone and bad, cf. 'The Bishop Orders his Tomb', 115 ff.
144 *Constance*: the wife of Heinrich VI and mother of Friedrich II. Cf. v. 407.
145 *Taurello's self*: opposite the next line SB has: 'Dug up at &':
149 *Are up and doing*: in contrast to the still figures which support the font at Goito (i. 410 ff.), Taurello's rather vulgar statues seem to gesticulate and clutch at you. *SB* has 'unlike the girls of stone'.
155 *the Isle*: Sicily.
156 *breathing-while*: as in Shakespeare, *Venus and Adonis*, 1142.
157 *Up-gathered on himself*: cf. Spenser, *Muiopotmos*, 397–8: 'Himselfe he close upgathered more and more / Into his den'.
157 *the Fighter*: like 'The Slave' (166), a suitable subject for a classically-minded sculptor of Browning's period, such as the American Hiram Powers. No specific originals have been traced, however.
163 *his over-match*: i.e. he is matched against an opponent who is too strong for him.

The Slave, no breath in her round mouth, watched
   leap
Dart after dart forth, as her hero's car
Clove dizzily the solid of the war
—Let coil about his knees for pride in him.
We reach the farthest terrace, and the grim   170
San Pietro Palace stops us.

                        Such the state

Salinguerra
contrived for a
purpose,

Of Salinguerra's plan to emulate
Sicilian marvels, that his girlish wife
Retrude still might lead her ancient life
In her new home: whereat enlarged so much   175
Neighbours upon the novel princely touch
He took,—who here imprisons Boniface.
Here must the Envoys come to sue for grace;
And here, emerging from the labyrinth
Below, Sordello paused beside the plinth   180
Of the door-pillar.

                 He had really left
Verona for the cornfields (a poor theft
From the morass) where Este's camp was made;
The Envoys' march, the Legate's cavalcade—
All had been seen by him, but scarce as when,—   185
Eager for cause to stand aloof from men
At every point save the fantastic tie
Acknowledged in his boyish sophistry,—

---

175 *1840–65* home—   177 *1840* He took who   180 *1840* Below, two
minstrels pause   181 *1840* ¶ One had really left   *1863,1865* ¶ He had really
left.   185 *1840* Looked cursorily o'er, but scarce as when,   *1863,1865* All had
been seen by him, but scarce as when,   188 *1840–65* sophistry,

---

168 *the solid*: the solid wall of warriors.
171 *San Pietro Palace*: in modern Ferrara the Via Salinguerra is near the Porta
S. Pietro.
174 *Retrude*: see note to ii. 910.
175 *whereat enlarged so much*: which prompted his neighbours to expatiate on
his new princely ways. *SB* has the words 'when he married the K's relative' (cf.
iv. 528) after 'home'.
178 *to sue for grace*: *SB*: 'what was like to be'.
180 *Sordello paused*: *1840* makes it clear that the disguised Palma was with
him, as noted by Domett: 'Sordello—& Palma disguised as a minstrel'. Opposite line 180 Domett refers to 'page 109', i.e. iii. 545–7.
185 *but scarce*: 'so cursorily' inserted, *SB*, which also has 'He had' before
'Looked cursorily' (*1840*). The reference is to his early days.

He made account of such. A crowd,—he meant   *Sordello ponders*
To task the whole of it; each part's intent   *all seen and heard.*
Concerned him therefore: and, the more he pried,
The less became Sordello satisfied
With his own figure at the moment. Sought
He respite from his task? Descried he aught
Novel in the anticipated sight
Of all these livers upon all delight?
This phalanx, as of myriad points combined,
Whereby he still had imaged the mankind
His youth was passed in dreams of rivalling,
His age—in plans to prove at least such thing
Had been so dreamed,—which now he must
     impress
With his own will, effect a happiness
By theirs,—supply a body to his soul
Thence, and become eventually whole
With them as he had hoped to be without—
Made these the mankind he once raved about?   *finds in men no*
Because a few of them were notable,   *machine for his*
Should all be figured worthy note? As well   *sake,*

190
195
200
205

---

189 *1840* crowd;   196 *1840* those livers   197 *1840* A phalanx as . . . .
combined   198 *1840–65* that mankind   200–1 *1840* to show at least the
thing|So dreamed, but now he hastened to impress   203 *1840* From theirs,
supply   206 *1840* mankind he was mad about?   208 *1840* Must all

---

190 *the whole of it: SB* inserts: 'to the uttermost development, & worth, not
want of worth,'.
194 *He respite: SB* inserts 'already' between these words, and 'no.' after
'task?'.
195 *Novel: SB* inserts 'Embarassing &' before this word.
196 *all delight?*: 'The vulgar Enjoyers': *SB*.
199 ∧ *His youth*: 'Which': *SB*.
200 ∧ *His age*: 'and', *SB*, which also seems to underline 'show', and adds 'had
been' at the end of the line.
201 *So dreamed, but* ∧ *now (1840)*: 'which': *SB*.
203 *theirs*: 'their happiness': *SB*.
205 *With*: underlined in *SB*. Whyte comments: 'This is the point where the
change from egotist to altruist begins to work in Sordello. He feels for the first
time the mute appeal made by human misery. The crowd which hitherto, since
they had refused to accept him on his own valuation, he had hoped to be
without, which he had up to this regarded as a clog not worthy of his genius, he
now feels to look to him for help. The miseries he has witnessed that morning
arouse his humanity'.
206 *these*: underlined in *SB*, with the note: 'These of the cavalcade &
march—'.

Expect to find Taurello's triple line
Of trees a single and prodigious pine.   210
Real pines rose here and there; but, close among,
Thrust into and mixed up with pines, a throng
Of shrubs, he saw,—a nameless common sort
O'erpast in dreams, left out of the report
And hurried into corners, or at best   215
Admitted to be fancied like the rest.
Reckon that morning's proper chiefs—how few!
And yet the people grew, the people grew,
Grew ever, as if the many there indeed,
More left behind and most who should
     succeed,—   220
Simply in virtue of their mouths and eyes,
Petty enjoyments and huge miseries,—
Mingled with, and made veritably great
Those chiefs: he overlooked not Mainard's state
Nor Concorezzi's station, but instead   225
Of stopping there, each dwindled to be head
Of infinite and absent Tyrolese
Or Paduans; startling all the more, that these
Seemed passive and disposed of, uncared for,
Yet doubtless on the whole (like Eglamor)   230
Smiling; for if a wealthy man decays

---

213 *1840* Of shrubs you saw,   214–15 *1840* report,|Fast hurried   217
1840 chiefs; how few!   219 *1840* as with many   220 *1840* succeed,   221
1840 their faces, eyes,   222 *1840* miseries,   223 *1840* Were veritably
mingled with, made great   224 *1840* no overlooking Mainard's   228
1840 startling too the more   230–1 *1840* Yet . . . . whole (quoth Eglamor)|
Smiling—for   *1863,1865* "Yet . . . . whole" (quoth Eglamor)|"Smiling—for

213 *Of shrubs you saw,* (*1840*): 'and, mixed up with great men,': *SB*.
216 *fancied*: imagined.
217 *proper chiefs*: 'Priests, captains, troubadours &c': *SB*.
218 *the people*: underlined in *SB*, with the note: 'domestic life of these—*so*
miserable—'.
224 *Mainard's state*: see note to iv. 43, and (for Concorezzi) note to iv. 95.
226 *each dwindled*: he realized that the true importance of such men derived
from the mass of ordinary people whom they represented.
228 *these*: the multitudes.
230 *Yet doubtless*: note revision. The meaning seems to be that as the true
importance of leaders derives from the great numbers of those whom they
lead, it is all the more surprising that the latter seem uncared-for; yet they put a
cheerful face on it, on the whole, inappropriate as it may appear.

And out of store of robes must wear, all days,
One tattered suit, alike in sun and shade,
'T is commonly some tarnished gay brocade
235 Fit for a feast-night's flourish and no more:
Nor otherwise poor Misery from her store
Of looks is fain upgather, keep unfurled
For common wear as she goes through the
  world,
The faint remainder of some worn-out smile
Meant for a feast-night's service merely.
240   While
Crowd upon crowd rose on Sordello thus,— *but a thing with a*
(Crowds no way interfering to discuss,   *life of its own,*
Much less dispute, life's joys with one
  employed
In envying them,—or, if they aught enjoyed,
245 There lingered something indefinable
In every look and tone, the mirth as well
As woe, that fixed at once his estimate
Of the result, their good or bad estate)—
Old memories returned with new effect:
250 And the new body, ere he could suspect,
Cohered, mankind and he were really fused,
The new self seemed impatient to be used
By him, but utterly another way
Than that anticipated: strange to say,
They were too much below him, more in
255 thrall
Than he, the adjunct than the principal.

---

232 *1840* store of such must wear all days 233 *1840* suit 234 *1840* fine
brocade 237 *1863,1865* fain to upgather, 240 *1863,1865* merely."
242 *1840* Crowds . . . . discuss 243 *1840* dispute 244 *1840* them, or, if
they enjoyed, *245 {Editors' emendation, based on *1840*.} *1840* There
lingered somewhat indefinable *1863–89* Where lingered something indefinable 248 *1840* estate,— 249 *1840* memories flocked but with a
new 254 *1840,1863* To that anticipated:

245 *There lingered*: the restoration of 'There' restores the sense, ruined by
'Where', which probably originated as a misprint.
250 *the new body*: cf. l. 203 above.
252 *The new self*: consisting of himself and mankind fused together. This is a
turning-point in his development.

What booted scattered units?—here a mind
And there, which might repay his own to find,
And stamp, and use?—a few, howe'er august,
If all the rest were grovelling in the dust?   260
No: first a mighty equilibrium, sure,
Should he establish, privilege procure
For all, the few had long possessed! He felt
An error, an exceeding error melt:
and rights hitherto While he was occupied with Mantuan chants,   265
ignored by him, Behoved him think of men, and take their wants,
Such as he now distinguished every side,
As his own want which might be satisfied,—
And, after that, think of rare qualities
Of his own soul demanding exercise.   270
It followed naturally, through no claim
On their part, which made virtue of the aim
At serving them, on his,—that, past retrieve,
He felt now in their toils, theirs—nor could leave
Wonder how, in the eagerness to rule,   275
Impress his will on mankind, he (the fool!)
Had never even entertained the thought
That this his last arrangement might be fraught
With incidental good to them as well,
And that mankind's delight would help to swell   280
His own. So, if he sighed, as formerly
Because the merry time of life must fleet,

257–9 *1840* scattered brilliances? the mind| Of any number he might hope to
bind| And stamp with his own thought, howe'er august,   260 *1840* rest
should grovel in   *1863,1865* rest were groveling in   261–2 *1840* equilibrium
sure| To be established,   263 *1840* For them himself had . . . . he felt
1863,1865 For all, the few had . . . . he felt   264 *1840–68* melt—   266 *1840*
men and of their wants   268–9 *1840* want that might be satisfied,| And, after
that, of wondrous qualities   270–1 *1840* exercise,| And like demand it
longer: nor a claim   272 *1840* part, nor was virtue in the aim   273–4 *1840*
them on his, but, past retrieve,| He in their toils felt with them, nor could
leave,   275 *1840* Wonder that in   276–82 *1840* will upon them, he the

257 *scattered units*: occasional 'brilliances' (*1840*) were no use: he must serve
mankind as a whole.
268 *might be*: underlined in *SB*.
269 *after that*: i.e. only after that. *1840* suggests that these qualities of his own
soul are relatively quite unimportant.
271 *And like demand it longer* (*1840*): *SB* changes to 'likely to'.
272–3 *which made . . . on his*: brackets round these words would clarify the
meaning.
281 *formerly*: an unrhymed line, due to revision.

'T was deeplier now,—for could the crowds repeat
Their poor experiences? His hand that shook
285 Was twice to be deplored. "The Legate, look!
"With eyes, like fresh-blown thrush-eggs on a thread,
"Faint-blue and loosely floating in his head,
"Large tongue, moist open mouth; and this long while
"That owner of the idiotic smile
"Serves them!"
290   He fortunately saw in time   *—a fault he is*
His fault however, and since the office prime *now anxious to*
Includes the secondary—best accept *repair,*
Both offices; Taurello, its adept,
Could teach him the preparatory one,
295 And how to do what he had fancied done
Long previously, ere take the greater task.
How render first these people happy? Ask
The people's friends: for there must be one good,

fool|Had never entertained the obvious thought|This last of his arrangements would be fraught|With good to them as well, and he should be|Rejoiced thereat; and if, as formerly,|He sighed the merry time of life must fleet, {No equivalent line for 280 in *1840*.}   283 *1840* now,   285 *1840* The   290 *1840* Serves them! He {No line division, *1840–65*.}   291 *1840* and the office   297 *1840* render then these . . . . ask   *1863,1865* render first these . . . . ask   *298 {Reading of *1840–68*}   *1888,1889* good

284 *His hand that shook*: for his poor physique, cf. v. 362 n.

285 *The Legate*: in contrast to himself, the idiotic-looking Legate has been serving mankind for a long time, strange as it seems.

290 *them!"*: 'The Pretor's insolence,—': SB.

291 *the office prime*: to 'render first these people happy' by establishing 'a mighty equilibrium' (261). Sordello believes that Taurello understands this office, which includes 'the secondary' office, 'the greater task' of calling into play the 'rare qualities/Of his own soul demanding exercising' (269–70).

297 *happy?* ∧ *Ask*: 'up to the average mark—& thence proceed to the further development. *His* way, to the second, nobody had tried, of course: but the first way, to the general happiness, all had been trying, Este & Salinguerra, but ineffectually, it would seem': SB.

298 *The people's friends*: 'Sordello's naïveté and utter ignorance of human nature is nowhere better portrayed than here', Whyte comments. 'With delicious simplicity he imputes without hesitation the purest motives of philanthropy alike to Kaiser and Pope, to Azzo and Taurello. He goes off hot foot to Taurello to get his advice on serving mankind, convinced in his own mind that the cause of all this struggle is "the best way of making the people happy." Poor Sordello!'

one ∧ *good*: 'immediate': SB.

One way to it—the Cause! He understood
The meaning now of Palma; why the jar   300
Else, the ado, the trouble wide and far
Of Guelfs and Ghibellins, the Lombard hope
And Rome's despair?—'twixt Emperor and
    Pope
The confused shifting sort of Eden tale—
Hardihood still recurring, still to fail—   305
That foreign interloping fiend, this free
And native overbrooding deity:
Yet a dire fascination o'er the palms
The Kaiser ruined, troubling even the calms
Of paradise; or, on the other hand,   310
The Pontiff, as the Kaisers understand,
One snake-like cursed of God to love the
    ground,
Whose heavy length breaks in the noon
    profound
Some saving tree—which needs the Kaiser,
    dressed
As the dislodging angel of that pest: 315

    299 1840 Cause! he   1863–68 Cause!—he   300–1 1840 Palma; else why
are|The great ado, ... far,   302 1840 These Guelfs . . . the Lombard's
hope   1863–8 Of Guelfs . . . the Lombard's hope   303 1840 Or its despair!
'twixt Emperor or Pope   305 1840 Of hardihood recurring still to
fail—   1863–8 Still hardihood recurring, still to fail—   307 1840
Deity—   1863–8 deity—   309 1840 His presence ruined troubling
thorough calms   310 1840,1863 Paradise—   1865,1868 paradise—   311
1840 as your Kaisers   312 1840 That, snake-like   313 1840 With lulling
eye breaks   314 1840 saving tree—who but the Kaiser drest 1863,1865 saving
tree—which needs the Kaiser, drest   315 1840 of the pest   1863–8 of that
pest,

    304 Eden tale: because, as 306–7 make clear, the contest between Ghibellin
and Guelf is like that between Satan and God in the Garden of Eden—or that
between God and Satan, according to one's point of view (that is why it is a
'shifting' tale).
    305 still to fail—: opposite this, and again opposite 307, SB has: 'What to do?'
    308 the palms: see Paradise Lost, iv. 139 and ix. 435.
    310 or, on the other hand: from the point-of-view of the Emperors and their
followers, the Pope is the serpent. Cf. Genesis 3:14: 'And the LORD God said
unto the serpent . . . thou art cursed . . .; upon thy belly shalt thou go'.
    314 Some saving tree: the noise of a bough breaking under the weight of the
snake saves Man by bringing 'the dislodging angel'.
    dressed: i.e. seen in the role of.
    315 that pest: cf. Paradise Lost, ii. 735.

Yet flames that pest bedropped, flat head, full
   fold,
With coruscating dower of dyes. "Behold
"The secret, so to speak, and master-spring
"O' the contest!—which of the two Powers
   shall bring
320 "Men good, perchance the most good: ay, it may
"Be that!—the question, which best knows the
   way."
And hereupon Count Mainard strutted past
Out of San Pietro; never seemed the last
Of archers, slingers: and our friend began
325 To recollect strange modes of serving man—
Arbalist, catapult, brake, manganel,
And more. "This way of theirs may,—who can
   tell?—
"Need perfecting," said he: "let all be solved
"At once! Taurello 't is, the task devolved
330 "On late: confront Taurello!"
                  And at last
He did confront him. Scarce an hour had past

since he apprehends its full extent,

316 *1840* Then? yet that pest bedropt,   *1863,1865* Then—yet that pest bedropt,   *1868* Then—yet that pest bedropped,   317 *1840* dyes; behold
319 *1840* Of the whole contest! which of them shall bring *1863,1865*
Of the contest! which of the two Powers shall bring *1868* "Of the contest!—
which of the two Powers shall bring   320 *1840–68* Men good—perchance the most good—   321 *1840* Be that; the question is which knows
the way. *1863,1865* Be that! the question, which best knows the way."
323 *1840* never looked the   325 *1868* man   327–9 *1840* And more: this
. . . . may, who can tell,|Need perfecting, said he: all's better solved|
At once: Taurello 'twas the   330 *1840* late—confront Taurello!
1863–8 late—confront Taurello!"   331 *1840* They did confront him.
Scarcely an hour past *1863–8* He did confront him. Scarcely an hour past

---

316 *bedropped*: covered with drops, as in *Paradise Lost*, x. 527.
317 *"Behold*: Sordello soliloquizes.
  321 *Be that*: SB seems to revise *1840* to 'Be that the question is, which knows
the way?'
  322 *Count Mainard*: 'of the Tyrol instrument of one cause, & the one [?
throne] to be *His*.' SB. Cf. 43 and note, above.
  323 *never seemed the last*: there seemed no end to.
324 *our friend*: Sordello.
  326 *brake*: the rack. For 'Arbalist' and 'manganel' see iv. 49 n. After 327 SB
has 'The Siege's incidents'.
  328 *Need perfecting, said he*: 'they have succeeded but indifferently as yet!' SB.
330 *at last*: 'a word from Oliero, and': SB.
  331 *confront him*: 'Palma in disguise & not making herself known to Salinguerra': SB.

When forth Sordello came, older by years
Than at his entry. Unexampled fears
Oppressed him, and he staggered off, blind, mute
And deaf, like some fresh-mutilated brute,   335
Into Ferrara—not the empty town
That morning witnessed: he went up and down
Streets whence the veil had been stript shred by
     shred,
So that, in place of huddling with their dead
Indoors, to answer Salinguerra's ends,   340
Townsfolk make shift to crawl forth, sit like
     friends
With any one. A woman gave him choice
Of her two daughters, the infantile voice
Or the dimpled knee, for half a chain, his throat
Was clasped with; but an archer knew the coat—   345
Its blue cross and eight lilies,—bade beware
One dogging him in concert with the pair
Though thrumming on the sleeve that hid his
     knife.
Night set in early, autumn dews were rife,
They kindled great fires while the Leaguers' mass   350

338 *1840* veil was stripped shred after shred,   *1863–8* veil had been stripped
shred by shred,   341 *1840* Its folk made shift to crawl and sit like friends
1863–8 Its folk made shift to crawl forth, sit like friends   343 *1840* Or
dimpled . . . . chain   345 *1840 proof* coat > coat—   346 *1840* lilies,   349
1840 dews fell rife,   350 *1840* And fires were kindled while the
Leaguer's   *1863,1865* They kindled great fires while the Leaguer's

332 *Sordello came*: '—as they gave way to the Legate—': *SB*.
older by years: such is the effect on an idealistic dreamer of the knowledge
imparted by this practical fighting-man.
340 *to answer Salinguerra's ends*: and clearly on his orders.
342 *any one.*: 'The newcomers brought food & hope': *SB*.
346 *Its blue cross*: the archer recognized that Sordello's coat bore the insignia
of the House of Romano. At i. 191 Verci explains that a blue cross was in Italy
the entitlement of a family descended from a crusader. On one side of their
shield the Family of Ecelin had eight lilies. Verci admits that this may seem
surprising, as lilies were usually a symbol of the Guelfs.
346 *bade beware*: the meaning is almost certainly that the archer bade Sordello
beware of a man who was following him with 'the pair', presumably the two
young girls whom their mother is offering him. This villain is strumming at
some instrument, but has a dagger concealed under his sleeve. Whyte supposes
that it is the bravo who is warned to beware.
348 *the sleeve*: cf. Chaucer, *Knight's Tale*, 1141.
350 *the Leaguers' mass*: the solemn mass celebrated by the members of the
Lombard League at their *carroccio*: cf. i. 317 n.

Began at every carroch: he must pass
Between the kneeling people. Presently
The carroch of Verona caught his eye
With purple trappings; silently he bent
355 Over its fire, when voices violent
Began, "Affirm not whom the youth was like
"That struck me from the porch: I did not strike
"Again: I too have chestnut hair; my kin
"Hate Azzo and stand up for Ecelin.
"Here, minstrel, drive bad thoughts away! Sing!
360   Take
"My glove for guerdon!" And for that man's
     sake
He turned: "A song of Eglamor's!"—scarce
     named,
When, "Our Sordello's rather!"—all exclaimed;
"Is not Sordello famousest for rhyme?"
365 He had been happy to deny, this time,—
Profess as heretofore the aching head
And failing heart,—suspect that in his stead
Some true Apollo had the charge of them,
Was champion to reward or to condemn,
370 So his intolerable risk might shift

*and would fain
have helped some
way.*

351 *1840–68* carroch—   352 *1840* Between that kneeling people: presently   356 *1840 proof* affirm>Affirm   *1840* Affirm   357 *1840–68* That,
striking from the porch, I did   359 *1840* Ecelin;   360 *1840* away; sing;
take   *1863,1865* away! sing! take   361 *1840* guerdon! and   *1863,1865* guerdon!" and   362 *1840* A.... Eglamor's!   363 *1840* Our Sordello's, rather!
all   *1863,1865* "Our Sordello's, rather!" all   364 *1840* Is ....
rhyme?   365 *1840* time;   366 *1840* head,   367 *1840* The failing
heart;   370 *1840 proof* To>So

356 *the youth*: Palma (cf. 373–5), who has fair hair and who is accompanying
Sordello disguised as a minstrel. Tiraboschi (*Storia della Poesia Italiana*, i. 56)
recounts, from Platina, the story that Ecelin's sister Beatrice, a young widow
who became enamoured of Sordello, followed him to Mantua 'in abito
d' umo': on p. 61 he suggests that Platina had written 'Beatrice' in error for
'Cuniza'. Here it seems that a bystander has recognized her resemblance to her
father, or has half-recognized her.
360 "*Here, minstrel*: Sordello is addressed, and offers to sing a song of
Eglamor's, only to find that one of his own is preferred.
368 *Some true Apollo*: a Ghibellin in the midst of Guelfs, he was in great
danger and would have preferred it if they had regarded some other poet as
their favourite, their Apollo.
369 *Was* ∧ *champion*: 'their': SB.

Or share itself; but Naddo's precious gift
But Salinguerra is
also pre-occupied;
Of gifts, he owned, be certain! At the close—
"I made that," said he to a youth who rose
As if to hear: 't was Palma through the band
Conducted him in silence by her hand.   375
   Back now for Salinguerra. Tito of Trent
Gave place to Palma and her friend, who went
In turn at Montelungo's visit: one
After the other were they come and gone,—
These spokesmen for the Kaiser and the Pope,   380
This incarnation of the People's hope,
Sordello,—all the say of each was said;
And Salinguerra sat,—himself instead
Of these to talk with, lingered musing yet.
'T was a drear vast presence-chamber roughly set   385
In order for the morning's use; full face,
The Kaiser's ominous sign-mark had first place,
The crowned grim twy-necked eagle,
    coarsely-blacked
With ochre on the naked wall; nor lacked
Romano's green and yellow either side;   390
But the new token Tito brought had tried
The Legate's patience—nay, if Palma knew

---

372 *1840 proof* certain:> certain! *1840* gifts returned, be certain! at   373
1840 I made that,   375 *1840* by the hand.   377 *1840* place, remember, to
the pair; who   *1863–8* place to Palma and her friend; who   378 *1840–68*
visit—one   379 *1840* other are they come and gone.   380–4 {not in
1840}   382 *1863* said,   *1865,1868* said   383 *1863–8* sat,   385–8 *1840* A
drear vast presence-chamber roughly set|In order for this morning's use; you
met|The grim black twy-necked eagle, coarsely blacked {Line 387 not in
1840.   *1863–8* as *1888* except 'coarsely blacked' in *1863*.}   389 *1840* naked
walls,   390 *1840* There green and yellow tokens either side;   391 *1840*
new symbol Tito

---

371 *Naddo's precious gift*: cf. ii. 500–2. *SB* comments, somewhat cryptically:
'he thought "if I have only sung a song!"'.
373 *a youth*: the disguised Palma.
376 *Tito of Trent*: 'The Kaiser's man,': *SB*. Cf. iv. 41–2.
378 *one*: 'the Popes' (i.e. the Pope's man): *SB*.
390 *green and yellow*: see note to ii. 909.
391 *the new token*: see l. 397 and 412. As the Pope's representative, Montelungo would have been angry at this sign of the Emperor's favour towards
Taurello, if the visit of Sordello and Palma had not so altered Taurello's
attitude that 'Afterward' (396) no change in him was to be seen.
392 *if Palma knew*: 'see page 162 (?)', notes Domett, referring to 788 ff. Palma
would have been astonished if she had realized that Taurello had been on the

What Salinguerra almost meant to do
Until the sight of her restored his lip
395 A certain half-smile, three months' chieftainship
Had banished! Afterward, the Legate found
No change in him, nor asked what badge he
    wound
And unwound carelessly. Now sat the Chief
Silent as when our couple left, whose brief
400 Encounter wrought so opportune effect
In thoughts he summoned not, nor would reject,
Though time 't was now if ever, to pause—fix
On any sort of ending: wiles and tricks
Exhausted, judge! his charge, the crazy town,
405 Just managed to be hindered crashing down—
His last sound troops ranged—care observed to
    post
His best of the maimed soldiers innermost—
So much was plain enough, but somehow struck
Him not before. And now with this strange luck
410 Of Tito's news, rewarding his address
So well, what thought he of?—how the success   *resembling*
With Friedrich's rescript there, would either   *Sordello in nothing*
    hush   *else.*
Old Ecelin's scruples, bring the manly flush
To his young son's white cheek, or, last, exempt
415 Himself from telling what there was to tempt?

---

396 *1840* banished? Afterward   398 *1840* carelessly! Now sate   401
1840 reject—   *1863–8* reject.   402 *1840* Though time, if ever, 'twas to pause
now—fix   407 *1840* His last of   409 *1840* before: and   411 *1840* of?
How   412 *1840* there   413 *1840 proof* flush,>flush   *1840* Ecelin's fiercest
scruple up, or flush   414 *1840* Young Ecelin's white

point of assuming the leadership of Romano himself, as authorized by the
Emperor. When he sees her again, however, the old half-smile (iii. 497) of a
man born to serve in second place returns to his features.
    396 *Afterward:* 'a minute': *SB.*   403 *On any:* 'Up [on] some': *SB.*
    404 *crazy:* decrepit.
    409 *before:* opposite 407–10 *SB* has: 'yet in the mind, He was triumphant,
thro' it'.
    411 *what thought he of?* ∧: 'The Past influenced him': *SB.*
    412 *rescript:* 'Edict of an emperour': Johnson.
    413 *or flush (1840):* 'into manliness': *SB,* which deletes 'fiercest'.
    415 *Himself . . . tempt?:* 'Himself from telling them what there was to have
tempted them, taking it himself?' *SB.*

No: that this minstrel was Romano's last
Servant—himself the first! Could he contrast
The whole!—that minstrel's thirty years just
    spent
In doing nought, their notablest event
This morning's journey hither, as I told—   420
Who yet was lean, outworn and really old,
A stammering awkward man that scarce dared
    raise
His eye before the magisterial gaze—
And Salinguerra with his fears and hopes
Of sixty years, his Emperors and Popes,   425
Cares and contrivances, yet, you would say,
'T was a youth nonchalantly looked away
Through the embrasure northward o'er the sick
Expostulating trees—so agile, quick
And graceful turned the head on the broad chest   430
Encased in pliant steel, his constant vest,
Whence split the sun off in a spray of fire
Across the room; and, loosened of its tire
Of steel, that head let breathe the comely brown
Large massive locks discoloured as if a crown   435
Encircled them, so frayed the basnet where
A sharp white line divided clean the hair;
Glossy above, glossy below, it swept
Curling and fine about a brow thus kept
Calm, laid coat upon coat, marble and sound: 440

---

418 *1840* whole! that minstrel's thirty autumns spent   *1863,1865* whole! that
minstrel's thirty years just spent   419 *1840* nought, his notablest   420
1840 as we told—   422 *1840* awkward youth (scarce dared he raise   423
1840 before that magisterial gaze)   424 *1840* —And   427 *1840* A youth
'twas nonchalantly   429 *1840 proof* agile, quick,>agile quick *1840*
agile   434 *1840 proof* comely, brown,>comely brown *1840* let see
the   435 *1840 proof* Large,>Large *1840* as a crown   439 *1840 proof* it
kept>thus kept

430 *And graceful*: SB inserts above this line: 'As a serpent's neck on the nicer
scales—'.
433 *tire*: head-dress.
436 *basnet*: also 'basinet', a light steel head-piece, terminating in a point
slightly raised above the head and enclosed in front with a visor. Cf. Scott,
Marmion, VI. xxi. 7.
440 *coat upon coat*: his hair seemed 'layered', so that his head looked like that
of a marble bust. We are told that Adelaide, who had magical powers, had been
on the lookout for a man of this appearance.

This was the mystic mark the Tuscan found,
Mused of, turned over books about.

   Square-faced,

How he was made
in body and spirit,

No lion more; two vivid eyes, enchased
In hollows filled with many a shade and streak
445   Settling from the bold nose and bearded cheek.
Nor might the half-smile reach them that
   deformed
A lip supremely perfect else—unwarmed,
Unwidened, less or more; indifferent
Whether on trees or men his thoughts were bent,
450   Thoughts rarely, after all, in trim and train
As now a period was fulfilled again:
Of such, a series made his life, compressed
In each, one story serving for the rest—
How his life-streams rolling arrived at last
455   At the barrier, whence, were it once overpast,
They would emerge, a river to the end,—
Gathered themselves up, paused, bade fate
   befriend,
Took the leap, hung a minute at the height,
Then fell back to oblivion infinite:
Therefore he smiled. Beyond stretched
460   garden-grounds

---

445 *1840–65* cheek;   449 *1840* bent—   451 *1840 proof* complete>
fulfilled *1840* As now: . . . . again; *1863,1865* As now . . . . again;   452
1840 Such in a series   454–9 {not in *1840*.}

---

446 *the half-smile*: his characteristic half-smile (cf. iii. 497, iv. 395) did not
reach his eyes, which never smiled.

447–8 *unwarmed, / Unwidened*: his eyes are cold and almost immobile.

450 *in trim and train*: sorted out and arranged.

451 *a period*: Taurello's life consists of a series of periods, each essentially
similar. Sordello's, on the other hand, consists of a number of 'rounds' (iii. 563
ff.), because his soul develops: that is the subject of the poem.

452 *life, ∧ compressed*: 'that life being': *SB*.

453 *serving for the rest*: below *SB* has: 'Struggles—for another end than the
great one proposed—the vanity of strife except for the pleasure of striving in
itself.'

454 *his life-streams*: note the addition in *1863*, to clarify the meaning. The
image is of a number of small streams failing to rise high enough (in spite of a
'leap') to join and form 'a river to the end'. There may be a reminiscence of 'a
tide in the affairs of men': *Julius Caesar* iv. iii. 216 ff.

460 *Therefore he smiled*: above this line, at the top of p. 149, *SB* has 'Saliens in
guerram', in a bold hand and underlined with a wavy line, no doubt to draw
attention to the meaning of 'Salinguerra', leaping into war.

garden-grounds: 'They were built—what for?—& ravaged—what for?' *SB*.

Where late the adversary, breaking bounds,
Had gained him an occasion, That above,
That eagle, testified he could improve
Effectually. The Kaiser's symbol lay
Beside his rescript, a new badge by way   465
Of baldric; while,—another thing that marred
Alike emprise, achievement and reward,—
Ecelin's missive was conspicuous too.

and what had
been his career of
old.

What past life did those flying thoughts
                    pursue?
As his, few names in Mantua half so old;   470
But at Ferrara, where his sires enrolled
It latterly, the Adelardi spared

---

462 *1840 proof* that> That   *1840* Procured him an occasion That   464 *1840*
Effectually; the   466 *1840* while   467 *1840* emprize, . . . reward,
469–70 *1840* ¶ What a past life those flying thoughts pursue! | As his no name

461 *the adversary*: by breaking into his territory the Guelfs had given him an
opportunity which he was in a position to take advantage of, as the Imperial
eagle on his wall bore witness. The revision from 'that' to 'That' is clearly for
emphasis.
465 *a new badge*: the Emperor had sent him a baldric as a sign of the power
which he might now exercise. But Ecelin's letter inhibited him. He cannot act
without authorization from the head of the House of Romano: cf. iii. 521 ff.
468 *Ecelin's missive*: *SB* has something like 'they had brought' after these
words.
469 *What past life*: 'The early life of Salinguerra': Domett.
470 *few names*: see ii. 917 n. 'He was born great—to *be* nothing': *SB*.
472 *the Adelardi*: in ch. xii of his *Histoire* (vol. ii, pp. 294 ff.) Sismondi
describes how 'Guglielmo Marchesella degli Adelardi, leader of the Guelf
party in Ferrara, . . . had the misfortune to see the last male heirs of his family
die, one after another: his brother and all his sons. One daughter of this brother
remained, a girl of tender years called Marchesella. He made him his heir, but
stipulated that if she died without issue his heirs should be his sister's children.
He then believed that the misfortune of his family could at least ensure peace
for his native country, by uniting the two houses which led the mutually
hostile parties. Salinguerra, son of Taurello, was the leader of the Ghibellins in
Ferrara. Guillaume was not content that his niece (aged only seven years)
should be destined to be Salinguerra's wife: he even put her in his care, and
charged her future husband with her education. Then he died. But the Guelfs
could not bear that the sole heiress of a family which had been so valuable to
them should be delivered to the family of their enemies . . . And so they found
means to surprise Marchesella and carry her off from the house of the Salinguerra family, and conducted her to that of the marquises of Este. They chose
Obizzo d'Este to be her husband, and first of all they put his family in
possession of all that belonged to the Adelardi'. The author of the *Chronica
Parva* gives the name of the girl as Lingueta. His passage is vivid, and he
comments that he himself has seen and read Guillaume's will, and that it is
deposited with him: 'Hoc testamentum vidi & legi, & hodie apud me est
depositum': Muratori viii. 481. Holmes discusses different versions of the
story: pp. 473 ff. The spelling 'Marchesalla' is erroneous.

No pains to rival them: both factions shared
Ferrara, so that, counted out, 't would yield
475   A product very like the city's shield,
Half black and white, or Ghibellin and Guelf
As after Salinguerra styled himself
And Este who, till Marchesalla died,
(Last of the Adelardi)—never tried
480   His fortune there: with Marchesalla's child
Would pass,—could Blacks and Whites be
            reconciled
And young Taurello wed Linguetta,—wealth
And sway to a sole grasp. Each treats by stealth
Already: when the Guelfs, the Ravennese
485   Arrive, assault the Pietro quarter, seize
Linguetta, and are gone! Men's first dismay
Abated somewhat, hurries down, to lay
The after indignation, Boniface,
This Richard's father. "Learn the full disgrace
490   "Averted, ere you blame us Guelfs, who rate
"Your Salinguerra, your sole potentate
"That might have been, 'mongst Este's
            valvassors—
"Ay, Azzo's—who, not privy to, abhors

473 *1840* Few means to   476 *1840* Ghibelin and Guelf,   *1863–8* Ghibellin
and Guelf,   478–9 *1840* died|—Last . . . . Adelardi,   480 *1840* there; but
Marchesalla's   481 *1840* Transmits (can Blacks . . . . reconciled *1868*
Would pass,—could Blacks . . . . reconciled,   482 *1840* Linguetta)   483
1840 grasp: each   486 *1840* Our first   489 *1840* proof learn>Learn *1840*
No meaner spokesman: Learn   490 *1840* Averted ere you blame us—wont
to rate   491 *1840* proof and, sole>and sole *1840* Salinguerra, and sole

477–8 *himself . . . died*: *SB* has 'The father' after each of these lines.
481 *Blacks and Whites*: the Guelfs in Florence divided into two parties, the
'Bianchi' and 'Neri', the former eventually identifying themselves with the
Ghibellins. The division, to which Dante refers (*Inferno* vi), in fact originated
later, in Pistoja in 1300.
484 *Already:* ∧ *when*: 'there's the first strife: to baffle it,': *SB*.
487 *lay*: allay.
489 *This Richard's father*: so revised in *1863*, to avoid confusion. *SB* has 'the
father' after line 488.
489–94 *"Learn . . . zealous."*: inverted commas added in *SB*.
489 *"Learn the full disgrace*: '"Before you blame us Guelfs", he said, "understand from what disgrace we have rescued you: this Taurello, who, had he
married Linguetta, would have become sole lord of your city, we reckon only a
vassal of Azzo of Este. Azzo himself, to be sure, abhors what we did, but we
were zealous for your welfare"': Duff.

"Our step; but we were zealous." Azzo then
To do with! Straight a meeting of old men: 495
"Old Salinguerra dead, his heir a boy,
"What if we change our ruler and decoy
"The Lombard Eagle of the azure sphere
"With Italy to build in, fix him here,

The original check   "Settle the city's troubles in a trice?   500
to his fortunes,   "For private wrong, let public good suffice!"
In fine, young Salinguerra's staunchest friends
Talked of the townsmen making him amends,
Gave him a goshawk, and affirmed there was
Rare sport, one morning, over the green grass   505
A mile or so. He sauntered through the plain,
Was restless, fell to thinking, turned again
In time for Azzo's entry with the bride;
Count Boniface rode smirking at their side;
"She brings him half Ferrara," whispers flew,   510
"And all Ancona! If the stripling knew!"
      Anon the stripling was in Sicily
Where Heinrich ruled in right of Constance; he
Was gracious nor his guest incapable;

494 *1840* Our step—but .... zealous. Azzo's then *1863,1865* Our
step—but .... zealous." Azzo's then *1868* "Our step; but .... zealous."
Azzo's then   496–7 {not in *1840*.}   498 *1863–8* sphere,   499–501 *1840*
in, builds he here?|This deemed—the other owned upon advice—|A third
reflected on the matter twice—   505 *1840* over the morass   509 *1840* at
his side;   *1863–8* at their side: 510 *1840* There's half Ferrara with her,
whispers flew,   511 *1840* knew!

494 *Azzo*: 'the father': *SB*.   498 *The Lombard Eagle*: Azzo.
499 *Italy*: i.e. the whole of Italy to choose from.
503 *amends*: 'said, after all he was a Mantuan & no Ferrarese': *SB*.
512 *in Sicily*: as Whyte points out, though with minor inaccuracies (pp.
14–15 and 200 n.), G. B. Pigna's *Historia de Principi di Este* (Ferrara, 1570)
describes Taurello's visit to Sicily in 1198: 'Salinguerra, finding himself
reduced to terms of equality with the other citizens, and being unable to
tolerate it, transferred himself, in the year 1198, to Cesare in Sicily. He revealed
to him the new incipient greatness which had presented itself to the Principi di
Este, and the danger threatening his affairs, every time the Estensi grew in
power': p. 130.
513 *Where Heinrich ruled*: 'Enters into Service (?) of Heinrich & marries his
daughter': Domett.
in right of Constance: Heinrich VI (1165–97) succeeded his father in 1189,
and heard of the death of the King of Sicily (his wife's nephew) at the same
time. In 1191 he was crowned Emperor (with his wife) in Italy. He then
proceeded to attempt to assert his right over the two Sicilies, but was not
successful for long.

515　Each understood the other. So it fell,
　　One Spring, when Azzo, thoroughly at ease,
　　Had near forgotten by what precise degrees
　　He crept at first to such a downy seat,
　　The Count trudged over in a special heat
520　To bid him of God's love dislodge from each
　　Of Salinguerra's palaces,—a breach
　　Might yawn else, not so readily to shut,
　　For who was just arrived at Mantua but
　　The youngster, sword on thigh and tuft on chin,
525　With tokens for Celano, Ecelin,　　*which he was in*
　　Pistore, and the like! Next news,—no whit　　*the way to*
　　Do any of Ferrara's domes befit　　*retrieve,*
　　His wife of Heinrich's very blood: a band
　　Of foreigners assemble, understand
530　Garden-constructing, level and surround,
　　Build up and bury in. A last news crowned
　　The consternation: since his infant's birth,
　　He only waits they end his wondrous girth
　　Of trees that link San Pietro with Tomà,
535　To visit us. When, as its Podestà
　　Ecelin, at Vicenza, called his friend
　　Taurello thither, what could be their end
　　But to restore the Ghibellins' late Head,

517 *1840* forgotten what　　518 *1840* He crept by into such　　519 *1840*
Over the Count trudged in a special heat　　521 *1840* Palaces;　　522 *1840*
else　　524 *1840* sword to thigh, tuft upon chin,　　*1863,1865* sword on thigh,
and tuft on chin,　　526 *1840* Pistore . . . . news: *1863,1865* Pistore . . . .
news,—　　*535 {Reading of *1840*}　*1840*　*proof* Podesta>Podestà
1863–1889 To visit Mantua. When the Podestà　　536 *1840* Regaled him at
Vicenza, Este, there　　537–40 {not in *1840*.}

519 *The Count*: Richard.
525 *Celano*: Rolandino states that in the March of Ancona 'the Counts of
Celano were men of great power and magnificence': Muratori viii. 182. Ecelin
is the Monk: for Bishop Pistore see above, ii. 336 n. The tokens are from the
Emperor.
527 *domes*: Johnson defines 'dome' as 'A building; a house; a fabrick'. For his
wife Retrude see ii. 910 n.
531 *A last news*: cf. 'a double news', vi. 795.
534 *Tomà*: cf. v. 283. Whyte (p. 188 n.) suggests that this refers to the
Bastione di S. Tomaso, beyond S. Vitale.
535 *To visit us*: we return to *1840*, because the sense was spoilt on revision.
Taurello is already in Mantua.
Podestà: 'Ecelin': SB. The revision makes this clear.

The Kaiser helping? He with most to dread
From vengeance and reprisal, Azzo, there   540
With Boniface beforehand, as aware
Of plots in progress, gave alarm, expelled
Both plotters: but the Guelfs in triumph yelled
Too hastily. The burning and the flight,
And how Taurello, occupied that night   545
With Ecelin, lost wife and son, I told:
—Not how he bore the blow, retained his hold,
Got friends safe through, left enemies the worst
O' the fray, and hardly seemed to care at first:
But afterward men heard not constantly   550
Of Salinguerra's House so sure to be!
Though Azzo simply gained by the event
A shifting of his plagues—the first, content
To fall behind the second and estrange
So far his nature, suffer such a change   555
That in Romano sought he wife and child,
And for Romano's sake seemed reconciled
To losing individual life, which shrunk
As the other prospered—mortised in his trunk;
Like a dwarf palm which wanton Arabs foil   560
Of bearing its own proper wine and oil,

*when a fresh
calamity destroyed
all.*

---

541 *1840* beforehand, each aware   543 *1840* A party which abetted him,
but yelled   545 *1840 proof* Taurello>Taurello,   546 *1840 proof* was
told:>were told: *1840* son, were told: 549 *1840–68* first—   550 *1840*
afterward you heard   553 *1840 proof* one,>one   *1840* plagues—this one
content   554,555 *1840* the other and estrange,|You will not say, his nature,
but so change   556 *1865,1868* child   557 *1840* sake was reconciled   558
1840 life, deep sunk,   559–61 *1840* A very pollard mortised in a trunk|Which
Arabs out of wantonness contrive|Shall dwindle that the alien stock may
thrive

---

542 *Of plots in progress* Λ: 'of the intended Italian Headship': *SB.*
543 *Both plotters*: Ecelin and Taurello.
546 *lost wife and son*: cf. ii. 333 ff. 'This is below the belt! Taurello did not lose
his child at Vicenza:' Duff. Perhaps 'lost' may be defended as ambiguous.
549 *hardly seemed to care*: Taurello Salinguerra retains something of this
carefree appearance: cf. i. 286 ff. and iv. 590 ff., below.
551 *Salinguerra's House*: he lost the desire of raising a family which should
become a power in the land. 'Ecelin came in front again': *SB.*
553 *A shifting of his plagues*: it was no longer Taurello that was Azzo's greatest
worry, but Ecelin (supported by Taurello): 'the first' (or former) is Taurello,
'the second' (or latter) Azzo. The House of Romano now became the focus of
all Taurello's loyalties.
559 *mortised*: strongly fastened into: here with the suggestion of grafting, as
the following lines make clear.

By grafting into it the stranger-vine,
Which sucks its heart out, sly and serpentine,
Till forth one vine-palm feathers to the root,
565 And red drops moisten the insipid fruit.
Once Adelaide set on,—the subtle mate
Of the weak soldier, urged to emulate
The Church's valiant women deed for deed,
And paragon her namesake, win the meed
570 O' the great Matilda,—soon they overbore
The rest of Lombardy,—not as before
By an instinctive truculence, but patched
The Kaiser's strategy until it matched
The Pontiff's, sought old ends by novel means.
575 "Only, why is it Salinguerra screens
"Himself behind Romano?—him we bade   *He sank into a*
"Enjoy our shine i' the front, not seek the   *secondary*
    shade!"   *personage,*
—Asked Heinrich, somewhat of the tardiest
To comprehend. Nor Philip acquiesced
580 At once in the arrangement; reasoned, plied
His friend with offers of another bride,
A statelier function—fruitlessly: 't was plain
Taurello through some weakness must remain
Obscure. And Otho, free to judge of both

562–3 {not in *1840*.}   564 *1840* that vine-palm . . . . root   565–8 *1840*
moisten them its arid fruit.| Once set on Adelaide, the subtle mate| And wholly
at his beck, to emulate| The Churches   569 *1840* To paragon   570 *1840* Of
its Matilda,—and they overbore   *1863–8* Of the great Matilda,—soon they
overbore   571 *1840* Lombardy—   572 *1840 proof* By that> By an   574
1840 proof Pontiff's> Pontiff's,   *1840* means: 575 *1840* Only, Romano
Salinguerra screens.   576–7 {not in *1840*.}   578 *1840* Heinrich was
somewhat   579 *1840* comprehend, nor   582–3 *1840* 'tis plain| Taurello's
somehow one to let remain   584 *1840* Obscure; and . . . . both,   *1863–8*
Obscure. And . . . . both,

566 *Once set on Adelaide* (1840): 'He began by Adelaide, a Tuscan, [word
illegible]': *SB*.
569 *her namesake*: Adelaide of Susa. Cf. iii. 488 ff. and n.
570 *the great Matilda*: see iii. 488 n.
577 *shine*: 'Brightness; splendour; lustre': Johnson.
578 *Heinrich* ∧ *was* (1840): 'who had entertained a decided opinion of the
young man': *SB*.
579 *nor* ∧ *Philip* (1840): 'even his successor': *SB*. Philipp von Schwaben
(c. 1180–1208), the youngest son of Friedrich I and brother of Heinrich VI.
584 *Otho*: Otto IV (c. 1174–1218) was elected anti-king (Gegenkönig) in

—Ecelin the unready, harsh and loth,   585
And this more plausible and facile wight
With every point a-sparkle—chose the right,
Admiring how his predecessors harped
On the wrong man: "thus," quoth he, "wits are
    warped
"By outsides!" Carelessly, meanwhile, his life   590
Suffered its many turns of peace and strife
In many lands—you hardly could surprise
The man; who shamed Sordello (recognize!)
In this as much beside, that, unconcerned
What qualities were natural or earned,   595
With no ideal of graces, as they came
He took them, singularly well the same—
Speaking the Greek's own language, just because
Your Greek eludes you, leave the least of flaws
In contracts with him; while, since Arab lore   600
Holds the stars' secret—take one trouble more
And master it! 'T is done, and now deter
Who may the Tuscan, once Jove trined for her,

589 *1840* thus, quoth he, wits   590 *1840* By outsides! Carelessly, withal,
his   593 *1840* A man who . . . . (recognise)   *1863* The man;—who . . . .
(recognise!)   *1865,1868* The man; who . . . . (recognise!)   595 *1840* qualities
are natural   598 *1840* Speaking a dozen languages because   599 *1865,1868*
least to flaws   600 *1840* In contracts, while, through Arab lore,
deter   601–2 {not in *1840*.}

opposition to Philip by a north-west German minority favoured by the Pope.
On the assassination of Philip in 1208 he was again elected king, and crowned
Emperor in Rome the following year. He quarrelled with the Pope, and was
excommunicated. In 1211 he was deposed in favour of Friedrich II. *SB* has
'when at last came' before this word.
  585 *the unready*: otherwise used 'Only as an epithet of Ethelred II', as OED
notes.
  587 *the right*: Ecelin.   588 *Admiring*: being astonished.
  590 *By outsides!*: *SB* adds: 'This is too clever for genius!—All the same to
Salinguerra!'
    his life: Taurello's.
  592 *surprise*: *SB* adds 'him:'.
  597 *the same*: *SB* adds: 'a little was better than none: one may better keep
doing something than nothing'.
  598 *Speaking the Greek's own language*: he learned to speak Greek because a
Greek will always get the better of you if you leave the slightest loophole in an
agreement.
  603 *the Tuscan*: Adelaide. Once Jove is in an astrologically favourable position for her, no one can keep her from joining Friedrich's power. Two
heavenly bodies are trined when they are 120° distant from each other, a highly
favourable aspect. Taurello no doubt fakes the 'evidence'.

From Friedrich's path!—Friedrich, whose
　　pilgrimage
605　The same man puts aside, whom he 'll engage
To leave next year John Brienne in the lurch,
Come to Bassano, see Saint Francis' church
And judge of Guido the Bolognian's piece
Which,—lend Taurello credit,—rivals Greece—
610　Angels, with aureoles like golden quoits
Pitched home, applauding Ecelin's exploits.
For elegance, he strung the angelot,
Made rhymes thereto; for prowess, clove he not
Tiso, last siege, from crest to crupper? Why
615　Detail you thus a varied mastery   *with the*
But to show how Taurello, on the watch   *appropriate graces*
For men, to read their hearts and thereby catch   *of such.*

---

604 *1840* path!   607 *1840* And see Bassano for Saint   608 *1840* —Profound on Guido   609 *1840* That, if you lend him credit,   *1863–8* Which,
lend Taurello credit,   611–12 *1840* exploits|In Painimrie. He . . . .
angelot;   616 *1840* But that Taurello, ever on

604 *Friedrich,* ∧ *whose*: 'the present emperor, finally': *SB*.
605 *The same man*: Taurello induced Friedrich to postpone the pilgrimage
which he had promised the Pope to undertake. Cf. i. 869 n. There is no
historical basis for attributing the delay to Taurello.
605–6 *engage / To leave*: elliptical: Taurello will guarantee that Friedrich will
let John Brienne down.
607 *Come*: infinitive, like 'see'. As Whyte points out (though with a wrong
reference), Verci relates an ancient tradition that Ecelin the Stutterer (the
Monk's father), having been preserved in a great storm as he returned from a
crusade, built a church in Bassano dedicated to the Virgin; and that this church
was later named after St. Francis: *Storia* i. 54. On the following page Verci tells
of an old inscription attributing the paintings in the church to 'Guidus
Bononiensis' and giving the date 1177.
And see Bassano (1840): *SB* has 'And Come' before these words.
610 *quoits*: the aureoles surround their targets, like quoits in a game: cf. ii.
615.
612 *the angelot*: see ii. 517 n.
613 *Made rhymes*: in Millot's *Histoire Littéraire des Troubadours*, iii. 436,
'Taurel' is mentioned among the minor troubadours as the author of a 'Tenson
avec Falconet'.
614 *Tiso*: as Whyte notes, this is Browning's invention. Rolandino
(Muratori, viii. 185) describes how Tisolinus, a nobleman of distinguished
parentage, was captured by the men 'of a certain town called Girzola', and
refused to surrender as his enemies included no one 'de sanguine Militari'. His
body was taken to Ferrara, 'and all the soldiers made a great lamentation, and
Salinguerra himself wept in sorrow, and had him honourably interred. That
took place in the year of Our Lord 1222'.
616 *But* ∧ *that Taurello (1840)*: 'to show how', *SB*, with 'that' scored through,
giving the text of *1863* and later editions.

Their capabilities and purposes,
Displayed himself so far as displayed these:
While our Sordello only cared to know   620
About men as a means whereby he 'd show
Himself, and men had much or little worth
According as they kept in or drew forth
That self; the other's choicest instruments
Surmised him shallow.

              Meantime, malcontents   625
Dropped off, town after town grew wiser. "How
"Change the world's face?" asked people; "as 't is
    now
"It has been, will be ever: very fine
"Subjecting things profane to things divine,
"In talk! This contumacy will fatigue   630
"The vigilance of Este and the League!
"The Ghibellins gain on us!"—as it happed.
Old Azzo and old Boniface, entrapped
By Ponte Alto, both in one month's space

---

621 *1840* means for him to show   622 *1840* men were much   624 *1863,*
1865 self; Taurello's choicest   625 *1840* Meantime malecontents   626
1840 wiser; how   627 *1840* face? said people; as   630 *1840* In talk: this
1863,1865 In talk! this   631 *1840* League,   632 *1840* Observe! accordingly,
their basement sapped,   {*1865* as *1888* except 'happed'}   633 *1840* Azzo and
Boniface were soon entrapped   634 *1840* Alto, and in

---

618 *purposes*: opposite this and the next two lines *SB* has: '*meant* to only & did
display *much & more* than he wanted'.
620 *While our Sordello*: Taurello and Sordello are opposites. Taurello's aim
was to achieve his ends through observing others (himself revealed only
cautiously, and in part—so that even his chosen instruments under-estimated
him), whereas Sordello was interested in others only in relation to himself and
his own powers. *SB* inserts 'who' after 'Sordello'.
622 *and* ∧ *men*: 'to whom': *SB*.
624 *That self*: 'displayed nothing, meaning the display to be the all in all': *SB*.
the other's: i.e. Taurello's. *SB* adds, 'he hoped,' after 'instruments'.
625 *shallow.* ∧ *Meantime*: 'Shallow? When': *SB*.
malecontents (*1840*): Johnson's spelling, revised in *1863*.
627 *said people* (*1840*): put in parentheses in *SB*.
627–8 *'t is now* / *It has been*: perhaps influenced by the formula at the end of
numerous prayers in *The Book of Common Prayer*: 'As it was in the beginning, is
now, and ever shall be'.
629 *Subjecting things profane*: the Guelf cause is all very well in theory, but the
obstinate resistance of the Ghibellins will tire out Este and the Lombard
League.
632 *their basement sapped* (*1840*): the foundation of their policy having been
undermined.
633 *Azzo and . . . Boniface*: '(the original offenders)': *SB*.
634 *one month's space*: 'of rage and mortification, let us hope': *SB*.

635 Slept at Verona: either left a brace
Of sons—but, three years after, either's pair
Lost Guglielm and Aldobrand its heir:
Azzo remained and Richard—all the stay
Of Este and Saint Boniface, at bay
640 As 't were. Then, either Ecelin grew old   *But Ecelin, he set*
Or his brain altered—not o' the proper   *in front, falling,*
       mould
For new appliances—his old palm-stock
Endured no influx of strange strengths. He 'd
       rock
645 As in a drunkenness, or chuckle low
As proud of the completeness of his woe,
Then weep real tears;—now make some mad
       onslaught
On Este, heedless of the lesson taught
So painfully,—now cringe for peace, sue
       peace
At price of past gain, bar of fresh increase
650 To the fortunes of Romano. Up at last
Rose Este, down Romano sank as fast.

---

636 *1840* sons—so three   639 *1840* St. Boniface,   640 *1840* As 'twere;
when either   641 *1840* not the   *1863–8* not of the   643 *1840* strengths:
he'd   646 *1840* proof made>make   *1840* weep—real tears! Now   647
1840 proof Este>Este,   648 *1840* So painfully—now cringe, sue peace, but
peace   649 *1840* price of all advantage; therefore cease   *1863,1865* price of
past gain,—much more, fresh increase   650 *1840* The fortunes of
Romano!   651 *1840* Este and Romano

---

635 *Slept at Verona*: 'Browning is not quite correct here', comments Whyte,
misquoting Maurisius: who records that Azzo and Count Richard died natural
deaths, within eight days of each other, not more than a month after the battle
of Ponte Alto in 1212: Muratori, viii. 23.
636 *either's pair*: each of them left two sons. According to the *Monachi
Patavini Chronicon* Azzo's sons were Aldrevandinus (or Aldubrandinus or
Oldrandinus), who was a young man, and Azzo, who was still a nursing infant;
while Count Richard left an elder son of his own name and a *younger* of the
name of William; Muratori, viii. 668.
637 *Guglielm and Aldobrand*: brackets round these words would clarify the
odd syntax.
639 *at bay*: 'plainly' [?]: *SB*.
640 *As 'twere*: '—put *them* down, & their houses are like *his*—The policy
begins to *show*': *SB*.
grew old: 'German self-inspection': *SB*.
642 *his old palm-stock*: at 558 ff. Taurello was a 'dwarf palm' into which a vine
has been grafted: here Ecelin is the palm, too old for grafting.
650 *Up at last*: 'in return': *SB*.

And men remarked these freaks of peace and war
Happened while Salinguerra was afar:
Whence every friend besought him, all in vain,
To use his old adherent's wits again.   655
Not he!—"who had advisers in his sons,
"Could plot himself, nor needed any one's
"Advice." 'T was Adelaide's remaining staunch
Prevented his destruction root and branch
Forthwith; but when she died, doom fell, for gay   660
He made alliances, gave lands away
To whom it pleased accept them, and withdrew
For ever from the world. Taurello, who
Was summoned to the convent, then refused
A word at the wicket, patience thus abused,   665
Promptly threw off alike his imbecile
Ally's yoke, and his own frank, foolish smile.
Soon a few movements of the happier sort

Salinguerra must
again come
forward,

Changed matters, put himself in men's report
As heretofore; he had to fight, beside,   670
And that became him ever. So, in pride
And flushing of this kind of second youth,
He dealt a good-will blow. Este in truth
Lay prone—and men remembered, somewhat
    late,
A laughing old outrageous stifled hate   67.

652–6 *1840* this sort of peace and war|Commenced while Salinguerra was afar:|And every friend besought him, but in vain,|To wait his old adherent, call again|Taurello: not he—who had daughters, sons,   658 *1840* Advice. . . . . staunch   *1863,1865* Advice." . . . . stanch   660 *1840* Forthwith; Goito green above her, gay   665 *1840* A word,—however patient, thus abused,| At Este's mercy through his imbecile|Ally, was fain dismiss the foolish smile,|And a few   671 *1840* So in   672 *1840* youth   673 *1840* blow.   674 *1840* Was prone—and you remembered,

654 *him*: Ecelin, as noted in *SB*.
658 *Adelaide's remaining staunch*: 'alone': *SB*.
660 *Forthwith*;, ∧ *Goito* (*1840*): 'but once she dead &': *SB*.
gay: gaily, heedlessly.
664–5 *refused* / *A word*: as Ecelin's weak and apologetic speech to Taurello is given at ii. 898 ff., this clearly means that he was given no opportunity of replying.
665 *abused*: 'indeed left': *SB*.   668 *a few movements*: 'already told': *SB*.
673 *blow:* ∧ *Este*: 'at Ferrara': *SB*. No doubt the capture of Count Richard.
675 *hate*: 'for stealing Linguetta?' Domett: '—burning his Son &c': Browning.

He bore to Este—how it would outbreak
At times spite of disguise, like an earthquake
In sunny weather—as that noted day
When with his hundred friends he tried to slay
680　Azzo before the Kaiser's face: and how,
On Azzo's calm refusal to allow
A liegeman's challenge, straight he too was
　　calmed:
As if his hate could bear to lie embalmed,
Bricked up, the moody Pharaoh, and survive
685　All intermediate crumblings, to arrive
At earth's catastrophe—'t was Este's crash
Not Azzo's he demanded, so, no rash
Procedure! Este's true antagonist
Rose out of Ecelin: all voices whist,
690　All eyes were sharpened, wits predicted. He
'T was, leaned in the embrasure absently,
Amused with his own efforts, now, to trace
With his steel-sheathed forefinger Friedrich's face
I' the dust: but as the trees waved sere, his smile
Deepened, and words expressed its thought
695　　erewhile.

---

676 *1840* bore that Este— 　　679 *1840* he offered slay 　　682 *1840* His hate, no doubt, would bear 　　684 *1840* *proof* up>up, 　*1840* Pharaoh, to survive 　　685 *1840* crumblings, be alive *1863–68* crumblings, and arrive 690–1 *1840* Each glance was sharpened, wit predicted. He|'Twas . . . . presently, 　　692 *1840 proof* now>now, 　　693 *1840 proof* forefinger.> forefinger 　　694 *1840* dust: and as

---

678 *that noted day*: see note to i. 819.

684 *the moody Pharaoh*: with primary reference to the embalming of the Pharaohs, 'earth's catastrophe' being the Last Day; but also cf. two phrases quoted in OED: 'this Pharaoh-like procrastination' and 'a Pharaoh stubbornness'. Although the latter is later than *Sordello*, it is clear that 'moody' here means that Taurello is stubborn in his hatred, which is directed against the whole house of Este and not merely against Azzo.

688 *Procedure!* ∧ : 'Thus then stood matters for the moment:' *SB*.

689 *Rose out of*: Domett underlines these words, and inserts a query in the margin. The meaning is probably that now that the Monk has withdrawn, Taurello stands forth as a more deadly hater of Este.

690 *predicted*: intransitive. Domett underlines 'He', writing 'Who?' in the margin and 'Salinguerra possibly (?)' below, a conjecture confirmed by Browning, who writes '(Sª.)'.

691 *absently*: after *1840*'s 'presently' *SB* has: 'after Sordello's departure'.

694 *dust:* ∧₁*and* (*1840*): 'in what he had begun [?as] a plan of Lombardy': *SB*.

695 *its thought erewhile*: the thought which had just occasioned his smile.

—*why and how,*
is let out in
soliloquy.

"Ay, fairly housed at last, my old compeer?
"That we should stick together, all the year
"I kept Vicenza!—How old Boniface,
"Old Azzo caught us in its market-place,
"He by that pillar, I at this,—caught each   700
"In mid swing, more than fury of his speech,
"Egging the rabble on to disavow
"Allegiance to their Marquis—Bacchus, how
"They boasted! Ecelin must turn their drudge,
"Nor, if released, will Salinguerra grudge   705
"Paying arrears of tribute due long since—
"Bacchus! My man could promise then, nor
        wince,
"The bones-and-muscles! Sound of wind and
        limb,
"Spoke he the set excuse I framed for him:
"And now he sits me, slavering and mute,   710
"Intent on chafing each starved purple foot
"Benumbed past aching with the altar slab:
"Will no vein throb there when some monk shall
        blab

696 *1840* ¶ Ay,   697 *1840* together all the year   *1863,1865* together, all the
year,   698 {Reading of *1868–89*}   *1840–65* kept Verona!—How   700
1840 I this pillar, each   702 *1840* Egging our rabble   703 *1840* to the
Marquis—   704 *1840* They caught us! Ecelin.... drudge;   *707 {Read-
ing of *1865,1868*}   *1840,1863* My man, ... wince,   *1888* My man .... wince
{colon inked in after 'wince' in Dykes Campbell copy.}   *1889* My man ....
wince: 708 *1840 proof* bones-and-muscles>bones-and-muscles!   *1840–65*
sound   712 *1840–68* slab—

696 *Ay,* (*1840*): Domett inserts double inverted commas, and notes: 'Salinguerra's Soliloquy to page 164', i.e. to line 848.
  698 *Vicenza!*: where Browning himself was confused (see textual notes
above) an editor must tread warily. The revised reading is retained because we
know from iv. 535 ff. that Ecelin and Taurello had been plotting in Vicenza,
and had been expelled from it by both Boniface and Azzo. In 703 'their
Marquis' might suggest Verona, but there does not seem to be any other
reference in the poem to an episode of this kind in Verona. The present passage
seems to lead on to 725.
  700 *He*: Ecelin the Monk.
  701 *In mid swing*: i.e. each of us was using words as if they were weapons with
which he was laying about him.
  703 *their Marquis*: Azzo.
  704 *us!* ∧ *Ecelin* (*1840*): 'we're without resource *now!*' SB.
  707 *My man*: the Monk.
  710 *he sits me*: Shakespearian: cf. 'He pluckt me ope his doublet': *Julius Caesar*
I. ii. 264–5.
  713 *Will no vein throb there*: 'He (?) *seems* to be running over Ecelin's probable
thoughts in the convent': Domett.

"Spitefully to the circle of.bald scalps,
"'Friedrich 's affirmed to be our side the Alps'
"—Eh, brother Lactance, brother Anaclet?
"Sworn to abjure the world, its fume and fret,
"God's own now? Drop the dormitory bar,
"Enfold the scanty grey serge scapular
"Twice o'er the cowl to muffle memories out!
"So! But the midnight whisper turns a shout,
"Eyes wink, mouths open, pulses circulate
"In the stone walls: the past, the world you hate
"Is with you, ambush, open field—or see
"The surging flame—we fire Vicenza—glee!
"Follow, let Pilio and Bernardo chafe!
"Bring up the Mantuans—through San
          Biagio—safe!
"Ah, the mad people waken? Ah, they writhe
"And reach us? If they block the gate? No tithe
"Can pass—keep back, you Bassanese! The edge,
"Use the edge—shear, thrust, hew, melt down
          the wedge,
"Let out the black of those black upturned eyes!
"Hell—are they sprinkling fire too? The blood
          fries
"And hisses on your brass gloves as they tear

715   Ecelin, he did all for, is a monk now,

720

725

730

---

715 *1840* "Friedrich's . . . . Alps"   717 *1840* world and the world's fret,   718 *1840* proof bar>bar,   *1840* drop   720 *1840–65* out—   725 *1840* flame—they fire   726 *1840* proof Pilia>Pilio   *1840* Bernardi chafe—   *1863,1865* Bernardo chafe—   729 *1840* And reach you? if . . . . gate—no tithe   *1863,1865* And reach us? if . . . . gate—no tithe

716 *brother Lactance . . . Anaclet*: imaginary monks. The *Biographie Universelle* contains articles on the scholar Lactantius and the anti-Pope 'Anaclet'.
719 *scapular*: a short cloak worn by the Benedictines and other religious orders.
725 *we fire Vicenza*: *SB* anticipates the revision to 'we'. Taurello is recalling the expulsion from Vicenza.
726 *Pilio and Bernardo*: imaginary characters: *chafe*: fume.
727 *through San Biagio*: there is still a Piazza S. Biagio in Vicenza, near the Ponte Pusterla (which spans the river Bacchiglione).
727 *safe!*: 'bring the rear up': *SB*.
727–8: between these lines *SB* has: 'What are we surprised? Have they a share & interest in the burning?'
728 *writhe*: follow a winding course.
729 *you?* (*1840*): *SB* anticipates the revision to 'us?'
No tithe: not one in ten.
731 *the wedge*: cf. 'Ivàn Ivànovitch', 126: 'An army they are: close-packed they press like the thrust of a wedge'.

"Those upturned faces choking with despair.   735
"Brave! Slidder through the reeking gate! 'How
    now?
"'You six had charge of her?' And then the vow
"Comes, and the foam spirts, hair's plucked, till
    one shriek
"(I hear it) and you fling—you cannot speak—
"Your gold-flowered basnet to a man who haled   740
"The Adelaide he dared scarce view unveiled
"This morn, naked across the fire: how crown
"The archer that exhausted lays you down
"Your infant, smiling at the flame, and dies?
"While one, while mine . . .
                              "Bacchus! I think there lies   745
"More than one corpse there" (and he paced the
    room)
"—Another cinder somewhere: 't was my doom
"Beside, my doom! If Adelaide is dead,
"I live the same, this Azzo lives instead
"Of that to me, and we pull, any how,   750

just when the   "Este into a heap: the matter 's now
prize awaits   "At the true juncture slipping us so oft.
somebody   "Ay, Heinrich died and Otho, please you, doffed

736 *1840* gate—how now! *1863,1865* gate—'how now?   737 *1840* You
. . . . her?   746 *1840* there   747 *1840* —Another . . . . somewhere— *1863,1865* "—Another . . . . somewhere—   748 *1840* doom: if
. . . . dead *1863,1865* doom! If . . . . dead   749 *1840–65* I am the
same,   750 *1840* pull any how   751 *1840–65* heap—   752 *1840*
oft;   753 *1840 proof* Otto,>Otho,

---

736 *Slidder*: 'To slide with interruption': Johnson. Cf. Dryden's *Aeneis*, ii.
749 and Pope's *Iliad*, xxi. 267.
    gate—how (*1840*): 'what's left of us'? *SB.*
    737 *her?*: Adelaide. For the 'vow' see iii. 424 ff.
    743 *The archer*. 'Sordello's father (?)', Domett.
    744 *smiling at*: *SB* substitutes 'born among'.
    745 *While one, while mine*: Taurello reflects bitterly that his own son was not
saved. Later he finds otherwise.
    747 *Another cinder*: the remains of his wife, Retrude.
    748 *my doom*: 'I was merely to destroy Este': *SB.*
    749 *this Azzo*: just as I now occupy the place that was Adelaide's, so Azzo's
son (of the same name) occupies that of his father.
    750 *and we pull*: and we destroy Este, one way or other. We now have the
perfect opportunity, so often missed in the past. *SB* inserts commas before and
after 'any how' (as do all eds. from *1863*) and adds: 'by my wearing this or his
wearing it'.
    753 *Heinrich died*: when Heinrich VI died in 1197, Friedrich's claim to the

"His crown at such a juncture! Still, if holds
755 "Our Friedrich's purpose, if this chain enfolds
"The neck of . . . who but this same Ecelin
"That must recoil when the best days begin!
"Recoil? that's nought; if the recoiler leaves
"His name for me to fight with, no one grieves:
760 "But he must interfere, forsooth, unlock
"His cloister to become my stumbling-block
"Just as of old! Ay, ay, there 't is again—
"The land's inevitable Head—explain
"The reverences that subject us! Count
765 "These Ecelins now! Not to say as fount,
"Originating power of thought,—from twelve
"That drop i' the trenches they joined hands to
　　　delve,
"Six shall surpass him, but . . . why, men must
　　　twine
"Somehow with something! Ecelin 's a fine
"Clear name! 'Twere simpler, doubtless, twine
　　　with me
770 "At once: our cloistered friend's capacity
"Was of a sort! I had to share myself

---

*754 {Reading of *1889*} *1840* juncture: let but hold *1863,1865* juncture! still,
if hold *1868,1888* juncture! Still, if hold {'s' added in ink after 'hold' in
DC} *755 {Reading of *1889*} *1840* let this chain enfold *1863–88* if this
chain enfold {'s' added in ink after 'enfold' in DC} 756 *1840* Ecelin? 757 *1840* begin— 758 *1840 proof* nought>nought; *1840* nought;
so the 759 *1840,1863* grieves! *1865* grieves 763 *1840 proof*
head—>Head— 764 *1840 proof* men!>us! 766 *1840* thought, *768
{Reading of *1840–68*} *1888,1889* why men 769 *1863,1865 Ecelin's*

throne lapsed almost immediately because of his tender age. In 1212, however,
he staked his claim anew against Otto IV, and two years later his position was
secure. In 1220 he was crowned Emperor in Italy. The words 'at such a
juncture!' must mean 'at so critical a juncture', not 'just after the death of
Heinrich'. By the time of his deposition Otto was bitterly opposed by the
Pope. Taurello is reflecting that one favourable opportunity for opposing the
Pope had been lost in the past: now that another offers, it must not be lost!
　756 *The neck of . . .: SB* has ', well,' inked in over the three points. Taurello
cannot name himself because of his temperamental inability to assume complete leadership.
　757 *That must recoil*: who was ill-advised enough to draw back.
　764 *The reverences*: exceptional as a plural.
　768–9 *men must twine / Somehow with something!*: we must unite in some way:
men cannot stand alone.
　772 *Was of a sort!*: i.e. was very limited.

"In fifty portions, like an o'ertasked elf
"That 's forced illume in fifty points the vast
"Rare vapour he 's environed by. At last   775
"My strengths, though sorely frittered, e'en
  converge
"And crown . . . no, Bacchus, they have yet to
  urge
"The man be crowned!

                    "That aloe, an he durst,
"Would climb! Just such a bloated sprawler first
"I noted in Messina's castle-court   780
"The day I came, when Heinrich asked in sport
"If I would pledge my faith to win him back
"His right in Lombardy: 'for, once bid pack
"'Marauders,' he continued, 'in my stead
"'You rule, Taurello!' and upon this head   785
"Laid the silk glove of Constance—I see her
"Too, mantled head to foot in miniver,
"Retrude following!

                    "I am absolved
"From further toil: the empery devolved
"On me, 't was Tito's word: I have to lay   790
"For once my plan, pursue my plan my way,
"Prompt nobody, and render an account
"Taurello to Taurello! Nay, I mount
"To Friedrich: he conceives the post I kept,

—himself, if it were only worth while, (margin note at lines 785-787)

775 *1840* by: at   777 *1840* crown—   781 *1840* came, and Heinrich   783 *1840* Lombardy; for,   784 *1840* Marauders, he continued, in   785 *1840* You rule, Taurello!   790 *1840* word: and think, to lay   794 *1840–65* Friedrich—

776 *frittered*: weakened by wear: cf. ii. 695.
777 *And crown . . .*: he hesitates, on the point of naming Ecelin.
778 *The man be crowned!*: SB adds: 'one man is a tree, one a shrub: That willow will not soar,'.
778 *That aloe*: that shrub would grow higher, if it had the courage; but, like me, it lacks the daring.
781 *asked in sport*: 'of the raw boy (crossbow)': SB. Cf. i. 837 ff.
784 *he continued*: bracketed in SB, 1840 having no inverted commas.
785 *You rule*: as Imperial Vicar.   786 *Constance*: Heinrich's wife.
787 *miniver*: a costly kind of fur.
788 *Retrude following!*: SB adds: 'Why how clear my course was! I had Retrude'. Now that he has lost her (the implication is), his course is far from clear.
793–4 *I mount / To Friedrich*: I am responsible to no one but the Emperor himself. He understands the importance of what I did.

795　　　"—Who did true service, able or inept,
　　　　"Who 's worthy guerdon, Ecelin or I.
　　　　"Me guerdoned, counsel follows: would he vie
　　　　"With the Pope really? Azzo, Boniface
　　　　"Compose a right-arm Hohenstauffen's race
800　　　"Must break ere govern Lombardy. I point
　　　　"How easy 't were to twist, once out of joint,
　　　　"The socket from the bone: my Azzo's stare
　　　　"Meanwhile! for I, this idle strap to wear,
　　　　"Shall—fret myself abundantly, what end
805　　　"To serve? There 's left me twenty years to
　　　　　　spend
　　　　"—How better than my old way? Had I one
　　　　"Who laboured to o'erthrow my work—a son
　　　　"Hatching with Azzo superb treachery,
　　　　"To root my pines up and then poison me,
　　　　"Suppose—'t were worth while frustrate that!
810　　　　　Beside,　　　　　　　　　　　　　*as it may be—but*
　　　　"Another life's ordained me: the world's tide　*also, as it may not*
　　　　"Rolls, and what hope of parting from the press　*be*
　　　　"Of waves, a single wave through weariness
　　　　"Gently lifted aside, laid upon shore?
815　　　　"My life must be lived out in foam and roar,
　　　　"No question. Fifty years the province held

---

795 *1840–65* Who　　　796 *1840* or I:　　　797 *1840 proof* The> Me　*1840–65*
follows;　　　800 *1840* Lombardy;　　　802 *1840* bone; *1863–8* bone:—
*807 {Reading of *1889*}　*1840–88* laboured overthrow {Altered in ink to
'laboured to o'erthrow' in DC}　　　810 *1840,1889* {some copies} Beside
*813 {Reading of *1840–68*} *1888,1889* wave though weariness {'though'
corrected to 'through' in some copies of *1889*}　　　814 *1840* That's gently
led aside,

---

797 *Me guerdoned*: absolute. 'Once I am rewarded, I shall give him my advice:
"if he really wants to compete with the Pope (I'll say) . . ."'
802 *my Azzo's stare*: just to think how astonished Azzo would be!
803 *this idle strap*: the baldric (iv. 464–6). The moment Taurello thinks of
accepting the power offered him by the Emperor, his characteristic half-
heartedness returns. His 'old way' is best: the game is not worth the candle.
811 *the world's tide*: Taurello seems to jump to another and opposite argument for not assuming the leadership: that there is no escape for him from the
'foam and roar' to which he has always been committed.
814 *laid upon shore?*: 'at Messina. I have watched such & fancied if one of
every million were not turned into *hills*': SB.
816–20 *Fifty years . . . Of him!*: Taurello muses on the transitoriness of the
name he will leave behind him, as if composing his own epitaph. His gardens

"Taurello; troubles raised, and troubles quelled,
"He in the midst—who leaves this quaint stone
    place,
"These trees a year or two, then not a trace
"Of him! How obtain hold, fetter men's tongues   820
"Like this poor minstrel with the foolish songs—
"To which, despite our bustle, he is linked?
"—Flowers one may teaze, that never grow
    extinct.
"Ay, that patch, surely, green as ever, where
"I set Her Moorish lentisk, by the stair, ·   825
"To overawe the aloes; and we trod
"Those flowers, how call you such?—into the
    sod; ·
"A stately foreigner—a world of pain
"To make it thrive, arrest rough winds—all vain!
"It would decline; these would not be destroyed: 830
"And now, where is it? where can you avoid
"The flowers? I frighten children twenty years
"Longer!—which way, too, Ecelin appears
"To thwart me, for his son's besotted youth
"Gives promise of the proper tiger-tooth: 835
"They feel it at Vicenza! Fate, fate, fate,
"My fine Taurello! Go you, promulgate

819 *1840* Those trees . . . . then, not *1863,1865* These trees . . . . then,
not   821 *1840* Like that Sordello with his foolish songs—   823 *1840* never
seem extinct;   826 *1840* aloes—   827 *1840* such?   828 *1840*
foreigner—and worlds of   830 *1840* decline— . . . . destroyed—   831
1840 is it—   835,836 *1840* tiger-tooth,|They prattle, at Vicenza!

will be regarded as merely curious, the trees he planted will not remain for
long.
    822 *despite our bustle*: in spite of the noise that men of action make during their
lives, the names of poets live longer, linked with their songs. Sordello's are like
flowers which never perish, even if they are carelessly handled.
    824 *that patch*: Taurello had planted an exotic mastic tree for Retrude (the
capital in 'Her' presumably expresses his love for her), yet this 'stately
foreigner' would not flourish, while the humble aloes (hardly worth calling
flowers) survived all our attempts to destroy them. Similarly (he reflects) his
own name may serve as a bogey to children for another twenty years at most
(and even as a bogeyman Ecelin III promises greatly to excel him!). Cf. ii. 965
ff.
    834 *besotted*: 'Intellectually or morally stupefied or blinded': OED sense 2.
The dreadful career of the future Ecelin the Tyrant is referred to.
    837 *promulgate*: he tells himself that fate ordains that he should publish the
Emperor's decree—and that the 'Prefect's badge' which he himself has been

"Friedrich's decree, and here 's shall aggrandise
"Young Ecelin—your Prefect's badge! a prize
"Too precious, certainly.   *—the supposition*
840   "How now? Compete *he most inclines to;*
"With my old comrade? shuffle from their seat
"His children? Paltry dealing! Don't I know
"Ecelin? now, I think, and years ago!
"What 's changed—the weakness? did not I
        compound
845 "For that, and undertake to keep him sound
"Despite it? Here 's Taurello hankering
"After a boy's preferment—this plaything
"To carry, Bacchus!" And he laughed.
                                Remark
Why schemes wherein cold-blooded men embark
850 Prosper, when your enthusiastic sort
Fail: while these last are ever stopping short—
(So much they should—so little they can do!)
The careless tribe see nothing to pursue
If they desist; meantime their scheme succeeds.
855   Thoughts were caprices in the course of deeds
Methodic with Taurello; so, he turned,—

---

839 *1840* Ecelin—our Prefect's   845 *1840* undertake preserve him
846–8 *1840* Say Taurello's hankering|After the boy's preferment—
this play-thing|To carry, Bacchus!   851 *1840 proof* short> short—
1840 Fails: for these   852 *1840* (Much to be done—so   854 *1840* Should
they desist;   856 *1840 proof* turned> turned,   *1840* so he turned,   *1863–8* so,
he turned,

---

given (a prize too precious for him) will help to aggrandize Ecelin III. Duff
takes 'Too precious' as meaning that Ecelin is unworthy of the badge, but the
following lines make it clear that Taurello considers himself unworthy of it.
Cf. *SB*: 'Had I been minded to take it, I could . . .'
   840 *Compete*: I cannot enter into competition with the Monk, as I should be
doing if I thrust his sons aside from their inheritance. That would be contempt-
ible. His weakness is no new discovery: I undertook to put up with that years
ago. I am not a boy, to be proud of wearing a baldric.
   842 *Don't I know*: 'what, he's weak?' *SB*.
   846 *Say Taurello's (1840): SB* revises to 'old Taurello's'.
   848 *Remark*: the poet addresses the reader. Taurello is a man of a temperament the opposite of that of the 'enthusiastic' Sordello. Men like Sordello are
always becoming discouraged at the thought that they cannot possibly do
more than a fraction of what they feel they ought to do, whereas men of the
world, carefree by comparison, go on in their usual way as if for lack of
anything else to do—and succeed.
   855 *Thoughts were caprices*: Taurello's real life consisted of a methodical series
of actions: thoughts were mere freaks or 'fancies' indulged in by the way.

Enough amused by fancies fairly earned
Of Este's horror-struck submitted neck,

being contented
with mere
vengeance.

And Richard, the cowed braggart, at his beck,—
To his own petty but immediate doubt   860
If he could pacify the League without
Conceding Richard; just to this was brought
That interval of vain discursive thought!
As, shall I say, some Ethiop, past pursuit
Of all enslavers, dips a shackled foot   865
Burnt to the blood, into the drowsy black
Enormous watercourse which guides him back
To his own tribe again, where he is king;
And laughs because he guesses, numbering
The yellower poison-wattles on the pouch   870
Of the first lizard wrested from its couch
Under the slime (whose skin, the while, he strips
To cure his nostril with, and festered lips,
And eyeballs bloodshot through the desert-blast)
That he has reached its boundary, at last   875
May breathe;—thinks o'er enchantments of the
       South
Sovereign to plague his enemies, their mouth,
Eyes, nails, and hair; but, these enchantments
       tried
In fancy, puts them soberly aside
For truth, projects a cool return with friends,   880

---

859 *1840* And Boniface completely at his beck,   867 *1840* Enormous water
current, his sole track   878 *1840 proof* And eye,> And nails,   *1840* And nails,
and hair;   879 *1840 proof* In infancy,> In fancy,   880 *1840* For truth, cool
projects, a return

---

862 *Conceding Richard;* |∧| *just*: 'yet enough warrant to kill Azzo': *SB*.
865 *enslavers*: Browning will have heard of the horrors of slavery from his
father, who '"conceived such a hatred to the slave-system in the West Indies"
. . . that he relinquished every prospect, . . . and came back, while yet a boy, to
his father's profound astonishment and rage': Kintner, ii. 1005–6.
870 *poison-wattles*: a wattle is a fleshy lobe pendent from the head or neck of
certain birds and other creatures. While lizards with wattles are common
enough in Africa, none of them is in fact poisonous, although they were often
believed to be so. The notion that the number of wattles could provide a clue to
a traveller's whereabouts is fanciful. The belief in the medicinal qualities of
lizard-skin was widespread.
875 *At last*: '& where he [? expands] & reigns': *SB*.
876 *May breathe*: 'in his kingship at its highest': *SB*.
878 *and hair* ∧: 'turn them into serpents or stones': *SB*.

The likelihood of winning mere amends
Ere long; thinks that, takes comfort silently,
Then, from the river's brink, his wrongs and he,
Hugging revenge close to their hearts, are soon
885 Off-striding for the Mountains of the Moon.
    Midnight: the watcher nodded on his spear,
Since clouds dispersing left a passage clear
For any meagre and discoloured moon
To venture forth; and such was peering soon
890 Above the harassed city—her close lanes
Closer, not half so tapering her fanes,
As though she shrunk into herself to keep
What little life was saved, more safely. Heap
By heap the watch-fires mouldered, and beside
895 The blackest spoke Sordello and replied
Palma with none to listen. "'T is your cause:
"What makes a Ghibellin? There should be˙
    laws—
"(Remember how my youth escaped! I trust
"To you for manhood, Palma! tell me just
900 "As any child)—there must be laws at work
"Explaining this. Assure me, good may lurk
"Under the bad,—my multitude has part

*Sordello, taught
what Ghibellins
are,*

---

881 *1840* winning wild amends   883 *1840* And from the river's brink
887 *1840–68* clear,   888 *1840* If any   889 *1840* Should venture   893 *1840*
saved   896 *1840* 'Tis your Cause—   *1863–8* "'Tis your Cause: 899
1840–68 Palma;   900 *1840* child)—laws secretly at work   902 *1840* bad;

881 *mere*: SB substitutes 'full, just' for the original 'wild'.
885 *the Mountains of the Moon*: a long range of mountains running across the
centre of Africa, just north of the equator, believed by the ancients to be the
source of the Nile. On maps of this period, such as *A New General Atlas* (1835),
they present a dramatic appearance, like a display of cumulus cloud drawn in
the middle of nowhere. Cf. Moore, *Lalla Rookh* ('Paradise and the Peri', 141),
and his note. The meaning is that Taurello becomes realistic in his plans, as the
escaped Ethiop does.
894 *mouldered*: cf. *The Ring and the Book*, iv. 79: 'But, when the wick shall
moulder out some day'.
896 *your cause*: Sordello, who has led a very sheltered youth, appeals to Palma
(who is one of the Ecelini) to explain to him what a Ghibellin is and stands for,
and why the contest with the Guelfs is of such importance.
902 *my multitude*: after his interview with Taurello, Sordello wants to be
reassured that the Ghibellins have the welfare of the people (whose cause he
himself has now espoused) at heart.

"In your designs, their welfare is at heart
"With Salinguerra, to their interest
"Refer the deeds he dwelt on,—so divest   905
"Our conference of much that scared me. Why
"Affect that heartless tone to Tito? I
"Esteemed myself, yes, in my inmost mind
"This morn, a recreant to my race—mankind
"O'erlooked till now: why boast my spirit's
          force,   910
"—Such force denied its object? why divorce
"These, then admire my spirit's flight the same
"As though it bore up, helped some half-orbed
          flame
"Else quenched in the dead void, to living space?
"That orb cast off to chaos and disgrace,   915
"Why vaunt so much my unencumbered dance,
"Making a feat's facilities enhance
"Its marvel? But I front Taurello, one
"Of happier fate, and all I should have done,
"He does; the people's good being paramount   920
"With him, their progress may perhaps account
"For his abiding still; whereas you heard

---

906 *1840* me: why   909 *1840* a recreant to that wide mankind   911 *1840*
—That force   912–14 *1840* same,| As though it bore a burden, which could
tame| No pinion, from dead void   915 *1840* —That orb consigned
to *1863,1865* —That orb cast off to   916 *1840* vaunt complacently my
frantic dance, *1863–68* vaunt so much my unincumbered dance,   918 *1840*
The marvel?   919–21 *1840* and what I should have done| He does; the
multitude aye paramount| With him, its making progress may account   922
1840 still: when . . . but you heard   *1863–68* still: whereas you heard

---

907 *that heartless tone:* lines 922 ff., below. *SB* has: '(talk wholly of familiar
material interests &c)'.
910 *why boast:* '(as I had been doing)': *SB.*
913 *which could tame (1840):* *SB* adds '& obstruct the flight of'. After the
following line there is a more helpful comment: '(*an angel to carry a world*—as in
Greek art)'.
916 *dance:* 'apart—': *SB.*
917 *facilities:* as if the ease of some achievement made it more marvellous.
918 *But I front Taurello:* but when I confront Taurello, who seems born under
a more fortunate star, a man who does all that I should have done (perhaps it is
precisely because the good of the People is paramount in his mind that he has
not risen further personally)—what do I hear?
920 *multitude* ∧ *aye (1840):* 'having been': *SB.*
922 *For his* ∧ *abiding:* 'comparatively': *SB*, which adds something like 'in the
way of realizations of my ideal—'.

"The talk with Tito—the excuse preferred
"For burning those five hostages,—and broached
925 "By way of blind, as you and I approached,
"I do believe."

         She spoke: then he, "My thought
"Plainlier expressed! All to your profit—nought
"Meantime of these, of conquests to achieve
"For them, of wretchedness he might relieve
930 "While profiting your party. Azzo, too,
"Supports a cause: what cause? Do Guelfs pursue
"Their ends by means like yours, or better?"
                      When

The Guelfs were proved alike, men weighed *and what Guelfs,*
  with men, *approves of*
neither.
And deed with deed, blaze, blood, with blood
  and blaze,
Morn broke: "Once more, Sordello, meet its
935   gaze
"Proudly—the people's charge against thee fails
"In every point, while either party quails!
"These are the busy ones: be silent thou!
"Two parties take the world up, and allow

923 *1840* His talk   926 *1840* I do believe.   926 *1840 proof* my> My   *1840*
My   927–30 *1840* Plainer expressed! All Friedrich's profit—nought| Of
these meantime, of conquests to achieve| For them, of wretchednesses to
relieve| While profiting that Friedrich.   931 *1840* what is it? Guelfs
pursue   932 *1840* better?   933 *1840* were shown alike, men ranged
with   935 *1840* once more,   938 *1840–65* ones—

923 *The talk with Tito*: cf. ll. 376–7 above.
926 *I do believe*: 'have [has?] been caring for the Multitude?': *SB*.
She spoke: after these words *SB* has: 'Ghibellinism & selfishness'. Although
we are not told what Palma says Sordello's reply shows that she confirms his
fear that Taurello is serving her interest while remaining indifferent to that of
the multitude. 'All Friedrich's profit' (*1840*) gives way to 'All to your profit'.
Taurello is merely working for the Ghibellin cause, and forgetting 'these' (the
common people) and their wretchedness.
932 *or better?*: 'No! said Palma—& showed the identity of the means, and
mediate ends': *SB*.
933 *were proved*: Domett unnecessarily deletes 'were' and substitutes 'had
been'.
934 *blood and blaze*: cf. ii. 464 and n., and vi. 693.
935 *"Once more*: Sordello soliloquizes. Domett underlines 'people's charge
against', with a query in the margin, perhaps not understanding that Sordello is
speaking (or musing).
937 *either party quails!*: it is not he who should be ashamed (he now reflects),
but the Ghibellins and Guelfs, who are mere busybodies.

"No third, yet have one principle, subsist   940
"By the same injustice; whoso shall enlist
"With either, ranks with man's inveterate foes.
"So there is one less quarrel to compose:
"The Guelf, the Ghibellin may be to curse—
"I have done nothing, but both sides do worse   945
"Than nothing. Nay, to me, forgotten, reft
"Of insight, lapped by trees and flowers, was left
"The notion of a service—ha? What lured
"Me here, what mighty aim was I assured
"Must move Taurello? What if there remained   950

Have men a cause   "A cause, intact, distinct from these, ordained
distinct from both?   "For me, its true discoverer?"

                                  Some one pressed
Before them here, a watcher, to suggest
The subject for a ballad: "They must know
"The tale of the dead worthy, long ago   955
"Consul of Rome—that 's long ago for us,
"Minstrels and bowmen, idly squabbling thus

Who was the   "In the world's corner—but too late no doubt,
famed Roman   "For the brave time he sought to bring about.
Crescentius?

            "—Not know Crescentius Nomentanus?" Then   960

---

941 *1840* same method; whoso   943 *1840* compose   944 *1840 proof*
Twixt . . . . Guelf's>'Twixt . . . . Guelf's,   *1840* 'Twixt us: the Guelf's, the
Ghibellin's to curse—   946 *1840* nothing; nay   950 *1840* Moved Salinguerra? If a Cause remained   951 *1840* Intact, distinct from these, and fate
ordained,   *1863,1865* A Cause, intact, distinct from these, ordained,   952
1840 For all the past, that Cause for me?¶ One pressed   954 *1840* ballad: he
must   958 *1840* corners—but too late, *1863–8* corner—but too
late,   959 *1840* about   960 *1840* Nomentanus?

---

940 *No third: Domett* has the following, almost certainly in Browning's hand:
'The charge your conscience prefers on the people's account (or,) what you feel
they might justly charge you with—the having neglected their cause'.
  942 *man's inveterate foes*: a very Shelleyan conception.
  948–9 *What lured / Me here*: SB has something like the following, perhaps to
amplify these words: 'after all Realizations failed (of my own)'.
  950 *Moved Salinguerra?* (*1840*): 'The growth of my own mind': SB.
  952 *that Cause for me?* (*1840*): 'to conceive & to realize?': SB.
  952 *Some one*: his identity does not matter, and is not revealed.
  954 *ballad:* |△| *he* (*1840*): 'he, their minstrel': SB.
  959 *the brave time*: 'O there was Rome once!'; SB.
  960 *Crescentius Nomentanus*: 'In the minority of . . . Otho III, Rome made a
bold attempt to shake off the Saxon yoke, and the consul Crescentius was the
Brutus of the republic': Gibbon, *The Decline and Fall of the Roman Empire*, ch.

He cast about for terms to tell him, when
Sordello disavowed it, how they used
Whenever their Superior introduced
A novice to the Brotherhood—("for I
965 "Was just a brown-sleeve brother, merrily
"Appointed too," quoth he, "till Innocent
"Bade me relinquish, to my small content,
"My wife or my brown sleeves")—some brother
      spoke
Ere nocturns of Crescentius, to revoke
970 The edict issued, after his demise,
Which blotted fame alike and effigies,
All out except a floating power, a name
Including, tending to produce the same
Great act. Rome, dead, forgotten, lived at least
975 Within that brain, though to a vulgar priest
And a vile stranger,—two not worth a slave
Of Rome's, Pope John, King Otho,—fortune
      gave

964 *1840* Brotherhood (for I   966 *1840* Appointed too, quoth he, till
Innocent   968 *1840* sleeves) out some one spoke   970–1 *1840* issued after
his demise|That blotted memory, and effigies,   973 *1840 proof*
same,>same   975 *1840* that man, though   976 *1840 proof*
stranger,>stranger *1840* stranger, fit to be a slave   977 *1840* Otho,

xlix (ed. of 1815, ix. 202–3): the side-notes gives the date 998. In the *Biographie
Universelle* Sismondi mentions that Pope John XV was exiled by Crescentius
'until he should have recognized the sovereignty of the people', commenting:
'so far as one can judge through the obscurity of the ages, the Roman republic,
administered until 996 by the consul Crescentius, enjoyed a great measure of
peace, an order and a safety which had long been unknown there'. In ch. iii of
his *Histoire des Républiques Italiennes* (i, 164) Sismondi gives a fuller account,
saying that Crescentius emboldened the Romans to shake the authority of the
Popes, 'which rested only on the belief of the nations in the sanctity of an
apostolic ministry, and which lost all its titles to their obedience once the
pontiffs renounced their virtues'. In opposition to Pope Gregory V, Crescentius set up a counter-Pope: if this attempt had proved successful, Sismondi
comments, 'the whole fate of Europe and that of religion could have been
changed. Italy would have been able to secure its independence' (p. 168).
  965–6 *merrily / Appointed*: well set-up (with a wife). Innocent III held strict
views on the celibacy of the clergy.
  968 *some brother spoke*: they always spoke of Crescentius when a novice
joined them, so that (in defiance of the edict issued after his death forbidding his
fame alike and effigies') he remained a potent memory and inspiration.
  969 *Ere nocturns*: before our evening devotions.
  972 *a floating power*: in *The Revolt of Islam*, 3093, we hear of the 'floating
shade' of departed hopes.
  977 *King Otho*: Otto III, Emperor 996–1002, made it his great aim to secure
the Emperor's right to nominate the Pope.

The rule there: so, Crescentius, haply dressed
In white, called Roman Consul for a jest,
Taking the people at their word, forth stepped   980
As upon Brutus' heel, nor ever kept
Rome waiting,—stood erect, and from his brain
Gave Rome out on its ancient place again,
Ay, bade proceed with Brutus' Rome, Kings
    styled
Themselves mere citizens of, and, beguiled   985
Into great thoughts thereby, would choose the
    gem
Out of a lapfull, spoil their diadem
—The Senate's cypher was so hard to scratch!
He flashes like a phanal, all men catch
The flame, Rome 's just accomplished! when
    returned   990
Otho, with John, the Consul's step had spurned,
And Hugo Lord of Este, to redress
The wrongs of each. Crescentius in the stress
Of adverse fortune bent. "They crucified

978 *1840* there: but Crescentius, haply drest   *1863,1865* there: so, Crescentius, haply drest   982 *1840* Us waiting; stept he forth and from his
brain   985 *1840* Themselves the citizens   986 *1840* Thereby, were fain
select the lustrous gem   *988 {Reading of *1840–68,1889*}   *1888* scratch
{exclamation mark inserted in DC.}   989 *1840* phanal, men too
catch   990 *1840* flame, and Rome's accomplished;   991 *1840* Otho and
John   992 *1840* With Hugo   994 *1840* They

981 *As upon Brutus' heel*: as Consul in 509 BC, Lucius Junius Brutus, founder
of the Roman Republic, made the people swear that they would never again
submit to kingly authority.
984 *Brutus' Rome*: cf. Cicero, *In Verrem*, III. v. 57. 147, on the celebrated
claim, 'Civis Romanus sum'.
985 *beguiled*: *1840*'s 'were' in the next line makes it clear that it was the Kings
who were beguiled, not Crescentius (as Whyte supposes). 968–8 remains
obscure, but cf. vi. 454 ff. The meaning seems to be that the Kings, genuinely
inspired by the ideal, prefer above all other privileges the precious 'gem' of
being Roman citizens, and so are content to diminish their personal splendour
('spoil their diadem') by living up to the difficult ideal of being merely equal
members of the Senate.|988|seems to mean that it is difficult to scratch 'the
Senate's cypher' even with a diamond.
989 *a phanal*: a beacon.   990 *Rome's ∧ accomplished*: 'all but': *SB*.
992 *Hugo*: '(always in Este')': *SB*. There was a historical Ugo of Este in the
tenth century.
994 *crucified*: accounts of the death of Crescentius, after he was treacherously
made captive, differ: according to Gibbon 'his body was suspended on a
gibbet, and his head was exposed on the battlements of the castle': loc. cit., p.
203.

995   "Their Consul in the Forum; and abide
"E'er since such slaves at Rome, that I—(for I
"Was once a brown-sleeve brother, merrily
"Appointed)—I had option to keep wife
"Or keep brown sleeves, and managed in the
    strife
"Lose both. A song of Rome!"
1000   And Rome, indeed,
Robed at Goito in fantastic weed,
The Mother-City of his Mantuan days,
Looked an established point of light whence rays
Traversed the world; for, all the clustered homes
1005 Beside of men, seemed bent on being Romes
In their degree; the question was, how each
Should most resemble Rome, clean out of reach.
Nor, of the Two, did either principle
Struggle to change, but to possess Rome,—still
Guelf Rome or Ghibellin Rome.
1010   Let Rome advance! *How if, in the*
Rome, as she struck Sordello's ignorance— *re-integration of*
How could he doubt one moment? Rome 's the *Rome,*
    Cause!
Rome of the Pandects, all the world's new
    laws—

---

995 *1840 proof* forum>Forum *1840* Forum *1863,1865* Forum,   996
1840 proof ere>e'er *1840* Such slaves at Rome e'er since,   1000 *1840*
Rome!   1002 *1840* of those Mantuan   1004 *1840* world; and all   1005
1840 men were bent   1007 *1840* reach   1008,1009 *1840* Herself; nor
struggled either principle|To change what it aspired possess—Rome, still
1863–8 Nor, of the great Two, either principle,|Struggled to change—but to
possess—Rome, still,   1010 *1840* For Friedrich or Honorius. ¶ Rome's
the Cause!   1011,1012 {not in *1840.*}   1013 *1840* The Rome of the old
Pandects, our new laws—

1000 *A song of Rome!*: the speaker repeats his request.
   And Rome, indeed: as a youth of Goito, and later in 'his Mantuan days',
Sordello had looked back to Rome as an ideal. Now, however, neither the
Guelfs nor the Ghibellins have the ambition of restoring Rome to its pristine
state.
   1008 *either principle*: 'of the great Two': *SB*.
   1010 *Rome's the Cause!* (*1840*): *SB* has a note which may read: 'Rome as it
struck Sordello's ignorance—'. Cf. textual notes.
   1013 *the Pandects*: 'A compendium . . . of Roman civil law made by order of
the Emperor Justinian in the sixth century': OED. The revival of the study of
Roman law was of the greatest importance to the development of European
civilization.

Of the Capitol, of Castle Angelo;
New structures, that inordinately glow,   1015
Subdued, brought back to harmony, made ripe
By many a relic of the archetype
Extant for wonder; every upstart church
That hoped to leave old temples in the lurch,
Corrected by the Theatre forlorn   1020
That,—as a mundane shell, its world late born,—
Lay and o'ershadowed it. These hints combined,
Rome typifies the scheme to put mankind
be typified the   Once more in full possession of their rights.
triumph of
mankind?   "Let us have Rome again! On me it lights   1025
"To build up Rome—on me, the first and last:
"For such a future was endured the past!"
And thus, in the grey twilight, forth he sprung
To give his thought consistency among
The very People—let their facts avail   1030
Finish the dream grown from the archer's tale.

1014–15 *1840* The Capitol turned Castle Angelo| And structures that
inordinately glow   1016–19 {not in *1840*.}   1021–3 *1840* As a black
mundane shell, its world late born|—Verona, that's beside it. These
combined,| We typify the scheme to put mankind   1024–5 *1840* rights| By
his sole agency. On   1026 *1840* Rome again—me, first   1027 *1840* Future
. . . . Past!   *1863,1865* Future . . . . Past!"   1030 *1840* The People's self, and
let their truth avail

1014 *Of the Capitol*: whereas in *1840* the Capitol gives way to Castle Angelo,
in the revised text the new Rome, even more splendid than ancient Rome, is to
add 'Castle Angelo' to its glories: it is to add religion to the secular excellence of
its predecessor.
1015 *New structures*: cf. *1840*. The brash new buildings are called to order (as it
were) by the dignity of the classical remains. The upstart new churches, built
within the Coliseum and intended to excel the ancient temples, are chastened
by the Coliseum, 'forlorn' as it is.
1022 —*Verona, that's beside it* (*1840*): the amphitheatre of Verona, the most
famous in Italy after the Coliseum, seems (in *1840*) to be no more than a
commonplace shell, created too late.
These hints combined: SB has a note which may read: 'make the *Rome*, that
ideal Rome'.
1025 *By his sole agency* (*1840*): Domett asks 'whose?' and Browning replies:
'(S².)', i.e. Sordello's.
1027 *was endured the past!*: 'Not Himself now—but the People's Ideal': SB.
1030–1 *avail* / *Finish*: as often, 'to' is omitted.
1031 *the archer's tale*: 'A day begins—which he will spend among the people,
in their way of life & wants': SB.

BOOK THE FIFTH.

Is it the same Sordello in the dusk
As at the dawn?—merely a perished husk
Now, that arose a power fit to build
Up Rome again? The proud conception chilled
So soon? Ay, watch that latest dream of thine
—A Rome indebted to no Palatine—
Drop arch by arch, Sordello! Art possessed
Of thy wish now, rewarded for thy quest
To-day among Ferrara's squalid sons?
Are this and this and this the shining ones
Meet for the Shining City? Sooth to say,   *Mankind triumph*
Your favoured tenantry pursue their way   *of a sudden?*
After a fashion! This companion slips
On the smooth causey, t' other blinkard trips
At his mooned sandal. "Leave to lead the brawls
"Here i' the atria?" No, friend! He that sprawls
On aught but a stibadium . . . what his dues
Who puts the lustral vase to such an use?
Oh, huddle up the day's disasters! March,

2 *1840* dawn?   3 *1840* power like to   6 *1840–65* Palatine,   8 *1840–65*
now—   9 *1840–65* sons—   11,12 *1840* say|Our favoured   15 *1840*
Leave   16 *1840* atria? No, friend.   17,18 *1840* stibadium suffers . . .
goose, Puttest our lustral vase   19 *1840* disasters—march

6 *Palatine*: the Palatine Hill, the site of the palace in Rome, and therefore the symbol of Imperial power. Cf. iv. 1000. Sordello's conception of Rome was a sort of new Jerusalem.
11 *the Shining City*: the ultimate source is no doubt 'the holy city, new Jerusalem' of Revelation 21:2. In the final paragraphs of the First Part of *The Pilgrim's Progress* Christian and Hopeful are met by 'the shining Ones' (or 'the shining men'), who escort them to the side of the river: cf. Revelation 7:9 and 4:4–5: Bunyan's earlier work, *The Holy City: or the New Jerusalem* has the same background. In 1879 Browning described Bunyan as 'the object of my utmost admiration and reverence' (*New Letters*, 251), and he had been so from his early childhood. See Maynard 134, 315, 378. Cf. *Paracelsus*, i. 588 ff.
14 *t'other blinkard*: the other short-sighted fool trips over his own sandal. 'Mooned' may mean either moon-shaped or decorated with moons.
15 *"Leave*: one of the ignorant revellers wishes to play the fool in the atria (courts) of the house: he is told he should lie down on one of the elegant semi-circular couches. What punishment is appropriate for a man who puts the vase for purified water to such base use?
19 *March*: be off with you, you renegades!

Ye runagates, and drop thou, arch by arch,   20
Rome!
        Yet before they quite disband—a whim—
Study mere shelter, now, for him, and him,
Nay, even the worst,—just house them! Any
    cave
Suffices: throw out earth! A loophole? Brave!
They ask to feel the sun shine, see the grass   25
Grow, hear the larks sing? Dead art thou, alas,
And I am dead! But here's our son excels
At hurdle-weaving any Scythian, fells
Oak and devises rafters, dreams and shapes
His dream into a door-post, just escapes   30
The mystery of hinges. Lie we both
Perdue another age. The goodly growth
Of brick and stone! Our building-pelt was rough,
But that descendant's garb suits well enough

Why, the work
should be one of
ages,

A portico-contriver. Speed the years—   35
What 's time to us? At last, a city rears
Itself! nay, enter—what 's the grave to us?
Lo, our forlorn acquaintance carry thus
The head! Successively sewer, forum, cirque—

---

22 *1840* Study a shelter,   23–4 *1840* Nay, even him, to house them! any
cave| Suffices—throw out earth.   30 *1840* That dream   36 *1840* us? and
lo, a city *1863,1865* us? at last, a city   38 *1840* So our   39 *1840* A head!
successively

---

20 *drop*: i.e. Sordello's 'Rome' is a mere dream.
   21 *Rome!*: 'another of Sordello's bubbles burst!': *SB*, which has also three
numbered remarks in the margin: '1. One must not see those mouths, those
eyes—pits for flies. 2. One would bring smiles into th[em?]. 3. One would do
the best they [? approve of].'
   22 *Study mere shelter*: let us reflect (for a whim) on the development of
architecture: that will illustrate what Sordello has so signally failed to understand, that Rome was not built in a day. Cf. *Prince Hohenstiel-Schwangau*, 1011
ff.
   him: 'humanity', *SB*, with other illegible words.
   26 *Dead art thou*: our generation has passed away.
   33 *building-pelt*: in *1840 proof* the letters 'lt' are queried by the printer:
Browning replies: '*Pelt*—a raw hide—all right'.
   35 *Speed the years*: cf. Carlyle's imaginative glimpse of the progress of
building in *The French Revolution*, Vol. I, I. ii. para. 6.
   37 *what's the grave to us?*: let us look into the future, ignoring the fact that we
shall be dead and buried.
   38 *our forlorn acquaintance*: poor old mankind now walks tall, proud of its
achievements.
   39 *cirque*: 'amphitheatre'. The word also occurs in 'Childe Roland', 133, *The*

40   Last age, an aqueduct was counted work,
      But now they tire the artificer upon
      Blank alabaster, black obsidion,
      —Careful, Jove's face be duly fulgurant,
      And mother Venus' kiss-creased nipples pant
45   Back into pristine pulpiness, ere fixed
      Above the baths. What difference betwixt
      This Rome and ours—resemblance what,
          between
      That scurvy dumb-show and this pageant
          sheen—
      These Romans and our rabble? Use thy wit!
      The work marched: step by step,—a workman
50   fit
      Took each, nor too fit,—to one task, one time,—
      No leaping o'er the petty to the prime,
      When just the substituting osier lithe
      For brittle bulrush, sound wood for soft withe,
55   To further loam-and-roughcast-work a stage,—
      Exacts an architect, exacts an age:
      No tables of the Mauritanian tree
      For men whose maple log 's their luxury!
      That way was Rome built. "Better" (say you)   *if performed*
          "merge   *equally and*
                                                        thoroughly;

40 *1840 proof* acqueduct> aqueduct   *1840* Last age that aqueduct   41 *1840*
And now   43 *1840* —Careful   47–8 *1840* ours? Resemblance what be-
tween|The scurvy . . . . and the pageant   49–51 *1840* rabble? Rest thy
wit|And listen: step . . . . fit|With each, nor too fit,— to one's task, one's
time,—   54–5 *1840* For bulrushes, and after, wood for withe|To further
loam and roughcast work a stage,   56 *1840* age,—   57 *1840* Nor
tables   58 *1840* maple-log's . . . . luxury,—   *1863–8* maple-log's . . . .
luxury!   59 *1840* And Rome's accomplished! Better (say you) merge

Ring and the Book, x. 417, *Red Cotton Night-Cap Country*, ii. 5, and *Fifine at the
Fair*, 110. 4.
      42 *Blank*: white, as in 'blank moon', *Paradise Lost*, x. 656: *obsidion*: a precious
stone, black but lustrous, which is hard to work: properly 'obsidian'.
      43 *fulgurant*: 'Flashing like lightning', OED, which cites only Henry More's
poem 'Resolution' (*Philosophicall Poems*, 1647, p. 314, l. 16: cf. note to i. 748
above), this passage, and *The Ring and the Book*, vi. 1600.
      48 *That scurvy dumb-show*: our miserable imitation and this glowing pageant.
'How has one grown up to the need of the [?] other': *SB*.
      50 *marched*: proceeded steadily.
      57 *the Mauritanian tree*: rare African wood.

"At once all workmen in the demiurge,   60
"All epochs in a lifetime, every task
"In one!" So should the sudden city bask
I' the day—while those we 'd feast there, want
     the knack
Of keeping fresh-chalked gowns from speck and
     brack,
Distinguish not rare peacock from vile swan,   65
Nor Mareotic juice from Cæcuban.
"Enough of Rome! 'T was happy to conceive
"Rome on a sudden, nor shall fate bereave
"Me of that credit: for the rest, her spite
"Is an old story—serves my folly right   70
"By adding yet another to the dull
"List of abortions—things proved beautiful
"Could they be done, Sordello cannot do."
     He sat upon the terrace, plucked and threw
The powdery aloe-cusps away, saw shift   75
Rome's walls, and drop arch after arch, and drift
Mist-like afar those pillars of all stripe,
Mounds of all majesty. "Thou archetype,

61–2 *1840* life-time, and all.tasks| In one: undoubtedly the city basks   63
1840 proof knack,> knack   *1840* those you'd feast there   65 *1840* Distinguish
not your peacock from your swan,   66 *1840* Or Mareotic . . . .
Cœcuban,   *1863–8* Nor Mareotic . . . . Cœcuban.   67 *1840* Nay sneer . . .
enough! 'twas   69 *1840* Us of   70–1 *1840* serves us very right| For
adding   72 *1840* List of devices—   73 *1840* cannot do.   78 *1840* Thou

60 *the demiurge*: the all-powerful Creator. The idea is Platonic: see, in particular, *Timaeus*, 28 ff.
62 *the sudden city*: in that case (comes the objection) the perfect city would make its brilliant appearance, but the inhabitants we would wish to place in it would not have learned enough to keep their clothes clean and untorn: they would still be too ignorant to distinguish between delicate dishes and wines. The revision of l. 65 suggests (falsely) that swan was regarded as a common dish and that there was a marked difference of quality between Mareotic wine and Cæcuban. David Watson's edition of Horace, which Browning owned (*New Letters*, 19), explains that '*Mareotick Wine*' is 'An exquisite kind of Wine, brought from a Region of Ægypt bordering upon the Lake *Mareotis*, not far from *Alexandria*' (*The Odes, Epodes, and Carmen Seculare . . . Translated into English Prose*, 1741, p. 154). It is quite clear that the Cæcuban in line 5 of the same Ode (I. xxxvii) is also a wine for special occasions.
basks (*1840*): 'as you conceived': SB.
67 '*Enough of Rome!*: Sordello concedes the point.
69 *her spite*: that of fate.
75 *aloe-cusps*: in botany the cusp is the 'sharp rigid point of a leaf': OED.
77 *of all stripe*: of every colour.
78 *Mounds of all majesty*: the majestic hills of this imaginary Rome.

"Last of my dreams and loveliest, depart!"
      And then a low voice wound into his heart: 80
"Sordello!" (low as some old Pythoness
Conceding to a Lydian King's distress
The cause of his long error—one mistake
Of her past oracle) "Sordello, wake!
"God has conceded two sights to a man—   85
"One, of men's whole work, time's completed
      plan,
"The other, of the minute's work, man's first
"Step to the plan's completeness: what 's
      dispersed
"Save hope of that supreme step which, descried
"Earliest, was meant still to remain untried   90
"Only to give you heart to take your own
"Step, and there stay, leaving the rest alone?
"Where is the vanity? Why count as one
"The first step, with the last step? What is gone
"Except Rome's aëry magnificence,   95
"That last step you 'd take first?—an evidence
"You were God: be man now! Let those glances
      fall!
"The basis, the beginning step of all,
"Which proves you just a man—is that gone
      too?

and a man can but do a man's portion.

79 *1840* depart!   81 *1840* Sordello (lower than a Pythoness   84 *1840* Sordello, wake!   85–92 {Not in *1840*.}   92 *1863–8* stay—   93 *1840* Where . . . . count you, one   95 *1840* Except that aëry magnificence—   96 *1940* That last step you took first? an evidence| You were . . . no matter. Let those glances fall!| This basis, this beginning step of all,| Which proves you one of us, is this gone too?

82 *a Lydian King*: when Croesus King of Lydia consulted the Delphic oracle he misunderstood its ambiguous reply: Herodotus i. 48 ff. Browning may first have found the story in *The Wonders of the Little World*, by Nathaniel Wanley, VI. x. 6 (ed. of 1788). On the importance of this book to Browning see particularly *Griffin and Minchin*, pp. 20–1.
   88   *dispersed*: i.e. lost.
   93 *Where is the vanity?*: 'God concedes two sights to mortals—one of the whole work, the other of their own work, the first step': *SB*. Cf. 85 ff. in the above text.
   96 *took* (*1840*): 'would have taken', *SB*, which adds: 'It was not *meant* to be taken—only [illegible] you [? had] to take your own *first* step'.
   97 *You were . . .* (*1840*): *SB* has 'God!' above the dots, and 'Be man &' before 'Let those glances fall!'

"Pity to disconcert one versed as you   100
"In fate's ill-nature! but its full extent
"Eludes Sordello, even: the veil rent,
"Read the black writing—that collective man
"Outstrips the individual. Who began
"The acknowledged greatnesses? Ay, your own
     art   105
"Shall serve us: put the poet's mimes apart—
"Close with the poet's self, and lo, a dim
"Yet too plain form divides itself from him!
"Alcamo's song enmeshes the lulled Isle,
"Woven into the echoes left erewhile   110
"By Nina, one soft web of song: no more
"Turning his name, then, flower-like o'er and
     o'er!
"An elder poet in the younger's place;
"Nina's the strength, but Alcamo's the grace:

---

101 *1840* ill-nature,   102 *1840* the veil's rent,   104 *1840–68* individual!   105 *1840* The greatnesses you know?—ay,   107–8 *1840* Close
with the poet—closer—what? a dim|Too plain form separates itself from
him?   109 *1840* Alcama's song   111 *1840* Of Nina's   112 *1840* name,
now,   113 *1840* An elder poet's.... place—   *1863,1865* An elder poet....
place—   114 *1840* Take Nina's strength—but lose Alcama's grace?
1863,1865 Nina's the strength—but Alcamo's the grace:

102 *the veil rent*: cf. Matthew 27:51.
103 *collective man*: 'For love, which scarce collective man can fill': Johnson,
The Vanity of Human Wishes, 361.
105 *The acknowledged greatnesses*: the great men whose identity is known to
us, and acknowledged.
106 *mimes*: probably in the sense of imitations (and hence poems), described
by OED as obsolete and rare. Cf. 'art-mimetic' in 'A Forgiveness', 122.
107–8 *a dim/. . . form*: that of an earlier poet whose identity is unknown to
us.
109 *Alcamo's song*: while the general sense is clear—that we can never find the
first 'whole and perfect Poet'—the detail has been confused from the first. In
1840 we have 'Alcama' and Nina: 'Alcama' is a man ('his', 112): the sex of Nina
is not indicated, but we may assume that Browning knew she was a woman.
Since Nina preceded 'Alcama' (we are told), we cannot be content with turning
over Alcama's name and admiring it as that of the first poet. In place of the
younger poet (Alcama) we find an elder (Nina). If we are content with Nina's
strength, dispensing with Alcama's grace, then we get 'no whole and perfect
Poet'. In *1863* Browning corrected 'Alcama' to 'Alcamo': the Sicilian poet
Ciullo d'Alcamo whom Tiraboschi (after a long discussion in ch. iii of his
Storia della Poesia Italiana) names as the first Italian poet. Tiraboschi regards the
(later) Sicilian Nina as possibly the first Italian poetess.
114 *strength . . . grace*: an antithesis that reminds us of Browning's reading in
Augustan literature: cf., e.g., Dryden's 'To my dear Friend Mr. Congreve', 19:
'Thus all below is strength, and all above is grace'.

115   "Each neutralizes each then! Search your fill;
   "You get no whole and perfect Poet—still
   "New Ninas, Alcamos, till time's mid-night
   "Shrouds all—or better say, the shutting light
   "Of a forgotten yesterday. Dissect
120   "Every ideal workman—(to reject
   "In favour of your fearful ignorance
   "The thousand phantasms eager to advance,
   "And point you but to those within your
       reach)—
   "Were you the first who brought—(in modern
       speech)
125   "The Multitude to be materialized?
   "That loose eternal unrest—who devised
   "An apparition i' the midst? The rout
   "Was checked, a breathless ring was formed
       about
   "That sudden flower: get round at any risk
130   "The gold-rough pointel, silver-blazing disk

115–21 *1840* then! gaze your fill;| Search further and the past presents you still| New Ninas, new Alcamas, time's mid-night| Concluding,—better say its evenlight| Of yesterday. You, now, in this respect| Of benefitting people (to reject| The favour   122 *1840* A thousand   123 *1840 proof* You>Refer you *1840* Refer you but . . . . reach)   124 *1840* who got, to use plain speech,   127–9 *1840* midst? the rout| Who checked, the breathless ring who formed about| That sudden flower? Get

---

115 *Each neutralizes*: 'You get no *whole* ideal Poet': *SB*.
117 *till time's mid-night*: until we can see no further back in time.
119 *Of yesterday* (*1840*): 'So with all other Ideals': *SB*.
Dissect: 'To divide and examine minutely': Johnson.
121 *In favour of*: out of consideration for.
122 *The thousand phantasms*: those of shadowy figures who can no longer be identified.
123–4 Between these lines *SB* has: 'If you will not take the step,—do you think none have done so?'
125 *materialized*: as at a seance, although OED has no example of this usage before 1880. Note the revision from 'plain speech' to 'modern speech'. Whyte (p. 16 n.) described this as one of the passages 'which will puzzle readers for many a long day to come'.
126 *unrest*: cf. *Prince Hohenstiel-Schwangau*, 2029–30: 'Nature prefers a motion by unrest, / Advancement through this force which jostles that'. Sordello could not be the first man to summon up an apparition to personify the Multitude, as a medium calls up an apparition of a magic lily. There may be Rosicrucian suggestions here.
130 *pointel*: pistil, of a lily (fleur-de-lys) symbolising France. This 'sudden flower' is made to appear as if by alchemy. Alchemists were believed to have

"O' the lily! Swords across it! Reign thy reign
"And serve thy frolic service, Charlemagne!
"—The very child of over-joyousness,
"Unfeeling thence, strong therefore: Strength by
    stress
"Of Strength comes of that forehead confident,   135
"Those widened eyes expecting heart's content,
"A calm as out of just-quelled noise; nor
    swerves
"For doubt, the ample cheek in gracious curves
"Abutting on the upthrust nether lip:

sums up in himself "He wills, how should he doubt then? Ages slip: 140
all predecessors. "Was it Sordello pried into the work
"So far accomplished, and discovered lurk
"A company amid the other clans,
"Only distinct in priests for castellans
"And popes for suzerains (their rule confessed   145
"Its rule, their interest its interest,
"Living for sake of living—there an end,—
"Wrapt in itself, no energy to spend
"In making adversaries or allies)—
"Dived you into its capabilities   150
"And dared create, out of that sect, a soul
"Should turn a multitude, already whole,

135–6 *1840* of a forehead confident,|Two widened   137 *1840*
noise,   138 *1840* The ample cheek for doubt, in   139 *1840* lip—   140
1840 slip—   142 *1840* and discovering lurk   147 *1840* end,   149 *1840*
allies);   *1863–8* allies),—   150 *1840* Dived he into   151 *1840* create out of
that sect   152 *1840–65* turn the multitude,

the power of reproducing a spectre of a flower in a glass vessel by heating it.
'Swords across it!' suggests the taking of a solemn oath. Charlemagne, here
taken as the first man to materialize or personify the Multitude, because he was
the founder of the Carolingian Empire, was born in 742. In 800 he was
crowned by the Pope, and proclaimed Emperor of the Romans the following
year. He died in 814.
    133 *over-joyousness*: Charlemagne's sword, 'Joyeuse', occurs in many of the
legends about him.
    134–5 *Strength by stress / Of Strength*: cf. *Paracelsus* v. 693 ff., and see note on
211, below.
    140 *Ages slip*: ages later someone (was it Sordello?) enquired what had been
done so far, and found a company of men differing from their fellows in being
ruled by priests and Popes instead of governors of castles and temporal
overlords. At first they lived to themselves, in their own manner, but then
someone (not Sordello but Hildebrand, as we find shortly) realized the possibility of making the sect act as the soul of a multitude of people.

"Into its body? Speak plainer! Is 't so sure
"God's church lives by a King's investiture?
155   "Look to last step! A staggering—a shock—
"What 's mere sand is demolished, while the
    rock
"Endures: a column of black fiery dust
"Blots heaven—that help was prematurely
    thrust
"Aside, perchance!—but air clears, nought 's
    erased
"Of the true outline. Thus much being firm
160   based,
"The other was a scaffold. See him stand
"Buttressed upon his mattock, Hildebrand
"Of the huge brain-mask welded ply o'er ply
"As in a forge; it buries either eye
"White and extinct, that stupid brow; teeth
165   clenched,
"The neck tight-corded, too, the chin
    deep-trenched,
"As if a cloud enveloped him while fought
"Under its shade, grim prizers, thought with
    thought
"At dead-lock, agonizing he, until
170   "The victor thought leap radiant up, and Will,
"The slave with folded arms and drooping lids

---

153 *1840* To some account? Speak   155 *1840* step: a staggering— *1863,1865* step! a staggering—   156–7 *1840* What's sand shall be
demolished, but the rock| Endures—   158 *1840* Blots heaven—woe, woe,
'tis prematurely thrust   159 *1840* Aside, that step!—the air clears— *1863–8*
Aside, perchance!—but the air clears,   160 *1840* outline? Thus much is firm
based— *1863–8* outline! Thus much being firm based,   161 *1840* scaffold:
see you stand   166 *1840* The neck's tight-corded,   168 *1840* Under it all,
grim   170 *1863,1865* thought leapt radiant

154 *a King's investiture*: the reference is to the war of investitures between the
papacy and the imperial power in the eleventh and twelfth centuries.
155 *Look to last step*: see what happened in the end.
A staggering: the conflict between Papacy and Imperial power.
156 *the rock*: Christ's Church.
162 *Hildebrand*: becoming Pope in 1073, as Gregory VII, Hildebrand condemned all forms of lay investiture two years later.
163 *brain-mask*: presumably countenance. The compound is not in OED.
168 *prizers*: prize fighters.   170 *leap*: like 'lean' (172), a subjunctive.

"They fought for, lean forth flame-like as it
   bids.
"Call him no flower—a mandrake of the earth,
"Thwarted and dwarfed and blasted in its birth,
"Rather,—a fruit of suffering's excess,   175
"Thence feeling, therefore stronger: still by
   stress
"Of Strength, work Knowledge! Full three
   hundred years
"Have men to wear away in smiles and tears
"Between the two that nearly seemed to touch,
"Observe you! quit one workman and you
   clutch   180
"Another, letting both their trains go by—
"The actors-out of either's policy,
"Heinrich, on this hand, Otho, Barbaross,
"Carry the three Imperial crowns across,
"Aix' Iron, Milan's Silver, and Rome's Gold—   185

*We just see
Charlemagne,
Hildebrand,*

---

173 *1840* —A root, the crippled mandrake   175 *1840* Be certain; fruit
1863,1865 Rather, a fruit   176 *1840* Whence feeling,   177 *1840 proof*
knowledge!>Knowledge!   178 *1840* For men   179 *1840,1863* seem to
touch,   180 *1840* Observe you: . . . . and we clutch   181 *1840 proof*
Another>Another,   184 *1840* May carry the Imperial

   172 *it*: the victor thought.
   173 *no flower*: whereas Charlemagne may be visualized as a 'sudden flower'
(129), Hildebrand resembles rather a mandrake root, ugly and stunted (yet
often associated with fertility, as in Genesis 30: 14–16). Whereas Charlemagne
represents Strength without feeling (having never suffered), Hildebrand, 'a
fruit of suffering's excess', is stronger still, as he knows feeling. Charlemagne
stands for 'Strength by stress/Of Strength' (134–5), Hildebrand for Knowledge 'by stress/Of Strength'. Cf. ll. 196 and 211 below.
   181 *their trains*: their successors.
   183 *Heinrich*: 'presumably Heinrich V' (Pettigrew). This makes good sense,
as he revolted against his father in 1104, compelled his abdication, and resumed
the struggle with the Papacy over the issue of investiture which had dominated
his father's reign. If the three great men in line 183 are mentioned in chronological order, however, then (since Otho is clearly Otho the Great, Emperor
962–7) and Barbarossa (Friedrich I) was Emperor from 1155 to 1190 (cf. i. 197),
the reference here may be to Heinrich I (876–936), the father of Otho the Great.
Although he was not crowned Emperor he extended the authority of the
Empire eastwards into Schleswig, Holstein, and Brandenburg. Duff suggests
Heinrich III, who was elected Deutscher König in 1026, and whose reign
marks the highest point of mediaeval Imperial power.
   184 *the three Imperial crowns*: commentators from Berdoe onwards have
noticed the confusion. It was the Italian or Lombard crown ('Milan's') which
was believed to include an iron nail from the Cross. The German crown
('Aix'') was made of silver; the Roman of gold.

"While Alexander, Innocent uphold
"On that, each Papal key—but, link on link,
"Why is it neither chain betrays a chink?
"How coalesce the small and great? Alack,
190　　"For one thrust forward, fifty such fall back!
"Do the popes coupled there help Gregory
"Alone? Hark—from the hermit Peter's cry
"At Claremont, down to the first serf that says
"Friedrich 's no liege of his while he delays
"Getting the Pope's curse off him! The
195　　　Crusade—
"Or trick of breeding Strength by other aid
"Than Strength, is safe. Hark—from the wild
　　　harangue
"Of Vimmercato, to the carroch's clang

---

186 *1840* As Alexander,　　187 *1840* On that the Papal keys—but,　　191–3
1840 The couple there alone help Gregory?|Hark—from the hermit Peter's
thin sad cry|At Claremont, yonder to the serf　　196 *1840–65* strength
197 *1840* Than strength, is safe: hark—　　*1863,1865* Than strength, is safe.
Hark—

---

186 *Alexander*: Alexander III (Pope 1159–81), who excommunicated Barbarossa.
　Innocent: Innocent III (Pope 1198–1216).
187 *On that*: on the other side, these men support the symbol of Papal
authority.
191 *The couple* (*1840*): 'Alex' & Inn!' SB.
192 *Alone?*: i.e. Is it only the Popes . . .? The meaning is clear in *1840*.
the hermit Peter: the *Biographie Universelle* describes him as 'the first preacher
of the Crusades' and comments that, 'inasmuch as he was the interpreter of the
dominant passions [of his age], he aroused the veneration and enthusiasm of
the nations'. According to the same source, Urban II charged him with the
duty of preaching the imminent delivery of Jerusalem. Modern historians
doubt whether he began preaching before the Council of Clermont in 1095.
Lecturing in 1838, Carlyle said 'It was a strange thing to see how Peter, a poor
monk, recently come home from Syria, but fully convinced of the propriety of
the step, set out on his mission through Europe . . . swaying all hearts and
burning them up with zeal, and stirring up steel-clad Europe till it shook itself
at his words . . . without any art at all, but with something far greater than art!
. . . belief! belief! belief!' *Lectures on the History of Literature*, ed. J. Reay Greene
(1892), 72–3.
195 *the Pope's curse*: see note to i. 200.
196 *Strength*: cf. l. 173 n.
198 *Vimmercato*: F. Stefanardo de Vimecarte, a Dominican chosen by the
Archbishop of Milan in 1292 to preach in favour of a crusade. The best-known
of his works is a poem, *De gestis in civitate Mediolani sub Oth. Vicecomiti, archiep.*,
printed by Muratori in *Rerum Italicarum Scriptores*, ix. 59–95, with details of his
life. The *Biographie Universelle* has an account of him.
　the carroch's clang: see i. 317 n.

"Yonder! The League—or trick of turning
      Strength
*in composite work
they end and
name.*
"Against Pernicious Strength, is safe at length.   200
"Yet hark—from Mantuan Albert making cease
"The fierce ones, to Saint Francis preaching peace
"Yonder! God's Truce—or trick to supersede
"The very Use of Strength, is safe. Indeed
"We trench upon the future. Who is found   205
"To take next step, next age—trail o'er the
      ground—
"Shall I say, gourd-like?—not the flower's
      display
"Nor the root's prowess, but the plenteous way
"O' the plant—produced by joy and sorrow,
      whence
"Unfeeling and yet feeling, strongest thence?   210
"Knowledge by stress of merely Knowledge?
      No—

199–200 *1840* strength|Against pernicious strength, ... length: *1863,1865*
strength|Against pernicious strength, ... length.   201 *1840* Albert's mak-
ing   202 *1865* St. Francis   *1868* St Francis   204 *1840* The use of strength
at all, is   *1863,1865* The very use of strength, is   205 *1840* future! Who shall
found   *1863,1865* Future! Who is found   206 *1840* Next step, next
age—trail plenteous o'er the ground   207–8 {Not in *1840*.}   209 *1840*
Vine-like, produced   210 *1840·* thence: 211 *1840 proof* knowledge>
Knowledge *1840* of Knowledge is it? No—

199 *The League*: see i. 110 n., above.   *Strength*: see l. 211 n., below.
201 *Mantuan Albert*: the bloodshed in Ferrara is said to have been brought to
an end for a short time in 1207, when a certain Alberto da Mantua preached
from the pulpit of the Duomo.
202 *Saint Francis*: of Assisi.
203 *God's Truce*: the 'Treuga Dei' was an arrangement by which (in theory)
fighting was to be permissible only on certain days of the week. It was first
introduced in southern France in the first half of the eleventh century.
205 *We trench upon*: we are anticipating.
207 *gourd-like*: the next step, to spread like a creeper instead of blossoming
like a flower or having the sheer strength of a mandrake, is not for Sordello. Cf.
1840, above. It is not possible for him, or any man of his time, to make a third
after Charlemagne and Hildebrand. The 'plenteous way/O' the plant' refers to
its fruit.
211 *Knowledge*: from 134–5 we have had a history of mankind in terms of
evolution from Strength to Knowledge. The first stage, represented by the
joyous but unfeeling Charlemagne, is 'Strength by stress / Of Strength', the
second, represented by Hildebrand, who had known suffering and therefore
feeling, is Knowledge worked by 'stress/Of Strength' (176–7), while the
ultimate goal—'Knowledge by stress of merely Knowledge' (211)—will come
only long after Sordello's time. Before that, but not very distinctly marked off
from the stage represented by Hildebrand, we find 'the trick of breeding
Strength by other aid / Than Strength' (196–7: the Crusades), the 'trick of

"E'en were Sordello ready to forego
"His life for this, 't were overleaping work
"Some one has first to do, howe'er it irk,
"Nor stray a foot's breadth from the beaten
     road.
"Who means to help must still support the load
"Hildebrand lifted—'why hast Thou,' he
     groaned,
"'Imposed on me a burthen, Paul had moaned,
"'And Moses dropped beneath?' Much done—
     and yet
"Doubtless that grandest task God ever set
"On man, left much to do: at his arm's wrench,
"Charlemagne's scaffold fell; but pillars blench
"Merely, start back again—perchance have been
"Taken for buttresses: crash every screen,
"Hammer the tenons better, and engage
"A gang about your work, for the next age
"Or two, of Knowledge, part by Strength and
     part

215

220

225

213 *1840* His work for   214 *1840* Some one must do before, howe'er it
irk: 215 *1840* No end's in sight yet of that second road: *1865,1868* Nor stay
a foot's breadth from the beaten road.   217 *1840* —why hast
Thou,   218–22 *1840* Imposed, my God, a thing thy Paul had moaned,|Thy
Moses failed beneath, on me? and yet|That grandest of the tasks God ever
set|On man left much to do: a mighty wrench—|The scaffold falls—but half
the pillars blench   *1863* {as *1888* except 'Doubtless,' in line 220.}

turning Strength / Against Pernicious Strength' (200: the Lombard League),
and 'God's Truce', 'a trick to supersede/The very use of Strength'. The
ultimate goal, 'Knowledge by stress of merely Knowledge', will be reached
when joy and sorrow, feeling and unfeeling, join. Ll. 227–8 make it clear that
the age after Hildebrand's is to be that 'of Knowledge, part by Stength and part
/ By Knowledge'. At 399 Taurello ironically agrees that he should 'turn Guelf,
submit our Strength . . . To the Pope's Knowledge', while at 968 he vainly
fancies that he and Sordello will together be 'free to break up Hildebrand,
Rebuild . . . Charlemagne—/But garnished, Strength with Knowledge'.
  216 *Who means to help*: it is through the Guelfs that mankind can be advanced.
  218 *Paul had moaned*: conceivably a very faint echo of Gregory VII's prayer to
the Apostles Peter and Paul on the occasion of his final excommunication and
deposition of Henry IV in 1080.
  224 *crash every screen*: even the great work of Hildebrand left much still to be
done. It was not enough to demolish 'Charlemagne's scaffold': 'crash' is
imperative (and transitive), like 'Hammer' and 'engage'.
  A tenon is the part of a piece of wood or stone which is fitted into another in
dove-tailing.
  226–7 *the next age* / *Or two*: an intermediate period.

"By Knowledge! Then, indeed, perchance may
      start
"Sordello on his race—would time divulge
"Such secrets! If one step's awry, one bulge   230
"Calls for correction by a step we thought
"Got over long since, why, till that is wrought,
"No progress! And the scaffold in its turn
"Becomes, its service o'er, a thing to spurn.

*If associates trouble
you, stand off!*

"Meanwhile, if your half-dozen years of life   235
"In store dispose you to forego the strife,
"Who takes exception? Only bear in mind
"Ferrara's reached, Goito's left behind:
"As you then were, as half yourself, desist!
"—The warrior-part of you may, an it list,   240
"Finding real faulchions difficult to poise,
"Fling them afar and taste the cream of joys
"By wielding such in fancy,—what is bard
"Of you may spurn the vehicle that marred
"Elys so much, and in free fancy glut   245
"His sense, yet write no verses—you have but
"To please yourself for law, and once could
      please
"What once apppeared yourself, by dreaming
      these

228–32 *1840* then—Ay, then perchance may start|Sordello on his race—but who'll divulge|Time's secrets? lo, a step's awry, a bulge|To be corrected by a step we thought|Got over long ago—till   233 *1840* and that scaffold *1863,1865* and the scaffold   235 *1840* Meanwhile, your some half-dozen   236 *1840* *proof* strife>strife—   *1840* Longer, dispose . . . . strife—   *1863–8* In store, dispose . . . . strife,   237 *1840* exception? 'Tis Ferrara, mind,   *1863–8* exception? Only bear in mind,   238 *1840* Before us, and Goito's   243 *1840* By wielding one in   245 *1840* in mere fancy   246–8 *1840* His sense on her free beauties—we have but|To please ourselves for law, and you could please|What then appeared yourself

235 *Meanwhile*: having explained the way in which Mankind progresses, the voice now delivers direct advice to Sordello. He must at least remember that he has left his Goito period behind, and has come to Ferrara. Before he was a whole man he could occupy his warrior-self by imagining himself a warrior, his other half by imagining himself a poet; but now that he has found that he is part of mankind, he must at least do something.
238 *Goito's left behind*: 'you agree:' *SB*.
241 *real faulchions*: commonly 'falchion': 'A broad sword more or less curved with the edge on the convex side': OED. For the contrast between reality and fancy, cf. i. 823 ff.
244 *spurn the vehicle*: cf. ii. 484 n.

"Rather than doing these, in days gone by.
250 "But all is changed the moment you descry
"Mankind as half yourself,—then, fancy's trade
"Ends once and always: how may half evade
"The other half? men are found half of you.
"Out of a thousand helps, just one or two
255 "Can be accomplished presently: but flinch
"From these (as from the faulchion, raised an
          inch,
"Elys, described a couplet) and make proof
"Of fancy,—then, while one half lolls aloof
"I' the vines, completing Rome to the tip-top—
260 "See if, for that, your other half will stop
"A tear, begin a smile! The rabble's woes,   *—should the new*
"Ludicrous in their patience as they chose   *sympathies allow*
"To sit about their town and quietly   *you.*
"Be slaughtered,—the poor reckless soldiery,
265 "With their ignoble rhymes on Richard, how
"'Polt-foot,' sang they, 'was in a pitfall now,'
"Cheering each other from the
          engine-mounts,—
"That crippled spawling idiot who recounts
"How, lopped of limbs, he lay, stupid as stone,
270 "Till the pains crept from out him one by one,
"And wriggles round the archers on his head

---

249 *1840* these: now—fancy's trade   250-1 {not in *1840*.}   252-3 *1840*
Is ended, mind, nor one half may evade| The other half: our friends are half of
you: 255 *1840* presently—   256 *1840* faulchion   257 *1840* Elys
258 *1840* fancy, —and, while   259 *1840* O' the grass completing
260 *1840* that, the other   261 *1840* smile: that rabble's   266 *1840* Polt-
foot, sang they, was in a pitfall now,   268 *1868* sprawling idiot

---

251 *fancy's trade*: vain imaginings. In the margin of *SB* we read: 'not recognized with impunity', with an illegible mark between the first two words. The
sense is no doubt that this cannot be ignored with impunity.
255 *but flinch*: if you refuse to do even the little which you can in favour of
indulging your fancy, then while you yourself ('one half') lie dreaming idly of
the New Jerusalem, mankind ('your other half') will not be comforted. That
would be as wrong as it would be to give up trying to lift a sword because it is
too heavy, or trying to write verse about your ideal woman because you can
get no further than the first couplet (?).
266 *'Polt-foot'*: club-foot.
268 *spawling*: spitting. Cf. 'Mr. Sludge, "The Medium"', 655.
269 *stupid as stone*: cf. ii. 938.

"To earn a morsel of their chestnut bread,—
"And Cino, always in the self-same place
"Weeping; beside that other wretch's case,
"Eyepits to ear, one gangrene since he plied   275
"The engine in his coat of raw sheep's hide
"A double watch in the noon sun; and see
"Lucchino, beauty, with the favours free,
"Trim hacqueton, spruce beard and scented hair,
"Campaigning it for the first time—cut there   28c
"In two already, boy enough to crawl
"For latter orpine round the southern wall,
"Tomà, where Richard's kept, because that
       whore
"Marfisa, the fool never saw before,
"Sickened for flowers this wearisomest siege: 28₅
"And Tiso's wife—men liked their pretty liege,
"Cared for her least of whims once,—Berta, wed
"A twelvemonth gone, and, now poor Tiso's
       dead,
"Delivering herself of his first child
"On that chance heap of wet filth, reconciled   29₀
"To fifty gazers!"—(Here a wind below
Made moody music augural of woe
From the pine barrier)—"What if, now the scene
"Draws to a close, yourself have really been

274 *1840* wretches' case   279 *1840* hacqueton and sprucely scented   283
1840 proof Tonià,> Tomà,   284 *1840* Marfisa. . . . before   286 *1840* Then
Tiso's   287 *1840* once, Berta,   291 *1840* To fifty gazers.   293 *1840*
barrier)—What   294 *1840* Draws to a shutting, if yourself have been

273 *Cino*: it is unclear whether he is the same as the Cino at i. 145 or the Cino
of iv. 91.
275 *plied*: worked, operated.
278 *Lucchino, beauty*: another imaginary character. The meaning is probably
'that young beau, Lucchino, free with his favours, who had still enough of the
boy in him to take a great risk to get some flowers for a wench he had never
even seen before . . . and who got cut in two, as a result'. A 'hacqueton' is a
jacket worn under mail: see *Ivanhoe*, ch. xxix.
283 *Tomà*: cf. iv. 534 n.   286 *Tiso's wife*: see iii. 302 n. and iv. 614.
293 *What if*: the voice asks Sordello whether he may not, after all, have been
the man who could have made the great advance for mankind—he who had
dreamed of the dignity of being a Roman consul as he idly picked purple
flowers at Goito or the stalks of dry aloes at Ferrara. A trabea was 'A toga
ornamented with horizontal purple stripes, worn as a state robe by kings,
consuls, and other men of rank in ancient Rome': OED.

295 "—You, plucking purples in Goito's moss
"Like edges of a trabea (not to cross
"Your consul-humour) or dry aloe-shafts
"For fasces, at Ferrara—he, fate wafts,
"This very age, her whole inheritance
300 "Of opportunities? Yet you advance
"Upon the last! Since talking is your trade,
"There 's Salinguerra left you to persuade:
"Fail! then"—

      "No—no—which latest chance secure!" *Time having been lost, choose quick!*

Leaped up and cried Sordello: "this made sure,
305 "The past were yet redeemable; its work
"Was—help the Guelfs, whom I, howe'er it irk,
"Thus help!" He shook the foolish aloe-haulm
Out of his doublet, paused, proceeded calm
To the appointed presence. The large head
Turned on its socket; "And your spokesman,"
310   said
The large voice, "is Elcorte's happy sprout?
"Few such"—(so finishing a speech no doubt
Addressed to Palma, silent at his side)

297 *1840* consul-feeling) or   298–9 *1840* Here at Ferrara—He whom fortune wafts|This very age her best inheritance   300 *1840* Yet we advance   302 *1840* persuade,   303 *1840* And then—¶No—. . . . secure!   *1863* Fail! then"—¶ "No—. . . . secure!"   *1865* Fail! then"—¶ "No—. . . . secure?"   304 *1840* Leapt up . . . . this   *1863,1865* Leapt up . . . . "this   305 *1840* The Past is yet redeemable whose work   *1863, 1865* The Past were yet redeemable; its work   306 *1840* Guelfs, and I,   307 *1840* Thus help!   310 *1840* And your spokesman,   311 *1840* voice, is   312 *1840* Few such

295 *purples*: 'A purple flower': OED, with no earlier example.
300 *Of opportunities?*: 'you were refined by the habit of idealizing, that you might be made know & feel beauty & good: the realizations *for yourself* were unsuccessful, in order that you might realize for *others*': SB.
Yet you advance: you still have one last opportunity!
303 *And then*— (*1840*): SB underlines 'then' and adds: 'to turn Guelf—could that be done, a *great* step. but you *will* not.'
Fail! then: 'If you fail, then . . .'   304 *this* ∧ *made*: 'one step': SB.
305 *work* ∧: 'amounted to this—': SB, deleting 'Was'.
306 *help the Guelfs*: at this stage in the historical process it is Hildebrand's work which is to be carried on, however much that may go against Sordello's instincts. The point is made so quickly and glancingly that readers have often missed it.
307 ∧ *Thus* (*1840*): 'Will': SB.
309 *the appointed presence*: that of Taurello.
310 *your spokesman*: Palma's.
311 *sprout*: son, offspring, as in *Ivanhoe*, ch. xxxii. For Elcorte see ii. 331 n.

"—My sober councils have diversified.
"Elcorte's son! good: forward as you may,   315
"Our lady's minstrel with so much to say!"
The hesitating sunset floated back,
Rosily traversed in the wonted track
The chamber, from the lattice o'er the girth
Of pines, to the huge eagle blacked in earth   320
Opposite,—outlined sudden, spur to crest,
That solid Salinguerra, and caressed
Palma's contour; 't was day looped back night's
          pall;

He takes his first   Sordello had a chance left spite of all.
step as a Guelf;
    And much he made of the convincing speech   325
Meant to compensate for the past and reach
Through his youth's daybreak of unprofit, quite
To his noon's labour, so proceed till night
Leisurely! The great argument to bind
Taurello with the Guelf Cause, body and mind,   330
—Came the consummate rhetoric to that?
Yet most Sordello's argument dropped flat
Through his accustomed fault of breaking yoke,
Disjoining him who felt from him who spoke.
Was 't not a touching incident—so prompt   335
A rendering the world its just accompt,
Once proved its debtor? Who 'd suppose, before
This proof, that he, Goito's god of yore,
At duty's instance could demean himself
So memorably, dwindle to a Guelf?   340

---

314 *1840* Our sober . . . . diversified: *1863,1865* —"My sober . . . .
diversified.   315 *1840* son!—but forward   316 *1840* say!   318 *1840* in a
single track   321 *1840* Opposite,   323 *1840,1863* Day looped back Night's
pall;   326 *1840–65* He meant should compensate the Past and
reach   329–31 *1840* At leisure! The contrivances to bind Taurello body
with the Cause and mind,|—Was the . . . . rhetoric just that?   334 *1840*
spoke:

---

315 *Elcorte's son!*: 'He despised, but he would listen—a success!': *SB*.
325 *the convincing speech*: the speech which was intended to be convincing.
326 *compensate*: stressed on the second syllable, as in Johnson.
327 *unprofit*: a rare word mainly found in religious writings, e.g. in Wycliffe
and the Wycliffite Bible.
333 *breaking yoke*: Cf. ii. 735 ff., and 341 ff., below.
335 *a touching incident*: ironical.

Be sure, in such delicious flattery steeped,
His inmost self at the out-portion peeped,
Thus occupied; then stole a glance at those
Appealed to, curious if her colour rose
345   Or his lip moved, while he discreetly urged
The need of Lombardy becoming purged
At soonest of her barons; the poor part
Abandoned thus, missing the blood at heart
And spirit in brain, unseasonably off
350   Elsewhere! But, though his speech was worthy
        scoff,
Good-humoured Salinguerra, famed for tact
And tongue, who, careless of his phrase, ne'er
        lacked
The right phrase, and harangued Honorius dumb
At his accession,—looked as all fell plumb
355   To purpose and himself found interest
In every point his new instructor pressed
—Left playing with the rescript's white wax seal
To scrutinize Sordello head and heel.
He means to yield assent sure? No, alas!
360   All he replied was, "What, it comes to pass
"That poesy, sooner than politics,
"Makes fade young hair?" To think such speech
        could fix
Taurello!

---

346 *1840–65* Lombardy's   348–9 *1840* thus . . . . heart,|Spirit in
brain,   352 *1840* That way, who,   354 *1840* accession,   355 *1840* himself took interest   358 *1840* head to heel: 359 *1840* Then means he . . .
yes, assent sure? Well? Alas,   *1863* Then means he yield assent sure? No,
alas!   *1865* Then means to yield assent sure? No, alas!   360 *1840* He said no
more than, So it comes to pass   362 *1840* hair: to think his speech

---

342 *His inmost self*: he admires himself, as he makes his speech.
347 *her barons*: great supporters of the Emperor: see iii. 271 n.
the poor part: his 'out-portion', which fails to be convincing because he is
excessively self-admiring and self-conscious.
353 *harangued Honorius dumb*: apparently unhistorical. Honorius III was the
Pope at this time: see i. 79–80.
362 *Makes fade young hair*: Sordello's prematurely aged appearance is frequently mentioned, e.g. at iv. 421. Cf. Shelley, *The Revolt of Islam*, 457 and
1666 ff.
To think: it would be absurd to think that such a speech as Sordello's could
win Taurello.

but to will and to   Then a flash of bitter truth:
do are different:

So fantasies could break and fritter youth
That he had long ago lost earnestness,   36
Lost will to work, lost power to even express
The need of working! Earth was turned a grave:
No more occasions now, though he should crave
Just one, in right of superhuman toil,
To do what was undone, repair such spoil,   37
Alter the past—nothing would give the chance!
Not that he was to die; he saw askance
Protract the ignominious years beyond
To dream in—time to hope and time despond,
Remember and forget, be sad, rejoice   37
As saved a trouble; he might, at his choice,
One way or other, idle life out, drop
No few smooth verses by the way—for prop,
A thyrsus, these sad people, all the same,
Should pick up, and set store by,—far from
    blame,   38

he may sleep on   Plant o'er his hearse, convinced his better part
the bed he has   Survived him. "Rather tear men out the heart
made.

"O' the truth!"—Sordello muttered, and renewed
His propositions for the Multitude.
    But Salinguerra, who at this attack   38
Had thrown great breast and ruffling corslet back
To hear the better, smilingly resumed
His task; beneath, the carroch's warning boomed;

363–4 *1840* ¶ Then a flash; he knew the truth:| So fantasies shall break   365
1840 he has long   366–7 *1840* power to express| Even the need of working!
Ere the grave   369 *1840* One such in . . . . toil   370 *1840* repair his
spoil,   371 *1840* Past—nought brings again the   *1863,1865* Past—nothing
would give the   372 *1840,1863* die: 376 *1840* As saved a trouble, suited to
his choice,   377 *1840* —One way or other   378–80 *1840* prop| A thyrsus
these sad people should, the same,| Pick up, set store by, and, so far from
blame,   382 *1840* Rather   383 *1840* Of the truth! *1863–8* Of the
truth!"—   385–6 *1840* who, the last attack, Threw himself in his ruffling
corslet back   388 *1840* Some task; beneath

369 *in right of superhuman toil*: as the reward of superhuman effort.
372 *Not that he was to die*: as he sees it at this moment.
379 *A thyrsus*: an ornamental staff carried by Dionysus and his votaries, such
as poets. Sordello wishes to do more for the sad Multitude than leave them a
few verses.
382 *tear men out*: tear out for men.
388 *task*: 'He had given Sordello quite time enough': *SB*.

He must decide with Tito; courteously
390   He turned then, even seeming to agree
With his admonisher—"Assist the Pope,
"Extend Guelf domination, fill the scope
"O' the Church, thus based on All, by All, for
     All—
"Change Secular to Evangelical"—
395   Echoing his very sentence: all seemed lost,
When sudden he looked up, laughingly almost,
To Palma: "This opinion of your friend's—
"For instance, would it answer Palma's ends?
"Best, were it not, turn Guelf, submit our
     Strength"—
400   (Here he drew out his baldric to its length)
—"To the Pope's Knowledge—let our captive
     slip,
"Wide to the walls throw ope our gates, equip
"Azzo with . . . what I hold here! Who 'll
     subscribe
"To a trite censure of the minstrel tribe
"Henceforward? or pronounce, as Heinrich
405   used,
"'Spear-heads for battle, burr-heads for the
     joust!'

---

392 *1840* Extend his domination,   393 *1840* Of the Church based   *1863–8*
Of the Church, thus based   *396 {Reading of *1863*} *1840* When sudden he
looked, laughingly *1865–89* When suddenly he looked up, laughingly   397 *1840* This . . . . friend's   399 *1840* Strength   401 *1840* To
. . . . Knowledge—letting Richard slip,   402 *1840* ope your gates,   403
1840 with . . . but no matter! Who'll *1863–8* with . . . what I hold here?
Who'll   406 *1840* "Spear-heads . . . . joust"

---

389 *Tito*: see iv. 41 n.

393 *on All, by All*: this may be regarded as one of the innumerable anticipations of Abraham Lincoln's 'Government of the people, by the people, for the
people' (1863).

394 *to Evangelical*: 'He had thought this, was unconvinced by this, despised
Sordello': *SB*.

398 *Palma's ends?*: '—So the young people arrange!' *SB*.

399–401 *our Strength . . . To the Pope's Knowledge*: see l. 211 n. above.

401 *our captive*: Count Richard.

406 *burr-heads*: spears reversed or otherwise rendered innocuous. Strictly a
burr is 'a broad iron ring on a tilting spear just behind the place for the hand':
OED.

"—When Constance, for his couplets, would
     promote
"Alcamo, from a parti-coloured coat,
"To holding her lord's stirrup in the wars.
"Not that I see where couplet-making jars   410
"With common sense: at Mantua I had borne
"This chanted, better than their most forlorn
"Of bull-baits,—that 's indisputable!"

Scorn flings cold   Brave!
water in his face, Whom vanity nigh slew, contempt shall save!
All 's at an end: a Troubadour suppose   415
Mankind will class him with their friends or
     foes?
A puny uncouth ailing vassal think
The world and him bound in some special link?
Abrupt the visionary tether burst.
What were rewarded here, or what amerced   420
If a poor drudge, solicitous to dream
Deservingly, got tangled by his theme
So far as to conceit the knack or gift
Or whatsoe'er it be, of verse, might lift
The globe, a lever like the hand and head   425
Of—"Men of Action," as the Jongleurs said,
—"The Great Men," in the people's dialect?
     And not a moment did this scorn affect

---

408 *1840* Alcama . . . . coat   410 *1840 proof* whose>where   411–12
1840 at Mantua we had borne|This chanted, easier than   413 *1840* Of bull-
fights, that's indisputable!   416 *1840* Mankind's to class   418 *1840* him in
some especial link?   419 *1840* tether's burst—   *1863,1865* tether
burst—   420 *1840* What's to reward or what to be amerced   422 *1840*
Deservingly, gets tangled   423 *1840* conceit his knack   424 *1840* be of
verse   426 *1840* Of—Men of Action,   427 *1840* —The Great Men,

---

407 *Constance*: the wife of Heinrich VI: see iv. 144 n. For Alcamo, cf. v. 109 n.
The incident is no doubt imaginary.
411 *With common sense*: Naddo's view: ii. 500.
413 *bull-baits*: see ii. 1013 ff.
420 *What were rewarded*: what good or bad effect could it possibly have
('amerced', literally punished or fined) if a wretched poet, in his endeavour
after visions, lost touch with reality to such a point that he came to believe that
a versifier could move the world, as men of action do? There is an implicit
allusion to the saying attributed to Archimedes, 'Give me somewhere to stand
and I shall move the world'.
427–8 Between these lines *SB* has: 'Salinguerras, Ecelins [?] roles &
Richards?'

Sordello: scorn the poet? They, for once,
430   Asking "what was," obtained a full response.   *arouses him at last,*
Bid Naddo think at Mantua—he had but   *to some purpose,*
To look into his promptuary, put
Finger on a set thought in a set speech:
But was Sordello fitted thus for each
435   Conjuncture? Nowise; since, within his soul,
Perception brooded unexpressed and whole.
A healthy spirit like a healthy frame
Craves aliment in plenty—all the same,
Changes, assimilates its aliment.
440   Perceived Sordello, on a truth intent?
Next day no formularies more you saw
Than figs or olives in a sated maw.
'T is Knowledge, whither such perceptions tend;
They lose themselves in that, means to an end,
445   The many old producing some one new,
A last unlike the first. If lies are true,
The Caliph's wheel-work man of brass receives
A meal, munched millet grains and lettuce leaves

---

431 *1840–68* Mantua,   433 *1840* His hand on   434 *1840* And
was   *435 *1840* Conjuncture? No wise; since . . . . soul   *1863* Conjecture?
Nowise; since, ... soul,   *1865–89* Conjecture? Nowise; since . . . .
soul,   436 *1840* whole: 438 *1840* plenty and, the same,   439 *1840*
aliment: 422 *1840* maw   443 *1840* —'Tis Knowledge . . . . tend,   *1863*
'Tis Knowledge, ... tend;   445–7 *1840* The Many Old producing some
One New, | A Last unlike the First. If lies are true, | The Caliph Haroun's
man   448 *1840* A meal, ay, millet

430 *a full response*: 'One of God's large ones': ii. 723.
431 *Bid Naddo think*: when a question was put to Naddo, he had merely to
consult his commonplace-book for an answer. Sordello, on the other hand,
was by no means ready for every situation.
434 *And was (1840)*: 'But was': SB.
435 *Conjuncture?*: the same error ('conjecture' for 'conjuncture': see textual
note above) occurred in *Colombe's Birthday*, v. 189. For Browning's comment
on this 'vile misprint' (which remained in 1888–9), see John Maynard in *Studies
in Browning and His Circle* (Fall 1974), p. 87. Cf. *Pauline*, 702–3 and *Paracelsus*, i.
767, v. 848.
within his soul: he was an original thinker who often found it impossible to
put his intuitions into words.
437 *A healthy spirit*: Sordello was a healthy spirit. When, in his search for the
truth on some matter, he reached a perception, he digested the 'aliment' his
spirit had required to arrive at it.
447 *The Caliph's wheel-work man*: Haroun-al-Raschid, the great Oriental
despot (*c*. 765–809), sent an embassy to Charlemagne in 807. Among many
remarkable gifts there are said to have been a number of automata: 'made of
wheels by an Egyptian sage': SB.

Together in his stomach rattle loose;
You find them perfect next day to produce: 450
But ne'er expect the man, on strength of that,
Can roll an iron camel-collar flat
Like Haroun's self! I tell you, what was stored
Bit by bit through Sordello's life, outpoured

and thus gets
the utmost out
of him.

That eve, was, for that age, a novel thing: 455
And round those three the People formed a ring
Of visionary judges whose award
He recognised in full—faces that barred
Henceforth return to the old careless life,
In whose great presence, therefore, his first strife   460
For their sake must not be ignobly fought;
All these, for once, approved of him, he
          thought,
Suspended their own vengeance, chose await
The issue of this strife to reinstate
Them in the right of taking it—in fact   465
He must be proved king ere they could exact
Vengeance for such king's defalcation. Last,
A reason why the phrases flowed so fast
Was in his quite forgetting for a time
Himself in his amazement that the rhyme   470
Disguised the royalty so much: he there—
And Salinguerra yet all-unaware

---

449 *1840–65* loose—   450 *1840* produce   *1863,1865* produce;   451 *1840*
proof don't⊳ne'er   454 *1840* Parcel by parcel through his life, outpoured   *456 {Editors' emendation}   *1840,1868–89* People .... ring,
1863,1865 people .... ring,   457–62 {not in *1840.*}   461 *1863* fought.
1865,1868 fought,   466 *1840* proved their lord ere they exact
467 *1840* Amends for that lord's defalcation.   469 *1840* for the time
470 *1840* that his rhyme   472 *1840* They full face to him—and yet unaware
1863,1865 And Salinguerra—and yet unaware   *1868* And Salinguerra yet
all unaware

454 *his life* (*1840*): 'Sordello's': *SB*.
456 *those three*: Sordello, Taurello and Palma.
464 *this strife*: 'whose object was, 1.' *SB*.
466 *He must be proved king*: 'I cannot remember the time', Browning wrote to
Ripert-Monclar (9 August 1837: Purdy Collection), 'when I did not . . . think
verse-making the finest thing in the world'. Even as a small boy he believed
'that "a poet" was the grandest of God's creatures.' Cf. i. 467 and 642, ii. 1001,
and below, ll. 471, 473 (*1840*), 506–8 and 515. See also *Pauline*, 20 and 474, and
Paracelsus, v. 412.

Who was the lord, who liegeman!

                      "Thus I lay

"On thine my spirit and compel obey

"His lord,—my liegeman,—impotent to build   475

"Another Rome, but hardly so unskilled

"In what such builder should have been, as
    brook

"One shame beyond the charge that I forsook

"His function! Free me from that shame, I bend

"A brow before, suppose new years to spend,—   480

"Allow each chance, nor fruitlessly, recur—

"Measure thee with the Minstrel, then, demur   *He asserts the*

"At any crown he claims! That I must cede   *poet's rank and*

"Shamed now, my right to my especial meed—   *right,*

"Confess thee fitter help the world than I   485

"Ordained its champion from eternity,

"Is much: but to behold thee scorn the post

"I quit in thy behalf—to hear thee boast

"What makes my own despair!" And while he
    rung

The changes on this theme, the roof up-sprung,   490

The sad walls of the presence-chamber died

Into the distance, or embowering vied

With far-away Goito's vine-frontier;

And crowds of faces—(only keeping clear

---

473 *1840* Who was the King and who . . . But if I lay   475 *1840* lord—Taurello? Impotent   478 *1840* that he forsook   479 *1840* His function! Set me free that shame I bend   480 *1840–65* spend,   *483 {Reading of *1840–65*}   *1868–89* any crowd he   484 *1840* As 'tis, my   485 *1840* Confess you fitter   487–9 *1840* behold you scorn the post|I quit in your behalf—as aught's to boast|Unless you help the world! And   494 *1840* faces (only

473–4 *Thus I lay / On thine my spirit*: Sordello insists that he is Taurello's natural lord. He is unable to build a new Rome (or ideal city), and acknowledges his shame at that: if only he had his opportunities again, and took them, then Taurello could not possibly have denied that he is a King among men! We note that he is nevertheless resigning his own rightful post to Taurello.

488 *boast*: 'In what you do': SB. Cf. *1840*: Taurello has nothing to boast about unless he helps the world.

490 *the roof up-sprung*: as if by magic, a suggestion enhanced by the Rosicrucian 'rose-light in the midst'. 'He began to reap the good of working on the real grounds': *SB*.

494 *faces*: those of the Multitude: 'Men, women, children': *SB*.

The rose-light in the midst, his vantage-ground   495
To fight their battle from)—deep clustered round
Sordello, with good wishes no mere breath,
Kind prayers for him no vapour, since, come
        death
Come life, he was fresh-sinewed every joint,
Each bone new-marrowed as whom gods anoint   500
Though mortal to their rescue. Now let sprawl
The snaky volumes hither! Is Typhon all
For Hercules to trample—good report
From Salinguerra only to extort?
        "So was I" (closed he his inculcating   505
A poet must be earth's essential king)
"So was I, royal so, and if I fail,
"'T is not the royalty ye witness quail,
"But one deposed who, caring not exert
"Its proper essence, trifled malapert   510

*basing these on
their proper
ground,*

"With accidents instead—good things assigned
"As heralds of a better thing behind—
"And, worthy through display of these, put forth
"Never the inmost all-surpassing worth
"That constitutes him king precisely since   515
"As yet no other spirit may evince
"Its like: the power he took most pride to test,

---

496 *1840* from) deep   498 *1840–68* death,   500 *1840,1863* Gods   501
1840–65 rescue: now   502 *1840* hither, Typhon's all   504 *1840* From
Salinguerra's   *505 {Indentation restored.}   *1840* ¶ So was I   *1863–89* "So
was I" {indented, *1868*}   505 *1840,1888,1889* inculcating   *1863–8* inculcating,   507 *1840* So . . . . fail   *508 {Editors' emendation, based on *1840.*}
1840 royalty . . . quail   *SB* quail>quail,   *1863–89* royalty, . . . quail,   512
1840 The herald of   515 *1840 proof* one>him   *1840,1863* King   516 *1840*
other creature may

---

502 *snaky volumes*: cf. Shelley, 'A Vision of the Sea', 141: 'the snake's
adamantine voluminousness'. L. 'volumen' means anything rolled up.
Is Typhon all: just as Hercules had many labours to accomplish, so Sordello
had more to do than merely to win Salinguerra's good opinion. Hercules
strangled two snakes while he was still in his cradle: killing Typhon was not
one of his exploits, but he did destroy the Hydra, often said to be the fruit of
Echidna's union with Typhon.
505 *inculcating*: stressed on the second syllable, as in Johnson.
510 *malapert*: presumptuously, frivolously.
513 *And* ∧ *worthy* (*1840*): 'who,' *SB*.
515–16 *constitutes . . . may*: altered to 'constituted' and 'might': *SB*.
517 *the power*: that of the dramatic poet.

"Whereby all forms of life had been professed
"At pleasure, forms already on the earth,
520   "Was but a means to power beyond, whose birth
"Should, in its novelty, be kingship's proof.
"Now, whether he came near or kept aloof
"The several forms he longed to imitate,
"Not there the kingship lay, he sees too late.
525   "Those forms, unalterable first as last,
"Proved him her copier, not the protoplast
"Of nature: what would come of being free,
"By action to exhibit tree for tree,
"Bird, beast, for beast and bird, or prove earth
            bore
530   "One veritable man or woman more?
"Means to an end, such proofs are: what the
            end?
"Let essence, whatsoe'er it be, extend—
"Never contract. Already you include
"The multitude; then let the multitude
535   "Include yourself; and the result were new:
"Themselves before, the multitude turn you.
"This were to live and move and have, in them,
"Your being, and secure a diadem   *recognizing true*
"You should transmit (because no cycle yearns   *dignity in service,*

---

520 *1840* power whose novel birth   521 *1840* proof—   522 *1840*
aloof,   523,524 {not in *1840*.}   525 *1840* forms . . . . first to last   526
1840 her copy, not   527 *1840* Nature: what could . . . . free   *1863* nature:
what could . . . . free   *1865* nature: what could . . . . free,   529 *1840* Bird,
beast   530 *1840* A veritable   531 *1840* proofs; and what the end?   532
1840 proof whatso'er>whatsoe'er   *1840* Your essence,   533 *1840,1863* contract!   534 *1840* multitude; now let   535 *1840* yourself, and the result is
new;   536 *1840* you;   537 *1840* have (in them)   539 *1840* That's to
transmit

---

522 *kept aloof*: 'what he longed to imitate,': *SB*.   526 *her*: nature's.
    protoplast: originator, creator, as in 'Abt Vogler' 34, *Fifine* 2165, and twice in
Parleyings ('Furini' 445, 'de Lairesse' 170).
    527 *what would come*: what good would it be if he were free to reproduce (by
his art) trees, birds, beasts and human beings as they already are?
    529 *Bird, beast* (*1840*): 'Bird, beast,' Domett.
    532 *extend*: underlined in *SB*.
    537 *to live and move*: 'For in him [the LORD] we live, and move, and have our
being': Acts 17:28.
    539 *no cycle yearns*: cf. Shelley, *Adonais*, xxvii, where Keats is addressed in
these words: 'Or hadst thou waited the full cycle, when / Thy spirit should
have filled its crescent sphere, / The monsters of life's waste had fled from thee

"Beyond itself, but on itself returns)   540
"When, the full sphere in wane, the world
        o'erlaid
"Long since with you, shall have in turn obeyed
"Some orb still prouder, some displayer, still
"More potent than the last, of human will,
"And some new king depose the old. Of such   545
"Am I—whom pride of this elates too much?
"Safe, rather say, 'mid troops of peers again;
"I, with my words, hailed brother of the train
"Deeds once sufficed: for, let the world roll
        back,
"Who fails, through deeds howe'er diverse,
        retrack   550
"My purpose still, my task? A teeming crust—
"Air, flame, earth, wave at conflict! Then, needs
        must
"Emerge some Calm embodied, these refer
"The brawl to—yellow-bearded Jupiter?
"No! Saturn; some existence like a pact   555
"And protest against Chaos, some first fact

541 1840 When   544 1840 Will,   545 1840,1863 King   547 1840
mid   549 1840 Once deeds sufficed: 550 1840 deeds diverse so e'er,
re-track   1863–8 deeds howe'er diverse, re-track   552 1840 conflict—see!
Needs must   553 1840 proof calm>Calm   1840 embodied   554–5 1840
(Saturn—no yellow-bearded Jupiter!)|The brawl to; some   1863–8 The brawl
to;—yellow-bearded Jupiter?|No! Saturn; some

like deer'. Browning is portraying the history of mankind as the history of its
Heroes, and arguing that each age limits itself to what is within the 'orb' of the
current Hero, progress coming about as the era of one Hero gives place to that
of another.
   541 o'erlaid: covered, influenced by Sordello.
   545–6 Of such / Am I: i.e. I am one of those proud orbs, those natural kings of
men: a statement somewhat confusingly placed. For the general conception, cf.
Keats, 'Hyperion', ii. 212: 'So on our heels a fresh perfection treads'.
   549 Deeds once sufficed: the age purely of action, and of men of action, has
passed or is passing. 'My purpose' (551) is that of all leaders of mankind, in
every age.
   let the world roll back: go back to the beginning of history, to the original
Chaos. Saturn first emerged as a principle of Calm, to be followed by Jupiter.
You will see the task on which I am or should be engaged as continuous from
the beginning. The revision from 'calm' to 'Calm' in 1840 proof is significant: cf.
'His dam held that the Quiet made all things': 'Caliban upon Setebos', 170. For
'retrack' (550) see also Paracelsus, v. 389.
   553–4 these refer / The brawl to: which 'Air, flame, earth [and] wave' all
acknowledge as arbitrator.

"I' the faint of time. My deep of life, I know
"Is unavailing e'en to poorly show" . . .
(For here the Chief immeasurably yawned)
    . . . "Deeds in their due gradation till Song
560   dawned—
"The fullest effluence of the finest mind,
"All in degree, no way diverse in kind
"From minds about it, minds which, more or
         less,
"Lofty or low, move seeking to impress
"Themselves on somewhat; but one mind has
565   climbed
"Step after step, by just ascent sublimed.
"Thought is the soul of act, and, stage by stage,
"Soul is from body still to disengage
"As tending to a freedom which rejects
570 "Such help and incorporeally affects
"The world, producing deeds but not by deeds,
"Swaying, in others, frames itself exceeds,
"Assigning them the simpler tasks it used
"To patiently perform till Song produced
575 "Acts, by thoughts only, for the mind: divest
"Mind of e'en Thought, and, lo, God's
         unexpressed

557 *1840* Time . . . my . . . . know, *1863–8* time. My . . . . know,   558
1840 show   560 *1840* Deeds   561 *1840* mind   563 *1840* From those
about us, minds . . . . less, *1863–8* From minds about it, minds . . . .
less   564 *1840* low, in moving seek impress   566 *1840* sublimed: 568
1840,1863 Is soul from body   574 *1840* As patiently

557 *the faint of time*: the dim past. OED cites this as its only example of the
absolute use of the adjective.
    My deep of life: my life even at its most intense. Cf. Shelley, 'Ode to Liberty',
ix: 'from the human spirit's deepest deep'.
    561 *effluence*: cf. *Adonais*, xlvi. 2: 'whose transmitted effluence cannot die'.
The thought is remarkably close to that of Shelley's *A Defence of Poetry*,
published in 1840 and therefore too late to have influenced *Sordello*: see, e.g.,
'Poetry is the record of the best and happiest moments of the happiest and best
minds': 9th para. from end.
    566 *by just ascent sublimed*: the meaning is probably that the mind of each regal
man is purified by the fact that he has ascended.
    572 *frames*: frames of mind: see ii. 671 n.
    575–6 *divest* / *Mind of e'en Thought*: 'As you take from thought the need of
expressing itself by (its own) *deeds*—i.e. *corporeal actions*. so take from mind the
need of expressing itself by thoughts—i.e. *mental actions*—& you have God's
naked wil[l]—So doing—the Germans get their pure Reason': *Domett*.

"Will dawns above us! All then is to win
"Save that. How much for me, then? where
  begin
"My work? About me, faces! and they flock,
"The earnest faces. What shall I unlock   580
"By song? behold me prompt, whate'er it be,
"To minister: how much can mortals see
"Of Life? No more than so? I take the task
"And marshal you Life's elemental masque,
"Show Men, on evil or on good lay stress,   585
"This light, this shade make prominent, suppress
"All ordinary hues that softening blend
"Such natures with the level. Apprehend
"Which sinner is, which saint, if I allot
"Hell, Purgatory, Heaven, a blaze or blot,   590
"To those you doubt concerning! I enwomb
"Some wretched Friedrich with his red-hot
  tomb;
"Some dubious spirit, Lombard Agilulph
"With the black chastening river I engulph!

whether
successively
that of epoist,

---

*577 {Reading of *1863,1865*}   *1840* Will dawns above us. But so much to
win   *1868–89* Will draws above us! All then is to win   578 *1840* Ere that! A
lesser round of steps within   *1863,1865* Save that! How much for me, then?
where begin   579 *1840* The last. About   580 *1840,1863* The earnest
faces!   583–5 *1840* No more? I covet the first task| And marshal yon Life's
elemental Masque| Of Men,   588–90 *1840* level: apprehend| Which evil
is, which good, if I allot| Your Hell, the Purgatory, Heaven ye wot,   591
1840 concerning: 592 *1840* tomb,   593 *1840* *proof* Agilulph—>
Agilulph   594 *1840–65* engulph;

---

580 *The earnest faces*: of the Multitude.
583 *I take the task*: cf. *1840*. I am prepared to attempt the first task, that of
portraying life as an 'elemental masque', with good and bad characters as in a
sort of Morality play.
590 *a blaze or blot*: a good or bad mark.
592 *Some wretched Friedrich*: the fiery tombs occur in *Inferno*, x, where
Friedrich II is mentioned at line 119. Agilulph (not in Dante) became King of
the Lombards in 590, when he was chosen as husband by the widowed Queen
Theodolinde: 'dubious' no doubt refers to his being a professed Arian. 'Some
unapproached Matilda' must refer to the same woman as 'the superb Matilda'
(iii. 491–2) and 'the great Matilda' (iv. 570), namely the celebrated Countess of
Tuscany. It is more evident why she should be destined for Heaven than for the
'languors of the planet of decline', presumably identical with 'the Swooning-
sphere' (v. 994), i.e. that of Venus. (Almost all the old commentators identify
the 'Matelda' who acts as Dante's guide through the Terrestrial Paradise with
this Countess Matilda). The 'black chastening river' is probably not the Styx,
which is one of the rivers of Hell, but the vast expanse of water which
surrounds Purgatory.

595   "Some unapproached Matilda I enshrine
"With languors of the planet of decline—
"These, fail to recognize, to arbitrate
"Between henceforth, to rightly estimate
"Thus marshalled in the masque! Myself, the
      while,
600   "As one of you, am witness, shrink or smile
"At my own showing! Next age—what 's to do?
"The men and women stationed hitherto   *dramatist, or, so to*
"Will I unstation, good and bad, conduct   *call him,*
                                                 analyst,
"Each nature to its farthest, or obstruct
605   "At soonest, in the world: light, thwarted, breaks
"A limpid purity to rainbow flakes,
"Or shadow, massed, freezes to gloom: behold
"How such, with fit assistance to unfold,
"Or obstacles to crush them, disengage
"Their forms, love, hate, hope, fear, peace make,
610   war wage,
"In presence of you all! Myself, implied
"Superior now, as, by the platform's side,
"I bade them do and suffer,—would last content
"The world . . . no—that 's too far! I
      circumvent
615   "A few, my masque contented, and to these
"Offer unveil the last of mysteries—
"Man's inmost life shall have yet freer play:

---

596 *1840 proof* splendours>languors   597 *1840* These . . . . recognise, *1863–8* These, ... recognise,   605 *1840* Light,   607 *1840* Or Shadow, helped, freezes   611 *1840* Myself   613–15 *1840* Bidding them do and suffer to content| The world . . . no—that I wait not—circumvent| A few it has contented,   616–17 *1840* mysteries|I boast! Man's life

---

597 *These* ∧ *fail* (*1840*): 'will you': SB. The exclamation-mark presumably indicates a challenge.
599 *Myself, the while*: cf. i. 22 ff.
603 *Will I unstation*: in the next age of poetry there will no longer be static characters: I shall take good and bad characters and allow some the maximum opportunity of development while I frustrate others from the beginning. When light meets an obstacle it reveals all the colours of a rainbow (if the obstacle is a prism), while if a shadow meets an obstacle it becomes blackness. Watch and you will see how men and women, given the opportunity to develop or 'obstacles to crush them', will reveal their qualities before your eyes!
612 *the platform's side*: cf. i. 30 n.

"Once more I cast external things away,
"And natures composite, so decompose
"That" . . . Why, he writes *Sordello!*

                             "How I rose,   620
"And how have you advanced! since evermore
"Yourselves effect what I was fain before
"Effect, what I supplied yourselves suggest,
"What I leave bare yourselves can now invest.
"How we attain to talk as brothers talk,   625
"In half-words, call things by half-names, no
    balk
"From discontinuing old aids. To-day
"Takes in account the work of Yesterday:
"Has not the world a Past now, its adept
"Consults ere he dispense with or accept   630
"New aids? a single touch more may enhance,
"A touch less turn to insignificance
"Those structures' symmetry the past has
    strewed
"The world with, once so bare. Leave the mere
    rude
"Explicit details! 't is but brother's speech   635

618–19 *1840* away|And Natures, varied now, so decompose   620,621
1840 That . . . but enough! Why fancy how I rose,|Or rather you advanced
since evermore   624–5 *1840* invest?|How we attained to   627 *1840*
aids—To-day   628 *1840* Yesterday—   631 *1840 proof* aids—>aids?
633 *1840–65* Past   634 *1840 proof* bare? Leave>bare: leave 1840 Your
world . . . . bare: leave   635 *1840* details, 'tis

---

619 *And natures composite*: having created characters which are real, not mere
symbols of good and evil, he will go further and analyse human character. For
'decompose' cf. 'Epilogue' to *Dramatis Personæ*, 100.
  620 *he writes* Sordello!: Whyte reverts to *1840* here, believing that these words
produce an anticlimax 'which ruins the whole speech and is only intelligible
when we remember the outcry as to Sordello's intelligibility which followed
its publication'. He complains that 'Browning sacrificed his art to his love of
sarcasm and a desire to laugh at his critics when he rewrote this line'. Cf. our
note to i. 4, however, and the passage about 'The childish skit or scoff' in
Sordello's poem 'Charlemagne' at iii. 632 ff. Browning is here emphasizing
that *Sordello* itself is 'but an episode' in his own poetic life.
  "*How I rose*: he reflects on the progress of his own poetry, and the advances
made by his audience.
  621 *And how have you advanced!*: cf. i. 25 ff. Now he (too optimistically)
envisages the possibility of the sort of relationship between poet and audience
regretfully put aside at i. 14 ff.
  624 *invest*: with attributes.   626 *balk*: hindrance.

"We need, speech where an accent's change gives
     each
"The other's soul—no speech to understand
"By former audience: need was then to expand,
"Expatiate—hardly were we brothers! true—
640 "Nor I lament my small remove from you,
"Nor reconstruct what stands already. Ends
"Accomplished turn to means: my art intends
"New structure from the ancient: as they   *who turns in*
     changed   *due course*
                                                         synthetist.
"The spoils of every clime at Venice, ranged
645 "The horned and snouted Libyan god, upright
"As in his desert, by some simple bright
"Clay cinerary pitcher—Thebes as Rome,
"Athens as Byzant rifled, till their Dome
"From earth's reputed consummations razed
650 "A seal, the all-transmuting Triad blazed
"Above. Ah, whose that fortune? Ne'ertheless
"E'en he must stoop contented to express
"No tithe of what 's to say—the vehicle
"Never sufficient: but his work is still
655 "For faces like the faces that select

638 *1840* audience—need was then expand,   639 *1840* were they
brothers!   640 *1840* my less remove   641 *1840* proof Wish> Nor *1840*
already: ends   645 *1840* Lybian God,   650 *1840* A seal   654 *1840*
sufficient—

637 *to understand*: i.e. to be understood.
639 *hardly were we brothers!*: I admit that we (you, my audience, and myself)
were hardly brothers then. As things are now, I neither lament that we are
much closer nor attempt to rewrite what I have already written.
644 *at Venice*: see the account of Dandolo and the plundering of Constantinople at iii. 131 n.
645 *Libyan god*: in Libya Jupiter was worshipped under the name of Ammon,
and represented in the likeness of a ram.
648 *their Dome*: that of 'St. Mark's [which] is constructed out of various
objects originally intended to illustrate [adorn] some other cult than that
which, by the superior power of the Christian symbol, has exclusively appropriated earth's homage': Browning to Furnivall, 27 March 1889: *Trumpeter*, p.
157.
649 *consummations*: highest achievements.
650 *A seal*: that of their supposed perfection, removed by the superiority of
the great Cathedral. Cf. *Paracelsus*, v. 711–12: 'So far the seal / Is put on life'.
651 *whose that fortune?*: what poet is destined to incorporate and transcend the
earlier masterpieces of poetry, as St. Mark's incorporates and transcends earlier
masterpieces of religious art and architecture?
653 *the vehicle*: cf. ii. 484 and 602 and v. 244.
655 *faces*: those of Mankind.

"The single service I am bound effect,—
"That bid me cast aside such fancies, bow
"Taurello to the Guelf cause, disallow
"The Kaiser's coming—which with heart, soul,
    strength,
"I labour for, this eve, who feel at length   660
"My past career's outrageous vanity,
"And would, as its amends, die, even die
"Now I first estimate the boon of life,
"If death might win compliance—sure, this strife
"Is right for once—the People my support."   665
    My poor Sordello! what may we extort
By this, I wonder? Palma's lighted eyes
Turned to Taurello who, long past surprise,
Began, "You love him—what you 'd say at large
"Let me say briefly. First, your father's charge   670
"To me, his friend, peruse: I guessed indeed
"You were no stranger to the course decreed.
"He bids me leave his children to the saints:
"As for a certain project, he acquaints
"The Pope with that, and offers him the best   675
"Of your possessions to permit the rest
"Go peaceably—to Ecelin, a stripe
"Of soil the cursed Vicentines will gripe,

656 1840 A single . . . . effect   1863,1865 The single . . . . effect,   657 1840
Nor murmur, bid me, still as poet, bow   1863,1865 And bid me cast aside such
fancies, bow   660 1840 proof for>for,   662 1840 would (as vain
amends)   664 1840 proof him—confident>Taurello—sure   1840 So death
might bow Taurello—sure this strife   665 1840 Is the last strife—the People
my support.   668–9 1840 who, as past surprise,|Began, You   670 1840 If
I say briefly? First   672–3 1840 decreed|Us both: I leave

658 the Guelf cause: the clearest statement of the aim which now seems to
Sordello the greatest which he can achieve, that of persuading Taurello to
espouse the Guelf cause.
662 (as vain amends) (1840): 'make some sacrifice': SB.
663 Now I first estimate: now that I for the first time appreciate what a blessing
life is, I would even be prepared to give it up if that would win Taurello over to
the Guelf cause.
666 My poor Sordello!: the narrator acknowledges the wildness of the preceding speech: 'we' expresses ironic commiseration on the part of the narrator.
669 "You love him: from one point of view, an exemplification of Taurello's
insight into human character: from another, an example of Browning's stac-
cato development of the story.
670 your father's charge: the charge laid on Taurello by the Monk.

This for one day:
now, serve as
Guelf!

"—To Alberic, a patch the Trevisan
680   "Clutches already; extricate, who can,
"Treville, Villarazzi, Puissolo,
"Loria and Cartiglione!—all must go,
"And with them go my hopes. 'T is lost, then!
   Lost
"This eve, our crisis, and some pains it cost
685   "Procuring; thirty years—as good I'd spent
"Like our admonisher! But each his bent
"Pursues: no question, one might live absurd
"Oneself this while, by deed as he by word,
"Persisting to obtrude an influence where
"'T is made account of, much as . . . nay, you
690   fare
"With twice the fortune, youngster!—I submit,
"Happy to parallel my waste of wit   *Salinguerra,*
"With the renowned Sordello's: you decide   *dislodged from*
"A course for me. Romano may abide   *his post,*
695   "Romano,—Bacchus! After all, what dearth
"Of Ecelins and Alberics on earth?
"Say there 's a prize in prospect, must disgrace
"Betide competitors, unless they style
"Themselves Romano? Were it worth my while
700   "To try my own luck! But an obscure place

---

682 *1840* Cartiglione, Loria—all go, *1863–8* Cartiglione, Loria!—all
go,   683 *1840* hopes!   687 *1840* Pursues—   *688 {Reading of
1840–68} *1888,1889* word 690 *1840* of much   691 *1840* youngster—
693 *1840* Sordello's—   694 *1840* me—   695 *1840* Bacchus! Who'd
suppose the dearth   697 *1840 proof* prospect>prospect, *1840* a thing in
698 *1840* competitors? An obscure place   699–700 {not in *1840*.}

681 *Treville*: cf. i. 252, where Cartiglion and Loria are among the fiefs of the
family. Verci iii. 183 gives the text of a letter (dated 1221) from Honorius III to
Ecelin the Monk commending his turning to religion and agreeing that he
should retain for himself Godego, 'Tresvillas cum Pudissolo, Villarazo, Lorlea
[*sic*], Ramone, Castilione', and other fiefs.
686 *his bent*: cf. ii. 120 and iii. 358.
687 *one might live*: Taurello reflects that it had proved possible for him to have
lived as futile a life as Sordello's, achieving nothing by action as Sordello had
achieved nothing by poetry.
690 *you fare*: you have twice as much good luck as I have!
694 *Romano may abide*: let the House of Romano look to its own fortunes!
698 *competitors*: for an instant Taurello seems to think of competing with the
House of Romano, on his own behalf—only to reject the notion.

"Suits me—there wants a youth to bustle, stalk
"And attitudinize—some fight, more talk,
"Most flaunting badges—how, I might make
    clear
"Since Friedrich's very purposes lie here
"—Here, pity they are like to lie! For me,   705
"With station fixed unceremoniously
"Long since, small use contesting; I am but
"The liegeman—you are born the lieges: shut
"That gentle mouth now! or resume your kin
"In your sweet self; were Palma Ecelin   710
"For me to work with! Could that neck endure
"This bauble for a cumbrous garniture,
"She should . . . or might one bear it for her?
    Stay—
"I have not been so flattered many a day
"As by your pale friend—Bacchus! The least help   715
"Would lick the hind's fawn to a lion's whelp:
"His neck is broad enough—a ready tongue
"Beside: too writhled—but, the main thing,
    young—
"I could . . . why, look ye!"
                                And the badge was thrown
Across Sordello's neck: "This badge alone   720
"Makes you Romano's Head—becomes superb
"On your bare neck, which would, on mine,
    disturb

701 *1840* youth, bustle, one to stalk   702 *1840 proof* talk> talk,   703 *1840*
badges—'twere not hard make clear   *1863,1865* badges—how, I might make
clear,   705 *1840* —Here—   706 *1840* Whose station's fixed unceremoniously   708 *1840–68* liegeman, ... lieges—   709 *1840* now!—   710
1840 self; Palma were Ecelin   711 *1840* For me and welcome! Could   713
1840 You should . . . or might one bear it for you? Stay—   716 *1840–68*
whelp—   718 *1840–68* Beside—   719 *1840* I could . . . why look
ye!   720 *1840 proof* act> badge   *1840* neck: this   721–2 *1840* Head—the
Lombard's Curb|Turns on your neck

709 *resume your kin*: take upon yourself the responsibilities of your House.
716 *a lion's whelp*: a phrase common in Shakespeare, as in *I Henry* IV. iii. 3.
147. The notion (in Shakespeare and others) that bears lick their cubs into shape
is also relevant here.
718 *writhled*: wrinkled. Taurello earlier commented on Sordello's careworn
appearance, e.g. at ll. 360–2 above.

"The pauldron," said Taurello. A mad act, *in moving,*
Nor even dreamed about before—in fact, *opens a door*
Not when his sportive arm rose for the nonce— *to Sordello,*
But he had dallied overmuch, this once,
With power: the thing was done, and he, aware
The thing was done, proceeded to declare—
(So like a nature made to serve, excel
In serving, only feel by service well!)
—That he would make Sordello that and more.
"As good a scheme as any. What 's to pore
"At in my face?" he asked—"ponder instead
"This piece of news; you are Romano's Head!
"One cannot slacken pace so near the goal,
"Suffer my Azzo to escape heart-whole
"This time! For you there 's Palma to espouse—
"For me, one crowning trouble ere I house
"Like my compeer."

                    On which ensued a strange
And solemn visitation; there came change
O'er every one of them; each looked on each:
Up in the midst a truth grew, without speech.
And when the giddiness sank and the haze
Subsided, they were sitting, no amaze,

---

723 *1840* My pauldron,   724 *1840* Nor dreamed about a moment
since—in fact *1863,1865* Not even dreamed about before—in fact,   728
1840 declare   730–1 *1840* well)|That he should make him all he said and
more: 732 *1840* any: what's *1863–8* any! What's   733 *1840* face? he
asked—ponder *1863,1865* face?" he asked—ponder   734 *1840* Head—
739 *1840* compeer.   740 *1840* And solemn visitation—mighty change
741 *1840* them—each looked on each—   742 *1840* speech,

---

723 *The pauldron*: the shoulder-plate of a suit of armour. Cf. l. 874.
726 *once*: 'after his old fashion': *SB*.
728 *to declare*: 'in his [? sudden] relief': *SB*.
734 *Romano's Head*: 'You put yourself in the right place,—no-one else will
stand there: I find you there, & take you': *SB*.
735 *One cannot slacken*: above this line, at the top of page 203, *SB* has: 'After
all, I have gone too [?] earnestly to work'.
739 *Like my compeer*: the Monk: cf. iv. 696. *SB* adds, in the margin: 'I will
make you all in all here—Keep your badge'.
742 *a truth grew*: namely the fact that Sordello is Taurello's son. At 732 we
heard that Sordello was studying Taurello's face, perhaps with some intuitive
dawning of recognition. We now hear that the true paternity of Sordello had
been confided to Palma by Adelaide, on her deathbed.
744 *no amaze*: there was no amazement: an absolute construction.

who is declared
Salinguerra's
son,

Sordello with the baldric on, his sire   745
Silent, though his proportions seemed aspire
Momently; and, interpreting the thrill,—
Nigh at its ebb,—Palma was found there still
Relating somewhat Adelaide confessed
A year ago, while dying on her breast,—   750
Of a contrivance, that Vicenza night
When Ecelin had birth. "Their convoy's flight,
"Cut off a moment, coiled inside the flame
"That.wallowed like a dragon at his game
"The toppling city through—San Biagio
    rocks!   755
"And wounded lies in her delicious locks
"Retrude, the frail mother, on her face,
"None of her wasted, just in one embrace
"Covering her child: when, as they lifted her,
"Cleaving the tumult, mighty, mightier   760
"And mightiest Taurello's cry outbroke,
"Leapt like a tongue of fire that cleaves the
    smoke,
"Midmost to cheer his Mantuans onward—
    drown
"His colleague Ecelin's clamour, up and down
"The disarray: failed Adelaide see then   765

---

746 *1840* Silent   747 *1840–68* thrill   *748 *1840* Nigh at its ebb, Palma
you found was still   *1863* Nigh at its ebb, Palma was found there still *1865,1868*
Night at its ebb, Palma was found there still   *1888,1889* Night at its
ebb,—Palma was found there still   750 *1840* breast,   751 *1840–68* contrivance that Vicenza night,   752 *1840* Her Ecelin had birth: their convoy's
flight   764 *1840* His colleague's clamour, Ecelin's, up, down

746 *though his proportions*: although he seemed to grow larger every moment.
747 *interpreting*: i.e. explaining, putting into words.
748–9 *still | Relating*: SB has, in the margin, '(The [? face] *through* the
disguise)'.
751 *that Vicenza night*: cf. ii. 322 ff. (the story as told to the youthful Sordello,
according to which he was said to be the son of Elcorte) and iv. 723 ff.
(Taurello's recollection).
755 *San Biagio*: cf. iii. 422 (and iv. 727). Here the reference is either to the
Porta S. Biagio or to a former church of the name (as Whyte suggests).
757 *Retrude*: Taurello's wife, now revealed as Sordello's mother.
762 *Leapt like a tongue of fire*: cf. Isaiah 30:27: 'his tongue [is] as a devouring
fire'.
765 *failed Adelaide see then*: '(mesmerism)': *SB*.

"Who was the natural chief, the man of men?
"Outstripping time, her infant there burst
   swathe,
"Stood up with eyes haggard beyond the scathe
"From wandering after his heritage
"Lost once and lost for aye: and why that rage,
"That deprecating glance? A new shape leant
"On a familiar shape—gloatingly bent
"O'er his discomfiture; 'mid wreaths it wore,
"Still one outflamed the rest—her child's before
"'T was Salinguerra's for his child: scorn, hate,
"Rage now might startle her when all too late!
"Then was the moment!—rival's foot had
   spurned

770

775

766–7 *1840* Chief, the Man of Men?|Outstripping time her Ecelin burst swathe,   768 *1840 proof* scathe,>scathe *1840* with haggard eyes beyond   770 *1840* aye—what could engage   *1863–8* aye—and why that rage,   771 *1840* Shape   772 *1840* Shape—   776 *1840–65* Rage, startled her from Ecelin—too late!   *1868* "Rage startled her from Ecelin—too late!   777 *1840* A moment's work, and rival's   *1863* Then was the moment! rival's   *1865* Then was the moment! a rival's

766 *chief . . . man of men*: note capitals in *1840*: according to Palma, Adelaide (helped by her magical powers) realised that Taurello Salinguerra, and not her husband the Monk, was the natural leader of men.
767 *burst swathe*: cf. Robert Blair, *The Grave*, l. 138: 'Like new-born infant wound up in his swathes'. Whyte suggests that 'This strange vision of Adelaide's may have been suggested . . . by a passage in Pietro Gerardo's *Vita d'Ezzelino III*'. All that Gerardo states, however, is that, wishing to know the future, and being very learned, 'she had recourse to Astrology, and found that her children were greatly threatened by the stars', but could see no more: p. [8v]. Duff offers this prose version: 'Her infant, turned to a youth, stood up in her view with eyes more haggard than the search after an inheritance lost for ever could have made them: why gave they forth such glances of rage and of keenly wounded feeling? Because his inheritance had gone to the son of his father's liegeman. She beheld a new shape—Taurello Salinguerra's son—gloating over the discomfiture of the familiar form of her own son; and, amid the many wreaths this new shape wore, the most glorious was the wreath that had been her son's before Taurello won it by his prowess and gave it to his child. Now, in her vision, as she beheld all this, she regarded her weakling husband with scorn and hate and rage; but these passions came too late to impel her to guard against calamity: the mischief was done. Then, she thought, looking back, still in vision, with this scene before her eyes, to the Vicenza night—then was the time to act—then she could have done something, and no rival's foot would ever have spurned her House to earth'.
768 *haggard eyes beyond the scathe* (*1840*): SB expands to 'malignant beyond what came from the scathe'.
776 *startled her from Ecelin* (*1840*): SB inserts 'III', meaning her son, the Tyrant. *too late!*: 'now' was the time!' SB.
777 ∧ *A moment's work* (*1840*): 'Had she taken': SB.

"Never that House to earth else! Sense
    returned—
"The act conceived, adventured and complete,
"They bore away to an obscure retreat   780

*hidden hitherto
by Adelaide's
policy.*

"Mother and child—Retrude's self not slain"
(Nor even here Taurello moved) "though pain
"Was fled; and what assured them most 't was
    fled,
"All pain, was, if they raised the pale hushed
    head
"'T would turn this way and that, waver awhile,   785
"And only settle into its old smile—
"(Graceful as the disquieted water-flag
"Steadying itself, remarked they, in the quag
"On either side their path)—when suffered look
"Down on her child. They marched: no sign
    once shook   790
"The company's close litter of crossed spears
"Till, as they reached Goito, a few tears
"Slipped in the sunset from her long black lash,
"And she was gone. So far the action rash;
"No crime. They laid Retrude in the font,   795
"Taurello's very gift, her child was wont
"To sit beneath—constant as eve he came
"To sit by its attendant girls the same

778 *1840–68* that brow to earth! Ere sense   779 *1840–65* adventured,   780 *1840* They stole away towards an   781 *1840* slain   782 *1840*
though   784 *1840* if you raised   786 *1840* smile   789 *1840*
path)   790 *1840* Downward: they marched: no sign of life once
shook   792 *1840 proof* Goito;>Goito,   794 *1840–65* rash—

---

778 *Never that brow to earth!* ∧ (*1840*): 'The temptation was too strong': SB.
780 *They bore away*: appalled by what she had seen in her vision, Adelaide
had had Sordello and his mother Retrude (who was not dead) conveyed to a
hiding-place.
787 *water-flag*: the yellow iris, that grows by the edge of rivers, as in *Marmion*,
vi. xxxvii.
790 *Downward* (*1840*): 'to her child': SB.
795 *No crime*: although moving the seriously injured Retrude was inhumane,
it could not be reckoned murder.
They ∧ *laid*: 'drew the child from underneath her and': SB.
the font: the font which played so important a part in the life of the youthful
Sordello (i. 410) thus turns out to be his mother's tomb. Cf. ii. 1002, iii. 1. At iv.
147 we gather that Taurello had had it conveyed to Mantua for Adelaide.
796 *was wont*: 'afterwards': SB.
797 *beneath*: 'a little nameless boy': SB.

"As one of them. For Palma, she would blend
800　"With this magnific spirit to the end,
"That ruled her first; but scarcely had she dared
"To disobey the Adelaide who scared
"Her into vowing never to disclose
"A secret to her husband, which so froze
805　"His blood at half-recital, she contrived
"To hide from him Taurello's infant lived,
"Lest, by revealing that, himself should mar
"Romano's fortunes. And, a crime so far,
"Palma received that action: she was told
810　"Of Salinguerra's nature, of his cold
"Calm acquiescence in his lot! But free
"To impart the secret to Romano, she
"Engaged to repossess Sordello of
"His heritage, and hers, and that way doff
"The mask, but after years, long years: while
815　　now,
"Was not Romano's sign-mark on that brow?"
Across Taurello's heart his arms were locked:　　*How the discovery*
And when he did speak 't was as if he mocked　　*moves*
　　　　　　　　　　　　　　　　　　　　　　　Salinguerra,

---

800 *1840* With this magific spirit to the end {*SB* corrects to 'magnific'}　801 *1840–65* first—　806 *1840* lived　808 *1840* fortunes: and,　810 *1840* nature, and his　812 *1840* Impart the　815 *1840 proof* mask>mask,　*1840* years!—while now *1863,1865* years!—while now,　816 *1840* brow?　817 *1840 proof* locked>locked:　818 *1840* And 'twas, when speak he did, as

---

799 *As one of them*: 'Do you remember how his life rolled by, meant there to live & die?' *SB*.

800 *this magnific spirit*: Sordello's, which Palma knew destined to rule her even before the day of the Love Court: cf. iii. 354 ff. Adelaide had terrified her into a promise never to reveal the truth to the Monk, however.

to the end (*1840*): 'that she had discovered and [?]': *SB*.

801 *scarcely*: only with great difficulty.

804 *A secret*: *SB* seems to revise to 'The secret', inserting 'that' between 'recital' and 'she' in the next line.

805 *at half-recital*: since Adelaide did not tell him that the child remained alive.

809 *received*: accepted and therefore connived at (which was criminal).

811 *But free*: but now that she was free (because of Adelaide's death) to tell Romano of the secret, she undertook to restore Sordello's rightful heritage to him (it was also hers), so putting aside the disguise which had been assumed for so many long years. Does not Sordello's brow proclaim that he is the true representative of Romano?

812 *the secret to Romano*: *SB* expands to: 'the secret to the Head of Romano, only, she had long ago silently'.

816 *on that brow?*: 'It was a strange, fit occasion to tell all': *SB*.

The minstrel, "who had not to move," he said,
"Nor stir—should fate defraud him of a shred   820
"Of his son's infancy? much less his youth!"
(Laughingly all this)—"which to aid, in truth,
"Himself, reserved on purpose, had not grown
"Old, not too old—'t was best they kept alone
"Till now, and never idly met till now;"   825
—Then, in the same breath, told Sordello how
All intimations of this eve's event
Were lies, for Friedrich must advance to Trent,
Thence to Verona, then to Rome, there stop,
Tumble the Church down, institute a-top   830
The Alps a Prefecture of Lombardy:
—"That 's now!—no prophesying what may be
"Anon, with a new monarch of the clime,
"Native of Gesi, passing his youth's prime
"At Naples. Tito bids my choice decide   835
"On whom . . ."
            "Embrace him, madman!" Palma cried,
Who through the laugh saw sweat-drops burst
      apace,
And his lips blanching: he did not embrace

---

819 *1840 proof* minstrel . . . . move>minstrel, ... move,   *1840* who had
not to move,   820 *1840* Not stir—should Fate   *1863* "Not stir—should
Fate   *1865* "Not stir—should fate   821 *1840* Of this son's infancy? much
less of youth   *1863–8* Of his son's infancy? much less of his youth!"   822
1840 this) which   824 *1840* —'twas better keep alone   825 *1840* idly meet
till now: 827 *1840* The intimations   828 *1840* Were futile—Friedrich
means advance   829 *1840* Rome—there stop—   832 *1840* —That's
now— no   833 *1840* Anon, beneath a monarch   836 *1840* On whom
. . . ¶ Embrace him, madman! Palma cried   838 *1840,1863* lips'

---

819 *had not to move*: *Domett* substitutes 'was' for 'had', in an unnecessary
attempt to clarify the meaning.
827 *All intimations*: the meaning seems to be that Taurello is so over-excited
and incoherent that he goes on ('in the same breath') to say that the seeming
promise ('intimations') of this memorable evening must be fallacious, as
Friedrich's advance is certain.
832 *"That's now!*: that is the plan at this moment: later, we shall see.
833 *a new monarch*: Friedrich II, who was born at Iesi, near Ancona. By 1214
his position as German King was secure. In 1220 he had his young son Heinrich
crowned as German King, and returned to Italy, where he was crowned
Emperor.
835 *At Naples*: in fact Friedrich did not spend his youth in Naples. 'When he
shall find such a deputy made to his hand': *SB*.
Tito: 'Friedrich's Pretor': iv. 41. Taurello is beginning to wander, in his
over-excitement.

Sordello, but he laid Sordello's hand
On his own eyes, mouth, forehead.

840   Understand,

This while Sordello was becoming flushed
Out of his whiteness; thoughts rushed, fancies
    rushed;
He pressed his hand upon his head and signed
Both should forbear him. "Nay, the best 's   *and Sordello the*
    behind!"   *finally-determined,*

845 Taurello laughed—not quite with the same
    laugh:
"The truth is, thus we scatter, ay, like chaff
"These Guelfs, a despicable monk recoils
"From: nor expect a fickle Kaiser spoils
"Our triumph!—Friedrich? Think you, I intend

850 "Friedrich shall reap the fruits of blood I spend
"And brain I waste? Think you, the people clap
"Their hands at my out-hewing this wild gap
"For any Friedrich to fill up? 'T is mine—
"That 's yours: I tell you, towards some such
    design

855 "Have I worked blindly, yes, and idly, yes,
"And for another, yes—but worked no less
"With instinct at my heart; I else had swerved,
"While now—look round! My cunning has   *—the devil*
    preserved   *putting forth*
"Samminiato—that 's a central place   *his potency:*

860 "Secures us Florence, boy,—in Pisa's case,
"By land as she by sea; with Pisa ours,
"And Florence, and Pistoia, one devours

---

844 *1840* Nay, the best's behind!   846 *1840* The . . . . thus you scatter,   847 *1840* The Guelfs   848 *1840* From—   *860 {Reading of 1863–8}   *1840* boy, in Pisa's case   *1888,1889* boy,—in Pisa's case.

839 *laid Sordello's hand*: so swearing fealty to him. Taurello is now aware 'Who [is] the lord, who liegeman', of which he had been unaware at 472–3.

847 *a despicable monk*: Ecelin.

853–4 *'T is mine— | That's yours*: as the side-notes make clear, this is the prompting of the Devil. Domett comments: 'Taurello's notion of overthrowing the Church'.

859 *Samminiato*: Hildebrand built the church of San Miniato al Monte on this hill overlooking Florence in 1080. Taurello points out that control of it ensures the defence of Florence against any attack by land, as control of Pisa ensures its defence from the sea.

"The land at leisure! Gloriously dispersed—
"Brescia, observe, Milan, Piacenza first
"That flanked us (ah, you know not!) in the
        March;   865
"On these we pile, as keystone of our arch,
"Romagna and Bologna, whose first span
"Covered the Trentine and the Valsugan;
"Sofia's Egna by Bolgiano 's sure!" . . .
So he proceeded: half of all this, pure   870
Delusion, doubtless, nor the rest too true,
But what was undone he felt sure to do,
As ring by ring he wrung off, flung away
The pauldron-rings to give his sword-arm
        play—
Need of the sword now! That would soon adjust   875
Aught wrong at present; to the sword intrust
Sordello's whiteness, undersize: 't was plain
He hardly rendered right to his own brain—
Like a brave hound, men educate to pride
Himself on speed or scent nor aught beside,   880
As though he could not, gift by gift, match men!
Palma had listened patiently: but when
'T was time expostulate, attempt withdraw
Taurello from his child, she, without awe
Took off his iron arms from, one by one,   885
Sordello's shrinking shoulders, and, that done,
Made him avert his visage and relieve

---

869 *1840* sure . . .   870 *1840* proceeded. Half of all this pure

864 *Brescia*: he is rapidly sketching out a plan of campaign. 'The March' is the Trevisan March: 'the Trentine and the Valsugan' are key passes.

869 *Sofia's Egna*: Sofia was the Monk's third daughter by Adelaide. She married Enrico da Egna. Verci tells us that the Castle of Egna was 'situated between Trento and Bolgiano': i. 110. Three pages later he mentions that Sofia was widowed young, and was married to Taurello by her father.

872 *sure to do*: 'One *personal* triumph & [? retrograding]': *SB*.

874 *pauldron-rings*: cf. 723 n.

876 *to the sword intrust*: although Sordello was a physical weakling, it was to the sword that his fortunes should be entrusted.

877 *Sordello's whiteness*: 'qy. connexion from p. *208*', wrote the printer above this, the first line of p. 209. '*All right*', Browning replies emphatically: *1840 proof*.

878 *He hardly rendered right*: Taurello realized his own military gifts but underestimated his other great gifts.

Sordello (you might see his corslet heave
The while) who, loose, rose—tried to speak,
   then sank:
890   They left him in the chamber. All was blank.
    And even reeling down the narrow stair
Taurello kept up, as though unaware
Palma was by to guide him, the old device
—Something of Milan—"how we muster thrice
895   "The Torriani's strength there; all along
"Our own Visconti cowed them"—thus the
   song
Continued even while she bade him stoop,
Thrid somehow, by some glimpse of
   arrow-loop,
The turnings to the gallery below,
900   Where he stopped short as Palma let him go.
When he had sat in silence long enough
Splintering the stone bench, braving a rebuff
She stopped the truncheon; only to commence
One of Sordello's poems, a pretence   *since Sordello,*
905   For speaking, some poor rhyme of "Elys' hair   *who began by*
"And head that 's sharp and perfect like a pear,   *rhyming,*
"So smooth and close are laid the few fine locks
"Stained like pale honey oozed from topmost
   rocks
"Sun-blanched the livelong summer"—from his
   worst
910   Performance, the Goito, as his first:
And that at end, conceiving from the brow
And open mouth no silence would serve now,

---

889 *1840* speak—   890 *1840* chamber—all   *891 {Indentation
restored.}   *1840* ¶ And . . . . the castle-stair *1863–89* And . . . . the narrow
stair {indented, *1863–8*}   893 *1840* Palma was guide to him,   894 *1840*
—how   895 *1840–65* there—   896 *1840* them—   905 *1840* Elys'
909 *1840* Summer—   *1863,1865* Summer"—

---

893 *the old device*: the old plan.
895 *The Torriani's strength*: the Torrianis or Della Torres were a prominent
Milanese family, traditional opponents of the Visconti.
898 *arrow-loop*: a narrow aperture through which arrows might be fired.
902 *Splintering*: tapping and damaging the stone bench with the cane which
was the symbol of his office (i. 289). Palma goes on to recite 'the Goito lay' (ii.
151 ff.) in an attempt to soothe Taurello.

Went on to say the whole world loved that man
And, for that matter, thought his face, tho' wan,
Eclipsed the Count's—he sucking in each phrase   915
As if an angel spoke. The foolish praise
Ended, he drew her on his mailed knees, made
Her face a framework with his hands, a shade,
A crown, an aureole: there must she remain
(Her little mouth compressed with smiling pain   920
As in his gloves she felt her tresses twitch)
To get the best look at, in fittest niche
Dispose his saint. That done, he kissed her brow,
—"Lauded her father for his treason now,"
He told her, "only, how could one suspect   925
"The wit in him?—whose clansman, recollect,
"Was ever Salinguerra—she, the same,
"Romano and his lady—so, might claim
"To know all, as she should"—and thus begun
Schemes with a vengeance, schemes on schemes,
    "not one   930
"Fit to be told that foolish boy," he said,

may, even from the depths of failure,   "But only let Sordello Palma wed,
"—Then!"
          'T was a dim long narrow place at best:
Midway a sole grate showed the fiery West,
As shows its corpse the world's end some split
    tomb—   935
A gloom, a rift of fire, another gloom,

---

916 *1840* spoke: the   919 *1840* aureole—   923 *1840* saint; that . . . .
brow—   924 *1840* Lauded . . . . now,   925 *1840* her, only   926 *1840*
him? whose   929 *1840* should—   930 *1840* not one   931 *1840*
boy,   932 *1840* But   933 *1840* —Then!

913 *that man*: Sordello, his son, whose praise delights Taurello.
915 *the Count's*: that of Count Richard.
922 *To get the best look at*: so that he could see her best.
924 *"Lauded her father*: Taurello is now glad that the Monk had thrown in his hand, so making it possible for Taurello to scheme on Sordello's behalf.
926 *whose clansman*: Taurello's second wife Sofia (or Sophia) was a daughter of the Monk by Adelaide. Cf. 869 n., above.
927 *the same*: similarly.
928 *Romano and his lady*: Romano's lady, and Taurello's too.
935 *As shows*: as a tomb split open on the Last Day reveals the scene to the corpse it has covered: a strange image, expressing a sinister sunset.

Faced Palma—but at length Taurello set
Her free; the grating held one ragged jet
Of fierce gold fire: he lifted her within
940 The hollow underneath—how else begin
Fate's second marvellous cycle, else renew
The ages than with Palma plain in view?   *yet spring to*
Then paced the passage, hands clenched, head   *the summit of*
    erect,   *success,*
Pursuing his discourse; a grand unchecked
945 Monotony made out from his quick talk
And the recurring noises of his walk;
—Somewhat too much like the o'ercharged
    assent
Of two resolved friends in one danger blent,
Who hearten each the other against heart;
950 Boasting there 's nought to care for, when, apart
The boaster, all 's to care for. He, beside
Some shape not visible, in power and pride
Approached, out of the dark, ginglingly near,
Nearer, passed close in the broad light, his ear
955 Crimson, eyeballs suffused, temples full-fraught,
Just a snatch of the rapid speech you caught,
And on he strode into the opposite dark,
Till presently the harsh heel's turn, a spark
I' the stone, and whirl of some loose embossed
    thong
960 That crashed against the angle aye so long
After the last, punctual to an amount
Of mailed great paces you could not but
    count,—

---

949 *1840–65* heart—   951 *1840* for: he,   *959 {Reading of
1840,1863,1889} *1865–88* embossed throng {Pencilled note in margin of
Dykes Campbell copy of *1888*: 'thong, surely'.}   962 *1840* count,

---

940 *The hollow*: i.e. into the small patch of bright light from the setting sun.
941 *Fate's second marvellous cycle*: cf. v. 539–40. Taurello is deluded.
945 *made out*: emanated from, was made by.
949 *hearten . . . against heart*: cf. 'hoping against hope'.
950–1 *when, apart / The boaster*: when each of the friends realizes very well,
when he is alone, that there is a great deal to worry about.
952 *Some shape*: Taurello is talking to himself, as if under the impression that
there is someone beside him.
953 *ginglingly*: 'gingle' is Johnson's spelling.

Prepared you for the pacing back again.
And by the snatches you might ascertain
That, Friedrich's Prefecture surmounted, left   965
By this alone in Italy, they cleft
Asunder, crushed together, at command
Of none, were free to break up Hildebrand,
Rebuild, he and Sordello, Charlemagne—
But garnished, Strength with Knowledge, "if we
    deign   970
"Accept that compromise and stoop to give

"Rome law, the Cæsar's Representative."
Enough, that the illimitable flood
Of triumphs after triumphs, understood
In its faint reflux (you shall hear) sufficed   975
Young Ecelin for appanage, enticed
Him on till, these long quiet in their graves,
He found 't was looked for that a whole life's
    braves
Should somehow be made good; so, weak and
    worn,
Must stagger up at Milan, one grey morn   980

---

963 *1840* again: 964 *1840* snatches might you ascertain   970 *1840*
if   972 *1840* Caesars' Representative.   *1863,1865* Caesars' Representative."   973 *1840* —Enough   *1863,1865* —Enough,   977 *1840* Him till,
these long since quiet   978 *1840* a long life's   979 *1840–65* good—

964 *you might ascertain*: i.e. from his barely-coherent monologue one might
make out a wild scheme to overcome Friedrich's Prefecture (cf. 835–6) so that
Taurello himself, Palma, and Sordello would enjoy complete power in Italy.
They would then be free to destroy the Papal power as established by Hildebrand (the Guelf ideal) and to rebuild Charlemagne's empire (the Ghibellin
ideal)—with this improvement, however, that instead of representing simply
'Strength by stress / Of Strength' (v. 134–5), like Charlemagne's original
power, the Strength would now be 'garnished' with Knowledge (cf. v. 211
n.)—if indeed they condescended so far as to grant Rome (the Papacy) some
moral power, as 'the Cæsar's Representative'.
974 *understood*: which, understood.
976 *Young Ecelin*: Ecelin the Tyrant, as he was to become, the son of the
Monk. His inheritance was a faint reflection of the mad flood of conquests of
which Taurello had dreamed. Attempting to achieve some part of these
conquests, Ecelin was fated to die at Milan one day when Taurello, Sordello
and Palma would all be dead. Domett underlines 'Him' and writes 'Salinguerra
(?)' in the margin: Browning corrects him: '(no—Young Ecelin)'. Duff makes
the same mistake as Domett.
977 *Him till (1840)*: 'Him on till, these long quiet': *SB*.

Of the to-come, and fight his latest fight.
But, Salinguerra's prophecy at height—
He voluble with a raised arm and stiff,
A blaring voice, a blazing eye, as if
985　He had our very Italy to keep
Or cast away, or gather in a heap
To garrison the better—ay, his word
Was, "run the cucumber into a gourd,
"Drive Trent upon Apulia"—at their pitch
990　Who spied the continents and islands which
Grew mulberry leaves and sickles, in the map—
(Strange that three such confessions so should
　　　hap
To Palma, Dante spoke with in the clear
Amorous silence of the Swooning-sphere,—
995　*Cunizza*, as he called her! Never ask
Of Palma more! She sat, knowing her task
Was done, the labour of it,—for, success
Concerned not Palma, passion's votaress.)
Triumph at height, and thus Sordello crowned—
1000　Above the passage suddenly a sound
Stops speech, stops walk: back shrinks Taurello,
　　　bids

---

981 *1840* To-Come, to fight　*1863,1865* To-Come, and fight　982 *1840*
And Salinguerra's　991 *1840* Grew sickles, mulberry leaflets in　993 *1840*
To Palma　994 *1840* Swooning-sphere.　995 *1840* Cunizza,　998
1840–68 votaress)　*999 {Reading of *1863–8*}　*1840* height, I say, Sordello
crowned— *1888,1889* neight {broken 'h'}, and thus Sordello crowned—

981 *the to-come*: the future, as in Shelley (thrice in *Hellas*, e.g.).
988 *run the cucumber*: i.e. join southern and northern Italy.
989 *at their pitch*: in his wild imaginings, Taurello believed himself in the
elevated position of the men who had in the past called the Morea after the
mulberry (Gk. μορέα) and Drepanum after a sickle (Gk. δρέπανον): Duff. Cf.
Paradise Lost viii. 198–9.
992 *three such confessions*: the previous confessions were those of Adelaide (v.
749 ff.) and (presumably) Sordello.
993 *Palma*: see i. 941 n. In *Paradiso* ix the amorous Cunizza, placed in the
planet Venus, addresses Dante and describes the position of Romano in the
Trevisan territory.
996–7 *her task / Was done*: she had loved Sordello and had done all that she
could for him.
999 *Triumph at height*: in Taurello's sanguine imaginings.
1000 *Above the passage*: 'Salinguerra's conversation interrupted': Domett.

With large involuntary asking lids,
Palma interpret. "'T is his own foot-stamp—
"Your hand! His summons! Nay, this idle damp
"Befits not!" Out they two reeled dizzily.   1005
"Visconti 's strong at Milan," resumed he,
In the old, somewhat insignificant way—
(Was Palma wont, years afterward, to say)
As though the spirit's flight, sustained thus far,
Dropped at that very instant.
                          Gone they are—   1010
Palma, Taurello; Eglamor anon,
Ecelin,—only Naddo 's never gone!
—Labours, this moonrise, what the Master
     meant:
"Is Squarcialupo speckled?—purulent,
"I 'd say, but when was Providence put out?   1015
"He carries somehow handily about
"His spite nor fouls himself!" Goito's vines
Stand like a cheat detected—stark rough lines,

1002 *1840* lids   1003 *1840* 'Tis   1005 *1840* Befits not. . . . . diz-
zily: 1007 *1840* old . . . . way   1010 *1840–68* instant. Gone they are—
{No line division. *1865* has 'instant,'}   1012 *1840* Ecelin, Alberic . . . ah,
Naddo's gone!   1013 *1840* —Labours this moonrise . . . . meant *1863–8*
—Labours, this moonrise, ... meant

1002 *asking lids*: cf. 'the asking eye' in Pope, *An Epistle to Dr. Arbuthnot*, 412.
1004 *damp*: 'Dejection; depression of spirit; cloud of the mind': Johnson.
1006 "*Visconti's strong*: cf. 896. Taurello starts talking of routine military matters, in his old fashion.
1010 *Gone they are*: the end of the story is here anticipated. Cf. *The Eve of St. Agnes*, 370 ('And they are gone—aye, ages long ago'). There may also be a reminiscence of Carlyle, *The French Revolution*, Vol. I, Book I, ch. ii, para. 5: '. . . Charlemagne sleeps at Salzburg, with truncheon grounded . . . They are all gone; sunk,—down, down, with the tumult they made . . .' Cf., too, Byron's *Lara*, ii. 598.
1011 *Eglamor anon*: see ii. 266.
1012 *Naddo's never gone!*: because he is the perpetual 'common sense' nagger.
1013 *moonrise*: as in Shelley, e.g. *The Revolt of Islam*, 751.
what the Master meant: what Sordello meant, perhaps by his conversation, his poetry, or something he had said about Squarcialupo. At ii. 783 ff. this minor jongleur (ii. 118) had revealed himself as an irritating critic of Sordello. Here it becomes evident that he was envious: cf. 'speckled vanity' in Milton, 'On the Morning of Christ's Nativity', 136, and 'assertions purulent of slander', cited in OED from *Fraser's Magazine*, xiv. 506 (1836).
1015 *when was Providence put out?*: perhaps proverbial.
1018 *like a cheat detected*: they had seemed to promise a great future for Sordello.

The moon breaks through, a grey mean scale
    against
The vault where, this eve's Maiden, thou
1020   remain'st
Like some fresh martyr, eyes fixed—who can
    tell?
As Heaven, now all 's at end, did not so well,
Spite of the faith and victory, to leave
Its virgin quite to death in the lone eve.
1025 While the persisting hermit-bee . . . ha! wait   *Just this*
No longer: these in compass, forward fate!   *decided, and*
                                              we have done.

1024 *1840* eve: 1026 *1840–65* longer—

1019 *scale*: perhaps in Johnson's last sense, 'Any thing marked at equal distances'.

1020 *this eve's Maiden*: the Caryatid by whom Sordello would or should have sat on this particular evening.

1023 *the faith and victory*: the faith and victory represented by Sordello's end.

1025 *hermit-bee*: solitary bee, a coinage of Browning's (repeated at vi. 621), perhaps by analogy with 'hermit bird'. Cf. *Pauline*, 439.

1026 *these in compass*: within range.

BOOK THE SIXTH.

THE thought of Eglamor 's least like a thought,
And yet a false one, was, "Man shrinks to
        nought
"If matched with symbols of immensity;
"Must quail, forsooth, before a quiet sky
"Or sea, too little for their quietude:"
And, truly, somewhat in Sordello's mood
Confirmed its speciousness, while eve slow
        sank
Down the near terrace to the farther bank,
And only one spot left from out the night
Glimmered upon the river opposite—
A breadth of watery heaven like a bay,
A sky-like space of water, ray for ray,
And star for star, one richness where they
        mixed
As this and that wing of an angel, fixed,
Tumultuary splendours folded in

At the close of a   To die. Nor turned he till Ferrara's din
day or a life,   (Say, the monotonous speech from a man's lip
Who lets some first and eager purpose slip
In a new fancy's birth—the speech keeps on

---

2 *1840* Man   3 *1840–65* immensity—   5 *1840* quietude: 7 *1840*
speciousness while evening sank   9 *1840–68* left out of the night   16 *1840*
die: nor   19 *1840–68* birth;

---

1 *least like a thought*: unlike the superficial Eglamor, Sordello is coming to
realize that Mankind is all-important: even the most generally-accepted of
Eglamor's beliefs, that men seem trivial beside the great objects of nature, was
false. Cf. the Epilogue to *Pacchiarotto*, st. 23, where, as an example of something
insipid, we have: "Thoughts? *"What is a man beside a mount!"* ".
    3 *symbols of immensity*: cf. *Endymion*, i. 299: 'Be still a symbol of immensity'.
    14 *an angel*: the scene resembles that presented by a dying or dead angel
which is recumbent, its wings folded and horizontal. See 565 and note.
    17 *(Say, the monotonous speech*: the speech is monotonous because 'its inform-
ing soul is gone', the speaker's original purpose having yielded (in his own
mind) to a fresh idea, even while he continues to talk of the idea which had been
so important to him a moment ago. Sordello's attention returns to the sound of
Ferrara, which now becomes significant to him again.

20   Though elsewhere its informing soul be gone)
     —Aroused him, surely offered succour. Fate
     Paused with this eve; ere she precipitate
     Herself,—best put off new strange thoughts
          awhile,
     That voice, those large hands, that portentous
          smile,—
25   What help to pierce the future as the past
     Lay in the plaining city?
                              And at last
     The main discovery and prime concern,
     All that just now imported him to learn,
     Truth's self, like yonder slow moon to
          complete
30   Heaven, rose again, and, naked at his feet,
     Lighted his old life's every shift and change,
     Effort with counter-effort; nor the range
     Of each looked wrong except wherein it
          checked
     Some other—which of these could he suspect,
35   Prying into them by the sudden blaze?
     The real way seemed made up of all the
          ways—
     Mood after mood of the one mind in him;   *past procedure is*
     Tokens of the existence, bright or dim,   *fitliest reviewed,*
     Of a transcendent all-embracing sense
40   Demanding only outward influence,

21 *1840* Aroused him,—surely offered succour; fate *1863,1865* —Aroused
him,—surely offered succour. Fate   23 *1840* Herself . . . put off strange
after-thoughts awhile,   *1863–8* Herself,—put off strange after-thoughts
awhile,   24 *1840* smile . . .   29 *1840* His truth, like   *33 {Reading of
1840.} *1863,1868–89* checked,   *1865* ch cked,   34 *1840* suspect

20 *informing soul*: Platonic: endowing with its form or essential character.
Pope uses the phrase in *An Essay on Criticism*, 76.
22 *ere she precipitate*: before the fatal die is cast, Sordello had best set aside the
thought of his new-found father and the tempting future he has offered him
and seek to discover what light 'the plaining city' of Ferrara may throw on the
future.
26 *plaining*: the word occurs in Browning's early poem, 'The Dance of
Death', 69.
37 *Mood after mood of the one mind*: 'Moods of my own Mind' is the heading
used by Wordsworth for some of the poems in his *Poems in Two Volumes*
(1807). Coleridge also used the phrase. Cf. i. 554, above.
40 *outward influence*: an influence from outside himself.

A soul, in Palma's phrase, above his soul,
Power to uplift his power,—such moon's
    control
Over such sea-depths,—and their mass had
    swept
Onward from the beginning and still kept
Its course: but years and years the sky above   45
Held none, and so, untasked of any love,
His sensitiveness idled, now amort,
Alive now, and, to sullenness or sport
Given wholly up, disposed itself anew
At every passing instigation, grew   50
And dwindled at caprice, in foam-showers
    spilt,
Wedge-like insisting, quivered now a gilt
Shield in the sunshine, now a blinding race
Of whitest ripples o'er the reef—found place
For much display; not gathered up and, hurled   55
Right from its heart, encompassing the world.
So had Sordello been, by consequence,
Without a function: others made pretence
To strength not half his own, yet had some
    core
Within, submitted to some moon, before   60
Them still, superior still whate'er their force,—
Were able therefore to fulfil a course,
Nor missed life's crown, authentic attribute.

42 *1840* power, this moon's control,   *1863,1865* power,—this moon's control,   *1868* power,—this moon's control   43 *1840* Over the sea-
depths,   *1863–8* Over the sea-depths,—   55 *1840* For myriad charms;
not   59 *1840* To strengths not   61 *1840* It still, superior still whate'er its
force,   63 *1840* Life's . . . . attribute—

41 *A soul . . . above his soul*: at iii. 317 ff. we heard how Palma had awaited
'some out-soul' to direct her, until she found it in Sordello. For many years he
himself had lacked a moon to sway the depths of his soul. Having been
'Without a function' (58), his great potential had been dissipated.
    43 *their mass*: that of the moods mentioned in 37, which are like the
eternally-moving depths of the sea.
    47 *amort*: (apparently) dead. Cf. Keats, *The Eve of St. Agnes*, 70.
    51 *in foam-showers*: at one moment his powers were like the sea dissipated in
showers of foam, at another they thrust onwards in a great concentrated wave.
    58 *others made pretence*: cf. 'A Grammarian's Funeral', 113–16: 'That low man
seeks a little thing to do, / Sees it and does it: / This high man, with a great thing
to pursue, / Dies ere he knows it'.
    63 *authentic attribute*: true identity, in terms of function, the crown of life.

To each who lives must be a certain fruit
Of having lived in his degree,—a stage,
Earlier or later in men's pilgrimage,
To stop at; and to this the spirits tend   *as more*
Who, still discovering beauty without end,   *appreciable in its*
Amass the scintillations, make one star   *entirety.*
—Something unlike them, self-sustained,
    afar,—
And meanwhile nurse the dream of being blest
By winning it to notice and invest
Their souls with alien glory, some one day
Whene'er the nucleus, gathering shape alway,
Round to the perfect circle—soon or late,
According as themselves are formed to wait;
Whether mere human beauty will suffice
—The yellow hair and the luxurious eyes,
Or human intellect seem best, or each
Combine in some ideal form past reach
On earth, or else some shade of these, some
    aim,
Some love, hate even, take their place, the
    same,
So to be served—all this they do not lose,
Waiting for death to live, nor idly choose
What must be Hell—a progress thus pursued
Through all existence, still above the food
That's offered them, still fain to reach beyond
The widened range, in virtue of their bond

65 *1840* degree, a stage   67 *1840* and to which those spirits tend   69 *1840*
scintillations for one star   70 *1840* afar,   77 *1840* Whether 'tis
human   82 *1840* place   83 *1840* That may be served—   *1863–8* And may
be served—   85 *1840* What Hell shall be— *SB* shall > must   87 *1840–68*
still towering beyond

65 *a stage*: whether or not it is an advanced stage in the pilgrimage of
Mankind.
67 *the spirits*: that class of lovers of beauty described at i. 483 ff.
69 *Amass the scintillations*: concentrate all the light in one bright star. *SB*
deletes 'scintillations for', substituting 'sparkles into'.
72 *winning*: persuading or 'getting' their one star to notice their souls, so that
one day, sooner or later, they may participate in this alien glory.
81 *shade*: reflection.
84 *Waiting for death to live*: unlike Sordello, or the Poet in *Alastor*, such men
find happiness on earth. Regal spirits are condemned to the Hell of a perpetual
pursuit of the Absolute.

Of sovereignty. Not that a Palma's Love,
A Salinguerra's Hate, would equal prove   90

*Strong, he needed
external strength:*

To swaying all Sordello: but why doubt
Some love meet for such strength, some moon
    without
Would match his sea?—or fear, Good manifest,
Only the Best breaks faith?—Ah but the Best
Somehow eludes us ever, still might be   95
And is not! Crave we gems? No penury
Of their material round us! Pliant earth
And plastic flame—what balks the mage his
    birth
—Jacinth in balls or lodestone by the block?
Flinders enrich the strand, veins swell the rock;   100
Nought more! Seek creatures? Life 's i' the
    tempest, thought
Clothes the keen hill-top, mid-day woods are
    fraught
With fervours: human forms are well enough!

---

89 *1840* Of sovereignty: not . . . . Love   91 *1840–65* Sordello: wherefore
doubt,   92 *1840* Love meet for such a Strength,   *1863* That Love meet for
such Strength,   *1865,1868* That love meet for such strength,   92 *1840* some
Moon's without   93 *1840* To match his Sea?—fear, Good so manifest,   *SB* [why] fear, Good ⟨so⟩ manifest,   94 *1840* faith?—but that the
Best   *SB* faith?—⟨but that⟩ [and yet] the Best   *1863* faith?—Ah, but the
Best   96 *1840* not: crave you gems? where's penury   *1863,1865* not! crave
we gems? no penury   97 *1840* us? pliant earth,   *1863,1865* us! pliant
earth,   98 *1840* The plastic . . . . Mage *SB* The plastic > And plastic
1863,1865 The plastic . . . . mage   100 *1840* strand and veins the
rock—   *1863,1865* strand, and veins the rock—   101 *1840* No more! Ask
creatures? Life in tempest, Thought *1863–8* Nought more! Ask creatures? Life's
i' the tempest, Thought {*1868* thought}   103 *1840* fervors . . . ah, these
forms . . . . enough—   *1863,1865* fervours: ah, these forms . . . . enough!

---

90 *Salinguerra's Hate*: of Azzo.   91 ⟨Λ⟩ *wherefore doubt* (*1840*): 'but': *SB*.
93 *or fear, Good manifest*: 'Why should we fear that, when Good can be seen
and served, only the Best should prove a deception? The answer is that the Best
is non-existent: it might be, yet never is': Duff.
98 *what balks the mage*: why cannot the magician (or alchemist) produce great
balls of jacinth (probably in the old sense, sapphire) or vast blocks of lodestone?
Because only small fragments of sapphire are to be found in nature, only veins
of lodestone occur in the rock. We are too apt to argue from the existence of the
Good to the actual existence of the Ideal or 'Best'.
101 *Seek creatures?*: in the same way we dream of human beings beyond all
actual men, and by associating them with natural forces and objects produce
the creatures of mythology. Cf. Wordsworth, *The Excursion*, iv. 851 ff.
103 *With fervors . . .* (*1840*): *SB* inserts 'now look on the sons of men:' above
the three points.

But we had hoped, encouraged by the stuff
105 Profuse at nature's pleasure, men beyond
These actual men!—and thus are over-fond
In arguing, from Good—the Best, from force
Divided—force combined, an ocean's course
From this our sea whose mere intestine pants
110 Might seem at times sufficient to our wants.
External power! If none be adequate,
And he stand forth ordained (a prouder fate)
Himself a law to his own sphere? "Remove
"All incompleteness!" for that law, that love?
115 Nay, if all other laws be feints,—truth veiled
Helpfully to weak vision that had failed
To grasp aught but its special want,—for lure,
Embodied? Stronger vision could endure
The unbodied want: no part—the whole of
• truth!
120 The People were himself; nor, by the ruth

even now, where can he perceive such?

105 *1840* Nature's pleasure, Men   *1863,1865* Nature's pleasure, men   106
1840 Men! and thus, perchance, are   *1863,1865* men! and thus, perchance,
are   *1868* men!—and thus, perchance, are   107 *1840–68* Good the   110
1840 Had seemed at   111 *1840–65* —External Power? . . . . adequate   *1868*
—External power? . . . . adequate   112 *1840* And he have been
ordained   113–15 *1840* A law . . . . sphere? the need remove|All incom-
pleteness be that law, that love?|Nay, really such be other's laws, though
veiled   *1863–8* A law . . . . sphere?—need to remove|All incompleteness, for
that law, that love?|Nay, if all other laws be such, though veiled   116
1840–68 In mercy to each vision that had failed   117–20 *1840* If unassisted by
its Want, for lure,|Embodied? stronger vision could endure|The simple
want—no bauble for a truth!|The People were himself; and by the ruth
1863–8 If unassisted by its want,—for lure,|Embodied? Stronger vision

104 *stuff*: OED mentions that, in relation to mining, the word means
'Material of rock, earth, or clay containing ore, metal, or precious stones'.
109 *intestine pants*: cf. Cowper, *The Task*, vi. 139: 'th' intestine tide'.
111 *External power!* (*1840*): 'Where is External Power? What if none be
adequate': SB.
113–14 *"Remove / All Incompleteness!"*: what if Sordello is to be a law to
himself, and it is to be his achievement to remove all incompleteness? SB
expands: '[What] if the need to remove / All incompleteness be that law, that
love? / Nay, If really such be all other mens' laws, though veiled, in their case'
&c.
115 *Nay, if*: what if the 'law' of other beings is limited to suit their weaker
vision, capable only of seeing 'special want', which has to be embodied so that
they can see it clearly? Sordello is musing vaingloriously, and wondering
whether he himself is capable of seeing the 'want' of all men 'unbodied'.
119 *no bauble* (*1840*): cf. v. 712, where the 'bauble' is the badge which Taurello
impulsively gives to Sordello, so making him 'Romano's Head' (721).
120 *The People were himself*: the whole truth which he desired to discover is

At their condition, was he less impelled
To alter the discrepancy beheld,
Than if, from the sound whole, a sickly part
Subtracted were transformed, decked out with
    art,
Then palmed on him as alien woe—the Guelf   125
To succour, proud that he forsook himself.
All is himself; all service, therefore, rates
Alike, nor serving one part, immolates
The rest: but all in time! "That lance of yours
"Makes havoc soon with Malek and his Moors,   130
"That buckler 's lined with many a giant's
    beard
"Ere long, our champion, be the lance
    upreared,
"The buckler wielded handsomely as now!
"But view your escort, bear in mind your vow,
"Count the pale tracts of sand to pass ere that,   135
"And, if you hope we struggle through the flat,
"Put lance and buckler by! Next half-month
    lacks
"Mere sturdy exercise of mace and axe
"To cleave this dismal brake of prickly-pear

---

could endure|The unbodied want: no bauble for a truth! The People were
himself; and, by the ruth   121 *1840* condition   122 *1840* Alter the discrepancy he beheld   123 *1840–68* Whole, a sickly Part   126 *1840–68* himself?   127 *1840* No: All's himself—   *1863–8* No! All's himself;   129 *1840*
That   132 *1840* Ere long, Porphyrio, be the lance but reared,   *1863,1865* Ere
long, O champion, be the lance upreared,   133 *1840* as now;   136 *1840*
through this flat,   137 *1840* buckler up—next   138 *1840* A sturdy . . . .
mace or axe

(as he supposes) that he and the People are one. He is just as capable of being
motivated by pity for their inferior condition as if he were deceived into
considering that his duty lay merely in succouring the Guelfs. The reading of
1840, 'No: All's himself' (127), makes it clearer that the Guelf cause is not
sufficient for him.
    127 *all service*: cf. *Pippa Passes*, Introduction, 190: 'All service ranks the same
with God', though the parallel is mainly verbal.
    128 *immolates*: SB adds: 'all the old ideals to realize—'.
    129 *in|At time!*: 'due': SB.
    "*That lance*: he imagines the People, or their advocate, addressing him
mockingly.
    130 *Malek*: see i. 841 n. He is on an imaginary crusade.
    133 *as now!*: as you are now imagining.   137 *lacks*: requires. calls for.

140

"Which bristling holds Cydippe by the hair,
"Lames barefoot Agathon: this felled, we 'll try
"The picturesque achievements by and by—
"Next life!"

             Ay, rally, mock, O People, urge   *Internal strength*
Your claims!—for thus he ventured, to the   *must suffice then,*
     verge,
Push a vain mummery which perchance

145

     distrust
Of his fast-slipping resolution thrust
Likewise: accordingly the Crowd—(as yet
He had unconsciously contrived forget
I' the whole, to dwell o' the points . . . one
     might assuage

150

The signal horrors easier than engage
With a dim vulgar vast unobvious grief
Not to be fancied off, nor gained relief
In brilliant fits, cured by a happy quirk,
But by dim vulgar vast unobvious work
To correspond . . .) this Crowd then, forth

155

     they stood.
    "And now content thy stronger vision, brood

140 *1840* That bristling   141,142 {Not in *1840*.}   143 *1840* Lames
barefoot Agathon.¶ Oh, People, urge   *1863,1865* Next life!"¶ Ay, rally,
mock, oh People, urge   144 *1840* ventured to the verge   147 *1840* No less:
accordingly the Crowd—as yet   *1863,1865* Likewise: accordingly the
Crowd—as yet   148 *1840–65* had inconsciously   149 *1840* To dwell
upon the points . . . one   *1863,1865* 'I the whole, to dwell o' the points . . .
one   150 *1840* horrors sooner than   151 *1840 proof* dull >dim   152
1840 off, obtain relief   155 *1840* To correspond—however, forth they
stood: *1863,1865* To correspond . . . this Crowd then, forth they
stood.   156 *1840* And now

140 *Cydippe*: a classical name, like *Agathon*, but without any specific allusion. Cf. Ovid, *Heroides*, xx-xxi.
143 ∧ *Oh, People* (*1840*): 'Poetry in good time': *SB*.
145 *a vain mummery*: a vain fancy.   146 *thrust*: thrust into his mind.
147 *(as yet*: so far he had forgotten the needs of Mankind in general and
concentrated on the needs of particular sections of humanity: it is (after all)
easier to mitigate the greatest sufferings than to come to terms with the vast
and ordinary sorrows of humanity, which are not to be imagined away or
helped or cured except by 'dim vulgar vast unobvious work'.
148 *forget* ∧: 'in its whole': *SB*.
149 *points . . . one might*: *SB* inserts ('for'.
151 *unobvious*: a favourite word of Jeremy Bentham's, as OED points out.
For Browning's knowledge of Bentham, see *Maynard*, p. 341.
156 *content*: imperative, not part of an absolute construction, as Duff supposes. Sordello imagines the Crowd bidding him look hard at them with what

"On thy bare want; uncovered, turf by turf,
"Study the corpse-face thro' the taint-worms'
      scurf!"
   Down sank the People's Then; uprose their
      Now.

These sad ones render service to! And how   160
Piteously little must that service prove
—Had surely proved in any case! for, move
Each other obstacle away, let youth
Become aware it had surprised a truth
'T were service to impart—can truth be seized,   165
Settled forthwith, and, of the captive eased,
Its captor find fresh prey, since this alit
So happily, no gesture luring it,
The earnest of a flock to follow? Vain,
Most vain! a life to spend ere this he chain   170
To the poor crowd's complacence: ere the
      crowd
Pronounce it captured, he descries a cloud
Its kin of twice the plume; which he, in turn,
If he shall live as many lives, may learn
How to secure: not else. Then Mantua called   175
Back to his mind how certain bards were
      thralled
—Buds blasted, but of breath more like perfume

---

157 *1840* want; the grave stript turf   158 *1840* scurf!   164 *1840* Have
been aware . . . . Truth   *1863,1865* Have been aware . . . . truth   165 *1840*
proof impart,>impart—   *1840* Truth   166–7 *1840* and of the captive
eased|Its captor look around, since   170 *1840–65* life's to . . . . chain,   *1868*
life to . . . . chain,   173 *1840* the plumage—he,   *1863,1865* the plume—
which he,   175 *1840* Secure—not otherwise. Then   *1863,1865* How to
secure—not else. Then   177 *1840* breaths more like perfumes

---

he believes to be his 'stronger vision' in order to see 'The unbodied want'
(118–19), if such is possible. He is challenged to uncover, layer by layer, the
misery of humanity, until he is looking at the decaying face of the corpse. For
'taint-worm' see 'Lycidas', 46. *SB* inserts 'beloved' before 'corpse-face'.
   159 *Down sank*: Sordello wonders how to serve Mankind in the present.
There is little he can possibly do. Even if he had recognized some partial truth
as a young man (not realizing how partial it was), some truth useful to
Mankind, what chance would there have been of his reaching a further truth,
and having it recognised by the crowd?
   173 *of twice the plume*: twice as splendid.
   176 *thralled*: enslaved, imprisoned. Cf. i. 663 and iv. 255.
   177 *Buds blasted*: cf. Milton, 'On the Death of a Fair Infant', 1: 'O fairest

Than Naddo's staring nosegay's carrion bloom;
Some insane rose that burnt heart out in sweets,
180 A spendthrift in the spring, no summer greets;
Some Dularete, drunk with truths and wine,
Grown bestial, dreaming how become divine.
Yet to surmount this obstacle, commence
With the commencement, merits crowning!
　　　Hence
185 Must truth be casual truth, elicited
In sparks so mean, at intervals dispread
So rarely, that 't is like at no one time
Of the world's story has not truth, the prime
Of truth, the very truth which, loosed, had
　　　hurled
The world's course right, been really in the
190 　　　world
—Content the while with some mean spark by
　　　dint
Of some chance-blow, the solitary hint
Of buried fire, which, rip earth's breast, would
　　　stream

178 *1840* carrion blooms *1863,1865* carrion bloom: 179 *1840* Could
boast—some rose that 180 *1840,1863* Spring, no Summer greets— *1865*
spring, no summer greets— 182 *1840* bestial 183 *1863,1865*
"Yet 185 *1840* Truth be casual Truth, 188–90 *1840* Truth, the
prime|Of Truth, the very Truth which loosed had hurled | Its course
aright, 191 *1840* Content 193 *1840–68* rip its breast,

flower no sooner blown but blasted'. The reference is to poets who die young,
yet leave behind them a perfume more fragrant than that of the ostentatious yet
decaying nosegay of a Naddo. Cf. iii. 217, above.
　179 *in sweets*: cf. Dryden, *Æneis*, xi. 417: 'the sweets of Life'.
　181 *Dularete*: an imaginary poet. As Whyte mentions, the name occurs in
Verci, as the nom-de-plume of a minor poet who wrote a tragedy.
　183 *Yet to surmount this obstacle*: merely to surmount this one obstacle—'the
obstacle placed in the way of the poetic genius by this expectation of
accomplishing all' (Duff)—is highly meritorious.
　185 *Must truth be casual truth*: Duff complains that 'The logic of this passage is
beyond recall'. While it is tempting to emend, however, it does not seem
necessary. The meaning appears to be that Sordello will deserve 'crowning' if
he is content to 'commence With the commencement'. Truth can only be
elicited by occasional men in apparently insignificant sparks, and this seems to
indicate that 'the prime Of truth' has in reality always lain buried 'in the
world'—that 'very truth' which, if it could have been released in one great
explosion, would have put the world to rights. In fact, however, the world has
had to be content with 'some mean spark', struck out by chance, yet a reminder
of the immense power which lies buried.
　191 ∧ *Content the while* (*1840*): 'which was': SB.

Sky-ward!

of which, try now
the inherent force!

          Sordello's miserable gleam

Was looked for at the moment: he would dash   195

This badge, and all it brought, to earth,—

    abash

Taurello thus, perhaps persuade him wrest

The Kaiser from his purpose,—would attest

His own belief, in any case. Before

He dashes it however, think once more!   200

For, were that little, truly service? "Ay,

"I' the end, no doubt; but meantime? Plain you

    spy

"Its ultimate effect, but many flaws

"Of vision blur each intervening cause.

"Were the day's fraction clear as the life's sum   205

"Of service, Now as filled as teems To-come

"With evidence of good—nor too minute

---

194 *1863,1865* Sky-ward!"   *196 {Reading of *1863–8*}   *1840* This badge
to earth and all it brought, abash *1888,1889* This badge. and all it brought, to
earth,—abash 198 *1840* purpose; would 199 *1840* His constancy
in 200 *1840,1863* it, however, 201 *1840* For, was that little truly service?
Ay— *1863,1865* For, were that little, truly service? "Ay— 203 *1840*
Effect, 204 *1840* Cause; 206 *1840–68* as filled as the To-come

---

194 *Sordello's miserable gleam*: this is the time for Sordello to bear witness to
the truth that he can perceive, miserably insignificant as it is in comparison
with the Truth in its entirety. He must reject the power which Taurello has
offered him and try to persuade him to urge Friedrich to cease opposing the
Pope.

196 *and all it brought*: underlined in *SB*, with a caret mark apparently indicating an intended insertion.

199 *His constancy* (*1840*): *SB* expands to 'His own constancy & preference'.

201 *truly service?*: would rejecting his opportunity of becoming Head of
Romano truly be a service to humanity? No doubt it would be, in the long run;
but what about the more immediate prospect? He sees its ultimate effect
plainly enough; but many obstacles hinder his vision of what lies between the
present and the ultimate goal. If his day's duty were as easy to see as the duty of
his whole life—if his immediate role were as evidently valuable as his future
role appears to be—all would be well. But in fact his day's service seems too
insignificant to constitute any real opposition to Evil. No doubt his life's work
is to help maintain the rule of the Guelfs; but he must be prepared to hate those
whom he used to love and love those whom he used to hate according to the
requirements of this general end. It would not be so difficult if those he had to
oppose were visibly branded as evil and those he had to support all wore visible
haloes. It would not be so difficult if the interests of the future never seemed to
conflict with those of the present, if the sum of good and evil in the future (at
least) were clearly indicated, as it is not in the present.

206 *To-come*: as at v. 981.

"A share to vie with evil! No dispute,
"'T were fitliest maintain the Guelfs in rule:
"That makes your life's work: but you have to
     school
210
"Your day's work on these natures
     circumstanced
"Thus variously, which yet, as each advanced
"Or might impede the Guelf rule, must be
     moved
"Now, for the Then's sake,—hating what you
     loved,
215
"Loving old hatreds! Nor if one man bore
"Brand upon temples while his fellow wore
"The aureole, would it task you to decide:
"But, portioned duly out, the future vied
"Never with the unparcelled present! Smite
220
"Or spare so much on warrant all so slight?
"The present's complete sympathies to break,
"Aversions bear with, for a future's sake
"So feeble? Tito ruined through one speck,
"The Legate saved by his sole lightish fleck?
"This were work, true, but work performed at
225
     cost
"Of other work; aught gained here, elsewhere
     lost.
"For a new segment spoil an orb half-done?
"Rise with the People one step, and sink—one?

208,209 *1840* evil! How dispute|The Guelfs were fitliest maintained in
rule?   210–12 *1840* That made the life's work: not so easy school| Your day's
work—say, on natures circumstanced|So variously, which   213–14 *1840*
impede that Guelf rule, it behoved|You, for the Then's sake, hate what Now
you loved,| 215 *1840* Love what you hated; nor if   *1863,1865* Loving old
hatreds! nor if   217 *1840* task us to decide—   *1863,1865* task you to
decide—   225 *1840–65* true—   226 *1840* work—. . . . lost—   *1863,1865*
work—. . . . lost.   227 *1840* half-done—   228 *1840* sink . . . one?

208 *How dispute (1840)*: 'the fact that': *SB*.   210 *school*: regulate.
210 *That*: 'to share knowledge': *SB*.
211 *work ∧.—say (1840)*: 'to take place': *SB*.
212 *yet, ∧, as*: 'according': *SB*.
223 *Tito ruined*: is Tito lost just because he is a Ghibellin (as 'Friedrich's
Pretor', iv. 41), the Papal Legate saved just because he is a Guelf?
227 *an orb half-done?*: is work half completed to be abandoned so that a
different task may be attempted?

"Were it but one step, less than the whole face
"Of things, your novel duty bids erase!   230
"Harms to abolish! What, the prophet saith,
"The minstrel singeth vainly then? Old faith,
"Old courage, only born because of harms,
"Were not, from highest to the lowest, charms?
"Flame may persist; but is not glare as staunch?   235
"Where the salt marshes stagnate, crystals
        branch;
"Blood dries to crimson; Evil 's beautified
"In every shape. Thrust Beauty then aside

How much of man's ill may be removed?

"And banish Evil! Wherefore? After all,
"Is Evil a result less natural   240
"Than Good? For overlook the seasons' strife
"With tree and flower,—the hideous animal
        life,
"(Of which who seeks shall find a grinning
        taunt
"For his solution, and endure the vaunt
"Of nature's angel, as a child that knows   245

229 *1840* Would it were one step— *1863,1865* Were it but one step—   230 *1840* things our novel   231 *1840* *proof* saith>saith, *1840* Harms are to vanquish; what? the Prophet saith, *1863,1865* Harms to abolish! what? the prophet saith,   233 *1840* courage, born of the surrounding harms, *1868* courage, only borne because of harms,   235 *1840* Oh, flame persists but . . . . stanch? *1863,1865* Flame may persist but . . . . staunch?   236 *1840–65* branch—   237 *1840–65* crimson—   238 *1840* shape! But Beauty thrust aside   239 *1840* You banish Evil: wherefore? After all *1863,1865* And banish Evil! wherefore? After all,   240 *1840* Is Evil our result   243 *1840* Of which   244 *1840* solution, must endure   245 *1840* Nature's

231 *Harms to abolish!*: can Evil be eliminated from human life? Are the sayings of prophets and the songs of poets of no avail? Are not ancient loyalties and ancient courage universally appealing and powerful (though they owe their very existence to evil that has been done in the past?)
235 *glare*: cf. *Paracelsus*, iii. 206–7: 'the false glare that confounds / A weaker vision'.
238–9 *Thrust . . . Evil!*: the meaning might be clarified by inserting inverted commas at the beginning and end of this injunction. The argument is that beauty is often the by-product of evil. Should we then disregard beauty, in order to get rid of evil? *SB* expands 'But . . . aside' to 'But, the Beauty of it thrust aside,'.
242 *the hideous animal life*: the doctrine of the struggle for existence and the survival of the fittest which was to be summed up a decade later by Tennyson in *In Memoriam*, 'Nature, red in tooth and claw' (st. lvi).
244–5 *the vaunt / Of nature's angel*: the boasting of Nature's messenger or witness (which he yet senses to be false).

"Himself befooled, unable to propose
"Aught better than the fooling)—and but care
"For men, for the mere People then and
    there,—
"In these, could you but see that Good and Ill
"Claimed you alike! Whence rose their claim
250   but still
"From Ill, as fruit of Ill? What else could knit
"You theirs but Sorrow? Any free from it
"Were also free from you! Whose happiness
"Could be distinguished in this morning's press
255   "Of miseries?—the fool's who passed a gibe
"'On thee,' jeered he, 'so wedded to thy tribe,
"'Thou carriest green and yellow tokens in
"'Thy very face that thou art Ghibellin!'
"Much hold on you that fool obtained! Nay
    mount
260   "Yet higher—and upon men's own account
"Must Evil stay: for, what is joy?—to heave
"Up one obstruction more, and common leave
"What was peculiar, by such act destroy

247 *1840* fooling—   248 *1840* Men, the varied People . . . . there, *1863*
Men, for the mere People . . . . there,—   249–50 *1840* Of which 'tis easy
saying Good and Ill|Claim him alike! Whence rose the claim   251 *1840* Ill,
the fruit of Ill—what   *1863,1865* Ill, as fruit of Ill—what   252 *1840* Him
theirs   253 *1840* from him! A happiness   *SB* A happiness>One happiness   255 *1840* miseries—   256–7 *1840* On one, said he, so wedded to his
tribe|He carries green   258 *1840* His very face that he's a Ghibellin—   *1863*
Thy very face that thou art Ghibellin!'—   259 *1840* on him that   260 *1840*
higher; and upon Men's   261 *1840* for what is Joy? To   *1863* for, what is
Joy?—to   263 *1840* peculiar—by this act   *1863,1865* peculiar—by such act

249 *Good and Ill*: there is the same mixture of good and evil in mankind
which we find in Nature, and it is that very mixture and its results which give
mankind a claim on your services.
253 *A happiness* (*1840*): revised to 'One happiness': *SB*.
254 *press*: 'Crowd; tumult; throng': Johnson.
257 *green and yellow tokens*: a fool had taunted him with the fact that his very
complexion marked him out as a Ghibellin. For 'The green and yellow' see ii.
909 and n.
259 *that*|∧|*fool*: 'happy': *SB*.
261 *what is joy?*: joy consists in removing one further obstacle to happiness,
so rendering frequent something that had before been rare: in a sense, therefore, joy destroys itself, by changing the situation in which it had been possible
for it to come into existence.

*How much of ill
ought to be
removed?*

"Itself; a partial death is every joy;
"The sensible escape, enfranchisement   265
"Of a sphere's essence: once the vexed—
    content,
"The cramped—at large, the growing
    circle—round,
"All 's to begin again—some novel bound
"To break, some new enlargement to entreat;
"The sphere though larger is not more
    complete.   270
"Now for Mankind's experience: who alone
"Might style the unobstructed world his own?
"Whom palled Goito with its perfect things?
"Sordello's self: whereas for Mankind springs
"Salvation by each hindrance interposed.   275
"They climb; life's view is not at once disclosed
"To creatures caught up, on the summit left,
"Heaven plain above them, yet of wings bereft:
"But lower laid, as at the mountain's foot.
"So, range on range, the girdling forests shoot   280

269 *1840* enlargement's to entreat,   *1863* enlargement to entreat,   274
1840 self; . . . . Mankind *1863,1865* self! . . . . mankind   275 *1840* Salvá-
tion—hindrances are interposed *1863,1865* Salvation by each hindrance
interposed;   276–8 *1840* For them, not all Life's view at once disclosed|To
creatures sudden on its summit left|With Heaven above and yet of wings
bereft—   *1863,1865* They climb, life's view is not at once disclosed|To crea-
tures caught up, on its summit left,|Heaven plain above them, yet of wings
bereft—   279 *1840* foot *1863,1865* foot,   280 *1840* Where, range
1863,1865 While, range

265 *The sensible escape*: joy consists in an escape of which we are conscious,
the freeing of the very essence of a sphere.
270 *complete*: 'Sordello's argument, framed to justify his desire to accept
Taurello's offer, is that Good only exists through the presence of Evil . . . It is
Hegel's doctrine of the implication of opposites': Whyte. Cf. Vol. I, p. 43 n,
above. The doctrine is to be found in the Stoic Chrysippus.
271 *"Now for Mankind's experience*: if I consider the matter (Sordello reflects),
am I not alone in having a boundless view? Yet was I not bored with my perfect
existence at Goito? For the rest of Mankind it is the very overcoming of
hindrances which gives salvation. They do not see everything at once, not
having been placed on the top of a mountain with a clear view of heaven (albeit
without wings): they are lower down, as if at the bottom of a mountain. Range
after range of forests girdles the slopes which separate me, with my clear view,
from the throngs who climb towards me, finding encouragement as they
conquer each peak and pierce each veil of mist.
278 *Heaven ∧ above (1840)*: 'plain': SB.
280 *the girdling forests*: cf. *Childe Harold's Pilgrimage*, iv. 1564–5: 'where yon
bar / Of girdling mountains intercepts the sight'.

"'Twixt your plain prospect and the throngs
    who scale
"Height after height, and pierce mists, veil by
    veil,
"Heartened with each discovery; in their soul,
"The Whole they seek by Parts—but, found
    that Whole,
285 "Could they revert, enjoy past gains? The space
"Of time you judge so meagre to embrace
"The Parts were more than plenty, once
    attained
"The Whole, to quite exhaust it: nought were
    gained
"But leave to look—not leave to do: Beneath
"Soon sates the looker—look Above, and
290   Death
"Tempts ere a tithe of Life be tasted. Live
"First, and die soon enough, Sordello! Give   *—if removed, at*
"Body and spirit the first right they claim,   *what cost to*
"And pasture soul on a voluptuous shame   *Sordello?*
295 "That you, a pageant-city's denizen,
"Are neither vilely lodged midst Lombard
    men—
"Can force joy out of sorrow, seem to truck

281–3 *1840* Between the prospect . . . . scale|Earnestly ever, piercing veil by veil,|Confirmed with . . . . soul   285–6 *1840* revert? Oh, testify! The space|Of time we judge   285 *SB* Oh,>No,   287 *1840,1863* The Parts,   288 *1840* it: for nought's gained   289 *1840* look—no leave   290 *1840* Above, then! Death   293 *1840* the bare right they claim   294 *1840* To pasture thee on   *1863–8* And pasture thee on   295 *1840–68* That thou,   296 *1840–68* Art neither   297 *1840–68* Canst force

---

284 *The Whole*: 'There is The Whole which they seek': *SB*.
285 *Could they revert? Oh, testify!* (*1840*): *SB* substitutes 'No,' for 'Oh,'.
293 *the first right*: Sordello is listening to the voice of temptation. Should he enjoy this present life, and luxuriate in the thought that while he is really a citizen of an ideal City he 'isn't doing too badly either' ('neither') as Leader of the House of Romano? *SB* notes, after 'denizen': 'Lord of the Ideal' and after 'Lombard men—' 'as King of Lombardy'. The 'pageant-city' is the ideal Rome of his dreams: cf. v. 11.
297 *seem to truck*: part of his 'voluptuous shame' will be the realization that he appears to be exchanging 'bright attributes' for base gains—will not he be able to win gold from the world's refuse, as an alchemist transmutes base metal into gold? Whatever he does, the common people will be no better off. (The form 'cruce' also occurs in 'In a Gondola', 33).

"Bright attributes away for sordid muck,
"Yet manage from that very muck educe
"Gold; then subject, nor scruple, to your cruce   300
"The world's discardings! Though real ingots
         pay
"Your pains, the clods that yielded them are
         clay
"To all beside,—would clay remain, though
         quenched
"Your purging-fire; who 's robbed then? Had
         you wrenched
"An ampler treasure forth!—As 't is, they crave   305
"A share that ruins you and will not save
"Them. Why should sympathy command you
         quit
"The course that makes your joy, nor will
         remit
"Their woe? Would all arrive at joy? Reverse
"The order (time instructs you) nor coerce   310
"Each unit till, some predetermined mode,
"The total be emancipate; men's road
"Is one, men's times of travel many; thwart
"No enterprising soul's precocious start
"Before the general march! If slow or fast   315

---

298 *1840–68* Thine attributes   300 *1840,1863* subject, nor scruple, to thy
cruce   *1865,1868* subject nor scruple, to thy cruce   301 *1840* The world's
discardings; think, if ingots pay   302 *1840* Such pains,   *1863–8* Thy
pains,   303–4 *1840* To all save thee, and clay remain though quenched|Thy
purging-fire; who's robbed then? Would I wrenched   *1863–8* To all save
thee,—would clay remain, though quenched|Thy purging-fire; who's robbed
then? Had you wrenched   305 *1840* An ample treasure forth!—As 'tis, why
crave   306–8 *1840* ruins me and will not save|Yourselves?—imperiously
command I quit|The course that makes my joy   309 *1840* Your
woe?   312 *1840* be emancipate; our road   *1868* be emancipated; men's
road   313 *1840* Is one, our times   315 *1840* march; if   *1863,1865* march! if

---

304 ∧ *Thy purging-fire* (*1840*): 'were': SB.
305 *they crave*: the Multitude makes demands on him which would destroy
his own chances of happiness but do nothing for their own.
306–7 SB has 'to give' after 306 (at the foot of p. 228) and 'to get?' at the top
of p. 229, above 307.
308 *remit*: 'To relax; to make less intense': Johnson.
311 *some . . . mode*: in some predetermined way.
314 *No enterprising soul*: like Sordello.

"All straggle up to the same point at last,
"Why grudge your having gained, a month
        ago,
"The brakes at balm-shed, asphodels in blow,
"While they were landlocked? Speed their Then,
        but how
"This badge would suffer you improve your   *Men win little*
320   Now!"   *thereby; he loses*
         His time of action for, against, or with *all:*
Our world (I labour to extract the pith
Of this his problem) grew, that even-tide,
Gigantic with its power of joy, beside
325   The world's eternity of impotence
To profit though at his whole joy's expense.
"Make nothing of my day because so brief?
"Rather make more: instead of joy, use grief
"Before its novelty have time subside!
330   "Wait not for the late savour, leave untried
"Virtue, the creaming honey-wine, quick
        squeeze
"Vice like a biting spirit from the lees
"Of life! Together let wrath, hatred, lust,
"All tyrannies in every shape, be thrust
335   "Upon this Now, which time may reason out

317 *1840* Why grudge my having gained a month ago   319 *1840 proof*
Speed you> Speed your   319–20 *1840* While you were landlocked? Speed
your Then, but how| This badge would suffer me improve my Now! *1863,1865*
{as *1888* except Now!' "}   323 *1840* Of this and more) grew up, that   324
1840 joy   326 *1840* at all his joy's   327 *1840* of that time because   328
1840 more—instead of joy take grief *1863,1865* more—instead of joy, use
grief   329 *1840* subside;   330 *1840* No time for the late savour—
1863,1865 Wait not for the late savour—   333 *1840* Of life—together
1863,1865 Of life!—together

316 *at last,* ∧ : 'seeing one arrived there,' *SB.*
317 *Why grudge*: why should they grudge the fact that you have reached the
cover of the bushes a month ago (when they were most fragrant, with the
asphodels in bloom) before they themselves could get a favourable
wind?—The 'asphodels' here may either be the mythical flower of the poets or
the genus of plants of that name found in southern Europe, particularly in
Apulia.
320 *This badge*: cf. v. 719 ff., and vi. 196.
324 *Gigantic*: instead of seeming brief, the remainder of his life, with its
potential for joy, seemed very great, as he faced his choice.
328 *use grief*: as a sort of condiment.

"As mischiefs, far from benefits, no doubt;
"But long ere then Sordello will have slipt
"Away; you teach him at Goito's crypt,
"There 's a blank issue to that fiery thrill.
"Stirring, the few cope with the many, still: 340
"So much of sand as, quiet, makes a mass
"Unable to produce three tufts of grass,
"Shall, troubled by the whirlwind, render
    void
"The whole calm glebe's endeavour: be
    employed!
"And e'en though somewhat smart the Crowd
    for this,   345
"Contribute each his pang to make your
    bliss,
"'T is but one pang—one blood-drop to the
    bowl
"Which brimful tempts the sluggish asp
    uncowl
"At last, stains ruddily the dull red cape,
"And, kindling orbs grey as the unripe
    grape   350
"Before, avails forthwith to disentrance
"The portent, soon to lead a mystic dance
"Among you! For, who sits alone in Rome?

---

336 *1840–65* doubt—   337 *1868* slipped   338 *1840* Away— . . . .
crypt *1863,1865* Away— . . . . crypt,   339 *1840–65* thrill!   340 *1840* Few
. . . . Many,   341 *1840* of dust as,   345 *1840* somewhat smarts   346
1840 Contributes each his pang to make up bliss,   349 *1840* So quick,
stains   350 *1840* orbs dull as   352 *1840* The mischief—soon *1863,1865*
The portent—soon   353 *1840* Among you! Nay, who

---

338 *at Goito's crypt*: at the font which he used to visit each evening.
340 *Stirring*: when they move, the Few always predominate over the Many.
A little sand, insufficient (without motion) to produce three tufts of grass, is
able to damage a whole wide glebe, when it is scattered by a whirlwind. 'Be
busy!' prompts the tempting voice.
348 *the sluggish asp*: the hooded serpent is eventually induced to raise its head
and stain its hood in the brimming bowl of blood. Its eyes change colour and
the portentous creature begins a 'mystic dance'.
353 *who sits alone in Rome?*: the significance of the rhetorical question is
obscure: Duff has 'who sits lonely when power is lying to his hand?' The
meaning is probably that the life which Salinguerra offers him in Rome would
be the opposite of his solitary life in Goito.

"Have those great hands indeed hewn out a
        home,
355   "And set me there to live? Oh life, life-breath,   *for he can*
      "Life-blood,—ere sleep, come travail, life ere   *infinitely enjoy*
        death!   *himself,*
      "This life stream on my soul, direct, oblique,
      "But always streaming! Hindrances? They
        pique:
      "Helps? such . . . but why repeat, my soul
        o'ertops
      "Each height, than every depth profoundlier
360   drops?
      "Enough that I can live, and would live! Wait
      "For some transcendent life reserved by Fate
      "To follow this? Oh, never! Fate, I trust
      "The same, my soul to; for, as who flings dust,
365   "Perchance (so facile was the deed) she chequed
      "The void with these materials to affect
      "My soul diversely: these consigned anew
      "To nought by death, what marvel if she threw
      "A second and superber spectacle
370   "Before me? What may serve for sun, what still
      "Wander a moon above me? What else wind
      "About me like the pleasures left behind,

354–6 *1840* home|For me—compelled to live? Oh Life,   356 *1840* —ere
sleep be travail,   357 *1840* This life to feed my   358 *1840* But alway
feeding! . . . . pique—   *1863,1865* But alway streaming! . . . . pique—   *1868*
But alway streaming! . . . . pique: 359 *1840* but wherefore say my   *360
{Reading of *1863*}   *1840* All height—than every depth profounder
drops?   *1865–89* Each height, then every depth profoundlier drops?   363
1840–65 Fate   364 *1840* The same . . . . dust   365 *1840 proof* checked>
chequed   *1840–65* Perchance—so facile was the deed,   367 *1840* That soul
diversely—   *1863,1865* My soul diversely—   368 *1840* why marvel   370
1840–65 Before it? . . . . sun—   371 *1840–65* me—what   372 *1840*
behind?

354 *great hands*: Taurello's: cf. l. 24 above.

    363 *I trust*: although I am not prepared to wait for a transcendent life prepared
for me by Fate after the present life, yet I am prepared to trust my soul to Fate in
another way. Perhaps fate threw a random cloud of circumstances into the void
to affect my soul in one way and another, just like a man flinging a handful of
dust: then when I die perhaps she will throw a more splendid cloud—a handful
of matter or circumstances from which another solar system will form itself for
me.

    365 *chequed*: chequered. As well as correcting the spelling, in the *1840 proof*,
Browning wrote 'chequed (*a different word*)' at the foot of the page (p. 231).

"And how shall some new flesh that is not flesh
"Cling to me? What 's new laughter? Soothes
   the fresh
"Sleep like sleep? Fate's exhaustless for my sake   375
"In brave resource: but whether bids she slake
"My thirst at this first rivulet, or count
"No draught worth lip save from some rocky
   fount
"Above i' the clouds, while here she 's
   provident
"Of pure loquacious pearl, the soft tree-tent   380
"Guards, with its face of reate and sedge, nor
   fail
"The silver globules and gold-sparkling grail
"At bottom? Oh, 't were too absurd to slight
freed from a
problematic   "For the hereafter the to-day's delight!
obligation,   "Quench thirst at this, then seek next
   well-spring: wear   385
"Home-lilies ere strange lotus in my hair!
"Here is the Crowd, whom I with freest heart
"Offer to serve, contented for my part
"To give life up in service,—only grant
"That I do serve; if otherwise, why want   390
"Aught further of me? If men cannot choose

373 *1840–65* what's new laughter—soothes   376 *1840–65* resource,
378 *1840–68* from the rocky   380 *1840* Of (taste) loquacious pearl   383
1840 At bottom—   *1863,1865* At bottom.   385 *1840–65* well-spring—
389 *1840* To give this life up once for all, but grant   390 *1840* I really serve;
391 *1840* me? Life they cannot chuse

373 *some new flesh*: he is contemplating some other state of being, 'Under a
cluster of fresh stars' (iii. 860), 'Above i' the clouds' (vi. 379).

376 *whether bids she*: does fate bid me seize the immediate pleasures or wait
for some uncertain and visionary after-life?

379 *Above i' the clouds*: 'Enjoy this world without troubling himself about the
next sphere': Domett.

380 *loquacious pearl*: pure water which babbles along in the brook. At i. 903
we hear how 'singing soft, the runnel slipped'.

tree-tent: cf. *Paracelsus*, ii. 471, 'the tent-tree by the wayside well'.

381 *reate*: 'A kind of long small grass that grows in water': Johnson.

382 *grail*: gravel. The other examples of this (poetic) word in OED are from
Spenser and from Henry More's *Philosophicall Poems* (1647), p. 224. For
Browning and More see i. 748 n.

389 *but grant (1840)*: 'so that I really serve': Domett.

391 *men*: i.e. other men. Domett emphasizes the sense of the *1840* version of
391–2 by underlining 'they' and 'I'.

"But set aside life, why should I refuse
"The gift? I take it—I, for one, engage
"Never to falter through my pilgrimage—
395 "Nor end it howling that the stock or stone
"Were enviable, truly: I, for one,
"Will praise the world, you style mere
          anteroom
"To palace—be it so! shall I assume
"—My foot the courtly gait, my tongue the
          trope,
400 "My mouth the smirk, before the doors fly ope
"One moment? What? with guarders row on
          row,
"Gay swarms of varletry that come and go,
"Pages to dice with, waiting-girls unlace
"The plackets of, pert claimants help displace,
405 "Heart-heavy suitors get a rank for,—laugh
"At yon sleek parasite, break his own staff
"'Cross Beetle-brows the Usher's
          shoulder,—why,
"Admitted to the presence by and by,
"Should thought of having lost these make me
          grieve   *and accepting life*
410 "Among new joys I reach, for joys I leave?   *on its own terms,*

392 *1840* But set aside—wherefore should I refuse   394–5 *1840* through
the pilgrimage—|Or end it   397 *1840 proof* antiroom   398 *1840* To the
true palace—but shall   *1863,1865* To the palace—be it so! shall   400 *1840*
My eye the glance,   401 *1840–65* What—with   405 *1840* for;   *407
{Reading of *1863–8*}   *1840* shoulder; why—   *1888,1889* shoulder,
—why   409–10 *1840* of these recurring make me grieve|Among new sights
I reach, old sights I leave?

395 *howling*: lamenting: conceivably with reference to Jeremiah 2:27.
397 *anteroom*: cf. Donne, *The Second Anniversarie*, 85–6: 'Think then, my
soul, that death is but a groom, / Which brings a taper to the outward room';
and *Easter-Day*, 752, in *Christmas-Eve and Easter-Day*: 'The earth, God's
antechamber'.
398 *shall I assume*: 'shall I put on the feelings proper to the next sphere before
its doors open!—while there is this one to enjoy?': Domett.
399 *My foot . . . the gait*: for the construction cf. iii. 76–7.
402 *varletry*: as in *Antony and Cleopatra*, v. ii. 56.
405 *get a rank for*: i.e. get them the positions at Court or elsewhere for which
they are pleading.
407 *Beetle-brows*: cf. *Balaustion's Adventure*, 1785: 'A churlish visage, all one
beetle-brow'.

"Cool citrine-crystals, fierce pyropus-stone,
"Are floor-work there! But do I let alone
"That black-eyed peasant in the vestibule
"Once and for ever?—Floor-work? No such
      fool!
"Rather, were heaven to forestall earth, I 'd say   415
"I, is it, must be blest? Then, my own way
"Bless me! Give firmer arm and fleeter foot,
"I 'll thank you: but to no mad wings
      transmute
"These limbs of mine—our greensward was so
      soft!
"Nor camp I on the thunder-cloud aloft: 420
"We feel the bliss distinctlier, having thus
"Engines subservient, not mixed up with us.
"Better move palpably through heaven: nor,
      freed
"Of flesh, forsooth, from space to space
      proceed
"'Mid flying synods of worlds! No: in heaven's
      marge   425

411–12 *1840* —Cool. . . . pyropus-stone—|Bare floor-work too!—But did
I let alone *1863,1865* —Cool. . . . pyropus-stone,|Are floor-work here!—But
did I let alone   415 *1840* Heaven to forestal Earth,   416 *1840* Must I be
blessed or you?   *1863–8* I, is it, must be blessed? Then,   *417{Read-
ing of *1868*} *1840* Bless me—a firmer arm, a fleeter foot,   *1863,1865* Bless me!
give firmer arm and fleeter foot,   *1888,1889* Bless me! Giver firmer arm and
fleeter foot, {corrected to 'Give' in some copies of *1889*}   419 *1840* greensward is too soft;   420 *1840* aloft—   422 *1840* us—   423 *1840*
Heaven— *1863,1865* heaven—   424 *1840* Of flesh   425 *1840* worlds—but
in Heaven's   *1863* worlds! No! In heaven's

411 *citrine-crystals*: citrine is 'a glassy variety of quartz having a wine-yellow
colour': OED. 'Pyropus-stone' is a deep-red gem. In heaven the floor is made
of rare and beautiful stones.
416 *I . . . must be blest?*: if I had to forego all preliminary pleasures of this life,
I should ask whether I really had to find myself in heaven. Cf. *Easter-Day*
570–5, in *Christmas-Eve and Easter-Day*.
420 *on the thunder-cloud*: among the gods.
422 *Engines subservient*: bodily organs, limbs, distinct from our souls.
425 *synods of worlds!*: Johnson's second definition of 'synod' is 'conjunction
of the heavenly bodies'. He quotes Boyle: 'the planets and stars have, according
to astrologers, in their great synods, or conjunctions, much more powerful
influences on the air than are ascribed to one or two of them out of that aspect'.
   in heaven's marge: as in old maps, which often have representations of such
figures as Titan and Sagittarius (the Centaur who had been transformed into a
constellation).

"Show Titan still, recumbent o'er his targe
"Solid with stars—the Centaur at his game,
"Made tremulously out in hoary flame!
   "Life! Yet the very cup whose extreme dull
"Dregs, even, I would quaff, was dashed, at
430   full,
"Aside so oft; the death I fly, revealed
"So oft a better life this life concealed,
"And which sage, champion, martyr, through
   each path
"Have hunted fearlessly—the horrid bath,
435 "The crippling-irons and the fiery chair.   *which, yet, others*
"'T was well for them; let me become aware   *have renounced:*
"As they, and I relinquish life, too! Let   *how?*
"What masters life disclose itself! Forget
"Vain ordinances, I have one appeal—
440 "I feel, am what I feel, know what I feel;
"So much is truth to me. What Is, then? Since
"One object, viewed diversely, may evince
"Beauty and ugliness—this way attract,
"That way repel,—why gloze upon the fact?
445 "Why must a single of the sides be right?
"What bids choose this and leave the opposite?
"Where 's abstract Right for me?—in youth
   endued

---

427 *1840* game   435 *1840* chair: 436 *1840–65* —'T was   437 *1840*
Life,   438 *1840* Life's secret but disclose   440–1 *1840* feel|—So much is
Truth to me—What Is then?   *1863,1865* feel|—So much is truth to me. What
Is, then?   444 *1840–65* repel,   446–7 *1840* Who bids choose this and leave
its opposite?|No abstract Right for me—

---

430 *was dashed*: by heroes in the past, whose goal was 'a better life'.
435 *the fiery chair*: in the margin *SB* has 'The supreme Good making [? pain]
for its [illegible]'.
436 *'T was well for them*: cf. *Easter-Day*, 40 ff. in *Christmas-Eve and Easter-Day*.
439 *Vain ordinances*: cf. Colossians, 2:20 : 'Wherefore if ye be dead with
Christ from the rudiments of the world, why, as though living in the world,
are ye subject to ordinances . . .?'
440 *I feel*: cf. *Pauline*, 277–9.
444 *why gloze*: why not face the truth? Cf. *Prometheus Unbound*, III. iv. 167:
'wrong, glozed on by ignorance'.
447 *in youth endued*: when I was young I always thought I knew where Right
lay, a Right which was to be pursued through each circle or phase of life, each
having an appropriate law: I thought I knew when it was right to rule
absolutely, as the Emperor did, when to yield implicit obedience like one of his

"With Right still present, still to be pursued,
"Thro' all the interchange of circles, rife
"Each with its proper law and mode of life,   450
"Each to be dwelt at ease in: where, to sway
"Absolute with the Kaiser, or obey
"Implicit with his serf of fluttering heart,
"Or, like a sudden thought of God's, to start
"Up, Brutus in the presence, then go shout   455
"That some should pick the unstrung jewels
        out—
"Each, well!"
                        And, as in moments when the past
Gave partially enfranchisement, he cast
Himself quite through mere secondary states
Of his soul's essence, little loves and hates,   460
Into the mid deep yearnings overlaid

Because there is a   By these; as who should pierce hill, plain,
life beyond life,   grove, glade,
And on into the very nucleus probe
That first determined there exist a globe.
As that were easiest, half the globe dissolved,   465
So seemed Sordello's closing-truth evolved
By his flesh-half's break-up; the sudden swell
Of his expanding soul showed Ill and Well,

451–2 *1840* in: thus to sway|Regally with   455 *1840* Up in the presence,
then go forth and shout   457 *1840 proof* well.>well! *1840* Were
well!¶ And, ... Past   *1863,1865* Each, well!"¶ And, ... Past   461 *1840*
the mid vague yearnings   463 *1840* And so into   464–5 *1840* Globe:|And
as that's easiest   467 *1840* In his .... break up—   *1863,1865* By his ....
break up—   *1868* By his .... break up;

serfs, and when to stand up boldly as a defiant hero, like the great Brutus. Ll.
456–7 are obscure, but cf. iv. 978 ff. The 'unstrung jewels' here may refer back
to 'the gem / Out of a lapfull, spoil their diadem'.
    457 *as in moments*: as when, in the past, he had sometimes felt liberated
momentarily. See ii. 379 ff.
    459 *secondary states*: e.g. 'little loves and hates' such as passionate support for
the Guelfs or Ghibellins. He penetrates beyond these to what is truly central,
like the fire at the centre of the earth, from which all originated. Cf. *Paracelsus*,
v. 653 ff.
    461 *the mid deep yearnings*: the yearnings deep in his soul. Cf. OED, 'mid',
B.l.b.
    467 *break-up*: Browning was particularly interested in the vision of life's
meaning which may present itself to a dying man. Cf. *Paracelsus* i. 765–9 and v.
487–8, 507–9. See Ian Jack, *Browning's Major Poetry* (1973), 198–200.
    468 *showed Ill and Well*: dying, Sordello 'perceived that ... all qualities

Sorrow and Joy, Beauty and Ugliness,
470   Virtue and Vice, the Larger and the Less,
All qualities, in fine, recorded here,
Might be but modes of Time and this one
    sphere,
Urgent on these, but not of force to bind
Eternity, as Time—as Matter—Mind,
475   If Mind, Eternity, should choose assert
Their attributes within a Life: thus girt
With circumstance, next change beholds them
    cinct
Quite otherwise—with Good and Ill distinct,
Joys, sorrows, tending to a like result—
480   Contrived to render easy, difficult,
This or the other course of . . . what new bond
In place of flesh may stop their flight beyond
Its new sphere, as that course does harm or
    good
To its arrangements. Once this understood,

---

472 *1840* Modes of Time . . . . Sphere,   474 *1840* As Time—Eternity,
as   475 *1840* Eternity shall choose

recognised on earth—might be merely modes of time and this one world of matter, and incapable of binding eternity (as they bind time) or mind (as they bind matter), if mind and eternity should choose to assert their attributes within a life conditioned otherwise than ours. These attributes, girt now with earthly circumstance, may in another sphere be girt quite differently—with a different good and a different evil, though with joys and sorrows still contrived, as they are here, to render easy or difficult a particular course of life under whatever takes the place of flesh, according as that course harms or benefits the arrangements of the new sphere in which it must be run, that these attributes may be prevented from flying beyond it': Duff. For 'urgent on', cf. Exodus 12:33. The second half of 474 is peculiarly confusing. *1840* is clearer. The unusual 'cinct' means 'surrounded', like 'girt'.

472 *Might be but modes of Time*: cf. Carlyle, *Sartor Resartus*, Book I, ch. viii, para. 5: 'the WHERE and WHEN, so mysteriously inseparable from all our thoughts, are but superficial terrestrial adhesions to thought; . . . the Seer may discern them where they mount up out of the celestial EVERYWHERE and FOREVER . . . Think well, thou too wilt find that Space is but a mode of our human Sense, so likewise Time; there *is* no Space and no Time: WE are—we know not what . . .'

475–6 *If Mind . . . within a Life*: a colleague agrees that the thought is 'of course extremely Hegelian', adding that 'it all begins to look just like Geist, the infinite, expressing itself in the finite'. We know that Browning did not in fact read Hegel (cf. Vol. I, 43 n, above), but some influence of German metaphysics here seems evident.

484 *understood*: was understood.

As suddenly he felt himself alone,   485
Quite out of Time and this world: all was
    known.
and with new
conditions of
success,
What made the secret of his past despair?
—Most imminent when he seemed most aware
Of his own self-sufficiency: made mad
By craving to expand the power he had,   490
And not new power to be expanded?—just
This made it; Soul on Matter being thrust,
Joy comes when so much Soul is wreaked in
    Time
On Matter: let the Soul's attempt sublime
Matter beyond the scheme and so prevent   495
By more or less that deed's accomplishment,
And Sorrow follows: Sorrow how avoid?
Let the employer match the thing employed,
Fit to the finite his infinity,
And thus proceed for ever, in degree   500
Changed but in kind the same, still limited
To the appointed circumstance and dead
To all beyond. A sphere is but a sphere;
Small, Great, are merely terms we bandy here;
Since to the spirit's absoluteness all   505

---

485 *1840 proof* alone>alone,   486 *1840* World,   487 *1840* of the
past   488 *1840* (Most   489 *1840* Of greatness in the Past—nought turned
him mad   *1863–8* Of his own self-sufficiency; made mad   490 *1840* Like
craving   491 *1840* Not a new . . . . expanded)—just   493 *1840* 'Tis Joy
when   494 *1840* On Matter,—let the Soul attempt sublime   *1863–8* On
Matter,—let the Soul's attempt sublime   495 *1840* beyond its
scheme   496 *1840* Or more   497 *1840* Sorrow to avoid—   498 *1840*
Employer . . . . Employed,   503 *1840* beyond: a sphere is but a
sphere—   *1863,1865* beyond. A sphere is but a sphere—   504 *1840–65*
here—

---

488 *when* ∧| *he*: SB moves 'in the Past' (*1840*) from the next line to a place
between these words.
490 *had*: SB seeks to clarify by underlining 'had', as well as 'new' (491).
492 *Soul on Matter*: when Soul exerts itself on Matter, in this temporal world,
Joy results when it is effective; but if the Soul attempts to change or purify
Matter beyond the present Scheme of Things (in a manner which would
interfere with the fulfilment of that Scheme) the result is Sorrow. 'Sublime' is
reminiscent of alchemy.
494 *let the Soul attempt* ∧| *sublime* (*1840*): 'to': Domett.
503 *A sphere*: cf. ll. 506–7, 'the present sphere we call / Life'. Domett
comments: 'there is great mastery of language & power of thought manifested
here in following out the subtle argument'.

Are like. Now, of the present sphere we call
Life, are conditions; take but this among
Many; the body was to be so long
Youthful, no longer: but, since no control
510   Tied to that body's purposes his soul,
She chose to understand the body's trade
More than the body's self—had fain conveyed
Her boundless to the body's bounded lot.
Hence, the soul permanent, the body not,—
515   Scarcely its minute for enjoying here,—
The soul must needs instruct her weak
    compeer,
Run o'er its capabilities and wring
A joy thence, she held worth experiencing:
Which, far from half discovered even,—lo,
520   The minute gone, the body's power let go
Apportioned to that joy's acquirement! Broke   *nor such as, in*
Morning o'er earth, he yearned for all it   *this, produce*
    woke—   *failure.*
From the volcano's vapour-flag, winds hoist
Black o'er the spread of sea,—down to the
    moist
525   Dale's silken barley-spikes sullied with rain,

---

506 *1840* like: now *1863,1865* like: now,   507 *1840–65* conditions—   508 *1840* Body   509 *1840–65* longer—   510 *1840* Body's
. . . . Soul,   511 *1840* It chose. . . . Body's   512 *1840* Body's   513 *1840*
Its boundless, ... lot— *1863,1865* Her boundless, ... lot: *1868* Her
boundless, ... lot.   514 *1840* So, the   515 *1840–65* Scarce the one
minute . . . . here, *1868* Scarce the one minute . . . . here,—   516 *1840*
instruct its weak   518 *1840* thence it holds worth experiencing—   *1863*
thence, the held worth experiencing— *1865* thence, she held worth
experiencing—   520 *1840* The minute's gone, the body's power's let
go   521 *1840* Apportioned to . . . . Broke, *1863,1865* That's portioned to
. . . . Broke   522 *1840 proof* woke>woke—   *1840* Say, morning o'er the
earth and all   523 *1840* vapour-flag to hoist   524 *1840* sea, to the low
moist   525 *1840 proof* rain>rain,

---

511 *trade*: business.

512 *had fain conveyed*: the soul would have liked to make the body permanent,
like itself.

518 *she*: the soul, which is unwilling to allow the body the joys which are
available to it, favouring only joys for which the body is insufficiently long-
lived.

521–2 *Broke / Morning*: when (for example) morning came . . .

523 *vapour-flag*: the cloud of smoke over the volcano. Browning saw Etna on
16 May 1838. Cf. *Sordello*, iii. 955 ff.

winds: which winds.

Swayed earthwards, heavily to rise again—
The Small, a sphere as perfect as the Great
To the soul's absoluteness. Meditate
Too long on such a morning's cluster-chord
And the whole music it was framed afford,—   530
The chord's might half discovered, what should
    pluck
One string, his finger, was found palsy-struck.
And then no marvel if the spirit, shown
A saddest sight—the body lost alone
Through her officious proffered help, deprived   535
Of this and that enjoyment Fate contrived,—
Virtue, Good, Beauty, each allowed slip
    hence,—
Vain-gloriously were fain, for recompense,
To stem the ruin even yet, protract
The body's term, supply the power it lacked   540
From her infinity, compel it learn
These qualities were only Time's concern,
And body may, with spirit helping, barred—
Advance the same, vanquished—obtain reward,
Reap joy where sorrow was intended grow,   545

---

526 *1840* to raise again—   527 *1840* (The Small *1863,1865* (The
Small,   528 *1840–65* absoluteness)—meditate   529 *1840* On such an
Autumn-morning's   530 *1840* afford,   531 *1840 proof* {lines 531–2 added,
in Browning's hand, as in *1840*: 'And, the chord's might discovered, what
should pluck / One string, the finger, was found palsy-struck.'}   533 *1840*
proof spirit,> Spirit,   *1840* And then what marvel if the Spirit, shown   534
1840 Body   535 *1840* Thro' its officious   536 *1840–65* contrived,   540
1840 proof term of joy,> Body's term, {as in *1840*}   541 *1840* From its
infinity,   543 *1840 proof* And therefore may,> The Body may,   *1840* That
Body may, with its assistance, barred—

---

528 *Meditate*: if he reflected too long on the rich harmony implicit in such a
collection of delights, then before he had fathomed the half of it he found
himself so weak that his finger was unable even to begin to play any part of it.
530 *framed afford*: framed to afford.
533 *no marvel*: it is in no way surprising if the Spirit—having seen a very sad
sight, that of the Body deprived of its proper goods and enjoyments (Virtue,
Good, Beauty) solely because of its (the Spirit's) presumptuously-offered
assistance—should wish unnaturally to protract its existence, so making it
learn that such goods and enjoyments are proper only to the sphere of the
Temporal, and that the Body may (if helped by the Spirit) advance and win
rewards—rewards which were never 'intended'.
534 *A saddest sight*: changed to 'This saddest sight' in *SB*.

Of Wrong make Right, and turn Ill Good
        below.
And the result is, the poor body soon
Sinks under what was meant a wondrous boon,
Leaving its bright accomplice all aghast.
550   So much was plain then, proper in the past;
To be complete for, satisfy the whole
Series of spheres—Eternity, his soul
Needs must exceed, prove incomplete for, each
Single sphere—Time. But does our knowledge
        reach
555   No farther? Is the cloud of hindrance broke
But by the failing of the fleshly yoke,
Its loves and hates, as now when death lets soar
Sordello, self-sufficient as before,
Though during the mere space that shall elapse
560   'Twixt his enthralment in new bonds perhaps?
Must life be ever just escaped, which should
Have been enjoyed?—nay, might have been   *But, even here, is*
        and would,   *failure inevitable?*
Each purpose ordered right—the soul 's no whit
Beyond the body's purpose under it.

546 *1840* Right. . . . below—   547 *1840 proof* Body,   *1840* Body   550
1840–65 Past;   553 *1840–68* Exceeded, so was incomplete for, each   554
1840 One sphere—our Time.   557 *1840* when they let soar   558 *1840* The
spirit, self-sufficient   559 *1840* Tho' but the single space   560 *1840* 'Twixt
its enthralment . . . . bonds   *1863–8* 'Twixt his enthralment . . . .
bonds,   561–4 *1840* Must Life be ever but escaped, which should | Have been

549 *its bright accomplice*: the soul.
550 *So much was plain*: Domett wrote 'beautiful, but query if true', with a
large question-mark, in the margin here: his last annotation.
551 *To be complete*: if his soul is to be wholly adequate to Eternity (the whole
series of spheres) then it is bound to be inadequate for any one sphere, i.e. Time.
552 *his soul*: 'had inevitably': *SB*.
557 *as now when death*: it becomes clear that he has just died. Cf. *Adonais*, xl:
'He has outsoared the shadow of our night'. We note that Browning makes
Sordello die at or about the age of 30, like Shelley, whereas the historical
Sordello is said to have lived to be an old man.—At l. 621 his heart appears to
give a posthumous beat.
559 *Tho' but*   (*1840*): 'during': *SB*.
560 *new bonds*: for all we know, it may be only for a short time that his soul is
self-sufficient again, before it comes under another jurisdiction in another life.
For ''twixt' = before, cf. 'betwixt and' in OED ('Betwixt', 3), said to be a
northern dialectical form.
563–4 *and a Soul's no whit | More* (*1840*): indistinctly altered in *SB*, perhaps to
'and had there been a Soul's purpose no whit Wider'.
564 *under it*: '—Agreeing like what he saw here—': *SB*.

Like yonder breadth of watery heaven, a bay,   565
And that sky-space of water, ray for ray
And star for star, one richness where they
    mixed
As this and that wing of an angel, fixed,
Tumultuary splendours folded in
To die—would soul, proportioned thus, begin   570
Exciting discontent, or surelier quell
The body if, aspiring, it rebel?
But how so order life? Still brutalize
The soul, the sad world's way, with muffled eyes
To all that was before, all that shall be   575
After this sphere—all and each quality

enjoyed? nay, ... would,|Once ordered rightly, and a Soul's no whit|More
than the Body's purpose under it| *1863–8* {as *1888* except 'it—' in line
564.}   565 *1840 proof* bay>bay,   *1840* ('A breadth of watery heaven like a
bay,   566 *1840* A sky-like space   570 *1840* To die) and which thus, far
from first begin   571–2 *1840* Exciting discontent, had surest quelled|The
Body if aspiring it rebelled.   573 *1840* Life?   574 *1840* world's
method—muffled eyes   575 *1840* before, shall after be   576 *1840* This
sphere—and every other quality   *1863–8* After this sphere—and every quality

    565 *Like yonder breadth*: it is to be desired that soul and body should harmon-
ize, as the sky and water harmonize (the sky looking like a bay, the bay looking
like the sky, ray and star mirroring each other and looking for all the world like
the multi-coloured wings of an angel that has lain down to die). In that event,
surely the soul would not render the body discontented but guide it aright? Ll.
565–6 virtually repeat vi. 11–12, while ll. 567–70 (first two words) exactly
repeat vi. 13–16. In its earlier occurrence the passage appears to describe the
evening scene which Sordello is contemplating, and which prompts him to
reflect that man is by no means dwarfed by nature, as Eglamor and others so
often say. Here the scene becomes a symbol of the power of man, if only body
and soul would work in harmony. Such are Sordello's reflections as he dies.
    570 *and which thus, far from first begin* (*1840*): altered in *SB* to 'and which thus
proportioned, far from first beginning'.
    573 ∧|*Still brutalize*: 'Proportion Soul to Body?': *SB.*
    574 *muffled eyes*: must ,we always treat the soul like a falcon or other
hunting-bird, hooding it so that it can see neither what went before the present
sphere of existence nor what will certainly follow it—so that it can only see
some supposedly unique and immutable qualities of Great, Good and Beauteous which alone it is permitted to pursue? May a soul never be allowed to see
All—'The Great Before and After' as well as the limited Present—yet volun-
tarily follow the single course which is prescribed for it, as the king-bird,
which is immeasurably ancient, yet submits to die at the prescribed
time?—There was an ancient belief that every ten years the eagle soars into the
'fiery region', plunges from there into the sea, moults its feathers, and acquires
new life. The reference is probably to the eagle rather than the phoenix (though
the legends are closely associated), since Psalm 103:5 is clearly relevant: 'thy
youth is renewed like the eagle's'. Harrison remarks that 'king-bird' applies
properly 'to one of the birds of paradise . . . or possibly to the eagle': loc. cit. p.
401 n.

Save some sole and immutable Great, Good
And Beauteous whither fate has loosed its hood
To follow? Never may some soul see All
— The Great Before and After, and the Small   80
Now, yet be saved by this the simplest lore,
And take the single course prescribed before,
As the king-bird with ages on his plumes
Travels to die in his ancestral glooms?
But where descry the Love that shall select   85
That course? Here is a soul whom, to affect,   *Or may failure*
Nature has plied with all her means, from trees   *here be success also*
And flowers e'en to the Multitude!—and these,
Decides he save or no? One word to end!
Ah my Sordello, I this once befriend   90
And speak for you. Of a Power above you still
Which, utterly incomprehensible,
Is out of rivalry, which thus you can
Love, tho' unloving all conceived by man—
What need! And of—none the minutest duct   95
To that out-nature, nought that would instruct

---

577 *1840 proof* immutable.>immutable *1840–68* Great and Good   579
1840 proof see all?   580 *1840* before and after   582 *1840 proof* before>
before,   584 *1840 proof* glooms>glooms?   586 *1840 proof* the Soul>a Soul
1840 Soul whom to affect   587 *1840–65* means—   588 *1840* flowers—
.... Multitude ... and these *1863,1865* flowers—. . . . Multitude!—and
these,   589 *1863,1865* end!"   590 *1840 proof* for>this   591 *1840* you. A
Power above him still *SB* you.>him.   592 *1840 proof* Which>
Which,   593 *1840 proof* therefore which>which thus *1840* thus he can
{lines 593 and 594 are printed, uncorrected, at the foot of p. 240 in the *1840*
proof, and in corrected form as the first two lines of p. 241}   594 *1840*
Man—   595 *1840 proof* of>of—   596 *1840 proof* out nature,>out-Nature,
{as in *1840*}

583 *the king-bird*: cf. Moore, *Lalla Rookh* ('Paradise and the Peri', note to l.
308).

586 *Here is a soul*: Sordello himself is a gifted soul, open to all the influences of
Nature, including that of his fellow-men. What will he do? In particular, will
he decide to 'save' his fellow-men, or not?

591 *you*: *SB* substitutes 'him'.

a Power above you: Duff surprisingly remarks that 'It is impossible to find in
this passage the slightest hint of Christian dogma'. The Christian reference of
602 seems unmistakeable. See Browning's own comment, in a letter to Ruskin,
cited at 625 n. below. *Pauline*, 818 ff. is more explicitly Christian.

595 ∧ *What need!*: 'of this,' *SB*, which inserts commas after 'none' and
'minutest'.

596 *out-nature*: cf. Palma's longing for 'some out-soul': iii. 317 ff. In *Paradise*
Lost Eve says to Adam: 'God is thy law, thou mine': iv. 637.

And so let rivalry begin to live—
But of a Power its representative
Who, being for authority the same,
Communication different, should claim   60
A course, the first chose but this last revealed—
This Human clear, as that Divine concealed—
What utter need!

when induced by   What has Sordello found?
love? Sordello
knows: Or can his spirit go the mighty round,
End where poor Eglamor begun? So, says   60
Old fable, the two eagles went two ways
About the world: where, in the midst, they
        met,
Though on a shifting waste of sand, men set
Jove's temple. Quick, what has Sordello found?
For they approach—approach—that foot's
        rebound   6
Palma? No, Salinguerra though in mail;
They mount, have reached the threshold, dash
        the veil
Aside—and you divine who sat there dead,

---

597 *1840 proof* live>live—   599 *1840 proof* Who . . . . same>Who, ...
same,   600 *1840 proof* different>different,   601 *1840 proof* the last>this
last   *1840* course the first chose and this   *1863–8* course, the first chose and
this   602 *1840 proof* To which all rivalry with this appealed >This Human
clear, as that Divine concealed—   603 *1840 proof* What utter>The utter {as
in *1840*}   604 *1840 proof* has his spirit gone>can his spirit go   *1840*
round   605 *1840 proof* At last, ends>At length, end   *1840* At length, end
where our souls begun? as says   *1863* End where poor Eglamor begun? as
says   *1865* End . . . . begun? as, says   *1868* End . . . . begun?— So, says
606 *1840* two doves were sent two ways   607 *1840* world—where in the
midst they met   608 *1840 proof* they set>men set   *1840* Tho' on   609
1840 proof found>found?   *1840* Jove's temple?   610 *1840–68* rebound
. .   613 *1840* dead

---

605 *End*: only to end (after experiences so much more profound than those of
ordinary men) 'where our souls begun?' (*1840*) or 'where poor Eglamor
begun?'—that is in appreciating the need for love.
606 *two eagles*: 'The City *Delphos* . . . is suppos'd to be in the middle of the
World; for when *Jupiter* sent forth two Eagles at the same time, one from the
East, the other from the *West*, they both met at that Place exactly, in Memory
whereof a Golden Eagle was there deposited': *An Historical Account of the
Heathen Gods and Heroes*, by Dr King, 5th ed. (1731), p. 75. SB changes 'doves
were sent' to 'eagles went'.
610 *that foot's rebound*: Salinguerra is moving so swiftly and lightly that his
step could be mistaken for Palma's.

Under his foot the badge: still, Palma said,
615 A triumph lingering in the wide eyes,
Wider than some spent swimmer's if he spies
Help from above in his extreme despair,
And, head far back on shoulder thrust, turns
     there
With short quick passionate cry: as Palma
     pressed
620 In one great kiss, her lips upon his breast,
It beat.
          By this, the hermit-bee has stopped
His day's toil at Goito: the new-cropped
Dead vine-leaf answers, now 't is eve, he bit,
Twirled so, and filed all day: the mansion 's fit,
625 God counselled for. As easy guess the word

---

616 *1840 proof* swimmer> swimmer's   618 *1840 proof* And> And,   619
1840 With short and passionate cry; as Palma prest   *1863,1865* With short,
quick, passionate cry: as Palma prest *1868* With short, quick, passionate cry: as
Palma pressed   620 *1840–65* kiss . . . . breast   621 *1840* By this
1863,1865 By this, {No line division.}   622 *1840* Goito—the new cropped
624 *1840 proof* fit!> fit   *1840* day—the mansion's fit   625 *1840* for; as

---

614 *the badge*: Sordello's last act had been to throw down the badge, rejecting
the power with which he had been tempted.
    616 *some spent swimmer*: possibly a reminiscence of portrayals of Leander.
    621 *the hermit-bee*: as at v. 1025. 'I once saw a solitary bee nipping a leaf round
till it exactly fitted the front of a hole; his nest, no doubt; or tomb, perhaps . . .
Well, it seemed awful to watch that bee—he seemed so *instantly* from the
teaching of God!': RB to EBB, Kintner, i. 357. Cf. *Pauline*, 439.
    623 *answers*: answers his purpose.
    625 *As easy*: we can no more find any fault in the bee's fulfilment of his task
than we can guess at God's instruction which enabled him to build his little
'mansion'. Unlike Sordello, the simple bee is not tortured by remembering the
maidens who support the font at Goito. In what has he failed?
    Browning quoted ll. 621–8, 780–9, and 853–70 in an interesting letter to
Ruskin on 1 February 1856, with the claim that this 'is certainly the first time in
my whole life that I ever quoted a line of my own'. He apologizes for 'the poor
quality of my verse' but quotes the lines to rebut a statement in the chapter 'Of
Modern Landscape' in *Modern Painters* in which Ruskin had written: 'There
never yet was a generation of men . . . who, taken as a body, so wofully
fulfilled the words "having no hope, and without God in the world" as the
present civilized European race': *Modern Painters*, vol. iii (1856), p. 259 (Cook
and Wedderburn ed., vol. v, p. 323). Browning replies: 'Of all my things, the
single chance I have had of speaking in my own person—not dramati-
cally—has been in a few words in the course of "Sordello" . . . . so I at once ask
myself—knowing what my faith was, & immeasurably deeper is—"Did I
then, if I needed to notice a natural object, really withhold my tributary
two-mites tho' they do but make a farthing?"': *A Letter from Robert Browning to
John Ruskin* (Baylor Browning Interests, no. 17: Waco, Texas, 1958).

That passed betwixt them, and become the
    third
To the soft small unfrighted bee, as tax

*but too late: an
insect knows
sooner.*

Him with one fault—so, no remembrance racks
Of the stone maidens and the font of stone
He, creeping through the crevice, leaves alone.   630
Alas, my friend, alas Sordello, whom
Anon they laid within that old font-tomb,
And, yet again, alas!
                    And now is 't worth
Our while bring back to mind, much less set
    forth
How Salinguerra extricates himself   635
Without Sordello? Ghibellin and Guelf
May fight their fiercest out? If Richard sulked
In durance or the Marquis paid his mulct,
Who cares, Sordello gone? The upshot, sure,
Was peace; our chief made some frank overture   640
That prospered; compliment fell thick and fast
On its disposer, and Taurello passed
With foe and friend for an outstripping soul,
Nine days at least. Then,—fairly reached the
    goal,—
He, by one effort, blotted the great hope   645
Out of his mind, nor further tried to cope
With Este, that mad evening's style, but sent
Away the Legate and the League, content

---

    628 *1840* so no   630 *1840* thro' .... alone—   631 *1840* Alas, my
friend—Alas Sordello! whom *1863,1865* Alas, my friend—alas Sordello,
whom   632 *1840* Anon we laid within that cold font-tomb— *1863,1865*
Anon they laid within that old font-tomb—   633 *1840* And yet again
alas!   637 *1840* fiercest? If Count Richard   644 *1840* least: then, fairly
reached the goal,   646 *1840* no further   647 *1840* With Este

---

634 ∧ *bring*: 'to': *SB*, which also deletes 'back'.
638 *the Marquis*: Azzo.
643 *an outstripping soul*: cf. Bunyan, *Holy Citie* (1669), p. 91: 'They out-stript
all the Prophets that ever went before them'.
644 *Nine days*: i.e. he was a nine days' wonder.
    fairly . . . goal: absolute: once the goal had been fairly reached.
645 *the great hope*: that of overthrowing the House of Este and perhaps going
even further, as he had dreamed of doing 'that mad evening': see v. 844 ff.
648 *the Legate*: the Papal legate, who represented the Lombard League.

No blame at least the brothers had incurred,
650 —Dispatched a message to the Monk, he heard
Patiently first to last, scarce shivered at,
Then curled his limbs up on his wolfskin mat
And ne'er spoke more,—informed the
    Ferrarese
He but retained their rule so long as these
655 Lingered in pupilage,—and last, no mode
Apparent else of keeping safe the road
From Germany direct to Lombardy
For Friedrich,—none, that is, to guarantee
The faith and promptitude of who should next
660 Obtain Sofia's dowry,—sore perplexed—
(Sofia being youngest of the tribe
Of daughters, Ecelin was wont to bribe
The envious magnates with—nor, since he sent
Henry of Egna this fair child, had Trent
665 Once failed the Kaiser's purposes—"we lost
"Egna last year, and who takes Egna's post—
"Opens the Lombard gate if Friedrich knock?")
Himself espoused the Lady of the Rock
In pure necessity, and, so destroyed
670 His slender last of chances, quite made void
Old prophecy, and spite of all the schemes
Overt and covert, youth's deeds, age's dreams,
Was sucked into Romano. And so hushed
He up this evening's work that, when 't was
    brushed

*On his
disappearance from
the stage,*

---

658 *1840* Friedrich,   660 *1840* dowry,   663–4 *1840* nor since he
sent| Enrico Egna this fair child had Trent   665 *1840* —we lost   667 *1840*
knock?)   669 *1840–65* and so destroyed   673 *1840* Romano: and   674
1840 that when,

---

649 *the brothers*: Alberic and Ecelin (the Tyrant).

654 *these*: the brothers.

660 *Sofia*: see v. 869 n. Her marriage to Enrico da Egna assured Friedrich of
the control of the Trentine Pass. When she was widowed, before 1224, she
married Taurello: Verci, i. 113–14. She is called 'the Lady of the Rock' because
the Pass was part of her dowry. The words "we lost . . . knock?" represent the
reflection which led Taurello to marry Sofia.

670 *last of chances*: of becoming a great man himself, and not simply a servant
of the House of Romano.

674 *this evening's work*: Sordello's death.

Somehow against by a blind chronicle   675
Which, chronicling whatever woe befell
Ferrara, noted this the obscure woe
Of "Salinguerra's sole son Giacomo
"Deceased, fatuous and doting, ere his sire,"
The townsfolk rubbed their eyes, could but
        admire   680
Which of Sofia's five was meant.
                                    The chaps
Of earth's dead hope were tardy to collapse,
Obliterated not the beautiful
Distinctive features at a crash: but dull
And duller these, next year, as Guelfs withdrew   685
Each to his stronghold. Then (securely too
Ecelin at Campese slept; close by,
Who likes may see him in Solagna lie,
With cushioned head and gloved hand to
        denote
The cavalier he was)—then his heart smote   690

---

677 *1840* Ferrara, scented this   678 *1840* And "Salinguerra's   681–2
1840 five he meant. The chaps|Of his dead hope {No line division after
'meant.'}   684 *1840* crash—scarce dull   *1863,1865* crash—but dull   685
1840 Next year, as Azzo, Boniface withdrew   *1863,1865* And duller, next year,
as Guelf chiefs withdrew   686 *1840* stronghold; then   687 *1840*
slept—close by   *1863,1865* slept—close by,

675 *a blind chronicle*: the *Chronica Parva Ferrariensis*, as Whyte noted (p. 12).
Lines 678–9 paraphrase the following sentence from the chronicle: 'Jacobus
Taurellus . . . his only son . . . was a source of lamentation to his friends and of
rejoicing to his enemies. According to Verci, i. 110, she bore her first husband
two sons, and Taurello one, Giacomo (i. 114).
680 *admire*: wonder.
681 *Sofia's five*: in his *Memorie di Ferrara* (5 vols., Ferrara, 1793), ii. 219, A.
Frizzi names five children of Taurello's, one being Sofia's and the others of
unspecified maternity. According to Verci, i. 110, she bore her first husband
two sons, and Taurello one, Giacomo (i. 114).
chaps: cheeks.
682 *earth's dead hope*: the Guelf cause, seen as man's hope of progress.
686 *securely*: free from care.
687 *at Campese*: according to Verci (i. 95) Ecelin the Monk died a little before
1235. He discusses where he was buried, and inclines to the view (implied by
Rolandino) that it was in Campese. Browning visited the reputed grave of the
Monk at Solagno or Solagna in 1838 (Griffin & Minchin, 96), but in fact Verci's
description of the tomb traditionally associated with him gives the details here
mentioned: 'on it [we see] sculptured a Benedictine Monk with his head resting
on soft cushions with gloves in his hand, which indicates his "signoria", and
other insignia of respect': i. 96. Verci emphasizes that the association of the
tomb with Ecelin is doubtful.

Young Ecelin at last; long since adult,
And, save Vicenza's business, what result
In blood and blaze? (So hard to intercept
Sordello till his plain withdrawal!) Stepped
695   Then its new lord on Lombardy. I' the nick
Of time when Ecelin and Alberic
Closed with Taurello, come precisely news
That in Verona half the souls refuse
Allegiance to the Marquis and the Count—
700   Have cast them from a throne they bid him
        mount,
Their Podestà, thro' his ancestral worth.
Ecelin flew there, and the town henceforth
Was wholly his—Taurello sinking back
From temporary station to a track
705   That suited. News received of this acquist,
Friedrich did come to Lombardy: who missed
Taurello then? Another year: they took
Vicenza, left the Marquis scarce a nook

the next aspirant
can press forward,

691 {Reading of 1868.}   1840 proof adult>adult,   *1840* Ecelin, conceive!
Long since adult,   *1863,1865* Ecelin at last!—long since adult,   *1888,1889* Ecelin at last; long since adult.   *692 1840 proof* And>And,   *693 1840* blaze? so
hard 'twas intercept   *1863,1865* blaze? ('t was hard to intercept   *694 1840
proof* option; stept>option! Stept   *1840* Sordello till Sordello's option!
Stept   *1863,1865* Sordello till his plain withdrawal.) Stept,   *1868* Sordello
. . . . withdrawal!) Stepped,   *695 1840* Its lord on Lombardy—for in the
nick   *1863,1865* Then, its new lord on Lombardy. I' the nick   *696 1840* Of
time when he at last and Alberic   *697 1840 proof* Close . . . . come>Closed
. . . . came   *1840* came precisely   *700 1840 proof* mount>mount,   *701
1840 proof* Pedestà>Podestà,   *1840* worth: *705 1840* suited: news   *706
1840 proof* Lombardy>Lombardy—{as in *1840*.}   *707 1840* Taurello? Yet
another year—

691 *Young Ecelin*: the Monk's son, Ecelin the Tyrant.
692 *Vicenza's business*: cf. v. 751–2.
693 *blood and blaze*: as at ii. 464 and iv. 934.
    intercept: stop him from pursuing his purpose: OED sense 2, described as
obsolete or rare.
697 *Closed with*: came to an understanding with, referring to his marriage to
Ecelin's sister Sofia.
699 *the Marquis and the Count*: Azzo and Count Richard.
700 *him*: Ecelin.
702 *Ecelin flew there*: Verci (ii. 110) quotes Maurisius, who writes that Ecelin
entered Verona 'with such speed as if he had been flying through the air'. For
the passage in Maurisius see Muratori, viii. 42–3.
704 *station*: a pre-eminent situation which did not suit his temperament.
705 *acquist*: acquisition, as in *Samson Agonistes*, 1755.
706 *Friedrich did come*: he joined Ecelin in Verona in 1236.
707–8 *they took / Vicenza*: Verci, ii. 118.

For refuge, and, when hundreds two or three
Of Guelfs conspired to call themselves "The
    Free,"   710
Opposing Alberic,—vile Bassanese,—
(Without Sordello!)—Ecelin at ease
Salinguerra's part   Slaughtered them so observably, that oft
lapsing to Ecclin,   A little Salinguerra looked with soft
Blue eyes up, asked his sire the proper age   715
To get appointed his proud uncle's page.
More years passed, and that sire had dwindled
    down
To a mere showy turbulent soldier, grown
Better through age, his parts still in repute,
Subtle—how else?—but hardly so astute   720
As his contemporaneous friends professed;
Undoubtedly a brawler: for the rest,
Known by each neighbour, and allowed for, let
Keep his incorrigible ways, nor fret
Men who would miss their boyhood's bugbear:
    "trap   725
"The ostrich, suffer our bald osprey flap
"A battered pinion!"—was the word. In fine,
One flap too much and Venice's marine

---

710 *1840* After conspired . . . . "the   *1863,1865* Of Guelfs conspired . . . .
"the   711 *1840* Alberic, these Bassanese,   716 *1840* page: 717 *1840* sire
was dwindled   721 *1840* professed—   722 *1840* brawler—   723 *1840*
neighbour, so allowed   725 *1840* who had missed . . . . bugbear—trap
1863,1865 who had missed . . . . bugbear—"trap   *1868* who had missed . . . .
bugbear: "trap   727 *1840* pinion—   *1863,1865* pinion'—

710 *"The Free"*: 'In his time', Maurisius writes in his chapter 'De Alberico de
Romano Eccelini fratre', 'certain men conspired against lord Alberico and his
following, and they called themselves "the party of free men". The other party
was called the "Masnada". They had gained in daring on account of the
ill-feeling between lord Ezzelino and lord Alberico. Their stupidity and pre-
sumptuousness rose to such a pitch that they threatened not merely the
Masnada but lord Alberico himself. Then lord Ezzelino acted wisely and
discreetly, in accordance with good sense and brotherly affection; he took no
notice of the previous quarrel, but captured Bassano by force and defeated the
traitors': Muratori, viii. 31.
713 *observably*: 'In a manner worthy of note': Johnson.
724 *nor fret*: he was no source of irritation to men who would (on the
contrary) have been sorry to lose the bugbear of their youth.
725–6 *trap | The ostrich*: 'Trap Ecelin', they said, 'but let our harmless old
osprey flap his ancient wings!' Cf. iv. 59, 63.
728 *marine*: shipping.

Was meddled with; no overlooking that!
730 She captured him in his Ferrara, fat
And florid at a banquet, more by fraud
Than force, to speak the truth; there 's slender
        laud
Ascribed you for assisting eighty years
To pull his death on such a man; fate shears
The life-cord prompt enough whose last fine
735   thread
You fritter: so, presiding his board-head,
The old smile, your assurance all went well
With Friedrich (as if he were like to tell!)
In rushed (a plan contrived before) our friends,
740 Made some pretence at fighting, some amends
For the shame done his eighty years—(apart
The principle, none found it in his heart
To be much angry with Taurello)—gained
Their galleys with the prize, and what remained
745 But carry him to Venice for a show?
—Set him, as 't were, down gently—free to go
His gait, inspect our square, pretend observe
The swallows soaring their eternal curve
'Twixt Theodore and Mark, if citizens
750 Gathered importunately, fives and tens,
To point their children the Magnifico,

---

730 *1840* We captured   732 *1840* truth—   734 *1840–1865* man—
fate *735 {Reading of DC and *1889*} *1840–88* threads   737 *1840* A great
smile your   740 *1840* fighting, just amends   741 *1840* —apart   743
1840 Taurello—gained   744 *1840* Our galleys   751 *1840* *proof*
Magnifico> Magnifico,

---

730 *She captured him*: Taurello was captured in 1240. Verci summarises the
accounts of the matter given by the various chroniclers: ii. 190 ff. Cf. Whyte,
pp. 13–14.
734 *fate shears*: cf. 'Lycidas', 75–6: 'Comes the blind Fury with th' abhorred
shears, / And slits the thin-spun life'.
736 *fritter*: weaken by fraying.
presiding: absolute: while he was presiding at . . . Cf. Carlyle, *The French
Revolution*, Vol. I, III. iii. 3: 'presiding that Bureau of his'.
738 *to tell!*: if it were not so.
746 *Set him . . . down*: accounts of Taurello's last days vary. The *Biographie
Universelle*, e.g., states that he died in prison.
746–7 *to go / His gait*: to go his way, as often in Scott.
749 *Theodore and Mark*: the names of the pillars in St. Mark's Square.

All but a monarch once in firm-land, go
His gait among them now—"it took, indeed,
"Fully this Ecelin to supersede
"That man," remarked the seniors. Singular!   755
Sordello's inability to bar
Rivals the stage, that evening, mainly brought

*who, with his
brother, played it
out,*

About by his strange disbelief that aught
Was ever to be done,—this thrust the Twain
Under Taurello's tutelage,—whom, brain   760
And heart and hand, he forthwith in one rod
Indissolubly bound to baffle God
Who loves the world—and thus allowed the
    thin
Grey wizened dwarfish devil Ecelin,
And massy-muscled big-boned Alberic   765
(Mere man, alas!) to put his problem quick
To demonstration—prove wherever 's will
To do, there 's plenty to be done, or ill
Or good. Anointed, then, to rend and rip—
Kings of the gag and flesh-hook, screw and
    whip,   770
They plagued the world: a touch of Hildebrand
(So far from obsolete!) made Lombards band

---

753 *1840* among us now—it took, indeed,   755 *1840* That man, ...
Singular   759 *1840* Was to be done, should fairly thrust   760 *1840* tutelage, that, brain   763 *1840* world—should thus allow the   765 *1840 proof*
massy> massy-   766 *1840* alas)   769 *1840* good: anointed,   772 *1840
proof* Lombard's>Lombards

---

752 *firm-land*: the mainland (as opposed to Venice). Cf. iii. 539, and *Fifine at
the Fair*, 1400.

757 *that evening*: the last evening of his life, when he decided not to accept the
temporal power which Taurello had given him: see v. 719 ff.

759 *the Twain*: Alberic and Ecelin the Tyrant. In the *Orlando Furioso* (iii. 33)
Ariosto describes Ecelin as 'immanissimo tiranno / Che fia creduto figlio del
demonio', a most atrocious tyrant, who will be reputed the very son of Satan.
As Whyte notes, both Aliprandi and Platina relate this story of his paternity.
Later Ariosto mentions Ecelin as being, like Attila, one of those 'whom God
inflicted upon us, to plague and torment us, after we had strayed too long from
the path of virtue': *Orlando Furioso*, xvii. 3.

762 *Indissolubly*: stressed on the second syllable, as in Johnson.

766 *his problem*: namely whether 'aught / Was ever to be done'.

771 *a touch of Hildebrand*: cf. *Henry V*, Prologue to Act IV, 47: 'A little touch
of Harry in the night'. Hildebrand stands for Knowledge 'by stress / Of
Strength' (v. 176–7).

Together, cross their coats as for Christ's cause,
And saving Milan win the world's applause.
775   Ecelin perished: and I think grass grew
Never so pleasant as in Valley Rù
By San Zenon where Alberic in turn
Saw his exasperated captors burn
Seven children and their mother; then, regaled
780   So far, tied on to a wild horse, was trailed
To death through raunce and bramble-bush. I   *and went home*
take   *duly to their*
                                                     reward.
God's part and testify that 'mid the brake
Wild o'er his castle on the pleasant knoll,
You hear its one tower left, a belfry, toll—
785   The earthquake spared it last year, laying flat
The modern church beneath,—no harm in that!
Chirrups the contumacious grasshopper,
Rustles the lizard and the cushats chirre
Above the ravage: there, at deep of day

---

779 *1840* children with their mother, and, regaled   781 *1840* bramble-
bush: 782 *1840–65* mid   783 *1840* on Zenone's knoll   785,786 {Not
in *1840*}   787 *1740 proof* grasshopper> grasshopper, *1840–65*
Cherups   789 *1840 proof* there>there,

773 *cross their coats*: wear the cross as a badge, as if upon a crusade: cf. i. 842.
774 *saving Milan*: Ecelin was captured and wounded when he attempted to
win Milan, a conquest which would have made him master of Lombardy.
777 *San Zenon*: as Whyte points out, 'San Zenone lies midway between
Bassano and Asolo, where the remains of the old castle still exist'. 'Valley Rù'
has not been found on maps of this area, but a valley of that name exists in the
province of Belluno, and there is a Monte Rua in the Euganean hills.
where Alberic: according to Verci (i. 197), in 1260 Alberic's 'six sons were cut
to pieces and his two daughters with their mother barbarously burnt alive. On
this same day Alberic was trailed at the tail of a horse until his body was torn to
pieces'. This was by S. Zenone. Various accounts are given by Rolandino and
others, as usual: see Muratori, viii. 358.
781 *raunce*: OED, citing no other example derives this from Fr. 'ronce',
bramble. Quarles has 'rance' = marble: *Divine Fancies*, IV. liii, and *Emblemes*, II.
x. 12.
781–2 *I take / God's part*: cf. 625 n. | 782 *brake*: bracken, thorns.
784 *toll*—: after this line, at the foot of p. 248, *SB* has: 'Spared by the
earthquake—the [? others] destroyed—'.
785 *The earthquake*: on 12 June 1836 a violent earthquake occurred in the
vicinity of Bassano and Asolo: 'last year' by poetic licence.
787 *the contumacious grasshopper*: cf. iii. 260, where Naddo is irritated by the
cicala.
788 *chirre*: 'To make the trilled sound characteristic of grass-hoppers, etc.':
OED. Cushats are wood-pigeons or ring-doves.
789 *at deep of day*: cf. 'June at deep', i. 901.

A week since, heard I the old Canon say   790
He saw with his own eyes a barrow burst
And Alberic's huge skeleton unhearsed
Only five years ago. He added, "June 's
"The month for carding off our first cocoons
"The silkworms fabricate"—a double news,   795
Nor he nor I could tell the worthier. Choose!
    And Naddo gone, all 's gone; not Eglamor!
Believe, I knew the face I waited for,
A guest my spirit of the golden courts!
Oh strange to see how, despite ill-reports,   800
Disuse, some wear of years, that face retained
Its joyous look of love! Suns waxed and waned,
And still my spirit held an upward flight,
Spiral on spiral, gyres of life and light
More and more gorgeous—ever that face there   805

Good will—ill The last admitted! crossed, too, with some care
luck, get second As perfect triumph were not sure for all,
prize: But, on a few, enduring damp must fall,
—A transient struggle, haply a painful sense
Of the inferior nature's clinging—whence   810
Slight starting tears easily wiped away,
Fine jealousies soon stifled in the play
Of irrepressible admiration—not
Aspiring, all considered, to their lot

---

790 *1840 proof* since> since,   793,794 *1840* Five years ago, no more: he
added, June's|A month   795 *1840 proof* doubled> double   *1840* fabri-
cate—   798 *1840* Believe I   799 *1840* courts: 801 *1840 proof* Disuse,>
Disuse,   806 *1840 proof* admitted—>admitted!   807 *1840 proof* all>all,
809 *1840* A transient

---

790 *A week since*: not to be taken literally: cf. 785 n. above.
792 *unhearsed*: exposed in its grave. Shakespeare has 'hearsed': *Hamlet*, I. iv.
47.
795 *a double news*: two items of news: cf. iv. 531.
797 *Naddo gone*: at v. 1012 we have been told that 'Naddo's never gone!': in
1840, however, the text there reads: 'ah, Naddo's gone!' At. v. 1011 (*1840*)
Eglamor is said to have gone.
799 *A guest my spirit*: when my spirit was enabled to visit the golden courts.
Knowing the secret of love, this minor poet keeps appearing as the narrator
holds his 'upward flight'. Eglamor's spirit still grieves for those condemned to
'enduring damp', but is not envious of the 'exclusive track' of greater souls. For
Eglamor's lack of envy see ii. 242 ff. Cf., also, 'the delight of the contented
lowness' with which the narrator of *Pauline* contemplates Shelley: l. 554 ff.
804 *gyres*: as in Cary, *Hell*, xvii. 93.

815　Who ever, just as they prepare ascend
　　　Spiral on spiral, wish thee well, impend
　　　Thy frank delight at their exclusive track,
　　　That upturned fervid face and hair put back!
　　　　　Is there no more to say? He of the rhymes—
820　Many a tale, of this retreat betimes,
　　　Was born: Sordello die at once for men?
　　　The Chroniclers of Mantua tired their pen
　　　Telling how *Sordello Prince Visconti* saved
　　　Mantua, and elsewhere notably behaved—
825　Who thus, by fortune ordering events,
　　　Passed with posterity, to all intents,
　　　For just the god he never could become.
　　　As Knight, Bard, Gallant, men were never
　　　　　dumb
　　　In praise of him: while what he should have
　　　　　been,
830　Could be, and was not—the one step too mean
　　　For him to take,—we suffer at this day
　　　Because of: Ecelin had pushed away
　　　Its chance ere Dante could arrive and take
　　　That step Sordello spurned, for the world's
　　　　　sake:

---

820 *1840* tale of this retreat betimes　　　823,824 *1840* Relating how a Prince
Visconti saved|Mantua　　825 *1840* thus by fortune's ordering events
1863,1865 thus, by fortune's ordering events,　　826 *1840 proof* intents,>in-
tents　*1840* posterity to all intents　　827 *1840* God . . . . become:　　829
1840 proof been>been,　　831 *1840* take,　　832 *1840 proof* Because
of—>Because of; {as in *1840*}.　　833 *1840* arrive to take

---

816 *impend*: hang over, hover benevolently over.

818 *and hair put back!*: cf. Keats, *The Eve of St. Agnes*, 36: 'With hair blown
back'.

821 *die at once for men?*: Browning's 'reading' of the story, as it is here told.

822 *The Chroniclers of Mantua*: according to Tiraboschi (op. cit., p. 64)
'Volterrano is the first to have called Sordello "Principe di Mantova", if
indeed, using the word "princeps" in the Latin sense, he did not only mean to
say that he was the chief among the citizens. And perhaps Leandro Alberti was
led into error by this same word: since he wrote more explicitly that he
[Sordello] was "il primo principe di Mantova dopo la Contessa Matilda". All
the later historians of Mantua who followed. . . have made Sordello "signor di
Mantova" . . .'

832–3 *had pushed away / Its chance*: the meaning seems to be that after Sordello
had disdained to take this all-important step forwards Ecelin made it impossible even for Dante to do so much for mankind—although he did a great deal.

He did much—but Sordello's chance was gone.   835
Thus, had Sordello dared that step alone,
Apollo had been compassed: 't was a fit
He wished should go to him, not he to it
—As one content to merely be supposed
Singing or fighting elsewhere, while he dozed   840
Really at home—one who was chiefly glad
To have achieved the few real deeds he had,
Because that way assured they were not worth
Doing, so spared from doing them
        henceforth—
A tree that covets fruitage and yet tastes   845
Never itself, itself. Had he embraced
Their cause then, men had plucked Hesperian
        fruit
And, praising that, just thrown him in to boot
All he was anxious to appear, but scarce
Solicitous to be. A sorry farce   850
Such life is, after all! Cannot I say

what least one may
I award Sordello?

He lived for some one better thing? this way—
Lo, on a heathy brown and nameless hill
By sparkling Asolo, in mist and chill,
Morning just up, higher and higher runs   855
A child barefoot and rosy. See! the sun 's

---

835 *1840 proof* gone>gone.   *1840* Sordello's step was gone.   836 *1840*
Thus had Sordello ta'en that   837 *1840 proof* He had been perfect
Phoebus—that bright fit>Apollo had been compassed—'twas a fit {as in
1840–68}   838 *1840 proof* to go>should go   839 *1840 proof* —Had
been>—As one   841 *1840* home—and who   842 *1840* he had   843
1840 proof he was> that way   845 *1840 proof* He'd be a tree of fruitage, which
yet tastes>A tree that covets fruitage and yet tastes   846 *1840* itself—had
1863,1865 itself: had   847 *1840* Our cause then, Men   848 *1840 proof*
well>just   849 *1840* appear   850 *1840* to be: a   851 *1840* is after
all—cannot   *1863,1865* is, after all! cannot   *852 {Reading of *1840*.}
1863–89 way.—   856 *1840* rosy—See!

---

837 *Apollo*: he would have become the perfect, god-like man of whom he
had dreamed as a boy. Cf. i. 897. Cf. *Paracelsus*, iv. 421–2: 'I had a noble
purpose, and the strength / To compass it'. The word 'fit' seems to mean
'opportunity'. Perhaps cf. *Coriolanus* III. ii. 33 (and III. ii. 2 with 1. 780 above).
    839 *to merely be supposed*: cf. Book I, e.g. 810 ff.
    845 *A tree*: a tree which wishes to bear fruit yet is uninterested in the fruit.
    847 *Hesperian fruit*: if he had espoused the cause of Mankind, men would
have tasted heavenly fruit.
    854 *sparkling Asolo*: cf. iii. 683 n.

On the square castle's inner-court's low wall
Like the chine of some extinct animal
Half turned to earth and flowers; and through
 the haze
(Save where some slender patches of grey
860 maize
Are to be overleaped) that boy has crossed
The whole hill-side of dew and powder-frost
Matting the balm and mountain camomile.
Up and up goes he, singing all the while
865 Some unintelligible words to beat
The lark, God's poet, swooning at his feet,
So worsted is he at "the few fine locks
"Stained like pale honey oozed from topmost
 rocks
"Sun-blanched the livelong summer,"—all
 that's left
870 Of the Goito lay! And thus bereft,   *This—that must*
Sleep and forget, Sordello! In effect   *perforce content*
He sleeps, the feverish poet—I suspect   *him,*
Not utterly companionless; but, friends,
Wake up! The ghost 's gone, and the story ends
875 I 'd fain hope, sweetly; seeing, peri or ghoul,
That spirits are conjectured fair or foul,
Evil or good, judicious authors think,

---

857 *1840* inner-court's green wall 858 *1840* —Like . . . . some fossil
animal 859 *1840 proof* flower;>flowers; *1840* thro' 860 *1840 proof*
There (save (when{?} grey) [where the{?}] patches of the maize> (Save where
some slender patches of grey maize 863 *1840* camomile: 867 *1840* the
few 868 *1840 proof* Showed>Stained 869 *1840* Sunblanched . . . .
summer.—All *1863–8* Sunblanched . . . . summer,"— all 871 *1840* Sordello . . . in 874 *1840–65* Wake up; the 875 *1840–65* sweetly—

858 *chine*: backbone. 863 *balm*: used generally for aromatic herbs.
866 *swooning*: growing faint because of his failure to compete with Sordello's
'Goito lay', as the boy sings it. Cf. Tennyson, 'The Lotos-Eaters' (in *Poems*,
'1833' for 1832), line 5: 'All round the coast the languid air did swoon'. For the
Goito lay see ii. 151 and v. 905. It is an imaginary poem, not one of the historical
Sordello's surviving compositions.
873 *Not utterly companionless*: i.e. I suspect that my readers are asleep too.
874 *The ghost's gone*: that of Sordello, called up by the poet. Cf. i. 20.
875 *peri or ghoul*: good or evil spirit.

According as they vanish in a stink
Or in a perfume. Friends, be frank! ye snuff

as no prize at all,
has contented me.

Civet, I warrant. Really? Like enough!   880
Merely the savour's rareness; any nose
May ravage with impunity a rose:
Rifle a musk-pod and 't will ache like yours!
I 'd tell you that same pungency ensures
An after-gust, but that were overbold.   885
Who would has heard Sordello's story told.

879,880 *1840* perfume: friends be frank: ye snuff| Civet, I warrant: really?
Like enough—   881 *1840* rareness—   882 *1840* rose—   883 *1840*
yours: 885 *1840* after-gust— . . . . overbold: *1863,1865* after-gust— . . . .
overbold.

878 *vanish in a stink*: a common belief: see, e.g., Joseph Glanvill, *Saducismus
Triumphatus* (ed. of 1689), pp. 365, 370. In *The French Revolution* (Vol. I, 1, i.
para. 6) Carlyle writes: 'as subterranean Apparitions are wont, vanish
utterly,—leaving only a smell of sulphur!'
879 *Friends*: as at i. 31.
880 *Civet*: i.e. a strong smell, too pungent, because *Sordello* is caviare to the
general. Cf. Bacon's *Sylva Sylvarum* [Century ix. 835], as quoted in Johnson:
'Some putrefactions and excrements do yield excellent odours; as civet and
musk'. Civet is obtained from the anal pouch of several animals of the civet
genus. Cf. vi. 177 above.
883 *musk-pod*: 'the receptacle in the musk-deer (or other animal) which
contains the musk': OED.

APPENDIX A

'Dramatis Personæ' and Browning's preface to the first edition of *Strafford*

DRAMATIS PERSONÆ.
(Theatre-Royal Covent Garden, May 1. 1837.)

Charles the First – – – – –	MR. DALE.
Earl of Holland – – – – –	HUCKEL.
Lord Savile – – – – – –	TILBURY.
Sir Henry Vane – – – – –	THOMPSON.
Wentworth, Viscount Wentworth, Earl of Strafford – – – – – –	MACREADY.
John Pym – – – – – –	VANDENHOFF.
John Hampden – – – – –	HARRIS.
The younger Vane – – – – –	J. WEBSTER.
Denzil Hollis – – – – –	G. BENNET.
Benjamin Rudyard – – – – –	PRITCHARD.
Nathaniel Fiennes – – – – –	WORREL.
Earl of Loudon – – – – –	BENDER.
Maxwell, *Usher of the Black Rod* – – –	RANSFORD.
Balfour, *Constable of the Tower* – – –	COLLETT.
A Puritan – – – – – –	WEBSTER.
Queen Henrietta – – – – –	MISS VINCENT.
Lucy Percy, Countess of Carlisle – –	HELEN FAUCIT.

Presbyterians, Scots Commissioners, Adherents of Strafford, Secretaries, Officers of the Court &c. Two of Strafford's Children.

PREFACE.

I had for some time been engaged in a Poem of a very different nature, when induced to make the present attempt; and am not without apprehension that my eagerness to freshen a jaded mind by diverting it to the healthy natures of a grand epoch, may have operated unfavourably on the represented play, which is one of Action in Character rather than Character in Action. To remedy this, in some degree, considerable curtailment will be necessary, and, in a few instances, the supplying details not required, I suppose, by the mere reader. While a trifling success would much gratify, failure will not wholly discourage me from another effort: experience is to come, and earnest endeavour may yet remove many disadvantages.

The portraits are, I think, faithful; and I am exceedingly fortunate in being able, in proof of this, to refer to the subtle and eloquent exposition of the characters of Eliot and Strafford, in the Lives of Eminent British Statesmen now in the course of publication in Lardner's Cyclopædia, by a writer whom I am proud to call my friend; and whose biographies of Hampden, Pym, and Vane, will, I am sure, fitly illustrate the present year—the Second Centenary of the Trial concerning Ship-Money. My Carlisle, however, is purely imaginary: I at first sketched her singular likeness roughly in, as suggested by Matthew and the memoir-writers—but it was too

1 *a Poem*: Sordello.
7 *considerable curtailment*: see pp. 10 ff.
14–15 *the Lives of Eminent British Statesmen*: see pp. 3 ff.
21 *Matthew and the memoir-writers*: *A Collection of Letters, made by Sir Tobie Matthews . . .; with a Character of Lucy, Countess of Carlisle*, 1660. When Miss Hickey queried the spelling of the name, Browning replied: 'I tried to be right at the time . . . with "Mathews" as, oddly enough, I originally had the name till Forster told me I was mistaken about it': *Checklist*, 83: 182. 'Mathews' is quoted in the long footnote on Lady Carlisle in the *Life*: 'This extraordinary woman, whom Dryden called the "Helen of her country", and from whom Waller borrowed a compliment for Venus, ("the bright Carlile of the court of heaven,") played a conspicuous part in the public affairs of the time. "She was thought to be as deeply concerned in the counsels of the court, and afterwards of the parliament, as any in England". After the death of Strafford she had become the mistress of Pym. Yet her passions were not extreme! Sir Toby Mathews lets us into her character:—"She is of too high a mind and dignity, not only to seek, but almost to wish, the friendship of any creature: *they whom she is pleased to chuse, are such as are of the most eminent condition, both for power and employments*; not with any design towards her own particular, either of advantage or curiosity; *but her nature values fortunate persons as virtuous*" . . .': p. 286 n. (p. 129 n.).

artificial, and the substituted outline is exclusively from Voiture and Waller.

The Italian boat-song in the last scene is from Redi's *Bacco*, long since naturalized in the joyous and delicate version of Leigh Hunt.

22 *Voiture*: Vincent Voiture's celebrated description is to be found in a letter to 'Monsieur Gourdon, at London', dated 4 December 1633, and by no means wholly corresponds to Browning's character: 'there is not any one of which may be said so much Good, and so much Ill . . . She is . . . a Person full of Enchantment, and there is not under the Heavens one that can command so much my Affection as she, did she but know what it is, and carry about her the sensitive Soul, as well as the rational. But considering her Temper, we can say no more of her than that she is the most charming of all those Things that are not good, and the most delightful Poison that ever Nature produc'd. I stand so much in Awe of her Wit, that it has almost hinder'd me from sending you these Verses; for I know she can judge what is good, and what ill in any Thing; and that all the Goodness which should have been in her Will, is diverted into her Judgment': *The Works of the Celebrated Monsieur Voiture*, translated by John Ozell (2nd ed., 2 vols., 1725), i. 167–8 (Letter xlix).

23 *Waller*: see in particular his poems 'The Country to my Lady of Carlisle' and 'The Countess of Carlisle in Mourning'. Herrick was one of many other poets who celebrated her charms: see his lines 'Upon a black Twist, rounding the Arme of the Countesse of *Carlile*'.

24 *Redi's* Bacco: Francesco Redi was well-known in England at this time: Elizabeth Barrett owned a copy of his *Poesie Toscane* before her marriage: *Sotheby Catalogue*, no. 1032. Hunt gives the Italian with his English version in his 1832 *Poetical Works*, p. 317. He translates: 'Oh what a thing / 'Tis for you and for me, / On an evening in spring, / To sail in the sea!'

APPENDIX B

The Berg Copy of *Strafford*

In the Berg Collection in New York Public Library there is an important copy of the first edition of *Strafford* (1837) which has on the title-page three inscriptions in Browning's hand: (1) 'Capt Pritchard from his most obliged friend RB. May-day, 1837': (2) 'To Frederick Locker from RB. Apr. 13. '69': (3) '(Corrected at London, 1862)'. It is evident that Browning used the copy which he had originally given to Pritchard when he was preparing *Strafford* for its second appearance, in the second of the three volumes of *The Poetical Works* published in 1863.

The revisions are almost all made in a soft pencil, though three or four appear to be in ink. While the majority are clear, others become clear only when we compare them with the *1863* printing; a few remain illegible. The Berg copy includes fewer than half of the revisions made in *1863*, and was evidently not sent to the printer: Browning must have marked up another copy, not known to survive, for his publisher. In the Berg copy Act I contains far more revisions than the remainder of the play, whereas in *1863* Acts I, II and V are all heavily revised throughout. Evidently Browning thoroughly revised Act I, Scene i in 1862, making alterations in almost all the speeches, and re-assigning some to different speakers. Nearly all these revisions appear in identical or slightly altered form in *1863*, together with some half dozen additional minor revisions. Act I Scene ii was also extensively revised in *1862*, about 100 lines being changed or added. Approximately half of these were further altered in 1863, in addition to some 36 revisions not indicated in 1862. Browning's 1862 revision became progressively less thorough, and less representative of the 1863 printing, up to the end of Act IV, which has only eight minor alterations; and though more changes were made in Act V, they were far fewer than the very numerous changes made in *1863*, where almost every line of Act V Scene ii is altered.

This uneven distribution of revisions in the Berg copy, along with the tentative form of some of the notes, and the further modification of many of its readings in later editions, means that it is not a reliable source of emendations. It is a pity, nevertheless, that Browning did not use some of its revisions: 'the pettiest of mistrust' improves the metre of II.ii.99. At the end of Act I the 1862 copy alters the name

'Strafford' to 'Wentworth' (I.ii.242, 245, 255); *1863* restores 'Strafford' in line 245 and 255, but omits the name altogether in l. 242,
producing a metrically unsatisfactory short line. We have used in our
text the *1862* reading 'ever', clearly preferable to 'even', in I.ii.33.

The general tendency of the 1862 revision is the same as that of
1863: in Act I, for example, Browning improves the style by removing repetitions and replacing colourless verbs; he gives additional
information in order to make past events clearer, but simplifies by
reducing the number of speakers; he emphasises the humanity and
suffering of Wentworth, and the opposing fanaticism of the Puritans, but he also adds a lengthy and dignified speech by Hampden
(I.i.235–252): this is his most substantial addition in Act I, and it
appears in almost the same form in *1863*. On the other hand, while
the minor revisions in Act V follow the same trend as those in *1863*,
its major revision—the drastic curtailment of the end of the play—is
not indicated at all in *1862*.

Some of the *1862* notes are merely suggestions for revision, and
obviously need the polishing they receive in *1863*: for example 'Abets
them as he told you, perhaps?' becomes 'Abets them,—as he
boasted, very like.' (I.ii.194). Other *1862* revisions are clearly
improved in their *1863* form—when, for instance, the 'forty' silver
pieces of I.ii.157 become 'thirty', linking Wentworth with the arch-
traitor to whom he has already been compared in the first scene. Less
satisfactory, however, is *1863*'s telescoping of I.ii.98, where the omission of a stage-direction leaves an ambiguous and perhaps perplexing line. *1863*, unlike *1862*, is also ambiguous at II.ii.124; and it fails to
use two interesting revisions in stage-directions: in *1862* Hollis's
Attendant is specifically 'the King disguised' at V.ii.58, and the
deletion of 'Hampden, Vane' from the stage-direction after V.ii.267
focusses attention on Pym alone. Here and in several other passages,
especially in Acts III and V, Browning's *1863* text ignores the *1862*
revisions and reverts to the readings of *1837*.

The following table excludes revisions in *1862* which duly
appeared in *1863*. It comprises revisions made in 1862 which were
modified in *1863*, and suggested revisions which Browning did not
adopt. Standardised abbreviations have been used for the names of
the speakers.

	1837	1862 ACT I	1863
i.40	That strangled agony bleeds	That strangled agony bleed	That strangled agony bleeds
i.73	—A man that England loved for serving her,	—Now, whom England loved for serving her, *	Now, one whom England loved for serving her,
i.88	And the same savage gesture! Now let England land	And the same gesture! Now shall England lie	And the same gesture. Now shall England crouch,
	Make proof of us. Voices. Strike him—the Renegade— Haman—Ahithophel— Hamp. (To the Scots.) Gentlemen of the North,	Or catch at us and rise?** Voices. —the Renegade! Haman—Ahithophel— Hamp. (To the Scots.) Gentlemen of the North,	Or catch at us and rise? Voices. The Renegade! Haman! Ahithophel! Hamp. Gentlemen of the North,
i.110	He would see—Pym and he were sworn, they say,	He would see—Pym and he being sworn, tis said,	He would see— Pym and he were sworn, 't is said,
i.114	he'd have Pym own	he'd have Pym see	he'd have Pym own
	A Patriot could not do a purer thing	A Patriot could not play a purer part,	A patriot could not play a purer part
i.129	praying God a space That he will not cast England quite away	praying God a space His anger cast not England quite away	praying God to spare His anger, cast not England quite away
i.134	Wentworth's come: he has not reached	Wentworth's come: nor sickness, care, The ravaged body, nor the wasted{?} soul {illeg.} waves which beat (set against) his ship	Wentworth's come: nor sickness, care, The ravaged body nor the ruined soul, More than the winds and waves that beat his ship,
		Could keep him from the King—He has not reached	Could keep him from the King. He has not reached
i.154	That, chronicling a Nation's great despair,	Which, chronicling a Nation's great despair,	That, chronicling a nation's great despair,
i.161	I'll do your bidding,	I'll do ⟨God's⟩ bidding,†	I'll do your bidding,
i.175	Hamp. And one name shall be dearer than all names:	{These 3 lines assigned to Vane.}	{These 3 lines assigned to Hampden}
i.180	Fiennes. We said that! There's no way beside!	Fiennes: We said it! There's no way beside!	{These words are part of the speech of 'Rudyard and others'}

* 'A man' lightly deleted, but nothing substituted.
** 'Fall' deleted in left-hand margin.
† Browning deleted 'your' and substituted 'God's', but deleted that too.

	1837	1862	1863
i.185	England rejects all Feltons;	England rejects the Feltons;	England rejects all Feltons;
i.187	That England will award me . . .	England awards me {altered to} Of England in her servants . . *	Of England in her servants—
i.196	Fresh argument	⟨Some⟩ argument**	Fresh argument
i.202	which Wentworth framed	he framed that clause	he framed such clause
i.211	That Wentworth . . . O will no one hope with me?	In Wentworth . . . but can no one hope with me?	To Wentworth: but can no one hope with me?
i.216	The People or the King? The People, Hampden, / Or the King . . . and that King—Charles! / Will no one hope? / Hamp. Pym, we do know you: you'll not set your heart / On any baseless thing: but say one deed / Of Wentworth's, since he left us . . . / (Shouting without) / Vane. Pym, he comes	The People or the King? . . . and that King—Charles! / Hamp.—Yes, Charles—who is one (describe for the {illeg.}) / Pym, all here know you: you'll not set your heart / On any baseless dream: but name one deed / Of Wentworth's, since he left us . . . / (Shouting without) / Vane. ⟨What?⟩ There! he comes	The People or the King? and that King, Charles! / Hamp. Pym, all here know you: you'll not set your heart. / On any baseless dream. But say one deed / Of Wentworth's, since he left us . . . . / (Shouting without.) / Vane. There! he comes,
i.225c	Vane Pym should have no friend! / Stand you firm, Pym! Eliot's gone, / Wentworth's lost, / We have but you, and stand you very firm!	Pym should have no friend! / Hampden is firm, and stand you also firm!	{Omitted. The lines formed part of a speech by Vane preceding Pym's 'And yet if 'tis a dream' (l. 225)}
i.225f	But . . I know not . . if you should fail . . O God! O God!	Yet . . I know not . . if you should fail . . O God! O God!	{Omitted.}
i.232	That violence, which something mars even Right	That violence, which something mars the Right	That violence, which something mars even right

* Browning deleted 'will' and added 's' to 'award', but then deleted 'That' and 'awards' also.
** Browning deleted 'Fresh', wrote 'Some' in the margin, then deleted it too.

	1837	1862	1863
i.239	{Absent*}	Have friend met friend	Has friend met friend
i.241	{Absent}	They spoke	We spoke
i.249	{Absent}	In drawing from our	In drawing out our
i.253	*Hamp.* Proceed to England's work: who reads the list? *A Voice.* "Ship-money is refused or fiercely paid	Proceed to England's work! Fiennes, read the list! We were in act to count them &c *Fiennes.* Ship-money is refused or fiercely paid	Proceed to England's work! Fiennes, read the list! *Fiennes.* Ship-money is refused or fiercely paid
i.260	We had a shadow of a Parliament: 'Twas well: but all is changed: they threaten us: They'll try brute-force for law—here—in our land!	We kept the shadow of a Parliament— 'Twas well: but all's changed: they change the first, They try brute-force for law—here—first of all!	We had a shadow of a Parliament In Scotland. But all's changed: they change the first, They try brute-force for law, they, first of all,
Scene ii ii.7	Shout for me . . . . they!—poor fellows. *Carl.* Did they shout? —We took all measures to keep off the crowd—	Shout for me . . . they! *Carl.* You come so strangely soon: On the King's bidding,—sooner than was hoped In spite of distance, sickness, obstacles—Did they shout? Yet we took measures to keep off the crowd—	Shout for me—they! *Carl.* You come so strangely soon: Yet we took measures to keep off the crowd—
ii.22	About us,—then the King will grant me.... Lady, Will the King leave these—leave all these—and say	About us,—then the King will grant me.... what? This, I hope That he for once put these aside and say	About us,—then the King will grant me— what? That he for once put these aside and say—
ii.33	Have even seemed to care for me: help me!	Have ever seemed to care for me: one word!	Have even seemed to care for me: one word!
ii.36	I know—I know—and Vane, too,	I know—I know—Old Vane, too,	I know, I know, and Vane, too, {'old Vane,' 1865.}

---

* *1837* lacks lines 235–252. The version written in the *1862* copy is substantially that of *1863*, with the exceptions listed here.

	1837	1862	1863
ii.62	Went. Pym and the People. Carl. Oh, the Faction!	Pym, the People. Carl. Oh, the Faction here!	Pym and the People. Carl. Oh, the Faction!
ii.71	These Vanes and Hollands—I'll not be their tool— Pym would receive me yet!—But then the King!— I'll bear it all. The King—where is he, Girl? Carl. He is apprised that you are here: be calm!	These Vanes and Hollands—I to⟨?⟩ be their tool— Who might be, even yet . . . But then the King!—Where is he? Carl. Just apprised that you are here:	These Vanes and Hollands! I'll not be their tool Who might be Pym's friend yet. But there's the King! Where is he? Carl. Just apprised that you arrive.
ii.96	And Weston's dead—and the Queen's English now— More English—oh, one earnest word will brush These reptiles from . . . (footsteps within.) The step I know so well!	Weston is dead—the Queen's ⟨grown⟩ half English now— More English—one decisive word will brush These insects from . . . (footsteps within.) The step I know so well!	Weston is dead: the Queen's half English now— More English: one decisive word will brush These insects from . . . the step I know so well!
ii.122	Have they, Pym . . . not dared—	Has the Council dared—	Have the Council dared—
ii.131	Pym— You're insolent! Pym. Oh, you misapprehend! Don't think I mean the advantage is with me:	Sir . . . . Pym. Oh, spare that gesture! you misapprehend! Nor think I mean the advantage is with me:	Sir! Pym. Spare me the gesture! you misapprehend! Think not I mean the advantage is with me.
ii.136	(Been) quite myself since then:	⟨Been⟩ quite myself since then:	Was quite myself since then:
ii.140	Forgive me: Savile, Vane, and Holland Eschew plain-speaking: 'tis a trick I have.	Forgive me: Savile, Old Vane, Holland Eschew plain-speaking: 'tis a trick I have.	Forgive me: Savile, old Vane, Holland here, Eschew plain-speaking: 'tis a trick I keep.
ii.154	I can't think, therefore, Charles did well to laugh When you twice prayed so humbly for an Earldom. Went. Pym . . . . . Pym. And your letters were the movingest!	I can't think, therefore, that its purchaser Did well to laugh you to such utter scorn When you twice prayed so humbly for the price The forty silver pieces . . I should say The Earldom, you expected—and expect— And may! Your letters were the movingest!	I can't think, therefore, your soul's purchaser Did well to laugh you to such utter scorn When you twice prayed so humbly for its price, The thirty silver pieces . . I should say, The Earldom you expected, still expect, And may. Your letters were the movingest!

	1837	1862	1863
	Console yourself: I've borne him prayers just now From Scotland	Console yourself: I've borne him prayers just now (what else should bring me think you in this place From Scotland	Console yourself: I've borne him prayers just now From Scotland
ii.164	False! a lie, Sir! .. Who told you, Pym?—But then The King did very well . . nay, I was glad When it was shewn me why;—I first refused it!	False, sir!—Who showed them you? Suppose it true, The King did well—most well . . nay, I rejoiced When it was shewn me; I refused the first!	False, sir!—Who showed them you? suppose it so, The King did very well . . nay, I was glad When it was shown me! I refused, the first!
ii.189	To aid us with your counsel: this Scots' League	To see a famous friend: nay, it is well To aid us with his experience: this Scots' League	To see an old familiar—nay, 't is well; Aid us with his experience: this Scots' League
ii.192	the Faction, too . . . Went. (Kneels.) Sire, trust me!	the Faction, too,— Of which your friend there is the head & front. Abets them as he told you, perhaps? Went. (Kneels.) Sire, trust me!	the Faction too, Whereof your friend there is the head and front, Abets them,—as he boasted, very like. Went. Sir, trust me!
ii.205	It is my comfort, mark you: all will be So different when you trust me . . as you shall! It has not been your fault,—I was away, Maligned—away—and how were you to know? I am here, now—you mean to trust me, now—	There is my comfort, mark you: all could be So different if you trusted me . . you shall! It has not been your fault,—I was away, Maligned—away—and how was the King to know?* But I am here, —he means to trust me, now—	There is my comfort, mark you: all will be So different when you trust me—as you shall! It has not been your fault,—I was away, Mistook, maligned, how was the King to know?— I am here, now—he means to trust me, now—
ii.215	You love me . . only rise!	Well {?} you love me! then rise!	You love me, Wentworth: rise!
ii.232	I know the faction, as They style it, . . Tutors Scotland! Charles. All their plans Went.	I know the faction, as They style it, tutors Scotland! All their plans	I know the Faction, as Laud styles it, tutors Scotland: all their plans

* Browning wrote 'mistook' in the margin, to the left of 'Maligned'.

	1837	1862	1863
ii.236	Of Scotland's treason; bid them help you, then! Even Pym will not refuse!	Of Scotland's treason; bid them help you, then! Ask England if Even Pym will not refuse!*	Of Scotland's treason; then bid England help: Even Pym will not refuse.
ii.238	Take no care for that: that's sure To prosper. *Charles.* You shall rule me: you were best Return at once:	Take no care for that: that's sure To prosper; I shall be there—So shall, *legally,* all be done.** *Charles.* you were best Return at once:	Take no care for that: that's sure To prosper. *Charles.* You shall rule me. You were best Return at once:
ii.242	Of Friends: yes, Strafford, while . . .	Of Friends: yes, Wentworth, while . . .	Of Friends: yes, while . . .
ii.245	Strafford, my brave friend, there were wild reports—	Wentworth, my good friend, there may have been	Strafford, my friend, there may have been reports,
ii.252	But you will not so very much dislike	{deleted: nothing substituted}	But you will not so utterly abhor
ii.255	Strafford, spare yourself—	Wentworth, spare yourself—	Strafford, spare yourself—
Scene i		*ACT II*	
i.13	Look up, dear Vane!	Look up, Vane!	Look up, friend Vane!
i.19	You'll grow one day A steadfast light to England, Vane! *Rud.* Ay, Fiennes, Strafford revived	You may grow one day A steadfast light to England, Vane! I'll hold, meanwhile, The light, to please you;— *Rud.* would you, in the case {?} Strafford revived	You may grow one day A steadfast light to England, Henry Vane! *Rud.* Meantime, by flashes I make shift to see Strafford revived
i.30	A sorer burthen	A heavier burthen	A sorer burden
i.46	The Parliament assembled: Rudyard, friends, He could not speak his mind! and Pym, who knows Strafford . . .	The Parliament assembled: Rudyard, friends, The measure is not his—and Pym, who knows Strafford . . .	The Parliament assembled. Pym, who knows Strafford . . .

* Browning wrote 'Ask England, if {?}' in the right hand margin after 'bid them help you, then!', possibly to replace part of this phrase.

** This is clearly a note to guide Browning in his revision of the line, not the line as revised. The words 'So shall . . .' seem to be arrowed to '*Charles*' and may be intended as a note for part of his speech, preceding or following 'you were best|Return at once'. The words 'You shall rule me' are deleted.

	1837	1862	1863
i.57	our House Would have consented to that wretched offer	our House Would have consented to that blessed offer	our House, I say, would have consented to that offer
i.60	If . . . say six subsidies, will buy it off, The House. . . . Rud. . . . Will grant them! Hampden, do you hear? Oh, I congratulate you that the King Has gained his point at last . .	If . . . say six subsidies, would buy it off, The House . . . would grant them! Rud. Hampden, do you hear? Congratulate with me! the good King Charles Has gained his point at last . .	If, say, six subsidies will buy it off, The House. . . . Will grant them! Hampden, do you hear? Congratulate with me! the King's the king, And gains his point at last—
i.110	Vane. Forgive me, Pym! Voices. This looks like truth—Strafford can have, indeed,	(Vane.) This {?} looks like {?} truth Forgive me, Pym!* Voices. This must be truth—Strafford can have, indeed,	Vane. Forgive me, Pym! Voices. This looks like truth: Strafford can have, indeed,
Scene ii			
ii.31	That I appointed, chooses	Its {?The} proper leader chooses	That I appointed, chooses
ii.99	When the least pique, pettiest mistrust, is sure To ruin me—and you along with me!	When the least pique, the pettiest of mistrust Is sure to ruin me—and you with me!	When the least pique, pettiest mistrust, is sure To ruin me—and you along with me!
ii.105	You say,	You'll say,	Say you,
ii.114	And if, thro' your own weakness, falsehood, Charles,	And if, thro' your own weakness, or ††	And if, through your own weakness, or what's worse,
ii.123	But your hideous heart— I had your heart to see, Charles! Oh, to have	but the face was masked? I had your heart to see, sir! Face of flesh,	What, the face was masked? I had the heart to see, sir! Face of flesh,
ii.152	Dear Pym! Come out of this unworthy place To our old room again! Come, dearest Pym!	Pym! Come out of this unworthy place To our old room again! Come, Pym!	Hence, Pym! Come out of this unworthy place To our old room again! He's gone.
ii.158	You have misreckoned, Strafford: time will . . . Perish	You have misreckoned, Strafford: time will teach us—Perish	You have misreckoned, Strafford: time shows. Perish,
ii.161	Of one whose prowess is to do the feat!	Of one whose prowess shall achieve the feat!	Of one whose prowess should achieve the feat!

* The words 'me, Pym' are half-circled, as if for transfer to the next line.
† Illegible words followed by a dash.

	1837	1862	1863
ii.179	His Squires are not the Giant's friends: well—well— Let us go forth!	His precious Squires are not the Giant's friends: Well, well! Let us go forth!	His Squires are not the Giant's friends. All's one: Let us go forth!
ii.214	And he will not, now:	And will never, now:	And he never will.
		ACT III	
Scene i			
i.47	I would you had not set the Scots on Strafford Till he had put down Pym for us, my lord!	I would you had not set the Scots on him, Till he had put down Parliament for us!	I would you had not set the Scots on Strafford Till Strafford put down Pym for us, my lord!
i.51	At once . . 'tis very urgent . . she would have	At once . . 'tis very urgent . . she desires	At once; 't is very urgent! she requires
Scene ii			
ii.32	What the king does. Strafford that serves you all—	What the king does! Strafford that saved you all—	What the King does. Strafford that lends his arm,
ii.45	Vane, find out the King!	Quick, Vane, find the King!	Vane, go find the King!
ii.169	From Savile and his lords, to Pym— I crush them, girl—	From Savile and his lords, to Pym—& his losels, I crush them, girl—	From Savile and his lords, to Pym And his losels, crushed!—
Scene iii			
iii.26	Friends, I've a kindness for you! Friends, I've seen you	Friends, I've a kindness for you! Friends you with the ruff,—there's no forgetting *that*— I've seen you	Friend, I've a kindness for you! Friend, I've seen you
iii.33	Came . . . just as we come!	Came . . . much as we come!	Came . . . just as we come!
		ACT IV	
Scene i			
i.115	Oh, draw the veil and save him!	Best draw the veil and save him!	Tear down the veil and save him!
Scene ii			
ii.45	Be kind This once! Glance at the paper . . if you will But glance at it . . .	Be wise This once! Glance at the paper . . if you will* But glance at it . . .	Be moved! Glance at the paper!

**'kind' is written above 'This once!'

1837	1862	1863
ii.174 The Oversight, pay for the Giant Sin	Dwarf Oversight, pay for the Giant Sin	The oversight here, pay for the main sin
ii.191 And left me, for a time.... *Vane (aside to* RUDYARD) Moved, is he not?	And left me, for a time.... *Vane (aside to* RUDYARD) Moved, at the last—	And left me, for a time . . . 'Tis very sad!
Scene ii	*ACT V*	
ii.19 We'll sleep safe there.	One sleeps safe there.	We sleep safe there.
s.d. after ii.58 *Enter* HOLLIS *and an Attendant.*	*Enter* HOLLIS *and the King, disguised—*	*Enter* HOLLIS *and an Attendant.*
ii.63 To solitude: and just	To the {illeg.} rest: and just	To solitude: and just
ii.72 At Wentworth. Or, a better project now—	At Wentworth. Garrard must be reengaged To write me . . . Or, a better project now—	At Wentworth. Garrard must be re-engaged My newsman. Or, a better project now—
ii.88 Who will advise the King, And yet	Who will advise the King, Be his Sejanus, Richelieu or what not, And yet	Who will advise the King, Turn his Sejanus, Richelieu and what not, And yet
ii.113 On the other side of the river! *Hollis (to his Companion)* Tell him all; I knew my throat would thicken thus . . . Speak, you! *Straf.* 'Tis all one—I forgive him. Let me have The order of release!	On the other side of the river! *Hollis (to his Companion)* Tell him all; Speak, you! *Straf.* 'Tis all one—he's the master. {?} Let me have The order of release!	On the other side of the river! Give at once His order of release!
ii.137 Still there is One who does not come—there's One That shut out Heaven from me . . . . *Hol.* Think on it then! On Heaven . . and calmly . . as one . . as one to die! *Straf.* Die? True, friend, all must die, and all must need	For there is One who does not come—the One That shut out Heaven from me . . . *Hol.* Now opens it then!* {Illeg.} gaze {?} On it . . and calmly . . that is as one to die! *Straf.* True, Hollis, all must die, and therefore need	For there is One who comes not. *Hol.* Whom forgive, As one to die! *Straf.* True, all die, and all need

* Browning deleted 'Think', and wrote 'Now opens it' in the right hand margin. In the following line 'it' is not clear: perhaps it should be read as "d'.

	1837	1862	1863
ii.174	And you've got Radcliffe safe—and Laud is here . .	And you've got Radcliffe safe—and Laud lies here . . turn is next	And you've got Radcliffe safe, Laud's turn comes next:
ii.227	Me . . no, not shame!	. . no, not shame!	Or, no, not shame!
s.d. after ii.267	PYM *is discovered with* HAMPDEN, VANE &c	PYM *is discovered with* &c.	PYM *is discovered with* HAMPDEN, VANE, etc.
ii.277	That yawns for him.	That waits for him.	Which waits for him.
ii.294	. . . Aye here I know I talk—and I will talk	. . . Aye here I know I talk—and I will talk dare & will	Ay, here I know I talk—I dare and must,
ii.303	Then, shall the meeting be!	Then, the meeting be!	Then, the meeting be!
303a	Then—then—then—I may kiss that hand, I know!	Then—then—then—I may take that hand, I know!	(303a omitted.)
ii.305	As well to die! Youth is the time—our youth,	As well to die! Youth is the true time—	As well die now! youth is the only time
ii.311	Best die. Then if there's any fault,	Then if there's any fault,	Best die. Then if there's any fault,
ii.312	Upon my downfall, Pym? Poor little Laud	Upon my downfall? Poor grey little Laud	Dies, smothered up. Poor grey old little Laud

APPENDIX C

A Summary of each Book of *Sordello*

BOOK THE FIRST

Before he begins to tell us the story of Sordello, and of the 'development of [his] soul', the poet comments on the method he is going to adopt. He would have preferred to tell the story

> By making speak, myself kept out of view,
> The very man as he was wont to do,

but complains that writers like himself, who elect what the public is pleased to regard as 'unexampled themes', seem to be obliged to comment on the action of their poems, to keep their readers on the right lines. In a semi-jocular passage, he claims to be writing for 'the dead, if fate denies the quick', but bids Shelley not to come near: 'this is no place for thee!'

At l. 73 'the past is hurled In twain' and (as if by the use of a zoom-lens) we are shown Verona, more than six hundred years ago. The Lombard League (which consists of Guelfs, or supporters of the Pope) is preparing to try to rescue Count Richard of Saint Boniface, an ally of Azzo VII who has been captured by the Ghibellins (or supporters of the Emperor). We hear confused voices, as in the opening scene of a play. First a Ghibellin speaks, then a Guelf, and then an envoy describes how Taurello Salinguerra, the brave and able supporter of the Ghibellin leader Ecelin, has recaptured Ferrara by one trick and Count Richard by another. To complete the historical introduction we are given an account of the 'Representative' of each side, Ecelin (the 'hill-cat') and Azzo (the 'lion').

We now hear how this very night, while the leading men are debating

> Concerning Richard and Ferrara's fate,

an unnamed man is to be seen reclining by a flickering lamp in a secret room, a man who has been profoundly influenced in some way by a remarkable woman who has just left him. The poet addresses Dante and tells him that this man is Sordello, his 'forerunner', and proclaims that he wishes to disentwine Sordello's fame from that of Dante, which has eclipsed it.

Immediately after this glimpse of Sordello at what we later learn to have been the turning-point in his life, the poet goes back 'some thirty years' and describes a little place near Mantua called Goito, where there is a castle. As if with a zoom-lens, again, the poet takes us into the castle, through mysterious 'corridors contrived for sin', 'Dusk winding-stairs, dim galleries', and brings us to a 'maple-panelled room' (which is strangely decorated) and thence to 'the main wonder', a vault in which there is a large font supported by finely-carved Caryatides. Every evening the youthful Sordello visits this font, sitting in turn by one of the carved figures of girls which support it, himself as still as stone, in this manner begging 'Pardon for them'. The reader is aware of something mysterious.

'A slender boy in a loose page's dress', the youth is described as 'a soul fit to receive Delight at every sense.' The poet gives an account of 'the regal class'

> Nature has broadly severed from her mass
> Of men, and framed for pleasure,

imaginative men who are keen lovers of beauty. He then distinguishes two categories within this class, those who are content to lose themselves in admiration of what they love, and those who are self-centred and regard everything which they recognize as desirable and admirable as merely an outward expression of ideas which have lain dormant within their own minds. They admire themselves and are content to dwell in their own thoughts. Sordello is a man in this second category, but his mind is enervated . . . Here the poet catches himself, just in time, before he anticipates the theme of the whole poem.

Sordello has been born at a critical time in history,

> With the new century, beside the glow
> And efflorescence out of barbarism,

and his youth has been passed calmly in 'this secret lodge of Adelaide's'. He is tended by 'Some foreign women-servants, very old', and is forbidden the northern side of the castle. His imagination plays round his surroundings, building airy castles of the kind that 'This world of ours' always lays low. As is natural in the circumstances, he is 'Selfish enough, without a moral sense', as he lacks anything to tell him that 'Others desired a portion in his joy'. As time passes, however, he yearns for recognition. Accordingly he does his best to imagine what people are like, drawing on the few he has met and what he has read and dreamed of mankind. How is he to become a focus of admiration? He reflects wryly that people will wish him to show 'Qualities strange, ungainly, wearisome' that he has been only too happy to do without, so far.

He now sets out to try to empathize with men, as he has hitherto done with the objects of nature, such as trees and flowers. He speculates, and at first dreams that he is as good as the powerful Ecelin—in his own mind. Realizing that this is only an absurd dream, however, he reflects that he is not yet adult, and falls back into his secluded life, although he is not 'careless as before'. He now cherishes the desire to be worshipped by the powerful of the world. Must he try to become like Friedrich, the Emperor—or like Eglamor, the famous poet? Or why not both? In his own mind, therefore, he is now 'Half minstrel and half emperor'. He imagines himself the perfect creature, let us use the old name Apollo. Where then is he to find his Daphne? Hearing of Palma, who is said to have scorned the love of the handsome and powerful Count Richard, he dreams of her. At this point circumstances impinge on his life, and he becomes involved in the affairs of his time, and in particular in the great struggle between the Guelfs and Ghibellins.

BOOK THE SECOND

In spring Sordello wanders forth, dreaming of Palma. He finds that he has come to Mantua, where a Court of Love is in progress. Count Boniface's best troubadour, Eglamor, sings a song about Apollo. Struck by its deficiencies, Sordello leaps up and sings a much better song, using the same incidents and characters. Among the spectators he sees Adelaide, and Palma, who murmurs to him and gives him her scarf. He swoons. When he recovers consciousness he finds himself at home, and the women-servants tell him that he is now Palma's minstrel. He spends a week in reflection, wondering how he is superior to Eglamor.

Now Eglamor's funeral procession comes in view. 'No genius rare', he was Sordello's opposite, a man who had enjoyed the celebrity of a poet, with the attendant pomp and trappings; yet he had recognized Sordello's superiority, and had died. Sordello pronounces an elegy over his corpse.

In May, 'my own month' as the narrator calls it, Sordello attempts to discover his parentage. He is told that he is an orphan, the son of a brave archer called Elcorte, and that he has been cared for in the old castle on the orders of Ecelin. This comes as a great shock, yet it serves to confirm his resolve to be different from other men, to become (indeed) the greatest of mankind, 'Monarch of the World!' The narrator apostrophizes Sordello with the warning that the world cannot be expected to take him at his own valuation. Sordello continues to dream, however, and (deciding to throw all his efforts into being a great poet) expects the world to acknowledge, from his poetry, what he *could* do in the world of action, if he cared.

Suddenly a letter from Naddo arrives, bidding him come to Mantua. Sordello goes there, produces a conventional poem, and has a great success. Surely, he reflects, it is now time to attempt something better:

> These lays of yours, in brief—
> Cannot men bear, now, something better?—fly
> A pitch beyond this unreal pageantry
> Of essences? the period sure has ceased
> For such: present us with ourselves, at least,
> Not portions of ourselves, mere loves and hates
> Made flesh; wait not!   (562–8)

So he seems to hear a voice admonishing him. As a preliminary, he starts experimenting with language. Failing in his endeavour, he condescends to write a popular poem on the exploits of Simon de Montfort.

Finding that his auditors are really only interested in that hero, and not in the poet who is singing of him, he becomes deeply frustrated. And so, 'poet no longer in unity with man, the whole visible Sordello goes wrong'. There is a conflict between the man in him, with his ordinary human desires, and the poet, with his wild and unattainable ambitions. He finds himself writing 'a crazy tenzon or sirvent' to please the crowd—only to discover that they have not (after all) any very high esteem for poets. Finding it more and more impossible to converse sincerely with ordinary men—he has to over-simplify, if they are to understand anything—he becomes more and more disillusioned. Naddo, meanwhile, is always at hand, professing to regard poets as the most gifted of mortals, yet constantly urging that there are 'matters one may probe Too deeply for poetic purposes': Sordello finds poetry more and more a source of frustration.

Now comes news of Adelaide's death, which has momentous consequences for the whole House of Romano. Ecelin II enters a monastery (hence his nickname 'The Monk'), dividing his territories between his sons Alberic and Ecelin (the future Ecelin III), and urging that the whole feud between Ghibellins and Guelfs should be brought to a close by a series of marriages (including one between Palma and Count Richard). He no longer wishes to plot against the Pope. Taurello Salinguerra arrives to try to dissuade him from taking this course, but too late. Ecelin is old and weary, and cannot be persuaded. Taurello therefore retreats to Mantua, where it is Sordello's honourable task to greet him with a song.

Seeking inspiration, Sordello wanders out; but finds none. He discovers that he has approached Goito by the one route which used to be forbidden him. With a sense of deep relief he returns to the castle, now in decay, and (hearing that Palma has left that very day) lies down 'Beside the Carian group reserved and still'. He reflects on his failure: is it through some fault in his Will that he has failed? In any event, both his own Body and Mankind have failed to answer the desires of his Will. He resolves to attempt to 'be king' again, and throws away his crown of laurels, apparently as a sign that he is abandoning poetry (or perhaps the attempt at popular poetry). The next day he is not to be found, when Taurello expects the usual song of welcome and praise.

BOOK THE THIRD

Back in his retreat in Goito, Sordello is happy for 'a sweet and solitary year'. Having failed to achieve ambitions which were Quixotic and ill-defined, he finds it a relief to have given up the struggle to implement his Will. Yet all is not well: 'he slept, but was aware he slept, So, frustrated'. One night there is thunder, followed by an earthquake. He reflects that such a convulsion and the sudden change which it brings with it is not possible for a man:

> No! youth once gone is gone:
> Deeds, let escape, are never to be done.

He meditates on his life so far, realizes that he should have embraced ordinary human experience (as the rungs of a ladder leading to higher things) instead of rejecting it, and regrets that he left Mantua.

Suddenly Naddo appears and tells him of the important political events outlined towards the end of Book the Second. He informs him that Count Richard is to marry Palma and then storm Ferrara. Naddo adds that Palma has sent for Sordello because (as Naddo wrongly assumes) she wants him to write a song celebrating her forthcoming marriage. To his surprise, Sordello immediately agrees to come.

In Verona this is a time pregnant with consequences for Christendom,

> Sure to receive, whate'er the end was, from
> The evening's purpose cheer or detriment.

Can the Emperor prevail over the Pope, and so 'restore The rule of Charlemagne'? This is the evening of which we have had a preliminary glimpse in Book I (77 ff.). We see Sordello and Palma sitting together like lovers, with 'locked fingers and linked arms'. As the people outside tumultuously prepare to send forces to join the Lombard League, she tells him how she has yearned for love, and how she realized, when he sang at the Love Court, that he was the 'out-soul' she was destined to follow and obey. She had then recognized her 'bent' and had decided to win him for herself—and for the House of Romano. She goes on to tell him how she had been with Adelaide when she died, and had heard much of Adelaide's plans for Romano—but breaks off when she is on the point of revealing that Sordello is in fact Taurello's son (a fact which is the key to much that is perplexing and obscure). She insists that it is important that the House of Romano should continue to prosper, however, and reveals how Taurello has played the role of 'Romano's angel', stopping her when she had been on the point of marrying Count Richard, and acting 'As Patron of the scattered family'. It is now for Sordello to take on that great responsibility, if he will:

> let Taurello's noble accents teach
> The rest! Then say if I have misconceived
> Your destiny, too readily believed
> The Kaiser's cause your own!

After a night's reflection Sordello resolves to be

> Gate-vein of this heart's blood of Lombardy,
> Soul of this body.

He realizes that he has been wrong to stand aside from life, and believes that he now has an opportunity to rescind 'The ignominious exile of mankind'. He has accomplished 'one round Of life': like Paracelsus, he 'achieves'. Yet we notice that he is immediately compared to Brennus, whose troops captured Rome yet failed to take its citadel.

At this point, after a strange, partly satirical allusion to his own poem, the poet decides to lay a spell on his characters for a while, and go to Venice. As the headnotes put it, 'Thus then, having completed a circle, the poet may pause and breathe, being really in the flesh at Venice'.

We are now given his musings 'on a ruined palace-step' in Venice. He meditates on the difference between the poetry of a minor poet like Eglamor and 'true works'—if indeed the latter are capable of being completed. Whereas Eglamor's poems are whole-hearted, because he is untroubled by any awareness of the potentialities of great poetry, a true poem always contains some hint that the poet regards this particular poem as merely 'an episode' in his own imaginative life. His audience, for ever awaiting 'the better lay' in which (as they suppose) he will share his fullest insight with them, is destined to be disappointed. They have foolishly trusted 'a sailor's promise, weather-bound'.

As the poet remains sitting outside the *palazzo*, he falls to thinking of women, and wonders who may be adorable enough to reclaim him and become his Queen (he does not have a Will like Sordello's). A 'sad dishevelled ghost' plucks at him and points. Reflecting on poverty, he tells us that the experience of Venice has led him to abandon his immature notion that all can and should become 'chiefs and bards':

> I ask youth and strength
> And health for each of you, not more.

He is confirmed in an old resolution that he should take Mankind as his mistress. He bids the poor woman (who typifies, as Browning explained in a letter, the most unfortunate of human beings) sleep on his shoulder, defying the censorious. He reflects on the casuistry to which men are prone, satirizes poets who make no true attempt to deal with the major issues of life, and (with a touch of irony) describes himself as a Moses who knows that he will never reach the Promised Land, although he tries to lead people in that direction.

What is the office of the poet, here on earth? Something which is a mere preliminary to what it will be in another life! The worst poets 'say they . . . have seen' something of man's condition: the better poets describe 'what it was they saw': while the best 'Impart the gift of seeing to the rest'. He seeks to prove to an interlocutor that he himself has the (essentially dramatic and psychological) gifts of the last category—so far as poets in this stage of existence can have them—and wishes him to 'take on trust' further truths which he himself 'behold[s]' but cannot make him see.

He understands how most people prefer men of action like Taurello, who 'carry on, a stage, The work o' the world', limited as their vision necessarily is. Readers of poetry should (in fact) attack those who are capable of great poetry yet neglect their duty. For his own part, he is making his attempt.

As the Book ends the poet salutes Landor, his 'patron-friend', and 'My English Eyebright' (Fanny Haworth), mentions that the appearance of 'the sad Dishevelled form' has renewed him and fortified his resolve to go on with the poem, and emphasizes that his subject is

> the fate of such
> As find our common nature—overmuch

Despised because restricted and unfit
To bear the burthen they impose on it—
Cling when they would discard it; craving strength
To leap from the allotted world, at length
They do leap,—flounder on without a term,
Each a god's germ, doomed to remain a germ
In unexpanded infancy, unless . . .

It must seem an unattractive theme, but his audience should not underestimate it. The Book ends with a strange simile from the life of 'John the Beloved' intended to enforce the moral that

What seems a fiend perchance may prove a saint.

BOOK THE FOURTH

We now return to Ferrara, racked by the struggle between the Ghibellins and the Guelfs. Taurello is holding Count Richard prisoner, and the Guelfs have arrived to treat for his release. People are gossiping apprehensively. Taurello's palace and the gardens he had built for his young bride are described at some length. (Richard is imprisoned there). We see Sordello standing beside the palace. He has been reflecting deeply on his relationship with mankind. In the words of Browning's own headings, he 'finds in men no machine for his sake, but a thing with a life of its own, and rights hitherto ignored by him—a fault he is now anxious to repair'. He wonders how he can serve men, instead of merely using them to exhibit his own genius. He reflects that even the Papal Legate, an absurd-looking man whom he despises, is of some service to mankind. He realizes that the first task is to render men happy (before proceeding to attempt to ensure their spiritual development), and resolves to become Taurello's pupil in this preparatory undertaking. He wonders about the struggle between the Guelfs and Ghibellins: where lies the true Cause which he should serve?—

. . . . Behold
The secret, so to speak, and master-spring
O' the contest!—which of the two Powers shall bring
Men good, perchance the most good: ay, it may
Be that!—the question, which best knows the way.

He hopes to learn from an interview with Taurello.
All we hear of this interview is the following:

. . And at last
He did confront him. Scarce an hour had past

> When forth Sordello came, older by years
> Than at his entry. Unexampled fears
> Oppressed him, and he staggered off, blind, mute
> And deaf, like some fresh-mutilated brute,
> Into Ferrara.

Later we learn that the tone in which Taurello had been talking to Tito, with whom he had been conversing when Sordello and Palma had arrived for the interview, had profoundly shocked the poet—

> The talk with Tito—the excuse preferred
> For burning those five hostages . . .

Sordello hopes that the subject had been brought up 'By way of blind', to prevent Palma and himself from hearing the real subject of the conversation.

In his shocked state Sordello wanders in Ferrara, which is in a terrible condition. A poor woman offers him the choice of her two young daughters. Recognized as a minstrel, he is asked to sing a song. At the end of it Palma appears and leads him away.

Having seen the Ghibellin and Guelf envoys, and Sordello (as spokesman for the People) in between, Taurello sits musing. Only the sight of Palma (it seems) has prevented him from assuming the leadership of the Ghibellins himself, under the Emperor. He looks young and fit, in contrast to the prematurely aged Sordello; yet he finds it impossible to take the final step to self-advancement, instead of remaining the servant of the House of Romano. He remembers his youth in Ferrara, how his friends had planned to marry him to Linguetta (a marriage which would have made him a great power in that city), and how the Guelfs of Ravenna had carried her off and he had been cheated. So it had happened that Linguetta had been married to Azzo of Este, and he himself had joined the Ghibellins. We hear of the later conflict between him and Azzo, and above all of the terrible night in Vicenza when he lost his wife and son (as he believes), yet behaved with great courage. It seems that the events of that night have led him to abandon all personal ambition:

> But afterward men heard not constantly
> Of Salinguerra's House so sure to be!

Instead it was in Romano that he 'sought . . . wife and child',

> And for Romano's sake seemed reconciled
> To losing individual life, which shrunk
> As the other prospered—mortised in his trunk.

Heinrich could not understand, but Otho does. Taurello becomes a

master of the art of understanding men— very different from Sordello, who

> only cared to know
> About men as a means whereby he'd show
> Himself, and men had much or little worth
> According as they kept in or drew forth
> That self.

Ecelin, however, fails Romano, and on his wife's death he withdraws
from the world. After further rumination Taurello is quite clear that
he cannot assume the leadership of the House of Romano. He reflects
that even Sordello may be better remembered than he, since his
songs will continue to be sung. From musing he turns to prac-
ticalities, and wonders whether he can pacify the Lombard League
without surrendering Count Richard.

Meanwhile Sordello anxiously asks Palma to explain the 'laws'
and to reassure him that

> . . . good may lurk
> Under the bad,—my multitude has part
> In your [the Ghibellins'] designs, their welfare is at heart
> With Salinguerra . . .

Shocked as he is by his interview with Taurello, he wants to be
certain that the Guelfs care more for the welfare of mankind than do
the Ghibellins. He concludes that a man who takes *either* side must
rank 'with man's inveterate foes'. 'Have men a cause distinct from
both?' He decides that 'Rome' is to be his Cause. At this point a
choric character appears and tells him the story of Crescentius,
which might serve him as a cooling-card; but he does not benefit
from the warning. For him

> Rome typifies the scheme to put mankind
> Once more in full possession of their rights.
> 'Let us have Rome again! On me it lights
> 'To build up Rome—on me, the first and last:
> 'For such a future was endured the past!'

What came of it all we are to hear—it seems that the archer's tale has
merely rendered Sordello more Quixotic than ever.

BOOK THE FIFTH

As a result of his experiences, Sordello's latest dream—'A Rome
indebted to no Palatine'—has vanished. Rome was not built in a day.

As he sits wistfully contemplating the wreck of his hopes, 'a low voice' winds into his heart, explaining that

> God has conceded two sights to a man—
> One, of men's whole work, time's completed plan,
> The other, of the minute's work, man's first
> Step to the plan's completeness.

When he imagined himself a god who could reach out towards the completed plan he had been deluded, but it is his duty to take his own single step. He must bear in mind that 'collective man Outstrips the individual'. If he considers the history of his own art he will see that it is impossible to find the first of poets: we are always conscious of dim forms in the background, whom we can only vaguely descry. In the history of mankind, similarly, he can hardly be foolish enough to believe that he is the first to 'materialize' the Multitude (in the jargon of modern spiritualism). Ignorant as he is, he knows of Charlemagne, who achieved Strength by stress of Strength. He knows of Hildebrand, who 'by stress Of Strength work[ed] Knowledge'. A period of three centuries had to elapse between these two great men. Things go by stages: the Crusades,

> Or trick of breeding Strength by other aid
> Than Strength:

the formation of the Lombard League,

> .   .   or trick of turning Strength
> Against Pernicious Strength:

and the 'Treuga Dei',

> .   God's Truce—or trick to supersede
> The very Use of Strength

—they are all to be regarded (by a sort of dialectic) as stages in the progress of mankind. The next step will be neither that of the beautiful flower (Charlemagne) nor that of the powerful root (Hildebrand), but that of a fruitful plant which will spread and spread. At this point in human development there is no possibility of achieving 'Knowledge by stress of merely Knowledge', which is the ultimate goal. Meanwhile,

> Who means to help must still support the load
> Hildebrand lifted.

Hildebrand had destroyed only the temporary part of Charlemagne's achievement. The next phase is that

> of Knowledge, part by Strength and part
> By Knowledge!

As for Sordello (the voice goes on), now that he has come to see that
Mankind is half himself, he must consider whether he may not be the
man to whom has been granted the greatest opportunity possible at
this point in history. He must try to persuade Taurello.

Eager to make the attempt, he goes to Taurello, by whose side
Palma sits silent. Speaking on her behalf as well as his own, he urges
Taurello to support the Guelf cause. Although the older man is
merely amused, Sordello does not lose confidence. As the spokesman for the People, he is indignant that Taurello does not recognize
himself as Sordello's natural subordinate. That was a new conception 'for that age'. He tells Taurello that 'A poet must be earth's
essential king', although he himself may not have succeeded. The
ultimate aim is that 'essence, whatsoe'er it be, [should] extend'. He
delivers a lecture on the progress of mankind: a lecture which fails to
hold Taurello's attention. In particular he talks of the importance of
the poet, as a king among men, and of the progress of poetry. In the
history of poetry (to quote from Browning's own headings)
'dramatist, or, so to call him, analyst' succeeds 'epoist' and is to turn
'in due course synthetist'. The kind of poetry he has in mind, dealing
with 'the last of mysteries—Man's inmost life' is illustrated by this
poem itself (or so the revised line 620 ironically suggests).

Almost raving (as it must seem to Taurello), Sordello concludes
that his own great task, as things have turned out, is to 'bow

> Taurello to the Guelf cause, disallow
> The Kaiser's coming—which with heart, soul, strength,
> I labour for, this eve, who feel at length
> My past career's outrageous vanity,
> And would, as its amends, die, even die
> Now I first estimate the boon of life,
> If death might win compliance—sure, this strife
> Is right for once—the People my support'.

Taurello's response is astonishing. He immediately comments that
it is clear that Palma loves Sordello, and adds that the Monk's
withdrawal has ruined his own hopes. He has lost thirty years of his
life even more certainly than Sordello has. But there is still a chance
for the House of Romano to remain mighty. He himself is not (now)
a supreme leader: if only Palma were Ecelin, to be persuaded by him!

And then he suddenly invests Sordello with the great power delegated to himself by the Emperor. Sordello is now the leader of Romano.

This utterly unexpected action has a sequel even more strange. As if by magic, Taurello realizes that Sordello is in fact his son, while Sordello recognizes that Taurello is his father. Palma has known of this (she confesses) since Adelaide's dying confession. She tells of the death of Retrude, Taurello's wife and Sordello's mother, and explains that Adelaide wished Sordello's identity to remain concealed because she had seen in a vision that Taurello was 'the natural chief, the man of men', and she wished her son (Ecelin, the future Tyrant) to inherit the leadership from his father. Retrude had been buried in the font which young Sordello had visited (quite ignorant of this fact) every evening.

Sordello remains silent, while Taurello talks in great excitement, intimating that it is not the Emperor Friedrich who is to benefit from all that he is planning, but Sordello himself. It is important to realize (as the head-notes emphasize) that such plans are the result of 'the Devil putting forth his potency: since Sordello, who began by rhyming, may, even from the depths of failure, yet spring to the summit of success, *if he consent to oppress the world*' (italics added). Sordello still remaining silent, Taurello talks more and more wildly. Palma quietly leads him down the stair, and tries to soothe him. He makes her sit on his knee, and dreams of the future—of what is to happen when Palma and Sordello are married, and he himself serves both. He believes that 'Fate's second marvellous cycle' is about to begin, although what he outlines is in fact a sinister adumbration of the course which Ecelin the Tyrant was later to pursue, however incompletely. Hildebrand's achievement is to be overthrown, Charlemagne's rule is to be restored, but in a new form.

'Salinguerra's prophecy at height', however, he and Palma hear a sudden sound from above. The Book ends with a sort of anticipation of the end of the whole poem.

BOOK THE SIXTH

We return to the moment when Taurello and Palma had left Sordello, and to his reflections as he watches the sun setting. Meditating on the power of Man, he hears 'Ferrara's din' outside, and wonders whether it can provide him with any guidance. 'Fate Paused with this eve':

> What help to pierce the future as the past
> Lay in the plaining city?

Looking back over his own life, he concludes that, having found no 'soul . . . above his soul' to guide him, and having been 'untasked of any love', he has 'missed life's crown, authentic attribute'. It is true that neither the Love which impels Palma nor the Hate which impels Taurello would have been sufficient for him; but surely *some* motivating power would have been right for him? The trouble is that 'the Best Somehow eludes us ever, still might be And is not!' Should he be 'a law to his own sphere?' No, he must make his attempt to serve Mankind, however inadequate the service open to him may seem. Should he fling down the badge which Taurello has given him, to show how he despises the limited earthly power which goes with it, and try to persuade him to change the Emperor's purpose? His 'life's work' is certainly to 'maintain the Guelfs in rule'; but what is his immediate objective to be? The more he reflects, however, the more incapable of decision he becomes, as he sees every side of the problem. Are old loyalties of no importance? Good and evil are inextricably mingled, are they not? It is the very struggle to rise which renders men happy. Had he himself not been sated by 'Goito with its perfect things?'. He is tempted to retain the badge and to derive personal happiness from the power it gives him. Perhaps this will not delay the progress of the People, which is bound to be very slow—and the ordinary pleasures of life await him. If we are to look on this world as a mere anteroom to a palace, why should he not enjoy its pleasures until the palace-doors of a higher existence open for him? He reflects that 'sage, champion, martyr' have been indifferent to such pleasures. But 'Where's abstract Right for me?' His 'closing-truth evolved By his flesh-half's break-up': that is to say that his final vision of the truth, as he died, was that the values of this life, 'Virtue and Vice, the Larger and the Less', may merely be 'modes of Time and this one sphere'. Why had he despaired in the past? Because he had failed to

> Fit to the finite his infinity.

He had refused to accept the limitations inherent in human life. And so, as morning breaks, 'death lets soar / Sordello'. The sound which Palma and Taurello had heard was that of his body falling on the floor of the room above them.

What Sordello had needed—the narrator comments, speaking for him 'this once'—was a Power above him, 'utterly incomprehensible', which he would have been able to love although he could not love 'all conceived by man'—and another Power which would have revealed the wishes of the former, 'This Human clear, as that Divine concealed.'

The narrator poses the question: 'what has Sordello found?' Was it simply the need for love, which 'poor Eglamor' had known from the beginning? When Palma and Taurello find him, with the badge under his foot, there is 'A triumph lingering' in his eyes, and as Palma kisses him his heart gives a final throb. Alas for Sordello, now dead!

Is it worth mentioning what happened to Taurello, and to the Ghibellins and Guelfs? Still loyal to the House of Romano, Taurello married the Monk's daughter Sofia 'In pure necessity', and so destroyed

> His slender last of chances, quite made void
> Old prophecy, and spite of all the schemes
> Overt and covert, youth's deeds, age's dreams,
> Was sucked into Romano.

He sank back into the secondary position which suited him. As the Guelfs withdrew, Mankind's hopes subsided; and in the end Ecelin the Tyrant and Alberic took over, evil men,

> Kings of the gag and flesh-hook, screw and whip,

and 'plagued the world'.

Taurello is allowed to grow old in Venice, free to walk about, a subject of curiosity to young and old alike. Sordello's refusal to take decisive action cost Mankind dear. In the end, however, 'a touch of Hildebrand' led to the downfall of Ecelin the Tyrant and of Alberic, when the Lombards banded together against them and saved Milan, so winning 'the world's applause'.

All this is now ancient history. They have all gone into the past, even Naddo. We have a strange final glimpse of Eglamor, whose face retains to the end 'Its joyous look of love'. As for Sordello, many stories are told of him, as 'Knight, Bard, Gallant'. The truth is that he failed to take the one step which he should have taken, and which would greatly have benefited mankind. By the time when Dante came on the scene and 'did much' for mankind Sordello's particular step was no longer to be taken. Sordello's life is bound to appear 'A sorry farce'. But what can be said in his favour?

It must be enough for him that his early song, 'the Goito lay', is still sung in the fields. 'So there you are (the poet says, addressing his readers): do you like the perfume left behind by the ghost I have raised for your benefit? You found it too strong, did you not? Caviare to the general?'

APPENDIX D

Quotations relating to *Sordello*

(See p. 160 and note, above)

Mrs. Conway 'hinted to Browning' that she would like to have an 'autograph' of his which might be sold at 'the Concord Bazaar for the benefit of the "freedmen"'. In response 'he took out a large bundle of papers,—manuscripts of his early poems ("Sordello" was in a separate wrapper); he removed the parchment wrapper of the poems, and showed us the sentences—Greek, Latin, English—with which it was covered. This parchment wrapper was duly forwarded to Mrs. Horace Mann, but who was the purchaser I know not'. Conway tells us that 'the sentences were irregular, some of them curving about to find room; one passage [unspecified] was all in capitals and run together like a single long word; the accents were hardly decipherable; no translations nor references to sources were given'. The passages are given here with the identifications and translations supplemented and corrected with the help of Dr Malcolm Lyons and others. Greek accents and obvious minor errors in Conway's transcription have been corrected. It should be noted that the important list of dates is given by Conway after the first two quotations.

(1) ᾿Αλλὰ πὰν τόλματον (καὶ) πένητα. . . . This is particularly obscure: the source is Longinus, *On the Sublime*, x, and it appears to be a quotation from Sappho. 'There is a *line* at the end of this Ode of *Sappho* in the original', observes William Smith in his well-known translation (3rd ed., 1752), 'which is taken no notice of in the translation, because the sense is complete without it'. The words might be construed to mean 'but to me (a poor man) all is to be dared'. The true text seems to be ἀλλὰ πὰν τόλματον ἐπεὶ καὶ πένητα (*Poetarum Lesbiorum Fragmenta*, ed. E. Lobel and D. Page, 31.17), 'But everything is to be endured, since a poor man (*accusative*) . . .'

(2) ᾿Ενικήσαμεν ὡς ἐβουλόμεθα 'We conquered as we wished'. the first line of a drinking-song quoted in Athenaeus, *Deipnosophistae*, xv. 694d (*Poetae Melici Graeci*, ed. D. L. Page, 888. 1.)

Here Conway prints the 'Venezia' note, as on p. 160 but inscribed within four lines making a square, with the following dates written beside it: 'Saturday, May 27, 1837 / Tuesday, June 18, 1837, July 30, 1837, Aug. 7. / Jan. 5, 1838, March 6, 27. / Feb. 23, 1840. ΘΔΕΑ'. The Greek letters are not any familiar abbreviation, but presumably express thankfulness: they could stand for some such words as Θεῷ

Δίδομεν Εὐχὰς Ἀρίστας. It seems likely that the dates all relate to *Sordello*, the last one perhaps recording the completion of proof-reading.

(3) Ἐξ ὧραι μόχθοις ἱκανώταται· αἱ ⟨δὲ⟩ μετ᾽ αὐτὰς
γράμμασι δεικνύμεναι ΖΗΘΙ λέγουσι βροτοῖς

'Six hours are enough for toil: those thereafter, expressed in writing, spell LIVE! to mortals'. *Greek Anthology*, x. 43 (with an allusion to the fact that the Greek letters representing the numbers 7,8,9,10 make up the imperative form of the verb 'to live').

(4) Ἥβα μοι, φίλε θυμέ. τάχ᾽ αὖ τινὲς ἄλλοι ἔσονται
ἄνδρες, ἐγὼ δὲ θανὼν γαῖα μέλαιν᾽ ἔσομαι

'Be young, my soul, soon there will be other men, while I shall be dead and merely black earth'. Theognis, *Elegies*, 877–8.

(5) Τεθνηκὼς ζωῶ φθεγγόμενος στόματι

'Dead, yet speaking with a living tongue'. Theognis, *Elegies*, 1230.

(6) Ὦ ἄνα . . . . . οὔποτε σεῖο
λήσομαι ἀρχόμενος οὐδ᾽ ἀποπαυόμενος,
ἀλλ᾽ αἰεὶ πρῶτόν τε καὶ ὕστατον ἔν τε μέσοισιν
ἀείσω· σὺ δέ μοι κλῦθι καὶ ἐσθλὰ δίδου

'O Lord, . . . never will I forget you, whether I am beginning or making an end, but shall always sing of you first and last and in the middle: do you listen to me and be favourable'. Theognis, *Elegies*, 1–4.

(7) Tu fulminibus frange trisulcis.

'Shatter with three-pronged lightning-bolts!' Seneca, *Hercules Oetaeus*, 1994.

(8) πάντη δ᾽ ἀθανάτων ἀφανὴς νόος ἀνθρώποισιν

'But the thought of the immortals is altogether secret unto men!' Solon, *Fragments*, 17.

(9) χοὕτως ἂν δοκέοιμι μετ᾽ ἀνθρώπων θεὸς ⟨εἶναι⟩

'And thus would I appear a god among men'. Theognis, *Elegies*, 339.

(10)   Ego quid sit ater
       Hadriae novi sinus et quid albus
                  Peccet Iapyx.

'I know from Experience what it is to be in the black Gulf of *Adria*, and what Danger attends the *Apulian* Winds'. Horace, *Odes*, III. xxvii. 18–20 (translated by David Watson in *The Odes, Epodes, and Carmen Seculare . . . Translated into English Prose*, 1741, a book owned by Browning: see *New Letters*, p. 19).

(11) Then I said, I will not make mention of him, nor speak any more in his name. But his word was in mine heart as a burning fire shut up in my bones, and I was weary with forbearing, and I could not stay. Jeremiah xx. 9.

(12) The Greek text of 1 Corinthians 14:8–9.
'For if the trumpet give an uncertain sound, who shall prepare himself to the battle? / So likewise ye, except ye utter by the tongue words easy to be understood, how shall it be known what is spoken? for ye shall speak into the air'.

(13) Ὡς παράξενοι χαίροντες ἰδεῖν τὸν ὁδὸν
    καὶ οἱ θαλαττεύοντες ἰδεῖν λιμένα
    οὕτω οἱ γράφοντες βιβλίου τέλος

'As travellers rejoice to see the road, and as seafarers rejoice to see the port, so do writers when they see the end of their book'.
Source unknown, but post-classical.

(14) Tomorrow, and Tomorrow and Tomorrow.
Macbeth, v. v. 19.

CORRIGENDA TO VOLUME I

p. xix, n^2: *for Pub. read Papers of the*
p. 68, note to 567: *for itself read* itself
p. 128, n^2: *for proela read* praela. The lines are the opening of Donne's poem, 'De Libro cum mutuaretur Impresso', and may be freely translated: 'Printed books are the usual thing, but manuscripts deserve to be more highly regarded'.
p. 241, textual note to 368: *for* < spare{?}> *read* < pure>
p. 275 The last four textual footnotes should be numbered 74, 75, 76, 77